THIRD EDITION

Human Resources Management

Wendell L. French
University of Washington

HOUGHTON MIFFLIN COMPANY   **Boston   Toronto**

Geneva, Illinois   Palo Alto   Princeton, New Jersey

Sponsoring Editor: Diane L. McOscar
Development Editor: Susan M. Kahn
Associate Project Editor: Susan Merrifield
Production/Design Coordinator: Sarah Ambrose
Senior Manufacturing Coordinator: Priscilla Bailey
Marketing Manager: Robert D. Wolcott

Cover Design: Len Massiglia

Figure Illustrations: Dartmouth Publishing, Inc.

Cover Image: Laszlo Moholy-Nagy: 1. "Composition AXXI," 1925; © 1993 ARS, New York/VG Bild-Kunst, Bonn

NOTE: The Ethical Dilemma in each chapter is drawn from real life, but the names and other facts have been changed. No reference to any specific company or individual is intended or should be inferred.

Library of Congress Catalog Card Number: 93-78694

ISBN: 0-395-47278-4

EXAMINATION COPY ISBN: 0-395-69089-7

123456789-RM-97 96 95 94 93

To Marjorie, Andrew, Thomas, and Amy,
and future adventures together

CONTENTS

v

Preface

As today's work world changes at a pace never before imagined, students, instructors, and managers are faced with the daunting task of keeping up with those changes. With this edition of *Human Resources Management*, I hope to help you meet that challenge. Building on the comprehensive, readable overview of previous editions, this edition has been thoroughly revised to be as contemporary, relevant, and accessible as possible. It has been written to help you address today's complex issues, such as globalism, diversity, downsizing, and many others.

This book is intended for anyone desiring a comprehensive overview of human resources management. It is specifically designed for college and university students and their instructors, but also has practical value for those already in business and industry.

This book requires no prerequisites and assumes no particular area of concentration, yet provides a solid foundation for human resources majors. It is relevant to any career track, whether managerial, professional, or entrepreneurial, and readers will find it directly applicable to understanding and influencing their current or future job environments.

The study of HRM deals with fundamental organizational processes that must be developed and managed effectively not only by HRM specialists but by all managers. Non-managers also have a big stake in HRM, and frequently are participants in managing these processes.

This text features up-to-date information on contemporary practice, issues, trends, and legislation. Some of the contemporary topics are self-managed teams, gain-sharing, the continuing rapid growth in the work force of women and minorities, international HRM, containment of health care costs, family and medical leave, the "glass ceiling," sexual harassment, managing diversity, and integrative labor-management bargaining. The book also includes historical perspectives on many aspects of HRM.

Contemporary Themes In Human Resources Management

Several themes in the book stem from my experience as a personnel director, professor, researcher, writer, administrator, and consultant. One theme is that management philosophy is an overriding factor in human resources management: What management believes about how organizational members, customers, and other stakeholders should be treated is a matter of crucial importance.

Other themes evident in the book are the importance of a systems perspective; the shortsightedness of inattention to the potential wisdom and skill of any organizational member; and the importance of simultaneous attention to a whole array of organizational configurations—two-person relationships, informal small groups, intact work teams (boss and subordinates together), intergroup relationships, and the total organization. Another theme is implicit throughout the book: At the heart of effective organizations is a dynamic integration of effective human resources management and effective technological management, broadly defined.

Organization of the Text

Part I of the book presents important background material, including definitions, history, and a survey of contemporary challenges facing those involved with managing human resources.

Part II presents a conceptual model of how HRM fits into the management and development of effective organizations. The last chapter in Part II, Chapter 6, begins an examination of the major HRM processes with human resources planning. Discussions of job and work design, staffing, training and development, performance appraisal and review, compensation and reward, protection and representation, and organization improvement follow in Parts III through VII. Drawing on the preceding concepts, the book then concludes with chapters on international human resources management and a look to the future.

Content New to the Third Edition

In addition to updated statistics and new real-world examples throughout the text, many content changes have been made to reflect contemporary issues facing human resources managers today:

- Chapter 1 includes new material on the roles of managers and employees in setting and upholding ethical standards. This coverage lays the foundation for later discussions of ethics, as applied to various HR functions and activities.

- Reflecting recent trends, Chapter 2 now includes material on how globalization has affected the development of management practice.

- A great deal of new ground is covered in Chapter 3, including an increased emphasis on valuing and managing today's diverse workforce; expanded coverage of economic and political environmental forces (inflation, energy costs, environmental concerns, globalization); coverage of the trend toward competitive strategies for productivity and quality improvement; and coverage of recent legislation, including the Older Workers Benefit Protection Act, Immigration Act of 1990, Americans with Disabilities Act, Civil Rights Act of 1991, Glass Ceiling Act of 1991, and the Family and Medical Leave Act of 1993.

- Following up on the earlier ethics coverage, Chapter 4 discusses values and ethics as they relate to management philosophy and organizational performance. Also included now are brief discussions of empowerment and of the time-honored "management systems" typologies: organic vs. mechanistic systems and Theory 1-4T.

- Chapter 6 incorporates up-to-date statistics and projections regarding the external labor market and demographic changes. It also provides information on how recent legislation and court cases—regarding sex discrimination, older workers, persons with disabilities, affirmative action, military leave, and child labor—affect HR planning.

- Self-managed teams are covered in Chapter 7 on Job Design and Analysis.

- Chapter 8 includes up-to-date material on new patterns in work scheduling, such as permanent part-time workers and telecommuting.

- The importance of cost considerations in recruitment is now mentioned in Chapter 9. This chapter also discusses internships as a recruiting method outside the organization, and defines new interview scenarios such as videotape and computer-assisted interviewing.

- The model for developing a skills training program in Chapter 11 has been revised to respond to reviewer comments. And a new section on multi-skilling has been added.

- Recognizing recent legislation and concerns regarding protected workers, Chapter 12 includes new material on developing employee potential of disabled workers, women, minorities, and the older worker. A new section on managing diversity has also been added.

- Chapter 13 discusses the growing importance of customer appraisals with the spread of TQM.

- In Part V, Compensation and Reward, a section on employee recognition programs has been added to Chapter 15, Incentive Plans. And a section on the recent Family and Medical Leave Act has been added to Chapter 16, Employee Benefits.

- To create a more logical structure, material on grievance-arbitration procedures in unionized settings has been moved to Chapter 18, Negotiating and Administering the Labor Agreement.

- The discussion of discrimination in Chapter 19 has been expanded to include harassment related to sex, age, race, and ethnicity. The issue of surveillance of employees in the workplace is also discussed in this chapter.

- Sections discussing circumstances under which employee participation is effective, employee support for participative approaches, study action teams, total quality management, and legal aspects of employee involvement programs have been added to Chapter 21.

- No HRM text would be up-to-date without recognizing today's global business environment. Chapter 22, International Human Resources Management, is new to this edition. It includes discussions of the rapid growth in multinational corporations, the phenomenon of culture shock, and dimensions along which differences in cultures can be contrasted. Descriptions of many widely different HR policies and practices around the world is an important feature of this chapter.

- The final chapter includes a new section on current ethical issues of concern to HR managers. It also projects current trends and offers some predictions about the nature of HRM in the future.

Special Features

In addition to an extremely accessible writing style, several features are designed to aid students in the learning process.

Each chapter begins with

- a chapter outline
- a list of learning objectives, and
- two short cases.

The cases are hypothetical composites of events that others or I have actually experienced across a wide variety of situations. Many readers will have had comparable experiences. Approximately half of these cases are new to this edition.

Two boxed inserts in each chapter,

- International Perspective and
- Contemporary Issues,

present real-life applications of HR policies or techniques, up-to-date information on personnel topics, or different points of view on HR issues. The boxes are drawn from a wide variety of sources, including professional journals, magazines, and national newspapers, such as *HRNews, HRFocus, HR Magazine, Across the Board, The Economist, Time,* and the *New York Times.* Topics include quality circles, corporate paternalism, blending cultures, Japanese-owned companies and Title VII, Karoshi, the EC's glass ceiling, teamwork, involvement, and participation.

To further illustrate the link between theory and application, each chapter has many in-text examples of actual HR practices in real-world organizations. Extensive use is also made of figures and tables for better visualization of theories, practices, and trends.

There are several important features at the end of each chapter:

- chapter summary
- ethical dilemma
- key terms
- review questions
- opening case questions
- comprehensive case

The Ethical Dilemma is a new feature that provides an opportunity for lively discussion and highlights the importance of recognizing and responding to potentially troubling ethical issues. In addition to the list of key terms, each term is introduced in bold face type and defined in the chapter. Each definition also appears in the *Glossary* at the back of the book.

The review questions are designed to reinforce students' understanding of the subject matter. Opening case questions move students to the next level of understanding by applying the opening case situation to chapter content.

The comprehensive cases cover current, major issues related to HRM. These are based on actual events and issues that have been given considerable attention by the media. Examples include "The Effects of NAFTA," "Self-Managed Teams," "The Benefits of Flexibility," "Downsizing without Layoffs," "Benefits for the Whole Family," "Drug Testing," "The Role of HR Managers in Total Quality Management," and "Managing Diversity." Discussion questions follow each case.

Teaching and Learning Supplements

Several important teaching and learning aids accompany the third edition of *Human Resources Management.*

- *Instructor's Resource Manual with Test Bank.* This volume includes an introduction and four parts.

  The Introduction includes an overview of the teaching/learning package and *team project.* The project involves organizing the class into two teams of students that will develop a management philosophy and key human resources policies and practices for a hypothetical company. Guidelines are provided to help facilitate the project.

  Part I contains the *chapter teaching aides:* chapter synopsis, chapter outline, learning objectives, lecture outline, suggested answer to the ethical dilemma, page references to the review questions, opening case questions and answers, and comprehensive case discussion questions and answers.

  Part II contains the *Test Bank* (by Judith Bulin, Monroe Community College). There are 1400 test items consisting of true/false, multiple-choice, completion, matching, essay, and case questions. Fifty percent of the questions are completely new or revised.

  Part III consists of the *Instructor's Supplement to Experiencing Human Resources Management* by Robert Lussier.

  Part IV contains 75 *transparency masters,* including both figures from the text and new illustrations and tables.

- A *Test Bank Data Disk* is available for the IBM PC or compatible computers and includes ASCII files for the Test Bank.

- *Experiencing Human Resources Management* by Robert Lussier (Springfield College), is a combination study guide and skill-building manual. This workbook includes valuable review and in-class materials. The contents include several types of objective questions as well as stand-alone skill-building exercises and application situations, and objective questions for each comprehensive case in the text.

Acknowledgments

There are many people who have contributed to the book and supplemental materials in important ways. In particular, I want to thank my wife, Marjorie, for her editorial help and constant support. On the Houghton Mifflin staff, I particularly want to thank Susan Kahn, Susan Merrifield, and Diane McOscar for their excellent editorial contributions and management of the total project. Thanks are also due to Bob Lussier for his important development of the exercise and activities manual and to Judy Bulin for her extensive and important contribution to the Instructor's Manual and Test Bank. I also want to thank the companies and human resources executives who were generous with their time and materials.

Thanks are also due to the following people for their insightful and helpful reviews or comments on parts or all of the manuscript:

Brendan Bannister
Northeastern University

Renato R. Bellu
CUNY-Kingsborough Community
   College

Lynda S. Clark
Maple Woods Community College

John W. Crim
Columbus College

Donald G. Gardner
University of Colorado

Charles N. Kaufman
University of South Dakota

Grace Klinefelter
Ft. Lauderdale College

James Klingler
Villanova University

John Kohl
University of Nevada, Las Vegas

Roger D. Lee
Salt Lake Community College

Eleanor A. Smith
Massachusetts Bay Community
College

Charles N. Toftoy
George Washington University

In addition to the above individuals, I would like to express particular thanks to:
Richard A. Engdahl, University of North Carolina, Wilmington, for his review of several chapters and his "Developing a Training Program" model in the chapter on skills training.

Robert W. Hollman, University of Montana, for his assistance with the chapter on performance appraisal and review, and

Fremont E. Kast, University of Washington, for his assistance in conceptualizing the chapter on international human resources management.

Other important persons in the entire project, of course, are the instructors and students who use the text, and I want to express my sincere appreciation to them. To all of these people, and to others who worked behind the scenes, I am most grateful.

Wendell L. French

CHAPTER 1

The Field of Human Resources Management

LEARNING OBJECTIVES

- Define human resources management and explain how it differs from the traditional view of personnel management.
- Identify the basic processes in human resources management.
- Describe the relationship between the human resources department and other managers within the organization.
- Explain the vital role of human resources management in modern organizations.

CASE 1.1   Martha Burke

Martha Burke, president and majority stockholder of Metro Publications, wrote "human resources director" on the agenda for the next department head meeting. Metro, formed three years before with only Martha and one assistant on staff, now employed almost 210 people — and things were getting complicated.

In the beginning, Martha herself had done all the recruiting and hiring, established the salaries, and reviewed the performance of all employees. As the company grew, however, she found it necessary to turn over some of these activities to department heads and supervisors. And that wasn't working as well as she had hoped.

In Martha's view, Metro Publications faced a number of serious problems. In the first place, some of the department heads were less careful than others. Some people were hired with insufficient experience or training, and it showed in their performance. Salaries varied widely from department to department. It seemed to Martha that certain department heads were overly generous, whereas others were downright stingy. It was also obvious that morale was high in some units and low in others. A minority employee who felt he had unfairly been passed over for promotion had threatened to bring a discrimination suit. Some employees seemed to be learning quickly; others were getting very little personal attention or training. There seemed to be no rhyme or reason to the pattern for employee time off. (Martha had recently issued instructions that no one could have more than a half-day off with pay in any one month, for whatever reason, but she knew that policy was too arbitrary.) Some very capable employees seemed to have too many menial tasks, and occasionally one would resign before Martha could nudge the department head into broadening that employee's job. On the other hand, some key people appeared to be overworked and under a good deal of stress. A few supervisors would let very capable people transfer to more responsible jobs; others would try to transfer only those people they didn't want. Sometimes it seemed that people with potential were let go; other times it seemed as though supervisors were protecting people who really weren't contributing much to the success of the organization.

These and other problems, all related to the management of people, had convinced Martha that Metro Publications needed a specialist in this area. As she wrote "human resources director" on the agenda, her thoughts ran along these lines: "I wonder how department heads will react to our bringing in a personnel director? I wonder what the person's exact responsibilities should be? Clearly, all of the department heads and supervisors have 'people' responsibilities. How do we make sure that this person's responsibilities are distinct from those of the other managers? How will we know if things are getting any better if we do hire a human resources director? I wonder whether this person should report to me or to the operations manager. Well, it's time we started sorting this out." ◄

CASE 1.2   More than Pizza

Perroni's, a small Italian restaurant near the university, was doing very well. The tables were typically full at both lunch and dinner, and there was usually a line of people waiting to get in on weekend evenings. Perroni's was popular with the college students and faculty members but drew customers from the broader community as well. Most people raved about the food, especially the pizza. But it seemed to Professor Jill Anderson that there must be other things going on behind the scenes, along with the good cooking, that contributed to the restaurant's success. She had some hunches, because her son Don, a sophomore at the university, worked at Perroni's as a busboy, or "busperson," as he put it. He appeared to like his job and the other employees. The hours he worked seemed to be ideal and the tips were good, although not as high as the waiters received. Jill teased him from time to time about being "the world's most overqualified busperson."

One evening, just before closing time, Jill came into Perroni's for some dessert. Don and two other employees, Manuel and Kim, joined her for a cup of tea. "What makes this such a good restaurant?" Jill asked. "I'm sure there's more to it than great pizza."

Manuel answered first. "It's the people that work here. Everyone's on the ball and we know we have to work together to make this place run right. We help each other out, too. We all work together to make the salads if the kitchen people are jammed up. We spend a lot of time training new people so that everyone's working procedures are consistent. We even work it out among ourselves what days and hours each of us will work during the upcoming week."

Don added, "That's all a big part of it, but there's more. The food-service help and the chefs really get along. Everyone agrees that pleasing the customer is the most important thing. Our chefs are the best around, but if a customer complains, we'll take the food right back to the kitchen. The chefs never get upset — they just get busy and do it over right. Happy customers mean bigger tips, and all the waiters give an equal share of their tips to the buspeople and the chefs. All of us make pretty good money here."

"Don't forget that the owner of this place is also a great boss," said Kim. "He pretty much leaves us alone during the shift, but he gets us together every now and then for a free dinner and asks us how the place might be run better. Once we figured out that the restaurant was losing money on several entrees, so we got him to raise the prices on those items, and no one complained. We saved his shirt! He even lets us take care of most of the hiring — we bring in friends we think will work well here. The boss really respects our judgment and no one seems to take advantage of that."

Jill thanked Don and his coworkers for their comments. "Very enlightening," she said. Their remarks confirmed some of her hunches about why the restaurant was doing so well, although she realized she needed to talk with more people, including the owner and the chefs, to get the whole picture. "Some of this informality, such as their hiring practices, might not work in a large organization," she thought. "On the other hand, some of it is super. One thing is clear — these people like each other. At least the ones I've seen and talked to act as if they do." ◀

T he issues Martha Burke faces at Metro Publications are basic concerns of all business and service organizations. From the smallest to the largest enterprise, fundamental activities pertaining to all the employees, or **human resources,** of an organization must be managed — and managed effectively. If these human resources are neglected or mismanaged, the organization is unlikely to do well and, in fact, may fail.

From a positive standpoint, it is people—human resources — that create organizations and make them survive and prosper. It is their efforts, talents, and skills in using other resources, such as knowledge, materials, and energy, that result in the creation of useful products and services.

In Case 1.2, it is clear that the employees were a critical factor in making Perroni's restaurant successful. In fact, the restaurant workers were Perroni's greatest resource. Management probably appreciated this, although we aren't given enough detail to know much about the role management played in this situation. If the owner doesn't know exactly why Perroni's is so successful, however, the restaurant could easily drift into practices that would cause it to fail. For Perroni's to be successful in the long run, the owner must continue to pay careful attention to the management of its human resources. Further, the owner must be skillful in integrating human resources with other important resources, including finances and technology — in this case, the technology involved in creating first-class manicotti and pizza.

What Is Human Resources Management?

Both opening cases deal with issues that pertain to human resources management. In Case 1.1, Martha Burke was aware all along that many "people activities" required attention in the day-to-day operations of Metro Publications: attracting talented people to the organization; choosing the most qualified candidates from among the applicants; orienting and training new employees; retraining experienced employees; motivating all employees and evaluating their performance; rewarding and compensating everyone on the staff; and sometimes disciplining, discharging, transferring, or promoting someone. These are all aspects of human resources management.

Martha also realized eventually that more thought and planning were needed for these activities. The lack of a clearly formulated management philosophy and the absence of carefully planned human resources policies and procedures were causing her considerable concern. These deficiencies were also costly to Metro Publications in efficiency and overall performance.

In Case 1.2, a number of human resources activities were going well at Perroni's, either by accident or by design. Capable people were being recruited and trained; standards of performance and expectations about people helping each other were high; work scheduling seemed to be satisfactory to everyone; the compensation system seemed to be working well; and management was listening and responding to employee suggestions. These are all key concerns of human resources management.

Human resources management is the term increasingly used to refer to the philosophy, policies, procedures, and practices related to the management of people

---

*The term *human resource management* (singular) is also used frequently. In this book, the plural *human resources management* is used because the employees of an enterprise are all different, each is unique, and we do not wish to imply uniformity and sameness. The terms *personnel and industrial relations*, *personnel and labor relations*, and *employee relations* are also frequently synonymous with *personnel management* or *human resource(s) management*.

within an organization. The term *personnel management* — or perhaps *modern personnel management* — means the same thing.* From time to time in this book, the term *human resources management* will be shortened to *HRM*. The top person will sometimes be referred to as the *HR director* or *HR executive*. The department will frequently be referred to as the HR department. (See *International Perspective* about Bell Helicopter on page 7.)

Changing Perspectives

Although *human resources management* is used within this book, and although terms like *human resources department*, *director of human resources*, and *vice president, human resources* are being used more and more, the more traditional terms are still widely used. For example, in thousands of contemporary organizations, the terms *personnel department*, *personnel director*, *vice president, personnel*, or *senior vice president, personnel* are extensively used and respected.

Changes in terminology reflect the increased significance associated with the management of people in organizations as well as the broader perspective from which the field is currently viewed. In the past, personnel management had a strong functional focus; that is, personnel specialists were primarily concerned with the administration of specific employee-related functions such as hiring, training, wage setting, and disciplinary action. A more modern view is that all personnel functions are interrelated; that is, each function affects the others. Moreover, how well these functions are managed has a tremendous effect on an organization's ability to meet its overall objectives. As these ideas have become more and more accepted, especially within the last twenty or thirty years, the view of "people management" has changed accordingly. It is now generally accepted that human resources management encompasses a dynamic, organization-wide perspective that is action-oriented and based on theory and research from many disciplines, and is necessarily interrelated with strategic planning. The terminology has gradually come to reflect these changes. But the terminology is not as important as what philosophy and policies are being put into operation and what practices are being established.

A broad-based view of human resources management has great practical value. With such a perspective, it is possible to understand the interrelationship of all human resources management activities and to appreciate how they contribute to the overall success of an organization. Within the organization, such an awareness increases the effectiveness with which human resources are used to achieve desired outcomes — outcomes that benefit employees and the organizations in which they work.

A Process-Systems View

A useful way to describe human resources management as it is practiced today is in *process-systems* terminology. The significance of the process-systems view is that it (1) takes into account the interdependence of all aspects of human resources management and (2) recognizes the relationship between human resources activities and organizational goals.

A **process** is an identifiable flow of interrelated events moving toward some goal, consequence, or end. An example in human resources management is the staffing process, a flow of events that results in the continuous filling of positions within the organization. These events will normally include such activities as recruiting applicants, making hiring decisions, and managing career transitions such as transfers and promotions.

Human resources management refers to the philosophy, policies, and practices related to the management of people within an organization. The partners at Kingston Technology believe their employees are the company's most important asset, thereby creating an environment where people care about the welfare of the company.

A **system,** on the other hand, is a particular set of procedures or devices designed to control a process in a predictable way. The staffing system of a given organization, for example, might include such devices and procedures as application blanks, interviews, reference checks, a six-month probationary period, a procedure for posting job openings within the organization, and procedures for applying for transfer. Thus, the term *process* refers to a combination of events that leads to some end result, and the term *system* identifies specific procedures and devices used to control those events.

According to the process-systems view, *human resources management is the systematic planning, development, and control of a network of interrelated processes affecting and involving all members of an organization.* These processes include

- Human resources planning
- Job and work design
- Staffing
- Training and development
- Performance appraisal and review
- Compensation and reward
- Employee protection and representation
- Organization improvement

To effectively manage these processes, human resources systems are planned, developed, and implemented through the combined efforts of all managers and human resources specialists — and frequently all employees — in an organization. Overall, the systems are intended to achieve organization-wide goals and contribute to organizational effectiveness and productivity.

International Perspective

HR Propels the Launch of a New Production Site

Staffing and training programs help Bell Helicopter move commercial operations to Canada

In 1984, Bell Helicopter Textron built a new production facility in Mirabel, Canada in anticipation of expected changes in international helicopter production regulations, such as having two engines when flying over cities or water. Those regulations never materialized. Bell Helicopter was faced with holding the keys to a new building and having to decide what to do with it.

Management decided to move production of all five models of commercial aircraft to the Canadian facility and leave the production of military aircraft in Texas, at the division's international headquarters. This decision put Bell Helicopter into a new international posture as a division. It also brought with it the problem of recruiting and training qualified personnel during a shortage of aircraft assemblers. The move from Texas to the Mirabel facility occurred in 1991. Initially, skilled technicians were hired in Canada to start production in the facility, but many left the company because of lack of challenge.

Bell Helicopter's HR team was faced with meeting four objectives: 1) quickly increasing personnel levels to meet the production plan and sales-forecasting requirements; 2) training the work force in aircraft assembly techniques; 3) reducing the production personnel turnover rate; and 4) strengthening the nontraditional organizational design on the shop floor.

Rather than scout for a new group of skilled workers, the HR department came up with a new plan — to identify and recruit recent high school students who met the following criteria: high math scores; employment experience in the manual trades; a sound understanding of written English and the ability to work in a team environment with the company's TQM philosophy. The

HR department, headed up by Charles Larocque, manager of HR at the Mirabel facility, recruited 240 high school graduates between January 1, 1989 and December 31, 1991. The recruits either had been unemployed or had unstable jobs. Fifteen percent were women. Ninety percent of the trainees lived within 15 miles of the facility.

The recruits entered one of two three-month programs in structural aircraft assembly or in electrical aircraft assembly. Bell Helicopter worked with local agencies and a school to develop, gather financing and hold training classes for trainees. After successfully completing the training period, 228, or 95% of the trainees were hired and integrated into the company's semiautonomous production teams.

It would have been easier for Bell Helicopter to hire skilled personnel at the outset, but it would have been more costly. Bell Helicopter hired the trainees at an average starting salary of $20,000, but the starting salary for most college graduates between 1989 and 1991 was $30,000. By the end of 1991, the number of employees had increased 83%, turnover had decreased 78%, productivity had risen 181% and sales had improved 280%. The training program provided a return on investment of $2.5 million within three years. The company's market share didn't increase, but the program did keep it from losing ground. Larocque says that to keep up with international competitors in France and Germany, and hold on to its one-third share of the market the company must invest heavily in training.

Source: Jennifer J. Laabs, "HR Propels the Launch of a New Production Site," *Personnel Journal*, January 1993. Reprinted by permission.

Key Processes and Systems

The fundamental processes in human resources management are shown in Figure 1.1, which follows the organization of this book in clockwise sequence. All the processes are linked in the diagram to depict the idea that they interact and are interdependent. What happens in one process tends to influence events in one or more of the others. For example, offering an unusually high salary in recruiting and hiring efforts (part of the staffing process) may cause serious problems in the management of the compensation and reward process. People already on the payroll may complain bitterly about what they are paid and press for a readjustment.

The quality of the design and management of the systems used to control and direct human resources processes is directly related to an organization's overall effectiveness. In some organizations, the human resources systems may be very primitive or haphazardly designed. In others, the systems used in human resources management can be so cumbersome that the organization is strangled by its own bureaucracy. Assume, for example, that you are a supervisor, you have a budgeted position for a typist, and you desperately need help; but you are required to write and rewrite a job description three times before your personnel requisition will be accepted for processing. Then you must wait until the job is advertised within your company for one month, and only after that can you accept outside applications. In this situation, you are certainly going to feel that something is wrong with the system. Systems in human resources management must be designed to further, not impede, the attainment of organizational goals.

A brief description of the fundamental processes in human resources management will help familiarize you with the scope and challenges of this field. The various chapters of the book will describe these processes in more detail and, in particular, will focus on systems that are used in their management.

Human Resources Planning

Human resources planning is the process of assessing the organization's human resources needs in light of organizational goals and making plans to ensure that a competent, stable work force is employed. The planning process includes an analysis of skill levels among employees and in the external labor market, of current and expected job openings, of plans for expanding or reducing staff throughout the organization, and of the external legal environment. The planning process, then, is closely related to the staffing process and depends also on the overall strategic plans of the organization.

The systems designed to control and direct the human resources planning process include such devices as computerized records of employees' skills and qualifications; forecasts of the numbers of employees with certain skills who are likely to leave over the next year; analysis of the extent to which affirmative action goals have been met; and confidential organization charts showing possible candidates for promotion to various executive positions. Human resources planning is the subject of Chapter 6.

Job and Work Design

Job and work design specifies the tasks to be performed by individuals and groups within the organization, and establishes the rules, schedules, and working conditions under which people perform those tasks. Through careful design, or circumstance, or both, events converge to create jobs to which people are assigned and the condi-

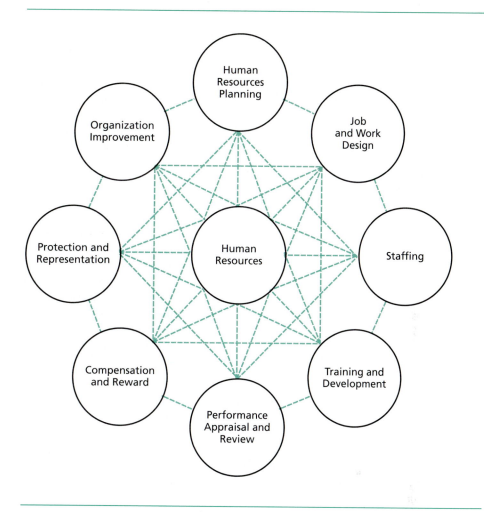

FIGURE 1.1   Major processes in human resources management

tions surrounding those jobs. Some of the systems used to help manage the process of job design include techniques such as time-and-motion study and work simplification, which aim to make jobs easy to learn and workers more efficient. Other job-design systems, such as job enrichment, involve techniques to restructure jobs to make them more interesting and challenging. Periodic discussions within a work team about the allocation of tasks can be considered a job-design system.

Job analysis, an outgrowth of job design, is the process of investigating the tasks and behaviors associated with a particular job. Various systems used in job analysis include observations of workers as they perform their jobs, interviews, and questionnaires. Typically the information obtained from job analysis is used to write job descriptions and to establish what is required of the person who will perform each job. In turn, job descriptions are useful in the staffing process, especially in recruiting, hiring, and training new employees. Job and work design and job analysis are discussed in Chapter 7.

Staffing

Staffing is the process that results in the continuous assignment of workers to all positions in the organization. This broad process includes the following activities: attracting qualified people to the organization; selecting from among candidates; bringing new people aboard and assigning and orienting them to their jobs; reassigning employees through transfer, promotion, or demotion; and ultimately managing employee separation through resignation, discharge, or retirement.

Some examples of systems used to manage the staffing process include school and college recruiting, advertising of job openings in newspapers and professional journals, skill tests, group interviews, and policies on transfers, promotions, and layoffs. This broad process and the systems frequently used in its management are discussed in Chapters 9 and 10.

Training and Development

The **training and development** process is a complex mixture of activities intended to improve the performance of individuals and groups within the organization. Some organizations, especially those that carry out complex and specialized operations and are confronted with rapid changes in technology, are heavily committed to training and development. Others view the process as a way to foster the career development of their employees at all levels. But almost all employees in any organization need some initial training, or orientation, when they start new jobs.

The systems that are used frequently in this process include skill development programs, coaching by a supervisor, general management courses, and training seminars. Training and development are covered in Chapters 11 and 12.

Performance Appraisal and Review

The **performance appraisal and review** process is the ongoing evaluation of individual and group contributions to the organization, and the communication of those evaluations to the persons involved. Such evaluations are made for a variety of purposes: to provide feedback about performance, to determine the need for training, to make decisions about pay increases, to select people for promotion, or to make judgments about the need for discipline.

The communication of appraisals (review) is part of this process, because how the appraisal is communicated will affect the extent to which it becomes a learning experience. Appraisals may be highly subjective or they may be highly systematic and based on carefully developed criteria and specific behavior. Some performance systems in current use are discussed in Chapter 13.

Compensation and Reward

The **compensation and reward** process is the flow of events that determines what wages, salaries, and incentives are paid and what supplemental benefits and nonfinancial rewards are provided. The presence or absence of rewards and recognition is important to employee morale and performance. Nonfinancial rewards, such as recognition and privileges, are particularly important in organizations staffed by unpaid volunteers. (One in every five Americans does some volunteer work.[1]) Some of the systems involved in the management of this process include job evaluation, plant-wide productivity plans, suggestion plans, and wage and benefit surveys. Compensation and other rewards are discussed in Chapters 14 through 16.

Protection and Representation

Most organizations have formal or informal ways to protect employees — to some extent, at least — from arbitrary and impulsive treatment and from physical danger and health hazards. In addition, individuals or groups may represent the interests of others, again either informally or in an organized, formal fashion. This broad process of **protection and representation** can be divided into three important subprocesses: the *accommodation process*, the *collective bargaining process* (found in unionized organizations), and the *health and safety management process.*

Accommodation

The *accommodation process* refers to the extent to which management listens and responds to — or accommodates — the needs, wants, and complaints (or grievances) of organization members. People working in organizations expect to be treated fairly; moreover, they feel they have the right to be heard and to be respected as individuals. Morale is severely affected when there is a sense of unfair treatment or when workers perceive that management does not care about their feelings, complaints, and suggestions. Systems for managing the accommodation process include questionnaires, suggestion boxes, an "open-door" philosophy, and formal grievance procedures. The effectiveness with which the accommodation process is managed varies within organizations and depends on a number of factors, such as prevailing leadership style and management philosophy. This topic is addressed throughout Part 2 and again in Chapter 19.

Collective Bargaining

The *collective bargaining process* refers to those events that establish a formal agreement between workers and management regarding such matters as wages and employee benefits, hours, working conditions, and grievance procedures. The process includes both the negotiation and the administration of the labor-management contract. The collective bargaining process and the systems used to manage labor-management relations are discussed in Chapters 17 and 18.

Health and Safety Management

The *health and safety management process* attempts to protect organization members from illness and physical dangers in the workplace. The process also includes the protection of the surrounding community from pollution and toxic substances. For many organizations, protecting the health and safety of human resources is a prime social responsibility that is reinforced by the increased awareness among workers and the general public of health and safety issues. Systems used in health and safety management are numerous and varied. Some examples are safety guards on machines, meetings with employees about safety, the availability of first-aid stations or dispensaries, the use of special equipment by technicians to monitor air purity, and stress-management programs. Health and safety management is discussed in Chapter 20.

Organization Improvement

The **organization improvement** process is the flow of events that determines the strategies by which organizations attempt to improve their effectiveness, increase employee satisfaction, or otherwise enhance the organizational environment. Such strategies vary in kind and effectiveness, as do the specific systems for managing this process. In general, the goal of these strategies and systems is to increase the level of cooperation, teamwork, and performance throughout the organization. The focus may be on organizational outcomes, such as product or service quality, or on the quality of the working life in the organization, or on both. The organization improvement process is discussed in Chapter 21, which will emphasize participative approaches and look at some of the conditions necessary for their success.

Who Manages Human Resources?

Every manager in the typical organization has major responsibilities in all of the processes normally included under human resources management as they relate to all employees under his or her authority. For example, in the area of staffing, the manager usually interviews the few "best" or "finalist" candidates referred by the human resources department and makes the final selection. In the area of appraisal, the manager conducts, at intervals, formal appraisals of each subordinate — using procedures developed by the human resources department in cooperation with top managers and monitored by that department. In the area of compensation, the manager makes final decisions about pay increases; these decisions must be in line with the formal plan establishing rules of progression (again, with rule compliance monitored by the human resources department) and with budgetary allocations approved by top management.

Nonsupervisory employees may also contribute to the management of the various human resources processes. For example, engineers in the design department of an aircraft manufacturing company might interview college graduates who are candidates for entry-level engineering jobs. Production workers who are members of self-managed work teams might participate in the selection and training of new team members. Shop stewards (officers of a union who are also employees of the company) are likely to be involved in processing grievances and in grievance hearings. All employees may be involved in making suggestions about the organization of tasks and the flow of work.

Top executives, including the HR executive, have a dominant role in establishing ethical standards for managing human resources, as well as for all organizational activities. In turn, managers and employees at all levels have important roles in influencing and upholding ethical standards. (See *Contemporary Issues* on page 13.)

Structure of the Human Resources Department

In organizations large enough to have a human resources or personnel department, the personnel director and his or her staff will play a key role in the design and monitoring of human resources systems. (Even in very small organizations, some person or persons — perhaps the president or owner or that person's assistant — will coordinate human resources activities for the entire enterprise.) Regardless of organization size, the fundamental human resources processes must be managed. Larger organizations are more likely to employ persons with specialized expertise to help design and implement human resources systems. A full-time specialist tends to emerge when organizations have about one hundred employees.

Figure 1.2 compares the typical human resources department in a small company employing approximately three hundred persons with the structure of that department in a corporation of several thousand employees. Responsibilities assigned to various human resources positions may be quite different in large and small companies. Table 1.1 lists activities that would most likely be allocated to the human resources department in a small company and in a large corporation. The activities are comparable, but in the smaller organization each personnel staff member is likely to have a wider variety of responsibilities. In larger corporations, more **specialization,** or expertise in a particular area, is permitted in each personnel job.

Contemporary Issues

Ethics: "Do Good, Do Well"

Here's what the record shows: It is nearly impossible to find an example of a company that got into financial trouble *because* it behaved ethically or in a socially responsible manner. Granted, some companies have failed in attempts to market what they believed were socially useful goods — but, then, many other companies have failed to find markets for trivial gadgets with no redeeming social value. Similarly, companies that have been totally indifferent to the social consequences of their actions have succeeded in accumulating great fortunes, and others that have been equally as insensitive to social questions have failed spectacularly.

So what is one to make of this "contradictory data"? Certainly, the lesson to be drawn from the BET nominees is not that virtue will lead to success, but rather that it is not the inevitable road to ruin that Seligmanites have claimed. Thanks to the Business Enterprise Trust, there are now numerous examples which illustrate that the choice of whether or not to do good is a moral, and not an economic, decision. One may either succeed or fail taking the high road, as one may either succeed or fail taking the low road. Given this reassuring knowledge that socially responsible behavior is on a different dimension from financial success, one might expect more business people to take the high road. For is it not the case that managers would much prefer the peace-of-mind of doing what they feel is morally right, as opposed to being compelled to do what is expedient?

Source: James O'Toole, "Do Good, Do Well: The Business Enterprise Trust Awards." Copyright 1991 by the Regents of the University of California. Reprinted from the *California Management Review*, Vol. 33, Spring 1991. By permission of the Regents.

Relationship with Other Departments

What organizational charts do not show is that human resources managers usually *share responsibility for personnel activities with other managers.* For example, human resources departments typically do not make the final hiring decisions for accounting or manufacturing departments. Rather, controllers or manufacturing directors, respectively, have the final say. But human resources departments typically do have major responsibility for designing and overseeing major components of the hiring system, including initial screening and referral.

Similarly, human resources departments are likely to do much of the human resources planning, most of the advertising and recruiting, and much of the interviewing. But these activities are usually performed in cooperation with other managers throughout the organization. The human resources staff typically does not have final decision-making authority over pay increases but is active in designing pay systems, administering those systems, and monitoring decisions made about pay to ensure that those decisions are based on uniform guidelines and are in agreement with the overall compensation plan. In short, human resources departments are typically responsible for the effective management of the various personnel systems, and their activities are usually conducted in cooperation with the management group. Most of the key human resources policy decisions are made jointly by the human resources director and other top managers.

This sharing of decision making — particularly where the various managers make decisions relating to one phase of a system and the human resources director

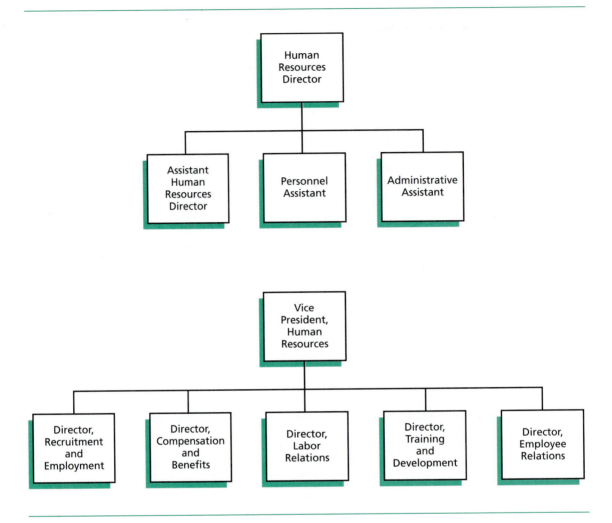

FIGURE 1.2 Structure of the human resources department in a small company (top) and in a large corporation (bottom)

makes decisions relating to another — can strain relationships. For example, to enforce agreed-upon policy, the personnel director might inform a department head that a subordinate's pay may not be increased beyond the top of the range unless there has been an appropriate increase in responsibilities. The department head may not like this restriction. Also, a personnel director might become too zealous in monitoring policy and be perceived as setting policies that do not have broad managerial support.

If there has been broad management participation in establishing human resources policies, these kinds of tensions are not likely to be very serious or very lasting. Nevertheless, because some managers may not appreciate the organization-wide implications of human resources decisions, the human resources director may need to conduct an ongoing effort to educate other managers about the unique role of the department.

TABLE 1.1 Responsibilities of the human resources department in a small company and a large corporation

SMALL COMPANY		LARGE CORPORATION	
Position	**Responsibilities**	**Position**	**Responsibilities**
Human Resources Director	Human resources planning Managerial/professional compensation Recruiting Labor relations Grievances	*Vice President Human Resources*	Executive committee Organization planning Human resources planning Policy Organization development
Assistant Human Resources Director	Wage and salary administration Recruiting Interviewing Orientation Training Reassignments Terminations Safety and health Special programs	*Director, Recruitment and Employment*	Recruiting Interviewing Testing Placement Terminations
Personnel Assistant	Testing Interviewing Job descriptions Job evaluation Training Employee benefits Employee services Suggestion plan	*Director, Compensation and Benefits*	Job analyses and evaluation Surveys Performance appraisal Compensation administration Bonus, profit-sharing plans Employee benefits
Administrative Assistant	Secretary to staff Word processing Records Interviewing	*Director, Labor Relations*	Negotiations Contract administration Grievance procedure Arbitration Health and safety Medical plans Cafeteria
		Director, Training and Development	Orientation Training Management development Career planning and development Quality circles Exit interviews
		Director, Employee Relations	EEO relations Contract compliance Staff assistance programs Employee counseling Outplacement

Rising Prominence of Human Resources Directors

The vital nature of human resources management and its overall impact in modern organizations are increasing the influence of human resources directors within those organizations. As will be seen in the next two chapters, both historical and environmental forces have created an urgent need for high-quality human resources management in contemporary organizations.

The typical reporting relationship between the human resources director and other members of top management, shown in Figure 1.3, indicates the responsibility and competence required of the human resources director today. Although the director may report to a vice president or executive vice president, a clear trend in the last two decades has been for a higher and higher percentage of human resources or personnel directors to report to the chief executive officer (CEO). Two-thirds to three-fourths of human resources or personnel directors now report to the CEO.[2] They are usually called *directors* or *vice presidents; vice president* is the most frequently used title in firms of more than 2,500 employees. In very large organizations, the personnel or human resources executive is frequently a *senior vice president*, for example at Motorola and United Air Lines.[3]

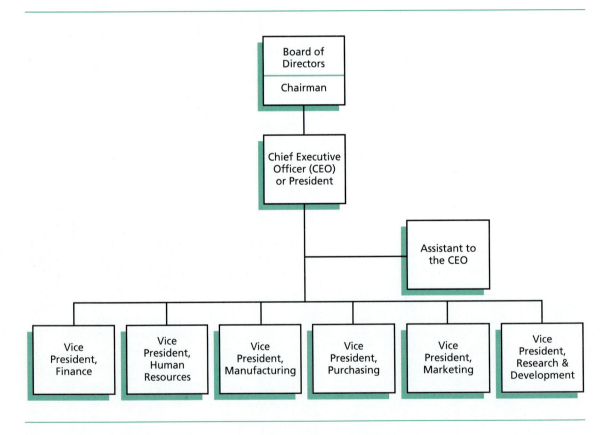

FIGURE 1.3 Reporting relationship of the human resources director to top management in a large manufacturing firm

*Strategic
Planning
and Human
Resources*

In most organizations, decisions about overall strategic planning and organizational change are the responsibility of the chief executive and immediate subordinates. These decisions have a direct impact on the way human resources will be used in achieving company goals. Using the expertise of human resources specialists throughout the planning process, therefore, can help minimize undesirable aspects of organizational change and maximize the achievement of organizational goals. For example, human resources executives have been heavily involved in overall strategic planning in such companies as Shell Oil Company, IBM, Amoco, AT&T, Chrysler Corp., United Technologies Corporation, Dow Chemical, and Marriott Corporation.[4]

Summary

People — human resources — create organizations and make them survive and prosper. If human resources are neglected or mismanaged, the organization is unlikely to do well.

Human resources management is a broad concept referring to the philosophy, policies, procedures, and practices used in managing people throughout the organization. Another definition: *human resources management is the systematic planning and control of a network of fundamental organizational processes affecting and involving all organization members. These processes include human resources planning, job and work design, job analysis, staffing, training and development, performance appraisal and review, compensation and reward, employee protection and representation, and organization improvement.* To further control and refine these processes, systems are continuously planned, developed, and implemented by management, frequently with the help of nonmanagement employees.

All managers are heavily involved in human resources management. In small organizations, a central figure, such as the owner or president, coordinates the organization-wide aspects of human resources management. In organizations large enough to have human resources (personnel) departments, that department plays a major role in the planning, development, and implementation of personnel systems.

Typically, key policy decisions in human resources management are made jointly by the human resources director and other top managers. Further, the human resources department typically makes decisions at various steps in personnel procedures (such as initial screening and referral), whereas other managers make decisions at other steps in those procedures (such as making a final selection from among several qualified candidates). Although this joint decision making can lead to strains in relationships, broad management participation in the development of human resources policies will tend to minimize these tensions.

The organization-wide impact of human resources management, coupled with the vital nature of the organizational processes involved, gives the human resources director a great deal of influence in today's organizations. A clear trend in the last twenty years has been for a higher and higher proportion of human resources executives (now two-thirds to three-fourths) to report to the chief executive officers of organizations and to hold the title of vice president. By and large, human resources directors in leading organizations are heavily involved in corporate strategic planning.

Ethical Dilemma

NOTE: The Ethical Dilemma in each chapter is drawn from real life, but the names and other facts have been changed. No reference to any specific company or individual is intended or should be inferred.

The chief financial officer (CFO) of rapidly growing SportsGear Factory wants to expand her control and influence in the corporation. She recognizes that executive compensation at SportsGear is highly correlated with the number of one's subordinates. Besides, she is more than annoyed that two of her fellow executives are hiring relatives and promoting them over equally qualified employees, and she wants to gain veto power over such hiring. She also wants more say in promotions throughout the company. SportsGear is now large enough to pull together the diverse human resources activities and to hire an HR director.

In meetings with the CEO and the board of directors about the structure of the organization, the CFO recommends that the new HR director and HR department report to her. Not divulging all her reasons, she makes the recommendation on the grounds that "so much money is at stake in these people matters."

What are the ethical issues involved, if any? (See Chapter 4 for a definition of ethics.) What are the pros and cons of the organizational arrangement that the CFO is recommending?

Key Terms

human resources	staffing
human resources management	training and development
process	performance appraisal and review
system	compensation and reward
human resources planning	protection and representation
job and work design	organization improvement
job analysis	specialization

Review Questions

1. Define *human resources management*, using process-systems terminology. How does this concept differ from the meanings sometimes associated with the more traditional term *personnel management*?
2. Identify and briefly describe the basic processes in human resources management.
3. In general terms, describe the respective roles in human resources management carried out by (a) the human resources department and (b) other managers.
4. Why is human resources management considered a vital aspect of the total management process?

Opening Case Questions

Case 1.1   Martha Burke

1. What were the problems facing Metro Publications that caused Martha Burke to consider hiring a human resources director?

2. What steps will Martha need to take to ensure a smooth transition after hiring a human resources director?

Case 1.2   More than Pizza

1. What are Don and his coworkers really saying about the success of Perroni's?
2. What are the advantages and disadvantages of the lack of a hiring system at Perroni's?

Comprehensive Case

HR in Growing Companies

There are days when I wish we had 35 employees again," says Janine Nierenberger, director of personnel for Spartan Motors, remembering a simpler time more than 10 years ago. Today the plant bustles with nearly 400 workers, and Nierenberger has little time to reminisce.

In a time of record business failures, a time in which *downsizing, rightsizing, retrenching* and other euphemisms have crept comfortably into our vocabulary, some companies are running in high gear. This growth is great news for CEOs and shareholders. HR executives, meanwhile, are taking deep breaths. They're up to their chins in applicant tracking, hiring, training, revamping benefits, and squeezing everything they can out of information systems. No one is really complaining; growth is exciting.

Still, it's a challenge for Spartan and companies like it. The Charlotte, Michigan-based manufacturer of chassis for fire trucks and motor homes is, in many ways, typical of the nation's growing companies. They're usually small enough and aggressive enough to move quickly with the market.

The little economic recovery the country has seen has been in smaller, growing organizations. "The *Fortune* 500 companies have lost a tremendous number of jobs during the last decade," says James Spoor, president of the Council of Growing Companies. "At the same time, the growth of our economy has come essentially from entrepreneurial companies that have fewer than 200 employees." In fact, Spoor notes, by the end of the decade, 85% of the U.S. work force will be working for companies with fewer than 200 employees.

Because these companies are so small and so numerous, they're hard to profile, explains Stanley Duobinis, senior vice president of the WEFA Group, an economic forecasting firm in Bala Cynwyd, Pennsylvania. Sometimes these firms are characterized by a few people who have a great idea, according to Duobinis. They develop the idea and market it, then find they can barely keep up with demand. "Once the product is accepted and all the hurdles are overcome, they can experience a huge expansion," he says.

More often, however, the growth is gradual — particularly for service firms that grow one contract at a time. Such companies may carve out a niche that the larger, national firms can't serve as well.

Because of the entrepreneurial nature of start-up companies, HR professionals are seldom involved from the beginning. When the company is run by a handful of people, that isn't a problem; as the company expands from a handful of employees to 40 or 50, and then to 200, however, chaos can reign without the exercise of human resources expertise.

"When I was hired in 1988, there really hadn't been anybody in HR," says Richard Shinton, HR manager of Exabyte Corp., a manufacturer of computer components and last year's third-fastest-growing public company, according to *Fortune*. "A secretary did most of the work, kept the records, and so forth. My first crisis was the day the vice president of engineering walked in and handed me 14 requisitions for engineers — and he wanted them tomorrow. Here in the Rocky Mountains, the kind of people we need can be hard to find."

In fact, some of these fast-growth companies are so innovative that there are no experts in their fields. They're forced to recruit from related industries to find the talent they need. Finding the necessary technical skill, however, is only half the challenge. Cooperation, flexibility and a work ethic are crucial to a small, fast-moving company.

"The HR executive has to identify people who are inherently positive, people who are team-oriented," says Spoor. Operating style, attitude and mental acuity mean more than the traditional kinds of hiring criteria. "Many growth companies look for the maverick, the person who isn't restrained by traditional views and approaches," he says. "In other words, they want someone willing to rethink the solutions to long-standing problems."

Staffing becomes increasingly complicated. A growing company doesn't stay small for long. Success breeds growth . . . and competition. "When you're a young, small organization, you need all-purpose people who have lots of practical skills," explains Marilynn Williamson, vice president of Drake Beam Morin, Inc. (DBM), a management consulting firm that specializes in companies in transition. "Very quickly, however, it becomes competitive. Then you need an entirely different type of person — somebody who's marketing-oriented and more aggressive — and who has more business background."

As important as business know-how, technical know-how, ingenuity, and a team-player attitude can be, the attribute that fast-growing companies consider most in hiring may be the ability to cope with change and ambiguity. At high-growth companies, jobs evolve and stretch as companies grow, and employees must be willing to change with them. Vice president of personnel of Babbage's, an entertainment-software chain found in shopping malls, Mike Ivanich says, "When you grow, everything changes — products, procedures, duties."

"Change is the way of life. Half or more of the products we sell in the stores today didn't even exist three years ago. You must hire people who are flexible," he explains.

Source: Excerpted from Rob Brookler, "HR in Growing Companies," *Personnel Journal*, 71, (November 1992). Reprinted by permission.

Discussion Questions

1. What are some of the crucial HR challenges facing a small but rapidly growing company?
2. What are some of the characteristics HR professionals look for in recruiting new employees for a small, growing company?

CHAPTER 2

A History of Human Resources Management

LEARNING OBJECTIVES

- Identify the major movements affecting the development of human resources management.
- Cite key legislation affecting labor-management relations.
- Identify the personnel specialists who were the forerunners of the modern human resources department.
- In general terms, describe the contributions of systems theory, sociotechnical systems design, and the behavioral sciences to contemporary human resources management.
- In general terms, describe how globalization has contributed to the development of human resources practices.

CASE 2.1	# Factory Work, 1815

In the manufacturing districts it is common for parents to send their children of both sexes at seven or eight years of age, in winter as well as summer, at six o'clock in the morning, sometimes of course in the dark, and occasionally amidst frost and snow, to enter the manufactories, which are often heated to a high temperature, and contain an atmosphere far from being the most favorable to human life, and in which all those employed in them very frequently continue until twelve o'clock at noon, when an hour is allowed for dinner, after which they return to remain, in a majority of cases, till eight o'clock at night.

The children now find they must labour incessantly for their bare subsistence; they have not been used to innocent, healthy, and rational amusements; they are not permitted the requisite time, if they had been previously accustomed to enjoy them. They know not what relaxation means, except by the actual cessation from labour. ◄

Source: Reprinted from Robert Owen, *Observations on the Effect of the Manufacturing System*, published in England *circa* 1815, p. 258.

CASE 2.2	# More Than a Technological System, More Than a Social System

Jack Stone, top candidate for the vacant position of director of personnel and industrial relations at HiPowr Diesels, was in a quandary. On the one hand, he was quite certain that he was going to be offered the job, the job paid well, and was a step up from his present position as assistant director of human resources at an electronics firm. Certainly, the job would be challenging, to say the least.

On the other hand, to Jack, HiPowr Diesels seemed like a throwback to the age of the dinosaurs. It wasn't entirely that people in the factory and offices seemed less than enthusiastic about their jobs — the new president of HiPowr had said as much in his interviews with Jack — the technology and layout of the plants and offices just seemed oppressive. For example, one of the first things that Jack had noticed in his several visits to the head office and plant was the frequent use of typewriters. Further, he saw a few instances of managers dictating to secretaries. "Haven't these people discovered word processors and, at least, dictating machines?" he said to himself.

His tour of the plant was a real downer. In the first place, the plant was shabbier and dirtier than Jack thought it ought to be. Secondly, people didn't seem to be excited about their jobs. The only really excited person was the company industrial engineer, who proudly described the new conveyer-belt and platform systems. The conveyer-belt system was a wonder of overhead belts and chains and cogs and hooks and continuously moving parts for diesel engines. It moved faster than the moving platforms on which the engines were being assembled. All the worker needed to do, if there was a need for a high-pressure copper fuel line, for example, was to reach overhead and pull one off a hook. "But," as a worker told Jack during a break in his plant tour, "the right parts are never overhead when you want them. You have to store up a supply of parts on the platform — which is too crowded already — or you'll get way behind and not make your quota. I wish they'd consulted with us before they installed this blankety-blank conveyer belt, let alone these platforms. The management is a group of idiots. It's a good thing most of us want to turn out high quality engines. But we could make even better ones."

Jack was to have at least one more interview before he and the president were to have a final interview. The more Jack thought about it, the more convinced he was that he didn't want the job unless the president and the rest of top management were willing to work with him on quite a number of things. Foremost in his mind was getting top management to sit down with employees to see how productivity and quality might be improved. In the offices, it was as though management wasn't paying enough attention to either improving technology or to the people. In the plant, in the case of the conveyer belt, maybe there was too much attention to technology — but it was one person's technology. He hadn't totally formulated the situation in his mind, but as he said to himself, "They're not developing and integrating a dynamic technological and social system. (But if I use words like that with the president, I wonder if he'll know what I'm talking about.) One thing I'm sure of, I'm not going to come in here and perpetuate the age of the dinosaurs. If top management wants me to team up with them to really change this place, I think I'll take the job — if they offer it to me. But maybe it's a different job than what we've talked about so far." ◀

The Industrial Revolution, which began in the mid-eighteenth century in England, was characterized by the development of machinery, the linking of power to machines, and the establishment of factories employing many workers. Extensive specialization of labor — that is, individual workers performing very narrow tasks, such as replacing bobbins on a sewing machine — was a key feature of the job design in these factories. Case 2.1 is a partial description of the terrible conditions under which children often worked during this era. In colonial New England, training in skilled craft work had been a possibility since the late 1600s, but this often meant that children as young as ten were being indentured for twelve or more years to a master in a particular trade. (See *Contemporary Issues* on page 25.)

In the early 1900s, children worked in factories for as many as twelve hours a day. Therefore, they were often exhausted with little time for schooling or play.

Contemporary Issues

Historical Perspective: Poor Children Indentured

In colonial New England, many youngsters less than 10 years old whose parents could not support them were indentured to masters who agreed to teach them a trade. This practice was legalized by the poor laws. The indenture quoted below, for example, required a youthful apprentice in 1676 to serve more than 12 years to learn masonry. As apprentices then were usually bound to masters until they were 21 years old, apprentice Nathan Knight apparently began his service when he was about $8\frac{1}{2}$ years. These were the conditions of his servitude:

> This Indenture witnesseth that I, Nathan Knight ... have put myself apprentice to Samuel Whidden, of Portsmouth, in the county of Portsmouth, mason, and bound after the manner of an apprentice with him, to serve and abide the full space and term of twelve years and five months ... during which time the said apprentice his said master faithfully shall serve.... He shall not ... contract matrimony within the said time. The goods of his said master, he shall not spend or lend. He shall not play cards, or dice, or any other unlawful game, whereby his said master may have damage in his own goods, or others, taverns, he shall not haunt, nor from his master's

business absent himself by day or by night, but in all things shall behave himself as a faithful apprentice ought to do. And the said master his said apprentice shall teach and instruct, or cause to be taught and instructed in the art and mystery as mason; finding unto his said apprentice during the said time meat, drink, washing, lodging, and apparel, fitting an apprentice, teaching him to read, and allowing him three months towards the latter end of his time to go to school to write, and also double apparel at end of said time ...

Even though this apprentice probably did not get a chance to go to school until he was about 20 years old, his master showed a sense of community and civic responsibility, for schooling of some sort — even though limited to reading and writing — was desperately needed in the Colonies. Although the school instruction for an apprentice at that time was inadequate, it may be considered another link with present-day apprenticeship, which provides technical classroom instruction to supplement on-the-job training.

Source: Excerpted from Bureau of Apprenticeship and Training, *Apprenticeship: Past and Present* (Washington, D.C.: U.S. Department of Labor, 1987), pp. 5–6.

But the consequence of grouping workers into shops and factories, and of the specialization of labor, was a gradual emergence of more systematic attention to the design of jobs, to the choice of workers for those jobs (selection), to the provision of pay and benefits (compensation), and to the welfare of employees both on and off the job. In the late 1800s, when unions were battling for recognition and violent strikes became a significant concern, these developments in management practices accelerated. By the early 1900s, as this chapter will demonstrate, many of the components of modern human resources management were falling into place.

The Scientific Management Movement

The **scientific management** movement of the late 1800s and early 1900s concentrated particularly on job design, selection, and compensation. The name most closely associated with this movement is Frederick W. Taylor. Working in the steel industry in the late 1870s, Taylor believed the same techniques used by scientists in the laboratory — experimentation, forming and testing hypotheses, and proposing theories based on research and testing – could be used by management to increase efficiency in the workplace.[1]

For Taylor, the science of management included systematic job design that began with observation, recording, and classification of job activities as they were typically carried out. Tasks could then be simplified and jobs made more efficient. Scientific selection involved choosing workers with the skills and capacities needed to carry out the now efficiently organized jobs. Scientific training and development meant training workers for particular tasks and was intended to replace the centuries-old practice of permitting workers to choose their own work methods and train themselves as best they could. By applying these principles, Taylor was able to raise the average worker's productivity at the Bethlehem Steel Corp. by over 300 percent.

Frank and Lillian Gilbreth were among the contemporaries of Taylor who extended his ideas. Frank Gilbreth analyzed workers' body movements by studying motion pictures of tasks being performed, and from these studies he formulated laws of efficient motion. This analytical approach to efficiency in industry, called **time-and-motion study,** was a forerunner of industrial engineering and the development of more effective automatic machinery.[2] Lillian Gilbreth is credited with one of the early books relating the principles of scientific management to psychology.[3] In general, the scientific management movement emphasized the importance of management planning down to the smallest details of factory operations. (The assembly-line techniques in Case 2.2 are an outgrowth of the scientific management movement's emphasis on efficiency.)

The Industrial Welfare Movement

In addition to directing attention to "scientific management" around the turn of the century, many firms were beginning to be involved in what has been called the **industrial welfare movement.** Industrial welfare work consisted of "voluntary efforts on the part of employers to improve, with the existing industrial system, the conditions of employment in their own factories."[4] Actually, the movement extended beyond the workplace to some aspects of the workers' lives off the job: "Management made available various facilities such as libraries and other recreational premises, offered financial assistance for education, home purchase and improvement, provided medical care and instituted hygienic measures."[5]

As an outgrowth of this movement, many business firms began to employ staff members called **social secretaries** or **welfare secretaries.** These people were employed to help with employee finances, housing, health, recreation, education, and other matters.[6]

Early Industrial Psychology

Applications of psychology to business and industry, or **industrial psychology,** began to emerge in the 1890s and early 1900s as psychologists studied selling techniques and ways of testing job candidates. The most notable industrial psychologist was Hugo Münsterberg, whose major contributions were (1) the analysis of jobs in terms of their physical, mental, and emotional requirements and (2) the development of testing devices for selecting workers. In his book *Psychology and Industrial Efficiency,* published in 1913, Münsterberg described his experiments for selecting streetcar operators at the Boston Elevated Railway Company. He wanted to test motormen candidates for their ability to discriminate between figures representing obstacles that were likely to move onto the streetcar track (people, horses, automobiles) and those that were likely to remain parallel to or off the track. The device he developed used a series of twelve cards that the subject moved by turning a crank. When the tests were completed, Münsterberg reported a strong correspondence between test performance and actual job performance.[7] Münsterberg also performed experiments in the telephone industry, successfully enough to claim that his tests helped to select better telephone operators.[8]

In addition to developing tests for measuring differences in attitude, industrial psychologists were developing the concept of statistical validity. Both Münsterberg and Edison D. Woods recognized the importance of comparing test scores with criteria for success to determine **predictive validity,** the extent to which a test accurately predicts job success or lack of it.[9] Before World War I, other personnel techniques were being developed, including reference checks, the use of rating sheets by interviewers, and comparison of applicants' ratings with ratings of successful workers.

The Human Relations Movement

What came to be called the **human relations movement** has been a major influence on modern human resources management. This movement is characterized by its focus on group behavior and workers' feelings as they relate to productivity and morale. Some of its beginnings were with a group of researchers in an industrial plant near Chicago.

The Hawthorne Studies

In 1924 researchers at the Western Electric Company's Hawthorne Plant near Chicago began some experiments to determine how lighting affected workers and their output. In one experiment, production increased when the lighting was improved, but in another it also increased when the lighting was severely reduced. After three years of experimentation with such "illogical" results, the researchers concluded that, in experiments involving people, it was impossible to change one variable (lighting) without affecting other variables such as worker interaction or worker-supervisor interaction. It became clear that it was human interaction that was affecting morale and motivation, which, in turn, were affecting production.[10]

Further inquiry and experimentation led researchers to conclude that productivity depended at least in part on the extent to which the employees became a team and cooperated wholeheartedly and spontaneously. Worker cooperation and enthusiasm seemed to be related to the interest in the work group shown by the supervisor and experimenters, the lack of coercion or force, and the extent to which workers participated in making decisions and changes that would affect them.[11] In short, the researchers came to view the industrial organization as a social system. Therefore, for several decades a great deal of research focused on group behavior and employee attitudes.

The Labor Movement

In a democratic society, it was probably inevitable that associations of wage earners, or **labor unions,** would arise to protect workers against some of the abuses of the Industrial Revolution and to improve their lot in life. Joint action by groups of workers began taking place as trade or labor unions spread from factory to factory and shop to shop. Eventually, labor unions won their greatest victory: the right to bargain collectively. **Collective bargaining** is the process in which union leaders, as representatives of workers, negotiate with employers over working conditions such as hours of work and compensation.

Even before the Industrial Revolution, collective **protests** and **strikes** — workers, as a group, refusing to work — were not unheard of. For example, in 1636 a group of fishermen in Maine protested against their wages being withheld.[12] In general, employers reacted to such collective action with outrage and attempts to thwart further organizing. In 1799 the Philadelphia Journeymen Cordwainers (shoemakers) attempted to bargain collectively with their employers, which resulted first in the employers locking their shops to keep out the workers — called a **lockout** — and then in a negotiated settlement between the union and the employers. Nevertheless, the union was taken to court, and in 1806 the Philadelphia Cordwainers were found guilty of "criminal conspiracy" to raise wages.

It was not until 1842 that the Massachusetts Supreme Court overturned the conspiracy doctrine. In *Commonwealth* v. *Hunt,* the court ruled that unions were not criminal per se and that labor organizations could have honorable as well as destructive objectives.[13]

The *Commonwealth* v. *Hunt* decision allowed unions to grow and prosper. One of the most important early unions was the Knights of Labor, formed as a national organization in 1869. From the beginning, this group emphasized the brotherhood of labor and sought to include all workers, both skilled and unskilled. Its early constitution included goals pertaining to workers' cooperatives, the eight-hour workday, the prohibition of child labor, and equal pay for women and men. **Boycotts** — refusing to buy from certain companies — were supported, but strikes were considered necessary only when other negotiating measures failed.

Partly as a result of widespread unemployment and wage cuts in the 1880s, the Knights of Labor became more and more involved in strike action. At first, most of the strikes were successful. Soon, however, the union grew too large to control its membership, unauthorized strikes involving sabotage occurred, and many business leaders used **strikebreakers** — nonunion workers who were willing to replace striking employees. By the 1890s the Knights of Labor were in decline.[14]

Meanwhile, the American Federation of Labor (AFL) had been organized in 1886 as an association of national craft unions. From the beginning, the AFL was pragmatic in seeking immediate improvements in wages and working conditions for the craft workers. Its officers were determined to avoid direct participation in politics and to reward its friends and punish its enemies regardless of political affiliation. These strategies served the union well, and it experienced slow but relatively steady growth, surviving the depressions of the 1890s and 1930s.[15]

By 1935, however, controversy had arisen within the AFL between leaders who favored craft unions and those who wanted to organize unskilled workers into industrial unions. This conflict resulted in the formation of the Committee for Industrial Organization. Originally the Committee intended to work within the AFL, but in 1937 the AFL expelled ten unions that were Committee affiliates. In 1938 the break was formalized when the Committee reorganized as the Congress of Industrial Organizations (CIO).

In 1955 power struggles and philosophical differences were put aside, and the CIO merged with the AFL to form the AFL-CIO. In addition to using collective bargaining to secure an improved standard of living for workers, the AFL-CIO increasingly turned to political action. Now an international organization, the AFL-CIO continues to lead the labor movement today. The current status of the labor movement is discussed in Chapter 17.

Violence in Labor Relations

Violence characterized many of the strikes of the second half of the nineteenth century. In the 1860s and 1870s the Molly Maguires, a secret society of miners of Irish descent, carried out terrorist activities, including beatings and murders of employers, in the coal fields of Pennsylvania. In 1886 a further example of the violence of this period occurred when police killed four people during a strike for an eight-hour workday at the McCormick Reaper Works in Chicago. At a resulting protest meeting in Haymarket Square in Chicago, a bomb was thrown into the ranks of police. Seven police officers and four workers were killed in the clash that followed.[16]

The turn of the twentieth century did not end this kind of violence. In 1913 open warfare broke out in the mining areas of the Colorado Fuel and Iron Corporation. The fighting reached a terrible climax when the Colorado state militia attacked a group of strikers at Ludlow. After firing machine guns at the tents in which workers' families were living, the militia doused the tents with oil and set them afire. Eleven children, two women, and six miners were killed. This incident has been called the Ludlow Massacre by historians.[17]

Violence continued to appear from time to time in American labor relations through the late 1930s. Early in 1937 U.S. Steel executives agreed to unionization, but the smaller steel companies refused to go along with U.S. Steel's lead, and violent strikes broke out. On May 30 ten people were killed and eighty wounded when police in South Chicago attacked marchers at a Republic Steel Company plant. The strike gradually dissipated, and the smaller steel firms were not organized until 1941.[18]

Government
and Labor:
1914–1959

The federal government's attitude toward the labor movement gradually changed from opposition to neutrality and finally to support of the concept of collective bargaining, including the right to strike. (Table 2.1 shows the sequence of significant laws and other government influences on labor relations starting with the Philadelphia Cordwainers of 1806.)

One of the most important laws was the Clayton Act, passed in 1914. This act limited the use of court orders, or **injunctions,** against workers and unions during labor disputes and legalized **picketing** (a line of workers carrying placards) and certain other union activities. The courts, however, tended to ignore or downplay the provisions of the Clayton Act until the passage of the Norris-LaGuardia Act in 1932, which essentially prohibited the use of injunctions in labor disputes. That act also made the **yellow-dog contract** illegal. A yellow-dog contract is an agreement between management and a worker under which the worker agrees not to join a union in exchange for continued employment.

The Wagner Act of 1935, also called the National Labor Relations Act, focused on labor's right to organize. The act allowed union employees to choose representatives who exercise exclusive bargaining rights for all employees in that union. It became an unfair labor practice for an employer to coerce or restrain employees in the exercise of their rights, to dominate or interfere with a labor organization, or to refuse to bargain collectively with a legal representative of the employees. The administration of the Wagner Act was given to the National Labor Relations Board (NLRB), which was created under the act.

But with the Taft-Hartley Act (Labor Management Relations Act) of 1947, Congress began to restrict union power. Certain union practices, such as sympathy strikes, refusals to bargain, and **closed shops** (situations in which the employer may hire only union members), were declared illegal. States were allowed to pass **right-to-work laws,** which permitted any state to outlaw **union shop provisions** in contracts as well. (In a union shop situation, all workers in a bargaining unit are required to become union members after a certain period of employment.)

Make-work (creating jobs with no substance or purpose) or **featherbedding provisions** (requiring the employer to hire unnecessary employees) in labor contracts were also deemed illegal. The act allowed the president of the United States to take action to postpone strikes or lockouts for eighty days when national health or safety was imperiled. The act also established the Federal Mediation and Conciliation Service, an independent department in the federal government with responsibility for helping unions and management reach agreements and avoid work stoppages.

In 1959 the Landrum-Griffin Act (Labor-Management Reporting and Disclosure Act) was passed to further protect employees and employers against arbitrary union power. This law included provisions for secret-ballot election of union officers, gave protection against embezzlement of union funds by union officials, and outlawed picketing to extort money from employers.

TABLE 2.1 **Significant laws and other government influences on labor relations 1806–1959**

LAWS, COURT DECISIONS, OR EVENTS	EFFECT ON LABOR RELATIONS
Philadelphia Journeymen Cordwainers tried for conspiracy (1806)	Philadelphia shoemakers found guilty of criminal conspiracy to raise wages and fined
In *Commonwealth* v. *Hunt*, Massachusetts Supreme Court rules on conspiracy doctrine (1842)	Union held to be legal organizations and conspiracy doctrine overturned
Clayton Act, 1914	Limits use of injunctions against unions during labor disputes and legalizes picketing
National War Labor Board created (1918)	Establishes "work councils" in factories during World War I
Railway Labor Act, 1926	Establishes collective bargaining, outlaws company unions, and provides for grievance and arbitration procedures in the railroad industry
Norris-LaGuardia Act, 1932	Essentially prohibits injunctions in labor disputes and makes the "yellow-dog" contract illegal
National Industrial Recovery Act, 1933	Gives most workers the right to organize and bargain collectively; later declared unconstitutional, but its labor provisions are written into the Wagner Act
Social Security Act, 1935	Establishes an unemployment compensation system, an old-age pension system, and various services for the blind and disabled.
Wagner Act, 1935	Allows union employees to choose representatives who exercise exclusive bargaining rights for all employees in the unions; specifies as unfair labor practices coercion or restraint by employers of employees in the exercise of their rights, dominating or interfering with a labor organization, or refusing to bargain; establishes the National Labor Relations Board
Fair Labor Standards Act, 1938	Establishes minimum wages and a maximum workweek beyond which overtime must be paid; outlaws employment of children under age sixteen in industries in interstate commerce, except that youths aged fourteen and fifteen may work limited hours in certain occupations
Taft-Hartley Act, 1947	Makes illegal certain union practices, such as refusal to bargain, sympathy strikes, and closed shops; allows states to pass right-to-work laws; makes illegal make-work and featherbedding provisions in labor contracts; establishes the Federal Mediation and Conciliation Service
Landrum-Griffin Act, 1959	Provides for secret-ballot election of union officers; gives union members protection from embezzlement by union officers; outlaws picketing to extort money

The Development of Human Resources Management as a Profession

Besides the growth of unions, the late nineteenth and early twentieth centuries witnessed the emergence of human resources management as a profession. The earliest developments came in the federal civil service.

The Federal Civil Service

The Civil Service Commission, established by the Pendleton Act of 1883, has had a major influence on the development of human resources management in the United States. Drawing many of its ideas from the British civil service system, the Pendleton Act established the use of competitive examinations for admission into public service; provided job security for public employees, including those who refused to engage in politics; prohibited political activity by the civil service; and encouraged a nonpartisan approach to employee selection. A commissioner was appointed to administer the act.[19]

The major effect of the Pendleton Act was to foster employees' appointment and career development in federal service on the basis of performance. Over the years this law has stimulated progressive personnel policies in private organizations as well. For example, around 1890 the Civil Service Commission was developing the forerunners of general intelligence tests and trade tests that became popular in private industry.

Personnel Specialists in Industry

Between 1900 and 1920, concurrently with developments in scientific management, industrial psychology, and the federal civil service, some companies began hiring specialists to assist with such matters as employment, safety, and training.

This trend was influenced by a number of management books published between 1899 and 1912 in Great Britain and the United States. Moreover, the first comprehensive text in the field appeared in 1920 — Tead and Metcalf's *Personnel Administration*.[20] Such publications stimulated interest in the field and encouraged the use of personnel specialists.

Several kinds of personnel specialists, in addition to the social or welfare secretary discussed earlier, were particularly evident shortly after the turn of the century. Companies such as The B. F. Goodrich Co. hired **employment agents** to centralize the recruiting and screening processes.[21] Some firms established departments of labor, as did the National Cash Register Company (now NCR Corp.) in 1901; the **labor department specialists** would respond to complaints from union employees and monitor working conditions and wage policies.[22] Some companies employed **wage,** or **rate, clerks** to set wage rates based on time-and-motion studies and analysis of job tasks.[23] Similarly, **pension administrators** were hired to manage the pension (retirement) and insurance plans that were proliferating in many railway and labor organizations.[24] A number of companies established training programs, staffed by **training specialists,** to teach employees new skills, particularly sales techniques.

In 1902 Maryland became the first state to pass a **workmen's compensation** (now **workers' compensation**) law, requiring employers to pay workers for lost time and injuries resulting from occupational accidents. The law was subsequently declared unconstitutional. But in 1911 the U. S. Supreme Court upheld the workers' compensation laws of several other states, and from then on **safety specialists** became very common in industry. Industrial firms wanted to reduce claims against themselves, and they depended on the safety specialist to help ensure safer working conditions in their plants. As a parallel development, physicians were employed by some companies to ensure that employees would be assigned jobs suited to their physical qualifications.[25]

The Emergence of the Personnel Department

As early as the 1880s, in some companies, a few specialized personnel activities were grouped into larger departments. But not until the second decade of the twentieth century did the modern personnel department emerge. In 1911 U.S. Steel created a Bureau of Safety, Sanitation, and Welfare. By 1918 International Harvester Co. had established a Department of Industrial Relations, and Ford Motor Co. had created a Sociological Department, which combined medical, welfare, safety, and legal aspects of employee relations. By the same year B. Kuppenheimer and Company had a Department of Industrial Relations that included subdivisions such as health, employment, grievances and discipline, and wage and rate setting.[26]

In 1917 Standard Oil of New Jersey approved a plan that provided for regular conferences between labor and management. At the same time the company established a retirement income plan, substantial insurance benefits, a safety program, and a medical division. To coordinate many of the new programs, Standard Oil created a personnel and training department.[27] In such ways were modern personnel departments born.

Systems Theory, Sociotechnical Systems Design, the Behavioral Sciences, and Industrial-Organizational Psychology

Since the late 1940s, and especially during the 1970s and 1980s, and to the present, human resources practitioners have drawn on the emerging knowledge from several sources. In particular, these sources have been systems theory, sociotechnical systems design, and the behavioral sciences, including industrial-organizational psychology.

Systems theory, by emphasizing the relationships among the parts of a totality, helps human resources managers understand how a change in one component of an organization can have repercussions throughout the firm. For example, if a company hires people with greater skills and more education than those it has hired previously, it may also need to upgrade its training program and pay more attention to opportunities for advancement in order to help meet the aspirations of both groups.

Sociotechnical system design focuses on the design of organizations and jobs toward improving the relationship between the technical systems of organizations and their social systems toward improving productivity, quality, and employee motivation and satisfaction. While the scientific management movement tended to emphasize the technical system, and the human relations movement tended to emphasize the social system, sociotechnical system design focuses on the interdependence between the two.[28] This field of inquiry and application has led to many improvements in manufacturing and mining, in particular, and to a greater understanding of how to design jobs.

The **behavioral sciences** — the social and biological sciences pertaining to human behavior — have provided especially important insights. Specifically, those aspects of the behavioral sciences that can be called **industrial-organizational psychology,** with emphasis on the dynamics of leadership, group behavior, and motivation, have had a tremendous impact on human resources management. (To a large extent, industrial-organizational psychology is an extension of early industrial psychology and the human relations movement.)

International Perspective

Quality Circles

Quality circles, one of the reasons . . . for Japan's success, are a technique of participative management that arose in Japan following World War II. To win their exports a better reputation in the world market, the Japanese focused on quality control. With the help of American experts like W. Edwards Deming and Joseph Juran in the early 1950s, the Japanese began by first implementing statistical quality control, then by expanding the responsibility for the control of quality throughout an entire company.

In 1961, Kaoru Ishikawa, an engineering professor at Tokyo University, with the backing of the Japanese Union of Scientists and Engineers (JUSE), suggested that small groups of workers be formed to address problems in their respective work areas. Ishikawa drew his inspiration, opti-

mism, and wisdom from many of the American organizational and behavioral specialists, including Likert, Maslow, Drucker, Argyris, McGregor, and Herzberg, whose writings were already well known in Japan. He was also influenced by Mogensen's "Work Simplification" programs in America, and by the Japanese tradition of interdependence that had derived from their limited space and rice-farming technology.

Because of the Japanese national emphasis on quality control, the early work groups focused primarily on quality, and these groups eventually came to be called quality control (QC) circles.

Source: Excerpted from William L. Mohr and Harriet Mohr, *Quality Circles: Changing Images of People at Work* (Reading, Mass.: Addison-Wesley Publishing Company, 1983), p. 13.

As will be evident throughout this book, systems theory, sociotechnical sytems design, and industrial-organizational psychology, in particular, are highly useful in contemporary job design, employee selection, in managing career transitions, and in appraisal and compensation, and other aspects of human resources management.

Professional Associations, College and University Curricula, and Publications

Providing impetus to the dissemination of knowledge and the development of the profession of human resources management has been the growth in membership of professional associations. Some of the large U.S. associations focusing on human resources management are the Society for Human Resources Management, the International Personnel Management Association, the Industrial Relations Research Association, the American Society for Training and Development, and the Personnel & Human Resources Division of the Academy of Management. (See also Chapter 23.) The gradually growing and now widespread inclusion of coursework on human resources or personnel management in the curricula of colleges and universities has greatly added to the dissemination and development of knowledge. University courses in the field go back at least to 1920 — Ordway Tead was teaching a course in personnel administration at Columbia University that year.

Professional journals and other publications in the field appeared at the end of World War I and in the early 1920s. They have increased in number and widened both their domestic and their international circulation. For example, *Personnel* — now called *HRfocus* — was first published in 1919, and the *Journal of Personnel Research* — now called *Personnel Journal* — appeared in 1922.[29]

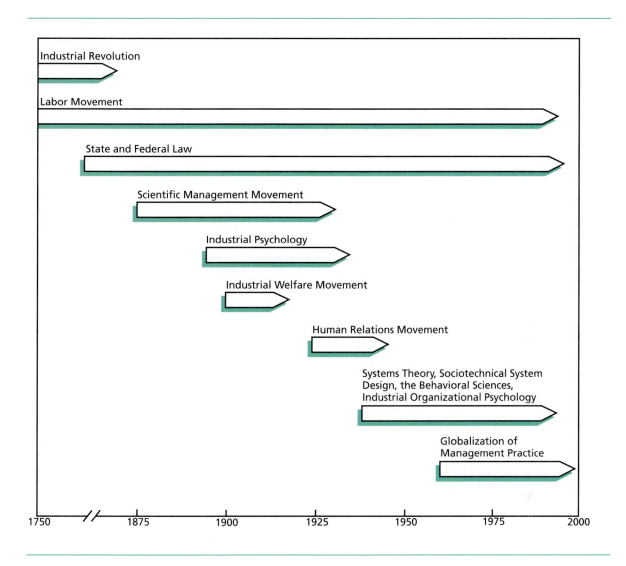

FIGURE 2.1   Approximate time lines: the development of human resources management

Globalization of Management Practice   With its roots in the developments of past decades, **globalization,** that is, intense international competition and interdependence among business firms and national economies, is dramatically evident in the 1990s. It is most apparent in the rapid proliferation of multinational corporations (MNCs — see Chapter 22). It has also greatly influenced the profession of human resources management and HRM practices through first-hand reports and published descriptions. The following are just a few of the foreign practices about which a great deal of information has been widely disseminated: research and practice relative to semiautonomous work teams in Great Britain and Sweden (see Chapter 7); the development of flextime in Germany and elsewhere in Europe (see Chapter 8); and the marrying of U.S. and

Japanese ideas into the quality circle movement in Japan and then in the United States (see *International Perspective* on page 34 and also Chapter 21). Figure 2.1 presents graphically the various events and movements that have brought about the development of human resources management.

Summary

Modern human resources management has emerged from six interrelated sources: (1) the scientific management movement, (2) the industrial welfare movement, (3) early industrial psychology, (4) the human relations movement, (5) the labor movement and the emergence of free collective bargaining, and (6) the development of human resources management as a profession.

Scientific management and early industrial psychology emphasized the proper design of tasks, selection and training of employees, and individual incentives. The human relations movement was mainly concerned with the feelings, interactions, and attitudes of employees and with the organization as a social system. The industrial welfare movement grew out of concerns about working conditions in factories and mills and other places of employment; it also grew out of concerns about the off-job lives of employees.

The establishment of workers' rights to organize and bargain collectively was a slow process, punctuated by violence. Nevertheless, strong unions and associations of unions emerged — most notably the AFL-CIO — and a series of federal laws established both the rights of unions and the rules under which unions must operate.

The emergence of human resources management as a profession began with developments in the civil service and the rise of personnel specialists in private industry. Eventually, the specialized personnel functions coalesced into a single personnel department. Since the 1940s, the profession has been strongly influenced by systems theory, sociotechnical systems design, and the behavioral sciences — industrial-organizational psychology, in particular — areas of inquiry that have application in virtually all aspects of human resources management. The growth of professional associations and publications focusing on human resources management, and the widespread college and university course offerings in HRM, have had a great influence on the field. The strong trend toward globalization and the rise of the multinational corporation have also contributed to the evolution of the field. The evolution of the profession continues today, worldwide.

Ethical Dilemma

Manuel Sanchez owns three Mexican food restaurants in the metropolitan area. All have a reputation for excellent food and good service. Manuel hires a number of teenagers, some who are fourteen and fifteen years of age. Most are desperate for jobs and are willing to work late at night. Manuel knows these hours are in violation of state and federal child labor laws, but he wants to help the young people. He also needs to pay minimum wages to maintain his current level of profitability. Manuel pays his employees in full for the time they work, but to protect himself, he requires the teenagers to sign time sheets showing that the hours worked are within the legal boundaries.

What ethical issues are involved? Is this a legal or an ethical problem? What is the difference, if any, between a legal issue and an ethical issue?

Key Terms

scientific management
time-and-motion study
industrial welfare movement
social, or welfare, secretary
industrial psychology
predictive validity
human relations movement
labor union
collective bargaining
protest
strike
lockout
boycott
strikebreaker
injunction
picketing
yellow-dog contract
closed shop

right-to-work laws
union shop provisions
make-work provisions
featherbedding provisions
employment agent
labor department specialist
wage, or rate, clerk
pension administrator
training specialist
workers' compensation (previously workmen's compensation)
safety specialist
systems theory
sociotechnical systems design
behavioral sciences
industrial-organizational psychology
globalization

Review Questions

1. What were the major movements since the late 1800s that have influenced the evolution of human resources management? Briefly describe each.
2. Explain why it is useful to go beyond viewing the organization as a technical system and also view it as a social system.
3. What were the key laws passed in the United States up through 1959 that had significant influence on labor-management relations? What was the impact of each law?
4. Identify the personnel specialists who were the forerunners of the modern human resources department.
5. In general terms, what have been the contributions of the behavioral sciences, systems theory, and sociotechnical systems design to contemporary human resources management?
6. How has globalization contributed to the evolution of the field?

Opening Case Questions

Case 2.1   Factory Work, 1815

1. What were some of the changes in the management of human resources brought about by the Industrial Revolution?
2. Briefly discuss some of the differences between general working conditions today and those prevalent in the early days of the Industrial Revolution.

Case 2.2   More than a Technological System, More than a Social System

1. In your opinion, what role, if any should a human resources director play in technological change in a company?
2. The inefficient overhead conveyor at HiPowr Diesels was in keeping with what historical developments in human resources management and out of phase with what other developments?

Comprehensive Case

Early Human Relations Research at Sears

During the 1940s, Sears, Roebuck and Company conducted human relations research in order to gain more insight into what its employees thought and felt about their jobs and about the company. The first employee survey results had been simple compilations of responses, counting how many people answered the question in different ways. This was of limited use for managers trying to understand employee interactions and attitudes.

Researchers found, however, that this same survey information became more meaningful when it was looked at alongside socially influenced factors such as an employee's age, sex, length of service, type of work, or level of authority, and other elements such as size of store, size and economic base of city, and geographical region. With the help of social scientists from the Committee on Human Relations in Industry at the University of Chicago, Sears began to apply the concepts of social anthropology, especially regarding class and status, to the design and interpretation of its employee surveys.

The revamped survey program combined questionnaires and nondirective interviewing. The questionnaires, administered to employees companywide, were diagnostic; they were meant to pinpoint areas of possible organizational trouble: a specific department, a category of employee, some company policy or practice, even a significant event. After researchers analyzed the questionnaires, they instructed trained interviewers, all members of the Sears personnel staff, to focus in on the areas of conflict the data signaled.

As the information yielded by these explorations into employee attitudes grew, their scope expanded. Originally referred to as "morale surveys," they were now called "organization surveys." The patterns they brought to light convinced Sears researchers that individual "morale" could not be determined apart from an overall understanding of human relations in the organizational structure.

Sears discovered that two kinds of factors influenced the morale of individual employees. Internal factors centered on the work environment: job status, work pressures, tensions arising from differences in job goals and interests and from hierarchical relationships, and changes in management, company policies, job methods, and reward systems. But factors external to the Sears environment, most of which managers could do nothing about, were also important. The survey found that

- Higher morale among women employees than among men could be explained by differences in social roles, expectations, and demands.
- Social roles related to race and ethnicity could affect morale.
- Higher morale in retail stores than in warehouses reflected greater ideological agreement between managers and salespeople than between managers and warehouse staff.
- Higher morale in the rural south than in the industrial north reflected more ideological affinity in the south.
- Morale varied inversely by size of work unit and by the size of the city in which the unit operated.

Managers were encouraged to view the survey process as a tool for understanding how the overall organization functioned and how internal and external factors influenced the attitudes and behavior of workers. They were invited to help interpret survey results and to develop solutions to identified problems.

By the late 1940s, Sears had grown to be a sizable company with numerous widely located retail outlets. Besides generating a body of useful, valuable knowledge, this survey program built for Sears a staff of well-trained and practical-minded personnel specialists who provided guidance for company management throughout the economic boom after World War II. Sears also established a reputation as an employer that responded to the needs and concerns of its employees.

Sources: James C. Worthy, "Human Relations Research at Sears, Roebuck in the 1940s: A Memoir," in *Papers Dedicated to the Development of Modern Management*, Daniel A. Wren, ed., The Academy of Management, 1986. Reprinted by permission. For a more detailed report on the original Sears, Roebuck and Company studies, see James C. Worthy, "The More Things Change, the More They Stay the Same," *Journal of Management Inquiry* 1 (March 1992): 14–38.

Discussion Questions

1. What were the various phases in the use of employee surveys at Sears over the years?
2. What findings emerged at Sears through the use of concepts from social anthropology?

CHAPTER 3

Contemporary Challenges in Human Resources Management

LEARNING OBJECTIVES

- Identify changes in the lifestyles, attitudes, and composition of the work force that affect human resources management today.
- Define "managing diversity" (or "valuing diversity").
- List eight criteria for analyzing the quality of work life in an organization.
- Describe the impact of economic conditions and international competition on the American work environment.
- Identify recent legislation and court decisions related to fair employment practices and worker protection and explain how they affect contemporary human resources management.

CASE 3.1   Meeting at the Country Inn

Doug McLennan, president of Southwest Telecommunications Equipment, had called a two-day meeting involving the top management group and its immediate subordinates, some forty people in all. The announced agenda was "cost-cutting" and "quality improvement." The meeting was held at a country inn featuring comfortable accommodations, excellent food, a swimming pool, and extensive trails for jogging or walking. The dress was casual.

The meeting started at 9:00 a.m. Coffee, tea, fruit juice, and sweet rolls were available, and before people settled down in their comfortable chairs there was much good-natured greeting and repartee. There was an undercurrent of tension, however. For example, one department head was overheard saying to another, "Well, I guess Doug is going to turn on the heat." Another comment was, "We're going to have to work a lot smarter."

Doug started the meeting with a few words of welcome and then talked about the purposes of the gathering. "I hope," he said, "that we can have a good exchange of ideas and points of view in the areas of quality control and cost reduction. I hope by the time we leave tomorrow we'll have formed some task forces to investigate and put into effect some of the more promising ideas." He then started talking about what he called "the realities."

"The reality is," Doug began, "that the Japanese and Germans are capturing a larger and larger share of our markets. Some of our East Coast competitors are moving up fast, too. Our products are very good, but theirs are almost as good and steadily getting better. I wouldn't admit that outside this room, but it's true. To compound the problem, the Japanese, in particular, are producing comparable items at substantially less cost. They've also developed a new transistor that's giving them an edge, and we can't find comparable ones on the market yet. We've got to find ways both to improve our products and to manufacture them at less cost. Let me show you some figures." He then displayed a series of charts portraying sales and cost trends, share of the market, and so on.

After a brief period of questions and discussion, Doug called on Beverly Shaw, vice president of human resources, to discuss the schedule for the rest of the meeting. Beverly explained that a series of small-group sessions was on the agenda for the rest of the day. Each group would discuss general topics of concern to the entire firm, such as "potential approaches to reducing costs" and "suggestions for improving productivity and quality in manufacturing." Groups were encouraged to brainstorm freely and to suggest where they felt task forces could explore and implement proposed solutions to specific concerns. In some sessions, people were assigned to groups according to their area of specialty in the firm; in other sessions, group membership cut across departmental lines. In every instance, the small groups reported the results of their deliberations to the total group for further discussion.

Among the task forces appointed before the end of the second day was one on training and development and another on recruitment and selection. Beverly Shaw was appointed to chair both. Although she felt a little defensive that there had been suggestions for improvement in "her" areas, she was also encouraged by the interest other managers had expressed in both training and selection — areas where she had been attempting to secure their support. She had been trying to interest the manufacturing people in helping develop better specifications for hiring new people, for example, and here was a chance to work jointly with them on that matter and others, since the manufacturing vice president was on both task forces. Beverly was also pleased that her assistant, Don Wills, was appointed to the task force on cutting costs in the offices because both she and Don had been concerned about inefficiencies in office procedures.

People were tired at the end of the two-day meeting, but generally pleased with the results. Doug had expressed his concerns, but he had not really "turned on the heat." No person or department had been scolded, and it was clear that Doug wanted to maintain a congenial, problem-solving approach to addressing issues. There had been some time for exercise and socializing, which was appreciated, and people were particularly pleased with the approaches to cost cutting and quality improvement. In closing, Doug thanked the members of the group for their participation and told them, "I want to get us all back together for a one-day meeting six weeks from now to report on progress." ◀

<table>
<tr><td>**CASE 3.2**</td><td></td></tr>
</table>

CASE 3.2   Tropical Bankcorp

Toby Marin, vice president of personnel, Tropical Bankcorp, was in the weekly meeting with his five unit managers. The agenda item was "recruitment and retention of high-performance tellers." Toby and his subordinates had reached the conclusion that too many of the brightest and quickest and most personable of the bank's tellers were being recruited away by other banks and other kinds of organizations. Further, too large a percentage of the best candidates were not accepting jobs at Tropical. "OK, gang, what's going on?" asked Toby. "What have you found out?"

Mary Ann Yates, head of training and development, was the first to speak up. "Reviewing the notes from several months of exit interviews, it looks to me as though we're not flexible enough to keep women with young families," she said. "They're going to banks that permit permanent part-time jobs or that subsidize child-care centers. Or they're going to other companies with flextime arrangements. A lot of women just can't cope with our 8:30 to 5:30 workday."

"It sure would be a pain in the neck to keep track of a lot of part-time people," responded Bill Young, head of compensation and benefits. "Besides, don't these people realize that they lose a lot of benefits if they are not regular employees? What I've been finding out is that they have to be practically full-time to get vacation benefits, for example."

"I'm sure they know they are losing benefits," responded Mary Ann, "but obviously, the jobs they went to seemed to fit their situations better than the jobs they had with us."

"Here's another angle," interjected Wendy Sanchez, head of recruitment and employment. "I found one bank that hires mothers nine months a year, when their kids are in school, and then hires college students to fill in during the summer. How they get college kids to give up going to the beach all summer long is a mystery to me."

Toby smiled, "That's an interesting idea. Let's come back to that and to Mary Ann's and Bill's comments after we've heard from the other two. We need to zero in on what the problem is before we go too far with solutions." ◀

These two cases suggest that forces outside the organization can have a major impact on human resources management. In Case 3.1, intense national and international competition was forcing the management group at Southwest Telecommunications Equipment to take a hard look at its management practices. Included in the practices to be examined were employee training and development and the way the company was recruiting and selecting new employees. In Case 3.2, the impact of external forces is also dramatic. In particular, the rapid growth in employment of women with small children and the desire to retain these employees are causing managers at Tropical Bankcorp to study the reasons for the high turnover among this group at Tropical.

Many environmental, organizational, and cultural influences affect human resources management today. Changing social and political trends and recent economic developments around the world help account for the growing importance of the human resources department to the organization. These trends and developments also intensify the importance of all managers' roles in selecting and managing human talent.

These influences, many of which represent ongoing challenges in contemporary human resources management, can be grouped into three major categories: (1) the changing work force, (2) the influences of the external environment, and (3) the regulatory measures — federal and state laws, court decisions, and administrative rulings — that govern human resources management.

The Changing Work Force

The American work force as a whole is different from what it was ten, or even five, years ago. Many of the changes have been occurring gradually over the years; some are very recent or still in process.

Diversity Lifestyles and life circumstances are changing. More and more people express concern about the appropriate balance of work with leisure and other aspects of their lives. Thus, they may be less willing to accept overtime assignments or to work long hours or weekends.

Further, there are growing numbers of single-parent families and families in which both spouses work. In 1987 two-thirds of the women aged twenty-five to fifty-four with children under age eighteen were in the labor force. A majority (55 percent) of women in this age group with children under the age of three were in the work force.[1] These trends create pressures on organizations to be flexible enough in working hours so that children can be picked up from school or taken to the doctor or dentist. They also create intense pressure on organizations and communities to provide day-care centers, including those for infants and toddlers. Lifestyle considerations also influence the organization's ability to recruit or transfer people. *Where people are willing to live and work is becoming a serious issue for a significant number of workers.*

Women The proportion of women in the work force has increased dramatically and will continue to do so. Women constituted only 40 percent of the total work force as recently as 1975; by the year 2005 they are expected to account for 47 percent of the labor force.[2] Projections indicate that by the year 2000 four out of five women aged twenty-five to fifty-four will be in the labor force. Further, women will constitute

Today's work force increasingly consists of women trying to balance the dual role of parent and provider.

between half and three-fourths of all entrants into the work force through the year 2000.[3]

Because women have traditionally carried the major burden of child rearing, the pressures mentioned above for flexible work scheduling, time off, and day-care centers are intensified. This also means that the "equal pay for comparable work" issue is going to be debated more frequently, and a larger number of people will be pressing for higher pay for women. Statistics show that during a recent thirty-year stretch women consistently earned about sixty cents for each dollar earned by men, although lately the figure has gone up to seventy-two cents.[4] This complex issue — comparable worth — is discussed in Chapter 14.

Minorities   The proportion of minority entrants into the labor force is changing. The overall labor force is projected to grow gradually between now and the year 2000, and black employment will grow slightly faster. The most dramatic changes, however, will be seen in the rapid growth in the number of Hispanic, Asian, and other workers. ("Other" includes Native Americans, Alaska natives, and Pacific Islanders.) The Hispanic labor force is expected to have grown 74 percent between 1987 and the year 2000, and the "Asian and other" work force by 71 percent.[5] These rapid changes have major implications for human resources management, including a need for greater cultural understanding in recruitment, selection, and promotion, a greater need for language training, and generally more awareness and appreciation of differing cultural backgrounds.

The term *minority* — to the extent that it is used in the United States to denote "nonwhite" or persons of color — begins to have less and less meaning in some areas, for example, parts of California, Texas, Florida, Alaska, and the entire state of Hawaii. As shown in *Contemporary Issues* on page 46, whites constitute only about 30 percent of the population of Hawaii.

Contemporary Issues

Data Picture Hawaii as Melting Pot
A Census Study Records the Islands'
Ethnic Diversity

There's a melting pot of cultures and ethnic backgrounds at the end of Hawaii's rainbow.

Hawaii was ranked the third highest area in population size in the country for the Chinese ancestry group, behind California and New York, according to federal census study records.

Hawaii, with 95,899 residents of Chinese origin, has 6.4 percent of the total 1.5 million Chinese-Americans living in the United States. California ranked first with 42.6 percent; New York was second with 15.7 percent.

Ancestry refers to a person's ethnic origin or descent, "roots," or heritage or the place of birth of the person or the person's parents before their arrival in the United States, officials said.

"Those larger states, like California and New York, have their Chinatowns," said Dr. Franklin Odo, director of the Ethnic Studies program at the University of Hawaii at Manoa. "These states have traditionally been strong magnets for Chinese immigrants."

A report released this week by the U.S. Census Bureau shows that about one-fourth (or 58 million) of the U.S. population considers itself to be of German or part-German ancestry.

Rounding out the top 10 are the Irish (38.7 million), English (32.7 million), African-American (23.8), Italian (14.7 million), American (12.4 million), Mexican (11.6 million), French (10.3 million), Polish (9.4 million) and Native American (8.7 million).

The Chinese make up the 25th largest population group, with 1.5 million, records show. Asian and Pacific ancestry groups are heavily concentrated in the Western part of the country. Nearly 90 percent of all Hawaiians, 72 percent of all Japanese and 55 percent of all Chinese live in the West.

"The percentage of whites in Hawaii is relatively small compared to other states," Odo said. "I think it's 30 percent white population in Hawaii.

"If you break that down into ancestry, well, you can see why Hawaii has such a small number of Germans and others."

Source: Devi Sen Laskar, "Data Picture Hawaii as Melting Pot," *Honolulu Star-Bulletin*, December 22, 1992, p. A-1. Reprinted by permission.

The Older Worker   The proportion of workers in the category that the U.S. Labor Department calls "prime age" (twenty-five to fifty-four)[6] is growing and will continue to grow through the year 2005 (see Figure 3.1). Meanwhile, the proportion of workers in the age group sixteen to twenty-four is declining. Consequently, employers will have a relatively smaller pool from which to draw new recruits and part-time workers. There may also be a greater need to retain or recruit more senior workers. The challenge for human resources managers is to keep abreast of all such trends and forces.

Managing Cultural Diversity   Current terms for managing these changes are **managing cultural diversity** and **valuing diversity**.[7] Included in the contemporary emphasis on valuing diversity are efforts toward more appreciation and understanding of the older worker and persons with disabilities, along with increased attention to women and minorities.

Social Conditions and Expectations   Among the most challenging problems in the management of human resources are current social conditions as they are reflected in workers' attitudes, values, and expectations.

Education   As shown in Figure 3.2, in 1975, 18 percent of workers between the ages of twenty-five and sixty-four had four or more years of college, and another 15 percent had completed one to three years of college. In all, about one-third of the work force had some college training. By 1990 about one-fourth of the work force had four or more years of college, and nearly one-half had some college training. One implication of this trend is that organizations need to look continuously to see whether talents are being used, whether jobs are sufficiently challenging, and whether there are avenues for advancement.

It is in the organization's interest to realize the optimal return from its human resources, as well as to make the organization an attractive place to work. In addition, the higher a person's education, the higher his or her expectations about challenging and interesting work. A survey in a large manufacturing organization found, for example, that employees with bachelors, masters, and doctorates ranked "challenging and interesting work" first in a group of thirteen factors. Employees with associate degrees ranked this item third, those with high school diplomas ranked it fourth, and those who had not completed high school ranked it thirteenth, the bottom of the scale.[8] Strategies for designing jobs to challenge and motivate workers are described in Chapter 7.

Participation   **Participation,** or employee involvement in organizational problem solving and decision making, is a key aspect of contemporary human resources management. More and more, employees want to participate in decisions about their work lives. For example, they want to be consulted before a major change is made in work schedules or in work assignments. People also want more freedom to question supervisory and management practices. They are less and less inclined to assume that "management knows best." Participation is introduced in Chapter 4 and discussed in various contexts throughout the text. Chapter 21 focuses on participative approaches to organization improvement.

Collective Action   There is a growing trend toward acceptance of collective action, such as unionization, among segments of the work force where collective action historically has not

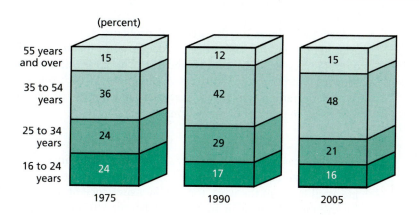

FIGURE 3.1   The changing age distribution of the labor force
Source: U.S. Department of Labor, *Occupational Outlook Handbook, 1992–93.*

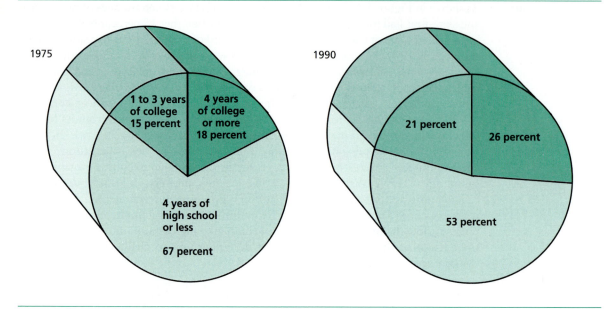

FIGURE 3.2   Workers aged 25–64 with a college background, 1975 and 1990

Source: U.S. Department of Labor, *Occupational Outlook Handbook, 1992–93.*
Bureau of Labor Statistics, Bulletin 2400, May 1992, p. 10.

been widely used. For example, unionization and strike action have been increasing, among nurses, government employees, teachers, professional athletes, and even physicians. As a result of these trends, human resources directors and other managers, as well as union leaders, have been paying more attention to human resources practices that might make organiztions vulnerable to unionization. Why workers join and form unions is discussed in Chapter 17.

Due Process   Partly as an outgrowth of the trends just discussed, members of the work force at all levels have higher expectations about **organizational due process,** that is, fair and orderly procedures for the airing of problems and complaints without fear of recrimination, and fair and orderly procedures for making decisions affecting the lives of employees (see Chapters 18 and 19). These expectations are being reflected in a growing acceptance of "progressive discipline," which relies on responsive, corrective action rather than severe penalties, and the use of grievance procedures in an increasing number of organizations.

Layoffs   Experience with job loss or the threat of job loss in recent years, stemming from such events as company mergers, acquisitions, or business downturns (or sometimes from just plain mismanagement) has undoubtedly had a great impact on many people at all levels in the work force. The experience of having lost a job, or of having survived a **reduction in force** (see Chapter 10), has probably influenced the attitudes of workers and managers in various ways. One consequence has been that many managers have begun to look more carefully at some of the options an organization may have when confronted with budget cutbacks. We will look at some of those options in Chapter 10.

The Environment   People are more aware of the fragility of the natural environment and of the interdependence of humans with their surroundings. Consequently, there are more pressures on organizations to follow environmentally sound practices, including more attention to health and safety, to the control and disposal of pollutants and toxic materials, and to transportation control so as to minimize traffic congestion and air pollution. Developing safe and healthful working conditions will be the topic of Chapter 20.

The Quality of Work Life   More and more employees and managers are interested in and concerned about the **quality of work life,** a concept that encompasses the entire range of organizational life — particularly as it is reflected in human resources management. Richard E. Walton provides us with eight criteria for analyzing the quality of work life in an organization:[9]

1. *Adequate and fair compensation.* One criterion is the extent to which "the income from full-time work meet[s] socially determined standards of sufficiency"[10] and the extent to which compensation is perceived as fair by the employee.

2. *Safe and healthy working conditions.* This criterion includes the extent to which working conditions minimize health and injury risks.

3. *Opportunity to use and develop human capacities.* To Walton, this criterion is the extent to which the job involves a whole task rather than fragments of tasks. In addition, it includes the extent to which the job involves planning activities as well as implementation activities, allows "substantial autonomy and self-control," and provides opportunity to use a wide range of skills.[11]

4. *Opportunity for continued growth and security.* This criterion includes the extent to which employees are encouraged to develop their capabilities rather than allow them to become obsolete, the extent to which there are opportunities for advancement, and the extent to which there is reasonable job security.

5. *Social integration in the work organization.* This criterion includes the extent to which there is freedom from prejudice and the opportunity for upward mobility in the organization. It also includes the extent to which organization members experience group support and a "sense of community" that extends beyond the immediate work group.

6. *Constitutionalism.* This criterion includes the extent to which the organization adheres to the concept of due process mentioned earlier and honors people's rights to privacy — for example, the right to withhold information about off-the-job behavior and family matters.

7. *Balanced role of work.* This refers to the extent to which the organization avoids interfering in an appropriate balance between work and other spheres of employees' lives, such as family life.

8. *Socially beneficial and responsible work.* This reflects the extent to which the employee sees the organization as being socially responsible in its products, its disposal of wastes, its employment practices, its dealings with underdeveloped countries, and so on.

Increasingly, people at all levels in the work force have higher expectations about these eight characteristics. In turn, these expectations influence how contemporary organizations are managed, and particularly how human resources are managed.

Influences of the External Environment

Many other forces, largely external to the organization, are having a major impact on human resources management. Like the trends we have already described, they tend to be interrelated.

Economic and Political Conditions

Economic and political conditions, both at home and abroad, have a strong influence on human resources management. In a strong, highly productive economy, organizations have greater financial resources for attracting workers with higher pay, for implementing training and development programs, and for funding other personnel programs. In contrast, a struggling economy plagued by high inflation and lower productivity intensifies the need for more cost-effective management of human resources. Current economic forces include the following factors.

Inflation, Energy Costs, and Environmental Concerns

Inflation, although relatively low in the late 1980s and early 1990s, periodically plagues the U.S. economy and is rampant in some countries, such as several in South America and in the former Soviet bloc of nations. Rising costs and prices can create a wide range of problems in human resources management, including difficulties in making decisions about starting salaries relative to the salaries of present employees and in allocating money between merit pay and across-the-board adjustments.

Control of oil prices by the Organization of Petroleum Exporting Countries (OPEC) and declining sources of energy have resulted in high energy costs and intensified pressures for conservation and production efficiency. Disasters such as Iraqi troops discharging oil into the Persian Gulf and setting Kuwait oil fields ablaze have joined major oil spills from tankers off the coasts of Scotland, France, Italy, and Alaska to contribute to the long-term rising costs of energy, as well as to serious environmental damage.

Higher energy costs, as well as environmental concerns, have affected working conditions. For example, many organizations attempt to be more conservative with office and plant heating in winter and with air conditioning in summer. Other forms of coping are prevalent; for instance, companies encourage employees to form car or van pools in order to save energy and to reduce congestion on roads and in parking lots.

Many companies, such as 3M and McDonald's have embarked on major programs to protect the environment and save energy. For example, 3M is investing in pollution controls at its manufacturing plants exceeding those required by law, and McDonald's is putting a major effort into recycling paper and plastic.[12] Such programs affect work rules, training programs, and company reputations. In turn, they can enhance organizations' ability to recruit new employees.

The importance of safety training and rigorous safety management, along with the need for improved technology, is obvious from the tanker disasters. Catastrophes such as the nuclear accident at Three Mile Island in 1979, the nuclear blast at Chernobyl, U.S.S.R., in 1986, and the poisonous chemical releases at Bhopal, India, in 1984, Texas City, Texas, in 1987, and Kumi, South Korea, in 1991 dramatize the human and economic costs when industrial organizations give little heed to the safety and health of their own employees, as well as to the safety and health of the people in the surrounding region. In some instances, such as the Chernobyl disaster, the human tragedies and economic costs continue to unfold. (See also Chapter 20).

Globalization   As mentioned in Chapter 2, international competition, cooperation, and the interdependence of business and industrial organizations — in other words, globalization — is intensifying. Competition is becoming more intense for many reasons, including increased management capability in many countries, heavy demand for energy and raw materials, and the availability of rapid transportation and communications. As of 1993, the newly formed European Economic Area, consisting of the European Community of twelve nations, plus Scandinavia and Austria (Swiss voters declined to join in late 1992), constitutes the world's largest trading bloc, accounting for 40 percent of world trade.

Although the European Community has had difficulty in establishing a common currency, the creation of this common market will increase efficiency and markets and intensify competition. However, it will also create opportunities for U.S. firms in terms of investments and joint enterprises.[13] The movement toward free trade among the United States, Canada, and Mexico, as represented by the North American Free Trade Agreement (if this agreement is ratified by Congress and the Mexican and Canadian legislatures), is likely to stimulate the economies of all three countries. But it may result in significant dislocations of workers in some industries and require extensive retraining programs.[14]

Rapidly increasing opportunities for entrepreneurship in East European countries such as Poland, Hungary, the Czech Republic, Slovakia, Latvia, Lithuania, and Estonia are stimulating both international competition and the development of joint enterprises and avenues of mutual cooperation. Also of major significance was the formation of the Commonwealth of Independent States (CIS) on January 1, 1992, a loose confederation of such former U.S.S.R. republics as Russia, the Ukraine, and Byelorussia.[15] The CIS is the culmination of the former U.S.S.R.'s fitful moves under President Mikhail Gorbachev toward **perestroika** (the restructuring of the Soviet economy in order to foster private enterprise) and **glasnost** (openness). The movement of these nations within the Commonwealth toward private ownership of property, entrepreneurship, and free enterprise is intensifying international competition and stimulating the formation of joint ventures across national boundaries.[16] This movement will have a considerable impact if military coups, ethnic rivalries, and regional wars do not derail it.

Japanese ownership in the United States, growing U.S. investment in plants in Europe, and European investment in U.S. firms also point to increasing globalization. (In 1991 the Japanese owned or had large investments in 1,435 manufacturing plants in the United States).[17] As Koh Sera of the Sumitomo Corporation, Tokyo, Japan says, "Globalization . . . looks at the whole world as being nationless and borderless."[18] Globalization can create some unexpected twists: the Ford Motor Co. announced in 1991 that Ford would build Japanese Nissan minivans in the United States.[19]

International competition and cooperation are linked to communication and transportation among nations. The jet airplane, the computer, the fax machine, and satellite communications have enormously increased the tempo of business trade and the sharing and dispersal of information. For example, commerce between Europe and the southern states of the United States requires only a few hours of travel between London and the Atlanta and Dallas airports. The stock market crash of 1987 and the turmoil in the international currency markets in 1992 made it clear that communications among the major stock and currency markets of the world — New York, Tokyo, London, Bonn, Hong Kong, and elsewhere — is almost instantaneous.[20] Further, there has been a widespread sharing of technology, some voluntary and some based on spying or smuggling in violation of U.S. or international law. Possible examples of the latter include the smuggling of helicopters into North Korea from California via a German exporter and Rotterdam,[21] the alleged pirating of American computer software by four Italian firms,[22] and the alleged selling of electron beam machines to China by Japan's Toshiba Corporation.[23]

An example of voluntary sharing of technology is The Boeing Co.'s alliances with the heavy-industry divisions of three Japanese firms, Mitsubishi, Kawasaki, and Fuji, to build the 777, a wide-body, long-range plane set for delivery to airlines in 1995.[24] Another instance of such cooperation is the agreement between international communication carriers to share undersea fiber-optic transmission circuits. Some of the firms involved in the accord are AT&T, British Telecommunications, Kokusai Denshin Denwa (Japan), France Telecom, Overseas Telecommunications Commission (Australia), and Deutsche Bundespost (Germany).[25]

Overall, this increased international competition and interdependence intensifies the pressure on executives, supervisors, and all employees to become more innovative, more efficient, more cost-conscious, and more quality-conscious, as well as more cross-culturally conscious, and more conscious of the environment. In turn, organization members, such as those at Southwest Telecommunications Equipment in Case 3.1, expect human resources management to become increasingly effective in helping with these matters.

Differential Industry Growth

For many reasons, including competition and technological innovations, employment is growing much more rapidly in some industries than in others. Figure 3.3 shows percentage changes in employment expected between 1990 and 2005 by major industry groups. Employment in manufacturing and mining industries is expected to decline slightly. On the other hand, employment in service industries — including temporary help, health care, government, banking, computer and data processing industries — is expected to increase by almost 35 percent.[26] Such shifts in employment have major implications for human resources management, including how much recruiting needs to be done and the kinds of training required.

Government Deregulation

In the last few years, federal legislation and decisions by the Supreme Court and federal agencies have drastically decreased or eliminated government regulation and control of a number of industries, including telecommunications, the airlines, banking and financial services, and the trucking and railroad industries. This **deregulation** has had many consequences, including increased competition among firms, and management pressures on unions for wage cuts and less restrictive work rules. Many new firms have sprung up, but many others have gone bankrupt or been purchased and absorbed by other companies, leading to extensive layoffs. The airline industry, in particular, has seen numerous bankruptcies and at least three carriers, Eastern Air Lines, Midway Airlines, and Pan American World Airways, have gone out of business entirely.[27] In many instances, employees with twenty or more years of experience have lost their jobs. Events such as these, of course, create major problems for human resources management. They challenge management to find ways to avoid the adverse consequences of layoffs, and, if layoffs cannot be avoided, to help employees make the necessary transitions.

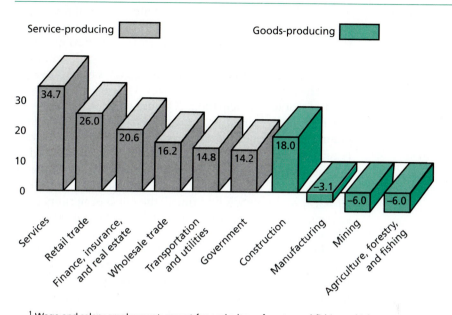

Service-producing ▢   Goods-producing ▣

Services	34.7
Retail trade	26.0
Finance, insurance, and real estate	20.6
Wholesale trade	16.2
Transportation and utilities	14.8
Government	14.2
Construction	18.0
Manufacturing	–3.1
Mining	–6.0
Agriculture, forestry, and fishing	–6.0

¹ Wage and salary employment, except for agriculture, forestry and fishing, which includes self-employment and unpaid family workers.

FIGURE 3.3   Projected percentage change in employment, 1990–2005
Source: U.S. Department of Labor, *Occupational Outlook Handbook, 1992–93.*
Bureau of Labor Statistics, Bulletin 2400, May 1992, p. 11.

Productivity and Quality Concerns

Finally, how to increase productivity and product quality are matters of deep concern to management, government, labor, and the public. Although there has been a resurgence in **productivity** (the total amount of worker output) from the slow rates of growth in the 1970s, growth in productivity has varied widely by industry. For example, in the communications industry, this rate was a plus 4.8 percent annually between 1979 and 1988, while the rate of growth in legal services and hotels for the same period was a *minus* 3.8 percent and 1.8 percent respectively.[28] By and large, white-collar productivity has grown much more slowly than productivity in manufacturing, where it has averaged 4.1 percent per year since 1979.[29] Overall, the average American worker produces more goods and services per year than the average German and Japanese worker, but the *growth* in productivity per year in the United States is substantially less than in Germany and Japan.[30] This suggests that other industrialized countries are rapidly catching up with the United States.

Concerns about such differentials, and about competitiveness in general, have greatly increased awareness of the importance of sustaining and improving productivity and quality. These concerns get translated into challenges for all areas of human resources management, including more effective work and job design and more effective selection, use, training, development, and motivation of employees.

Innovations in Management and Technology

Successful management practices in other areas of the world, such as Japan and Europe, are affecting the use of human resources in the United States. For example, Japanese success in combining American statistical quality control techniques with American group dynamics approaches led to the invention of the **quality circle,** in which groups of workers meet to discuss ways to improve products and work methods. This, in turn, influenced many U.S. organizations to experiment with this form of worker participation. (Quality circles are discussed in Chapter 21.) As another example, many American firms have adopted the Japanese practice of maintaining low inventories of parts ("just-in-time" inventory systems, or JIT) and requiring suppliers to maintain very high quality standards. One implication is that the suppliers now expect higher-quality work from their employees. Another example is flextime, an innovation that came out of West Germany. Originally called *Gleitzeit*, meaning "gliding time," the concept permits employees to set their own starting and stopping times within broad boundaries.[31] (Flextime is discussed in Chapter 8.)

Technological innovations are also creating rapid change, particularly in certain industries. The transistor, the laser beam, the personal computer (including the laptop, notebook, and pocket versions),[32] the cellular telephone, the fax machine, and the robot all exemplify innovations that have changed the nature of products and the way work is organized. For instance, computers and robots are helping build the General Motors' new Saturn cars and have contributed to a restructuring of the traditional assembly line, making possible more flexible working assignments and giving workers substantial responsibility for quality control.[33]

Regulatory Measures

Since attention will be paid throughout this book to the influence of federal legislation, court decisions, presidential executive orders, and administrative rulings, we will mention them only briefly here. Table 3.1 lists a number of recent laws, court decisions, and executive orders that have had, and continue to have, a profound effect on human resources management. Generally, these apply to all categories of employees, including supervisors, professionals, and executives, who work for employers with fifteen or more employees. Similar state laws and regulations may affect even smaller organizations.

Major Laws

In particular, the Equal Pay Act, the Civil Rights Act, the Age Discrimination in Employment Act, the Equal Employment Opportunity Act, the Americans with Disabilities Act, and the Civil Rights Act of 1991 have given women, minorities, older workers, and persons with disabilities greater protection against **discrimination,** or employment decisions based on prejudice in human resources practices. A 1965 executive order required that firms having federal contracts establish **affirmative action** programs — programs designed to raise the levels of minority and female employment. (See Chapter 6 for a more detailed definition.) The Occupational

Safety and Health Act helped establish mandatory safety and health standards for work organizations, and the Employee Retirement Income Security Act (ERISA) was designed to protect employees covered by private pension plans.

Minorities and Affirmative Action

A Supreme Court decision in 1971 (*Griggs* v. *Duke Power Company*) was aimed at reducing discrimination against minorities caused by educational requirements or testing practices. The Court found that the employer unlawfully discriminated against blacks by requiring a high school education or successful completion of an intelligence test as a condition for employment in certain jobs.

A 1979 decision (*Steelworkers* v. *Weber*) provided additional support of affirmative action programs by permitting companies and unions to adopt quotas jointly to eliminate racial imbalance in the work force. A 1984 decision modified this support, however, by saying that courts may not interfere with seniority systems to protect newly hired minorities against layoffs (*Firefighters Local Union No. 1784* v. *Stotts et al.*).[34]

Late in 1991 Congress passed a civil rights act, which reversed a number of Supreme Court decisions — for example, *Wards Cove Packing Co.* v. *Atonio* (1989) and *Martin* v. *Wilks* (1989) — and amended the Civil Rights Act of 1964, as well as segments of other laws. In particular, the Civil Rights Act of 1991 allows complainants to seek compensatory and punitive damages (previously available only to racial and ethnic minorities) in cases involving intentional discrimination based on sex, religion, or disability. Either party can demand a jury trial. (Damages are limited to $50,000 for employers of a hundred or fewer employees and range up to $300,000 for employers of more than five hundred workers.) In addition, the new civil rights law prohibits **race-norming** or other discriminatory adjustment of test scores or cutoff points on the basis of race, color, religion, sex, or national origin. The act also codifies the concepts of "business necessity" and "job related" stated in the *Griggs* v. *Duke Power Company* case.[35]

The Civil Rights Act of 1991 includes the Glass Ceiling Act of 1991, which established a commission to study artificial barriers to the advancement of women and minorities and to make recommendations for increasing their opportunities and developmental experiences in management. (The **glass ceiling** refers to the invisible barriers to advancement confronting women and minorities.) The Glass Ceiling Act also established a national award for "diversity and excellence in American executive management" to be given annually to one or more organizations that deserve special recognition for promoting opportunities and developmental experiences for women and minorities.[36]

Women's Benefits and Rights

As shown in Table 3.1, a 1978 law and 1983 Supreme Court decisions focused on personnel practices relating to the pay and benefits of female employees. The 1993 Family and Medical Leave Act provided unpaid leave rights in larger organizations for both women and men in the case of family or medical emergencies. (See Chapter 16 on Employee Benefits.) The 1978 Pregnancy Discrimination Act required employers to provide pregnant workers with the same group health or disability benefits as other workers. In *Newport News Shipbuilding and Drydock Co.* v. *EEOC*, the Supreme Court held that employers must treat male and female employees equally in providing health insurance for spouses. In *Arizona* v. *Norris*, the court ruled that employer-sponsored retirement plans could no longer pay women smaller benefits

TABLE 3.1 **Recent laws, Supreme Court decisions, and executive orders affecting human resources management**

LAW, COURT DECISION, OR EXECUTIVE ORDER	EFFECT ON HUMAN RESOURCES MANAGEMENT
Equal Pay Act, 1963	Prohibits discrimination on the basis of sex in wage payments for jobs that require equal skill, effort, and responsibilities under similar working conditions in the same establishment.
Civil Rights Act, 1964	Title VII prohibits employment or membership discrimination by employers, employment agencies, and unions, based on race, color, religion, sex, or national origin; act creates the Equal Employment Opportunity Commission (EEOC).
Executive Order 11246 (1965)	As amended by Executive Order 11375, prohibits discrimination based on race, color, religion, sex, or national origin in government contracts; also requires federal contractors to develop affirmative action plans to raise the level of minority and female employment in their firms.
Age Discrimination in Employment Act (ADEA), 1967	Prohibits discrimination against persons aged forty to sixty-five in such matters as hiring, job retention, compensation and other terms, conditions, and privileges of employment.
Occupational Safety and Health Act (OSH Act), 1970	Authorizes the secretary of labor to establish mandatory safety and health standards.
Griggs v. *Duke Power Company* (1971)	U.S. Supreme Court rules that the employer unlawfully discriminated against blacks by requiring a high school education or successful completion of an intelligence test as a condition of employment in certain jobs.
Equal Employment Opportunity Act, 1972	Amendments to the Civil Rights Act permit the EEOC to bring enforcement actions in the federal courts.
Vocational Rehabilitation Act, 1973	Requires federal contractors to take affirmative action to employ and promote qualified handicapped persons.
Employee Retirement Income Security Act (ERISA), 1974	Prescribes eligibility rules, vesting standards, and an insurance program for private pension plans.
Vietnam Era Veterans' Readjustment Assistance Act, 1974	Protects the employment rights of all disabled veterans and sets forth obligations of employers to military reservists and National Guard members called to active duty.
Amendments to Age Discrimination in Employment Act (1978)	Extends protection until age seventy for most workers and without upper limit in federal employment.
Pregnancy Discrimination Act, 1978	Requires employers to give pregnant workers the same group health insurance or disability benefits given other workers and makes it illegal to fire or refuse to employ a woman because of pregnancy.

TABLE 3.1 **Recent laws, Supreme Court decisions, and executive orders affecting human resources management** *(Cont.)*

LAW, COURT DECISION, OR EXECUTIVE ORDER	EFFECT ON HUMAN RESOURCES MANAGEMENT
Steelworkers v. *Weber* (1979)	Supreme Court endorses right of employers and unions to jointly adopt quotas to eliminate racial imbalance in a work force through affirmative action.
Washington County v. *Gunther* (1981)	In case involving female guards alleging sex discrimination in pay, Supreme Court holds that such suits were not barred under Title VII of the Civil Rights Act merely because the plaintiffs were performing work similar to but not identical with that performed by male guards.
Newport News Shipbuilding and Drydock Co. v. *EEOC* (1983)	Supreme Court rules that employers must treat male and female employees equally in providing health insurance for their spouses.
Arizona v. *Norris* (1983)	Supreme Court rules that employer-sponsored retirement plans may no longer pay women smaller benefits than men, despite studies showing different life expectancies for the sexes.
NLRB v. *Bildisco & Bildisco* (1984)	Supreme Court rules that employers filing for reorganization in federal bankruptcy court may temporarily terminate or alter collective bargaining agreements even before the judge has heard the case.
Firefighters Local Union No. 1784 v. *Stotts et al.* (1984)	Supreme Court rules that courts may not interfere with seniority systems to protect newly hired black employees from layoffs.
Retirement Equity Act, 1984	Broadens conditions under which spouses receive retirement benefits and further amends ERISA through such provisions as allowing pension plan members to take maternity or paternity leave of up to one year without loss of service credit for the period.
Immigration Reform and Control Act, 1986	Makes it illegal for employers to hire illegal immigrants; requires proof of legal authorization to work from all employees hired after November 6, 1986; imposes record-keeping requirements on employers; and provides for stiff fines for hiring undocumented workers and for paperwork violations.
Amendments to Age Discrimination in Employment Act, 1986	Bars most mandatory retirement programs.
Amendments to Public Contracts (Walsh-Healey) Act, 1986	Removes requirement of overtime payments beyond eight hours in one day in government contract work, thus encouraging compressed workweek schedules.

TABLE 3.1   **Recent laws, Supreme Court decisions, and executive orders affecting human resources management** *(Cont.)*

LAW, COURT DECISION, OR EXECUTIVE ORDER	EFFECT ON HUMAN RESOURCES MANAGEMENT
Johnson v. *Transportation Agency* (1987)	Supreme Court rules that employers may implement affirmative action plans to correct sex discrimination.
Worker Adjustment and Retraining Notification Act (Plant Closings Bill), 1988	Requires businesses with a hundred or more employees to give at least sixty days' notice when closing a facility or operating unit or making significant reductions in a work force or in working hours. Each employee and state and local government agencies must be notified.
Employee Polygraph Protection Act, 1988	Bars most private employers from using polygraph tests in screening applicants and from testing current employees unless there is a reasonable suspicion of theft.
Drug-Free Workplace Act, 1988	Requires employers with federal contracts to establish policies and procedures to create a drug-free workplace and to make a good-faith effort to maintain a drug-free workplace.
Older Workers Benefit Protection Act, 1990	Requires that waivers of ADEA rights be "knowing and voluntary" and codifies the "equal benefit or equal cost" principle.
Immigration Act, 1990	Authorizes larger numbers of immigrants to enter the United States on the basis of unique expertise, training, and experience.
Americans with Disabilities Act (ADA), 1990	Makes it illegal to discriminate in human resources practices against individuals with known physical or mental limitations who can perform the essential functions of the job, and requires employers to make "reasonable accommodation" for disabled applicants and employees.
UAW v. *Johnson Controls* (1991)	Supreme Court rules that employers may not bar women of childbearing age from certain jobs because of potential risk to fetuses.
Civil Rights Act, 1991	Allows compensatory and punitive damages in cases involving intentional discrimination based on sex, religion, or disability — previously available to racial and ethnic minorities. Either party to a case can demand a jury trial. Prohibits "race-norming" or other discriminatory adjustment of test scores or cutoff points on the basis of race, color, religion, sex, or national origin. Codifies the concepts of "business necessity" and "job related" stated in *Griggs* v. *Duke Power Co.* Includes the Glass Ceiling Act of 1991.

TABLE 3.1 **Recent laws, Supreme Court decisions, and executive orders affecting human resources management** *(Cont.)*

LAW, COURT DECISION, OR EXECUTIVE ORDER	EFFECT ON HUMAN RESOURCES MANAGEMENT
Glass Ceiling Act, 1991	Establishes a Glass Ceiling Commission to study and make recommendations concerning elimination of artificial barriers to the advancement of women and minorities and concerning increasing opportunities and developmental experiences of women and minorities in management; establishes a national award for "diversity and excellence in American executive management."
Family and Medical Leave Act, 1993	Requires larger employers to give workers unpaid leave up to 12 weeks for family or medical emergencies.

than men, despite actuarial studies showing different life expectancies for the sexes. A 1984 amendment to ERISA broadened the conditions under which spouses, whether male or female, receive retirement benefits and provided that participants in a retirement plan could take maternity or paternity leave for up to one year without loss of service credit under the pension plan. In 1987, in *Johnson* v. *Transportation Agency*, the Supreme Court upheld voluntary affirmative action plans designed to correct discrimination based on sex.

In 1991 the Supreme Court ruled in *UAW* v. *Johnson Controls* that employers could not bar women of child-bearing age from specified jobs because of potential danger to fetuses. This decision, supported by women's rights groups, was seen by many employers as creating a number of costly problems. One perceived problem is the possibility of lawsuits over damage to unborn children; another is the creation of a competitive disadvantage relative to foreign firms if U.S. companies cannot use certain chemicals.[37] An advantage to employees is that the ruling will probably push firms to enhance safety and health protections for workers. (See also Chapter 20.)

Older Workers In 1990 Congress passed the Older Workers Benefit Protection Act, which amended the Age Discrimination in Employment Act (ADEA). The original law, with subsequent amendments, had prohibited discrimination against persons aged forty and over in such matters as hiring, job retention, and compensation, as well as other aspects of employment. The Older Workers Benefit Protection Act was passed partly because of allegations that in numerous instances older workers were being coerced into signing releases of claims against firms in return for severance payments. The new law requires that waivers of ADEA rights be "knowing and voluntary." Further, the new law affirms the "equal benefit or equal cost" principle, under which an employer must provide to older workers benefits at least equal to those provided younger workers, unless the employer can prove that the cost of providing an equal benefit is greater than for younger employees.[38]

Persons with Disabilities

The Americans with Disabilities Act (ADA), passed in 1990, makes it illegal to discriminate in any employment practices against individuals with known mental or physical limitations who can perform the essential functions of the job. This includes "job application procedures, hiring, firing, advancement, compensation, training, and other terms, conditions and privileges of employment," and "applies to recruitment, advertising, tenure, layoff, leave, fringe benefits, and all other employment-related activities." The law also requires employers to make **"reasonable accommodation"** for disabled applicants and employees.[39] "Reasonable accommodation" is interpreted to mean "any modification or adjustment to a job or the work environment that will enable a qualified applicant or employee with a disability to perform essential job functions." The law applies to private employers, state and local governments, employment agencies, and labor unions. Effective in 1992, it covers employers with twenty-five or more employees. Beginning July 26, 1994, employers with fifteen or more employees will be covered.[40]

Immigration

In 1986 the Immigration Reform and Control Act was passed, and gradually took effect, with full implementation in 1988. Under this law, employers are prohibited from hiring illegal immigrants and are required to fill out a form known as the I-9 for all new employees. The law, enforced by the Immigration and Naturalization Service, requires proof of legal authorization to work, retention of I-9 forms for at least three years, and stiff fines for hiring undocumented workers and for paperwork violations.[41] One of the most difficult aspects of the law is how an employer can comply with the law and at the same time avoid violating the Civil Rights Act. (Solutions, or partial solutions, to this dilemma will be discussed in Chapter 9.)

A newer law, the Immigration Act of 1990, is particularly significant in that it makes it substantially easier for U.S. organizations to employ uniquely qualified professionals from abroad. As shown in *International Perspective* on page 61, under this law, three times as many professionals can be admitted than before, providing they offer unique training, experience, and expertise. It is anticipated that employers will be able to secure permanent residency for qualified workers — including those who are to be transferred within international firms — without extensive delays.[42]

Overtime Pay

In 1986 The Public Contracts (Walsh-Healey) Act was amended to permit work schedules beyond eight hours in one day without requiring daily overtime payments. This permitted government contractors to experiment with alternative work schedules, such as the four-day, forty-hour week. The requirement of overtime pay at the rate of time and one-half for work beyond forty hours in one week was kept in the law.[43]

Labor Relations and Plant Closings

A 1984 Supreme Court decision (*NLRB* v. *Bildisco & Bildisco*) gave companies filing for reorganization under the bankruptcy laws the freedom to alter or terminate a labor agreement temporarily, even before a federal judge hears the case, providing the employer has made a "reasonable" effort to negotiate a more favorable contract with the union.[44]

Also, as shown in Table 3.1, in 1988 Congress passed the Worker Adjustment and Retraining Notification Act, or the "Plant Closings Bill." This law requires firms of 100 or more employees, excluding part-time employees, to provide sixty

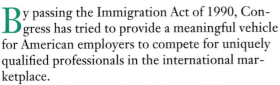

Skilled Workers Find Easy Access

By passing the Immigration Act of 1990, Congress has tried to provide a meaningful vehicle for American employers to compete for uniquely qualified professionals in the international marketplace.

The legislation makes fundamental changes to the selection system for individuals authorized to enter the U.S. for employment, either on a temporary or permanent basis. It also features a new classification and quota system for allocating immigrant visas, which will affect all individuals seeking permanent residency status in this country. The legislation amends a broad range of immigration-related issues, affecting most areas of immigration and nationality law.

Employment-Based Permanent Visas

Those seeking to enter the U.S. as immigrants based on employment opportunities in this country may do so in larger numbers under the new law as long as they present unique expertise, training and experience.

With increased availability of immigrant visas for the most experienced and accomplished workers, it is anticipated that employers will be able to obtain permanent residency status on behalf of certain workers without the extensive delays which now plague the system. In particular, those in the U.S. as intracompany transfers of international firms will have easier access to permanent residency.

The new law does not include automatic transition for those processing for immigrant status based on employment through the current system. Thus, any individual who is currently processing based on employment but does not receive an immigrant visa prior to September 30, 1991, will be required thereafter to comply with additional petitioning procedures to obtain a visa under the new system.

Priority will be given to workers who can document extraordinary ability in their field, to experienced researchers and professors and to managers and executives with international firms. These workers will not be required to obtain prior certification from the Labor Department regarding availability of equally qualified U.S. workers, and "extraordinary ability aliens" will not be required to have an employer sponsor.

Professionals with advanced degrees or extensive experience or accomplishments that will benefit the U.S. economy will be eligible for permanent resident status based on an offer of employment and a certification from the Labor Department. In limited circumstances, a waiver of the employer sponsor and certification prerequisites will be available.

All other workers, including domestics, skilled workers and professionals with undergraduate-level training, will be allocated immigrant visas after the sponsoring employer obtains a certification from the Labor Department, under a new certification procedure, which verifies a shortage of qualified U.S. workers for the position offered. Immigrant visas for unskilled workers such as domestics will be restricted, requiring approximately twice the current waiting period.

days' advance notice of the closing of a facility or operating unit with 50 or more workers. The law also requires sixty days' notice if, during any thirty-day period, the employer lays off 50 to 499 workers and these layoffs constitute 33 percent of the employees at one site. Similarly, if 500 or more workers are laid off from a single site during any thirty-day period, the sixty days' advance notice is required. The same notice is required if work hours are reduced more than 50 percent during each month of any six-month period.[45]

Polygraph Testing

The Employee Polygraph Protection Act was passed in 1988. This law, which stemmed from congressional concerns about accuracy and privacy, outlaws the use of polygraph tests by most private employers in screening job applicants. **Polygraph testing** is a form of testing in which the examiner measures a subject's physiological changes (such as heart rate) in reaction to a structured set of questions.[46] Present employees may also not be tested with the polygraph except when there is a reasonable suspicion of theft or other incident resulting in economic loss to the firm. Federal, state, and local government employers are exempted from the law, and private security firms and drug companies may administer polygraph tests to applicants and employees.[47]

Drug Abuse

Congress passed another law which is having far-reaching implications, at least for federal contractors. As a subsection of the Anti-Drug Abuse Act of 1988, the Drug-Free Workplace Act of 1988 requires federal contractors to establish policies and procedures to ensure that their organizations are free of drug abuse and to make a good-faith effort to sustain a drug-free working environment. Among the requirements of contractors are the publishing of company rules about the possession and use of controlled substances; the establishment of a drug-free awareness program; and, in the event an employee is convicted of violating any criminal drug statute in the work setting, administering appropriate discipline or requiring participation in a rehabilitation program.[48]

Implications for Human Resources Management

Thus, most aspects of human resources management, including work rules, recruitment, selection, promotion, separation, training and development, performance appraisal, compensation, labor relations, and health and safety management, are affected by federal legislation, regulations, and rulings. Almost all aspects of human resources management — including the questions that can be asked in an employment interview — are now potential areas for litigation. We will go into more detail in subsequent chapters.

Summary

Many environmental, organizational, and cultural influences affect human resources management. We have grouped these forces into three major categories: the changing work force, influences of the external environment, and regulatory measures.

Members of today's work force have more education, higher aspirations about participation, and more expectations about due process in the work situation. Some segments of the work force are more likely to find collective action such as unionization acceptable than in the past. Because lifestyles and life circumstances are changing, there is more concern about the balance between work and leisure. The increasing proportions of minorities and older workers in the work force present major challenges in education and understanding.

The large increase in the number of women in the work force, including mothers, has given rise to expectations and pressures about work schedules and day-care centers and has intensified concerns about male-female pay differentials. "Valuing diversity," or "managing cultural diversity," is a major theme of the 1990s, and it pertains to many categories in the work force — women, minorities, immigrants, older workers, and persons with disabilities. There are also more pressures on organizations to avoid layoffs, to follow environmentally sound practices, and to be concerned about the quality of working life.

Influences on human resources management from the external environment are many. Some of the more salient external influences, which tend to be interrelated, are the high cost of energy, inflation, differential industry growth, intense national and international competition (globalization), successful management practices in other countries, government deregulation of several industries, technological innovations, and widespread concerns about productivity and product quality.

Federal legislation and presidential executive orders have had, and continue to have, a profound effect on human resources management. In particular, the Equal Pay Act, the Civil Rights Act, the Age Discrimination in Employment Act, the Equal Employment Opportunity Act, the Americans with Disabilities Act, and the Pregnancy Discrimination Act have given women, minorities, older workers, and handicapped workers greater protection against discrimination in human resources practices. The Family and Medical Leave Act provided more opportunity for emergency leave for both men and women.

An executive order in 1965 required affirmative action programs in firms having federal contracts. The Occupational Safety and Health Act (OSH Act) helped establish mandatory safety and health standards for work organizations, and the Employee Retirement Income Security Act (ERISA) was designed to protect employees covered by private pension plans. The Immigration Reform and Control Act was designed to curb the employment of illegal immigrants, but the Immigration Act of 1990 authorized larger numbers of immigrants to enter the United States on the basis of unique qualifications. Amendments to the Walsh-Healey Act permitted federal contractors to schedule longer work days without paying overtime, thus encouraging such schedules as the four-day, forty-hour week. The Employee Polygraph Protection Act stemmed from congressional concerns about the accuracy of polygraph testing and employee privacy. The Worker Adjustment and Retraining Notification Act was designed to give employees in larger organizations advance notice of layoffs or major reductions in hours of work. The Drug-Free Workplace Act required federal contractors to establish policies and procedures to ensure and maintain work settings free of drug abuse.

In recent years Supreme Court decisions have also had a major influence on human resources management. Many decisions have been aimed at reducing discrimination and eliminating racial imbalance in the work force. Many others have dealt with the disparate treatment of men and women in job opportunities, pay, and benefits.

Ethical Dilemma

Sally Veneti is a whiz at computers. Lately, she has found that she can access the medical records and salary history of other employees using the personal computer on her desk. She has begun to pass on the information to friends at work with comments such as, "This is confidential, but Margaret Jones is making $4,000 a month in that low-level job of hers." Or "Did you know that Mr. McKinnon had a lung removed a while back?"

What are the ethical issues involved?

Key Terms

managing cultural diversity
valuing diversity
participation
organizational due process
reduction in force
quality of work life
perestroika
glasnost
deregulation

productivity
quality circle
discrimination
affirmative action
race-norming
glass ceiling
reasonable accommodation
polygraph testing

Review Questions

1. What are some of the major changes in the lifestyles and attitudes of the work force that affect human resources management today?
2. List and briefly explain eight criteria for analyzing the quality of work life in an organization.
3. Describe the impact of economic conditions and international competition on the internal environment of American organizations.
4. Identify the major federal laws and executive orders related to fair employment practices and worker protection that have been issued since 1960. How has each affected human resources management?
5. Identify significant Supreme Court decisions related to fair employment and worker protection issued since 1960. How has each affected human resources management?

Opening Case Questions

Case 3.1   Meeting at the Country Inn

1. Why do you think Doug McLennan chose to hold the planning session at the country inn? What made it more conducive to his purpose than holding the meeting in Southwest Telecommunications Equipment board room?
2. What impact could such a meeting have on the managers' perceptions of their quality of work life?
3. From a human resources perspective, how can Southwest Telecommunications Equipment compete in the national and international markets and still be sensitive to cost reduction?

Case 3.2   Tropical Bankcorp

1. What changes in the work force and the labor market seem to be contributing to the turnover at Tropical Bankcorp?
2. What kind of flexible working arrangements might work well in a bank? What might be some of the problems with such arrangements?

Comprehensive Case

The Effects of NAFTA

As technology has made geographical distance less of an economic factor, political boundaries have become the most important barrier standing in the way of the development of a truly global economy. Around the world, countries are torn between protectionist and free market philosophies. On the one hand, most nations strive to protect their own businesses and retain their own national identity, often by imposing tariffs and trade restrictions. On the other, they also want to reduce trade barriers, encourage exports, and allow their citizens access to the best goods at the lowest prices.

The countries of Europe have bonded together in the European Community, although progress toward a truly unified Europe has been slowed by disagreements about everything, from the standardization of electrical plugs to the rates of currency exchange. In North America, meanwhile, Mexico, Canada, and the United States have been negotiating the North American Free Trade Agreement (NAFTA), which would turn the three countries into a huge single economic market. Because of the uncertainty about the effects of NAFTA, however, the agreement has become the center of political and economic controversy.

No one disputes that the agreement, if ratified by legislatures in all three countries, would create the largest free-trading entity in the world, with more than 360 million people doing some $6 trillion in business. It is also clear that easy access to inexpensive Mexican labor would help at least some large American and Canadian companies to be more profitable. A number of American manufacturers, from the Big Three automakers to typewriter maker Smith Corona, have already taken advantage of low Mexican wages by moving manufacturing and assembly plants south across the border. Mexican factory workers typically earn $10 to $20 a day, as little as one-tenth the wages of their counterparts in the United States. When Smith Corona moved its manufacturing opera-

tions from Cortland, New York, to Mexico, it calculated that it could reduce its labor costs by four-fifths, and the savings would pay for the move within a year. Similarly, American car manufacturers save an average of $700 per vehicle when they use Mexican rather than American labor.

Such cost savings for big businesses were one of the chief reasons that the Bush administration backed the NAFTA. With fewer restrictions on international trade, more companies could take advantage of cheap labor and expanded markets, therefore improving, at least theoretically, the overall health of American business. But though Bill Clinton was influenced by this reasoning, he also listened more closely to those who worried about the loss of American jobs and the deterioration of the environment.

Environmental issues concern many opponents of free-trade agreements because, under the agreements, one country's or state's tough environmental regulations might be seen as a "restriction of trade" and be invalidated by the agreement. In a free-trade bloc, environmental standards might legally be forced to sink to the level mandated by the least restrictive member country. American environmentalists point out that some American companies have already taken advantage of Mexico's loose environmental regulation by building just south of the border plants that are so environmentally harmful that they would never be allowed in the United States.

An even more widespread concern about the NAFTA is that it will take hundreds of thousands of jobs away from workers in the United States. If the trickle of U.S. companies moving their operations south becomes a flood after the agreement is ratified, the companies' gain may come at the expense of their American employees. Unions and laid-off employees have fought against such moves and in some cases have won support from their elected representatives.

Proponents of the NAFTA acknowledge that the agreement may mean the loss of some American jobs in the short run, but they argue that it will be good for the entire country in the long run. They assert that moving manufacturing operations to Mexico while keeping white-collar jobs in the United States, as Smith Corona has done, is better than moving an entire company to Asia, an alternative that many businesses have chosen. NAFTA's supporters say that the movement of manufacturing jobs to areas with low standards of living is inevitable, and in the long run it is good for Americans to get out of low-skill jobs. They predict that the money going to newly hired Mexican workers will one day return to the United States, as those workers spend their pesos on goods bought from their neighbors to the north. This expansion of a major market for American goods, coupled with the lower consumer prices that should result from companies' ability to use less costly labor, should mean a healthy long-term prognosis for the American economy.

NAFTA's supporters point to the success of Ford Motor Co.'s Hermosillo, Mexico, plant. Because the plant lowers the cost of making Mercury Tracers, it saves American consumers money. At the same time, it helps Mexican workers take a big step from the Third World to the First. Like other companies that have moved south, Ford has found that young Mexican workers without previous automaking experience take quickly to the quality-oriented Japanese-style approaches that all automakers are now using. The result? Hermosillo's cars win awards for high quality, pleasing both the Mexican workers and American car buyers. The challenge for those politicians who debate and implement NAFTA is to find ways to encourage more Hermosillos without creating jobless ghost towns in America's rust belt.

Sources: Douglas Harbrecht and Geri Smith, "A Noose around NAFTA," *Business Week*, February 22, 1993, 37; Stephen Baker, "Detroit South," *Business Week*, March 16, 1992, 98–103; Keith Bradsher, "Global Issues Weigh on Town As Factory Heads to Mexico," *New York Times*, September 1, 1992, A1; Stephen Baker, "'Free Trade Isn't Painless,'" *Business Week*, August 31, 1992, 38–39; James R. Owen, "Congress May Block Passage of Free Trade Pact," *Seattle Post-Intelligence*, December 7, 1992, p. A3.

Discussion Questions

1. What are the potential positive aspects of NAFTA?
2. What are the potential negative aspects of NAFTA?
3. What are some of the implications for HR departments?

CHAPTER 4

Factors in Organizational Performance

LEARNING OBJECTIVES

- Identify factors in the external and internal environment of an organization that influence organizational outcomes.
- Describe the outcomes that can be used to measure organizational performance.
- Explain how the structure of an organization channels behavior.
- Explain the significance of management philosophy for human resources management.
- Define ethics.
- Define the catalyst role of the human resources director.
- Characterize effective leadership.
- Define organizational culture and its components and indicate how it can be assessed.
- Define organizational climate and explain the role of human resources management in measuring it.
- Describe a System 1 organization and a System 4T organization.
- Contrast mechanistic and organic systems

CASE 4.1   Glacier Valley Bank

Mary Sue had never worked so hard in her life, but she was enjoying her job as a loan officer at Glacier Valley Bank. It was clear that the president of the bank and Mary Sue's supervisor expected all employees to be particularly sensitive to customer needs. The slogan "the customer comes first" was not a cliché but a reality in the organization, although there were few rules or official guidelines about how to comply with the slogan. The bank officers and supervisors went out of their way to compliment employees when a particularly difficult customer problem was solved well or to pass along customers' expressions of appreciation. Good customer service was also frequently recognized in performance reviews. Further, the open layout of the bank and its decor contributed to the pleasant atmosphere and to the ease with which employees could help customers and each other.

There was a story told from time to time among employees about how the president had opened the bank during a severe blizzard that closed most of the businesses in town so that an elderly lady could get an important document out of her safe deposit box. The president, so the story went, had picked up the woman in his four-wheel-drive Jeep, taken her to the bank, allowed her to get the document, and driven her home again. The story was told with some awe, and usually in the context of reminding new employees of the importance of going out of their way to help customers. This didn't mean the bank was easy on loans, but it did mean it would go to great lengths to help a customer solve a problem.

Mary Sue felt she was quite free to use her own initiative and judgment to solve customer problems, and she liked this freedom. Another thing she liked about working at the bank was that when problems needed to be solved or changes in procedure were necessary, everyone involved was consulted, and solutions and decisions were usually based on opinions and recommendations agreed to by the group. Even job candidates were interviewed by members of the group in which they might be employed. The president believed strongly in employee participation because, as he said from time to time in branch meetings, "Involved people are committed people." ◄

CASE 4.2   George's Style

George was tough in meetings. He was the head buyer at Sheldon-Saxon, a large department store in a resort city in Florida. At his regular Thursday morning supervisors' meeting, he always questioned individual supervisors relentlessly. Anyone expected to give a report had better be ready and fully informed or George would be quick to respond with caustic interrogation and sarcastic remarks. Two or three such episodes in a row would almost guarantee such treatment indefinitely, no matter how hard the supervisor tried to reverse the trend. Usually, the person would eventually be eased out of the department, through either transfer or discharge. George was even tougher on the supervisors and even more sarcastic at meetings now that the company was experiencing a severe cash-flow problem.

On several occasions, subordinates had complained about George's behavior to the vice president, who was his superior. When they did so, they were rebuffed with comments like, "We back up our managers here," or "If you can't stand the heat, you should get out of the kitchen." As a result, department members stopped going to George's boss with complaints. Most people were aware through the company grapevine that, under this particular vice president, leadership style varied a great deal from unit to unit. A common problem, however, seemed to be that managers at George's level were unskilled in running meetings. It was generally known that a few departments were much happier places. For example, a buyer who had transferred to the Advertising and Public Relations Department, which reported to a different vice president, commented that her new department seemed like a "happy family" compared with the "chain gang" atmosphere in George's unit.

Tomorrow would be Thursday, and Al, one of the more senior supervisors, was due to give a report. He wasn't ready, but it wasn't his fault. On Monday, George had given him a rush project that had simply eaten up most of his time. Now, with just a few hours to go, Al did not have all the figures he needed to prepare the thorough, sensible progress report he was expected to give. "I could talk to George now and tell him what's happened," Al thought, "but he's likely to give me a lecture on time management and tell me that the world won't wait for the slow folks."

Al stewed about the matter for a while and then telephoned another supervisor. "Sharon, the Dictator has me caught between a rock and a hard place. Maybe I'm going to have the flu tomorrow. At any rate, can you meet me in the cafeteria? I need some advice." ◄

T hese two situations give some idea of the factors people consider when evaluating how they feel about their jobs and indicate how these factors are tied to perceptions of the environment within a particular organization. Mary Sue enjoys her job and can identify several reasons why: the supportive approach of management toward employees and customers, the spontaneous rewards for effective customer service, and the involvement of all employees in making decisions and changes. Al feels intimidated by George's leadership tactics, in spite of the fact that he does his best to perform promptly the tasks George assigns him. When assignments conflict, George's tendency to be unsupportive and sarcastic makes it difficult for Al to discuss the conflict with him. Instead, he ponders the idea of calling in sick to avoid George's criticism, and rather than finishing his progress report, he schedules a break with a friend to elicit some support.

This chapter and the next explain how the factors that contribute to an individual's job satisfaction are intertwined with human resources management activities and influence the overall success of an organization. This chapter describes how human resources management affects and is affected by key features of the organization's environment. Chapter 5 discusses individual and group motivation and performance and suggests how human resources management can strengthen both. The discussion begins with an overview of factors related to organizational performance — factors that must be well managed if an organization is to be successful.

A Model of Organizational Performance

Figure 4.1 is a model of the factors to which management must pay attention if the organization is to survive and prosper. The model groups these factors into three categories: from left to right, the external environment, the internal (or organiza-

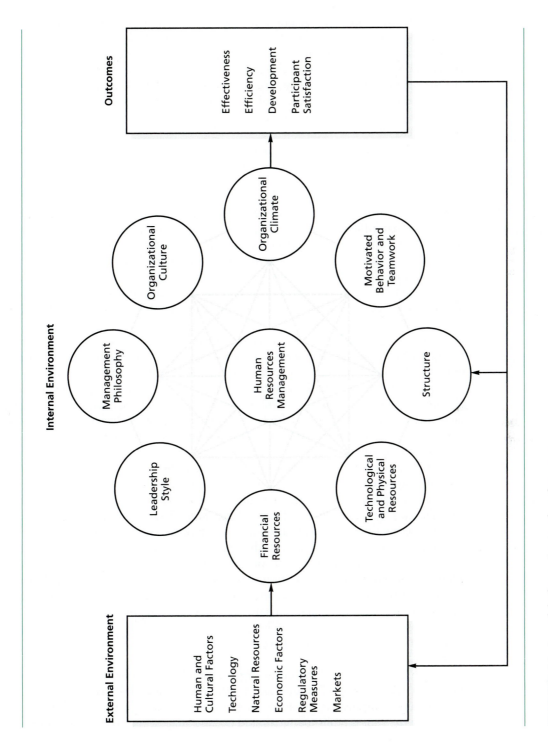

FIGURE 4.1 A model of organizational performance

tional) environment, and outcomes. These categories are linked by large arrows to indicate that extensive influences flow from the factors on the left to the center and then to the right side of the diagram.

There are reciprocal, or return, influences as well, which are suggested by the arrows at the bottom of the diagram. For example, the executives of an organization (part of the internal environment) may influence regulatory measures (a factor in the external environment) by lobbying of government officials or may support educational and training programs in the community in order to have a steady source of qualified people to employ. The organization's effectiveness (an outcome) in producing goods and services of the quality and price desired in the marketplace influences consumers and creates a level of demand (market response) in the external environment.

A brief description of the three groups of factors shown in the model will clarify what is involved in efforts to improve organizational performance.

The External Environment

The factors shown in the left-hand side of the model are realities of the external environment that influence activities within the organization. Management may have only limited control over these factors, but as Chapter 3 showed, the external environment has a strong impact on organizational life and on human resources policies and procedures in particular. Understanding and coping with the external environment is an important part of any effort to improve organizational performance, and human resources specialists — and managers in general — must constantly adapt their activities to these factors.

Among the many human and cultural factors that affect organizational performance are technical and managerial skills and abilities. Knowledge about the Japanese and German management practices mentioned in Chapter 3 would be an example. Values people hold about the treatment of others and about the products of a given organization are other human and cultural factors. Still others are attitudes about work and leisure, attitudes about collective action (such as whether one is willing to help form a union), and attitudes about participation in decision making and problem solving.

Another external factor is the technology available in the society. This includes not only equipment, such as the microcomputer or the robot, but also techniques for using the equipment, and the theoretical and applied knowledge behind it.

The cost and availability of natural resources is another important external factor affecting what the organization does and how well it performs. Economic factors of importance include markets (the number of people wanting a certain product), the purchasing power that people have, the level of employment and unemployment, and the competition that exists for markets and resources. Regulatory measures — laws, court decisions, and administrative regulations — also influence how organizations function and have particularly strong implications for human resources management. (The previous chapter listed numerous laws and other regulatory measures that have a direct influence on practices in human resources management.)

Finally, markets for whatever the organization is producing or wants to produce will affect the firm's profitability and long-term survival. In successful organizations, determining market needs and user reactions is a high-priority activity that serves as a basis for establishing goals and making adaptations to suit market preferences. One of the common characteristics among America's fastest growing companies is that they all focus on "what their customers really want."[1]

The Internal Environment

The factors shown in the center of the model are aspects of the organization's internal environment, over which management and employees together have a great deal of control. In particular, management has extensive control over the organization's human resources policies and practices; the financial, technological, and physical resources it uses; its structure; management philosophy; and leadership style. Factors that are managed less directly include organizational culture, organizational climate, and motivated behavior and teamwork. These concepts tend to overlap, as we will see.

"Human resources management" appears at the center of the model because the effective use of human resources is of primary importance to the organization's survival and long-term success. People form the organization, and people manage the processes that create the product or service for which the organization is in business. In fact, how well these human resources are managed is probably the most critical factor in an organization's overall performance.

The internal factors are connected by dotted lines to symbolize that they all tend to affect or interact with each other; these interactions are discussed in detail later in this chapter. For now, it is enough to say that, for an organization to be highly successful, *all* these internal factors must be intelligently and harmoniously managed.

Outcomes

The factors shown in the right-hand side of Figure 4.1 are **organizational outcomes,** or consequences. These outcomes represent four measures of performance that are useful in evaluating the success of an organization.

Effectiveness, perhaps the most important outcome, can be defined as the extent to which organizational goals are achieved. An example of effectiveness in a successful organization is the production and sale of high-quality bicycles that meet the profit and market goals established by top management. In evaluating effectiveness, it is important to assess the extent to which the goals of individual workers and of groups of workers are in line with overall organizational goals. Thus, individual effectiveness is the extent to which an individual contributes to the attainment of organizational goals, and group effectiveness is the extent to which group goals are achieved in the context of reaching the organization's goals.

Efficiency involves weighing a desired outcome against the resources used to achieve that outcome. It is the ratio of outputs to inputs, or benefits to costs. An organization can be effective in meeting major goals and, at the same time, terribly inefficient (that is, very wasteful). Or an organization can be efficient in doing something other than achieving its goals, in which case it is ineffective.[2] In 1982 and 1983, when U.S. Steel was losing $1.5 billion in its steel operations, numerous managers were resisting cost-cutting measures, including the termination of unnecessary employees at all levels. This prompted the manager of the company's Fairfield Works to remind supervisors that "Fairfield is a profit center, not an employment center."[3] In this case, the plant had become efficient at hiring and retraining unnecessary people rather than in reaching its goals, which included making a profit.

Development is the extent to which individual employees, groups of workers, and the total organization are developing in their capacity to meet future opportunities and challenges. This outcome is very important to the long-term survival of the organization. It is quite possible to reach short-term goals, such as attaining a certain level of profits, but to so seriously deplete human resources that the organization falters and ultimately goes bankrupt. This can happen if insufficient attention is paid to such matters as hiring, training, and giving people the opportunity to assume broader responsibilities. Development also includes the extent to which financial, technological, and physical resources are improved or increased.

Participant satisfaction refers to employees' positive emotional response to their work and jobs. The satisfaction of individuals is important, but so is the collective satisfaction of individuals in groups and in the organization as a whole. High performance is not likely to result from focusing solely on employee satisfaction, but ignoring this factor is to risk some highly negative consequences, such as inability to retain valuable employees or to recruit desired talent.

To contribute effectively to overall organizational success, top executives, all managers and supervisors, and, ideally, all employees need to maintain an awareness of *all* the factors identified in Figure 4.1. Human resources management, as a field of study and as a professional area of practice, must be especially concerned with these factors and their interrelationships. Factors in the external environment must be accommodated, perhaps even influenced; the internal factors must be intelligently and harmoniously managed; and the outcomes must be evaluated continuously to determine the extent to which the organization is successful.

Of particular significance is the way factors in the internal environment influence the design and implementation of human resources systems. It is therefore worthwhile to examine these internal factors one at a time.

The Role of Human Resources Management

The knowledge, skills, and values of managers and of all members of an organization — and the extent to which these are used — will have a major influence on the organization's effectiveness. The way in which these dimensions of knowledge, skills, and values are melded into high motivation and teamwork in the pursuit of organizational goals is particularly important.

Thus, human resources management involves not only individual performance, but the performance of people in twos, such as the interaction of a supervisor and a subordinate, or an employee and a customer; in groups, such as work groups, task forces, and project teams; and between groups or units, such as the interactions between manufacturing and marketing personnel. Further, it is necessary to think not only about the quality of those relationships, but also about how they are influenced by human resources management. For example, at the Glacier Valley Bank, described in Case 4.1, good customer relationships were recognized and rewarded through the performance appraisal system, thus reinforcing effective employee-customer interactions. The Sheldon-Saxon department store, discussed in Case 4.2, desperately needed some kind of an appeal procedure supported by top management — or at least an agreed-upon leadership style — that would permit subordinates to raise and resolve serious concerns. Human resources management in that organization was deficient in that regard, and the organization was that much less effective.

Motivated Behavior and Teamwork

Motivated behavior represents the extent to which individuals will put their abilities to use on the job, and **teamwork** refers to people's willingness and ability to work together to achieve organizational goals. Group and intergroup behavior (relationships among various groups) are significant aspects of teamwork.

Motivated behavior is an important component of the model because the desire and willingness of employees to expend effort to reach and sustain high levels of performance are a critical factor in organizational success. The nature of motivation, what motivates individuals and groups, and what organizations can do to enhance individual and group motivation are complex issues that are dealt with in detail in the next chapter. For now, be aware that motivated behavior and teamwork are complex phenomena that result from the interplay of many forces, including all other features of the internal environment shown in Figure 4.1.

Technological and Physical Resources

In addition to the central resource — people — there are other resources organizations use that affect overall performance. For example, the technology an organization uses will influence its effectiveness and efficiency. If an automobile manufacturer can reduce the costs of welding body frames by 10 percent over a two-year period by using robots, such a step may help the company stay in business. (But how the company handles the displacement of those employees who previously did the welding — a human resources matter — may also have both short- and long-term consequences for profitability and survival.)

Financial Resources

Financial resources obviously are important to organizational success. If the owner or managers of a company cannot raise the money they need to buy necessary equipment and supplies or to employ skilled workers, the organization will be ineffective and may not survive. If cash flow is insufficient to make payments on debt or to meet payrolls, or is insufficient to conduct an effective marketing effort, an organization can quickly find itself in dire circumstances. Conversely, a strong, ongoing cash position can provide an organization with many opportunities, including a stable salary and benefit structure that permits recruitment of people with important skills necessary for long-term growth and profitability.

Structure

Structure is another major internal factor that is crucial to organizational performance. **Structure** refers to all the arrangements in an organization through which the activities and behavior of its employees are directed toward desired goals. In most organizations, mechanisms for channeling activities and controlling behavior will include these kinds of formal arrangements:

- *Management systems:* procedures and devices for channeling organizational activities such as planning, goal setting, staffing, purchasing, marketing, accounting, communicating, and the like. (This concept overlaps the next three concepts.)
- *Job design:* the grouping of tasks into particular jobs to establish the way work is to be carried out and the specific requirements of the jobs to be performed.
- *Organizational hierarchy:* the grouping of workers into units (such as departments and divisions) and levels to determine who is held accountable to whom. (See Figure 4.2 for an example of an unorthodox organizational chart showing reporting relationships at the Erie Insurance Group.)
- *Layout and physical arrangements:* the design of the workplace itself, the technology and equipment made available for completing tasks, and other characteristics of the organization's physical environment.
- *Work rules and regulations:* the standardized procedures for controlling, rewarding, and punishing employees' behavior.

All these mechanisms for organizing the workplace affect the interaction among employees and the level of cooperation or conflict among individuals and groups in the organization.

Further, structure strongly affects the overall environment of the organization, which can be a positive or negative influence on desired organizational outcomes. Technology and physical arrangements influence structure in the sense that plant equipment and layout put people in close proximity to some workers while preventing interaction with others. It is difficult to interact face to face with someone who is stationed on the other side of a loud metal-cutting saw or enclosed high up on a mobile crane. A dangerous, excessively noisy, or unpleasant physical environment can have negative effects on efficiency and employee satisfaction. At Glacier Valley Bank in Case 4.1, the open layout of the bank made it easy for employees and customers to interact, a condition favorable to the bank's business.

Some kinds of organization activities require more structure than others. For example, an automobile assembly plant requires more structure than the advertising department of the same company. But not all manufacturing plants need to be structured according to traditional assembly-line technology, in which a worker performs one or a very small number of tasks over and over again. Alternatives in job design, such as job rotation or the formation of self-managed work teams (see Chapter 7) responsible for planning and directing their own work, can minimize structure, with positive effects on organizational outcomes.

The degree of structure in an organization is in part a consequence of management philosophy. If a plant manager holds a pessimistic set of assumptions about people, he or she is likely to impose more rules and regulations than if an optimistic set of assumptions is held. (See the discussion of Theory X and Theory Y that follows.) Further, many human resources policies and practices (such as standards for performance evaluation and procedures for handling employee complaints and grievances) channel behavior and so become part of the organization's structure. These policies and practices may be a reflection of a well-thought-out management philosophy, or they may partly shape the structure of the organization without any deliberate planning.

Structure, then, constrains or channels behavior. The design of personnel policies and procedures should take into account the existing structure of the

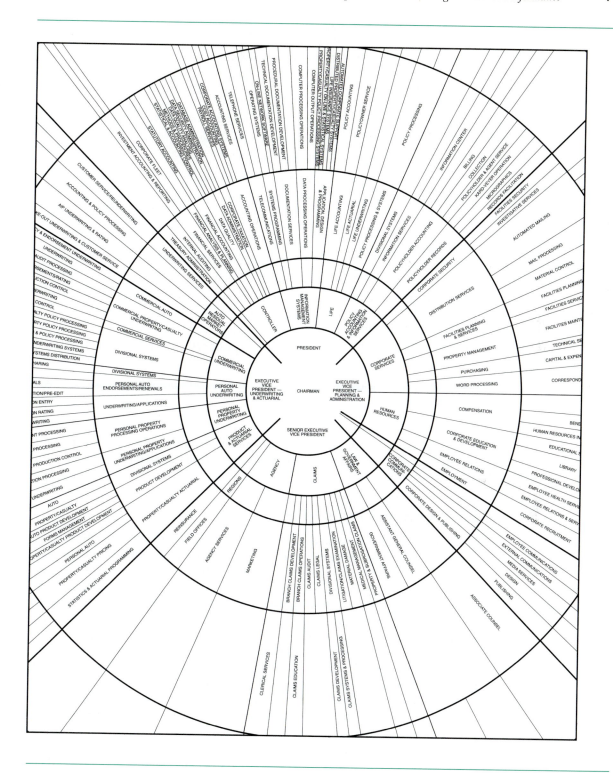

FIGURE 4.2 Partial organization chart of the Erie Insurance Group.
© Erie Insurance Group, Erie, PA. Reprinted with permission.

Contemporary Issues

Tandem's Core Values

Tandem pursues its philosophy the way it pursues its quarterly reports. There are two areas that constitute the philosophy that's passed on to Tandem employees: visions and values. The company's visions are essentially its business goals in terms of products and marketing. At the heart of Tandem's philosophy, however, are its values, which define *how* the company achieves its visions.

The importance that Tandem places on its values was present when the company opened its doors in 1974, but it wasn't until 1988 that these values actually were articulated. That year, the philosophy group worked with hundreds of employees in focus groups to figure out the company's values. Repeatedly, 11 items kept reappearing, and today make up Tandem's core values. They include:

- Respect for people and their diversity
- Importance of the individual
- Fairness
- Honesty and trust
- Open and effective communication
- Hard work
- Flexibility
- Innovation and creativity
- Quality in all we do
- Shared success.

Source: Diane Filipowski, "The Tao of Tandem," *Personnel Journal*, 70 (October 1991):75. Reprinted by permission.

organization, and all managers should be concerned with whether the structure imposed on the workplace enhances or inhibits organizational performance.

Management Philosophy

A key feature of the environment in any organization is **management philosophy**, the set of ideas and beliefs held by the executives about how people should be managed. Examples of different management philosophies can be seen in Cases 4.1 and 4.2. At Glacier Valley Bank, the president's statement that "involved people are committed people" was a strong message to managers and supervisors throughout the organization. It conveyed the president's underlying belief that employee participation in important matters was critical to the organization's success. At Sheldon-Saxon, the vice president's repeated statements that "we back up our managers here" (which also means "we are not going to act on any subordinate's complaints") and "if you can't stand the heat, get out of the kitchen" (which probably means something like "we expect you to accept whatever higher management says and does, and if you can't, get out") were expressions of powerful philosophical attitudes that governed much subordinate behavior.

The philosophy of top management is particularly important because managers and supervisors down through the organization react and adapt to the signals higher management gives off about acceptable supervisory behaviors. For example, if top management believes strongly that employees are to be told exactly what to do with no questions asked, this belief will tend to be acted out down through the organization. If, in contrast, top management believes strongly that employees should have considerable voice in matters concerning their jobs and working conditions, middle- and first-line managers will tend to act on this philosophy. Certainly, different management philosophies have very different consequences, particularly for morale and employee development.

Values   Underlying management philosophy are the values held by executives and other managers and supervisors. A **value** is something that is prized or esteemed. An example is Tandem's emphasis on "respect for people and their diversity" in *Contemporary Issues* page 78.

Ethics   **Ethics** is an extremely important aspect of management philosophy. Ethics can be defined as *the moral values, rules or standards governing the conduct of a particular group, profession, or culture.* Ethics pertains to the rightness and wrongness in human behavior.[4] One way to consider the ethics of a given action or inaction is to assess the extent of its constructive, or helpful, consequences as against its destructive, or harmful, consequences to others, relative to both the short term and the long term. What is deemed ethical and unethical depends on the values held by individuals, groups, and the broader society. Corporate philosophy statements frequently include statements about values or ethics.

A 1991 survey of 1,078 respondents — mostly human resources vice presidents or directors — found that the most serious ethical problems faced by today's human resources professionals have to do with managers making personnel decisions based on factors other than performance. Dealing with favoritism and bias were reported as the most serious ethical problem areas.[5] (More details of this survey will be reported in Chapter 23.)

Beliefs and Assumptions About People: Theory X and Theory Y   Douglas McGregor dramatized the impact of management philosophy by analyzing the assumptions managers make about people in organizations. He described two sets of assumptions, Theory X and Theory Y, that are qualitatively different and lead to distinct leadership behaviors and human resources policies and practices.

A **Theory X** set of assumptions essentially holds that the average person dislikes work and responsibility, has little ambition, and primarily wants security. Managers who subscribe to Theory X believe that most people need to be directed, controlled, coerced, and threatened with punishment to get them to work toward organizational goals. A **Theory Y** set of assumptions involves a more positive view of human nature. Theory Y contends that work is as natural as play or rest, that people will exercise self-direction in working toward goals to which they are committed, and that commitment stems from the rewards associated with attaining those goals. In addition, Theory Y asserts that people can learn to accept and seek responsibility and that most people have more creativity and ingenuity than is usually recognized.[6]

McGregor also described how each of these management philosophies leads to different human resources practices. For example, under Theory X, performance appraisal is very much a top-down process, in which the superior communicates a judgment of the subordinate's performance based on standards established by management. Under Theory Y, performance appraisal can involve more employee participation, with real give-and-take in the review process. Such an approach is far more likely to help both the superior and the subordinate develop their capacities. Compensation practices also reflect different managerial assumptions. Traditional wage plans are consistent with Theory X, whereas participative incentive systems, in which employees share the benefits of increased profits or savings, reflect Theory Y assumptions.

According to McGregor, Theory X underlies traditional "principles of management" that have tended to dominate managerial literature, as well as much of the managerial strategy in business and industry. Theory Y, on the other hand, is consistent with recent research in behavioral science and shows promise of stimulating much more individual growth and development than has been possible under Theory X.[7]

Corporate Philosophy Statements

In most organizations, management philosophy must be inferred from what managers say and do. In some organizations, however, philosophy statements have been developed and published, and these serve as guides to managerial behavior throughout the organization.

For example, at Hewlett-Packard Co., the statement of corporate objectives includes the following remarks about "Our People":

> *Objective:* To help HP people share in the company's success which they make possible; to provide employment security based on their performance; to ensure them a safe and pleasant work environment; to recognize their individual achievements; and to help them gain a sense of satisfaction and accomplishment from their work.
>
> We are proud of the people we have in our organization, their performance, and their attitude toward their jobs and toward the company. The company has been built around the individual, the personal dignity of each, and the recognition of personal achievements.
>
> Relationships within the company depend upon a spirit of cooperation among individuals and groups, and an attitude of trust and understanding on the part of managers toward their people. These relationships will be good only if employees have faith in the motives and integrity of their peers, managers and the company itself. . . .
>
> HP selects and manages its businesses with a goal of providing long-term employment for its people and opportunities for personal growth and development. In return, HP people are expected to meet certain standards of performance on the job, to adjust to changes in work assignments and schedules when necessary, and to be willing to learn new skills and to apply them where most critically needed. This flexibility is particularly important in our industry where rapid technological change and intensifying worldwide competition compel us all to continually seek better ways to do our jobs.[8]*

Although formal statements of management philosophy do not guarantee that managers will behave accordingly, experience suggests that there is often strong consistency among management philosophy statements, personnel practices, and leadership style. In any event, whether written down or inferred, management phi-

---

*Courtesy of Hewlett-Packard Co.

losophy does seem to have considerable influence on human resources policies and practices.

Implications for the Human Resources Director

Management philosophy is a powerful influence in the organizational environment and can dramatically affect the design of human resources systems. But if the top management group is unaware of its own philosophy, management practices at all levels may be unguided or whimsical and will certainly be less than optimally effective. This suggests a special responsibility for the human resources director: that is, he or she may serve as a *catalyst*, one who initiates a discussion within the executive group to reach agreement about management philosophy. It is the human resources director who can raise questions such as the following:

- What is our philosophy of management and what assumptions about people underlie it?
- If we disagree on philosophy, how can we reconcile these differences?
- If our philosophy is inadequate or incorrect, what should it be?
- How can we translate our philosophical attitudes into concrete organizational objectives?
- Do our present human resources policies and supervisory procedures reflect this philosophy?
- How can we communicate our management philosophy effectively?

Dealing directly with such issues can help unify management efforts within an organization.

Leadership Style

Leadership is the process of influencing the behavior of others in the direction of a goal or set of goals or, more broadly, toward a vision of the future. A constructive leadership style, which provides vision and direction and furthers cooperation and productive group effort, is essential to effective organizational performance.

As described by John Kotter, leadership can be distinguished from management, although the concepts overlap and the division may be somewhat artificial. According to Kotter, management involves "planning and budgeting," "organizing and staffing," and "controlling and problem solving." In contrast, leadership involves "establishing direction," which includes developing a vision and strategies for getting there; "aligning people," which includes communicating the direction and securing cooperation; and "motivating and inspiring," which, according to Kotter, often requires "appealing to very basic, but often untapped, human needs, values, and emotions."[9] Both effective leadership and effective management are essential, according to Kotter, if organizations are to be successful for the long term.[10] What we mean by effective leadership is consistent with Kotter's view and includes *both* strong leadership and strong management.

The Nature of Effective Leadership

Although the nature of effective leadership has been debated extensively over the years — and is still being debated — there is substantial agreement about most of the following conclusions.

Traits and Behaviors

It was once believed that certain personal traits, such as intelligence, physical attractiveness, and self-confidence, differentiated leaders from nonleaders. A massive amount of research was conducted in an attempt to identify special leadership traits. However, as researchers found that they were only modestly successful in identifying consistently useful leadership traits, they began to turn their attention to the actual behaviors and actions of leaders. The goal became one of gaining insight into the different factors affecting successful and less successful leadership.[11]

It is now generally believed that *effective leadership requires a mixture of traits and behaviors.* Effective leadership requires intelligence, drive, alertness, and insight regarding the tasks to be performed and the feelings of the persons performing the tasks.[12] Effective leadership requires behaviors such as giving instructions, suggesting new procedures, supplying information, and providing encouragement and support. Another way of saying this, based on years of research, is that effective leadership requires an appropriate blend of **production-centered behavior,** such as assigning tasks, establishing deadlines, and reviewing deficient work, and **employee-centered behavior,** such as being friendly and approachable, listening to subordinates, and involving them in planning or decision making.[13]

Situational Forces

A second conclusion about leadership is that *the appropriate blend of leadership behaviors depends on various conditions or forces present in the situation.* Among these might be the nature of the tasks to be performed or the technology being used. For example, some kinds of manufacturing require more structure and less participation than do research laboratories.[14]

One analysis of leadership, now considered a classic, advances the idea that effective leadership requires assessing the forces in the situation before choosing an appropriate leadership style. Leadership behavior is seen on a continuum from maximum use of authority by the manager — for example, the manager simply makes a decision and announces it — to considerable freedom for subordinates (see Figure 4.3).[15]

Forces that a manager should consider in deciding how to lead are seen as falling into three categories: forces in the manager, forces in the subordinates, and forces in the situation (see Table 4.1). The manager should consider his or her personal qualities: his or her feelings, values, and leadership strengths. Does he or she feel sufficient trust in subordinates? How well does he or she accept uncertainties? The manager should also consider the forces influencing subordinates. How knowledgeable are they about the situation or the problem? Are they interested in solving problems and are they able and willing to take on responsibility? Other important considerations include their need for independence, their understanding of and identification with the goals of the organization, and their expectancies about sharing in decision making. Once all of these factors have been identified and analyzed, the manager must consider forces in the situation itself. What are the skills needed to address the situation, and what are the time constraints, if any? How well do the subordinates work together as a group? Another important factor is the organization itself. How do the values and traditions of the organization influence the situation? Careful analysis of all of these forces is important in determining the most appropriate leadership approach.[16]

Interaction and Participation

A third conclusion, widely shared, and implied by the discussion thus far, is that *effective leadership is an interactive process.* Leadership does not occur in isolation but in interaction with others. Thus, it is important to understand and improve on those interactions. An important aspect of this interactive process is participation.

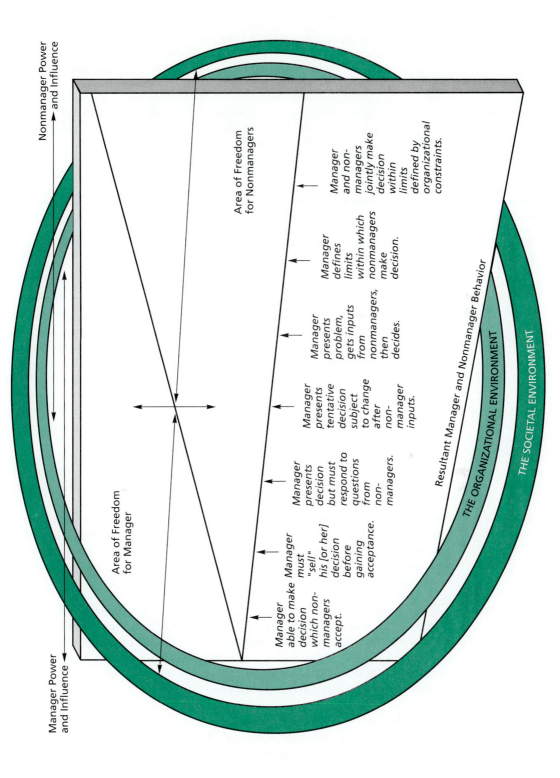

FIGURE 4.3 Continuum of manager–nonmanager behavior

TABLE 4.1 Forces influencing leadership style

FORCES IN THE MANAGER	FORCES IN THE SUBORDINATES	FORCES IN THE SITUATION
Own value system	Need for independence	Values and traditions of the organization
Confidence in subordinates	Readiness to assume responsibility	How effectively the subordinates work together
Own leadership inclinations	Tolerance of uncertainty	The nature of the problem
Tolerance of uncertainty	Degree of interest in the problem	Time pressure
	Understanding and identification with the goals of the organization	
	Knowledge and experience	
	Expectations about participation	

Source: Reprinted by permission of the *Harvard Business Review*. An exhibit from "How to Choose a Leadership Pattern," by Robert Tannenbaum and Warren Schmidt (May/June 1973). Copyright © 1973 by the President and Fellows of Harvard College; all rights reserved.

A fourth conclusion about leadership that can be drawn from research and theory is that *participation by subordinates in attempts to remove barriers to productivity, quality, and cooperation tends to have beneficial results in terms of organizational outcomes.* These outcomes include productivity and satisfying human needs for autonomy, a sense of accomplishment, and interaction with others in accomplishing tasks.[17] Some research studies reach less optimistic conclusions about participation,[18] but there is an explanation for this variance. Participation is of different kinds and quality. Therefore, studies that do not define and describe the exact nature of that participation are bound to produce mixed results.[19] A major review of the research on participation concludes with these summary remarks:

> Decades of research show conclusively that given half a chance — with competent implementation under appropriate circumstances — participative management can assuredly benefit organizations in terms of hard criteria of performance and productivity.... Participative management also has important benefits for workers, in terms of satisfying the ... primary human work needs of autonomy, ... the opportunity to derive feelings of accomplishment from the completion of meaningful work, and interaction with others in the context of accomplishing a task.[20]

These findings are reinforced by a joint study by U.S. and Soviet scholars and managers, which concludes as follows: "Over the years, the Soviets' use of a centralized hierarchy and a directive management style has tended to generate resentment and weakened worker commitment." Clearly, as the Soviet and East European experience has shown, a high degree of reliance on authoritarian leadership practices tends to result in many dysfunctional consequences.[21]

Team Versus One-on-One Leadership

A fifth conclusion about leadership — a point that is not widely recognized in the literature — is that *it is important to make a distinction between a team leadership style and a one-on-one form of leadership.* Much of the research and theory on leadership and participation does not make this distinction. Some managers meet frequently with their subordinates as a group; others seldom, if ever, do so. Some managers

A decrease in the time needed for new-product development is only one of the benefits of meetings of cross-functional teams.

think of their subordinates as an interdependent team; others think of them as a collection of individuals who report to a common superior. Figure 4.4 diagrams these two forms of leadership.

The dynamics of these two styles of leadership are quite different. To illustrate, a group of people whose jobs are interdependent and who never get together to discuss mutual problems must rely on their supervisor to be the link between them. Or they must rely on informal communications among peers. In both circumstances, the people who might well contribute to the solution of some problem are probably not all present. Never meeting together might make some sense if there is so much conflict between two or more subordinates that they have to be kept apart; yet this absence of group discussion occurs in some organizations even when there is no such conflict. In contrast, in a team leadership approach, there are relatively frequent meetings of **intact work teams** — formal leader and subordinates together — in which matters of mutual concern are discussed. Both approaches are used in most organizations, but in widely varying proportions. (The formal leader is the person who has been assigned or elected to the role of leader or supervisor. Sometimes called "positional leader.") As we will see in the discussion of characteristics of effective groups in Chapter 5, task behaviors are those that relate directly to the task, whereas maintenance behaviors have to do with the emotional life of the group. An example of a maintenance behavior is "gatekeeping," that is, making certain that no one is left out of the discussion — a responsibility that group members can exercise as well as the formal leader. In short, effective team leadership is a shared process.

Shared Leadership

A sixth conclusion about leadership comes out of the group dynamics field: *effective group or team leadership requires a sharing of responsibility between the formal leader and all of the members of the group in carrying out effective task and maintenance behaviors.*

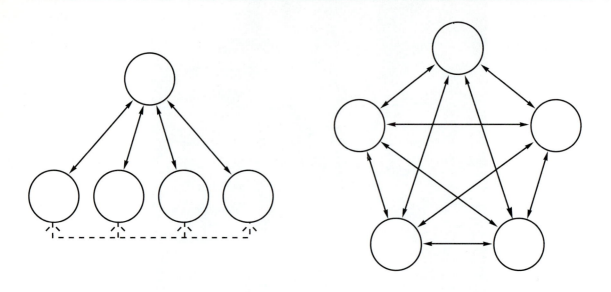

FIGURE 4.4 One-on-one (left) and team (right) leadership patterns

Empowerment   Finally, there is a seventh conclusion with which many managers, trainers, and authors would concur. It has to do with empowerment. **Empowerment** is the enhanced autonomy, creativity, and productivity of subordinates, achieved through training, delegation, involvement, and support. In short, empowerment is the consequence of many of the leadership behaviors discussed above.

Implications for Directors   These conclusions about leadership have implications for several areas of human resources management.

Staffing   Selection and promotion practices need to take into account the traits and behaviors required for successful leadership in the particular setting. For example, in selecting supervisors, fewer participatory skills may be required if the job is supervising workers on an assembly line rather than several self-managed work teams. Someone supervising untrained workers is likely to need greater skills in assigning tasks, training, and reviewing deficient work than someone supervising highly skilled subordinates.

Training and Development   Programs in training and development need to help supervisors and managers acquire a range of leadership skills that can be used under changing circumstances. Participatory leadership skills, in particular, are important in today's organizations. In addition, to the extent that organizational performance depends on effective team leadership and interaction, all team members should be trained in effective team behaviors. Many contemporary organizations have recognized this. For example, factories in which self-managed teams are used tend to involve all team members in team skills training, including group decision making. Organizations that use quality circles tend to give quality circle groups some training in group dynamics and team decision making.

General Design of Personnel Systems

Personnel systems can be designed — either deliberately or by accident — in such a way that they reinforce a one-on-one leadership pattern or a team leadership style. For example, recruitment and selection procedures might focus only on technical training, or they might have an additional focus that includes searching out candidates who have abilities and interests in teamwork. An appraisal system might be so controlling that it creates resentment among subordinates and becomes an obstacle to effective interaction. On the other hand, the system might be designed so that it encourages mutual problem solving. An individual incentive system might get in the way of a team leadership approach by encouraging dysfunctional competition among employees. By contrast, a plantwide productivity plan that makes extensive use of task forces and shared rewards would tend to reinforce a team leadership pattern.

Interaction with Other Managers

Finally, the human resources director and his or her professional staff need to exercise effective leadership in planning, developing, and managing the various human resources systems in the organization. Because authority in human resources matters is shared with others, effective interaction with top managers and supervisors at all levels is essential.

Organizational Culture

Another factor in the internal environment that is crucial to organizational performance is **organizational culture,** a broad concept that includes management philosophy. This concept is widely discussed in business and industry today, but frequently it is not well defined.

Organizational culture consists of those values, beliefs, assumptions, myths, norms, goals, and visions that are widely shared in the organization. We have already defined *value* as something that is prized or esteemed. A *belief* is a conviction that something is true. To illustrate, Edward M. Carson, formerly president of the First Interstate Bank of Arizona and subsequently president of First Interstate Bankcorp, articulated the belief that "people are a bank's most valuable assets, and if you treat them right, you'll be successful."[22] Although this belief is part of management philosophy, it becomes a facet of organizational culture when all employees come to hold this belief and act accordingly. An *assumption* is something that is taken for granted and is similar to a belief, although it is less likely to be stated with such certainty. It may not be stated at all but simply held in people's heads. An example was the assumption held by the executives and employees of Continental Illinois National Bank just prior to its near collapse in 1984 that "we're too big and important to go under."[23] A *myth* is a legendary or traditional story that may be true, half-true, or fictional and recurring. An example was the commonly repeated story within Allied armies before World War II that the Maginot Line — a line of concrete fortifications across the border between France and Germany — was impregnable. A *norm* is an unwritten rule or standard about how people should behave. For example, well-rehearsed stand-up presentations using flip-chart displays appear to be the norm at IBM for presenting proposals or analyses of problems.[24] A *goal* is a stated purpose or desired result toward which people aspire. (See Figure 4.5 for a statement of the multiple "Company Goals" of Knight-Ridder, Inc.) A **vision** is a broad image or view of what organization members want the organization to be like in the future. In sum,

COMPANY GOALS: The basic operating goals of the company are: to achieve systematic and orderly profit growth, to diversify via acquisition and entrepreneurial startups in the media/communications field, to meet the varied and complex needs of its customers, and to maintain the highest standards of professionalism and editorial quality. The company is dedicated to serving the communities where it operates, providing its employees with opportunities to make their lives more productive, and rewarding and enhancing the investment of the company's shareholders.

FIGURE 4.5 Multiple goals of Knight-Ridder, Inc.
Source: Courtesy of Knight-Ridder, Inc.

the cluster of values, beliefs, assumptions, myths, norms, goals, and vision that are widely shared in an organization make up that organization's culture.

Organizational culture is somewhat difficult to pin down or measure, but can often be inferred from immersion in it and observation of what people say, write, and, in particular, do. At Glacier Valley Bank, the high priority given customer needs was not only spoken about and acted on, but was also reinforced by the reward system. From time to time the president articulated his belief that "involved people are committed people," and we can infer that this belief was widely shared in the organization. An underlying assumption undoubtedly was that employee commitment is related to organizational success. Another aspect of the bank's culture could be sensed in the story about the president opening the bank for the elderly woman during a blizzard. Whether accurate or not, the story conveyed the high value bank employees placed on service to customers.

Overlap with Management Philosophy The concept of organizational culture, although broader than the concept of management philosophy, overlaps it in two ways. First, organizational culture includes management philosophy — the latter consisting largely of management's assumptions, beliefs, and values. Second, management philosophy has a profound effect on the culture of the organization, largely because subordinates tend to be strongly influenced by the way management thinks. In reviewing the policy statements of the Dana Corporation, for example, one can assume that the company has a strong culture reflecting its management philosophy (see Figure 4.6).

Variability Organizations, and sometimes subdivisions within them, can differ markedly in their cultures. We can infer, for example, that the culture of Glacier Valley Bank was distinctly different from the culture at Sheldon-Saxon. The culture at Glacier Valley Bank was pervasive throughout the organization. Attention to customer and employee needs was reflected in all the bank's practices and even its atmosphere. At Sheldon-Saxon there was apparently no consistent culture. Depending on the department and its manager, the culture could be open and employee-centered or

 **POLICIES**

EARNINGS

The purpose of the Dana Corporation is to earn money for its share holders and to increase the value of their investment. We believe the best way to do this is to earn an acceptable return by properly utilizing our assets and controlling our cash.

GROWTH

We believe in steady growth to protect our assets against inflation.

We will grow in our selected markets by implementing our market strategies.

PEOPLE

We are dedicated to the belief that our people are our most important asset. Wherever possible, we encourage all Dana people within the entire world organization to become shareholders, or by some other means, own a part of their company.

We believe people respond to recognition, freedom to participate, and the opportunity to develop.

We believe that people should be involved in setting their own goals and judging their own performance. The people who know best how the job should be done are the ones doing it.

We believe Dana people should accept only total quality in all tasks they perform.

We endorse productivity plans which allow people to share in the rewards of productivity gains.

We believe that all Dana people should identify with the company. This identity should carry on after they have left active employment.

We believe facilities with people who have demonstrated a commitment to Dana will be competitive and thus warrant our support.

We believe that wages and benefits are the concern and responsibility of managers. The management Resource Program is a worldwide matter–it is a tool that should be used in the development of qualified Dana people. We encourage income protection, health programs, and education.

We believe that on-the-job training is an effective method of learning. A Dana manager must prove proficiency in at least one line of our company's work – marketing, engineering, manufacturing, financial services, etc. Additionally, these people must prove their ability as supervisors and be able to get work done through other people. We recognize the importance of gaining experience both internationally and domestically.

We believe our people should move across product, discipline, and organizational lines. These moves should not conflict with operating efficiency.

We believe in promoting from within. Dana people interested in other positions are encouraged to discuss job opportunities with their supervisors.

We believe in providing programs to support the Dana Style. We encourage professional and personal development of all Dana people.

PLANNING

We believe in planning at all levels.

The Policy Committee is responsible for developing the corporate strategic plan.

Each operating unit within its regional organization is responsible for a detailed five-year business plan. These business plans must support the corporate strategic plan and market strategies. These plans are reviewed annually.

Commitment is a key element of the Dana Management Style. This commitment and performance will be reviewed on a monthly basis by the appropriate regional operating committee and on a semi-annual basis during Mid-Year Reviews.

ORGANIZATION

We discourage conformity, uniformity, and centralization.

We believe in a minimum number of management levels. Responsibility should be pushed as far into the organization as possible.

Organizational structure must not conflict with doing what is best for all of Dana.

We believe in an organizational structure that allows the individual maximum freedom to perform and participate. This will stimulate initiative, innovation, and the entrepreneurial spirit that is the cornerstone of our success.

We believe in small, highly effective, support groups to service specialized needs of the Policy Committee and the world organization at large as requested. We believe in task forces rather that permanent staff functions.

We do not believe in company-wide procedures. If an organization requires procedures, it is the responsibility of the manager to create them.

CUSTOMERS

Dana is a global company focused on markets and customers. We compete globally by supplying products and services to meet the needs of our customer in our selected markets.

We are dedicated to the belief that we have a responsibility to be leaders in our selected markets.

We believe it is absolutely necessary to anticipate our customers needs for products and services of the highest quality. Once a commitment is made to a customer, every effort must be made to fulfill that obligation.

It is highly desirable to outsource a portion of our production needs. Outsourcing increases our competitiveness and protects the stability of employment for our people. It also protects our assets and assures performance to our customers.

Dana People throughout the organization are expected to know our customers and their needs.

COMMUNICATION

We will communicate regularly with shareholders, customers, Dana people, general public, and financial communities.

It is the job of all managers to keep Dana people informed. Each manager must decide on the best method of communication. We believe direct communication with all of our people eliminates the need for a third party involvement. All managers shall periodically inform their people about the performance and plans of their operation.

CITIZENSHIP

The Dana Corporation will be a good citizen worldwide. All Dana people are expected to do business in a professional and ethical manner with integrity.

Laws and regulations have become increasingly complex. The laws of propriety always govern. The General Counsel and each General Manager can give guidance when in doubt about appropriate conduct. It is expected that no one would willfully violate the law and subject themselves to disciplinary action.

We encourage active participation of all of our people in community action.

We will support worthwhile community causes consistent with their importance to the good of Dana people in the community.

The Policy Committee
Dana Corporation

Approved by the Board of Directors
Dana Corporation

10/28/69   Rev. 12-1-87

FIGURE 4.6 Dana Corporation's policy statements reflect management philosophy

Source: Dana Corporation, Toledo, Ohio.

department and its manager, the culture could be open and employee-centered or oppressive and authority-centered.

The Need for Analysis   Whether a particular cultural aspect of an organization is beneficial or harmful depends on the extent to which that aspect is useful throughout the organization. In Case 4.2, the beliefs or assumptions about people that caused George to belittle an humiliate his staff may have satisfied George's power needs, but they were very harmful to departmental morale and productivity.

It is important for the people in an organization — the top managers and the human resources people, in particular — to be analytical and concerned about the culture of their organization. Specifically, it is important to keep in mind questions like these:

- How is the basic culture of the organization — the shared values, beliefs, assumptions, myths, norms, goals — affecting the organization's performance?

- How widely shared are these factors? For example, is there a strong, organization-wide consensus about goals and vision? Or are the goals and vision in the heads of just a few persons? Or is there a lack of clarity or considerable dissension about these matters, or both?

- In what way is the culture being reflected in human resources policies and practices?

- Are personnel policies and practices inadvertently creating a certain kind of culture?

- Are personnel policies and practices congruent with — or inconsistent with — the desired broader culture of the organization?

- Which aspects of that culture are useful and beneficial, and which hinder organizational success?

The reason it is important for human resources directors — and all managers — to be concerned and analytical about organizational culture is that people and organizations can become victims of organizational culture rather than masters of it. Unless organization members understand and actively shape the culture, highly dysfunctional aspects can emerge.

There is a practical means of measuring some aspects of organizational culture. Culture can be examined through in-depth interviews, discussions, and observations that reveal values, beliefs, assumptions, and so on, but some aspects can also be measured through the use of "organizational climate" questionnaires.

Organizational Climate

Organizational climate, another major factor in organizational performance, is heavily influenced by, and interacts with, the human resources practices in organizations. **Organizational climate** can be defined as *the measurable, collective perceptions of organization members about those aspects of their working life that affect their motivation and behavior —in particular, the culture of the organization, the prevailing leadership style, the degree of structure, and the personnel policies and practices.*[25]

Climate Surveys Questionnaires used to measure individual perceptions of the prevailing climate in the organization are called **climate surveys.** Although climate is usually measured for the entire organization or a major division, scores are typically calculated by departments as well so that management can assess the climate in different units. The human resources department ordinarily coordinates the entire procedure, from obtaining or designing the questionnaire to administering the questionnaire and tabulating the results to helping managers and groups use the results in constructive ways.

Although climate surveys vary in content, a typical one would ask employees to indicate their perceptions or feelings about these categories:*

1. *Structure:* the feeling that employees have about the constraints on the group, how many rules, regulations, procedures there are; is there an emphasis on "red tape" and going through channels, or is there a loose and informal atmosphere?
2. *Responsibility:* the feeling of being your own boss; not having to double-check all your decisions; when you have a job to do, knowing that it is *your* job.
3. *Reward:* the feeling of being rewarded for a job well done; emphasizing positive rewards rather than punishments; the perceived fairness of the pay and promotion policies.
4. *Risk:* the sense of riskiness and challenge in the job and in the organization; is there an emphasis on taking calculated risks, or is playing it safe the best way to operate?
5. *Warmth:* the feeling of general good fellowship that prevails in the work group atmosphere . . . the prevalence of friendly and informal social groups.
6. *Support:* the perceived helpfulness of the managers and other employees in the group; emphasis on mutual support from above and below.
7. *Standards:* the perceived importance of implicit and explicit goals and performance standards; the emphasis on doing a good job; the challenge represented in personal and group goals.
8. *Conflict:* the feeling that managers and other workers *want* to hear different opinions; the emphasis placed on getting problems out in the open, rather than smoothing them over or ignoring them.
9. *Identity:* the feeling that you belong to a company and you are a valuable member of a working team; the importance placed on this kind of spirit.[26]

It would be interesting to conduct climate surveys in the Korean companies described in *International Perspective* on page 92. We would probably find employees giving high scores to "warmth," "support," and "identity." But it is also possible that scores might be substantially less favorable on "structure," "responsibility," "risk," and "conflict," depending on where these organizations fall on the System 1–4T continuum to be discussed later in the chapter.

If climate surveys containing such categories were used in the organizations described in the cases at the beginning of this chapter, they would probably reveal wide differences. Employees of Glacier Valley Bank would probably indicate that there was an emphasis on rewards rather than punishment; that there was considerable warmth and support; that standards of performance were high, at least with

---

*From George H. Litwin and Robert A. Stringer, *Motivation and Organizational Climate*. Boston: Division of Research, Harvard Business School, 1968. Reprinted by permission of Harvard Business School Press.

International Perspective

Corporate Paternalism: Company Knows Best

Perhaps the most dominant principle guiding Korean management — sometimes stated, sometimes not — in large and small companies alike has been familism, both literally (since ownership and upper management is frequently passed on from father to son) and figuratively, in that employers oversee and control employees' lives like good parents. This latter quality, also called corporate paternalism or even corporate welfarism, can blanket every aspect of a worker's life. Blue-collar workers might receive low-cost dorm rooms (or, if they are married, apartments), meals, and free medical care. Managers might be given meals, homes, cars, various family allowances, and college scholarships for their children. At the Hyundai Motor Company in Ulsan, 45 percent of the workers live in a company village that includes a library, public bath, barbershop, athletic fields, and playgrounds — even a billiard hall. The company also built condominiums, which it sold to the employees at cost, and maintained dorms at popular beaches, which it rented to employees for a nominal fee.

But this paternalism can go beyond simple benefits and perquisites. Some managers will make a special effort to look after their workers, particularly the young women, by watching their health, diet, family problems, and future plans, especially with respect to education. If a young woman who usually sends money home decides to take her full wages, management may ask why.

Supervisors will often visit an employee's home when there is illness or a death in the family or celebrate a child's "100th day" after birth; they will also attend and occasionally officiate at employees' weddings.

The sense that they are part of a corporate family is important to workers, for a simple reason. According to a public relations manager at Lucky-Goldstar, "Korean workers select a company, first of all, on the basis of office atmosphere. Money comes second. Because we spend so much time in the office, we see our fellow workers more than we see our real families. So the office must be like a family, too." Indeed, the hours for a Korean worker, both blue- and white-collar, can be so long that there is little time for anything else. This is a source of frustration, and complaints that work takes too much time from family life are common.

Koreans have attempted to graft some of the family feeling — if not outright paternalism — onto their American operations. Managers will attend office parties, visit sick employees (or even their employees' sick family members), and make a sincere effort to know their workers personally. At Samsung's color television plant in New Jersey, management celebrates Thanksgiving by giving its employees a buffet lunch.

Source: Excerpted from Robert P. Kearney, "Managing Mr. Kim," *Across the Board* 28 (April 1991):43–44.

respect to customer relations; and that employees had strong feelings of identification with the bank. In Case 4.2, on the other hand, George's subordinates would probably indicate on a climate questionnaire that there was too much structure, that they did not feel as if they were their own bosses, that punishment was emphasized more than positive rewards, that playing it safe was the best way to operate, that support was lacking, and that conflict was suppressed.

The consequences of unfavorable climate characteristics include using job time to confer with peers in order to cope, high stress, looking for another job, considering reporting in sick, reduced communications with superiors, and considerable job dissatisfaction. We can infer that the likely consequences of the favorable climate characteristics in Case 4.1 were open problem solving, loyalty, cooperation among peers and across groups, enhanced motivation and satisfaction, and high-quality customer service. We can also infer that top management, with the assistance — or perhaps the leadership — of the human resources department, had formulated a conscious strategy to create and maintain the favorable climate that existed in the bank.

Measures of organizational climate, to a large extent, can be considered measures of the organizational outcome we have called "participant satisfaction." Thus, organizational climate is both an important internal variable to be closely monitored by management and, at the same time, a reflection of participant satisfaction, an organizational outcome important in its own right.

Two Typologies

It can be useful to have one or more typologies — a systematic classification of types — of organizations in mind so that different organizations can be contrasted in terms of such broad aspects as culture, climate, leadership style, and so on. We have found two typologies to be particularly useful: Burns and Stalker's concepts of mechanistic and organic systems and Likert and Likert's concepts of "Systems 1 through 4T."

The typology of Scottish authors Tom Burns and G. M. Stalker includes some dimensions of structure, leadership style, management philosophy, and organizational culture. At least some aspects of culture can be inferred from their typology — in particular, values, beliefs, and norms. The typology of Rensis and Jane Likert, researchers at the University of Michigan, focuses largely on leadership style and organizational climate, but it also stresses the organizational outcome of participant satisfaction. Implicit in the Likert typology are cultural factors such as values, beliefs, assumptions, and norms. We will first consider mechanistic and organic systems and then move on to Systems 1–4T.

Mechanistic and Organic Systems

Burns and Stalker contrast two managerial systems: **mechanistic systems** and **organic systems.** Neither type is necessarily found in a pure form, but both are readily identified in the experience of most people. They represent the opposite ends of a continuum, and are not seen as a dichotomy. The two types of systems can be found in various mixtures in organizations, and their application depends a great deal on the particular technologies being used. This section highlights some of the features of each.

Mechanistic Systems

Burns and Stalker see the mechanistic form of organization as appropriate to stable conditions and having the following characteristics:

1. A high degree of task differentiation and specialization, precise delineation of responsibilities and methods to be used.

2. Extensive reliance on each managerial level for coordination, control, and communications.
3. A tendency for the top people to control incoming and outgoing communications, and to be very conservative about giving out information within the system.
4. Extensive emphasis on vertical interactions between superiors and subordinates, with the activities of subordinates mainly governed by these interactions.
5. Insistence on loyalty to superiors and to the organization.
6. A high value placed on knowledge, skill, and experience of particular relevance internally to the organization, in contrast to more general knowledge, skill, and experience.[27]

Another characteristic, though not explicit in Burns and Stalker's model, is also one of the key characteristics of mechanistic systems:

7. A one-on-one leadership style, as described earlier in the chapter.[28]

Organic Systems   By contrast, organic systems are seen by Burns and Stalker as appropriate to rapidly changing conditions and have the following characteristics:

1. A continuous reassessment of tasks and assignments through interactions with others.
2. A network of authority, control, and communication stemming more from expertise and commitment to the total task than from reliance on the omniscience of the chief executive or the authority of the managerial hierarchy. The lead on projects is taken by the most informed and capable person, and this is usually decided by consensus.
3. A tendency for communications to be very open and extensive.
4. The encouragement of a communications pattern and style that are diagonal (between people of different rank and across functional groups) and lateral (across the organization at the same rank), as well as vertical. The style is also consultative and information-giving rather than a command style.
5. More emphasis on commitment to the organization's mission, progress, and growth than on obedience and loyalty.
6. A high value placed on expertise relevant to the commercial and technological milieu of the organization.[29]

Finally, there is yet another characteristic that is central to organic organizations:

7. A team leadership style, with an emphasis on high participation and considerable attention to interpersonal, group, and intergroup processes. One-on-one interaction is frequent, but systematic attention is paid to bringing the relevant people together to work on matters of mutual interdependence and concern.[30]

Which of these management systems is best? Space is lacking to analyze the research in detail, but some highlights can be provided. In a study done in South Essex, England, Joan Woodward discovered that successful firms of the "large-batch production" type (large-batch or assembly-line production) tended to be mechanistic, while successful firms of the unit or "small-batch" production type tended to be organic.[31] In another study, Paul Lawrence and Jay Lorsch found that the production units of six organizations had a much more formalized structure than the research laboratories in the same firms.[32] Jay Lorsch and John Morse determined, in a sample of four manufacturing plants and six research laboratories, that the two more effective manufacturing plants tended to be mechanistic while the two less effective plants were perhaps too organic. It was just the reverse in their sample of six research laboratories, where the more effective labs tended to be organic, and the less effective labs tended to be mechanistic. However, an organic characteristic was present in *all* of the successful firms: the capability of people to bring problems to the surface and work them through.[33]

In short, it appears that the mix of organic and mechanistic traits for optimal effectiveness depends in large measure on the type of product and the production technology used, both across companies and within companies. Note, however, that Burns and Stalker believed that the mechanistic form of organization was appropriate to stable conditions and the organic to rapidly changing conditions. Most industries in the 1990s find themselves in the latter situation. Besides, skill in surfacing problems and working together to reach solutions — an organic characteristic — needs to be present in all organizations. Historically, many, if not most, industries have been too mechanistic, and the thrust of many of the managerial changes in recent years has been to strengthen and add organic characteristics. (Job enrichment and self-managed teams, discussed in Chapter 7, are only two of many possible examples.)

Systems 1–4T   Another typology which can be useful in analyzing organizations, and which somewhat parallels Burns and Stalker's concepts, is Rensis and Jane Likert's descriptions of "management Systems 1–4T." In this typology, Rensis and Jane Likert describe four management systems that vary in terms of three major dimensions: leadership, organizational climate, and employee satisfaction. Each of these three categories has a number of subdimensions. For example, the leadership category includes managerial support, managerial interaction facilitation, and peer support. The subdimensions are converted into a hundred or more questionnaire items (the total questionnaire is called the Survey of Organizations), which are answered anonymously by employees.[34]

The dimensions of the survey can be identified in the descriptions of Systems 1, 2, 3, and 4. We will consider Systems 1 and 4, which are at the ends of the continuum.

In the System 1 type of organization, control, goal setting, and decision making are concentrated at the top. There is practically no seeking of subordinates' ideas, and subordinates are not involved in decisions related to their work. In general, little or no confidence is shown in subordinates. Threats, punishment, and fear are used extensively, and cost and productivity data serve as a means of policing and punishment. Communication is largely downward. There is little lateral communication and upward communication is minimal and frequently distorted. Mistrust, hostility, and dissatisfaction dominate, and there is considerable resistance in the informal system to the directives of the formal organization. Teamwork hardly exists at all, and motivation is low, except at the top.

System 4 is the most participative and is highly group-process oriented. As viewed by organization members, goals are established through participation and many decisions are made by consensus. Group interaction is facilitated by superiors who are the "linking pins" between work groups and by task force members from various relevant units. A high level of confidence is shown in subordinates: their ideas are sought as a matter of course, and they are fully involved in decisions related to their work. Communication flow is downward, upward, and lateral, and there is little distortion. No use is made of coercion or fear; high motivation stems from extensive involvement, group goals, and compensation systems developed through participation. Cost, productivity, and other control data are used for self-guidance and problem solving. Favorable attitudes prevail. People at all levels feel responsible for achieving the organization's goals, and there is little or no covert resistance to unit goals and policies. Teamwork is evident throughout the organization.[35]

When variables such as "the levels of performance goals" and the "level of technical competence" are added to the typology and these scores are also high, Likert and Likert refer to this condition as **System 4T**, the *T* standing for "Total model."[36]

Each of the Systems 1–4 works, although there is considerable evidence to show that System 1 organizations usually pay a heavy price in terms of employee resistance of all kinds and in low morale and commitment. Further, there is a good deal of research indicating that, over the long term, high scores on organizational climate and other dimensions of the questionnaires discussed on the preceding pages tend to be associated with organizational productivity, profitability, and excellent labor relations.[37] In general, and increasingly, managers and employees alike have the expectation that organizations can profitably shift toward Systems 3 or 4 (or 4T). (The reader will note that System 4 is congruent with the optimistic philosophy of Theory Y, as described earlier, and System 1 tends to be congruent with Theory X philosophy, which is more pessimistic about human nature.)

Summary

This chapter has presented a model of the factors that are considered crucial in organizational performance. These factors fall into three categories: external, internal, and outcomes. All are interrelated, and influence or are influenced by human resources management.

The external factors are human-cultural factors, technology, natural resources, economic factors, regulatory measures, and markets. The internal factors are human resources management; financial, technological, and physical resources; structure; organizational climate; motivated behavior and teamwork; organizational culture; management philosophy; and leadership style. The extent to which the organization attains success on measures of organizational performance (outcomes) — effectiveness, efficiency, development, and participant satisfaction — depends heavily on how well the internal factors are managed and how well the organization accommodates to and uses such external factors as available human skills and capabilities, available technology and natural resources, and regulatory measures.

In the internal environment of an organization, human resources management is central, affecting in particular the motivation and teamwork of the employees. Technological and physical resources also affect performance and employee relations, and adequate financial resources are necessary to maintain good employee policies.

The various kinds of structure — management systems, job design, organizational hierarchy, layout and physical arrangements, and work rules and regulations — constrain and channel behavior. Structure affects interactions among employees and, in turn, efficiency and employee satisfaction. It is important to be alert to the degree to which various structuring mechanisms — including those in human resources management — strengthen or inhibit individual and organizational performance.

Management philosophy about how people should be managed has a powerful effect throughout the organization. Management based on Theory X, a negative view of people's motives, will be distinctly different from management based on Theory Y, a positive view. The human resources director can serve as a catalyst, initiating discussion within the top management group of the consequences of different philosophies and helping management agree on which philosophy is desirable for the organization. Values and ethics are extremely important aspects of management philosophy.

Effective leadership — the process of influencing individual and group behavior toward the attainment of organizational goals and vision — requires a mix of traits and behaviors appropriate to the conditions or forces present in the situation. Leadership is an interactive process; it can be thought of as a one-on-one process or as a team matter or both. Participation by subordinates tends to have beneficial results, provided the appropriate conditions are present; the leader and subordinates must share responsibility for carrying out task behaviors and behaviors relating to the emotional life of the group. These assertions have a number of implications for human resources management in the areas of staffing, training and development, and the design of personnel techniques and programs generally.

Organizational culture is another internal factor crucial to organizational performance, and one that interacts with human resources management. Human resources directors — and all managers — should be concerned and analytical about organizational culture because people and organizations need to be masters of that culture rather than victims of it.

Organizational climate is the measurable collective perceptions of employees about the culture, leadership style, structure, and personnel policies and practices of an organization. The human resources department usually assists the organization in the use of climate surveys. Research indicates that how people perceive the organization is related to organizational performance.

Two typologies, Burns and Stalker's mechanistic and organic systems and Likert and Likert's Systems 1–4T, are seen as helpful in analyzing organizations across major aspects of organizational culture, climate, and structure. While the organic, Systems 4T managerial approaches tend to have many positive consequences, the mix of characteristics has to fit such variables as the production technology used, the particular unit of the organization, and the qualifications of organization members. Managers and human resources professionals need to be aware of and proactive about the type of managerial system being created through various human resources policies and practices.

Ethical Dilemma

Frank Levy, vice president of purchasing of Acme Retail, has told his department heads that he wants more openness and frank participation in their regular meetings with him, both as a group and individually. He has asked their involvement in reducing the number of purchasing division employees by 10 percent, and they have worked with him to tackle the problem. He has not disclosed to them that he plans to lay off at least three department heads — probably the older, highest salaried department heads — when the 10 percent quota is reached.

Is Frank's approach ethical? Why or why not? Discuss the pros and cons of how he is proceeding.

Key Terms

organizational outcomes	Theory X
effectiveness	Theory Y
efficiency	leadership
development	production-centered behavior
participant satisfaction	employee-centered behavior
motivated behavior	intact work teams
teamwork	empowerment
structure	organizational culture
management systems	vision
job design	organizational climate
organizational hierarchy	climate surveys
layout and physical arrangements	mechanistic systems
work rules and regulations	organic systems
management philosophy	Systems 1–4T
value	System 4T
ethics	

Review Questions

1. Identify factors in the internal environment of an organization that influence organizational outcomes.
2. List, and briefly explain, the outcomes that can be used to measure organizational performance.
3. How does structure channel behavior in an organization? Give examples.
4. Discuss the impact of management philosophy on human resources management.
5. Define ethics. Describe how the ethics of an action might be evaluated.
6. Describe the catalyst role of the human resources director.
7. Describe some of the behaviors that characterize effective leadership.
8. Define organizational culture and its components. How can organizational culture be assessed?
9. Define organizational climate. How can it be measured?
10. Describe a mechanistic system and contrast it with an organic system.
11. Describe the characteristics of a System 1 organization and a System 4 organization. What is meant by System 4T?

Opening Case Questions

Case 4.1 Glacier Valley Bank

1. What is the basic management philosophy of Glacier Valley Bank?
2. Is the president of the bank a Theory X or Theory Y manager? Explain your answer.

3. What are the implications of the bank's philosophy for the human resources department?
4. What is the organizational climate of the bank?

Case 4.2 George's Style

1. What style of leadership does George demonstrate?
2. What might happen to George's division if he continues in his leadership style?
3. What impact does George's leadership style have on Al?

Comprehensive Case

Autocrats Not Welcome

Some of the most respected and progressive management concepts of the 1980s — quality circles, employee ownership, participatory management, and profit sharing — emphasized the importance of blurring the distinction between executive and employee. Yet during the Reagan era, many people in the business world extolled the virtues of business leaders who were "tough," "action-oriented," and "decisive" and who could make the difficult decisions that would lead to "downsizing" to a "lean and mean" organization. The ideal American organization seemed schizophrenic — a team of supportive equals led by a ruthless, insulated despot.

More recently, many companies have begun to realize that the tough, autocratic, driven leader is incompatible with the kind of organization they are trying to create, even if such a leader seems to be helping the organization be more profitable. Sunbeam-Oster, for instance, fired Chairman Paul B. Kazarian in December 1992 even though Kazarian's restructuring of the company had turned the company around, from losing millions in 1990 to posting a $47 million profit in 1991. In fact, just before Sunbeam fired Kazarian, it had rewarded him with a large bonus to reflect the company's strong financial standing. But the board of directors had lost confidence in Kazarian because of his poor relationships with people both inside and outside the company. The managing director for one of Sunbeam's advertising agencies said, "He sure made a lot of people nuts," while a former Sunbeam executive described the company's culture under Kazarian as like a "military barracks."[1] By firing Kazarian, Sunbeam seemed to be making a statement that such an atmosphere — though perhaps necessary during the company's restructuring — was not appropriate for a company that wanted continued growth.

In reassessing leadership styles, many organizations are now looking at successful mavericks and developing new paradigms of the leader as listener, healer, even "servant." The most radical of these alternative leadership ideas, "servant leadership," was developed by Robert K. Greenleaf and his think tank, the Center for Applied Ethics. Servant leaders are "nice guys" who somehow don't finish last, who make their way through the organizational meat grinder to come out on top. To them, profit is not the only goal; providing employees with meaningful, fulfilling work may be just as high a priority. They listen, take surveys and polls, and try to lead the organization in ways that will please customers and employees. Rather than use their exalted positions for self-promotion, they tend to be self-effacing, and instead of acting quickly and ruthlessly and then turning their backs, they try to help and to heal, to treat employees as human beings, and to make decisions for the long-term good of the organization and its people.

The late Sam Walton, one of America's richest people and head of the phenomenally successful Wal-Mart Stores, was one such leader. He believed that the real boss is the customer, that employees and suppliers are partners, and that managers are servants. He and his company focused not on short-term profits but on long-term goals. Wal-Mart managers are allowed to make mistakes, and change is encouraged rather than feared. The continuing success of Wal-Mart, despite Walton's death in 1992, demonstrates the value of his principles.

Another very successful company that has challenged traditional views of leadership is Ben & Jerry's Homemade, Vermont-based makers of premium ice cream. From top to bottom, the company reflects, in the words of its mission statement, "a deep respect for individuals, inside and outside the company, and for the communities of which they are a part." The company makes decisions by first considering the effect of a proposal on the employees, before looking at the "bottom line." The company conducts "rate-the-boss" surveys every year and endeavors to keep its organizational structure as flat as possible.

General Electric Co. is a much more traditional company than Ben & Jerry's or Wal-Mart, but in 1992 it too was calling for an end to autocratic management. CEO John F. Welch, Jr., wrote in a letter to stockholders that GE "cannot afford management styles that suppress and intimidate" employees. The company has sent executives to learn from Wal-Mart and now insists that managers focus not just on making profit but on sharing the company's values — thinking globally, listening to customers, battling bureaucracy.

Arnold Brown, chairman of a consulting firm specializing in trend analysis and change management, attributes the reassessment of leadership styles to a pervasive disgust with what he calls leaders' "imperial arrogance." According to Brown, people are sick of executives' multimillion dollar compensation, bloated sense of self-importance, and isolation from workers and stockholders alike. He contrasts the behavior of Sam Walton, who would visit stores unannounced to talk and *listen* to customers and employees, with that of the former General Motors chair, Roger Smith, whose inaccessibility became the subject of the film *Roger and Me*. As Brown sees it, executives like Smith who surround themselves with security guards and public relations experts are doomed to lose touch with the people they are supposed to lead and serve; such remoteness means that the leaders cannot respond quickly and efficiently, as any business must if it is to stay competitive.

Servant leaders are successful because they respond to very basic and universal human needs. People want to feel valued and important. As J. C. Penney's former CEO Donald Seibert puts it,

they want to be "insiders." Consultant Pat McLagan compares the tendency of some American companies to revert to Rambo-style leadership in difficult times with what happened in the Soviet Union. Although not as extreme, perhaps, as in the Soviet Union, some American companies are heavily bureaucratic, operate from the top down, stifle dissent, and get more repressive and dictatorial when times get tough. Without a shift in the way they think about leadership, many American organizations may soon follow the Soviet Union into the history of failed enterprises.

1. Quoted in Geoffrey Smith, "How to Lose Friends and Influence No One," *Business Week*, January 25, 1993, p. 42.

Sources: Arnold Brown, "The Naked Emperors," *Across the Board* 29 (June 1992):13–14; James C. Hyatt and Amal Kumar Naj, "GE Is No Place For Autocrats, Welch Decrees," *Wall Street Journal*, March 3, 1992; p. B1; Walter Kiechel III, "The Leader As Servant," *Fortune*, May 4, 1992, p. 121; Walter Kiechel III, "When Management Regresses," *Fortune*, March 9, 1992, pp. 157–162; Jennifer J. Laabs, "Ben & Jerry's Caring Capitalism," *Personnel Journal* 71 (November 1992):50–57; Donald V. Seibert, "People Want to be Insiders," *Across the Board* 29 (September 1992):27; Geoffrey Smith, "How to Lose Friends and Influence No One," *Business Week*, January 25, 1993, pp. 42–43; Wendy Zellner, "Mr. Sam's Experiment Is Alive and Well," *Business Week*, April 20, 1992, p. 39.

Discussion Questions

1. Describe the leadership style of the leader who becomes "servant." Contrast this with managerial behavior that is autocratic.
2. If management style in an organization shifts from highly autocratic to more of a "servant" mode, what are some of the implications for human resources management?

CHAPTER 5

Motivation and Performance of Individuals and Groups

LEARNING OBJECTIVES

- Summarize the key theories of motivation and their implications for human resources management.
- Describe the relationship among motivation, performance, and satisfaction.
- Give several reasons why human resources management should be concerned with employee dissatisfaction.
- Explain the importance of work groups in the modern organization.
- Identify the role of human resources management in the development of effective work groups.
- Explain the consequences of excessive intergroup conflict and competition in the organization, and discuss the implications for human resources management.

CASE 5.1   The Merger

Tom Nelson was a young, college-trained, and ambitious purchasing agent at Lake-view General Hospital in upstate New York. Until recently, he had been sure his superiors considered him an excellent employee. His pay increases had been substantially above average, and his boss frequently complimented him on his work. He had been highly motivated and displayed the same enthusiasm for his job that he showed in his competitive handball and volleyball games. Tom liked the area and hoped to stay, having aspirations to move up the ladder to the top administrator's job.

Lately, however, Tom sensed that all was not well. The hospital had been purchased by a private, profit-oriented organization, and there were frequent directives from corporate headquarters that things should be done differently. Some were reasonable, but others seemed to Tom to decrease efficiency and were very irritating. The corporate vice president in charge of purchasing had visited only once, and that brief visit had left the impression that the corporation was going to do most of the talking and very little listening. Tom's boss seemed subdued and preoccupied, and now seldom commented on Tom's work. There had been some speculation that the purchasing function might be consolidated with the purchasing department of another hospital owned by the same corporation. This possibility was not unreasonable, because the other hospital was only fifteen miles away. Tom wondered whether he would soon be out of a job.

Tom's coping with the situation took several forms. For one thing, he stopped making proposals that would increase efficiency. Further, he triple-checked his work to make sure there were no mistakes. He had a reputation for being accurate, but now accuracy was becoming almost an obsession. He also stopped volunteering for task forces that the hospital had traditionally used to tackle procedural problems involving several departments.

Tom was aware of the reasons for his changed attitudes and behavior. "If I make a mistake, they'll build up a file to use against me so they can lay me off; if I don't, somebody in headquarters will get the credit anyway; I'm not going to give headquarters any excuse to criticize my work," Tom thought. "And I'm not going to waste my time improving the efficiency of this place when those fools at corporate systematically make things worse. I'm going to lie low for a while and concentrate on my handball game." ◄

CASE 5.2   Solving Customer Problems at Hydraulic Systems Corporation

Sharon Yee, manufacturing director at Hydraulic Systems Corporation, had a problem. Jack Korman, marketing director, had just phoned with reports from three field representatives. Several newly installed hydraulic activators were malfunctioning, customers were complaining, and the company might lose some important business if the problems weren't corrected immediately.

"How soon can you get the field reps plus some of our customers' engineers together with two or three of my manufacturing people?" Sharon asked Jack.

"That would depend on where they meet. Denver is central, and one of the customer problems is there. I'll call the customer to see if we can set up a meeting at their Denver plant tomorrow, and we'll fly the others in," responded Jack.

"Let me know," said Sharon. "If you'll give me the names of the reps, I'll have my people get on the phone with them to do some preliminary work before they leave for Denver, and I'll ask my assistant, Joe Stevens, to arrange an agenda with your staff."

After they had hung up, Sharon thought to herself, "I'm glad we've got a company-wide bonus plan. It doesn't create cooperation between the marketing staff and my people, but it sure helps."

The meeting with the customers was held in Denver the next day. Three hours beforehand, the marketing and the manufacturing departments met together to share information on the nature of the problem and to plan how to make the meeting with the customers as productive as possible. Joe Stevens presided at both meetings.

At the preliminary meeting, Joe first presented a tentative sequence of items for discussion and then rearranged it, on the basis of suggestions from both the marketing reps and the manufacturing people. The first agenda item was "Field reps' information about the problem." During this part of the meeting, the manufacturing people mostly listened to the field reps' reports and asked questions for clarification. There was no effort to find out who was at fault, no blaming of one department by the other, and no sarcasm. As the meeting went on, it was clear that each department was using the other as a resource to solve a shared problem. The mood seemed to be, "We've got a problem that needs to be solved together, and everyone in both groups has a contribution to make."

This mood carried over into the meeting in Denver with the customers. By early evening there was agreement that the manufacturing department knew how to correct the products already sold and eliminate the problem in future production runs. Everyone at the meeting was satisfied with the outcome. Before adjourning, the Denver customer said, "I know a good steak house. You can't leave until morning anyhow, so please be our guests."

"Oh, no," replied Joe. "We created the problem and you helped us solve it. The steaks are on us, but we'll let you pick the place."

After the group had arrived at the restaurant and ordered, Joe telephoned Sharon long distance to tell her the results of the meeting. Sharon was pleased and said she would call Jack first thing in the morning. She also commented, "When you get back tomorrow, we'll want to send a short note thanking the people who met with you. Once again, Joe, you've done a first-rate job in running a problem-solving session, and it's really appreciated. Have a good trip back." ◄

T hese situations suggest that individual motivation and job satisfaction are influenced by many of the organizational factors shown in Figure 4.1 in the preceding chapter. In turn, motivation and satisfaction have a direct influence on organizational performance.

At Lakeview General Hospital, in Case 5.1, Tom Nelson's motivation and performance were influenced by organizational climate factors such as increased "red tape"; by changes in leadership style that included less support, less recognition, and less listening; and by a perception that management's concern with financial resources might cost him his job. Although his way of coping may not have been constructive for himself and for the hospital, it was certainly understandable, given the circumstances.

At Hydraulic Systems Corporation, in Case 5.2, a high level of cooperation existed between the sales and manufacturing departments. Problems were addressed by everyone in both departments for the benefit of customers and employees alike. Human resources systems — specifically the company-wide bonus plan — and supportive leadership behavior reinforced employee participation and effective problem-solving behavior within and among separate groups. The strong group skills displayed by Joe Stevens suggest that Hydraulic Systems had supported group dynamics or leadership training, or that people like Sharon Yee or other top managers were excellent role models, or both.

The motivation and performance of individuals and groups within an organization are the major topics of this chapter. First, the complex process of individual motivation and the relationships among motivation, performance, and job satisfaction are explored. Next, how dissatisfaction affects the worker and the workplace is investigated. Finally, the chapter discusses group behavior, which also has a strong effect on individual motivation and organizational outcomes. Throughout, the role of human resources management in enhancing motivation, performance, and satisfaction in the organization is emphasized.

Individual Motivation

What motivates people? How do we motivate our employees? How can we get people to do a better job? Why did she quit? Why is he so upset? Questions like these, and the answers arrived at by management, underlie many of the personnel policies and practices in a given organization. But the reality is that asking these questions is far easier than answering them.

Motivation may be defined as the desire and willingness of a person to expend effort to reach a particular goal or outcome. Individual motivation is a consequence of many forces operating simultaneously in the person and in the person's environment. Motivated behavior in the organizational setting is just as complex. As we saw in the last chapter (Figure 4.1), motivated behavior results from the interplay of many factors, including organizational culture, leadership style, structure, and human resources policies and practices. The individual personality traits, skills, and attitudes that a person brings to the job also play a large part in motivation.

There is no single, generally accepted theory of what motivates people in the workplace, but reviewing several contemporary theories is helpful in understanding the concept. These theories also have important applications for human resources specialists and managers for a significant reason: *enhancing motivation can lead to improved performance and greater organizational success.*

Need Theories   It is fairly widely accepted that a good deal of motivation has its origins in certain basic needs. Need theories of motivation are based on the assumption that basic wants or requirements govern much of people's behavior. Abraham H. Maslow, in particular, has been identified with the development of a need theory of motivation. Other researchers, such as Clayton P. Alderfer, have revised and extended Maslow's ideas. Another theorist, David C. McClelland, has focused largely on three needs: achievement, power, and affiliation. A brief review of the major need theories will help you understand the complex process of motivation.

Need Hierarchy Theory   According to Maslow, individuals are motivated by the desire to fulfill particular needs that are shared by all people:

1. **Physiological needs** include the basic requirements for food, water, and sleep.
2. **Security or safety needs** include shelter, clothing, and ways of defending oneself.
3. **Belonging and affection needs** include the desire to relate to other people and to give and accept love, care, and cooperation.
4. **Esteem needs** include the desire for self-worth, independence, and achievement and for recognition and respect from others.
5. **Self-actualization needs** include the desire for growth, development, and self-fulfillment and the urge to realize one's potential.[1]

Maslow's theory states that for each individual these needs emerge in a particular order, and that needs at one level must be satisfied before a person is motivated to satisfy needs at the next higher level. A person's physiological and security needs must be satisfied before the "higher" needs for esteem and self-actualization can predominate. Maslow's priority ordering, or *hierarchy*, of needs is shown in Figure 5.1.

In essence, Maslow believed that a strongly felt need for accomplishment and growth can emerge only with the satisfaction of the more basic needs. (This could

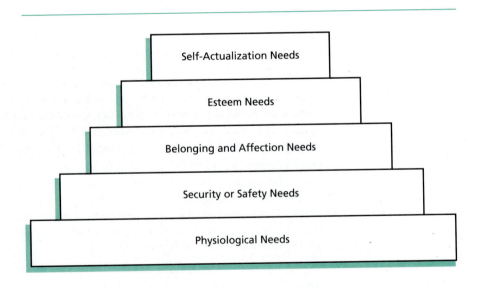

FIGURE 5.1 Maslow's need hierarchy

partly explain why Tom Nelson in Case 5.1 had temporarily abandoned working up to his potential — he was preoccupied by unmet security needs.) Maslow acknowledged, however, that there can be reversals in this hierarchy. A notable example is the martyr who is willing to give up everything in the service of a particular ideal or value.

The major implication of Maslow's theory for human resources management is that policies and practices in the organization, including leadership style, must pay attention to all these needs if the organization hopes to have people working up to their full potential. For example, making supervisors and managers work such long hours that they do not get enough sleep probably reduces their desire for achievement and creativity. Being arbitrary and capricious about employees' job security interferes with cooperation, initiative, and other desirable behaviors. On the other hand, paying exclusive attention to the more basic physiological and security needs and ignoring the needs for achievement and self-esteem would defeat organizational purposes. Thus, the human resources director and all managers would be wise to examine periodically the extent to which organizational practices further or impede fulfillment of human needs and the extent to which there is an appropriate balance in need fulfillment.

ERG Theory   Alderfer, a researcher interested in further testing and explaining Maslow's ideas, identified three categories of needs: existence, relatedness, and growth (ERG).

1. **Existence needs** relate to material desires and include the essential requirements for food, clothing, and shelter.
2. **Relatedness needs** are the desires for human relationships that are satisfied through interaction with families, coworkers, work groups, superiors, subordinates, friends, and friendship groups.
3. **Growth needs** are the needs to be creative and productive and to be most fully what one can be.

Although these categories parallel the needs in Maslow's hierarchy, ERG theory states that two or more needs can operate simultaneously as motivating forces and that the emergence of relatedness and growth needs does not require satisfaction of the existence needs. Further, inability to meet relatedness or growth needs can increase the motivation to satisfy existence needs. For example, failure to earn a promotion and thereby meet growth needs could result in greater concern about working conditions, pay, and benefits. In addition, ERG theory suggests that relatedness and growth needs may become more intense in an organization where there is ample opportunity to meet them.[2]

An implication of ERG theory is that in designing and managing human resources policies and practices one must assume that all employees have the potential for continued growth and development. This in turn suggests, for example, the desirability of ongoing opportunities for training, for transfer or promotion, and for developing interaction skills.

Need for Achievement, Affiliation, and Power   The work of McClelland and his colleagues focuses on the need for achievement, affiliation, and power.

1. **The need for achievement** is the need to excel and to strive for accomplishment and success.

2. **The need for affiliation** is the need for social contact, for approval, and for mutual support.
3. **The need for power** is the need to influence others and situations, to be dominant, to control.[3]

Basically, McClelland concluded that, although the need for achievement is the main motivator for those who wish to start and develop their own small businesses, the need for power is the crucial motivator of top executives in larger, more complex organizations. Further, to be successful in a large organization, a manager should have a greater need for power than for affiliation. These conclusions were tempered by the observations that the most successful managers exercise their power in a controlled and disciplined way in behalf of others and the organization, not themselves, and that they create a strong sense of team spirit among their subordinates.[4]

One implication for human resources management is that training for supervisors and managers with strong achievement or power needs should include training in effective interpersonal and group skills to help ensure that their leadership behaviors and peer relationships will contribute to effective teamwork.

Motivation-Hygiene Theory

Frederick Herzberg developed a theory of motivation based on factors that produce job satisfaction and dissatisfaction. Although controversial, the *motivation-hygiene theory* has stimulated a great deal of research focusing on ways of improving performance through a clearer understanding of motivation and satisfaction.

Herzberg tested this theory in a study of engineers and accountants in several firms. He found that the key factors in motivation and satisfaction are achievement, recognition, work itself, responsibility, and advancement. These factors are called **motivators:** their presence increases job satisfaction and motivation, but their absence does not lead to dissatisfaction. A second group of factors, called the **hygiene factors,** includes company policy and administration, supervision, salary, interpersonal relations with the supervisor, and working conditions. Herzberg claimed that if these factors are negative or absent, dissatisfaction results. The presence of positive hygiene factors by themselves, however, does not lead to satisfaction and motivation.[5] (See Table 5.1.)

TABLE 5.1 Motivators and hygiene factors*

MOTIVATORS	HYGIENE FACTORS
Achievement	Company policy and administration
Recognition for achievement	Supervision
Work itself	Salary
Responsibility	Interpersonal relations
Advancement	Working conditions

*According to Herzberg, the presence of motivators in the work environment increases job satisfaction and motivation, and the presence of positive hygiene factors prevents job dissatisfaction. Both groups of factors meet employee needs, but only the motivators lead to superior effort and performance.

Source: Based on Frederick Herzberg, *Work and the Nature of Man* (Cleveland: The World Publishing Company, 1966). Reprinted by permission.

The motivation-hygiene theory is an intriguing one because it takes into account a great variety of factors affecting motivation and satisfaction. But logic and the researcher's own work suggest that, in reality, these factors do not operate separately from one another in a given person. For example, the desires for advancement and for recognition — considered motivators — are probably both connected to feelings and attitudes about salary — a hygiene factor. In addition, the research indicates that some factors, such as salary, appear to be associated with *both* satisfaction and dissatisfaction. Finally, research has shown that both categories of factors serve to motivate. In one study of managerial and professional workers, the hygiene factors were as frequently associated with self-reports of high performance as were the motivators.[6]

In spite of this controversy, Herzberg's theory has great value for managers and human resources professionals, for it identifies a wide range of factors involved in motivation and satisfaction. The theory has also had a major influence on job design in many organizations because it has made managers more aware of the importance of such matters as job challenge and responsibility in motivation. Some of these job redesign projects, in which employees are given significantly more responsibility for planning and control, are described in Chapter 7.

Reinforcement Theory

This theory, based largely on the work of B. F. Skinner, focuses on influencing behavior through rewards and punishments, or **reinforcement.** The process of shaping behavior through reinforcement is called **behavior modification,** or *operant conditioning.* This approach to motivation has both commonsense and controversial aspects.

Basically, the theory says that if a desired behavior is followed immediately by some reward, the person will be motivated to repeat that behavior. But if the consequence of the behavior is displeasing to the person, he or she is less likely to repeat that behavior. According to the theory, the shorter the time between the behavior and the reinforcement, the more likely it is that the behavior will be influenced. Further, punishment can be useful in eliminating undesired behavior; but it can also cause negative side effects such as aggression, which makes it less effective than positive reinforcement.[7]

A major implication of this theory for human resources management, as well as for the direct supervision of people, is that an emphasis on rewards will tend to be more effective than an emphasis on punishments. Further, this theory has led managers in many organizations to pay more attention to recognizing and praising good work.

Chapter 15, "Incentive Plans," describes particular positive reinforcement programs that some companies have used. A controversial aspect of some of these programs is whether praise per se is adequate or whether, in addition, adjustments need to be made in the compensation plan.

Equity Theory

The word **equity** refers to the quality of being just or fair. Determining what is fair or unfair treatment is an ongoing challenge for all managers and human resources specialists. Equity theory provides some insight into how people perceive fairness and unfairness and the consequences of these perceptions. A basic assumption of equity theory is that people want to be treated fairly and that individuals within an organization tend to compare their own contributions and rewards with the contributions and rewards of others.

To feel fairly treated on the job, one must perceive that what one puts in (for example, education, seniority, skill, effort, job performance, and loyalty) corresponds with personal outcomes (such as pay, privileges, job satisfaction, recognition, and opportunity). (See Figure 5.2 for an illustration of equity theory.) One must also feel that one's contributions and outcomes are in line with the contributions and outcomes of others. If a person believes that he or she produces far more than another but that they both are paid the same, a case of inequity exists and the person may try to do something to correct it. This might take a number of forms, including complaining, slowing down, being absent frequently, or quitting. The theory also suggests that if people perceive that personal outcomes are too high relative to what they put in and, in turn, too high in comparison with what others contribute and receive, they will feel motivated to bring the situation into psychological balance by such mechanisms as rationalization, more productivity, or higher-quality work.[8] The theory can also be extended to perceived fairness or unfairness of punishment.

A number of studies give some support to these assertions. Experiments have found that people will alter their performance in predictable ways if they feel underpaid or overpaid. If they feel underpaid, they tend to reduce the quality or quantity of production or to be more likely to engage in theft. In the case of supervisors who feel underpaid, there is more of a tendency to be tightfisted with subordinates. If employees feel overpaid, they tend to increase quality or output, depending on the pay system. If one feels overpaid, however, it is easier to convince oneself that the pay is justified than if one feels underpaid.[9]

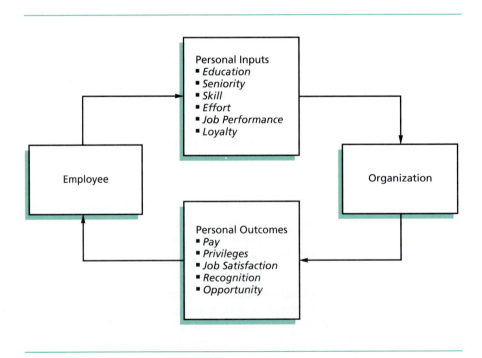

FIGURE 5.2 Equity theory: a fair balance between contributions and outcomes

A major problem in applying equity theory is that different people and different groups have differing perceptions of what is just or fair. Because perceptions can differ about which contributions have the most merit, which performance behaviors are worth the most, and which rewards have the most value, there can be considerable disagreement over the proper allocation of rewards and penalties. Many of the problems in wage and salary administration stem from such differing perceptions.

Expectancy Theory
In recent years, a number of authors and researchers have developed a theory of motivation called *expectancy theory*. According to this theory, motivation is a function of an individual's "expectancy" that a certain amount of effort will lead to a certain level of performance that, in turn, will lead to desired outcomes or rewards. Each potential outcome has a **valence,** which is its degree of attractiveness or value to a specific individual. These valences vary for different people because of individual needs and perceptions. To be highly motivated, a person must want the rewards that are available, must believe that these rewards are linked to performance, and must believe that his or her own effort can result in the necessary performance.[10]

Consider the case of Anita Green, an employee of a typical organization. If Anita believes that doing very good work will result in higher pay, and she very much wants higher pay to buy a new car, she is likely to be motivated to do high-quality work. For Anita, higher pay has a positive valence, or high attractiveness. But to be highly motivated Anita must also believe that her hard work will result in high performance. Therefore, Anita's motivation is a function of her expectancy that her effort will lead to performance that will result in desired outcomes.

Job Satisfaction

Job satisfaction can be defined as a person's emotional response to aspects of work (such as pay, supervision, and benefits) or to the work itself. The word *morale* is often used interchangeably with satisfaction, but morale frequently has more of a group or organizational connotation.

Like motivation, job satisfaction is a complex notion that manifests itself in different ways in different people. Whether job satisfaction is high or low depends on a number of factors, including how well a person's needs and wants are met through work, working conditions themselves, the extent to which an individual defines himself or herself through work, and individual personality traits.[11]

Job satisfaction has been an important part of human resources management ever since the Hawthorne studies (see Chapter 2), when it was thought that a firm correlation existed between satisfaction and performance. At that time, high satisfaction was thought to be a *cause* of high performance. It was assumed that management could improve performance simply by satisfying workers through pleasant working conditions, adequate rewards, and the like. Now, however, it is generally accepted that this cause-and-effect relationship is an incorrect view of the connection between satisfaction and performance.

Modern theory and research suggest that focusing solely on satisfying workers will not result in high performance and productivity. The relationship may be the other way around: high performance may cause high job satisfaction, which is reinforced by the rewards that accompany performance. In other words, performance leads to rewards that in turn produce satisfaction.

The Motivation-Performance-Satisfaction Relationship   Figure 5.3 depicts the relationship of motivation, performance, and satisfaction as suggested by recent research about job satisfaction and by theories of individual motivation. Note that the diagram includes some factors in organizational performance that were discussed in the last chapter and illustrated by Figure 4.1.[12]

From left to right, individual needs and goals (box 1) are fundamental driving forces in motivation. The extent and direction of an individual's motivation (box 2) are influenced by factors in the organizational environment such as leadership style, group norms and support, intergroup behavior, and human resources policies and practices (box 3). Individual motivation is further influenced by the desirability of the rewards (valence) and by the expectancy that effort will lead to the performance that will produce the desired outcomes (box 4). The effort that is expended (box 5), coupled with the individual's skills and abilities (box 6), results in performance (box 8). However, the technology that is in use, the support services that are provided (such as the proper raw materials or parts supplied at the right time), and the

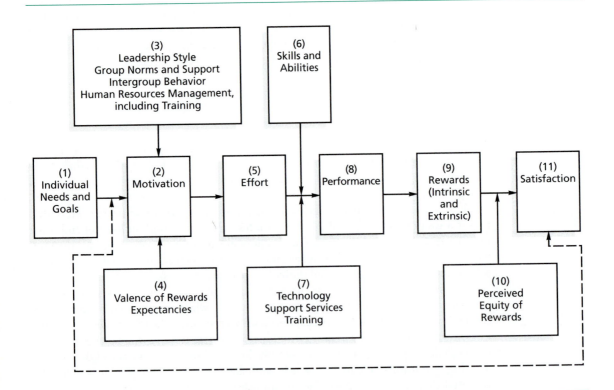

FIGURE 5.3 The motivation-performance-satisfaction relationship

Source: Adapted from David A. Nadler and Edward E. Lawler III, "Motivation: A Diagnostic Approach," pp. 26–38, and Edward E. Lawler III, "Satisfaction and Behavior," pp. 39–50, both in *Perspectives on Behavior in Organizations*, eds. J. Richard Hackman, Edward E. Lawler III, and Lyman W. Porter (New York: McGraw-Hill, 1977). Reprinted by permission of the author.

training given the person (box 7) are also factors in the level of performance. Performance leads to rewards of both an intrinsic and an extrinsic nature (box 9). **Intrinsic rewards** are internal reinforcements such as feelings of accomplishment and self-worth; **extrinsic rewards** are external reinforcements such as pay, recognition, or promotion.[13]

Job satisfaction (box 11) stems from performance and the accompanying rewards but is influenced by the extent to which the individual perceives the rewards as equitable (box 10). An arrow is drawn from box 11 back to boxes 1 and 2 because job satisfaction or dissatisfaction affects need fulfillment, future goals, and ongoing motivation.

Consequences of Dissatisfaction

Job satisfaction does not necessarily lead to better job performance. But what is the link, if any, between high dissatisfaction and performance? It seems reasonable to assume that a person who is highly dissatisfied on the job is less likely to perform at peak levels. Equity theory suggests that workers who are frustrated in attempts to attain some desired outcome will either aim for alternative goals (for example, giving up on the idea of being promoted to supervisor and aiming to become elected union steward) or exercise some kind of defensive behavior in an attempt to reduce the tension (for example, complain to coworkers).

Defensive Behavior

Research and experience confirm the link between high dissatisfaction and certain behavioral reactions. For example, in a study of eighty-two employees at various levels in several organizations, it was found that frustration can have extremely negative consequences for organizational goals. Such self-reported behaviors as interpersonal arguments, complaining about the supervisor or organization to people outside, ignoring the supervisor, considering quitting, purposely damaging or defacing equipment, doing work incorrectly, taking undeserved breaks, or using drugs appeared with considerable frequency.[14]

Sabotage

The deliberate damaging of equipment or products — **sabotage** — by employees represents one of the more costly possible consequences of organizational frustrations. For example, deliberate damage to automobiles by employees in automobile assembly plants and sabotage of navy helicopters and jet airplanes have been documented.[15] It may be, however, that high job dissatisfaction is only one of several factors leading to sabotage. Other factors, such as an individual's psychological tendency toward extreme behaviors, may also be operating. Nonetheless, satisfying workers must be part of an effort to reduce sabotage in an organization.

Absenteeism

Failure to report to work — **absenteeism** — also appears to be associated with job dissatisfaction. A review of the literature on factors associated with job attendance concluded that job satisfaction was one of the major influences on attendance, although only one of many factors. Another major influence, for example, was ability to attend, that is, the extent to which illness or accidents, family responsibilities, and transportation problems did not interfere with coming to work.[16]

Turnover

An Australian study of **turnover** — frequently calculated as the ratio of the number of employee separations during a month to the number of employees on the payroll at the middle of the month — found that one factor was dissatisfaction. This study determined that high turnover was part of a broader set of problems, including lowered production and quality, higher costs, low satisfaction with superiors, work anxiety, absenteeism, and accidents. The researchers concluded that long-term solutions to turnover are to be found in "identifying and remedying specific issues producing dissatisfaction as well as more substantive programs of organization development or other forms of planned change."[17]

Implications for Managers and Human Resources Specialists

Although the connections between satisfaction and attendance and satisfaction and turnover are rather complicated, the costs of absenteeism and turnover provide ample reason for managers and human resources specialists to be concerned with job satisfaction. Although not all turnover or absenteeism can or should be prevented, it is obvious that high levels of both can be extremely costly to an organization. Further, high dissatisfaction tends to be costly in many other ways. When workers perform below their full potential, the organization suffers from reduced effectiveness and efficiency. Top managers would be wise to assess satisfaction levels in their organizations — by unit, by level, and by job category. One way to do this is to use climate or satisfaction surveys at intervals and then to take appropriate remedial action.

Group Influences on Performance

The discussion until now has considered motivation and performance on an individual basis. But in the organizational setting, most individuals are members of work groups. A **work group** is a number of persons, usually reporting to a common superior and having some face-to-face interaction, who have some degree of interdependence in carrying out tasks for the purpose of achieving organizational goals.

While we will use the terms somewhat synonymously, it is important to make a distinction between "groups" and "teams." A **team** is a form of group, but has some characteristics in greater degree than ordinary groups, including a higher degree of commitment to common goals and a higher degree of interdependence and interaction. Authors Jon Katzenbach and Douglas Smith define "team" as follows:

> A team is a small number of people with complementary skills who are committed to a common purpose, set of performance goals, and approach for which they hold themselves mutually accountable.[18]

This distinction will become particularly relevant in later chapters when we discuss such topics as "self-managed teams."

The development of effective work groups (including teams) is an important part of human resources management. Groups affect individual behavior, motivation, and performance just as individuals can affect the way groups function. Moreover, group behavior is partly a function of organizational culture, climate, leadership style, and other aspects of the organization's environment. Finally, the extent to which group goals are consistent with organizational goals is a key factor in the overall success of an organization.

Formal Versus Informal Groups

Formal groups are groups established by management, such as work groups, special committees, and task forces. But there are numerous other group configurations in organizations that have not been established by management. These are usually

Work groups tend to meet a number of human needs such as the needs for affiliation, cooperation, and esteem.

called **informal groups** and form spontaneously as a result of proximity or similarity of work, mutual interests, mutual need fulfillment, or combinations of these reasons. For example, four people who work on the same floor of the building but in different departments may eat lunch together regularly. Six people, all from different work groups, may ride to work together and develop strong friendships. Informal groups are sometimes called "shadow groups" because they tend to be invisible to management, yet they can influence the organization powerfully — for example, by transmitting information or affecting attitudes.

Individual Needs and Organizational Goals

Work groups and informal groups tend to meet a number of human needs, such as the needs for affiliation, cooperation, and esteem. Groups are a source of identity, support, and friendship for individual workers, who might otherwise feel lost in a large organization. Work groups, then, play an important role in meeting the emotional needs of individuals. Clearly, groups meet many human needs in the Mexican culture, as illustrated in *International Perspective* on page 117.

In addition, work groups and other formal groups fill several important functions in helping the organization meet its task objectives. Because most jobs are interdependent, groups help get the work done. They also help orient new members to specific job procedures and to the organization's environment and help train them. Moreover, probably a high proportion of work groups in today's organizations participate to some extent in decision making and goal setting that affect organizational outcomes. How well work groups perform such functions, however, depends to a great extent on factors in the internal environment, including leadership style, human resources practices such as orientation and training, and organizational climate.

Group Control over Production

A number of studies over the years have shown that work groups have considerable control over productivity. Many studies have demonstrated that groups of workers can defend themselves against what they consider unreasonable or unfair performance standards.

For example, the Hawthorne studies described in Chapter 2 found that workers in the bank wiring observation room had a standard for output considerably below that set officially by management and that this norm was enforced by pressure from the group. One of the ways pressure was exerted was through a game called "binging," in which one worker would strike another on the upper arm if verbal persuasion was not sufficient to get that person to reduce production.[19]

Another study showed that, in general, the higher the standards of performance established informally by work groups, the higher the production of those groups. Members of these work groups were absent or late for work less often and were less likely to leave the job early in comparison with groups that held lower standards of performance.[20]

Research also indicates that the members of a very unified and cooperative, or cohesive, group will conform closely to the standards set by the group, whether the standards are high or low. Groups that lack cohesiveness, however, tend to show considerable variation in productivity among members. A high degree of cohesiveness seems to lead to high productivity when the attitude of the group toward the company is favorable. If there are good relations among management, union, and employees, the cohesive group sets high standards of performance. If not, a cohesive group tends to show lower-than-average productivity.[21]

Work banking is another illustration of how workers and work groups can control production. **Work banking,** which has been frequently documented, is the hiding of present production in order to demonstrate productivity up to some standard or quota at some future time. Motives for work banking might include having finished items to pull out when one is feeling ill and needing to slow down, wishing to take it easy at intervals, or protecting oneself against conditions affecting production over which one has no control. Robert Schrank, author of *Ten Thousand Working Days*, gives an example of work banking in a machine shop where propeller shafts for cargo ships were being manufactured:

> We walked to the back end of the plant, out onto the loading platform. There I could not believe my eyes. I saw two guys burying a thirty-foot propeller shaft in the backyard. I burst out with, "What the hell are you guys doing?" They said, "Hey fellows, you watch us be heroes at the end of the month when the boss gives us that we-need-to-break-quota b.s."[22]

Characteristics of Effective Groups

Group dynamics theory and research have important things to say about the characteristics of groups that are highly effective in attaining their goals. The degree to which group goals are consistent with broader organizational goals will of course be a function of a number of factors, including management philosophy and leadership style, organizational climate, and the reward system. For example, if management does not talk about the importance of departments cooperating with each other, does not exert leadership in this direction, and does not reward cooperation, groups are more likely to pursue their own narrower objectives at the expense of total organizational performance.

International Perspective

Blending the Best of Both Cultures

It doesn't take most North American managers very long to realize that employees in Mexico have a different attitude toward work. According to a summary of bicultural preferences by The McFletcher Corp., an international consulting and research firm, North Americans generally favor taking the initiative, having individual responsibilities and taking failure personally.

Mexicans are comfortable operating in groups and the group shares both success and failure.

North Americans are competitive, have high goals and live for the future. Mexicans tend to be cooperative, flexible and enjoy life as it is, now.

"In Mexico, the priorities are family, religion, then work," says Alfonso Martin del Campo, general manager of Motorola's semiconductor products sector in Guadalajara, Mexico. Employers respect these priorities and look for ways to support family activities.

During the year, the Guadalajara plant hosts family dinners to celebrate the anniversaries of employees who have worked there five, 10, 15 and 20 years. There's also an annual Christmas dinner for employees and their families, and a dinner to celebrate Mother's Day.

Guadalajara Motorola plant employees may borrow the company clubhouse on weekends for weddings, baptisms, anniversary parties and other family celebrations. On weekends employees play soccer on the company's park-like grounds while families visit with friends as they cheer for the players.

Each year Motorola hosts a family day on which everyone can tour the plant, watch videos of workers, enjoy entertainment and food, then play sports until it's time to go home.

"US Americans are oriented towards *doing*," says Eva S. Kraus in her book, *Management in Two Cultures: Bridging the gap between US and Mexican managers.* "Getting things done is a virtue on which most US Americans place a high value. In other cultures a higher value may be placed on *being* which emphasizes the intrinsic quality of the individual."

The typical workday in Mexico is from 8 a.m. to 5:30 p.m. The Motorola plant rents a bus and provides transportation to many of the employees. "When the plant was built 20 years ago it was very far away from the city," says del Campo, "and employees needed the bus to get to work. There's a law in Mexico that once you give a benefit you can't take it away, so the bus still picks up employees every day."

Minimum wage, 11,000 pesos, or about $4 a day, is so low many companies voluntarily pay more. Mexican companies traditionally don't offer retirement benefits, although del Campo says some are beginning to. Medical benefits are offered.

Because many employees prefer to eat their main meal in the middle of the day, the Motorola cafeteria offers two lunch menus that it subsidizes 70%. A grill serves steaks or fish, for which employees pay the regular price. In a spirit of cooperation, managers serve the luncheon meals.

The most successful North American companies in Mexico seem to be those that blend the best from both cultures and it's working at Motorola. In 1989, after implementing the organizational effectiveness change model, the company won the American Chamber of Commerce of Mexico National Training Award.

Source: Excerpted from Kent Banning and Dick Wintermantel, "Motorola Turns Vision to Profits," *Personnel Journal*, 70 (February 1991):55. Reprinted by permission.

Some of the conclusions from group dynamics theory and research about the characteristics of highly effective groups follow. There are important implications for human resources policies and practices.

1. Group members, including the formal leader, are skilled both in group task behaviors and group maintenance behaviors. **Group task behaviors** are those that directly relate to performing the task, such as initiating, information giving, and summarizing. **Group maintenance behaviors** are those that pertain to the emotional life of the group and its development, such as harmonizing, gatekeeping (bringing all members into discussions), and encouraging. Effective group leadership is seen as a shared process; effective group and leadership behaviors are not assumed to be the sole responsibility of the formal leader.[23]

These conclusions have particular implications for training and management development in organizations: training in group skills needs to be supported and encouraged. They also have implications for supervisory selection and leadership style: supervisors and managers need to run meetings in such a way that these behaviors can be used. To illustrate, group members cannot use their group skills if the formal leader dominates the discussion.

2. Group members and the leader trust each other and have high confidence that each can carry his or her share of the load. This has implications for personnel selection: additions or replacements should have the skills and attitudes (or the potential) needed to help the group carry out its mission. Conversely, if the human resources department, through inattention to transfer practices, permits a group to become a "dumping ground" for unqualified people, the group and the organization are likely to pay a high price in terms of group performance.

3. Meetings have a problem-solving, supportive atmosphere. When there are differing points of view, issues are worked through to everyone's satisfaction rather than solved by forcing methods of decision making, such as lining up support behind the scenes and then taking a formal vote. This has implications for leadership style and training in group problem-solving approaches.

4. The leader is influential in setting the supportive, problem-solving tone of the work group by his or her own behaviors. Again, this has implications for supervisory selection and training.

5. Group members and the leader actively help each other develop skills of a technical, interpersonal, and group nature. At the group level, this means sharing information and suggestions, and mutual training. At the level of human resources systems, it means making training programs available for upgrading technological and human relations skills and rewarding people for being effective trainers, both within their groups and in formal programs.[24]

What is known about effective groups, the influence of groups on individual motivation and job performance, and the influence of management practices on group behavior makes it clear that human resources management must be concerned about groups. By extension, intergroup theory and research can also shed light on how relations between groups affect organizational performance.

Intergroup Behavior

Relationships among groups in an organization can contribute extensively to organizational performance or can inhibit or even destroy it. High-quality communications and cooperation, in particular, can enhance organizational outcomes, whereas conflict that is not managed or that escalates can have a severe dampening effect. Excessive competition among groups is similar to unmanaged conflict in its consequences.

Conflict and Competition

Conflict in the organization consists of opposing behaviors between two or more people or groups who have incompatible goals. A certain level of conflict can be healthy from time to time if it serves to raise issues, thus leading to problem solving, a restructuring of goals, or a redefinition of purpose. An example of conflict might be two department heads each trying to get the other fired by withholding and distorting information. Unless a dialogue takes place — probably with the help of a neutral third party — the costs to the organization in efficiency and effectiveness are likely to be considerable.

Competition, on the other hand, may involve common goals and a good deal of common interest, along with limited opposing behaviors. An example might be two groups set up by management to develop a prototype of some instrument, with the winning group given the go-ahead to manufacture and market the winning design. This kind of competition can have favorable outcomes, provided all the competitors have reasonable job security, all benefit from the gains that are made, and all are given recognition for their contributions.

When competition and conflict within an organization are mismanaged or excessive, there are predictable negative consequences. Some of these, as indicated by research on conflict and competition between groups, are as follows:

1. Although both groups take pride in their accomplishments, each makes favorable evaluations of "our" group and negative evaluations of the other.

2. Each group has distorted perceptions and judgments about the other group. The performance of the other group is frequently underestimated; the performance of one's own group tends to be overestimated.

3. Each group sees the other as the "enemy," people make disparaging remarks within their own group about the other group, and contact with the other group is frowned on. Considerable energy is used to outwit the "enemy."

4. If one of the groups has grossly inadequate resources, members may become discouraged and demotivated. There is likely to be considerable friction within the group, and members may have difficulty dividing the tasks.

5. Information is used to erode the position of the other group and to enhance one's relative position rather than to clarify matters or solve problems. For example, in talking with superiors who have control over resources needed by both groups, one group may be quick to pass on negative information about the other group but fail to mention compliments or favorable information they have heard.[25]

Managing Conflict and Developing Cooperation

What we know about competition and conflict between groups strongly suggests that management philosophy and practices, including human resources policies and procedures, should contribute to cooperation, effective communication, and problem solving across groups. This assertion can be stated negatively: management must be careful that it does not consciously or unconsciously create policies and practices that produce unnecessary competition and conflict and their negative consequences.

Contemporary Issues

Aspirations Statement (Levi Strauss & Co.)

We all want a Company that our people are proud of and committed to, where all employees have an opportunity to contribute, learn, grow and advance based on merit, not politics or background. We want our people to feel respected, treated fairly, listened to and involved. Above all, we want satisfaction from accomplishments and friendships, balanced personal and professional lives, and to have fun in our endeavors.

When we describe the kind of LS&CO. we want in the future, what we are talking about is building on the foundation we have inherited; affirming the best of our Company's traditions, closing gaps that may exist between principles and practices, and updating some of our values to reflect contemporary circumstances.

What Type of Leadership Is Necessary To Make Our Aspirations a Reality?

New Behaviors: Leadership that exemplifies directness, openness to influence, commitment to the success of others, willingness to acknowledge our own contributions to problems, personal accountability, teamwork and trust. Not only must we model these behaviors, but we must coach others to adopt them.

Diversity: Leadership that values a diverse work force (age, sex, ethnic group, etc.) at all levels of the organization, diversity in experience, and a diversity in perspectives. We have committed to taking full advantage of the rich backgrounds and abilities of all our people and to promote a greater diversity in positions of influence. Differing points of view will be sought, diversity will be valued and honesty rewarded, not suppressed.

Recognition: Leadership that provides greater recognition — both financial and psychic — for individuals and teams that contribute to our success. Recognition must be given to all who contribute, those who create and innovate and also those who continually support the day-to-day business requirements.

Ethical Management Practices: Leadership that epitomizes the stated standards of ethical behavior. We must provide clarity about our expectations and must enforce these standards through the corporation.

Communications: Leadership that is clear about Company, unit, and individual-goals and performance. People must know what is expected of them and receive timely, honest feedback on their performance and career aspirations.

Empowerment: Leadership that increases the authority and responsibility of those closest to our products and customers. By actively pushing responsibility, trust and recognition into the organization, we can harness and release the capabilities of all our people.

Source: Courtesy Levi Strauss & Co.

There are some specific implications for various human resources managers who wish to maximize cooperation and minimize the negative consequences of conflict and competition:

1. Recruitment and selection — attract and employ people who are oriented toward collaborative relationships and already have well-developed group and intergroup skills or who have strong potential in these areas.

2. Promotion — use effective group and intergroup skills as one criterion for promotion.

3. Training and management development — provide training for all supervisors and team members in group and intergroup skills and the underlying theory.

4. Performance appraisal and review — make group and intergroup skills an area for review and coaching. Hold supervisors and managers accountable for cooperation across the organization.

5. Compensation and rewards — recognize effective group and intergroup behaviors and include these areas in pay-increase decisions. Design compensation systems so that there are no rewards for withholding cooperation and so that cooperation is rewarded. (At Levi Strauss & Co. there is a conscious effort to give rewards for the contributions of teams; see *Contemporary Issues* on page 120.)

6. Organization improvement strategies — use conflict-management techniques, such as intergroup problem-solving workshops.

Developing cooperation in the organization, of course, must be the example set by top management. The actual style and behavior of top management will largely set the tone for the entire organization.

Summary

Individual motivation — the desire and willingness of a person to expend effort to reach a particular outcome — is a consequence of a complex interplay of factors. These factors include intraorganizational elements, such as those discussed in Chapter 4, and intrapersonal elements, such as needs and expectations.

Among the various need theories of motivation are Maslow's need hierarchy theory; Alderfer's ERG theory; and McClelland's achievement, affiliation, and power theory. Maslow and Alderfer both assert that motivation springs from basic needs of all human beings, but they have different views on the extent to which the more basic needs must be satisfied before the self-actualization or growth needs emerge. McClelland sees the need for achievement as the main motivator of entrepreneurs, whereas the need for power is crucial for top executives of large, complex organizations.

Herzberg's motivation-hygiene theory holds that some factors in the work environment serve as motivators and some serve as hygiene factors that prevent dissatisfaction. Reinforcement theory holds that if a desired behavior is followed immediately by some reward a person will be motivated to repeat that behavior. Equity theory focuses on the consequences of perceived fairness or unfairness. Expectancy theory holds that motivation is a function of an individual's expectation that a certain amount of effort will lead to a certain level of performance, which, in turn, will lead to desired outcomes or rewards.

Satisfaction may be usefully thought of as an outcome rather than a cause of performance. Job satisfaction, according to contemporary theory, stems from performance and accompanying rewards. Dissatisfaction can lead to several behaviors that hinder performance. Efforts to improve performance by simply improving pay, benefits, or working conditions may not succeed.

Work groups, both formal and informal, are important to understanding human resources management because they are important in meeting individual needs and organizational goals. (Teams are work groups with a high degree of commitment to common goals, high interdependency, and mutual accountability.) Work groups have a great deal of control over productivity through such means as restriction of production and work banking. Members of a cohesive group will conform to standards set by the group, whether high or low. If the attitudes in a cohesive group are favorable to management, the group tends to set high standards of performance.

Effective groups tend to have members and leaders who are skilled both in task behaviors — behaviors that bear directly on the task to be done — and in group maintenance behaviors — those behaviors associated with managing the emotional life of the group. Effective groups tend to have members who trust each other; their meetings tend to have a problem-solving, supportive atmosphere, and group members actively help each other in developing skills of a technical, interpersonal, and group nature. Further, these conditions are actively influenced and supported by the leader.

Relationships between units in an organization can contribute to or seriously detract from organizational effectiveness. Conflict or excessive competition between two groups (or two people) that is not brought out in the open and managed properly will have negative consequences. Management practices, particularly in the areas of management philosophy, leadership style, and human resources policies and procedures, can contribute greatly toward managing conflict in constructive ways.

Ethical Dilemma

Laura Fischer is vice president for marketing in a large hospital and medical supply company. Her style is strictly down to business, with no small talk. She is meticulous about establishing an agenda and circulating it before meetings with department heads. Besides her information items, most meeting agendas require reports from department heads on one project or another. Laura is relentless in pursuing "hard facts," and woe to any department head who is not well prepared. The meetings have an inquisitorial tone, with her assistant and some department heads also zeroing in on the weaknesses they see. Privately, department heads are expressing great frustration with the meetings. There is some indication to employees in the division that the stress level is very high, and speculation that some of the ulcer cases and heart attacks have not been coincidences.

Discuss Laura's style in terms of ethics.

Key Terms

motivation	absenteeism
motivators	turnover
hygiene factors	work group
reinforcement	team
behavior modification	formal group
equity	informal group
valence	work banking
job satisfaction	group task behaviors
intrinsic reward	group maintenance behaviors
extrinsic reward	conflict
sabotage	competition

Review Questions

1. List and briefly explain the key theories of motivation. What are their implications for human resources management?
2. Describe the relationship among motivation, performance, and satisfaction.
3. Why should human resources management be concerned with employee dissatisfaction? Provide several reasons.
4. Explain the importance of work groups in organizations. In what ways are they related to organizational outcomes?
5. Identify the characteristics of effective work groups.
6. Discuss the role of human resources management in the development of effective work groups.
7. Explain the consequences of excessive intergroup conflict and competition in the organization. What are some of the implications for human resources management?

Opening Case Questions

Case 5.1 The Merger

1. Discuss the motivation-performance-satisfaction relationship in Tom's situation.
2. What could the human resources department have done to ensure continued good performance on the part of employees?
3. What can the human resources department do now?

Case 5.2 Solving Customer Problems at Hydraulic Systems Corporation

1. What human resources practices led to the successful problem-solving session between the marketing and manufacturing people at Hydraulic?
2. Discuss what might have happened if the marketing and manufacturing employees came into the meeting blaming each other and feeling very competitive.

Comprehensive Case

Motivating High-Tech Employees

High-tech companies can succeed only if they can recruit and retain scientists and engineers to create and design the companies' products. Since creativity and perseverance are critical to most research and development work, technical employees need to be motivated not just to stay with the company but to do the rapid, imaginative work that will keep the company ahead of its competitors. Motivating such employees is, therefore, a top priority for research-oriented companies.

But the traditional motivational systems that most companies rely on don't always work for engineers and programmers. Although many of the stereotypes of the "techy nerd" are unfounded, technical people do seem to be different from the rest of us in certain key ways. Most importantly, the opportunity to advance their careers by rising to the top seems to motivate few technical wizards. Instead, they thrive on technical challenge. They become research scientists or engineers or programmers because they have a love and a talent for solving certain kinds of technical problems. Many tend to work obsessively on such problem solving and are happy only if they are busy piecing together some puzzle.

Most American companies have not been designed to encourage such people. In many companies, the chief motivator is the chance for promotion, with an accompanying pay raise. But even in technology-oriented companies, promotion usually means taking the technical wizards out of the worlds they know and putting them behind desks. Some technically oriented people are happy to manage others, but in many cases the move from researcher to manager benefits no one. The researcher may not have the people skills necessary for a management position, and removing the best and most experienced researchers from R&D departments saps those departments of some of their best resources.

To avoid such problems, some companies are providing other channels for technical advancement. In order to motivate good researchers to stay in the lab, Bausch & Lomb created slots for research vice presidents, with pay and responsibilities befitting the title. The company expects 10 percent of its research staff eventually to opt for this career track. For the same reason, General Electric Co. has established a high-level position of chief technical officer to make clear that technical workers are represented in the corporate structure.

While these parallel career tracks seem to be working for some companies, others have begun recognizing the benefits of having technically oriented people in the company's main chain of command. Managers need to understand, to some extent, what their employees are doing; therefore, it seems only logical that a technology-oriented company would develop as many technologically literate managers as possible. Many analysts attribute the phenomenal success of software maker Microsoft Corp. to the fact that CEO Bill Gates is himself an ace programmer. His employees know better than to try to confuse him with technical mumbo jumbo. Technical people are inclined to respect one of their own.

Another strategy for keeping technical people lively and motivated is to help them to move out of the traditionally isolated "research ghetto." Engineers who talk regularly with salespeople and customers develop a better sense of what people need their products to do, and they find it rewarding to hear how their creations are changing people's lives. Engineers with good communication skills or business sense are particularly in demand, and many value the chance to use their nontechnical skills.

Those employees who continue to devote themselves solely to technical problems will usually be more motivated if they are challenged with more responsibility and made to feel that their jobs are integral to the effective functioning of the company. Companies like 3M develop reputations as innovators by encouraging new ideas and initiative at every level. The company hands out individual bonuses and throws parties and awards ceremonies to celebrate employee innovation.

Even on the factory floor, employees will work harder if they feel that what they are doing is important and if they can take pride in the quality of their work. Baldor Electric, a maker of custom industrial motors, involved its lathe operators in the pursuit of a better product simply by giving them more accurate tools with which to measure the work that they do. A medical instrument manufacturer, the Stryker Corporation, is among a number of companies that have found that motivation increases and defects decrease when the assembly line is eliminated and employees are allowed to work on an entire product and control its manufacture.

As American companies come to rely ever more heavily on technology, they may begin to resemble more closely their Japanese competitors. At the moment, the CEOs of about two-thirds of Japan's top manufacturing companies have backgrounds in science or engineering, while only one-third of American CEOs have such expertise. As a result, American companies are known for their financial and legal solutions to problems, whereas Japanese companies look for technical solutions. Gradually, American high-tech companies may find that the best way to motivate their technical people is to make sure that there are plenty of avenues to any of the top jobs.

Sources: Mark Alpert, "Engineers," *Fortune*, September 21, 1992, pp. 87–95; Henry Eason, "Keeping Good People," *Nation's Business*, (July 1984):37–39; Alan Farnham, "Baldor's Success: Made in the U.S.A.," *Fortune*, July 17, 1989, pp. 101–105; "Managing Innovation," *Business Week*, special 1989 issue, "Innovation in America," pp. 104–134.

Discussion Questions

1. What approaches are being used by the companies in this Comprehensive Case to motivate high-tech employees?
2. Analyze the motivational approaches used by these companies in the light of the need theories of motivation. To what extent are the approaches congruent or at odds with need theories?

CHAPTER 6

Human Resources Planning

LEARNING OBJECTIVES

- Define human resources planning and describe the two major steps in the planning process.
- Explain how human resources planning is related to the overall strategic plan of the organization.
- Explain the relationship of human resources planning to the staffing process.
- Indicate why an understanding of the external labor market is so important in human resources planning.
- List several key federal laws and discuss their implications for human resources management.
- Define affirmative action and explain its essential role in the planning process.
- Explain why the human resources department plays a major role in human resources planning.

CASE 6.1   A Can of Worms

Quality Chemicals, a medium-sized manufacturer of varied chemical products, had closed the year with impressive sales. But Alan Corelli, personnel director, was worried about the future prospects of the firm. He knew that several top executives would retire within the next two or three years, which meant that a number of key positions would need to be filled soon. But where would the replacements come from? Some talented employees reported to these older executives, but most were relatively young and inexperienced. In fact, Alan's impression was that very few departments had any employees who could be promoted immediately to upper-level management positions. He figured that executives would have to be recruited from outside the organization, as he himself had been a year ago.

Alan also knew that the company's strategic plans for the next five years included more aggressive research, manufacturing, and marketing of pharmaceuticals and reagent-grade chemicals. He was aware, however, that the company's present strengths were in manufacturing and that it probably had too few employees with technical research skills.

Alan had recently mentioned his concerns about future staffing to the president of the company, who had said, "I'm beginning to be worried, too. It seems we need some concrete plans for making sure we're employing the right people in the right jobs at the right time, particularly at the management levels. And I don't see many women moving into management jobs. How come? I know we've got some really bright ones in the company. You're our people specialist. How about coming up with some recommendations on how to proceed?" "I will," said Alan. "I'll try to get back to you in a few days."

The first thing Alan did was to sketch out an overall organizational chart. He then prepared a detailed chart for each division, with names of all employees down through the first level of supervision. Beside each name, he tried to make some notations about whether the person was immediately promotable, potentially promotable, or not likely to be promotable. But he soon realized he didn't know the work of some people well enough to make an accurate classification and he would need to involve top and middle management in this evaluation process. He was also convinced that training and development opportunities were important in promotability and that there should be some kind of plan to expose potentially promotable employees to those opportunities.

"An effective training program is going to take some bucks," Alan thought. "I wonder if there's any money in the budget for a management development program. And what about the pros and cons of promoting from within versus hiring from the outside? I wonder if there is a consensus among top management on that."

When he began to make notes on employees in the research labs, he became painfully aware that he had little insight as to what talent currently existed among the research staff and what additional skills were needed in the chemical engineering side of the business. The more he thought about the matter of human resources planning, the more complicated it became. "This is a can of worms," he said to himself. "I'll need lots more information before I can make any intelligent recommendations."

The "few days" grew to six weeks before Alan met with the president again about staffing concerns. By this time Alan had talked with at least fifty people at all levels of the organization and had developed a lengthy report containing a dozen categories of recommendations. One of the recommendations was that human resources planning committees be appointed in research and development, manufacturing, marketing, and administration. Alan also proposed that he serve as an adviser to each committee. The main job of these committees would be to make a preliminary assessment of the potential management and technical talent in each unit and to develop broad recommendations on training and development needs. Alan also recommended that a small corporate committee be appointed to develop the overall philosophy and strategy.   ◀

CASE 6.2   The Morning News

Friday morning the newspapers announced that Eastern Seaboard Savings Bank had been purchased by New World Savings. It was a shock to Eastern Seaboard's employees, partly because they feared that they would become subordinate to New World Savings. Would there be layoffs? Transfers? What would happen to their benefits? Would this mean new bosses? A new chain of command? Employees at New World Savings were also shocked, but they were less worried since their bank had bought out the other.

The whole transaction had occurred so fast that even Steve Carroll, vice president of human resources of New World Savings, had not come to grips with most of the implications. He had been in on part of the secret discussions and had been appalled at how financial considerations had almost totally dominated negotiations. For one thing, despite Steve's urging, the top executives of New World had not discussed their philosophy about the treatment of people in the newly acquired bank. Were Eastern Seaboard employees to be full-fledged associates in this merger, or were they to be second-class citizens from the outset?

Steve had many other concerns. "This is a human resources planning challenge in spades," Steve said to his assistant, Clare Underhill. "We don't even know which branches are going to be merged, let alone which functions are going to be consolidated." New World's CEO had announced that "a few" branches and functions would be merged and that Eastern Seaboard's CEO would become executive vice president of the combined company. There were no specifics beyond that. "And if anybody is to be laid off, we've got to be careful we don't find ourselves with a rash of discrimination suits," Steve added.

"That's right," Clare replied. "Further, we know very little about their employee benefits. We're going to have to merge theirs with ours. And there is the whole matter of appraisal procedures and compensation policies. I have a hunch that Eastern Seaboard has been way behind many of our practices."

"To say nothing about leadership style," said Steve. "My impression is that they've had a fairly autocratic approach to dealing with employees. They do have a suggestion system and an open-door policy, but I've heard that hardly anyone uses either. I haven't much idea as to the skill levels in that bank — for example, I wonder if they have any hotshots on computers and information systems. We could use some help there."

"And then there's the delicate question of their personnel director and department," remarked Clare. "How good are they? And what have they been up to? Do we merge with them? That's kind of a scary thought."

"Obviously, we have our work cut out for us," said Steve. "I suspect that no one has the answers to most of these questions and that we're going to be called on to give lots of advice. The first thing I've got to do is to find out what's on the boss's mind. He's called a meeting of all the vp's for eleven o'clock. I hope I can get people to talk a little about philosophy — I'm going to push the notion that we should try to get everyone on the same team, and fast." ◄

As Alan Corelli found out in Case 6.1, human resources planning is a complex process. Once one looks into the matter, it quickly becomes clear that all personnel processes are related to human resources planning. The promotability of managers to higher positions, for example, is tied in with the effectiveness of the recruitment and selection procedures used when these people were originally hired, their training and development opportunities, the kind of leadership and performance reviews they have experienced, the opportunities for mobility in the organization, and management philosophy about such matters as whether the organization should make every effort to promote from within. As Alan became aware, human resources planning must be tied to the strategic plans of the organization.

In Case 6.2, Steve Carroll and Clare Underhill are faced with a huge human resources planning challenge, stemming from the acquisition of one savings bank by another. All aspects of human resources management of both companies will need to be reviewed sooner or later. Some, like top-executive philosophy about layoffs, must be dealt with immediately. Depending on the outcome of those deliberations, civil rights and other legal aspects of downsizing will need to be addressed promptly.

As Steve and Clare are aware, human resources planning must be attuned to the realities of the external environment. Laws, court decisions, immigration policies, and administrative rulings enforcing equal employment opportunity have a major influence on human resources planning in most organizations today. Other influential factors in the environment are economic, social, and political conditions; changing skill levels in the labor force; market conditions and competition; and technology.

This chapter presents the broad scope of human resources planning and the basic considerations involved in any planning effort. The first part of the chapter reviews key aspects of human resources planning and explains how this process relates to overall organizational planning and to the staffing process in particular. The second part of the chapter describes forces in the external environment that affect human resources planning and staffing. This discussion focuses on the external labor market and the legal background against which all planning decisions must be made.

What Is Human Resources Planning?

In Chapter 1, **human resources planning** was defined as the process of assessing the organization's human resources needs in the light of organizational goals and making plans to ensure that a competent, stable work force is employed. For example, companies need to recruit employees with certain abilities and knowledge, to create training programs for developing particular skills or to provide development opportunities for present and potential managers, and to ensure compliance with government legislation regarding equal employment opportunity and affirmative action.

Relationship to Strategic Planning

The starting point of effective human resources planning is the organization's overall purpose, or mission, frequently written in the form of a **mission statement.**[1] From this is derived the **strategic plan**, or plan for conducting the business as profitably and successfully as possible. Part of strategic planning is the development of organizational goals and objectives. (See Figure 6.1.) An **organizational goal** is a long-term, broad purpose or aim, and an **organizational objective** is a short-term purpose or aim.

According to the former chairman of General Electric Co.,

> Strategy is trying to understand where you sit today in today's world. Not where you wish you were and where you hoped you'd be, but where you are. And it's trying to understand where you want to be.... It's assessing with everything in your head the competitive changes, the market changes that you can capitalize on or ward off to go from here to there. It's assessing the realistic chances of getting from here to there.[2]

Strategic plans are as unique as the organizations that develop them, but underlying most organizational strategies is the determination of some unfulfilled need for products or services that the organization can satisfy. Supplying these products or services then becomes part of the organization's goals.

Relationship to Organizational Goals

The process of identifying organizational goals is usually based on careful research into market need, existing competition, and cost and profit estimates. Most manufacturing organizations, for example, are constantly seeking to improve their products or to develop new ones. Progress in research and development can make an organization's current products obsolete almost overnight. This means that strategic plans and organizational goals must be periodically reassessed and adjusted.

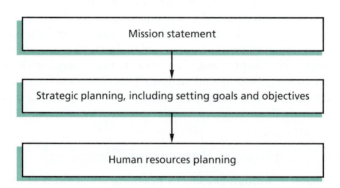

FIGURE 6.1   Typical developmental sequence from mission statement to human resources planning

To a great extent, organizational goals influence the nature of all managerial processes and of human resources management in particular. This means that the structure of the organization, the specific jobs to be performed, the financial and technological resources needed, and the qualifications and numbers of people employed will consistently reflect organizational goals.

Relationship to Organizational Culture and Climate

To be effective, human resources planning must also be conducted in the light of the desired organizational culture and climate. More and more top executive groups are describing the culture and climate they want in their organizations. As was pointed out in Chapter 4, management philosophy and organizational culture and climate dramatically affect the design of human resources programs.

Aspects of the Planning Process

Human resources planning, then, is the ongoing planning of the organization's human resources philosophy, policies, and programs in the context of the overall strategic plans and the changing conditions within and outside of the organization. Clearly it is a much more complex and broader process than a personnel director sitting at a desk drawing an organization chart and making notes, as Alan Corelli started out doing in Case 6.1. That was a good start, but as Alan found out, it was only a start.

Needs Forecasting and Program Planning

Figure 6.2 depicts this broad-based view of human resources planning. The figure isolates two major steps in the process: needs forecasting and program planning. **Needs forecasting** is the process of determining an organization's future demand for human resources. This forecast, or prediction, of needs is derived from a broad information base that includes, among other things, a careful analysis of external conditions; present and potential skill levels within the organization; organizational considerations such as job design, management philosophy, and budget; the need for temporary, part-time, or other contingent workers (see Chapter 8) and projected staff reductions and transfers (reallocations) throughout the organization.[3]

Program planning is done once the forecast of human resources needs is completed. According to James W. Walker, **program planning** takes place in two areas: performance management and career management. **Performance management** includes the planning of broad organizational matters (such as performance standards and quality of work life) and of specific human resources management processes, including performance appraisal and compensation. **Career management** involves the planning of staffing policies and systems, including recruitment, selection, training, and management succession.[4] Figure 6.3 is a form used in succession planning. **Succession planning** is the process of anticipating future managerial staffing needs and making plans for the development of managers to meet those needs.[5]

Relationship to the Staffing Process

Human resources planning, then, is closely linked to the staffing process, which results in the assignment of workers to all positions in the organization. Indeed, human resources planning is the first step in the staffing process. (See Figure 6.4.) To function smoothly and efficiently, organizations must be able to anticipate and cope with staff vacancies due to retirement, promotion, resignation, and so on. Plans must be made to manage these internal shifts or losses in human resources, as well as the deliberate expansion or reduction of particular departments. But the planning process is not strictly confined to staffing changes within the organization. Human

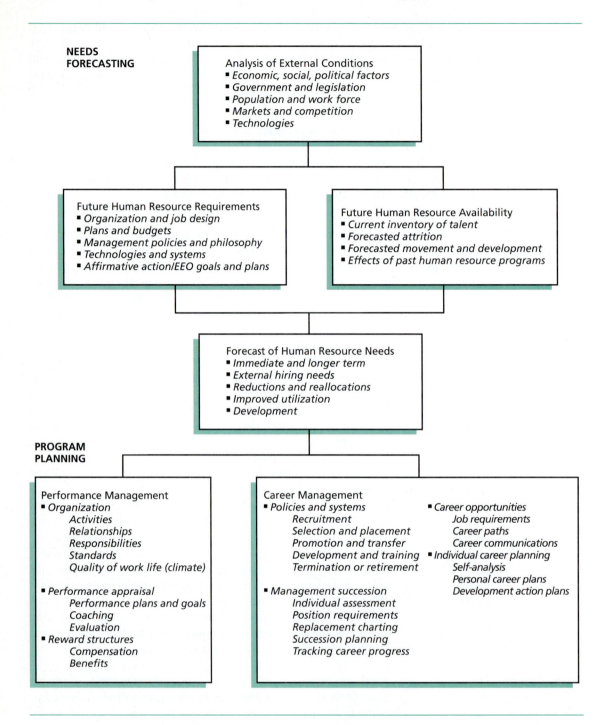

NEEDS FORECASTING

Analysis of External Conditions
- *Economic, social, political factors*
- *Government and legislation*
- *Population and work force*
- *Markets and competition*
- *Technologies*

Future Human Resource Requirements
- *Organization and job design*
- *Plans and budgets*
- *Management policies and philosophy*
- *Technologies and systems*
- *Affirmative action/EEO goals and plans*

Future Human Resource Availability
- *Current inventory of talent*
- *Forecasted attrition*
- *Forecasted movement and development*
- *Effects of past human resource programs*

Forecast of Human Resource Needs
- *Immediate and longer term*
- *External hiring needs*
- *Reductions and reallocations*
- *Improved utilization*
- *Development*

PROGRAM PLANNING

Performance Management
- *Organization*
  Activities
  Relationships
  Responsibilities
  Standards
  Quality of work life (climate)
- *Performance appraisal*
  Performance plans and goals
  Coaching
  Evaluation
- *Reward structures*
  Compensation
  Benefits

Career Management
- *Policies and systems*
  Recruitment
  Selection and placement
  Promotion and transfer
  Development and training
  Termination or retirement
- *Management succession*
  Individual assessment
  Position requirements
  Replacement charting
  Succession planning
  Tracking career progress
- *Career opportunities*
  Job requirements
  Career paths
  Career communications
- *Individual career planning*
  Self-analysis
  Personal career plans
  Development action plans

FIGURE 6.2 The human resources planning process

Source: Human Resource Planning, by James W. Walker. Copyright © 1980 by McGraw-Hill, Inc. Used with the permission of McGraw-Hill Book Company.

MANAGEMENT SUCCESSION PLAN

Organization _____   Date _____

| Probability of Vacancy: |
| Within 1 Year............A |
| 1 to 3 Years...............B |
| Beyond 3 Years..........C |

Position Incumbent		(A) Ready Now	(B) Ready 1–3 Years	(C) Ready Beyond 3 Years	Contingency Plan

FIGURE 6.3   Management succession plan form

resources planning must also be responsive to rapidly changing forces in the external environment, such as market demand, changes in the labor market, technological innovations, and regulatory measures.

Consequences of Inadequate Planning

One example of inadequate planning is the case of an organization caught in a severe budget crisis for which management sees only one solution — to lay off large numbers of employees. Careful planning for such a crisis during better times might have resulted in a series of alternatives, making layoffs unnecessary. The first step might be to curtail hiring and allow retirements and resignations to reduce the payroll. In some cases, the effect might be great enough to permit the organization to survive the crisis without further action. If a hiring freeze is not adequate, the organization might induce voluntary retirements by offering financial incentives to those people within a few years of retirement. (The organization would need to analyze the probable consequences for various units, however, before offering the early retirement possibility. In Case 6.1, an early retirement offer might seriously deplete the management ranks.) The merits of nontraditional staffing methods (such as permanent part-time work and job sharing) and other approaches to reducing the work force can also be evaluated as part of the human resources planning process. (Planning for potential crisis situations will be discussed in more detail in Chapter 10.)

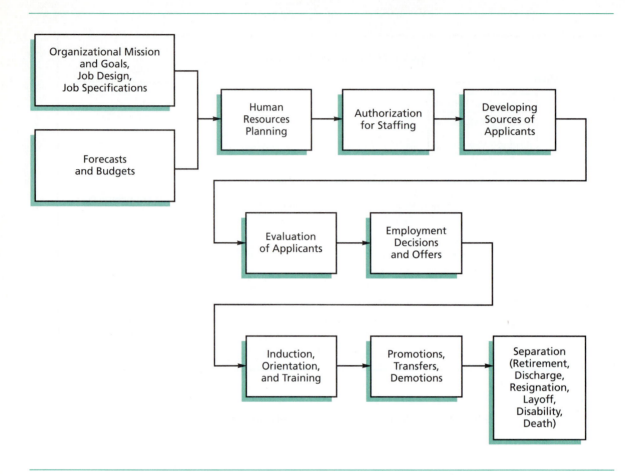

FIGURE 6.4   Human resource planning: the first step in the staffing process

Many other problems can occur if human resources planning is haphazard or neglected. For example, planning should take into account staff reductions in all parts of the organization and should be tied into any system for transferring employees. Staff reductions might be contemplated by top management because of declining sales or increased automation, including the use of computers or robots. However, it would be obvious mismanagement to lay off people in one part of the organization if their critical skills are needed in another area.

In addition, effective human resources planning requires careful monitoring of attrition rates in various units. **Attrition** is the voluntary separation of employees from the organization through resignation and retirement. Such data not only provide information for planning recruiting and hiring but can give some clues about morale as well. If the resignation rate in a department is high, the human resources staff can discreetly inquire about the reasons. Once the causes are understood, corrective action can be taken.

Budgetary Considerations

Human resources planning should also take into account budgetary allocations for staffing; in addition, staffing budgets must be based on a realistic appraisal of human resources requirements. Obviously, hiring should not occur at a faster rate than the overall budget permits. There may be times when the organization cannot afford to employ workers with certain skills because of limited financial resources. Planned expenditures for wages and salaries must be balanced against plans for adding machinery and increasing inventories. It is important that the human resources department work closely with the accounting and finance departments during the planning process and that this collaborative planning be based on realistic marketing, income, and cost projections.

The Labor Agreement

An organization's labor agreement is also a major consideration in staffing decisions. Typically, the labor contract contains provisions regulating transfers, demotions, discharges, bidding on job openings, and layoff procedures. For example, many labor contracts require that seniority be a factor in layoff procedures and that recall of laid-off employees be based on reverse order of layoff. In addition, rules in the labor contract concerning transfers and promotion will affect which jobs are filled from the outside. If the contract requires the posting of a job in order to give union members an opportunity to apply for it, the net effect may be that higher-level jobs are filled from within and that new employees are hired into lower job classifications. Strikes, of course, are emergency situations requiring planning for such matters as the proper shutdown of equipment, protection of plant equipment and property, and whether to continue operations with nonstriking employees.

Data Collection and Monitoring

If continual and high-quality planning is to take place, data on individuals such as skill level, job title, pay grade, date of birth, and department must be systematically collected, processed, and interpreted. Computer programs can be particularly helpful in large and medium-sized organizations to manage data involving hundreds, if not thousands, of employees under several pay plans and in numerous skill classifications and pay grades. Charts and tables can be helpful in visualizing trends in the external labor market. The low cost of a personal computer with a printer and the availability of useful programs can enable even the smallest organizations to have an important human resources planning and record-keeping tool.[6]

The External Labor Market

Understanding the external labor market is extremely important in human resources planning. Because of the need for continuous and adequate staffing, every enterprise depends on the quality and quantity of human resources external to it. Thus, the quality of training and education in the broader society is of great consequence to each organization.

Occupational Employment Projections

Innovations in technology and science, in particular, tend to have a dramatic and often immediate impact on skill and talent needs. Obsolete products, equipment, or work methods can create surpluses of skills in a relatively short time. For example, optical character reading and voice recognition technologies are expected to greatly reduce the demand for typists, word processors, and data entry keyers by the year

2005.[7] Shortages of certain skills in the external labor market may suggest the need to develop specialized internal training programs, to redesign certain jobs, or to encourage educational institutions to expand programs in some of these skills. Skill surpluses may suggest reductions in these programs.

Figure 6.5 suggests that the demand for workers through 2005 will vary widely among different occupational groups. Employment in the broad category of "technicians and related support occupations" is projected to grow the most rapidly — by 37 percent. This category includes workers who provide technical assistance to scientists, engineers, and other professional workers, as well as those who program and operate technical equipment. Included in this category are paralegals, one of the fastest-growing occupations. The next most rapidly growing category, "professional specialty occupations," includes engineers, computer specialists, health diagnosing and treating occupations, lawyers, and social and recreation workers. Employment in this broad category is expected to grow by 32 percent.[8]

It should be noted, however, that these projections are based on percentage of change, not absolute numbers. For example, while the number of paralegals will grow by 85 percent by 2005, the growth in absolute numbers will be 77,000 workers. This is in contrast to retail service workers, a category that will grow by only 24 percent, but in absolute numbers will grow by 887,000 workers.[9] Thus, it is important to look at both the rate of growth and the absolute numbers. It should also be noted that these statistics reflect national trends and that regional and local trends may be

FIGURE 6.5   Employment change by occupational group

Source: U.S. Department of Labor, Bureau of Labor Statistics, *Occupational Outlook Handbook, 1992–93,* Bulletin 2400, May 1992, p. 12.

different. Human resources specialists need to track trends at all three levels to accurately forecast skills available in the external labor market.

Demographic Changes and Equal Employment

Over the years, attitudes of both managers and employees in many organizations have tended to suppress the employment of minorities in certain jobs, particularly supervisory and white-collar positions. Members of minority groups have commonly been employed as unskilled laborers or relegated to production and maintenance jobs. Similarly, women have been traditionally underemployed in a wide range of occupational categories. Although these situations are gradually being corrected, much remains to be accomplished. For example, although blacks and Hispanics have increased their share of white-collar and skilled jobs in the last two decades, they are still poorly represented in some job categories, particularly in professional, technical, managerial, and sales occupations. (See Table 6.1.)

Today all organizations share the need to eliminate from the workplace **discrimination,** or employment decisions based on racial, ethnic, sexual, age, or other kinds of prejudice. Fairness and justice alone make eliminating discrimination a compelling matter, but changing demographics add urgency to this issue. For example, as of 1990, one American in four defined himself or herself as Hispanic or nonwhite. If present trends in birthrates and immigration persist, it is anticipated that by the year 2000 the Hispanic population will have increased a further 21 percent, the Asian population 22 percent, the black population 12 percent, and the white population 2 percent. Hispanics will constitute one out of six Americans by 2050.[10] Organizations that fail to fully utilize the talents of all segments of society will increasingly be at a competitive disadvantage, particularly as skilled labor becomes harder to find.

Federal Legislation and Regulations

In the past thirty years, legislation protecting employees and job applicants from discrimination has made **equal employment opportunity,** or equal consideration regardless of such personal characteristics as sex, race, and age, the single most important requirement of all human resources planning efforts. These efforts must, at the very least, ensure compliance with existing legislation; in addition, human resources planners must stay informed about current litigation and new court decisions that provide organizations with guidelines for improving their equal opportunity programs.

This section describes in some detail the antidiscrimination laws, major court cases, and changing social attitudes affecting all planning and staffing decisions in human resources management today. The underlying theme of this discussion is that a firm commitment to equal employment opportunity is advantageous to any organization because (1) discriminatory hiring practices have systematically excluded much-needed skills and talents from the workplace and (2) discrimination suits are costly to the organization in terms of court-enforced financial settlements and public image. In an organization committed to thorough, high-quality human resources planning, much can be done actively to improve job opportunities for women, minorities, the disabled, and those aged forty and over. In turn, such planning efforts can have positive effects on overall organizational performance. The

TABLE 6.1 Employed civilians, by occupation, sex, race, and Hispanic origin: 1983 and 1991 (selected statistics)

Occupation	1983 Total employed (1,000)	Percent of total Female	Black	Hispanic	1991 Total employed (1,000)	Percent of total Female	Black	Hispanic
Total	100,834	43.7	9.3	5.3	116,877	45.6	10.1	7.5
Managerial and professional specialty	23,592	40.9	5.6	2.6	31,012	46.3	6.3	3.7
Executive, administrative, and managerial[1]	10,772	32.4	4.7	2.8	14,954	40.6	5.7	4.0
Officials and administrators, public	417	38.5	8.3	3.8	511	45.9	11.3	3.6
Financial managers	357	38.6	3.5	3.1	481	44.7	4.0	3.2
Personnel and labor relations managers	106	43.9	4.9	2.6	126	57.6	5.7	3.1
Purchasing managers	82	23.6	5.1	1.4	112	33.9	2.9	2.2
Managers, marketing, advertising and public relations	396	21.8	2.7	1.7	514	30.6	2.1	2.9
Administrators, education and related fields	415	41.4	11.3	2.4	541	55.2	8.5	4.2
Managers, medicine and health	91	57.0	5.0	2.0	199	65.0	6.2	4.1
Managers, properties and real estate	305	42.8	5.5	5.2	448	46.0	6.3	5.8
Management-related occupations[1]	2,966	40.3	5.8	3.5	3,951	50.8	7.4	4.4
Accountants and auditors	1,105	38.7	5.5	3.3	1,446	51.5	7.6	3.7
Professional specialty[1]	12,820	48.1	6.4	2.5	16,058	51.6	6.7	3.4
Architects	103	12.7	1.6	1.5	127	17.1	2.1	4.4
Engineers[1]	1,572	5.8	2.7	2.2	1,846	8.2	3.6	2.4
Aerospace engineers	80	6.9	1.5	2.1	103	8.7	1.9	3.1
Mathematical and computer scientists[1]	463	29.6	5.4	2.6	923	36.8	6.3	2.9
Natural scientists[1]	357	20.5	2.6	2.1	438	26.1	3.3	3.6
Health diagnosing occupations[1]	735	13.3	2.7	3.3	849	18.1	2.6	3.6
Physicians	519	15.8	3.2	4.5	575	20.1	3.2	4.4
Dentists	126	6.7	2.4	1.0	150	10.1	1.5	2.7
Health assessment and treating occupations	1,900	85.8	7.1	2.2	2,376	86.2	7.2	2.9
Registered nurses	1,372	95.8	6.7	1.8	1,712	94.8	7.1	2.4
Pharmacists	158	26.7	3.8	2.6	187	36.8	3.4	3.2
Dietitians	71	90.8	21.0	3.7	71	93.7	19.1	6.8
Therapists[1]	247	76.3	7.6	2.7	340	77.9	7.2	4.8

TABLE 6.1 Employed civilians, by occupation, sex, race, and Hispanic origin: 1983 and 1991 (selected statistics) *(Cont.)*

Occupation	1983				1991			
	Total employed (1,000)	Percent of total			Total employed (1,000)	Percent of total		
		Female	Black	Hispanic		Female	Black	Hispanic
Teachers, college and university	606	36.3	4.4	1.8	773	40.8	4.8	2.9
Teachers, except college and university[1]	3,365	70.9	9.1	2.7	4,029	74.3	8.6	3.7
Counselors, educational and vocational	184	53.1	13.9	3.2	222	64.4	15.5	3.7
Librarians, archivists, and curators	213	84.4	7.8	1.6	212	81.1	5.8	2.6
Librarians	193	87.3	7.9	1.8	194	83.0	6.1	2.4
Social scientists and urban planners[1]	261	46.8	7.1	2.1	386	53.5	6.7	3.5
Economists	98	37.9	6.3	2.7	116	45.7	5.1	3.2
Psychologists	135	57.1	8.6	1.1	230	60.3	7.8	3.8
Social, recreation, and religious workers[1]	831	43.1	12.1	3.8	1,124	51.0	15.1	5.9
Social workers	407	64.3	18.2	6.3	603	68.0	21.9	7.2
Recreation workers	65	71.9	15.7	2.0	106	76.3	16.3	7.2
Clergy	293	5.6	4.9	1.4	331	9.3	5.4	4.3
Lawyers and judges	651	15.8	2.7	1.0	772	18.9	2.8	1.6
Technical, sales, and administrative support	31,265	64.6	7.6	4.3	36,086	64.7	9.3	6.0
Sales occupations	11,818	47.5	4.7	3.7	13,958	48.8	6.6	5.5
Supervisors and proprietors	2,958	28.4	3.6	3.4	3,739	34.3	4.3	4.9
Sales representatives, finance and business services[1]	1,853	37.2	2.7	2.2	2,344	42.1	5.0	3.7
Administrative support, including clerical	16,395	79.9	9.6	5.0	18,334	80.0	11.4	6.6
Financial records processing[1]	2,457	89.4	4.6	3.7	2,389	91.0	6.2	5.6
Service occupations	13,857	60.1	16.6	6.8	15,986	59.8	17.2	11.2
Precision production, craft, and repair	12,328	8.1	6.8	6.2	13,162	8.6	7.8	8.6
Operators, fabricators, and laborers	16,091	26.6	14.0	8.3	17,172	25.2	15.0	12.0

[1]Includes other occupations, not shown separately.

Source: Bureau of the Census, U.S. Department of Commerce *Statistical Abstract of the United States, 1992*, 112 th Edition, pp. 392–394.

impact of other legislation, such as the Plant Closing Bill (1988), the Immigration Reform and Control Act (1986), and the Immigration Act (1990), was discussed briefly in Chapter 3. The Family and Medical Leave Act (1993) will be discussed in Chapter 16.

The Civil Rights Acts and the Equal Pay Act

Title VII of the Civil Rights Act of 1964, as amended by the Equal Employment Opportunity Act of 1972 and supplemented by the Civil Rights Act of 1991, and other legislation, prohibits discrimination in employment on the basis of race, color, religion, sex, national origin, or disability. Title VII applies to private employers of fifteen or more persons, state and local government, educational institutions, employment agencies, and labor unions. There are certain exemptions, such as the U.S. government (covered under executive orders) and Indian tribes.

Occasionally, exceptions to the law have been made where religion, sex, age, or national origin (but not race or color) have been considered a **bona fide occupational qualification** (BFOQ). An early example of a BFOQ might have been a French restaurant hiring a French cook (which was an early congressional interpretation[11]), but this may no longer be permissible. Exceptions to the Civil Rights Acts are rare; they have usually been related to religious or sex discrimination and applied to such occupations as church ministers and restroom attendants.[12] A notable recent exception is the case of Japanese subsidiaries in the United States. Because of a reciprocal treaty with the United States, these foreign units may discriminate in favor of Japanese nationals at the executive levels. (See *International Perspective* on page 141.)

The Equal Employment Opportunity Commission (EEOC), an independent federal agency composed of five members, was created by the Civil Rights Act of 1964 to investigate charges of discrimination and to resolve problems "by informal methods of conference, conciliation, and persuasion." Originally, court action beyond this step had to be undertaken by the party charging discrimination if these informal methods did not solve the problem. Amendments made to the law in March 1972 now permit the EEOC itself to bring lawsuits against employers in the federal courts. This means that the EEOC is free to seek court orders to enforce its decision. In addition, the EEOC prepares written guidelines that translate Title VII requirements into legal employment practices. Although these are guidelines, not binding laws, they can be used as standards for evaluating the extent to which an organization is complying with Title VII. (See Chapter 9 for a discussion of the "Uniform Guidelines on Employee Selection Procedures," issued jointly by the EEOC and other federal agencies.)

In many parts of the country, appropriate local agencies are given a period of time in which to process discrimination charges before the EEOC steps in for further action. Most states have fair employment practice laws and enforcement agencies to which the commission defers for initial action.

Title VII specifies certain penalties for organizations found guilty of discrimination. These include the court ordering the organization to stop engaging in the unlawful practice, the reinstatement or hiring of employees with or without back pay, and the payment of reasonable attorney's fees.[13] As stated in Chapter 3, these provisions have now been enlarged under the Civil Rights Act of 1991, which allows jury trials and punitive and compensatory damages in cases of intentional discrimination based on sex, religion or disability. (Other laws had previously allowed damages in cases involving ethnic or racial minorities.)[14]

International Perspective

Court Rules Japanese-Owned Company Not Bound by Title VII

The Seventh Circuit Court of Appeals has ruled that Japanese subsidiaries operating in the U.S. may legally prefer Japanese citizens over U.S. citizens and Title VII prohibitions against discrimination on the basis of national origin do not apply.

According to the ruling in *Fortino v. Quasar Co.*, Title VII is preempted by a treaty between Japan and the U.S. which permits companies of either country to prefer their own citizens for executive positions in subsidiaries based in the other country. This ruling clarifies a 1982 Supreme Court decision (*Sumitomo Shoji America Inc. v. Avagliano*) and gives Japanese-owned firms the right to exclude U.S. citizens from the top tier of management.

While it is not clear to what extent Japanese-owned firms can invoke treaty rights to opt out of Title VII provisions, even a conservative reading of the case suggests important ramifications for employment policy and foreign investment.

First, the court's decision creates a legally enforceable "glass ceiling" for U.S. employees working in Japanese-owned firms and, presumably, for those working in any foreign-owned firm whose home country has negotiated similar treaty language. Foreign-owned companies that invoke treaty rights to block American access to upper-level positions send a signal to employees that while blue collar careers are encouraged, white collar careers are not.

Second, for the last decade many economists and policy makers have argued that increased foreign investment is good for the United States because it creates jobs. This case, by automatically excluding U.S. workers from those jobs that afford the highest income potential, underscores the point that jobs created by foreign investment are not necessarily a simple substitution for jobs created by domestic investment. Quasar and its parent Matsushita Electric, may have had an interest in establishing precedent, but using the court ruling to justify what will still be perceived as discrimination against Americans will merely provide fodder for those policy makers that would curtail foreign investment and foreign trade.

Finally, the case comes at a time when the U.S. is in the midst of a debate over, as Robert Reich says in his latest book *The Work of Nations*, "who is us?" Who is really an "American" firm: Corporation A which is headquartered in the U.S. but most of its work force and production facilities are off-shore or Corporation B which is based abroad but has significant operations and employees in the U.S.? Reich argues that the truly "American" firm, the one that deserves support from policy makers and consumers, is Corporation B because the United States is enriched not by firms that merely repatriate profits but by those that employ and train its citizens. The Quasar ruling, to the extent that it is applied, throws a wrench in Reich's argument: companies that employ Americans but erect a "glass ceiling" for them do not seem to qualify as "us" regardless of investments in training and employment.

Source: Issues in HR (March/April 1992), 1–2. Reprinted with the permission of *Issues in HR* published by the Society for Human Resource Management Alexandria, VA.

The Equal Pay Act of 1963 prohibits discrimination on the basis of sex in wage payments for jobs that require equal skills, effort, and responsibility under similar working conditions in the same establishment. This act, along with the Civil Rights Act of 1964, has extensive effects on human resources planning and decision making in thousands of organizations today. The Civil Rights Act of 1991 adds to the importance of human resources planning in eliminating discrimination and in avoiding costly lawsuits.

The impact of the two Civil Rights acts and the Equal Pay Act can readily be seen in court awards and in out-of-court settlements. For example:

- The Burlington Northern Railroad and the EEOC agreed to a $50 million settlement to resolve charges of racial bias in hiring, initial assignment, transfer, testing and training, discipline, and promotion. The award included $10 million in back pay, and the organization was required to give priority consideration in hiring to black applicants who had previously been rejected.[15]

- The Ponderosa steak-house chain agreed to pay over $1 million to 221 women who charged that the firm had discriminated against them in pay and managerial promotions.[16]

- Settling a discrimination complaint, Honda of America Manufacturing agreed with the EEOC to pay 370 blacks and women $6 million in back pay and to offer them jobs. Those receiving the award had previously applied for employment and had been turned down.[17]

- A San Francisco federal court ended lengthy litigation between the now defunct Pan American World Airways, Inc., and the Independent Union of Flight Attendants by approving a $2.3 million settlement to more than 100 Pan Am flight attendants who were forced to resign or were discharged, suspended, or denied promotion because of the airline's weight policy. The court found that Pan Am's policy relied on "sex-based stereotypes prohibited by Title VII." Pan Am also agreed to pay the union's attorney's fees of $400,000.[18]

- Price Waterhouse, a large accounting firm, was ordered by an appeals court to promote a woman to partnership. Although she was considered an outstanding worker, the woman had been denied the promotion because she was considered overbearing and abrasive and referred to by coworkers as "macho." In addition to the partnership, the court ordered the company to provide back pay with interest, totaling some $370,000.[19]

- In a case that had extended over a sixteen-year period, the State Farm Life Insurance agreed to pay $157 million to 814 Californian women who had been refused jobs as sales agents in the company. A federal district judge had previously ruled that the company was liable for intentional sex discrimination in the recruitment, selection, and hiring of agents in California.[20]

Overcoming Sex Discrimination

As several of the above cases demonstrate, the Civil Rights Act of 1964 has been a major influence in combating discrimination based on sex. At first, the ban on discrimination on the basis of sex was referred to as a "sleeper" in the original Civil Rights Act. Most of the congressional debate surrounding the act centered on racial discrimination, and the provision about sex was introduced by opponents in an attempt to defeat the bill. Alleged discrimination on the basis of sex, however, now constitutes a high percentage of the cases filed with the EEOC. Many of the recent cases culminating in consent settlements involved charges of discrimination against women in hiring, pay, and promotion. In response to these court-ordered settlements and to pressure from organized women's groups, many traditional employment practices are being altered dramatically.

Among these changing practices is the growing use of nonsexist terminology in job labels to avoid implications of discrimination in recruiting and hiring. For example, the *Dictionary of Occupational Titles* (DOT), published by the U.S. Department of Labor, has changed many of the job titles listed there.[21] To illustrate, *airplane stewardess* has been changed to *airplane flight attendant, surveying axman* to *surveying brush clearer, brewmaster* to *brewing director, bus boy* to *dining room attendant, fisherman* to *fisher, foreman* to *supervisor, governess* to *child mentor, new car salesman* to *new car associate,* and *salesman* to *salesperson.*

Some discrimination complaints are being filed by men seeking jobs traditionally held by women. For example, the Supreme Court declined to reverse a circuit court of appeals ruling that an airline's refusal to hire a male flight attendant was in violation of the Civil Rights Act.[22] Since that decision, an increasing number of men have been employed as flight attendants. To illustrate, Pacific Southwest Airlines agreed to pay $275,000 in back wages and offer flight attendant jobs to males and to blacks and Hispanics of both sexes.[23]

The most dramatic change in employment practices, however, is the placement of women in jobs traditionally filled by men. Today, women are employed as police officers, police chiefs, blacksmiths, coal miners, boilermakers, truck drivers, army paratroopers, locomotive engineers, surveyors, hog buyers, firefighters, fire chiefs, baseball umpires, zoo keepers, commercial airline pilots, military officers, and astronauts. Women are commanding Coast Guard and navy ships,[24] and in the Gulf War, women helicopter pilots were part of the spectacular advance of the army's 101st Airborne Division.[25] Women may now fly all kinds of combat aircraft.[26] But in spite of the growing number of women in the overall work force and the increase in female employees in traditionally male jobs, statistics from the U.S. Department of

Organizations must ensure that the various rights of female workers are protected, including protection against sexual harrassment. This is especially challenging for women in careers typically occupied by men.

Labor indicate that women are still substantially underrepresented in certain occupations.

The entry of women into the work force is associated with certain changes in stereotyped attitudes and mythical assumptions about working women. For example, the notion that most women were working "just for pin money" was long ago refuted by a University of Michigan study, which revealed that one-third of working women surveyed were the sole wage earners in their households. The same study found that most women were just as concerned about opportunities for self-actualization and promotion as were men.[27]

Findings like these have clear implications for the planning and design of all human resources management programs. Organizations must be concerned with satisfying the particular needs of female workers to reduce dissatisfaction and turnover and to enhance their contributions to organizational performance. Skill training and career development programs for female workers are one way of reaching this goal. Organizations must also make some accommodation to the fact that women still carry much of the responsibility for child care in our society. Flexible work schedules and the provision of day-care services by some organizations are indications that this accommodation is beginning to take place. Organizations must also ensure the various rights of female workers, beyond rights in hiring, pay, and promotion. These additional rights include protection against sexual harassment (see Chapter 19) and rights under the Pregnancy Discrimination Act (see Chapter 3).

Older Workers

(Before reading this section, you may wish to test yourself concerning your views of the older worker. See *Contemporary Issues* on page 145.)

Certain stereotypes and distorted attitudes about older workers also exist. One is that the older worker is less productive. A research study involving a random sample of semiskilled assemblers in a factory, found this to be untrue. In the sample, productivity increased with age.[28] Other myths hold that the older worker costs the firm more in absenteeism, illness, insurance, pensions, workers' compensation, and so on. None of these assumptions may be true in a given firm. Indeed, many employers have found the older worker to have greater experience and better retention rates, and to be more satisfied with the job and the organization.[29] (Erroneous assumptions about older workers will be discussed further in Chapter 12.)

The Age Discrimination in Employment Act of 1967 (ADEA) was designed to protect older workers against age discrimination in hiring, retention, promotion, compensation, and other conditions of employment. Essentially, the act makes it illegal to base salary decisions on age, to pass over older employees for promotions, and to discharge or impose retirement on older workers in order to replace them with younger workers or to lower costs of pension benefits. This act applies to any employer subject to Title VII and is enforced by the secretary of labor. Amendments to the ADEA in 1978 banned involuntary or **mandatory retirement** before age seventy by private employers of twenty or more people and at any age for most occupations in the federal government. Later amendments banned mandatory retirement at any age.

In 1990, the Older Workers Benefit Protection Act amended the ADEA to require that waivers signed by older workers in early retirement situations be "knowing and voluntary." The amendments also affirmed the "equal benefit or equal cost" principle, under which an employer must provide older workers with benefits equal

Contemporary Issues

Understanding Older Workers: Test Yourself!

How do you view older workers? The Conference Board surveyed executives in 363 companies about their views on common perceptions of older workers compared with younger workers. Test your own attitudes.

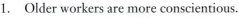

1. Older workers are more conscientious.
    True   False
2. Older workers tend to be less productive.
    True   False.
3. Older workers tend to have greater loyalty to the company.   True   False
4. Older workers tend to be less creative.
    True   False
5. Older workers have fewer accidents.
    True   False

6. Older workers are less likely to keep up with new developments in their fields.
    True   False
7. Older workers have better job morale.
    True   False
8. Older workers have better judgment.
    True   False
9. Older workers have lower turnover rates.
    True   False
10. Older workers tend to be more difficult to supervise.   True   False
11. Older workers have more absences.
    True   False

Answers to "Test Yourself"
1. True 2. False 3. True 4. False 5. True 6. False 7. True 8. True 9. True 10. False 11. False

Source: *Working Age* 7 (September/October 1991):1. © 1991 American Association of Retired Persons. Reprinted with permission.

---

to those of younger workers, unless the employer can prove that the cost is greater. (See Chapter 3).

There are a few exceptions to the provisions of the ADEA. For example, mandatory retirement at age sixty-five is permitted for those executive or policy-making employees who have held their positions for at least two years and whose annual retirement benefits attributed to employer contributions total at least $44,000. Further, through 1993, the prohibition of mandatory retirement policies did not pertain to certain firefighting and law enforcement personnel or to tenured university faculty members.[30]

Occasionally, age is considered a bona fide occupational qualification, although this exemption is interpreted narrowly by the secretary of labor. An example of a BFOQ given by the government is a young actor required for a youthful role. In addition, employers may override age criteria when applying the terms of bona fide (nondiscriminatory) seniority systems and the legal provisions of company benefit plans. For example, the age provisions of a retirement plan are no excuse to refrain from hiring an individual, but an employer is not required to place the individual under the plan if his or her age bracket has been excluded. Finally, nothing in the act prevents an employer from disciplining or discharging an older worker as long as these activities are taken for valid job-related reasons.

Lawsuits involving charges of age discrimination are on the increase. In 1989, employers paid out almost three times as much in settlements pertaining to EEOC age discrimination suits than in settlements pertaining to EEOC race or job bias suits.[31] In a recent case, Pan American World Airways, Inc., settled an age discrimination suit by more than 90 pilots who had been forced to retire at age sixty. The $17.2 million award included a consent decree requiring the airline to allow pilots to qualify for flight engineer assignments as they approached age sixty.[32] The Equitable Life Assurance Society of the United States agreed to a $12.5 million settlement in a case involving 363 former employees. All were over forty years of age and had been fired, according to the company, as part of a cost-cutting plan.[33] Honda of America Manufacturing agreed to pay nearly half a million dollars in back wages to 85 employees to settle charges that the automaker discriminated against them when they first applied. The workers, who were forty years of age or older, were hired in 1986 but had applied in 1984 and 1985.[34]

Many other firms have been sued by managers who have been fired, forced into early retirement, or passed over for promotion. Some of the firms that have either lost age discrimination suits or settled out of court include Sandia National Laboratories, Atlantic Container Line, Textron, Connecticut General Life Insurance, ITT Corp., The Standard Oil Company of California, Sears, Roebuck and Co., American Express Company, and Monarch Paper Company.[35]

Clearly, human resources planning needs to accommodate to the ADEA to avoid charges of discrimination based on age. Beyond that, however, it is important that the organization develop personnel policies and practices that will enhance and maintain the motivation and morale of employees of all ages, including those forty and over.

Persons with Disabilities

A few years ago, it was estimated that roughly 18 percent of the country's noninstitutional population aged eighteen to sixty-four had some form of disability. This percentage represented a larger group of workers than any one racial minority.[36] Out of this huge group, only about 15 percent of the employable disabled were working.[37]

Employer attitudes are a major factor in the underemployment of those with disabilities. One study showed employer attitudes to be less favorable toward the disabled than toward any other minority, including ex-convicts.[38] In addition to prejudice, there are other barriers to employing those with disabilities, such as overly strict job requirements, inappropriately designed jobs, and improper physical facilities.

Concern for the employable disabled has led to the passage of two federal laws prohibiting discrimination against the physically impaired. The Rehabilitation Act of 1973, Section 503, requires employers with government contracts of over $2,500 to take positive steps to enhance employment and promotion opportunities for qualified individuals with disabilities. Section 504 requires every institution in the country getting federal assistance, such as colleges and hospitals, to take steps to ensure that such individuals are not discriminated against in employment.[39]

The Americans with Disabilities Act (ADA) of 1990 extended the Civil Rights Act of 1964 to outlaw discrimination against any applicant with a disability that "substantially limits" his or her mental or physical capacity, provided the person is qualified to perform the "essential functions" of the job. Further, the ADA requires employers to make "reasonable accommodation" for disabled applicants and employees, provided such accommodation does not create an "undue hardship" for the employer. The ADA applies to private employers, state and local governments, employment agencies, and labor unions. The law covers all aspects of human resources management, including recruitment, employee benefits, training, and separation. (See also Chapter 3). This law became effective July 1992 for employers with twenty-five or more employees and July 1994 for employers of fifteen or more employees.[40]

A wide variety of physical and mental disabilities have been determined to be protected handicaps under federal law. Among these conditions are visual impairment, high blood pressure, heart conditions, diabetes, dyslexia, epilepsy, posttraumatic stress disorder, AIDS, and sensitivity to smoke.[41]

The hiring of persons with disabilities requires very careful planning by individual organizations. Disabled workers have special needs, and advance planning is necessary to place them in appropriate jobs, to restructure jobs when feasible, and to make changes in the physical plant. Further, special training programs may be warranted in many instances.

A survey found that the most frequent modifications in physical facilities made for disabled employees were, in this order, designated parking spaces, special restroom equipment, wheelchair ramps, handrails, widened access areas, lowered drinking fountains, and modified elevator equipment. The most frequent measures taken to enhance job performance were providing special workstation equipment (such as amplifiers, headsets, or large computer screens), job restructuring, flexible work schedules, and the provision of readers or interpreters.[42] Meeting these challenges should be an integral part of the overall human resources planning process.

Affirmative Action

A crucial element in the human resources planning process is the need for **affirmative action.** Affirmative action has been defined as "a remedial concept that requests employers and labor unions to take positive steps voluntarily to improve the work opportunities of women, racial and ethnic minorities, persons with disabilities, and Vietnam veterans who have been deprived of job opportunities."[43] Under Executive Order 11246, affirmative action plans are legal requirements of federal contractors and subcontractors having 50 or more employees or a federal contract worth more than $50,000. This order is enforced by the Office of Federal Contract Compliance Programs (OFCCP), Department of Labor.[44] Affirmative action plans are also required under the Rehabilitation Act of 1973, under the Vietnam Era Veterans Readjustment Assistance Act of 1974 (which protects the employment rights of all disabled veterans), and under Executive Order 11478 (which calls for affirmative action in federal agencies). More than 95,000 companies employing 27 million workers are covered by the federal affirmative action program.[45]

Besides federal contractors, organizations that receive federal grants, such as hospitals, universities, and day-care centers, are required to have affirmative action programs. Further, many companies and government agencies have voluntary affirmative action programs, using guidelines issued by the EEOC and influenced by Supreme Court rulings.

Under the various executive orders and legislation, contractors are required to develop and administer affirmative action plans with specific goals and timetables for raising the level of minority and female employment in their firms. Typically, the long-term goal is to raise minority and female employment to a level comparable to the percentage of minority and female workers in the local work force. Voluntary affirmative action programs, however, may include higher interim goals or targets. Such interim goals can upgrade overall employment prospects for minority and female workers more quickly.[46]

Once these goals and timetables have been established, employers develop and administer specific programs to meet them. As part of this process, employers are advised to review *all* existing employment practices. In this way they can identify and remove barriers to equal employment opportunity and make changes that will increase employment and advancement opportunities for minorities and females. Thus, the goals established in affirmative action plans will directly affect recruitment, hiring, training, and all other aspects of human resources management.

An example of the impact of affirmative action regulations is the 1980 consent agreement between Uniroyal and the Department of Labor, in which the company agreed to establish special hiring goals for minorities and women and to pay $5.2 million in back pay to 750 women workers.[47] In the same year, Firestone Tire & Rubber Co. was barred from doing business with the federal government until the company could demonstrate that it was complying with affirmative action regulations.[48]

The legality of affirmative action was upheld by the U.S. Supreme Court in 1979. In *Steelworkers* v. *Weber*, the court ruled that affirmative action programs implemented voluntarily by employers and unions to enhance employment opportunities for minorities are legal. In this case, Brian Weber, an employee of Kaiser Aluminum & Chemical Corp., had been passed over for a training program in favor of black employees with less seniority. The company had made its trainee selections under a union-management agreement establishing a 50 percent quota for black trainees until the proportion of black employees corresponded to the proportion of blacks in the local labor force. One implication of this ruling is that employers can establish "race-conscious" affirmative action programs unilaterally or in cooperation with unions in order to correct imbalances in a work force.[49] Similarly, in the 1986 *Local 93* v. *City of Cleveland* case, the Supreme Court approved an affirmative action plan of promotions for firefighters using a one-to-one ratio of blacks to whites to increase the level of minority employment in upper-level jobs. In 1987, in *U.S.* v. *Paradise*, the Court upheld a one-to-one ratio for promoting black state troopers in Alabama.[50]

In *Johnson* v. *Transportation Agency* in 1987, the Supreme Court ruled that both public and private employers may voluntarily implement affirmative action plans to correct sex discrimination. The Santa Clara County, California, transportation agency had promoted Diane Joyce, with an interview score of 73, over Paul Johnson, who had scored 75 on the interview. Paul Johnson sued the county, and ultimately the case reached the Supreme Court. The Court upheld the promotion, which was made under an affirmative action plan to correct a "manifest imbalance" in the work force.[51]

The *Weber* and later decisions do not guarantee that all aspects of affirmative action programs will be approved. In 1984, the Supreme Court ruled in *Fire Fighters Local 1784* v. *Stotts* that a bona fide seniority system cannot be overridden in a layoff situation to protect an affirmative action program. In that case, nonminority City of Memphis employees with more seniority than minority employees had been laid off or demoted. The union and the city went to court on behalf of the nonminority employees and ultimately prevailed. In writing for the majority, Justice White cited a 1964 memorandum issued by congressional sponsors of Title VII that said, "Title VII does not permit the ordering of racial quotas in business or unions."[52] In a related case in 1986, *Wygant* v. *Jackson Board of Education*, the Court ruled that the

U.S. Constitution barred the school district from laying off white teachers with more seniority than blacks who remained at work.[53]

The Civil Rights Act of 1991 reversed several 1989 Supreme Court decisions that had the potential of curtailing affirmative action programs. Further, the new Civil Rights Act permits victims of intentional sex, religious, and disability discrimination to seek compensatory and punitive damages up to $300,000.[54] (See also Chapter 3.) This is likely to encourage firms to strengthen affirmative action programs, which, in general, are well accepted in corporate America.[55]

The extensive dissent within the Supreme Court in some of the above decisions and the disagreements between the executive branch and Congress about quotas suggest that the whole issue of quota systems has not been finally resolved. Human resources planners, as well as managers in general, will need to be alert to ongoing changes in the laws, court decisions, and administrative rulings affecting affirmative action efforts. (As will be discussed in Chapter 12, human resources planning in many organizations is shifting from an emphasis on compliance and affirmative action to an additional emphasis on valuing diversity.)

Military Leave

The 1990–1991 war in the Persian Gulf prompted employers to review federal laws and their personnel policies pertaining to military leave. Thousands of military reservists and National Guard members were called to active duty during that crisis.

Under the Vietnam Era Veterans' Readjustment Assistance Act of 1974, reservists and guard members who go on active duty, either voluntarily or because they are called, have certain rights, provided they satisfactorily complete military duty and apply for reinstatement within 90 days of their discharge from service. These rights are as follows:

- He or she must be returned to the former position or to a position of equal seniority, pay, and status unless the employer's circumstances are so changed that this is impossible. This guarantee extends for four years, unless extended by the federal government.

- He or she must be given the seniority, pay, and status "as the person would have enjoyed if such person had continued in such employment continuously." This position could be the previous position, a better position, a lesser one, or no position at all depending upon the circumstances of the employment relationship.[56]

Employers are not required to make up any difference between the person's civilian pay and his or her military pay. However, during the Gulf War, numerous employers continued employee benefits and made up the difference in pay for a period of time, for example, 30 to 120 days.[57]

Child Labor

Until recently, child labor abuses have not been much of an issue in the United States since the passage of the Fair Labor Standards Act (FLSA) in 1937 and its amendments. However, the rapid growth of fast-food establishments, in particular, has coincided with a renewed concern about the exploitation of child labor.

In 1990, Secretary of Labor Elizabeth Dole ordered compliance officers to investigate fast-food chains, pizza parlors, and other businesses that typically hire teenagers, and found nearly 43 percent in violation of the law. In a three-day sweep, the compliance officers found 1,400 out of 3,400 businesses in violation. Most of the children working illegally were fourteen- and fifteen-year-olds who, under the

FLSA, may not work from 7 p.m. to 7 a.m., during school hours, or for more than eighteen hours per week. The typical violation involved a fourteen- or fifteen-year-old working until 10 p.m. at a restaurant. In addition, a substantial number of sixteen- and seventeen-year-olds were found working in jobs considered too hazardous for this age group, such as operating meat-slicing machinery and paper-bailers. Many of the companies found in violation of the law were immediately cited, with fines estimated at $1.8 million. One conclusion by Secretary Dole was that employers should consider paying higher wages if they have difficulty attracting workers of legal age.[58]

In 1992, the New York State Labor Department found 130 children illegally employed in New York City factories during the first six months of the year. One factory worker was seven years old and two were eight years old.[59] Child labor has not disappeared. (The most extensive abuses are in India — see Chapter 22.)

Role of the Human Resources Department

Typically, the human resources department has a major role in human resources planning. One study of 477 firms found that the personnel department was responsible for all or some of the human resources planning and forecasting in 94 percent of them and was assigned all or some responsibility for EEOC compliance and affirmative action in 98 percent.[60]

These assignments are appropriate because the personnel department is normally at the center of an information network on labor-market conditions, skill levels in various departments, mobility patterns within the organization, departmental wage and salary structures, and federal and state legislation and court rulings. To make its maximum contribution to organizational effectiveness, the personnel department must take the initiative in becoming actively and responsively involved in matters of human resources planning.

Teamwork among the total executive group in human resources planning, however, is extremely important. One study compared firms that were leaders in productivity with a random sample of other large firms. The study found that the human resources department of a leading firm was *three times* more likely to be working with line managers in such matters as succession and compensation-system planning than the human resources department in an average firm. Further, when human resources executives were queried about the role their department played in the corporation, many more executives in the leading firms reported that their departments participated in business decisions and contributed to their company's achievement of its strategic goals than did executives in average firms.[61] Clearly, effective human resources planning is a collaborative effort that is closely related to the strategic planning of the organization.

Summary   Human resources planning requires ongoing analysis of the organization's human resources needs in the light of the organization's strategic goals, staffing needs, and the desired organizational culture and climate, as well as the external labor market and legal environment. The planning of specific human resources programs — such as recruitment, training, promotion, and compensation — to meet those needs can then follow.

Effective human resources planning should take into account the present and anticipated financial condition of the organization, as well as the changing human resources needs within its various departments. It is an important coordinating function that ensures that the valuable human resources of the organization are carefully nurtured and developed. Systematic data collection and interpretation are essential to this process.

Federal legislation, Equal Employment Opportunity Commission rulings, and court decisions have a major impact on both human resources planning and specific program design. In particular, the Civil Rights Act of 1964 and the new Civil Rights Act of 1991, the Equal Pay Act, the Age Discrimination in Employment Act, the Equal Employment Opportunity Act, the Rehabilitation Act, the Vietnam Era Veterans' Readjustment Assistance Act, and the Americans with Disabilities Act are having a profound influence on recruitment, hiring, promotion, training, discipline, compensation, and separation practices. Other laws, such as the Immigration Reform and Control Act, the Plant Closing Bill, the Pregnancy Discrimination Act, the Older Workers Protection Act, and the Immigration Act are also having an impact on human resources planning and management.

Affirmative action requires employers and labor unions to take positive steps to improve the work opportunities of minorities, women, persons with disabilities, and veterans. The goals established in affirmative action plans will directly affect recruitment, hiring, training, and all other aspects of human resources management. Specific methods for implementing affirmative action mean that the human resources specialists must keep informed of changing government policy and legal actions in this area.

The human resources department has a major role in human resources planning. Ideally, effective human resources planning is a collaborative effort, involving all managers in the organization. Further, human resources planning must be closely related to the organization's overall strategic planning.

Ethical Dilemma

Ralph Magnus is a new employment interviewer in the human resources department at Diesel Trucks, Inc. One interviewee, Susan Garber, who was subsequently hired, disclosed to him that she is a single parent and that she suffers from epilepsy, which she controls with medication. A few weeks later, Ralph and two former college buddies, one from the accounting department and one from manufacturing, were having lunch and talking about new women employees whom they considered particularly attractive. During the conversation, Ralph casually mentioned that Susan is a single mother and that she is epileptic.

Are there ethical issues involved? If so, what are they? What action, if any, would you take with Ralph if you were director of human resources?

Key Terms

human resources planning
mission statement
strategic plan
organizational goal
organizational objective
needs forecasting
program planning
performance management

career management
succession planning
attrition
discrimination
equal employment opportunity
bona fide occupational qualification
mandatory retirement
affirmative action

Review Questions

1. Define human resources planning and describe two major steps in the planning process.
2. Explain how human resources planning is related to the overall strategic plan of the organization.
3. How are human resources planning and the staffing process related?
4. Why is an understanding of the external labor market important in human resources planning?
5. What federal laws and regulations have had the most impact on human resources planning and in what way?
6. What is affirmative action? How does affirmative action affect human resources planning?

Opening Case Questions

Case 6.1   A Can of Worms

1. Now that Alan Corelli has set up committees to assess the promotability of the company's present employees, what other steps in human resources planning should he take?
2. What options are available to Quality Chemicals to prepare current employees for the key positions that Alan may soon need to fill?

Case 6.2   The Morning News

1. For human resources planning purposes, what information would seem to be the most crucial for Steve and Clare to obtain as soon as possible?
2. To what extent has human resources planning been part of the negotiation and acquisition process? What should have been different, if anything?

Comprehensive Case

Recruiting and Keeping Hispanic Employees

The rapid growth of the Hispanic population in the United States means that even organizations that resist affirmative action and ignore the benefits of an ethnically diverse work force will soon find themselves hiring more Hispanic workers. The Hispanic-American population is increasing at about four times the rate of the overall American population; about 40 percent of the 19 million new Americans expected by the end of this decade will be Hispanic. Already, Hispanics represent a sizable minority in certain cities, accounting for 23 percent of the inhabitants in Los Angeles and 28 percent in Miami. Hispanic women constitute one of the fastest-growing labor force groups; the number of Hispanic women in the work force rose by 67 percent between 1980 and 1991. Demographers predict that by 2050 about one out of every six Americans will be Hispanic, double the current percentage.

These figures are impressive, and the growth rate of the Hispanic population is expected to continue because of emigration from the Caribbean and Central and South America and because the fertility rate is higher for Hispanics than for other groups of Americans. Companies cannot afford to overlook the amount of talent that these numbers represent.

Yet for many employers, finding, hiring, and retaining Hispanic employees requires a willingness to see through stereotypes and a sensitivity to cultural differences. The term *Hispanic* actually lumps together people of distinctly different backgrounds and cultures — those from Mexico, Cuba, Puerto Rico, and Central and South America. These diverse peoples are united by their use of the Spanish language, and it is language differences that sometimes cause difficulties in the workplace.

Language is one of the major reasons that Spanish-speaking workers have much higher on-the-job injury rates than do their white and African-American peers. Few companies offer training in Spanish, and some Hispanic workers are reluctant to ask for help or to complain about problems because they fear discrimination or, in some cases, because they are illegal aliens. A company dedicated to providing a safe workplace for its employees may need either to provide job and safety training in Spanish or to help Spanish-speaking employees learn English.

Although language barriers can pose some real problems, widespread Hispanic stereotypes are more likely to make companies reluctant or unable to hire Hispanic workers. Hispanic students score lower on some standardized tests than do their white peers, leading some people to believe that Hispanics are uneducated, unqualified, or less intelligent than other Americans. But when the numbers are adjusted to account for the effects of socioeconomic background, the achievements of Hispanic students are comparable to those of white students. For example, more than 90 percent of students from Hispanic families with incomes over $48,000 finish high school — just slightly below the 94 percent graduation rate for whites in the same income bracket.

Some employers also complain that they simply cannot find qualified Hispanic employees. This may indeed be a real problem for companies trying to hire Hispanics in particular parts of the country; almost three-quarters of Hispanic-Americans live in Florida, New York, California, or Texas. But there are now organizations dedicated to keeping track of Hispanic college students (the Hispanic Association of Colleges and Universities) and professionals (the Consortium to Identify and Promote Hispanic Professionals), as well as magazines such as *Hispanic Business* and *Hispanic*, which can help organizations learn about Hispanic people and cultures. Employers who want to hire Hispanics can also intensify their recruiting of community college graduates. More

Hispanics go to two-year rather than four-year colleges because community colleges tend to be less expensive and closer to home.

Hispanics are also often stereotyped as unwilling to leave their communities. To the extent that some truth underlies this generalization, employers should learn from it. Hispanics who feel isolated in an organization would naturally be reluctant to leave their communities, and employers can combat such isolation through outreach programs. Experts in Hispanic recruitment also encourage companies to develop alliances with educational institutions and contact potential employees while they are still in school. But employers must avoid being overzealous about Hispanic recruiting, projecting unrealistic images of the ethnic makeup of their work force and the possibilities for advancement.

Some organizations will need to adjust their human resources policies to attract and retain Hispanic employees. But as people of Spanish-speaking origins become an increasingly important factor in the United States, companies that make the adjustment will see their efforts pay off.

Sources: Peter T. Kilborn, "For Hispanic Immigrants, a Higher Job-Injury Risk," *New York Times,* February 18, 1992, pp. A1, A11; Fabian Linden, "Latin Beat," *Across the Board* 28 (June 1991):9–10; Karen Matthes, "Attracting and Retaining Hispanic Employees," *HRfocus* 69 (August 1992):7; "Women and Minorities," *Monthly Labor Review* 115 (August 1992):2.

Discussion Questions

1. The term *Hispanic* refers to what groups of people?
2. What are some of the negative stereotypes of Hispanics? How accurate are these stereotypes?
3. What are the implications for the HR department if a company wishes to effectively utilize Hispanic workers?

CHAPTER 7

Job Design

LEARNING OBJECTIVES

- Define job design and describe the major considerations involved in establishing job content.
- Identify the goal of job enrichment and describe some of the positive and negative results associated with individual and team approaches.
- Describe self-managed teams and the situations in which they are being utilized.
- List the purposes of job analysis and describe the common methods for obtaining information about job content.
- Indicate the importance of accurate job descriptions and of appropriate job specifications.
- Define performance standards and explain how they are developed.
- Describe the responsibilities of the human resources department with respect to job design and job analysis.

CASE 7.1

High Seas Autopilots

High Seas Autopilots was different from any place Vivian had ever worked. Mostly it was better. She liked the people. She liked the job. And she liked herself.

Before Vivian was hired, she had been interviewed by her present work group and had spent two hours watching the group at work. Now that she was aboard, she was working with the team assembling autopilots from start to finish. She had learned three of the jobs and was looking forward to learning the others, particularly those involving electrical connections. Her pay was increasing as she learned new tasks, which she liked, but she also liked the variety of jobs, and she liked working as part of a team. Her group planned its own production and ordered the necessary parts. The team also established its own production goals and quality standards every three months, after meeting with the supervisor and the production manager.

It seemed to Vivian that her supervisor was more a consultant and troubleshooter than a boss. He worked with several other groups in the same way but was usually available when Vivian's group needed him.

The group members got along very well with each other. It didn't take long before Vivian was being invited to the homes of the others on social occasions.

Vivian had some contact with the people in the front office in addition to the production manager. For example, on two occasions the employment manager dropped by. Once she chatted privately with Vivian to ask her how the orientation to the job had been and whether the training was going all right. The other time she dropped by to ask whether Vivian's pay increases were coming through properly. Somehow this helped make Vivian feel she was important to the company. ◀

CASE 7.2

What Is This Team Thing, Anyway?

Vince Vigano was upset. By most counts he was a first-rate manager, or "general plant supervisor," which was his title. Now, after many years of successful managing, he was being told to do things differently. It was the concept of "team management" that was throwing Vince.

Vince already saw himself as a good team player, cooperating with his boss to get things done well and quickly. He didn't see himself as a tyrant or a dictator overseeing his 14 supervisors and their 160 people, but he did see himself as a person who got subordinates to move fast to achieve the results that he and his boss expected. He also prided himself on running a clean and safe plant — a "taut ship," as he called it, although that was a navy term, not army, where he had served twenty years.

The word had come down that the company wanted the work force — in the form of work teams, in particular — to make many more decisions and to become much more involved in quality and production problems. The company also wanted work teams to interview candidates for job openings. But to Vince, the company was asking the employees to do what he and his supervisors had always done.

Vince reacted defensively. In the two-hour, weekly supervisory training sessions, he gave the training people a hard time, with comments like "I've heard all of this before" or "The way things really work in the plant is like this. . . ." And then he would describe how difficult it was to run a plant. Sometimes he would refer to "the way we used to do it in the army." Occasionally, one of the other general plant supervisors would argue with Vince and defend the team concept, but Vince was a likable guy with a strong personality, so his peers mostly just listened. His subordinate supervisors chose not to argue with him, and some of them openly agreed with him.

Vince's boss, the director of manufacturing, had heard of Vince's defensiveness from several sources over a period of several weeks. Some of it he had experienced directly from Vince in the form of pointed questions in staff meetings. In a quick conversation with the company personnel director, Vince's boss remarked, "I've really got my hands full with Vigano on this team thing. I may have to transfer him or let him go, and I sure hate to do it." The personnel director replied, "The training people tipped me off that Vince was dragging his feet. Let's meet tomorrow and talk this thing through. Maybe we can plan a strategy to salvage the situation." ◄

These cases describe several issues related to job design, an important concern of human resources management. **Job design** is the process of determining the specific tasks and responsibilities to be carried out by each member of the organization.

Effective job design is a complex process that must be viewed from several standpoints. Meshing jobs with organizational goals, maximizing employee motivation, achieving performance standards, and matching a worker's skills and abilities with job requirements are all key considerations in job design. Ignoring any of them can reduce organizational effectiveness, efficiency, or worker satisfaction.

Case 7.1 describes a situation in which Vivian was part of a self-managed team and where things were going well. In this team, members learned a variety of tasks and took turns performing all jobs related to the assembly of autopilots. In this case, broadening the tasks assigned to individual workers and allowing the work group to participate in planning and managing its own operation had positive effects on worker motivation and satisfaction.

In Case 7.2, things were not going so well, at least for Vince. He was very resistant toward redesigning jobs to give his employees more autonomy. In particular, he was resistant to delegating to work teams the responsibilities that he had always thought were management activities.

Together, these cases suggest that there can be many positive consequences from job redesign, but that changing to new ways of doing things is neither easy nor painless. Strategies in job design and the purposes of job analysis are the main topics of this chapter. The chapter begins with an overview of the basic considerations in job design and then describes a contemporary approach to job design known as job enrichment. Some approaches to job design focus on individual jobs, whereas others focus on the total work performed by a team. The need for careful job analysis, accurate job descriptions, and appropriate job requirements (or specifications) — all of which are a direct reflection of job design — are explored next. Throughout this chapter, it will be evident that job design and analysis are closely related to most, if not all, of the major processes in human resources management. Although human resources departments typically do not play a direct role in job design and redesign or in setting performance standards, they can make an important contribution in these areas. Their activities relating to job analysis, job descriptions, and job specifications, however, are much more direct and immediate.

Considerations in Job Design

Job design is a fundamental organizational process with many implications for human resources management. As stated earlier, job design is the complex flow of events that establishes the responsibilities assigned to each member of the organization and the physical circumstances in which each employee carries out those responsibilities.

There are two major components of the responsibilities established through job design. One component is **job content.** Job content is the set of activities to be performed on the job, including the duties, tasks, and job responsibilities to be carried out; the equipment, machines, and tools to be used; and the required interactions with others.

The other major component of the responsibilities established through job design is the set of **organizational responsibilities** attached to the job, that is, the responsibilities relating to the overall organization that each employee is expected to carry out, such as complying with rules and work schedules. Examples are filling out time sheets, following safety procedures, and adhering to the established schedule of the workday.

Another aspect of job design is the set of physical working conditions surrounding the job. Examples of working conditions are the extent to which there is comfortable temperature versus extremes of hot or cold, or excellent lighting versus poor lighting, or safe conditions versus hazardous conditions. Such working conditions are part of the design of the job.

Job Content   Establishing the content of a job is the central thrust of job design and is closely related to other human resources management processes. To illustrate, job content determines the skills and abilities the organization must seek in its recruitment and selection efforts. If the job of production supervisor requires several years of on-the-job welding experience with various kinds of metals, a firm is unlikely to recruit applicants from a vocational school. In turn, job content is a major factor in the training that is conducted. Welders who work with aluminum will require different training from welders who work with steel, and the training for both kinds of welding will be different from that needed by aircraft electrical assemblers. Performance appraisal will focus largely on how well the person is carrying out the content of the job. What the person is paid is likely to reflect several factors in the job's content, such as its complexity and the level of responsibility involved. And job content will frequently be a major bargaining issue in negotiations between management and labor unions. For example, the union may insist that a pipefitter should not do any kind of electrical work.

There are various ways to examine job content. For example, Ernest J. McCormick and others have designed a questionnaire that includes some 190 *job elements* that, in turn, can be used to analyze jobs. (These are discussed in the "Job Analysis" section of this chapter.) Authors J. Richard Hackman and Greg R. Oldham, on the other hand, suggest that job content can be viewed in terms of five *core job characteristics:*

- ***Skill variety:*** the degree to which a job requires a variety of different activities in carrying out the work, involving the use of a number of different skills and talents of the person. . . .
- ***Task identity:*** the degree to which a job requires completion of a "whole" and identifiable piece of work, that is, doing a job from beginning to end with a visible outcome. . . .
- ***Task significance:*** the degree to which the job has a substantial impact on the lives of other people. . . .
- ***Autonomy:*** the degree to which the job provides substantial freedom, independence, and discretion to the individual in scheduling the work and in determining the procedures to be used. . . .
- ***Job feedback:*** the degree to which carrying out the work activities required by the job provides the individual with direct and clear information about the effectiveness of his or her performance. . . .[1]*

These core job characteristics can occur in different mixes in different jobs. For example, a mechanic may be employed to tear down and rebuild automobile engines (high task identity) but may be subject to extensive direction from a supervisor and prevented from using efficient methods by the outmoded tools available in the shop (low autonomy). Another job may be high on autonomy but inadequate in skill variety and task identity. In turn, these job characteristics are related to certain individual and organizational outcomes.

Emergency Medical Technicians have an inherent "task significance" factor in their work. The knowledge that their job has a substantial impact on other people is a source of professional and personal satisfaction.

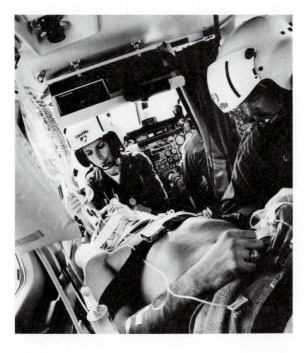

*Adapted from Hackman/Oldham, *Work Redesign*, © 1980, Addison-Wesley Publishing Co., Inc., Reprinted with permission of the publisher.

Individual and Organizational Outcomes

Recently, there has been a good deal of theorizing and research about the consequences for employees of job design and, in particular, job content. The argument is that people have become better educated and their expectations about job satisfaction have increased, but pressures for efficiency have resulted in jobs that are too specialized and narrow and thus less challenging and less meaningful. Although most experts would agree that there are, indeed, job design problems in today's organizations, there is substantial disagreement about the extent of the problems. Some observers see worker dissatisfaction in American organizations as a major crisis; others recommend careful diagnosis of morale and productivity on an organization-by-organization basis.[2]

Hackman and Oldham have suggested the latter approach and believe the important question is this: "How can we achieve a 'fit' between persons and their jobs that fosters *both* high work productivity and a high-quality organizational experience for the people who do the work?"[3] They propose that organizations analyze jobs using the five core job characteristics described earlier and then redesign jobs to maximize worker motivation.

According to Hackman and Oldham, these core job characteristics are associated with certain psychological states in the worker. As shown in Figure 7.1, skill variety, task identity, and task significance are related to "experienced meaningfulness of the work." Job autonomy is related to "experienced responsibility for outcomes of

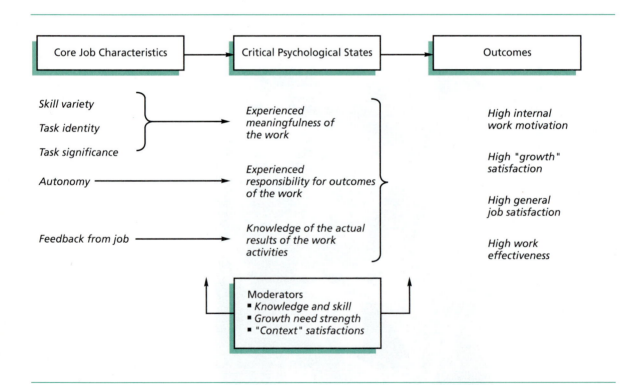

FIGURE 7.1 The complete job characteristics model

Source: J. Richard Hackman and Greg R. Oldham, *Work Redesign.* © 1980 Addison-Wesley Publishing Company, Inc. Reprinted with permission.

the work." Feedback from the job is related to the psychological state of "knowledge of the actual results of the work activities." In turn, these psychological states are associated with high work motivation, high satisfaction with the job and with one's growth on the job, and high work effectiveness. Thus, the five job characteristics are important dimensions to consider in designing new jobs or in redesigning existing jobs to increase motivation and improve performance.

As shown at the bottom of Figure 7.1, certain factors can moderate or minimize some of these outcomes. One is knowledge and skill. A significant deficiency in either can lead to less than desirable performance and a sense of failure. Another factor that can moderate these outcomes is the strength of the person's need for growth; that is, if a person has a low need to learn and develop, the presence of the core job characteristics is less likely to lead to high motivation and high job satisfaction. On the other hand, if a person has a high need to learn and develop, the presence of the core job characteristics is more likely to lead to high motivation and high job satisfaction. In addition, dissatisfaction with the "context" of the job, such as with pay, job security, coworkers, or supervision, is likely to minimize the favorable consequences of designing more complex and challenging jobs.[4]

The five core job characteristics shown in Figure 7.1 can be measured by the **Job Diagnostic Survey (JDS),** a well-researched instrument that has been used in a wide variety of job redesign projects. The survey is used to determine whether there is a need to redesign work and whether doing so is feasible, given the existing structure of the jobs and existing conditions in the organization. Some of the conditions that need to be considered are provisions of the labor-management contract; how constraining the present technology is and how committed the organization is to it (if the company has invested millions of dollars in assembly-line equipment, it is not likely that there will be much enthusiasm for a job redesign project); and to what extent budgeting, auditing, inventory, and other control systems would constrain job modification.[5]

Job Enrichment and Self-Managed Teams

A planned program for enhancing job characteristics is typically called **job enrichment.** We can define job enrichment as the process of enhancing the five core job characteristics for the purpose of increasing worker motivation, productivity, and satisfaction. This concept is different from **job enlargement,** which is the addition of more and different tasks to the job. (Job enlargement is called **horizontal restructuring** when it involves broadening the scope of the job to include tasks that previously preceded or followed in the flow of the work.)

Job enrichment, to use Hackman and Oldham's categories, involves increasing skill variety, task identity, task significance, autonomy, and feedback from the job. This process is sometimes referred to as **vertical restructuring** because it usually includes the addition of some activities previously performed by the supervisory level above, including some of the planning. Thus, job enrichment usually involves adding tasks from the level above, whereas job enlargement adds tasks from the same level.

Contemporary job enrichment programs have their historical base in Abraham Maslow's need hierarchy theory and Frederick Herzberg's motivation-hygiene theory (discussed in Chapter 5). These theories suggest that factors pertaining to the job itself, such as job challenge, independence, and responsibility, are powerful motivators. Some forms of job enrichment stem from notions that worker participation in production planning and quality control has positive effects on productivity and satisfaction. Some approaches focus on the jobs of individual workers, whereas others focus on the tasks and responsibilities of work groups, or teams, with considerable emphasis on the interactions among group members. Team approaches have emerged mostly from experiments in job design in the United States, England, and Sweden.

Individual Approaches
The job enrichment efforts of Robert Ford at AT&T and of Frederick Herzberg and colleagues in various places exemplify the focus on the individual job. At AT&T, some jobs were restructured both horizontally and vertically; that is, both the number of tasks and the degree of responsibility associated with a job were increased. In addition, more routine or monotonous tasks were automated or added to lower job classifications. Overall, the aim was to create more meaningful jobs for individual workers (see Figure 7.2).

For example, at the Indianapolis office of the Indiana Bell Telephone Co., where all the directories for the state were compiled, the production of each direc-

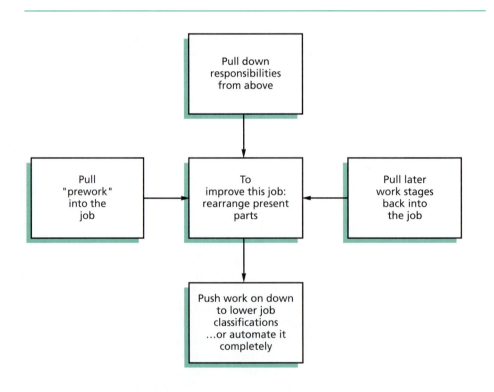

FIGURE 7.2   Steps in improving a job

Source: Reprinted by permission of the *Harvard Business Review.* An exhibit from "Job Enrichment Lessons from AT&T" by Robert N. Ford (January/February 1973). Copyright © 1973 by the President and Fellows of Harvard College; all rights reserved.

tory required twenty-one separate steps, including manuscript verification, keypunch, and keypunch verification. Each employee performed very few tasks for each directory. Through a job enrichment effort, each employee became responsible for one or more directories, performing all of the twenty-one production steps.[6] In general, these kinds of job enrichment efforts have had positive results, including higher production, lower absenteeism, and a reduction in the number of employees needed.[7]

Any reduction in the number of employees through such programs needs to be handled through normal attrition (normal retirements and resignations) or transfer rather than through layoffs. The policy needs to be understood ahead of time or employees will resist job enrichment. The human resources department can play an important role in helping top management develop and communicate information about such policies and in making certain that the spirit of the policies is being carried out.

Herzberg and his colleagues have taken a similar approach to enriching individual jobs. For example, in a British firm the jobs of laboratory technicians were modified to increase workers' involvement in planning and control. Specifically, the technicians were authorized to make their own materials, equipment, and maintenance requests and were encouraged to write the final reports on each of their experiments. In another of Herzberg's job enrichment projects, the position of sales representative was redesigned. Some people were given freedom to plan the frequency of their sales calls and were provided with technical assistance from the service department "on demand." They were also authorized to settle customer complaints up to a certain amount of money on the spot and were given suggested ranges within which prices could be quoted.[8] Thus, in both projects, employees were provided with broader, more complete jobs that included greater responsibility for planning and control.

Team Approaches

The team approach to job enrichment is a way of giving more responsibility and control to work groups in an effort to improve productivity, satisfaction, or performance. As described by M. Scott Myers, job enrichment can take the form of *more planning and more controlling* by individual workers, and *more team interaction.* (See Figure 7.3.) Myers describes how, at Texas Instruments, Incorporated, the jobs of electronic assemblers, which involved "intricate assembling, bonding, soldering, and welding operations," were enriched. First, the assemblers were given training in how to improve working methods and procedures and were encouraged to suggest improvements in the manufacturing procedures in their department. Second, work groups consisting of five to twenty-five assemblers were formed, and each elected a team captain to a six-month term. Each week the team captain solicited work improvement ideas from team members, recorded suggestions on a standard form, crediting each contributor, and presented recommendations to the supervisor and superintendent. After these weekly meetings with management, the team captain gave team members feedback on the extent to which their ideas would be adopted.[9] In other writings, Myers describes problem-solving and goal-setting meetings of these natural work groups, which he sees as a part of a broad job enrichment process.[10]

Self-Managed Teams

A job enrichment approach similar to the one at Texas Instruments has had a significant impact on a number of industries. It has led, for example, to modification of

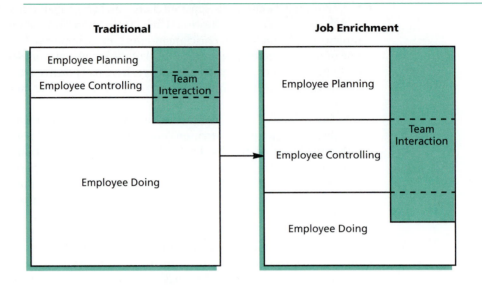

FIGURE 7.3 Impact of job enrichment on job design
Source: Based on interpretations of M. Scott Myers, *Every Employee a Manager* (New York: McGraw-Hill, 1970), pp. 55–95.

the traditional assembly line in the European automobile industry and in a number of American auto firms. Two of the largest automakers in Sweden, Volvo and Saab-Scania, some years ago experimented with team production methods in which a **self-managed team** (or self-directed team)* — a work group that essentially manages itself with minimal supervision — is responsible for assembling some major component such as an engine. Under this system, the average supervisor oversees two groups of twenty subordinates and works with two team leaders, who are responsible for production scheduling and material handling. The supervisor serves more as a consultant and a teacher than in the past, and the teams are given considerable freedom to organize their own work.[11]

The forerunners of the Swedish automobile industry experiments were studies by the Tavistock Institute in England. These experiments are often referred to as **sociotechnical programs** because they represent efforts to link social aspects of the factory and mine with the technology. One of the earliest experiments, in British coal mining, involved broadening the scope of jobs and building a team approach to coal production, supplemented by pay incentives.[12] Another Tavistock project, in a weaving mill in India, took the same thrust in terms of broadening tasks and creating self-managed work groups.[13]

Since these early Tavistock and Swedish experiments, the use of self-managed teams has spread widely in American industry. For example, self-managed teams are used at the General Motors Corp.'s Spring Hill, Tennessee, factory, which produces the Saturn automobile. At the Saturn plant, teams of assembly workers do far more

*Such teams are also called high-performance teams or superteams. The term *cross-functional teams* implies the bringing together of specialists from different functions, such as accounting, engineering, marketing, manufacturing, and so on.

than mechanical assembly and shoulder a wide range of responsibilities, including interviewing prospective team members, choosing equipment, and dealing with suppliers.[14] Similarly, self-managed teams are used at Pitney Bowes, Stamford, Connecticut, manufacturer of high-tech postage meters; at the San Diego Zoo; and at Steelcase's facility in Grand Rapids, Michigan.[15] Experimentation with self-managed teams started at Microsoft Corp. in Redmond, Washington, in 1993.

The common elements of self-managed teams have been the creation of work teams responsible for the production of an entire item or a "whole" task, including the allocation of work, quality control, and product improvements. Typically, team members are paid according to the number of tasks they can perform or the number of skills mastered — such remuneration is called **skills-based pay** — and they also help screen applicants when the team has vacancies. Team leader positions are sometimes created in these self-managed teams, and sometimes not. Case 7.1 provides an example of a self-managed team.

Benefits and Limitations

Generally, although not always, individual approaches to job enrichment have had positive results. For example, in the Herzberg project in a British firm described earlier, the technicians involved in the project improved the quality of their technical reports in comparison with those of the control groups. The sales representatives increased sales 19 percent over the previous year, whereas the sales of the control group declined 5 percent.[16] Results at AT&T included such outcomes as a reduction in the number of employees needed (from 120 to 74 in the Illinois Bell directory-compilation unit) and higher production and lower absenteeism at the Chesapeake & Potomac Telephone Company.[17]

Similarly, team approaches to job enrichment usually have had mixed to positive results. At Texas Instruments, management reported reduced turnover and more cooperation.[18] At the Volvo plant, turnover declined dramatically and work quality went up; at the Saab-Scania plant, turnover and absenteeism decreased, while productivity and quality remained high and worker satisfaction increased.[19] In the British coal-mining project, productivity, safety, and morale all improved significantly, and results in the Indian project were favorable.[20] At a General Foods Corporation pet-food plant, quality rejects, turnover, accidents, and absenteeism were significantly below the norms of other plants. There was some erosion of these gains in later years, however, and the company had difficulty extending the program to other plants, partly because of lack of top management understanding and support.[21]

Productivity at General Mills, Inc., plants using self-managed teams was reported to be 40 percent higher than at its other plants.[22] Diebold reported doubling productivity in one year through shifting to self-managed work teams.[23] Positive results have also been reported at the GM Saturn plant, at Pitney Bowes, and at Steelcase.[24]

Not all of these gains can be attributed to job enrichment. Job enrichment — particularly of the self-managed team variety — typically involves changes in plant layout, technology, selection, training, compensation, and the role of the supervisor. Thus, most of the crucial factors in organizational performance shown in Figure 4.1 tend to be altered.

Supervisor and middle-management resistance is common in job enrichment efforts when the process does not take into account the interests of people at this level. (Case 7.2 is an example of this.) Realistically, managers can see the possibility that their responsibilities might be reduced, or that a layer of supervision might be eliminated entirely. Thus, top management, including the human resources director, must take a broad view of the possible impact of job enrichment and team approaches and develop procedures for these people that will enhance cooperation. Examples would be training supervisors in team leadership skills, and top management handling any resulting overstaffing at middle-management levels through normal attrition or transfer to other company operations.

It should be noted that effective teams are crucial to quality improvement efforts in today's organizations. We discuss this further in Chapter 21. (See also *Contemporary Issues* on page 167.)

Role of the Human Resources Department

Although job design affects almost every aspect of human resources management, the role of the human resources department in the actual design and redesign of jobs is usually indirect. Unless the human resources department has on its staff job design specialists who act as consultants to managers, that department will play largely supporting roles.

One important role it can play is in diagnosing organizational problems. This diagnosis might occur through informal contacts, interviews with supervisors and employees, discussions with supervisors and managers during training sessions, or questionnaires. If a need for job redesign in some units becomes evident, human resources specialists can provide preliminary design information and bring together the right people to discuss the feasibility of job redesign.

A second role is in training and management development, where both internal and external specialists can be recruited to provide information on job redesign methods. Where the self-managed team concept is emphasized, a great deal of training needs to be conducted with potential and present team members on such matters as effective team functioning, problem solving, and leading meetings.

A third role, and an extremely important one for the human resources director and his or her staff, is to assist in the planning and implementation of job redesign programs to ensure that sound human resources policies and practices are developed and followed. For example, what happens to any organizational members whose jobs are significantly altered or eliminated through a job redesign project will need to be thought through. This includes people at supervisory and middle-management levels. Implications for the wage and salary structure will need to be assessed. For example, if some unit, such as manufacturing, moves in the direction of self-managed teams, the organization will probably want to develop policies and practices related to skills-based pay.

Finally, the human resources department will need to be prepared to modify job descriptions, job specifications (the qualifications needed to perform a job), and recruitment practices, and perhaps to adjust pay scales. Job analysis plays an important role in all these activities.

Job Analysis

Job analysis is the systematic investigation of job content, the physical circumstances in which the job is carried out, and the qualifications needed to carry out job responsibilities. The categories of information usually obtained in job analysis in-

Contemporary Issues

Teamwork, Involvement, and Participation

The team is the key enabling mechanism within quality. A team culture results in greater communication across functions and departments, and it reduces adversarial relationships among disparate functions.

Employee involvement compels managers to create an environment conducive to participation. Managers are expected to be coaches, counselors and resource people. They have to recognize employees for their efforts and offer them encouragement, not punishment. The shift toward participative management has been difficult for some managers who were socialized in an authoritarian culture. Unable to adapt, these people become both cultural and economic casualties. Involvement and empowerment have created

difficulties for some workers as well. Unionized employees in the United States are traditionally suspicious of moves made by management to increase productivity and introduce quality circles. For Americans, with their heightened sense of individualism and a heterogeneous work force, teams have to be built and facilitated. People learn how to work in teams.

This raises the relationship between quality and learning. The total quality company is a learning and teaching organization. Continuous quality improvement requires continuing training, retraining and skill upgrading.

Source: Excerpted from Larry Schein, "The Culture of Service Quality," *Total Quality Management*, The Conference Board, Report Number 963, 1991, p. 11. Reprinted by permission.

---

clude what activities are performed, and how, when, and why; the machines, tools, or equipment used; what interactions with others are required; the physical and social working conditions; and the training, skills, and abilities required on the job.[25] Although the terminology and specifics may vary from one job analysis approach to another, most include comparable categories. This information can be used to develop written job descriptions and to establish what is required of the person who will perform the job.

Job analysis is becoming an increasingly important part of human resources management. Equal Employment Opportunity Commission (EEOC) rules and recent court decisions require that all selection, promotion, and compensation decisions be based on job-related criteria, not on vague or subjective standards. This means organizations must be able to verify the job-relatedness of all personnel devices and techniques, such as job requirements, application blanks, interviews, tests, and performance appraisals. Careful job analysis serves as the foundation for developing devices and techniques that will stand this scrutiny. Furthermore, to comply with the Americans with Disabilities Act, organizations need to be able to identify essential job functions. (See Chapter 6.) Broadly speaking, careful job analysis is good management in itself if the results are used to improve the effectiveness of staffing, appraisal, training, reward, and other practices.

The person doing the job analysis, often called a job analyst, may be a member of the human resources department staff, a member of the unit where jobs are being analyzed, a member of an industrial engineering group, or an outside specialist hired on a project basis. Figure 7.4 is a job description for a job analyst and for a personnel recruiter. Various techniques are used in job analysis, including observation, interviews, questionnaires, and **critical incidents,** which are records that describe either very good or very poor employee performance.

One of the most popular devices used in job analysis is the **Position Analysis Questionnaire (PAQ).** This questionnaire requires the analyst to rate the job against approximately 190 job elements, usually on a 0- to-5-point scale.[26] Table 7.1 shows the major categories and subcategories measured by the instrument.

Although the PAQ has been thoroughly researched and allows statistical comparisons among jobs, it is very lengthy and requires college-graduate reading ability. Thus, some people find it difficult or frustrating to use.[27] But it can be a helpful tool in determining salary ranges for particular jobs. Because the total PAQ points for

---

166.267-018 JOB ANALYST (PROFESS. & KIN.) ALTERNATE TITLES: PERSONNEL ANALYST

Collects, analyzes, and prepares occupational information to facilitate personnel, administration, and management functions of organization: Consults with management to determine type, scope, and purpose of study. Studies current organizational occupational data and compiles distribution reports, organization and flow charts, and other background information required for study. Observes jobs and interviews workers and supervisory personnel to determine job and worker requirements. Analyzes occupational data, such as physical, mental, and training requirements of jobs and workers and develops written summaries, such as job descriptions, job specifications, and lines of career movement. Utilizes developed occupational data to evaluate or improve methods and techniques for recruiting, selecting, promoting, evaluating, and training workers, and administration of related personnel programs. May specialize in classifying positions according to regulated guidelines to meet job classification requirements of civil service system and be known as Position Classifier (government ser.).

166.267-038 PERSONNEL RECRUITER (PROFESS. & KIN.)

Seeks out, interviews, screens, and recruits job applicants to fill existing company job openings: Discusses personnel needs with department supervisors to prepare and implement recruitment program. Contacts colleges to arrange on-campus interviews. Provides information on company facilities and job opportunities to potential applicants. Interviews college applicants to obtain work history, education, training, job skills, and salary requirements. Screens and refers qualified applicants to company hiring personnel for follow-up interview. Arranges travel and lodging for selected applicants at company expense. Performs reference and background checks on applicants. Corresponds with job applicants to notify them of employment consideration. Files and maintains employment records for future references. Projects yearly recruitment expenditures for budgetary control.

FIGURE 7.4 Job descriptions for a job analyst and a personnel recruiter

Source: U.S. Department of Labor, Employment and Training Administration, *Dictionary of Occupational Titles,* 4th ed., rev. 1991, p. 111.

TABLE 7.1 Categories measured by the Position Analysis Questionnaire (PAQ)*

INFORMATION INPUT	INTERPERSONAL ACTIVITIES
Sources of job information: Use of written materials Discrimination and perceptual activities: Estimating speed of moving objects	Communications: Instructing Interpersonal relationships: Serving/catering Personal contact: Personal contact with public customers Supervision and coordination: Level of supervision received

MEDIATION PROCESSES

Decision making and reasoning: Reasoning in problem solving
Information processing: Encoding/decoding
Use of stored information: Using mathematics

WORK SITUATION AND JOB CONTEXT

Physical working conditions: Low temperature
Psychological and sociological aspects: Civic obligations

WORK OUTPUT

Use of physical devices: Use of keyboard devices
Integrative manual activities: Handling objects/materials
General body activities: Climbing
Manipulation/coordination activities: Hand-arm manipulation

MISCELLANEOUS ASPECTS

Work schedule, method of pay, and apparel: Irregular hours
Job demands: Specified (controlled) work pace
Responsibility: Responsibility for safety of others

*The Position Analysis Questionnaire (PAQ) is copyrighted by the Purdue Research Foundation, West Lafayette, Indiana.

Source: Ernest J. McCormick, Paul R. Jeanneret, and Robert C. Mecham, Position Analysis Questionnaire, © 1969 by Purdue Research Foundation, West Lafayette, Indiana 47907. Reprinted by permission.

jobs tends to correlate highly with actual salaries paid, the questionnaire is often used to determine the relative worth of various jobs.[28]

Job Descriptions and Job Specifications

Job descriptions, sometimes called position descriptions, are written summaries, usually one or two pages long, of the basic tasks associated with a particular job. Job descriptions usually have a label, called a "job title," and they frequently include a section describing the qualifications needed to perform the job. These qualifications are called **job specifications.** (See Figure 7.5 for an example of a job description that includes job specifications.)

Purposes   Job descriptions and specifications can be very useful for a number of purposes, as shown in Figure 7.6. But if they are written and filed away, they can be a waste of time.

JOB DESCRIPTION

Job Title	RESEARCH ASSISTANT	Branch	
Job Number	3135-I	Division	ECONOMIC RESEARCH
Salary Grade	9	Department	
Date		Section	

JOB DUTIES

Compiles industrial and economic data by: obtaining current and comparative statistics relative to trends in production, commerce, employment, etc., from newspapers, periodicals, publications of government agencies, trade associations, and other standard sources; maintaining a set of statistical records for the department concerning industries and areas of the region; selecting and classifying for the department library pertinent articles from the above-mentioned sources; digesting suitable material on national and regional economic developments; plotting acquired statistics and developing informative graphs, tables, and charts; preparing special statistical and other reports.

Also computes department's own seasonally adjusted employment data series. Furnishes various industrial and economic data to bank and other officials.

Prepares the Weekly Business Briefs by gathering and assembling data and writing original copy to provide a digest of regional and national business news for the Bank's staff, officers, and customers. Uses own judgment in selecting articles of significance. Submits material for final approval.

Also researches and prepares section for the Summary of Regional Industries. Researches and prepares local business section for the Metropolitan Real Estate Research Report. Prepares statistical data for charts and tables in the quarterly and annual issues of the Summary. Prepares statistical data and writes a section on local home price trends for the Metropolitan Real Estate Research Report. Prepares special reports on various subjects as requested.

Assists in maintaining research library; assists Economist in developing new statistical series and ideas for charts; assists other staff members with miscellaneous functions.

The Research Assistant, under general supervision, is engaged primarily in the acquiring of pertinent, factual data relative to varied industries, their trends and any other significant details. In large part this material provides the basis for analysis, opinions, and recommendations by the Economist, although some of the analysis is included in the duties of the Research Assistant.

JOB REQUIREMENTS

Education	A broad knowledge of a technical workfield applicable to duties such as economics and business theory, and an understanding of statistical methods and the application and analysis thereof. Equivalent to college degree in Economics or Business Administration.
Experience	Job requires practical experience in statistical methods and analysis and a period to acquire a knowledge of various information sources. Time — six months to a year.
Resourcefulness	Job requires judgment and initiative in determining sources of information and judgment in selection of significant data and application of statistical formulas to develop informative results. Under general supervision.
Responsibility	Considerable care is required since most errors are difficult to locate. Reports and publications are distributed beyond the bank and relied upon as being correct and indicative of trends. Work must be prepared promptly, and deadlines met.
Contacts	Routine staff contacts plus frequent public contacts by telephone and occasionally in person requesting or furnishing information. Courtesy and tact are required.
Supervision	Does not supervise.
Mental Effort	Requires considerable care and attention due to the concentration required for the selection, development, and analysis of economic information.
Physical Effort	Medium office position. Job requires frequent use of calculator and adding machine. Also requires frequent referral to department library and occasional trips to public library and other outside offices for information.
Job Conditions	Average office conditions.

FIGURE 7.5 Job description from a large bank

Used with permission.

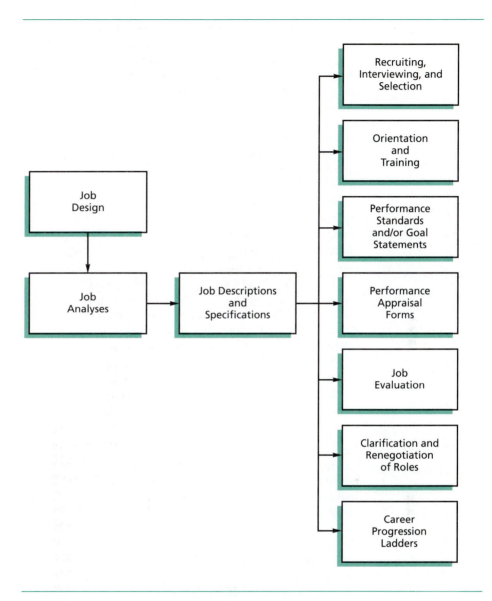

FIGURE 7.6 Potential uses of job analyses and job descriptions

First, job descriptions are helpful throughout the recruiting and selection process. They can be used in writing advertisements for job openings and in writing letters to people or organizations that are in a position to refer candidates. They provide the recruiter, the selection interviewer, and the interviewee with a basic outline of the job for which candidates are being considered.

Job descriptions are also useful in orienting and training new employees. They can provide an overview of the activities that need to be carried out, which can be explained to the employee in more detail by the supervisor and training people. The job description is not likely to list *all* the duties of a job, however, and both the supervisor and the new employee will need a clear understanding of the responsibilities not covered.

Job descriptions are also used in the development of performance standards (discussed later in this chapter). Performance standards expand the job description and establish, in measurable terms, how well the job is to be performed. Job descriptions are also relevant to the development of performance appraisal (or merit rating) forms, which are frequently designed to include some of the major categories covered in the job description.

Job descriptions and specifications can also provide basic information needed for job evaluation. **Job evaluation** is the process of determining the relative worth of jobs within an organization to establish wages and salaries.

In addition, job descriptions can contribute to a dialogue between supervisor and subordinate or to a group discussion when it is necessary to clarify mutual expectations. This process can result in a renegotiation of responsibilities and a better understanding of what can and should be expected of workers holding particular jobs.

Finally, job descriptions can be used to think through and develop the avenues for transfer and promotion that lead to advancement in the organization. This process can culminate in the development of **career progression ladders** (to be discussed further in Chapter 10), which depict possible career paths and advancement opportunities for individual employees.

Some organizations have two descriptions for each job. A lengthy, detailed version may be used in training and in job evaluation, and a shorter version may be used in human resources planning and in recruiting and interviewing.

The Importance of Accurate Job Descriptions

The need for job descriptions that accurately reflect actual job content is clear when we consider the weight given to job descriptions by applicants and recruiters. Potential applicants may make themselves available for interviews or screen themselves out of consideration according to how the job is described in an advertisement or bulletin board posting. Recruiters, particularly in large firms, may not have a detailed knowledge of the actual job other than what is written in the job description; and they may make inappropriate judgments or provide misleading information if the job description is not accurate.

Furthermore, inaccurate job descriptions can reduce the effectiveness of training or result in the development of unrealistic performance standards. For example, if some of the more significant parts of the job are not included in the job description, any training designed according to that job description may neglect those important aspects. Or performance standards may be developed for the less important aspects, but no clear standards may be developed for the more significant parts of the job. These problems demonstrate the importance of gathering information systematically, writing job descriptions carefully, and checking the accuracy of the job description with both the job incumbent and the supervisor. *Because jobs tend to change over time — sometimes rapidly — it is important that job descriptions and specifications be updated periodically.* Furthermore, procedures need to be established to ensure a reanalysis of a job when it appears that job responsibilities have changed significantly.

The Importance of Valid Job Specifications

Government regulations state that job specifications should be related to actual job requirements. One Supreme Court case in particular has had a broad impact on job specifications. Drawing on the Civil Rights Act and rulings by the Equal Employment Opportunity Commission, the U.S. Supreme Court ruled in the *Griggs* v. *Duke Power Company* case (discussed briefly in Chapter 3) that an employer had unlawfully discriminated against blacks by requiring a high school education or passage of an intelligence test as conditions of employment or advancement in certain jobs. The thrust of the Court's argument was that these specifications were not significantly related to job performance. The Court went on to say the following:

> The facts of this case demonstrate the inadequacy of broad and general testing devices as well as the infirmity of using diplomas or degrees as fixed measures of capability. History is filled with examples of men and women who rendered highly effective performances without the conventional badges of accomplishment in terms of certificates, diplomas, or degrees. Diplomas and tests are useful servants, but Congress has mandated the common-sense proposition that they are not to become the masters of reality.[29]

This decision makes it imperative that job specifications be consistent with the activities detailed in the job description and with the actual duties of the job. Careful review and discussion of job descriptions will sometimes reveal that certain job specifications are unnecessary. For example, not all jobs require a high school diploma, and many do not require a college degree. In all cases, careful job analysis is the most reliable method for ensuring the validity of job specifications.

There are circumstances in which job specifications are realistic but management wishes to reduce the qualifications required for a particular job. If an organization wishes to expand its employment of disadvantaged minorities, if there is a shortage of certain skills in the labor market, or if labor costs have risen dramatically, it may be necessary to reduce the proportion of employees with certain degrees or certificates. In such cases, there is often a conscious plan to restructure jobs — usually several simultaneously — to permit the hiring of people with lower skills. For example, the high cost of physician care might prompt the creation of a nurse practitioner or a physician's assistant position to absorb the more routine aspects of medical care. The creation of new skilled positions, however, often requires the development of special training programs, the cooperation of one or more unions, and, as in the case of health care institutions, compliance with licensing regulations.

Thus, several questions should be asked periodically about job specifications. Are they too high? Too low? Are people being hired who are underqualified or overqualified, or who have the wrong skills? Do these factors result in job dissatisfaction or substandard performance? Are present job specifications unnecessarily screening out disabled or otherwise disadvantaged people? Is the quality of the work force too low? Are job specifications screening out too many people who would make good candidates for promotion? Job specifications, then, need to be evaluated in terms of whether they accurately reflect job content.

Performance Standards

Whereas job descriptions are statements of *what* activities are to be performed, **performance standards** make explicit *the quantity and/or quality of performance expected in the basic tasks set forth in the job description.* Usually, performance standards are statements of what is considered acceptable and attainable performance on a particular job. Thus, they follow from job design and content and are logical extensions of job descriptions. Some organizations are very systematic in developing written performance standards for each job; others may rely on informal communications or occasional memoranda between subordinates and superiors.

Some performance standards may be dysfunctional. For example, an unwritten standard in many Japanese firms appears to be that one should work extraordinarily long hours to demonstrate loyalty to one's company. *Karoshi*, or death from overwork, is one consequence. (See *International Perspective* on page 175.)

Performance standards for production jobs have been fairly common since the development of scientific management and time-and-motion studies around the turn of the century. Most often these standards are written in terms of the number of units to be produced in a certain period. Typically, these standards are used in connection with incentive systems under which bonuses are paid for production above and beyond the standard rate.

The use of performance standards for managerial and professional positions is of more recent origin and, to a large extent, has been upstaged by interest in management by objectives (MBO), which will be discussed in Chapter 13. Whereas performance standards tend to establish acceptable performance by the average incumbent of a particular job, management by objectives tends to be more future oriented in that it involves setting goals or objectives leading to higher levels of performance. In practice, the two may be hard to distinguish because they can blend together easily.

Figure 7.7 is a partial list of performance standards for a managerial position. The full document included nine major categories subdivided into forty-one more specific standards. (If this document were closer to an MBO format, we would see more statements of objectives and target dates by which they are to be achieved.)

Purposes   One purpose of developing performance standards is to establish guidelines against which actual performance can be measured. This has benefits for both the person holding the job and the one or more superiors who evaluate that person's performance. The more the employee understands what is expected, the more likely it is that he or she will be able to carry out the responsibilities of the position successfully. In turn, the superiors' performance appraisal can be much more objective and relevant if based on statements of what is expected.

The advantage of written performance standards, contrasted with informally communicated standards, is that the organization is more likely to be thorough about their development. Further, having things in writing is a convenient way to share and retrieve information. Most, if not all, organizations, however, will have some performance standards that are not written down. For example, if the president of a company has indicated that he or she wants and expects the sales department to gross $8 million in sales in the coming year, that statement really becomes a performance standard for the sales manager, whether or not it is put in writing. Similarly, targets that have been communicated with respect to safety, reduction in scrap, increases in new accounts, and so on are implicit — if not explicit — performance standards for the jobs involved. Unless each person has specific standards relating to his or her part in reaching that target, however, there may be a tendency to "let the other person do it."

International Perspective

Karoshi

You got to the office this morning at about 7:30, worked through lunch, and finally, at about 8:15 p.m. you're headed home.

You're so tired you could die, right?

Just be glad you're not Japanese!

The Japanese workforce is facing a lethal problem called Karoshi, which means death from overwork. As numerous families are filing lawsuits charging that overwork caused the death of a family member, Japan is determining how to deal with this dilemma.

On average, Japanese workers spend as many as 200 more hours a year at work than do their American counterparts, and 500 more hours than the Europeans. The Japanese salarymen may literally be killing themselves on the job. Loyalty to the company is measured by time at one's desk. By demanding that workers put in extraordinary hours of overtime, Japanese companies are actually seeing less productivity. As a result the government, in a year long campaign has urged a shift away from long hours and limited vacation time toward a more balanced lifestyle, and greater productivity. Sony Corporation's CEO mandates that all employees must take an annual vacation, whether they want to or not.

An entrepreneurial Bellevue, Washington firm, Priority Management Systems, opened an office in Tokyo last July. Its training programs stress the importance of a balance between the personal and professional aspects of one's life. A growing shortage of skilled workers in Japan is forcing companies to lessen the demands they put on workers. Priority Management president and founder, Dan Stamp, says companies also have to equip employees with essential management skills so they deal with the stresses of a constantly changing, highly-automated workplace.

Source: Excerpted from John P. Young, "From the Editor," *Academy of Management EXECUTIVE*, 5 (February 1991):4. Reprinted by permission.

Another purpose in developing performance standards can be to enhance motivation and commitment. If the supervisor and the employee genuinely work together to write performance standards, the employee's participation can contribute to the fulfillment of needs for affiliation, recognition, and autonomy. In addition, the outcome is likely to be commitment to the standards established and increased motivation to reach them.

Procedures Procedures for developing performance standards vary widely. In a highly directive approach, the superior may simply write the standards and inform the employee. In a participative approach, there will be much more interaction between the supervisor and the employee. A participative procedure might be something like the following:

1. The supervisor solicits the cooperation of subordinates in developing performance standards and the procedure to be followed in writing them.
2. Each subordinate writes tentative standards for each aspect of his or her job and provides the supervisor with a preliminary draft.

Compliance with performance standards is adequate when:
1. Medical treatment for occupational injuries or disease, first aid treatment for certain non-occupational conditions, and other care as necessary for the industrial health program is provided.
   (a) There is no increase in Workers' Compensation claims due to inadequate medical care within the Division.
   (b) The medical reviews of employee Workers' Compensation claims are completed within seven days.
   (c) The number of dispensaries is adequate to handle the treatment of the plant population, considering the geographic location of the area the dispensary will serve, the number of employees that can adequately be handled per shift by a nurse (50 calls), and the hazards of the area.
2. We have recommended and developed industrial health policies.
   (a) Incidence of occupational disease as noted by Workers' Compensation claims and our frequency rates is 1 per 400 employees per month or less.
   (b) Evidence that health programs are being adequately engaged in as indicated by current procedures and current physicians' program manuals.
   (c) There are no reported employee terminations due to environmental factors that the Medical Section has failed to correct by preventive medical plans.
   (d) The Corporate Director of Health and Safety approves and supports our program.

FIGURE 7.7   Performance standards for medical director

Used with permission.

3. Each subordinate meets with the supervisor to discuss the tentative standards and to reach agreement on the final document.
4. The standards are used by the employee to track how well he or she is doing and by the supervisor and employee to appraise the employee's performance. In work groups where jobs are interrelated and interdependent, it can be productive to involve the entire group in a team approach to developing standards.

Performance standards are written in quantitative terms whenever possible, but in practice some job aspects are difficult to quantify, and qualitative statements must be used. An example of a qualitative statement is "uses tact in dealing with customers," although one could argue that the quantitative version "receives no complaints about lack of tact during the year" might be a more useful statement. Obviously, it is easier to develop performance standards for jobs that have a readily measured result than for jobs that have a high interpersonal component.

This process is almost identical to the MBO process described in a later chapter. The essential difference is that performance standards may tend to focus on the minimum required performance, while focusing on objectives is more future oriented and perhaps challenges employees to "stretch" themselves more in terms of creativity and productivity. (See Chapter 13.)

Problems   One of the pitfalls in developing performance standards, or goal statements in an MBO program, is that management may not pay enough attention to the *process* of developing the standards or goals. If standards are imposed on members of the organization in an autocratic and dictatorial manner, the whole process is likely to be resisted. On the other hand, if subordinates understand the overall goals to be achieved and participate in setting their own standards, they are likely to set them reasonably high and be committed to meeting them.

In a unionized situation, a potential problem can be union-management relationships. In some situations, unions have cooperated with management in establishing standards based on approaches such as time-and-motion study. In other situations, unions have resisted the development of standards. In particular, in the absence of an incentive pay system of some kind, unions have tended to resist managerial attempts to increase performance beyond what is considered "a fair day's work." However, intense foreign competition and periods of high unemployment in some industries have prompted some unions to be more flexible in working with management to raise standards for productivity and quality.

One of the most serious problems with performance standards is related to one of the five core job characteristics described previously — autonomy. If the standards are seen as overly restrictive and oppressive, motivation and morale are likely to be low. These conditions are likely to be accompanied by such costly outcomes as considerable job stress and high absenteeism and turnover. For example, many organizations with large data-processing requirements, such as insurance firms, banks, and credit-card companies, have developed computer programs to monitor the extent to which employees working at video display terminals meet production standards. In one company, management might believe the system to be efficient, but a claims processor has a different view: "The girls at work call it a sweatshop. Most of them figure they won't last more than two years."[30]

In some instances, management has restored some autonomy to employees with good results. For example, at a Ford Motor Co. plant, a button was installed that allows an employee to shut down the entire assembly line at any time. Shutdowns by employees occur on average twenty times a day for ten seconds each, for a total of a little over three minutes. With this approach, defects dropped from seventeen to less than one per car in ten months.[31] Similarly, employees at a GM Buick plant can halt production by pulling a cord at their workstations.[32]

Role of the Human Resources Department

The human resources department must be concerned about job analysis, job descriptions and specifications, and performance standards because of their major impact on almost all aspects of human resources management. That department will typically have a major role in the planning and coordination of the systems used; that is, the department will be involved in determining what job analysis procedures are used, making sure that the information obtained through job analysis is used to write appropriate job descriptions and specifications, and then using job descriptions and specifications for the various purposes shown in Figure 7.6. These purposes include uses in recruitment, orientation and training, performance appraisal, performance standards, and job evaluation.

In some instances, the human resources department employs job analysts to analyze jobs and write job descriptions; in other instances, analysts are employed by an industrial engineering group and work cooperatively with the human resources staff.

(Industrial engineers typically help the organization in such matters as the selection of the tools, machines, and equipment; plant layout; and development of performance measures and standards.) Frequently, the human resources department trains selected members from various units to write job descriptions and then coordinates and monitors the overall effort.

The human resources department is ordinarily *not* involved in writing performance standards for jobs outside its own department. That department may train supervisors and other employees in how to develop standards, but the actual development and writing of the standards is a matter between the various supervisors and managers and their subordinates.

The human resources department can play a major role in encouraging discussions between superiors and subordinates at all levels about the optimal level of autonomy versus control. In view of what is known about job design — and about characteristics associated with high motivation and performance, in particular — it is clear that performance standards can be used in ways that demotivate rather than motivate. Part of the solution lies in increasing the employee's participation in developing the standards and in using them to monitor his or her own performance. In particular, if the supervisor tries to control behavior through punishment, the consequences are likely to be negative.

Summary

Job design is the process of determining the specific tasks and responsibilities to be carried out by each member of the organization. It has many implications for human resources management. Both the content of one's job *and the ability to influence content and level of performance* affect a person's motivation and job satisfaction. Further, job content has a direct relationship to the qualifications needed on the job (job specifications), to the recruitment and training needed, to the development of performance standards, to what is reviewed in performance appraisal, and to compensation.

There are various ways to examine job content. Hackman and Oldham have provided a useful method based on five core job characteristics: skill variety, task identity, task significance, autonomy, and job feedback. Job enrichment, using Hackman and Oldham's terminology, is the enhancement of the five job characteristics.

There has been considerable experimentation in recent years with team approaches to job enrichment, including the concept of self-managed teams. The use of self-managed teams is growing rapidly. Job enrichment efforts, particularly team approaches, frequently involve many organizational changes, including changes in technology, plant layout, selection, training, and compensation. Most, or all, of the crucial factors in organizational performance tend to be altered.

The human resources department's role in job design is usually indirect, although job design influences almost every aspect of human resources management. The department may diagnose organizational problems that suggest job redesign, incorporate information on job design in training and management development programs, and help plan job redesign programs to ensure that sound human resources policies and practices are developed. Further, the department will need to be prepared to modify job descriptions and job specifications and to modify recruitment, selection, training, compensation, and other practices to be consistent with any job redesign program.

Job analysis is the systematic investigation of a job's content. Careful job analysis is necessary for the development of accurate job descriptions and appropriate job specifications. In turn, these documents are important in recruitment, orientation, and training; in the development of performance standards; in performance appraisal; in determining relative job worth (job evaluation); and in developing promotion ladders. The development of job descriptions can promote a useful dialogue between a supervisor and a subordinate — or a team of subordinates — about their respective roles and can help in restructuring those roles as needed.

Government regulations, supported by the *Griggs* v. *Duke Power Company* case, require that job specifications be job related to guard against discrimination against minorities, women, the disabled, and other protected groups. Management should periodically examine job specifications to see whether they are furthering organizational goals and whether they are appropriate in light of legal requirements.

Performance standards can be considered an extension of job descriptions. Usually, performance standards are statements of what is considered acceptable, and they are frequently written in quantitative terms. The purposes of performance standards include communicating expected levels of performance and establishing guidelines against which performance can be measured. Written standards are useful for communicating and retrieving this information. MBO programs may be more future oriented and may serve to "stretch" employees more than performance standards.

The human resources department typically plays a major role in helping plan the systems to be used in job analysis and in developing job descriptions, job specifications, and performance standards. Specialists in that department may be assigned to conduct job analyses and write job descriptions in cooperation with managers, supervisors, and employees. The human resources department is not involved in the actual writing of performance standards but plays a diagnostic, training, and monitoring role.

Ethical Dilemma

Debbie Schuler, aged sixteen, is employed as a part-time waitress and hostess at Craig's Steak & Fish House. State law prohibits employers from allowing employees below the age of eighteen to serve alcoholic beverages to customers. Because the restaurant is short-handed and customers are usually impatient about being served, the waitresses of Debbie's age frequently serve beer and wine to customers. The owner, Craig, has seen this occurring, and the manager is fully aware of the practice. Debbie is concerned, wondering if she is going to get into trouble with the state. She has considered going to the manager about the matter, but is fearful that she might lose her job as a result.

What are the ethical issues? What should Debbie do? What should her employer do?

Key Terms

job design
job content
organizational responsibilities
Job Diagnostic Survey (JDS)
job enrichment
job enlargement
horizontal restructuring
vertical restructuring
self-managed team
sociotechnical program

skills-based pay
job analysis
critical incidents
Position Analysis Questionnaire (PAQ)
job descriptions
job specifications
job evaluation
career progression ladders
performance standards

Review Questions

1. Define job design.
2. What is job content?
3. What are the core job characteristics as described by Hackman and Oldham and with what psychological states are these characteristics associated?
4. What is job enrichment?
5. Give an example of an individual approach to job enrichment and a team approach to job enrichment. What are some benefits and limitations of each approach?
6. Typically, what are the common elements in the use of self-managed teams?
7. What is job analysis and what are its purposes?
8. Discuss the importance of accurate job descriptions and appropriate job specifications.
9. What are performance standards? How are they developed?
10. Discuss the responsibilities of the human resources department with respect to job design and analysis.

Opening Case Questions

Case 7.1 High Seas Autopilots

1. What effects do job design and the team approach have on Vivian's need fulfillment?
2. What are the benefits of allowing the team to establish its own production goals and quality standards?

Case 7.2 What Is This Team Thing, Anyway?

1. What are some of the basic elements of the self-managed (or self-directed) team concept?
2. What are some likely reasons that Vince Vigano is upset and defensive? What could management have done (or do now) to help make the transition less painful for Vince?

Comprehensive Case

Self-Managed Teams

In their constant search for ways to increase productivity without raising costs, American companies are turning increasingly to self-managed teams. Although fewer than ten percent of American businesses now use such teams, some analysts predict that that number could rise to 40 or 50 percent by the end of the decade. When these teams are given appropriate training and are supported by top management, they can improve morale and change the way employees view their companies, as well as significantly increase productivity.

Although most companies find it easiest to institute self-managed teams in a new facility, some of the greatest successes of self-managed teams have come in reversing the fortunes of old, unproductive plants. For example, in the mid-1980s Chrysler Corp. was ready to close down its New Castle, Indiana, plant. The plant was the company's oldest, the equipment was run down, worker morale was low, and absenteeism was high. Employees stayed home when they felt like it, took long breaks when machinery broke down, and sometimes even sabotaged the work they were supposed to be doing, out of spite toward the company.

All that changed in 1986, when the company began breaking the work force up into teams that do everything from assigning tasks and ordering parts to dealing with poor attitudes or attendance. Workers became "technicians," supervisors became "team advisers." As a result, the number of defects and union grievances has tumbled, and the absenteeism rate is less than half of what it used to be.

Part of the secret in the success of self-managed teams is the feeling of power that workers gain from them. At the General Motors Corp. Saturn plant, teams control their own budget and hiring and play a major role in the company's drive to make the plant more efficient. Because of Saturn's no-layoff policy, the teams don't have to worry that their waste-cutting or labor-saving suggestions will cost team members their jobs; teams have even been known to figure out ways to pack more work into their own schedules. Such control over their own jobs has developed an intense sense of commitment among most workers, and the result is that the plant's products are the highest-quality American cars, with defect rates as low as those of GM's top Japanese rivals.

Not everyone works well in such teams, of course, and changing to a team orientation requires careful planning, extensive training, and scrupulous selection of team members. GM hasn't instituted Saturn-type teams at its other plants partly because it is difficult to change the way veteran workers interact; at the Saturn plant, the company had a chance to screen employees to find the most self-motivated team players. The food giant, General Mills, Inc., used to hire roughly one in five job applicants. In staffing its new team-run cereal factory in Georgia, however, the company screened four thousand applicants to find just one hundred employees.

Employees' resistance to the team concept isn't the only kind of barrier that companies must overcome. Some employees find that the added responsibility, while it does give them more control and a sense of power, also increases their worries. People who used to leave their job at the office now find themselves mulling over problems at night. Besides, most self-managed teams require each worker to learn all the tasks for which the team is responsible. So instead of just knowing how to run a machine, an individual may need to know how to repair it, order parts for it, and plan its use and maintenance. Some workers resist taking on so many different tasks.

Management's commitment to the teams is crucial, and differences between management and workers can look even more stark when the workers take on more responsibility in teams. At the Saturn plant, for instance, the pay gap between workers and managers is likely to cause more friction when the two groups share some responsibilities. When management pressured workers into an increase in production, which led to an increase in defects, workers staged a slowdown to protest. Open communication is important to the teams' success, and everyone, including managers, must be willing to listen to criticism and suggestions from team members.

Management can be particularly helpful to teams by being as specific as possible about what the team is supposed to do. Giving a team a mandate to "improve quality" may not be enough. Specifying that the team's goal is to reduce the number of production defects by 25 percent within a year may get better results.

These kinds of goals are part of the strategic planning process. If possible, the team should have a hand in setting such goals, as well as in developing mission statements, creating training programs, and establishing recruitment strategies. Team members may need many different kinds of training: in communication skills, in doing all the different tasks that the team is responsible for, in problem solving, in using statistical tools that measure the quality of a process, and in the just-in-time principles that underlie most production-oriented teams.

Starting to rely on teams may require a substantial change in the organization's priorities.

Besides spending more on training, the organization may also need to invest more in research and development. A project team involving engineers, production people, and marketers may take more time and money to perfect a new product's design, but with such team input early in the process, the product should need fewer changes and revisions and should reach the market sooner than would conventionally created products. Companies should not shift to self-managed teams casually, and they should recognize possible problems from the outset. But as more and more companies are discovering, the potential rewards are huge.

Sources: Constance Hamilton, "Training Is a Vital Link in the Process," *HRfocus* 69 (September 1992):4–5; Joan S. Lublin, "Trying to Increase Worker Productivity, More Employers Alter Management Style," *The Wall Street Journal*, February 13, 1992, B1; Louis S. Richman, "America's Tough New Job Market," *Fortune*, February 24, 1992, pp. 52–61; Jana Schilder, "Work Teams Boost Productivity," *Personnel Journal* 71 (February 1992):67–71; David Woodruff, "Saturn," *Business Week*, August 17, 1992, pp. 86–91; and David Woodruff, "Where Employees Are Management," *Business Week*, *Reinventing America*, 1992, pp. 66.

Discussion Questions

1. What are the tasks of team members at the Chrysler New Castle and GM Saturn plants?
2. What are some of the problems or challenges in making the self-managed team concept work successfully?

CHAPTER 8

Work Rules and Schedules

LEARNING OBJECTIVES

- Identify the factors that affect the level of control in an organization.
- Explain why work rules are necessary in an organization.
- Specify the consequences of restrictive work rules for employee morale and organizational effectiveness.
- Discuss the considerations involved in administering work rules.
- Cite the usual steps in progressive discipline.
- List the advantages and disadvantages associated with each of the following work schedules: regular work schedule, overtime work, shift work, the compressed workweek, flextime, permanent part-time work, job sharing, and telecommuting.
- Describe the role of the human resources department in managing work rules and schedules.

CASE 8.1 Several Subcultures at Simply Scrumptious

Jenny Forsythe, CEO of Simply Scrumptious Desserts, is meeting with Jules Jacobsen, SSD's human resources vice president. "I appreciate what you're telling me, Jules. If I hear you right, we've gone overboard in terms of flexibility, to the point of having several subcultures in our factories and offices who are mad at each other. Or more accurately, mad at us. We have the regular, full-time people; we have the permanent part-timers; we've got the people who are on flextime and those who are not; and there's the four-day week people; and then the temporaries. Not to mention the summer interns."

"That's right," Jules responds. "It isn't exactly a crisis, but the volume of grumbling suggests that some attention to quality and to customers is being sacrificed through this internal bickering."

"What do you suggest?"

"Partly it's a matter of communicating the whole story. But I think we have to listen to our employees in some systematic way to get a real fix on the problems. It's probably mostly a matter of people perceiving something as unfair: "Group A gets such and such, and we don't;" or "Why wouldn't the same practice work in our department?" Maybe we ought to set up some focus groups — or sensing groups, or whatever they're called — and do some hard listening. Of course, in several plants we have the unions to contend with. We'd have to get their cooperation."

"Sounds like you're on the right track, Jules. How about talking with a few of the other top management people and then presenting an action plan at our team meeting in a couple of weeks? I'd like to have all of our employees share my conviction that Simply Scrumptious is a terrific company and that it's in all of our interests to pull together. Most people probably believe that, but maybe we need to do some tuning up." ◀

CASE 8.2 Just a Bundle of Laughs

You had to admit that Charlie Shearson was funny a lot of the time. Charlie, an estimator in the purchasing department at Jones Manufacturing, was an accomplished storyteller and usually had a new joke to tell when you ran into him in the cafeteria or in the hallways. He was also a great practical joker — he had smuggled a dried fish into a coworker's desk during the holidays, causing a great deal of laughter and commotion, and had poured orange dye into the water cooler on Halloween, much to the consternation of some people who didn't know whether the water was fit to drink.

Bill James, Charlie's supervisor, had cautioned him about both incidents, telling him that not everyone thought his pranks were funny and that they were interfering with work.

This time Bill was furious. It was St. Patrick's Day, and Charlie had obtained three or four green plastic derbies and was sailing them across the work area. One of them went out a window — directly above the president's office — and another hit Bill right in the chest. There was laughter from coworkers when the first hat went out the window, but dead silence when the other hat hit Bill. Everyone looked at Bill uneasily. Bill didn't need any encouragement. He had had it up to the eyeballs with Charlie.

"You're fired," he shouted. "That's the last time you'll horse around here. Go pick up your paycheck." Charlie looked shocked, shrugged his shoulders, picked up a few things from his desk, and walked out.

The next day, the personnel and labor relations director telephoned Bill to tell him Charlie had filed a grievance, or formal complaint, through the union, protesting the discharge, and asked Bill to drop by his office. "I'll be there in a few minutes," Bill said. He leaned back in his chair and pondered the situation. "I'll bet I'll have to take that clown back," he thought. "I haven't got any warnings in the file, and I gave him a pay raise last time around. The union will claim it was a trivial matter, and that he's too good a worker to fire over such an incident."   ◀

These cases concern work rules and schedules — matters of considerable importance to how people feel about their jobs, how they feel about management, and how they get the work done. In Case 8.1, the human resources vice president and the CEO are concerned that their company may have moved so far in the direction of creating flexible working arrangements that tensions between various categories of workers are beginning to develop. Management may have solved some problems only to create others.

In Case 8.2, Charlie Shearson's pranks may have been more of a liability than an asset to the company, but an absence of rules about horseplay or Bill James's failure to document previous warnings may now result in Charlie being reinstated. Maybe Charlie *should* be reinstated. At any rate, the company is now faced with a series of meetings with the union as the matter goes through grievance proceedings. If Charlie's grievance ultimately goes to an arbitrator, the arbitrator may order him reinstated with back pay.

From what is known about such matters as motivation, equity, employee control over productivity, and the necessity for the coordination of work, it is clear that these incidents are anything but trivial. The effective management of work rules and schedules is an important factor in job performance and satisfaction. This chapter is about work rules and what organizations do when rules are violated. The chapter also discusses various ways of scheduling the workday and workweek, and the role played by the human resources department in these matters.

Control Versus Freedom

A broad question about work rules and schedules is whether organizations (through union-management agreements or other means) should control employees' behavior tightly — whether they should have **restrictive work rules** — or whether they should provide maximum freedom in the workplace. The answer depends on many factors, including the size and complexity of the organization; management philosophy; work-group norms (unwritten rules or standards of behavior); the technology, equipment, and materials used by the organization; and social or cultural norms and attitudes.

The organization's size and complexity are factors in the design of work rules and schedules. For example, a retail organization of eight people, all working in one large room in a small building, is not likely to need an elaborate set of rules governing work. Requirements about such matters as working hours and overtime and how much tardiness can be tolerated are set by the owner and communicated directly to workers. By and large, problems are handled informally. Everybody knows who is there and who is not, and who is working hard and who is taking it easy. Rare cases of discipline are handled by the owner. By contrast, a large aerospace manufacturer with thousands of employees at several locations — some of them in different states — requires a fairly elaborate set of rules and regulations. One of the reasons is that, with thousands of employees, all kinds of problems and dilemmas occur, and no one person can keep track of all the incidents and precedents. A company of this size and complexity has had thousands of such incidents, leading to a gradual codification of rules and regulations. This codification, in general, makes everyone's life easier. For example, the small firm may never have experienced a **garnishment,** a legal proceeding in which a creditor of some employee gets a court order requiring the company to turn over some fraction of that employee's wages to that creditor. The large company, on the other hand, may have experienced this nuisance many times and will have established rules, consistent with federal and state law, about what discipline, if any, is to be meted out to the employee if a garnishment occurs. (The Family Support Act of 1988 requires employers to garnish the wages of non-custodial parents for child support effective January 1994.)[1]

Management philosophy will have a major influence on work rules. A Theory X management philosophy, for example, will probably contribute to trying to solve problems by issuing edicts and restrictive work rules. A Theory Y philosophy will probably influence a manager to be more willing to discuss problems thoroughly with subordinates before taking any action.

Work-group norms influence work rules in two ways. First, the norms help determine the necessity for rules. For example, if group norms across the organization are that no one takes a break longer than fifteen minutes, there may be no need for a formal rule about this. On the other hand, if employees are casual about returning from breaks, with some people chronically staying a half-hour or so, and discussions and warnings have not corrected the problem, supervisors and managers are likely to want to start imposing rules.

In addition to influencing the need for rules, group norms are themselves informal rules governing behavior. Work groups develop their own attitudes and standards and put considerable pressure on members to conform. These standards may be consistent with or contradict those of management. Obviously, if group norms are in opposition to formal work rules, there will be an uneasy tug-of-war going on between management and employees, with employees attempting to circumvent rules and supervisors trying to enforce them.

Technology, equipment, and materials also affect work rules and schedules. A huge machine that stamps out automobile bodies will require the presence of a full crew, and because of its noise and potential danger, will require rules about wearing protective devices, how close one can get to the machine, and who can operate it. Some equipment and materials require swift and strict enforcement of safety regulations. Obviously, smoking must be prohibited in an area where liquid hydrogen or aviation gasoline is piped from one tank to another. Under such circumstances, smoking, or the use of welding torches, or any grinding that would produce sparks, cannot be tolerated for an instant.

Social or cultural norms and attitudes also influence work rules and schedules. For example, giving employees more flexibility in starting and stopping work has become much more acceptable as executives have come to realize that such programs may be partial solutions to traffic congestion in metropolitan areas and in and around plant parking lots. As another example, growing concern about the adverse effects on health of smoking has led an increasing number of organizations to develop rules that permit smoking in designated areas only. Attitudes in society about this particular issue are resulting in local and state laws requiring organizations to establish rules about smoking. In 1984, for example, San Francisco put into effect an ordinance that requires employers to "accommodate, insofar as possible, the preferences of nonsmokers and smokers and, if satisfactory accommodation cannot be reached, to prohibit smoking in the office work place."[2] Since then, numerous states and municipalities have passed laws regulating smoking in the workplace.

The Purpose of Work Rules

Organizations typically have rules pertaining to such matters as starting and stopping work, total hours to be worked, rest periods, fighting and intoxication on the job, refusal to carry out instructions from a superior (**insubordination**), smoking in hazardous areas, and recording time worked. One purpose is to ensure reasonable predictability of employee behavior beyond that provided by group norms so that the organization can function without undue disturbance. Another purpose is to protect employees from hazardous conditions.

It is easy to visualize the consequences to an organization if unpredictable work schedules, unsafe practices, rough horseplay, intoxication, stealing, and falsification of records were condoned. Unless minimum standards of conduct are enforced, work will be seriously disrupted.

Reasonable work rules help fulfill human needs for security, order, predictability, and avoidance of physical harm. Since most people understand that these needs will not be satisfied in a chaotic environment, they are willing to accept a minimum number of rules. In Case 8.2, Charlie Shearson's practical jokes, although humorous to some people, were probably a serious irritation to others. Certainly, they interfered with work. Most employees would probably agree with rules that give supervisors authority to discipline employees whose behavior gets too far out of line. As another example, people in military organizations will accept a high degree of control when it is related to survival in combat and to unit security. Mine workers understand the importance of strict rules about the firing of explosives. People in a manufacturing plant will ordinarily understand the interdependence of their jobs and will accept fairly rigorous rules pertaining to stopping and starting work.

Restrictive Work Rules

If work rules are too restrictive or confining, they can frustrate the fulfillment of human needs and interfere with organizational effectiveness. Rules limiting socializing on the job can frustrate needs for affiliation and cooperation. Rules that limit job scope, whether management- or union-imposed, can frustrate needs for autonomy and self-actualization. Rules that are seen as arbitrary and punitive tend to result in defensive — and sometimes aggressive — employee behavior.

For example, at a Kaiser Aluminum & Chemical plant in West Virginia, workers were divided into eighteen crafts, such as carpenters and electricians, and were prohibited by the union contract from doing work of any craft but their own. This held true even if workers in a particular craft had run out of work and other crafts were short-handed. The company and the union agreed to reduce the eighteen categories to twelve, thus expanding the kinds of work to which employees could be assigned.[3]

Administering Work Rules

When enterprises are small, the chief executive has the major responsibility for the development of work rules and schedules. As organizations become larger and more complex and the human resources department is created, the personnel director is usually expected — in cooperation with other managers — to suggest revisions in work rules and schedules to top management. Supervisors are then responsible for enforcing the rules. The more work rules are supported by group attitudes and norms, the more enforcement becomes a responsibility shared by all employees.

If management can engage supervisors and employees in problem solving rather than issue directives, it is more likely that work rules will be developed that are practical and have broad support. Some rules, of course, are so fundamental to organizational survival — such as rules against theft and rules prohibiting smoking near flammable materials —that most employees expect management to have established them long ago.

Just as the organization requires rules to operate, the employee needs information about those rules and an understanding of the consequences of violating them. Work rules are typically listed and described in employee handbooks (see Figure 8.1), and information is provided during orientation sessions at the time of employment. Organizations sometimes post work rules on bulletin boards and will almost always post warning signs in hazardous areas.

Violation of Work Rules

Work rules serve as control devices in that they represent standards of behavior that ensure a reasonable level of conformity throughout the organization. An employee's failure to conform to the rules can lead to disciplinary action. **Disciplinary action** is the penalty or punishment associated with violation of a rule. A few organizations give positive rewards for above-average compliance in such matters as attendance or on-time arrival, but this practice is not widespread.

The following list illustrates some offenses that can lead to disciplinary action in business, industrial, and other organizations.

- Dishonesty, deception, or fraud, including computer fraud
- Unexcused absence
- Repeated tardiness
- Excessive absence
- Leaving work without permission
- Alcohol or drug abuse
- Possession of liquor or illegal drugs
- Theft of property, including trade secrets
- Sleeping on the job
- Failure to report injuries
- Failure to meet quality or quantity standards
- Safety-rule violations
- Use of abusive or threatening language

Time cards

Time cards are a record of an employee's regular working time, overtime, absences, and special situations. In order to make sure that non-exempt employees are fully and fairly compensated, those who are paid weekly are asked to submit a time card, signed by the supervisor and the employee, to the Payroll Department by noon on Thursday. Non-exempt employees who are paid monthly should submit a signed time card to the Payroll Department by noon of the last working day of the month. Exempt employees are not required to submit time cards.

Payday

If you are paid weekly, you will receive your paycheck every Thursday. If you are on a monthly pay schedule, you will be paid on the 12th day of each month. If the 12th falls on a Saturday or a Sunday, you will be paid the Friday before.

If you are absent from work on payday, your check will be held in the Payroll Department for you to pick up on your return. If you know that you will be on vacation and want to receive your paycheck in advance, you must make arrangements through the Payroll Department at least two weeks beforehand.

You may elect to have your pay deposited directly in your bank account. If you arrange for direct deposit, you will receive a statement of your earnings and deductions on payday.

Payroll deductions

When you are hired, we ask you to fill out federal and state withholding forms and certain benefit forms. The Payroll Department makes standard deductions for state and federal taxes and for F.I.C.A. (social security). Other deductions which may affect your paycheck are based on your requests, deductions for life or accident insurance, long term disability insurance, credit union, United Way, MBTA passes, and the like. If you suspect that a deduction is incorrect or if you wish to change a deduction, you should contact the Human Resources or Payroll Departments.

FIGURE 8.1 Sample page from an employee handbook

Source: Reprinted by permission of Houghton Mifflin Company.

- Discourtesy to customers
- Willful damage to material or property
- Fighting
- Horseplay
- Gambling
- Insubordination
- Carrying concealed weapons
- Sexual harassment
- Age, racial, or national origin harassment
- Working for a competitor
- Violation of grooming or dress code

The last item is probably the most controversial. For example, Continental Airlines, Inc., discharged a female part-time sales agent for not wearing makeup foundation and lipstick, but offered to reinstate her with back pay after there was considerable negative publicity about the matter.[4] Safeco's policy of requiring all its male white-collar employees to literally wear white collars and white shirts has been challenged at the insurance company's annual meeting.[5]

Some of the offenses appearing on the list require further definition in specific organizations. For example, what is meant by "excessive absence" and "repeated tardiness" needs to be defined so that employees and supervisors both know what standard is being applied. (In one study, about two-thirds of the manufacturing firms surveyed defined what was meant by those terms in their particular companies. Tardiness up to ten times per year was within the acceptable range for about half the firms.)[6]

Some offenses are difficult to detect and measure, and enforcement techniques, such as random drug testing, can be controversial in terms of employee relations or in terms of legality. (For example, although courts tend to approve urine testing when there is a "reasonable individualized suspicion" that an employee's performance is being affected by drugs, courts are divided on random or across-the-board drug testing.[7] See Chapter 20 for further reference to substance abuse and testing.)

A number of offenses may not be considered serious enough for **discharge** — permanent dismissal from the organization — the first time, but repeated offenses are more likely to involve discharge. Rule violations frequently considered serious enough to warrant immediate discharge are theft, falsifying the employment application or work records, possession of illegal drugs or weapons, divulging trade secrets, physical assault, or deliberate damage to material or property.[8]

Lighter penalties for violations of less serious infractions include oral or written **warnings, demotion,** or **disciplinary layoff.** A warning informs an employee that a more severe penalty (frequently specified) will be applied at the next infraction of the rules. A demotion is a reduction in job responsibilities, usually accompanied by a reduction in hourly pay or salary. In a disciplinary layoff, the employee is temporarily separated from the organization and the payroll, typically for a few days or weeks. **Docking** of pay — simply not paying for the time missed — for absenteeism or tardiness is a frequent practice. At least one organization — General Motors Corp. — reduces supplemental benefits for excessive absenteeism. Absenteeism by a few workers at the company had become so expensive that GM and the United Auto Workers agreed to cutting a violator's benefits — profit-sharing, health insurance, and bereavement pay — by 20 percent or more if the person's unexcused absences exceeded 20 percent for a six-month period. This was in addition to lost wages for the employee during the unexcused periods.[9]

Automatic application of penalties for offenses varies widely. There is growing sentiment that the circumstances of each case, including any organizational factors that may have contributed to the offense, should be considered in meting out discipline.

Documentation

Careful **documentation** of employee violations of work rules is important in administering discipline and in defending any disciplinary action if there is a challenge through court or grievance procedures.[10] Further, to ensure consistency in the handling of disciplinary cases, the human resources department would be wise to keep records of serious incidents and the surrounding circumstances, and what action was taken, in order to advise supervisors and managers about how to handle future cases and to recommend any needed policy changes.

Progressive Discipline

The principle of **progressive discipline** is widely accepted in the administration of work rules. In essence, progressive discipline means that management responds to a first offense with some minimal action, such as an oral warning, but to subsequent offenses with more serious penalties, such as disciplinary layoff or discharge. A sequence of disciplinary actions might be as follows:

1. Oral warning
2. Written warning stating consequences of future offenses
3. Disciplinary layoff or demotion
4. Discharge

The details of progressive discipline procedures will vary from firm to firm. An interesting step used by some companies is the **decision-making leave.** If disciplinary discussions have not resulted in the desired changes, the employee is placed on a one-day, paid leave during which the employee is instructed to think through his or her commitment to the organization and willingness to solve the immediate problem. The employee is expected to return the next day with a decision either to "change and stay or quit and find more satisfying work elsewhere." Upon return, if the employee has elected to stay, he or she immediately meets with the supervisor to set specific performance goals and to develop an action plan. The supervisor expresses confidence in the employee, but the employee is warned that failure to meet expectations will result in termination. The conversation is written up in memo form and a copy goes into the employee's file.[11]

The overall goal of progressive discipline is to correct problems early and avoid the last-resort step of discharge. The seriousness of discharge is reflected in the label often given to discharge by union members and officials: "capital punishment." The wide acceptance of the progressive discipline principle probably stems in part from arbitrators' decisions made under grievance and arbitration provisions of union-management contracts. Arbitrators have typically examined both the correctability of a situation and the seriousness of an offense in comparison with the penalty imposed and have generally advocated progressive discipline procedures.[12]

Although Bill James, in Case 8.2, had cautioned Charlie Shearson about his practical jokes, he probably should have given Charlie a written warning after the water cooler incident. Although it is true that Charlie had engaged in intolerable horseplay, the union might take his grievance all the way to arbitration, and an arbitrator might hold that a written warning, or perhaps a disciplinary layoff, should have been administered before the company resorted to discharge.

Responsibility for Discipline

The supervisor is usually considered to be responsible for discipline in his or her unit. Many business firms, however, require each discharge case to be reviewed by higher authority before the discharge is made final. For example, a supervisor may be required to bring a recommendation for termination to the department head for review. The human resources department is usually involved in this review of the substance of the case and also usually monitors the procedures followed to make sure they are in accord with company policy. Federal civil service regulations, as well as most state and local civil service regulations, require all dismissals to be reviewed.[13]

Legal Ramifications

Although the principle of the right to discharge has been well established in the United States, increasingly discharges of employees are being affected by the Civil

Rights Act, Age Discrimination in Employment Act, the Americans with Disabilities Act, EEOC rulings, and court decisions. For example, in an early case, 160 older management and nonmanagement employees of Standard Oil Co. of California were terminated during a reduction in force; they complained that they were being separated to make way for younger replacements. The U.S. Department of Labor sued on their behalf, and the outcome was an agreement that Standard Oil of California would reinstate the workers and pay them $2 million.[14] (For more on the legal aspects of discharge, see Chapters 10 and 19.)

The Workday and Workweek

Work schedules, like work rules, are a major condition surrounding jobs. "Work schedules" refers to matters such as starting and stopping times, the number and length of work breaks, how work beyond the regularly scheduled day or week is administered, whether the work is done on company premises or at home, and whether the employee is full-time or part-time. Like work rules, work schedules have a significant influence on the satisfaction, and frequently the performance, of employees, and how they are administered and changed is important. From the standpoint of management, work schedules are necessary to coordinate and control work. Further, a certain amount of uniformity is required to meet employee expectations of equitable treatment. Work schedules can be more flexible, however, than has been traditionally assumed in many organizations.

As pointed out in *Contemporary Issues* on page 194, the work schedule for paid employment is not the total workday for a huge proportion of the population. More and more companies are trying to assist employees in balancing the demands of the job with the demands of the home and family.

Traditional Work Schedules   The typical business and industrial workday and workweek have changed a great deal over the years. For example, in 1835, the workday in the Philadelphia Navy Yard was sunrise to sunset, with time off for breakfast and other meals. During the summer, this meant an extremely long and exhausting day, although for a short period in December and early January working hours dropped to slightly fewer than 8. In late June 1835, employees actually worked 11 hours and 54 minutes, *not including time off for meals*. In 1836, the workday was reduced to 10 hours the year around, largely through pressures from shipyard mechanics of the National Trades' Union who had already obtained this concession from private shipyards in the Philadelphia area.[15] Presumably, employees worked these long hours six days per week, since the average weekly hours worked in 1840 has been estimated at 78.[16]

About 150 years later, the typical workday in American business and industry was roughly 8 hours per day for a five-day workweek. In June 1990, the weekly hours worked by production or nonsupervisory employees in the private sector averaged 34.5, down from about 40 hours per week in 1950. There were some differences among industries, however. For example, the average of the weekly hours for workers in wholesale trade was 38.1, in retail trade 28.8, and in manufacturing 40.8 hours.[17] The low figure in retail trade partly reflects the widespread use of part-time workers in that industry.

Various forces have probably contributed to this decline in working hours. One clear factor is pressure from labor unions. Another is that, with rising real wages, it has become possible to have both a higher living standard and additional leisure.[18]

Overtime Work

Overtime work is work performed beyond the regularly scheduled workday or workweek as defined by the organization or by law. Since the Fair Labor Standards Act was passed in 1938, most employers in interstate commerce have been required to pay time and one-half the regular rate of pay for hours worked beyond forty in one week, except to those employees who are exempt from the law.

Employees to whom overtime payments must be made are called **nonexempt employees** — that is, employees who are protected by the laws. Production, maintenance, and clerical workers are usually nonexempt employees. In contrast, bona fide executive, administrative, and professional employees, including outside sales personnel and certain other special categories, as defined by the U.S. Department of Labor, need not be paid overtime and thus are called **exempt employees.**[19] An interesting inclusion in the exempt class, based on wage level, is the category of systems analysts, computer programmers, software engineers, and other "similarly skilled" computer workers providing they are paid 6.5 times the minimum wage and are paid by the hour. Computer workers earning more than $27.63 per hour are considered exempt employees and are not entitled by law to overtime pay, although company policy may include them.[20]

One effect of these laws, of course, has been to discourage management from scheduling workweeks longer than forty hours. Another effect has been to spread jobs across the population. The laws were originally passed during a period of high unemployment and were intended to spread the available work, as well as to protect workers from exploitation.

Shift Work

Shift work is usually considered to be regular employment that occurs sometime between 7 p.m. and 7 a.m. There has been a significant increase in shift work in the world over the past thirty years, in part because continuous-process operations, in which machines or procedures are run continuously, have been widely adopted in industries such as steel and petrochemicals, where starting and stopping on a daily basis is prohibitively expensive. Other factors in the growth of shift work include the economic necessity to maximize the use of capital equipment (machinery, vehicles, buildings, and so forth) and the growth of "round-the-clock" service industries, such as transportation and medical care.[21]

There are many variations of shift work, depending on whether the organization is operating twenty-four hours a day and seven days a week, and on the circumstances and history of the particular enterprise. For example, the day shift might be 8:00 a.m. to 4:30 p.m., with a half-hour unpaid lunch period; the afternoon shift from 4:15 p.m. to 12:15 a.m. (sometimes called the "swing shift"); and the night shift from midnight to 8:15 a.m. (sometimes called the "graveyard shift"). In some circumstances, organizations employ part-time workers on a four-hour shift (sometimes called the "twilight shift") at the end of a regular eight-hour day. "Split shifts" are sometimes used when there are peak workloads at widely different times of the day. In these circumstances, an employee may be scheduled to work two different partial shifts with an interval of several hours between the two periods. (Nuclear submarines in the U.S. Navy have an eighteen-hour-day schedule, with six hours of work, six hours of sleep, and six hours on watch. In contrast, crews on most surface ships are on a four-hours-on and four-hours-off schedule.)[22] A few years ago, it was

Contemporary Issues

24-Hour Employees

For many people, 5 p.m. is the end of the workday. They go shopping, out to dinner or to the gym to work out. But for a larger number of working men and women with families, their workday is nowhere near finished. They go home to another shift — a shift of soccer practice, car pools, care for an elderly relative, orthodontist appointments, school events, in addition to marketing, cleaning and errands. Millions of workers go home to several hours of additional work — to a "second shift," in the words of Arlie Hochschild, in her book of the same name.

With the "traditional" family (a family in which the mother is not employed outside the home) accounting for less than 7% of all American families, there's simply more and more to do everyday — both at the workplace and at home. According to many experts, progressive companies are wrestling with the fact that their employees have lives outside the workplace and that their personal concerns often create additional demands on their time at work. Recognizing the employee as a 24-hour human being and translating that into the corporate culture is an enormous undertaking that requires a serious, long-term commitment by the company.

Balancing work and family, and being sensitive to time demands are complex issues that affect some of the most basic assumptions we hold about the workplace: Are traditional work schedules counterproductive in some cases? Is the workplace an appropriate sphere for family problems — and solutions? Is the traditional view of employees too narrow and rigid for today's society?

A more holistic view of employees is crucial if companies are to attract and retain talented individuals. What's now being referred to as a "life cycle" approach to employees goes far beyond dependent care referrals.

A life cycle view of an employee means that the corporate culture responds to an individual's changing needs throughout that employee's life, recognizing in a fundamental way that the employee's personal life strongly influences his or her effectiveness at work, and that the corporation must play an active role in alleviating some of the external pressure. For example, employees don't stop having child care concerns when their children reach elementary school age or become teenagers. Their concerns simply change.

A few pioneer companies already have begun to explore this complex arena. Some businesses are experimenting with ideas and programs that may seem radical to us today: new forms of flex time, career breaks and sabbaticals; phased retirement; and exhaustive employee surveys they will use as scaffolding for future strategic planning.

Some companies even contract with frequently used services — such as banks, dry cleaners, barber shops and hairdressers — to open retail outlets when they design or relocate their offices. The key is that services and programs are part of an integrated approach to solving this overwhelming problem.

estimated that on any one day in the United States, nearly one worker in six was working hours other than a regular day schedule. About half of these shift workers were employed on afternoon shifts, and the others worked on night shifts.[23] At about the same time in the United Kingdom, although schedules varied widely, the typical practice was to rotate employees across shifts. A worker might be on the day shift for a week, the afternoon shift for a week, and then on the night shift for a week before rotating back to the day shift.[24] (This clockwise sequence, by the way, seems to work better than the reverse, according to **chronobiologists,** scientists who study the biological rhythms of the human body.)[25] In many organizations, however, the workers on a given shift stay on that shift unless they apply and are selected for another schedule.

Research has found that certain conclusions can be drawn about the effects of shift work on employees, although the data are partially contradictory. Generally speaking, people experience both advantages and disadvantages with shift work.

Some of the benefits of shift work are that it permits some workers to find employment they might not otherwise find, to hold down two jobs, or to attend school. Other benefits that appeal to some people are the relaxed work pace and greater freedom from supervision sometimes found on shift work. Further, night work seems to fit the biological rhythms of some people better than day work. In addition, shift work usually pays more than day work. Shift premiums vary from a few cents per hour to substantial amounts, with the median differential at about 10 percent.[26]

Some of the drawbacks of shift work, according to a review of the research, are the negative consequences frequently experienced in terms of health, relationships with other people, leisure activities, and safety.[27] Shift workers may experience difficulties in sleeping or digestion and appetite problems. They may regret that they have less time to spend with children, spouses, and friends because of their varying schedules. Research shows that shift workers have problems in meshing their schedules with family members and friends.[28] There is contradictory evidence as to whether shift workers have more accidents than day workers, but there is enough laboratory and other data to suggest that shift work, for some people, may be a contributor to accidents. Laboratory studies show that disturbances in the twenty-four-hour body cycles (called **circadian cycles**) tend to be associated with an increase in reaction time and errors.[29]

In addition to being alert to the health, family, social, recreational, and safety consequences of shift work, management needs to pay attention to the integration of afternoon and night shift workers with the people and activities on a day schedule. This integration is important both for the morale of shift workers and for effective coordination and cooperation between shifts. Without attention to this integration, misunderstanding and conflict can arise between workers and supervisors on one shift and workers and supervisors on another. Examples of typical problems between shifts are complaints that the people on the previous shift do not clean up properly, do not maintain the equipment properly, misplace tools, and so on. One way cooperation and integration between shifts can be furthered is for daytime managers to meet periodically with shift employees. Another device is for shifts to overlap so there can be sufficient communication and coordination between the supervisors and employees of the adjoining shifts. The human resources staff can do much to assist in this integration by helping establish such mechanisms and, in cooperation with the appropriate managers, by systematically assessing how employees see the level of cooperation and help between shifts.

New Patterns in Work Scheduling

Recent years have seen a great deal of experimentation with different kinds of work schedules, such as the compressed workweek, flextime, permanent part-time work, peak-time work, job sharing, and telecommuting, and temporary employment, all of which are discussed below. The reasons for this experimentation include changing lifestyles and desires for more leisure time, attempts to minimize traffic problems, the development of the personal computer, and attempts by management to increase both morale and productivity. Some, if not all, of the experimentation is based partly on pragmatic attempts by managers to reduce costs.

Compressed Workweek

The **compressed workweek** is a work schedule in which the employee works the same number of hours per week as previously but completes them in fewer days. The workweek declined by nearly twenty hours between 1901 and shortly after World War II and then leveled off at about forty hours.[30] The typical pattern then became a five-day, forty-hour workweek. This five-day week is gradually being modified by the appearance of the four-day, forty-hour workweek, in which the employee works for ten hours each day, four days per week. This concept is being tried or considered by a number of firms in the United States and elsewhere. One survey of 120 firms found 20 percent using a compressed workweek for at least part of the work force.[31] The federal government has encouraged federal agencies to experiment with the compressed workweek and other forms of work schedules through the Federal Employees Flexible and Compressed Work Schedule Act of 1978.[32]

A four-day workweek does not necessarily mean that the plant or company operates only four days a week. Rather, it means that the individual employee's work commitment is for only four days, and typically for ten hours per day. Under different programs, however, the total number of hours worked per employee varies from as low as thirty-two to as high as forty-eight. In addition, not all employees in such organizations are on a four-day schedule. Frequent starting points for such programs are in units such as data-processing departments that may already be using afternoon or night shifts or hospital nursing staffs where round-the-clock shift work is necessary.[33]

Companies using the four-day week generally reported desirable consequences, including increased morale, reduced absenteeism, enhanced recruiting, improvements in traffic flow, and increased productivity. Reported difficulties included resistance of working mothers to ten-hour shifts, complaints from parents that they were not spending enough time with children, less effective service to customers, scheduling and coordination problems, and worker fatigue.[34]

One obstacle to adopting the four-day week can be union adherence to the idea that any work in one day beyond eight hours should be paid at overtime rates. Various state laws may also be obstacles, although a number of states have modified their laws to encourage compressed workweek schedules. At one time, the Walsh-Healey Act was a problem for the compressed workweek because of its requirement of overtime pay beyond eight hours. Amendments to that law and the Contract Work Hours and Safety Standards Act now allow for compressed workweek schedules of forty or fewer hours to fall within the definitions of "normal workdays" and "normal workweeks" so that overtime payments are not required.[35]

Flextime

Increasingly, **flextime** (sometimes called flexitime, flexible hours workweek, variable working hours, or *gleitzeit* — gliding time) is being adopted by organizations around the world. Flextime is a schedule under which employees may choose when to arrive at work and when to depart and which includes a *core time* when everyone must be on the job. For example, employees may be free to arrive anytime between

7:00 and 10:00 a.m. and leave between 3:00 and 6:00 p.m., but all must be on company premises between 10:00 and 3:00 (see Figure 8.2). Further, there are usually rules about the total number of hours that must be worked during one week (for example, forty) or during two weeks (for example, eighty). Typically under flextime, all employees fill out time sheets or punch the time clock.

In 1985, about 12 percent of all workers in the United States were on flexible schedules.[36] A 1989 survey found one-half of the 196 companies that responded to be using some kind of a flextime program.[37] Some of the U.S. firms that have adopted the concept are Hewlett-Packard Co., Digital Equipment Corp., Corning Glass Works, TRW Inc., Conoco Inc., Metropolitan Life Insurance Co., and Control Data Corp.[38] Thousands of firms in Europe have also adopted some version of flextime, and in England, Parliament has authorized its use for Britain's half-million civil servants. Very few programs appear to have been terminated.[39]

Flextime is a substantial departure from traditional management practices. It may require a change in management's attitudes about the control of worker behavior. Further, successful application also requires solving problems that are unique to each situation.

Some of the advantages to flextime appear to be as follows:

- Employees can adjust their schedules to spend more time with their families.
- Employees and work units can manage their own schedules within limits to adjust to their own particular lifestyles.
- Stress over concern about tardiness beyond one's control (for example, traffic jams) is reduced.
- Peak traffic times can be avoided, and less time is spent commuting.
- Personal matters such as dentist or doctor appointments can be attended to more easily.
- Tardiness almost disappears.
- Deceptive use of sick leave diminishes.[40]

Some of the disadvantages of flextime appear to be as follows:

- There can be a lack of availability of employees during the flexible work periods at the beginning and end of the workday. This can adversely affect customers, suppliers, and fellow employees.

7:00 A.M.	9:00 A.M.	11:30 A.M.	1:30 P.M.	4:00 P.M.	6:00 P.M.
Flexible Period	Core Period	Flexible Lunchtime (30 Minutes)	Core Period	Flexible Period	

FIGURE 8.2 Example of a flextime schedule

- There is an increased need to coordinate within and between units as to time availability and to ensure coverage of vital functions such as staffing switchboards.
- Time reporting becomes more burdensome because employees may vary their hours and carry over hours.[41]
- There can be abuses, such as some employees taking extended lunches, which occurred in some federal agencies. (As a result, Congress gave agency heads the authority to restrict or end flextime if continuation does not appear to be in the public interest.)[42]

Generally favorable results from flextime have been reported by both European and American organizations. The research studies that have been conducted report generally increased job satisfaction and either no change or an improvement in job performance.[43]

Permanent Part-Time Work

Permanent part-time workers constitute one category of what can be called **contingent workers,** workers who are on the payroll of an organization in a part-time or temporary capacity, or who are subcontractors, consultants, or "leased" employees. Leased employees are those that are "rented" long term from a temporary help agency.[44] A 1989 study found 91 percent of 521 responding organizations using contingent workers of some kind.[45]

Increasingly, organizations are revising their work rules and employment practices to use **permanent part-time employees.** Such employees are frequently used to solve some operating problem such as the need for adequate coverage during peak hours. *Part-time* can mean some reduced proportion of the regular day or fewer days per week, or both, or fewer weeks or months per year. The word *permanent* can mean certain employees working part-time for an extended number of years or can connote the organization's ongoing allocation of a proportion of its payroll budget to part-time positions.

An example of widespread use of permanent part-time workers is the use of **peak-time employees** in banks and savings and loan institutions. For example, The Provident Bank in Cincinnati and the Western Savings & Loan Association in Phoenix supplement their staffs with part-time tellers at peak periods, such as noon hours and Friday afternoons. Typically, such employees are paid a significantly higher hourly wage than regular employees, but they receive no supplemental benefits except those required by law if they work more than one thousand hours per year.[46]

There are many variations in part-time work. For example, the Shawmut Bank of Boston has employed about a dozen people for a nine-month work year with summers off, a program that attracts women who want to spend substantial time with their children in the summers. They are replaced by college students during their three-month break.[47] Western Airlines uses many part-time ticket agents and baggage handlers to cover maximum staffing needs early and late in the day.[48]

According to estimates, one-half to three-fourths of all business firms use permanent, part-time employees, although the proportion of the work force involved is usually only from 2 to 7 percent.[49] This trend was further stimulated by federal legislation enacted in 1978 and by laws or policies in thirty-five states encouraging public agencies to employ permanent part-time workers, who are entitled to certain benefits and advancement opportunities ordinarily reserved for full-time people.[50]

Men are increasingly requiring flexible or part-time schedules to allow time for child care as well as time to pursue other responsibilities or interest.

Many of the regular part-time workers in the work force are women — and sometimes men — who need to be employed less than full-time in order to take care of children or to pursue other responsibilities or interests. In particular, women returning from maternity leave tend to be interested in part-time work arrangements for several months or even several years. A frequently found work schedule is 9:30 a.m. to 2:30 p.m. Others who are employed part-time in relatively large numbers are students.

Some firms report low turnover, ease in recruitment, and high productivity as advantages in using part-time employees. Further, part-time workers usually receive fewer employee benefits than full-time employees, and thus their use reduces labor costs. Disadvantages include increased complexity of supervision, increased administrative costs, and from the employee's point of view, fewer benefits.[51] Although part-time workers' job satisfaction has been found to be high in many instances, a study of fifty-five stores in a Midwest retail chain found part-time workers' job satisfaction to be lower than that of full-time workers.[52]

Job Sharing One version of the use of part-time employees is the concept of **job sharing,** in which a job is split into two four-hour segments and shared, for example, by two people who want to devote more time to families or other interests. Another version involves one person working full days for part of a week and the other person working the other days. Job sharing obviously requires coordination and compatibility between the two people to ensure continuity and effective performance from day to day. Organizations frequently find that the total performance from the two half-time employees exceeds what ordinarily would be expected from one full-time employee.[53] (The concept of job sharing should not be confused with the concept of work sharing, which is a reduction in hours or days worked by a large group of employees, usually in order to spread the work and avoid layoffs with a budget cutback. For example, an entire plant may work thirty hours per week as opposed to the usual forty hours.)[54]

An example of job sharing occurred at United Air Lines, Inc. during a period of financial difficulty in 1980. Rather than simply lay off junior flight attendants, the company approached the Association of Flight Attendants for recommendations about how to reduce the payroll. The union proposed, and the company accepted, a temporary job-sharing program under which two flight attendants could agree to share a job for a four-month period. Volunteers, in pairs, worked out their own schedules, and pay was allocated between the two in proportion to the amount of time flown.[55] Control Data employed young minority mothers and teenagers in a job-sharing arrangement. Young mothers were employed from 9 a.m. to 3 p.m. while their children were in school; teenagers came to work after school from 3 to 6 p.m. The system was so successful that Control Data extended it to other inner-city plants.[56]

According to both employers and employees who have participated in job sharing, some of its advantages in addition to the extra performance, include the energy and enthusiasm the employees bring to the job and employer accessibility to a wider range of applicants. For example, the pool of applicants can include retirees, students, people whose family responsibilities prohibit full-time work, and people who simply want more free time.

Job sharing has two main disadvantages. First, if the two people who are involved do not communicate and cooperate well, the costs in inefficiency can be considerable. Usually, this has not been a problem. The other disadvantage is the potentially increased costs of supplemental benefits. For example, state unemployment insurance and social security taxes may cost more for the two people than if only one person were employed.[57]

Telecommuting

Telecommuting is one form of **home-based work,** or working at home for an employer. It is predicted that **telecommuting** — working at home through the use of computer and word processor equipment linked by telephone to the home office — will involve as many as 15 million workers in the United States by the mid-1990s. Organizations like Aetna Life and Casualty Co., Investors Diversified Services, The Chase Manhattan Bank, N.A., and Blue Cross and Blue Shield have experimented with the idea with small numbers of employees.[58] In 1981, J.C. Penney Company, Inc., began employing several telephone sales associates to work in their homes, and within a few years the program was greatly expanded. In 1986, California's Pacific Bell instituted a telecommuting program involving more than two hundred employees.[59]

However, nationwide, the number of persons involved by 1989 was still not large. A survey of employed persons by *The Wall Street Journal* found only 3 percent of the respondents working at home full-time, although it should be noted that some 35 percent of the respondents completed part of their work at home. Examples would be people who finish reports on their home computers at night or on weekends.[60]

Typically, the telecommuter is in a nonmanagerial role, but some managers have found they can increase their productivity by working part-time at home using a computer linked to the home office. It appears that full-time telecommuters are paid differently from regular employees: they are often paid by the project — frequently grossing more than their colleagues back at the office — but sometimes are ineligible for supplemental benefits. Examples of jobs in which telecommuters are frequently found are computer programming, financial analysis, processing insurance claims or catalogue orders, and word processing.[61]

The advantages of telecommuting are several:

- Parents with small children or persons with disabilities can work at home.
- People who dislike commuting can avoid the traffic and time spent commuting.
- Employees save what it would ordinarily cost to commute to work.
- Employees can schedule their own hours.
- Employees can work some days at home and some days at the office, depending on the nature of the tasks to be done.
- Substantial increases in employee productivity have been reported.
- Telecommuters may earn more gross pay.
- Employers have a larger pool of potential employees from which to recruit.

But there are disadvantages:

- Telecommuting diminishes the ties between employee and supervisor and coworkers.
- The company of others helps meet some basic human needs; telecommuting decreases face-to-face interaction. (Some telecommuters have reduced the sense of isolation by meeting colleagues for lunch periodically; some firms have telecommuters work in the office one or two days per week.)
- Telecommuting requires changes in management style: supervisors must rely on the honor system or piecework compensation systems and plan to stay in touch with the employee because there is no longer the informal office contact.
- Telecommuters usually do not receive health and pension benefits.
- There is concern among some telecommuters and employees who are potential telecommuters that they may "stagnate" at home, losing touch with the company information and influence network and missing out on promotions.
- Some unions believe there is the potential for exploitation in the case of individually negotiated piecework arrangements, leading to wide disparities in compensation for telecommuters, similar to the problems that led to the outlawing of home work in the garment industries in the early 1940s. This is not considered a major problem.
- Weight gains because of easy access to the refrigerator are reported by some telecommuters.[62]

In general, it appears that telecommuting will increase. Its application is limited largely to information-manipulating or information-creating jobs, such as writing, financial analysis, typing letters and statistical tables, computer programming, and data processing.

Temporary Employees   The use of temporary workers appears to be growing. To illustrate, according to Secretary of Labor Robert Reich, 90 percent of the jobs created in February of 1993 were temporary jobs and held by people who would rather have had full-time, regular positions. Further, it was reported that, at that time, fully one-third of American workers were contingent employees with temporary, part-time, or contract jobs, usually with no benefits nor job security. While these practices provide flexibility and lower costs (at least short term) for employers, many are arguing that these trends are running counter to increased emphasis on employee involvement and the development of high-performance organizations.[63]

Role of the Human Resources Department

The human resources department has important and ongoing roles relative to work rules, disciplinary procedures, and work schedules. One role is to diagnose continuously the effects on employee morale and performance. This can be done through extensive and frequent informal contacts with employees, supervisors, and managers, and through more systematic procedures, such as climate surveys that are tailored to include questions about these areas.

Another important role — frequently overlooked by human resources departments and by managers in general — is anticipating and understanding the impact that a change in a rule or practice will have on other parts of the system. For example, when four University of Tennessee employees became telecommuters for several months, they and their supervisors felt that their work was as good as or better than before, but the employees left back at the office felt that they were put under more pressure to answer phones and help out with rush jobs.[64] Ideally, the human resources department works with managers to anticipate such side effects caused by the changes and helps alleviate problems if they occur.

Monitoring compliance with local, state, and federal laws pertaining to working hours and overtime is also an important role for the human resources department. Violations have the potential of being very expensive. For example, in 1991, ITT-Rayonier, based in Hoquiam, Washington, was ordered by a federal district court to pay ninety-one mechanics in its pulp mills $28 million in back wages for uncompensated "on call" hours in violation of the Fair Labor Standards Act. In addition, the company was assessed an equal amount — $28 million — as a penalty for failing to comply in good faith with the overtime laws.[65] ITT appealed, and the Ninth Circuit Court reversed the judgment, finding that time spent waiting for work is compensable only if the time is spent primarily for the benefit of the employer. In this case, the mechanics were free to pursue a wide variety of personal activities while on call and thus were not entitled to overtime compensation.[66] Human resources departments, therefore, must carefully evaluate the degree to which employees are restricted in their activities under a call-in policy. More broadly, HR departments must monitor all activities that might be considered time worked and thus might subject the organization to lawsuits for back pay and penalties. (In China, some of this monitoring is done by a Communist party secretary to ensure that party ideology is maintained. See *International Perspective* on page 203.)

Finally, human resources specialists, and all managers, must treat all employees — day-shift employees, afternoon- and evening-shift workers, part-time

International Perspective

Working in China

The Lun Feng stuffed-toy factory is one of about 1,000 Guangdong manufacturing operations that together employ more than 2 million people. As one of approximately 10,000 joint ventures established since 1979, most along the coast, Lun Feng represents both the promise and the problems that have accompanied Deng's economic reforms.

To upgrade Lun Feng for state-of-the-art stuffed-toy manufacture, which means loading an empty building with sewing machines, Lun Feng's Hong Kong joint-venture partner lent the factory's nominal owner, the town of Kai Kong, more than $1 million. Since then, Lun Feng has been on his own.

It is possible for a non-Communist to be a factory manager in China, but most managers are still card carrying party members. Even so, there is always a party secretary to enforce Communist discipline. Before Deng's reforms, there was no question that the Communist secretary dominated, even if he was functionally illiterate in basic business precepts. Since 1984, though, Beijing has directed that party secretaries leave operations to the factories' designated managers — a direct slap at Leninist ideology, which holds that since the party is the only body capable of enforcing the will of the workers, factories must be under party control.

On the ground, however, where nothing is ever simple, the power relationship varies from place to place. "It is nothing more than a normal battle for control," admits a factory party secretary in Ji-nan. "I don't know much about what my factory actually does, but that doesn't mean I don't want to be the boss." At Lun Feng, Deng's system

works fairly well. Only after Tiananmen did the secretary actively meddle, but then just to direct that the radio be tuned to a mainland station rather than one in Hong Kong. The music the workers listen to all day is the same, but the news is different.

There seem to be three keys to Lun Feng's success. The first is its location on the Kai Kong River, which allows the factory to ship its goods by sea and not by the country's notoriously awful roads.

Lun Feng's second ace is electricity. Across China, electric power is in such short supply that even favored state-owned operations must shut down for two or three days a week. Lun Feng beat the power problem with money. For about $3 million, the factory installed five auxiliary diesel generators. With eleven workers maintaining the equipment 24 hours a day, eight seconds is the longest Lun Feng has been without power.

Then there are "the girls," about 3,000 of them, who work from 7:30 in the morning until 11 at night six days a week. None I speak with are over 19. Almost all are from Hunan province. Most stay no more than two years and then return home to marry. They earn close to $200 a month, an almost unheard-of wage in China.

As troublesome as it can sometimes be to have a mercurial government as one's business partner, greater problems arise from a mismatch of position and personnel. Most jobs are assigned by the government, often with little regard for a person's qualifications or preferences.

Source: Excerpted from Michael Kramer, "Free to Fly Inside the Cage," *Time*, October 2, 1989, p. 68. Copyright 1989 The Time Inc. Magazine Company. Reprinted by permission.

people, and telecommuters — as valuable resources. Achieving high morale and motivation in these groups, as well as strong organizational performance, requires this kind of effort.

Summary

Factors that influence the design of work rules and schedules are management philosophy; work-group norms; the technology, equipment, and materials used by the organization; and social and cultural norms and attitudes. Work rules and schedules are necessary in organizational life to ensure coordination and reasonable predictability of employee behavior. Work rules are also necessary to protect employees from hazardous conditions and inequities in treatment.

Work rules that are too strict or confining will impede the fulfillment of such human needs as those for affiliation, cooperation, autonomy, and self-actualization and may lead to subterfuge and resentment. Rules that are too lax may lead to inefficiencies as well as morale problems. Work rules that tend to protect jobs, such as lines of demarcation between crafts, may provide job security in the short run but, if too restrictive, may have serious consequences for organizational effectiveness and survival in the long run.

Management needs to be clear about the consequences of rule violations. The principle of progressive discipline is advocated as good practice in most discipline cases. Supervisors ordinarily have responsibility for discipline in their units. However, most organizations require review by higher authority before a discharge can be made final. Increasingly, the right to discharge is being affected by federal law, EEOC rulings, and court decisions.

The typical workday in the United States is slightly less than eight hours; the workweek is typically five days. Overtime payments of time and one-half for hours worked beyond forty in one week to nonexempt employees are required under the Fair Labor Standards Act.

Shift work has advantages for some people, but negative consequences are also frequently experienced. Management needs to pay special attention to the problems of shift workers and to make sure that they and their work activities are integrated with the work and the people on day schedules.

There has been substantial interest in and experimentation with different kinds of work schedules in recent years, including the compressed workweek, flextime, permanent part-time work, job sharing, and telecommuting. All of these practices have advantages and disadvantages, and their applicability depends on specific circumstances of the organization and the job. Temporary work appears to be growing, and some believe that this trend is running counter to the development of high-performing organizations.

The human resources department plays important roles with respect to work rules, discipline, and work schedules. Two of these roles are to diagnose continuously the effects of current rules, procedures, and schedules on employee morale and performance and to make suggestions for changes. Cooperation with other managers and sensitivity to employee needs and problems are important to the success of the human resources department in these matters. Monitoring compliance with laws pertaining to working hours and overtime is also an important function that has major cost implications.

Ethical Dilemma

Sharon is a superb worker but has some difficulty getting to work on time, sometimes arriving forty-five minutes late. Her boss, Andy, is uneasy about this since company policy is to dock the pay of nonsupervisory employees for tardiness beyond five minutes. Allowing employees to make up the time is not permitted. But Sharon frequently and willingly works beyond quitting time when the work piles up. Andy, therefore, does not dock her pay for tardiness, although the situation is very irritating to him. He does not talk about the matter with his other subordinates.

What are the ethical issues involved, if any? What are the consequences of allowing this situation to continue? What should Andy do?

Key Terms

restrictive work rules	nonexempt employees
garnishment	exempt employees
insubordination	shift work
disciplinary action	chronobiologists
discharge	circadian cycles
warnings	compressed workweek
demotion	flextime
disciplinary layoff	contingent workers
docking	permanent part-time employees
documentation	peak-time employees
progressive discipline	job sharing
decision-making leave	home-based work
overtime work	telecommuting

Review Questions

1. Discuss several organizational factors that influence the extent of control over the behavior of employees.
2. Explain why work rules are necessary in organizations.
3. Discuss the consequences of overly restrictive work rules.
4. What is progressive discipline? Cite the usual steps in progressive discipline.
5. Who should have responsibility for discipline in organizations? Discuss.
6. Discuss the advantages and disadvantages of shift work, the compressed workweek, flextime, permanent part-time work, job sharing, and telecommuting.
7. Discuss the role of the human resources department in managing work rules and schedules.

Opening Case Questions

Case 8.1 Several Subcultures at Simply Scrumptious

1. If management creates several categories of employees through flexible work arrangements — for example, the categories mentioned in the case — what kinds of work rules or conditions might cause tensions between these groups?

2. Discuss some possible ways to minimize friction in the management of different categories of employees.
3. Using ERG theory and equity theory (from Chapter 4), develop a few general principles that could be useful in managing such subgroups.

Case 8.2 Just a Bundle of Laughs

1. Does Bill have any grounds for firing Charlie since he has no warnings on file? Explain.
2. If you had been Charlie's coworker and were asked to testify at the grievance proceedings, how would you handle the situation?

Comprehensive **Case**

The Benefits of Flexibility

Most companies that experiment with nontraditional work arrangements — job sharing, flexible schedules, and telecommuting — do so to help employees cope with some of the difficulties of modern life. The stay-at-home housewife or househusband is becoming rarer, but someone still needs to take Junior to ballet lessons or drive Grandma to the doctor. In the past decade, as the number of families with a parent at home has dwindled, the number of workers responsible for an aging relative has doubled. Even the environment has become a factor in work schedules, since every employee who works at home usually means one fewer car adding to the city's smog.

What many organizations that moved away from the nine-to-five week have found, however, is that new schedules can increase productivity, morale, and efficiency. Flexible job arrangements also often require managers to be creative, well organized, and flexible themselves. More and more, these arrangements are being viewed not as Band-Aid solutions to crises, but as innovative ways to increase the use of employees' potential.

Those interested in nontraditional work schedules often must overcome the perception that someone who isn't in the office from nine to five every day isn't doing as much work as other employees. But in reality a well-managed program of flexible schedules or telecommunting can increase productivity. Ironically, by staying at home during "work" hours, employees are able to make a clearer distinction between work time and personal time. Someone on a four-day, ten-hour schedule can use the day off to get the car fixed and have the pooch's nails trimmed, rather than doing such chores on expanded lunch hours. With more control over personal distractions, employees can more conscientiously devote their work hours to work.

Some companies that have experimented with alternative schedules have seen immediate rewards. When a ten-person department at Xerox Corp. moved to flexible schedules, productivity rose 10 percent while absenteeism dropped. Companies like Automatic Data Processing and The Travelers Companies, which are known as innovators in work schedules, find that the ability to control their work time attracts talented employees and reduces turnover. A stable work force, in turn, tends to produce a stable customer base. A study in Arizona showed that 80 percent of the supervisors surveyed felt that telecommuting increased productivity and two-thirds felt that it improved their departments' efficiency. It should come as no shock to any student of human behavior that people work best when they are most comfortable.

Many people involved in flexible scheduling find that it yields more subtle but important changes in their own skills and attitudes. People who no longer have the luxury of wandering into a colleague's office every time they have a question find that they become more organized, direct, and concise when they go to their telephone or terminal to get their question answered. Managers responsible for employees who aren't always around find that they learn to focus more on objectives and results rather than on how employees are reaching those results.

Such gains, of course, require flexibility on the managers' part and attention to a number of potential problems. Arranging meetings may be difficult if all the necessary participants are on different schedules. Fairness becomes a major issue: should employees without children or aging relatives be asked to work steadier hours than colleagues with more complicated personal lives? If one employee gets permission to work three twelve-hour days in order to spend long weekends with a sick parent in another state, should another employee be given the same schedule in order to ski on weekdays?

Job sharing, in which two people share one full-time position, can create its own set of problems, especially in service industries. Customers may want to deal with just one person, and may be frustrated when told "She's not in today." Both the individuals themselves and their supervisors need to communicate clearly and follow established procedures so that the daily or weekly transitions from one employee to another don't create constant chaos.

Now that the time clock has disappeared in many businesses and the forty-hour work week is being divided up in creative ways, many long-standing assumptions about work are being challenged. Some unions and labor laws were originally created to free workers from the tyranny of twelve-hour shifts, yet now some experts are advocating such shifts as a safe and healthy way to meet business needs and fulfill employee desires. At the same time, employees who years ago would have given anything to escape the world of office politics and snooping bosses now find that they are lonely working home alone and opt to spend more time at the office than they need to. As lifestyles continue to change along with employee and employer needs, it is likely that the number of alternative work schedules will continue to grow.

Sources: Shari Caudron, "Working at Home Pays Off," *Personnel Journal* 71 (November 1992):40–49; Richard M. Coleman, "Twelve-Hour Shift Schedules: What You Need to Know," *HRfocus* 69 (May 1992):16–17; Sue Shellenbarger, "Managers Navigate Uncharted Waters Trying to Resolve Work-Family Conflicts," *The Wall Street Journal*, December 7, 1992, B1, B4.

Discussion Questions

1. What are some of the positive aspects of telecommuting or other forms of working at home? What are some of the problems?
2. What are some of the positive aspects of flextime? Job sharing? What are the problems with each?

CHAPTER 9

Recruitment and Selection

LEARNING OBJECTIVES

- Define the recruitment process and describe the organizational and environmental factors that affect it.
- Identify the basic methods of recruitment and the roles played by different types of managers.
- Explain how and why organizations attempt to recruit specific groups such as women, minorities, and persons with disabilities.
- Define the selection process and identify the roles of the human resources staff and other managers.
- Explain the concepts of reliability, validity, and job relatedness and their relation to selection standards.
- Describe the main sources of information about job applicants.
- Identify the advantages and difficulties of testing procedures.
- Explain the different types of interviews, the problems that an interviewer must confront, and the characteristics of an effective interview.

209

CASE 9.1   New Components in the Electronics Business

Electrotech, Inc., was a small electronics firm founded by two young and ambitious engineers. For the five years of its existence, the company had specialized in the design of circuits for complex industrial and scientific applications. Now, though, Electrotech was changing almost overnight. Jim Odrobina, one of the founders, had patented a small component, known as the QT-48, that had proved extremely useful in the circuits the company designed. As word of the device spread, other firms began to order QT-48s for their own uses. Lately, the orders had rolled in much faster than the company could fill them. Then last week had come the clincher: Jim had returned from a trip to Washington with the news that the Defense Department wanted eighty thousand of the components and would probably order hundreds of thousands in the next year!

The implications were obvious. To meet such demand, the company would have to add an entire manufacturing department, different from all of the firm's other departments. Moreover, as a government contractor, Electrotech would be subject to many new rules and regulations. Beth Ann McNulty, human resources director, was especially concerned about government rules regarding equal employment opportunity (EEO) for such groups as women, minorities, and the disabled. In general, she felt that the question of finding *people* for the new jobs was being somewhat overlooked in all the excitement about machinery and robot arms and huge contracts. Today, after clearing her desk, Beth poured herself a fresh cup of coffee and began to list the major personnel problems:

- To begin with, where would the new manufacturing workers come from? Electrotech was located in a suburban town with little manufacturing industry. Would employment agencies in nearby cities be much help? For the less skilled positions, could Beth use the placement offices of regional vocational-technical schools? Where should she advertise?

- The surrounding suburban towns were almost all white, but the region as a whole contained sizable black and Hispanic communities. Would the federal or state government require the firm to recruit in these communities? If so, how could it best be done?

- According to the basic plan being developed, the supervisors for the manufacturing department would be chosen from among the current managerial-level employees — people who could be trusted, in Jim Odrobina's view. But would engineers make good managers of a manufacturing line? Wouldn't it be better to recruit from outside?

- Could some of the new jobs be designed to suit the disabled? Wouldn't this be necessary, in fact, to establish equal employment opportunity?

- And, finally, a subject close to Beth's heart: What about women employees? Currently, all but two of the engineers were men. All but three of the secretaries and clerks were women. Beth had excused this situation on the grounds that women engineers were hard to find, but now she believed, for both ethical and legal reasons, that the proportion of female employees — especially in high-level positions — would have to be increased as the company expanded.

In the heady atmosphere of the company's tremendous boom, Beth didn't want to be a lonely critic. Yet she felt that the personnel problems had to be confronted squarely or the results could be disastrous. She was glad she had convinced Jim Odrobina to convene a meeting of department heads so they could all discuss the hiring program. Beth drank another cup of coffee as she prepared her notes for the meeting. She was going to acquaint these engineers with the basic facts of EEO; she would recommend that a firm of outside consultants be hired to develop an affirmative action program; and she would offer her own plan for recruiting supervisors. Most of all, she hoped to convince everyone that recruiting and selecting the right people would require cooperation and commitment from every manager in the organization. ◀

CASE 9.2

It's Only Common Sense, Isn't It?

Budget Office Supplies was moving toward self-directed teams in its numerous retail outlets. Teams were organized by product specialty, such as computers and computer supplies, fax machines and telephones, office furniture, and so on.

The new teams were assigned responsibility for scheduling work and selecting team members, as well as for managing inventory and customer relations. Although the human resources department did most of the recruiting and, along with supervisors, had an important role in preliminary screening, the teams had considerable autonomy in selecting new members. An attempt was made to reach consensus on the employment of a given candidate, with all team members, the supervisor, and the human resources department in agreement.

Initially, team members were trained in interviewing techniques by the training department. Role playing was used extensively. Team members were also taught what they could ask in an interview and what was prohibited by state and federal law. However, selection-interview training was not extended to new people who had been added to teams. Mistakes were becoming more frequent.

In the most recent set of interviews, half of the fax and telephone department team had talked with four candidates while the other half of the team was waiting on customers. The latter subgroup would then talk with the same candidates in a second interview. Let's listen in on the conversation among the team members who had just finished the interviewing.

Yoshi: "Mitch, you asked the two women candidates if they had children. You can't do that under state law. We're likely to have a discrimination suit on our hands."

Mitch: "I was just trying to find out if they would have problems getting to work. Besides, if they have kids, they'll be on the phone all of the time."

Carolyn: "What kind of assumptions are you making, Mitch? I've got two kids — one in kindergarten and the other in the fourth grade — and I'm seldom on the phone. Besides, I do more than my fair share of the work."

Mitch: "Well, I was just trying to use some common sense."

Yoshi: "Common sense or not, assumptions or no assumptions, what you asked is just plain illegal."

Carl: "Maybe we ought to get our employment office people to meet with us and give us a refresher course on what we can ask and can't ask. The rules are kind of hazy in my mind at this point."

Mitch: "I'd go for that."   ◄

The staffing process — putting the right people in the right positions at the right times — is one of the most critical tasks any organization faces. The quality of the work performed can be only as high as the capabilities of the people performing it. This chapter examines the two initial stages in staffing an organization. **Recruitment** is the process of finding qualified people and encouraging them to apply for work with the firm. **Selection** is the process of choosing among those who do apply. Together, these two facets of human resources management supply the lifeblood of the organization.

The Recruitment Process

Ideally, the recruitment process should ensure that, for every position available in the firm, there is a sufficient number of qualified applicants. As Beth Ann McNulty realized in Case 9.1, these applicants should include members of both sexes and various social groups such as minorities and disabled workers. Especially for larger organizations, recruitment is a complex and continuing process that demands extensive planning and effort.

Organizational Factors   Many factors pertaining to the organization itself affect the success of the recruitment program. Probably the most important factor is the company's reputation in terms of its products or services. Overall, the company projects a certain image to the community at large, and this influences its ability to attract qualified workers. In many cases, good advertising and successful public relations efforts can increase community knowledge of the company, raise public appreciation, and thus make a dramatic impact on recruitment.

Relations with labor unions can be critical to public perceptions of the firm, as can the company's reputation for offering high or low wages. Subtle elements in the organizational culture and climate are also important. Since many people hear about job possibilities from friends or relatives already working at the firm, attitudes about the company are passed along through this informal network. For instance, if current employees are confused by the leadership style or annoyed by what they perceive as lack of recognition for their efforts, their casual comments may discourage their friends from applying.

Cost is an important factor in recruitment. A small firm, for example, may not have the resources to interview candidates at colleges outside the region or to pay the travel expenses of candidates who might be invited from outside the area. To illustrate, the average cost of recruiting an exempt employee in 1990 was $6,900, and this did not include relocation costs, which can be substantially larger.[1] Each firm will need to analyze the costs involved in alternative methods of recruitment.

Environmental Factors

In addition to factors within an organization, the external environment influences recruitment success in a variety of ways. Most obviously, the condition of the labor market affects the supply of qualified applicants. If a firm cannot find enough skilled applicants in the immediate area, it may need a regional or national search program. Competition from other companies can reduce the pool of qualified workers or raise salary expectations beyond what the firm is willing to pay.

Economic trends can influence both the number of people pursuing certain occupations and the demand for their services. While computer scientists are in demand, steel and textile workers may face layoffs. In this century, the rapid pace of technological change has accelerated these trends. Not only do products become obsolete from one year to the next, but manufacturing processes and the skills needed to carry them out can undergo similar change. Since the labor market may not keep pace with these developments, special training programs may be necessary. Organizations can encourage colleges and vocational schools to offer courses in new specialties. At times, however, a firm may need to restructure some of its jobs to adapt them to the people available.

Social attitudes about particular types of employment will also affect the supply of workers. If a job is considered uninteresting, oppressive, or low in status, applicants will shun it unless the wages are extremely attractive.

In some industries, unions may control the supply of applicants. In the garment and construction trades, for example, potential employees are often referred by the union hiring hall. Although discrimination against nonunion members is illegal, the union can evaluate applicants in terms of work experience and acquired skills, and under these conditions the applicants who are referred will usually be union members.

Finally, federal and state regulations concerning equal employment opportunity and affirmative action set the framework within which a recruitment program must function. Later sections of this chapter discuss responses to the legal environment.

Managerial Roles

Responsibility for the overall recruitment process normally is assigned to human resources managers. They are responsible for designing and implementing a recruitment program that will meet the company's personnel needs while complying with all legal requirements. This responsibility includes finding sources of applicants; writing and placing advertisements; contacting schools, agencies, and labor unions; establishing procedures to guarantee equal employment opportunity; and administering the funds the firm has budgeted for recruitment.

But these goals probably would not be attained without the cooperation of other managers, who are in the best position to predict the needs of their own departments. They are responsible for deciding how tasks should be accomplished and what kinds of people are needed to fill each type of position. They can often anticipate retirements, resignations, and other kinds of vacancies and can determine whether any of their current staff members are ready for promotion. Typically, when a vacancy occurs, the appropriate supervisor or manager completes a personnel requisition form, which usually requires higher management approval. (See Figure 9.1, the Erie Insurance Group's request-for-personnel form.)

ERIE
INSURANCE
GROUP

An Equal Opportunity Employer

HR USE ONLY			

REQUEST FOR PERSONNEL

POSITION DATA

JOB TITLE

NUMBER OF EMPLOYEES NEEDED ►

SALARY RANGE ►

REQUESTOR

DATE

☐ DIVISION   (LIST)
☐ BRANCH OFFICE
☐ DISTRICT CLAIMS OFFICE
☐ DISTRICT SALES OFFICE

DEPARTMENT   (LIST)

SECTION

UNIT

CHOOSE ONE ►   ☐ Full Time   ☐ Part Time   ☐ Temporary   ☐ Contract Labor   And Complete The Appropriate Section Below

IF FULL TIME OR PART TIME ►   List Work Schedule if Other Than 8:00-4:00 Monday-Friday

☐ REPLACEMENT   Who is Being Replaced ?

☐ ADDITION   List Reason(s) for Addition

IF TEMPORARY OR CONTRACT LABOR ►   List Work Schedule if Other Than 8:00-4:30 Monday-Friday

REASON NEEDED

DATE NEEDED   HOW LONG NEEDED

POSITION REQUIREMENTS

EXPERIENCE

EDUCATION

SKILLS

REQUEST APPROVAL

IMMEDIATE SUPERVISOR

APPROVED BY (DEPARTMENT MANAGER)   DATE

APPROVED BY (DIVISION OFFICER/BRANCH MANAGER)   DATE

WHO WILL INTERVIEW (NOT APPLICABLE FOR CONTRACT LABORERS)?   EXTENSION

ARE THERE ANY DATES AND TIMES THE INTERVIEWER(S) IS NOT AVAILABLE FOR INTERVIEWING?

HR B-13 6/89 (R)

FIGURE 9.1 Example of a personnel requisition.   *Source:* Courtesy of the Erie Insurance Group.

Recruiting Within the Organization

For positions above the entry level, the best source of applicants may be the organization itself. Recognizing this, most firms follow a deliberate practice of recruiting from within.

Methods Finding qualified applicants within the organization is the main goal of the internal recruiting effort. There are several methods for locating these applicants. Among the most common are job posting, referrals, and skills inventories. Assessment centers are used by some larger firms to recruit and evaluate present employees who might be candidates for supervisory positions; these centers will be discussed in Chapter 10.

Job Posting Perhaps the most common method of finding applicants, **job posting** involves announcing job openings to all current employees. Bulletin board notices or printed bulletins can be used for this purpose. Some firms have developed computerized job posting systems so that employees can obtain information on their computer screens.[2] In some companies the personnel or human resources office publishes a monthly newsletter that lists the positions available. The announcements carry information about the nature of the position and the qualifications needed, and any employee who is interested may **bid** on the job — that is, enter the competition for it. Job posting can help ensure that minority workers and other disadvantaged groups become aware of opportunities to move up in the organization. For this reason, courts and federal agencies have frequently required job posting and bidding as part of the settlement of discrimination cases. Job posting systems were found in three-fourths of the firms surveyed in one study.[3]

College student wearing "unemployed" graduation cap. Although a college degree is a definite advantage in the eyes of recruiters, new college graduates are having a tougher time finding appropriate employment than graduates in previous decades.

Employee Referrals

Another way to find applicants within the organization is through **employee referrals** by other departments. Informal communications among managers can lead to the discovery that the best candidate for a job is already working in a different section of the firm. In some cases, referrals are made through "support networks" established by certain groups of employees; in recent years women's groups have had a noticeable influence in this area.

Skills Inventories

Many firms have developed computerized **skills inventories** of their employees. Information on every employee's skills, educational background, work history, and other important factors is stored in a data base, which can then be used to identify employees with the attributes needed for a particular job.

Advantages and Disadvantages

The chief advantage of recruitment from within the organization is that the employee is already known. His or her performance in the job will usually be more predictable than that of an outsider. In addition, less general training and orientation will be required, and less time will be needed for the person to adapt to the work environment. Especially for higher-level positions, external recruitment searches can be costly and difficult, and for this reason recruiting from within is often the more cost-effective option. Internal recruitment also serves to raise employee morale and improve the organizational climate.

In some cases, however, it may be impossible for a firm to fill a position with a member of its own staff. In other cases, especially in smaller companies, internal recruitment may be possible but inadvisable. If filling a gap in one department means creating an equally critical gap in another, the best course may be to recruit immediately from the outside. Moreover, if opportunities for advancement are few, promoting an individual who is not clearly the most qualified, nor the group's choice, may cause resentment. Obviously, the use of internal recruitment should be tied closely to long-range planning for career development.

Even for large organizations, an overreliance on internal recruitment can be harmful. Without occasional new blood from the outside, management may become stagnant, out of touch with the competition and the marketplace. Some firms may deliberately "raid" their competitors' staffs to bring in fresh ideas and to find out what competitors are doing. A major task in establishing an effective recruitment program is to decide the proper balance between internal and external recruiting.

Recruiting Outside the Organization

Finding qualified applicants from outside the organization is the most difficult part of recruitment. The success of an expanding company or one with many positions demanding specialized skills often depends on the effectiveness of the organization's recruitment program. Typically, the external recruitment process makes use of a variety of methods.

As in internal recruiting, employee referrals can be an important source of applicants. To encourage referrals, many firms offer incentive programs, which may include cash bonuses. In addition, labor unions can be a key source for applicants skilled in a particular craft. Under some contracts, the company may be required to give the union first notice of job openings; even when this is not required, doing so may help the company maintain good labor-management relations.

Often, however, a firm must take a more active recruitment role, mounting advertising campaigns, contacting a variety of placement agencies, or sending recruiters into the field to seek out qualified candidates. (For examples of innovative external recruiting methods, see Figure 9.2.)

Advertising

Advertising may range from the simplest "Help Wanted" ad to a nationwide, multimedia campaign. Whatever form it takes, it has the advantage of reaching relatively large numbers of potential applicants. An organization whose job openings are not rigidly defined may want to advertise widely in order to attract responses from people of many backgrounds. Normally, however, the most useful advertisement is one that specifies the exact nature of the job, the qualifications required, and the salary range. In all instances, the advertising medium should be selected carefully, with the target audience in mind. Ninety-seven percent of firms surveyed in one study used newspaper advertising as a recruiting tool.[4]

Placement Agencies

Educational institutions, ranging from high schools to universities, generally have placement offices to assist their graduates in finding work. Some universities and technical programs have their own newsletters to alert students and graduates to work opportunities, and an enterprising recruiter will take full advantage of this resource.

State placement agencies are another source of referrals. According to one study, more than 70 percent of the companies surveyed made use of the state employment service.[5] In most states the agency responsible for job placement is known as the **Job Service,** though the department to which it belongs may have any variety of titles, such as Department of Human Resources, Department of Employment, or Department of Labor and Industry. These agencies are partially funded by the United States Employment Service (USES) under the Wagner-Peyser Act of 1933.

The Department of Defense (DOD) is another source of referrals. Through a program called Operation Transition, the DOD assists any of the approximately 300,000 people discharged from the four military branches each year. Through a touch-tone telephone system, called the Defense Outplacement Referral System, employers may access minirésumés completed by military personnel stationed around the world. Once registered for this program, employers may advertise job openings on an electronic bulletin board, called Transition Bulletin Board, which is used by personnel at more than 350 bases worldwide.[6]

Both educational institutions and state Job Services provide referrals without charge either to the applicant or to the prospective employer. The DOD charges only a modest amount for the on-line time used. In contrast, private employment agencies, which are in business to earn a profit, charge a commission that is payable if and when an applicant is hired. Usually, the new employee is responsible for paying the fee, which can be as high as 20 percent of a year's wages. Sometimes a company will offer to pay the applicant's agency fee in order to make the position more attractive, and on occasion a firm may itself sign a contract with an agency.

A particular type of private agency, known as the **executive search firm,** has come into prominence recently. These agencies specialize in searching out top-level executives to fill critical corporate positions. Their clients are employers, not job

Telerecruiting Phone calls to potential candidates, with names obtained from mailing lists of professional associations, schools, and mailing list companies.

Direct Mail Using lists from above sources.

Point-of-Sale Recruiting Messages (posters, literature, messages on the back of cash register tapes) Useful if customers are potentially qualified applicants.

Talent Scout Cards One organization in need of customer-oriented service staff gave its managers "talent scout" cards inviting prospective candidates to apply for jobs. Managers were asked to distribute the cards to exceptionally friendly, helpful customer service personnel they encountered while doing their own shopping.

Posters Displayed on community bulletin boards, parks, laundromats, banks, etc.

Door Hangers Useful for recruiting in a specified geographical area.

Radio Alone or to refer candidates to open houses or large newspaper ads.

Billboards Fixed highway displays or electronic billboards with varying messages.

Hotlines and 800 Numbers Telephone lines with either recorded job vacancy messages or live interviewers. Live lines are increasingly being made available on Sundays, when most newspaper ads appear and candidates have the time to follow up on openings.

Information Seminars On job hunting skills, or on topics specific to one's industry, such as new developments in artificial intelligence. The latter may attract qualified professionals who would be reluctant to attend an open house or job fair, where the recruiting purpose was more explicit.

Welcome Wagon, Relocation Consultants, Realtors These organizations are aware of newcomers to the community. Increasingly, spouses of individuals transferred into the community are seeking work, and can be located through these sources.

Referral Programs Employee referral systems are common, but now some firms are encouraging their customers and suppliers to refer candidates as well.

Outplacement Firms and Local Layoffs Skilled employees who have lost their jobs through no fault of their own may be found by contacting outplacement firms and by monitoring the local paper for layoffs at other establishments in the community.

FIGURE 9.2 Innovative External Recruiting Methods
Source: Compiled from Catherine D. Fyock, "Expanding the Talent Search: 19 Ways to Recruit Top Talent," *HR Magazine*, July 1991, pp. 32–35.

seekers, and their sizable fees are generally payable whether or not any suitable candidates are found. Because they may lure the right executive away from another company, these firms have been derisively referred to as "headhunters"; yet many large corporations have come to rely on them. A substantial number of chief executive officers are now being recruited in this way.[7]

**Field
Recruiting**

Companies interested in recruiting new college graduates generally do more than simply contact school placement offices. They send recruiters to the campus itself to tell students what the company can offer and to screen potential applicants. The recruiting trip is coordinated with the placement office, which arranges facilities, helps to publicize the visit, and perhaps does an initial screening of the students. The company may also run notices in the student newspaper and other local publications that students are likely to read.

This sending of recruiters out into the environment is called **field recruiting.** For positions above the entry level, firms often engage in a different type of field recruiting. An engineering firm in the Midwest, for example, might send recruiters to a West Coast city where engineers have recently been laid off. An ad in the local paper would invite prospective applicants to meet the company's respresentatives at a certain hotel on a certain date. Often the best locations for field recruiting are meetings of professional associations, where members of particular professions gather to conduct seminars and present research papers. The associations themselves may maintain lists of members seeking work.

Internships

Placement directors, students, and recent college graduates tend to agree that the internships offered by many organizations constitute one of the most effective recruiting strategies. Internships usually involve employment the summer before graduation from college, and, of course, require a prior recruitment and selection process. Internships give the student a unique opportunity to experience a company firsthand; they also provide managers with an excellent opportunity to further assess the student's capabilities and potential. However, internships are time-consuming and expensive to operate, and they require considerable planning and supervision so that the student is engaged in meaningful work.[8]

**Unsolicited
Applicants**

Recruitment is an active and often aggressive process. To find the best candidates for employment, organizations get out and search for them. From time to time, however, excellent applicants turn up unexpectedly. In fact, a Department of Labor study found that, from the employee's point of view, direct application to the employer was the most likely means of obtaining a job.[9] A high proportion of firms (91 percent) consider walk-in applicants an important source of recruits, particularly for office-clerical and production positions.[10]

Generally, an unsolicited applicant will have to be told that no appropriate positions are currently available. By the time a position does become open, the applicant may have accepted work elsewhere. Nevertheless, carelessness in handling unsolicited applications can cost a firm some valuable employees, and a cold or haughty attitude in the personnel department can have a chilling effect on public attitudes toward the organization.

Recruiting Specific Groups

A network of laws and regulations helps to prevent discrimination in employment on the basis of race, color, religion, sex, national origin, age, or physical disability. Most firms, except the smallest, are covered by these government restrictions, and compliance with the law is a major concern in recruitment. An ad for a "salesman" would constitute sex discrimination in recruiting; a campaign to recruit only "recent" college graduates might leave the company open to charges of age discrimination. To comply with affirmative action guidelines, firms with government contracts are required to seek *actively* to develop sources of applicants in the legally protected groups.

Women

In recent decades the proportion of women in the workplace has grown steadily. By the year 2000, women are expected to make up 47 percent of the labor force in the United States.[11] Yet women are still underrepresented in many occupations and professions that have been traditionally held by men. Engineering is one example, as Case 9.1 shows; others are mechanics, industrial sales, and many types of administrative or managerial jobs. A major part of many recruitment programs is an effort to draw women into positions such as these.

For women advancing to managerial positions the organizational obstacles have been especially severe. The invisible barrier to advancement that confronts women and minorities is referred to in the media and also in the Civil Rights Act of 1991 as the **glass ceiling** (or the **glass wall** in the case of the lateral mobility).[12] Assumptions that women are too "emotional" to make rational decisions under pressure or that they will leave the company if they decide to have children are among the stereotypes that have prevented fair consideration of personal qualifications.

Some companies have found that career-planning and assertiveness-training programs can help to develop female managerial candidates while benefiting many male candidates as well.[13] Women's support networks have grown up within organizations and throughout major cities; these can nurture and encourage women managers and also provide useful referrals.

Men for Jobs Traditionally Held by Women

As a counterpoint to hiring women in roles once reserved for men, many firms have begun to hire men for jobs traditionally performed by women. The legal actions cited in Chapter 6 opened the position of flight attendant (originally "stewardess") to males; in addition, a significant number of men are now being hired as telephone operators, nurses, and secretaries.

Minorities

The most useful sources in recruiting minorities, according to one study, are — in order of most frequent use — referrals by employees, colleges and universities, advertising in targeted media, community agencies, private employment agencies specializing in the particular group, and the U.S. Employment Service.[14] When the recruitment campaign involves advertising, the ads may be most effective if they appear in minority media — a local newspaper for the black or Hispanic community, for example. Campus recruiting may take on an extra dimension as companies work with educational institutions to develop courses that will help minority students learn marketable skills. Some firms sponsor scholarships for minority undergraduates. Summer job programs can also help; a company that hires minority students for summer work will gain some word-of-mouth advertising in the community and a head start in screening and developing potential full-time employees.

Among minority groups, the hard-core unemployed are a particularly difficult segment to reach. Alienated from the majority culture, they may pay little attention to advertising campaigns, avoid private employment agencies that will charge them a fee, and perhaps even ignore the state Job Service. They may be convinced from the outset that they are essentially unemployable, and they may treat any recruitment initiatives with suspicion. Under these circumstances, referrals from current minority employees may be a company's best entry into the community. The firm can also work through community agencies, neighborhood groups, and churches — any local organizations that are available.

Older Workers and Persons with Disabilities

In Chapter 6, the role of the Age Discrimination in Employment Act (ADEA) in limiting employment discrimination based on age was discussed. The principal beneficiaries have been employees and applicants aged forty and over.

To guarantee equal opportunity for older workers, organizations must be careful to word job advertisements so as not to discourage older workers from applying. Organizations should guard, too, against the promotion of stereotypes that older workers are less energetic or are "set in their ways." Companies may also find a neglected source of talent in older workers already on the staff.

Publicity for persons with disabilities has increased in recent years, yet the disabled may face more discrimination than any other group. Their problems are compounded by the physical obstacles they must overcome in the buildings where they work.

The physical needs of handicapped people must be considered in advance. Jobs and equipment can be redesigned with worker disabilities in mind. The term **reasonable accommodation** has been used to describe the efforts a company should make to adjust its physical facilities and job specifications. Reasonable accommodation has been defined in the law as "any modification or adjustment to a job or the work environment that will enable a qualified applicant or employee with a disability to perform essential job functions."[15] (See Chapter 3.)

The Selection Process

Once an effective recruitment program has supplied enough job applicants, the organization faces the task of choosing the best ones for specific jobs. The selection process involves judging candidates on a variety of dimensions, ranging from the concrete and measurable (for example, years of experience) to the abstract and personal (for example, leadership potential). To do this, organizations rely on one or more of a number of selection devices, including application forms, reference checks, tests, physical examinations, and interviews. Any of these devices must satisfy strict requirements of relevance and legality, and their effects on the individual applicant and the organization as a whole must be considered carefully.

In almost all organizations, the human resources department is responsible for designing the selection system and managing its everyday operation. Human resources managers, in cooperation with other managers, largely set the overall strategy; they are likely to be influential in deciding, for example, whether the department should focus on choosing people who are best qualified for current vacancies or those who have the greatest long-term potential. The personnel managers also decide how the guidelines for equal employment opportunity should be met, and whether the company needs outside legal assistance in formulating its affirmative action plan.

Typically, **screening** of particular applicants to determine who will then be sent to department heads or other managers — or to team members, as in Case 9.2 — for final evaluation is performed by the human resources department. The eventual hiring decision usually comes from the supervisor or manager in whose department there is an opening. But in most organizations, the final steps of the selection process are coordinated with the human resources staff, which controls such matters as salary scales and benefits.

As team members were reminded in Case 9.2, and as we are seeing throughout this chapter, there are legal constraints on the use of recruitment and selection devices. In Case 9.2, Mitch was asking a question in an employment interview that was illegal. This case has obvious implications for the training of anyone involved in selection interviewing.

Determining Selection Standards

The particular standards to be used in selection — the criteria against which an applicant will be evaluated — need to be chosen with care. To allow an accurate prediction of a candidate's success on the job, they must satisfy several requirements: they must be reliable and valid and they must be job related.

Reliability and Validity

The **reliability** of a test or other selection device refers to the consistency of the results it produces. If the same person can score high on a test one week and low the next week, the test is not reliable. A device's **validity,** on the other hand, is the degree to which the scores or rankings it provides relate to success on the job. Obviously, reliability and validity are closely connected. If a selection device is not highly reliable — if an individual's score can vary significantly — then it cannot have a high degree of validity.

Although these two concepts apply to all selection devices, their meaning is clearest in relation to tests. This section focuses on how they relate to testing procedures, but their importance for other selection devices should be kept in mind.

Reliability is usually measured in one of three ways:

- The *repeat*, or *test-retest*, approach, in which the procedure is administered to the same individual a second time
- The *alternate-form* method, in which two forms of the same test are given
- The *split-half* procedure, in which a test is divided into two parts

With each method, the device will be considered reliable if a high correlation is found between the two sets of scores.

The means of determining validity are not so clear-cut. There are three general methods, but they tend to overlap, and in a particular situation they may all be appropriate.

Criterion-related validity refers to the correlation between scores on the selection device and ratings on a particular criterion of job performance. As an example, for the position of millwright, employees' scores on a test designed to measure mechanical skill could be correlated with performance in repairing machines in the mill. If the correlation is high, the test can be said to have a high degree of validity, and its use as a selection device would be considered appropriate. Because the validity of job criteria themselves can be called into question, however, validation studies must be designed very carefully.[16]

Criterion-related validity is normally expressed as a correlation coefficient. A coefficient of 1.00 represents perfect correlation between the test results and the job criterion; a coefficient of zero indicates the total absence of a correlation. In practice, validity coefficients for single tests rarely exceed 0.50.

Another kind of validity is **content validity,** which refers to the correspondence between the behaviors measured by the test and the behaviors involved in the job. For a secretarial position, a typing test would have high content validity if the secretary had to produce many letters a day. But for a job as administrative assistant involving minimal typing, the same test would have little content validity. This is the simplest kind of validity to determine, but it cannot apply to tests that measure learning ability or general problem-solving skills.

The third kind of validity, **construct validity,** pertains to tests that measure abstract traits in the applicant's makeup. For a position as a teller or management trainee, a bank might wish to test its applicants for "numerical aptitude." An aptitude is not a specific criterion or feature of behavior; rather, it is a concept created to explain a large group of behaviors. To prove that the numerical test had construct validity, the bank would need to show (1) that the test did indeed measure the desired trait and (2) that this trait corresponded to success on the job.

In evaluating a particular test, any combination of the three types of validity may be useful. Careful validation studies can not only help a firm comply with the law but also improve business efficiency. One study estimated that widespread use of more valid selection devices for a single occupation, computer programming, could increase productivity by hundreds of millions of dollars.[17]

Job Relatedness and Uniform Guidelines

For selection standards to have **job relatedness,** they must be relevant to actual performance on the job. If, for example, a secretarial position requires extensive typing, a test of typing speed would be job related, and it would be reasonable to set a minimum standard in terms of words per minute. The law does not discourage the use of testing and measuring procedures if they are relevant to the job and if they are reliable and valid.

To help employers develop legally acceptable selection standards, the Equal Employment Opportunity Commission (EEOC) cooperated with three other federal agencies to develop the **Uniform Guidelines on Employee Selection Procedures.** Issued in 1978, these guidelines may themselves be reinterpreted and revised over the years, but they provide a useful reference for all organizations to consult.

The guidelines include a **bottom-line principle,** according to which the judgment of adverse impact will be made on the basis of a firm's entire selection process. As long as the overall selection process does not produce an adverse impact, federal agencies will generally not challenge particular components of it. For example, a specific test that has an adverse impact on minorities may be ignored if the company selects a high enough percentage of minorities by other means.

The guidelines give detailed explanations of job relatedness and validity, and they describe the technical requirements for each of the three methods of validation. A fundamental principle underlying the guidelines is the concept of **adverse impact,** a term used by the Supreme Court in the 1971 case of *Griggs* v. *Duke Power Company* (see Chapter 7). (This concept appears to mean the same as "disparate impact" used in the Civil Rights Act of 1991.) Briefly, the concept can be understood as follows: if a hiring practice has an adverse impact on any legally protected group, this is prima-facie evidence (if uncontested, establishes a fact) of discrimination; therefore the practice is illegal unless it can be justified by "business necessity." However, if a procedure has no adverse impact, it is generally assumed to be legal.

The guidelines provide that adverse impact will usually be determined with a rule of thumb known as the "four-fifths" or "80 percent" rule:

> A selection rate for any race, sex, or ethnic group which is less than four-fifths (4/5) (or eighty percent) of the rate for the group with the highest [selection] rate will generally be regarded by the Federal enforcement agencies as evidence of adverse impact, while a greater than four-fifths rate will generally not be regarded by Federal enforcement agencies as evidence of adverse impact.[18]

Supreme Court decisions in 1989 seemed to call into question a number of assumptions underlying *Griggs* v. *Duke Power Company* and the guidelines. However, the Civil Rights Act of 1991 reversed these decisions and appears to restore the earlier assumptions by an addition to the earlier Civil Rights Act. The law now reads as shown in Figure 9.3 on page 225.

These zigs and zags in the law suggest that human resources professionals and other managers need to be alert to changes in employment law. As attorneys who track such changes in employment law have noted, "Employers are cautioned that federal law governing employment decisions remains in constant flux."[19]

Sources of Information About Applicants

Depending on the recruiting methods used, an organization may have several informal sources of information about applicants, as well as more formalized sources. For example, an employee might say, "I understand you are talking to Marcia Y. from the ABC company; she's really good at this work." But the major sources of information about applicants are usually standard ones: application forms, interviews, reference checks, physical examinations, and/or tests. Application blanks and interviews are almost universally used by employers, while the mixture of other devices used varies from organization to organization.

This section discusses application forms, reference checks, and physical examinations. In later sections, we will consider selection tests and selection interviews.

Application Forms   The application form is a sheet or small booklet with blanks to be filled in by the applicant. Its purpose is to supply the organization with basic information about the candidate's background: education, work experience, previous salary, and so forth. (See Weyerhaeuser Company's application form, Figure 9.4.) The applicant's résumé may cover much of the same ground, but the application form has the advantage of a standardized format, which allows managers throughout the organization to glean the relevant information at a glance. (This information is sometimes called **biodata,** that is, biographical data.)[20]

Studies have shown that background data such as educational level and work experience are generally good predictors of job performance. By correlating specific items on the form with measures of success on the job, researchers have assessed the

SEC. 105. BURDEN OF PROOF IN DISPARATE IMPACT CASES.

(a) Section 703 of the Civil Rights Act of 1964 (42 U.S.C. 2000e-2) is amended by adding at the end the following new subsection:

"(k)(l)(A) An unlawful employment practice based on disparate impact is established under this title only if —

"(i) a complaining party demonstrates that a respondent uses a particular employment practice that causes a disparate impact on the basis of race, color, religion, sex, or national origin and the respondent fails to demonstrate that the challenged practice is job related for the position in question and consistent with business necessity; or

"(ii) the complaining party makes the demonstration described in subparagraph (C) with respect to an alternative employment practice and the respondent refuses to adopt such alternative employment practice.

"(B)(i) With respect to demonstrating that a particular employment practice causes a disparate impact as described in subparagraph (A)(i), the complaining party shall demonstrate that each particular challenged employment practice causes a disparate impact, except that if the complaining party can demonstrate to the court that the elements of a respondent's decisionmaking process are not capable of separation for analysis, the decisionmaking process may be analyzed as one employment practice.

"(ii) If the respondent demonstrates that a specific employment practice does not cause the disparate impact, the respondent shall not be required to demonstrate that such practice is required by business necessity.

"(C) The demonstration referred to by subparagraph (A)(ii) shall be in accordance with the law as it existed on June 4, 1989, with respect to the concept of 'alternative employment practice'.

"(2) A demonstration that an employment practice is required by business neces-sity may not be used as a defense against a claim of intentional discrimination under this title.

"(3) Notwithstanding any other provision of this title, a rule barring the employment of an individual who currently and know-ingly uses or possesses a controlled sub-stance, as defined in schedules I and II of section 102(6) of the Controlled Substances Act (21 U.S.C. 802(6)), other than the use or possession of a drug taken under the su-pervision of a licensed health care profes-sional, or any other use or possession authorized by the Controlled Substances Act or any other provision of Federal law, shall be considered an unlawful employ-ment practice under this title only if such rule is adopted or applied with an intent to discriminate because of race, color, religion, sex, or national origin."

(b) No statements other than the inter-pretive memorandum appearing at Vol. 137 Congressional Record S 15276 (daily ed. Oct. 25, 1991) shall be considered legislative history of, or relied upon in any way as leg-islative history in construing or applying, any provision of this Act that relates to Wards Cove — Business necessity/cumula-tion/alternative business practice.

SEC. 106. PROHIBITION AGAINST DISCRIMINATORY USE OF TEST SCORES.

Section 703 of the Civil Rights Act of 1964 (42 U.S.C. 2000e-2) (as amended by section 105) is further amended by adding at the end the following new subsection:

"(l) It shall be an unlawful employment practice for a respondent, in connection with the selection or referral of applicants or candidates for employment or promotion, to adjust the scores of, use different cutoff scores for, or otherwise alter the results of, employment related tests on the basis of race, color, religion, sex, or national ori-gin.".

FIGURE 9.3 Excerpts from the Civil Rights Act of 1991

Please answer all questions. If one does not apply, insert or check "NA".

If additional space is required to adequately answer any question, please indicate by an asterisk (*) and identify the supplemental information on a separate sheet.

In reading and answering these questions, please keep in mind that none of the questions are intended to imply limitations, preferences or discrimination based on age, sex, marital status, race, creed, color, national origin or existence of any sensory, mental or physical handicap that does not interfere with the performance of the position for which you are applying.

PERSONAL BACKGROUND

NAME (PLEASE PRINT) Last | First | Middle Initial

PRESENT ADDRESS (Street, Rfd, Box) | CITY | STATE & ZIP CODE | TELEPHONE

SOCIAL SECURITY NO. | DATE AVAILABLE FOR EMPLOYMENT

HAVE YOU THE LEGAL RIGHT TO WORK IN THE U.S. ? ☐ Yes ☐ No

HIRE IS SUBJECT TO VERIFICATION THAT APPLICANT MEETS LEGAL AGE AND U.S.WORK PERMIT REQUIREMENTS.

MAJOR FIELDS OF EMPLOYMENT INTEREST OR POSITION DESIRED
1) 2)

SALARY REQUIREMENT $ | GEOGRAPHIC REFERENCES 1) 2) | WILLING TO RELOCATE ☐ Yes ☐ No

PROFESSIONAL LICENSES AND CERTIFICATES

HOW DO YOU FEEL ABOUT WORKING EVENINGS, WEEKENDS, OR HOLIDAYS IF REQUIRED BY THE NATURE OF THE WORK?

HAVE YOU BEEN CONVICTED OF A FELONY OR BEEN RELEASED FROM A PRISON OR OTHER DETENTION FACILITY WITHIN THE PAST SEVEN YEARS?(If Yes, Detail Briefly.)* ☐ Yes ☐ No

* A CONVICTION WILL NOT NECESSARILY BAR AN APPLICANT FROM EMPLOYMENT.

IF APPLYING FOR A POSITION WHICH REQUIRES YOU TO DRIVE, PLEASE COMPLETE THE FOLLOWING

POSSESS A VALID DRIVER'S LICENSE? ☐ Yes ☐ No | DRIVER'S LICENSE NO. | LICENSE EVER RESTRICTED, SUSPENDED, REVOKED?(If Yes, Explain) ☐ Yes ☐ No

IN THE EVENT OF EMERGENCY, NOTIFY:

NAME | ADDRESS | TELEPHONE

FAMILY OR PERSONAL PHYSICIAN | TELEPHONE | HOSPITAL REFERENCE

EDUCATIONAL BACKGROUND

NAMES AND LOCATIONS OF HIGH SCHOOLS, COLLEGES, UNIVERSITIES, SPEC. PROGRAMS	ADDRESS OF SCHOOL	FACULTY REFERENCE	DATES FROM	DATES TO	DIPLOMA/ DEGREE EARNED	GRAD. DATE	COLLEGE	GRADE PT AVG A=4.0
H.S.					Yes ☐ No ☐		Major / Minor	
1.								
2.								
3.								

HIGH SCHOOL OR COLLEGE HONERS, PUBLICATIONS, PROFESIONAL SOCIETIES, ATHLETICS AND OTHER EXTRA-CURRICULAR ACTIVITIES WHICH MAY RELATE TO THE JOB YOU ARE APPLYING FOR (INDICATE POSITIONS HELD).

TECHNICAL SKILLS

SPECIALIZED TECHNICAL SKILLS (i.e. COMPUTER PROGRAMMER/LANGUAGE, EQUIPMENT OPERATION, SPECIAL TOOLS OR MACHINES USED)

APPLICANTS FOR SECRETARIAL/CLERICAL WORK PLEASE CHECK MACHINES YOU CAN OPERATE:

☐ Typewriter ☐ Power Keyboard ☐ Ten Key Adding Machine Typing Speed
☐ Calculator ☐ Switchboard ☐ Key Punch Shorthand Speed
☐ Machine Transcription ☐ Teletype Others (Explain)

BUSINESS EXPERIENCE/PREVIOUS EMPLOYMENT

Please start with your most recent position. If there are references or prior employers whom you do not want us to contact without your permission, *please circle their names.* Include U.S. military if it occurred during the last three position held. Please account for at least the last five years.

COMPANY (1) | ADDRESS

KIND OF BUSINESS | EMPLOYED FROM: TO:

POSITION | MONTHLY COMPENSATION OR HOURLY RATE $

NATURE OF WORK | NUMBER SUPERVISED

NAME OF SUPERVISOR | POSITION OF SUPERVISOR

REMARKS (State clearly your reasons for leaving or desiring to change from this position)

COMPANY (2) | ADDRESS

KIND OF BUSINESS | EMPLOYED FROM: TO:

POSITION | MONTHLY COMPENSATION OR HOURLY RATE $

NATURE OF WORK | NUMBER SUPERVISED

NAME OF SUPERVISOR | POSITION OF SUPERVISOR

REMARKS (State clearly your reasons for leaving or desiring to change from this position)

COMPANY (2) | ADDRESS

KIND OF BUSINESS | EMPLOYED FROM: TO:

POSITION | MONTHLY COMPENSATION OR HOURLY RATE $

NATURE OF WORK | NUMBER SUPERVISED

NAME OF SUPERVISOR | POSITION OF SUPERVISOR

REMARKS (State clearly your reasons for leaving or desiring to change from this position)

CONT. ON BACK OF THIS SECTION

FIGURE 9.4 Weyerhaeuser Company application form *Source:* Courtesy of the Weyerhaeuser Company.

APPLICANT FLOW DATA SHEET

As a Federal contractor and/or subcontractor, Weyerhaeuser Company must compile statistical data on the sex, minority, handicapped and veteran status of job applicants. If you wish to provide this statistical information, please indicate below. This data will be removed from the application and entered only on an applicant flow log. If you do not wish to provide this information, your status will be summarized into an "unknown" category and will not jeopardize you as a prospective employee. However, information on your prior status as an applicant and the positions you are applying for are important in considering you for any upcoming positions.

Have you filled out an application earlier this calendar year? ☐ Yes ☐ No

Date of this application: MO DAY YR

POSITIONS APPLYING FOR

Name   Last   First   Initial

STATISTICAL INFORMATION

Sex
1 ☐ Male
2 ☐ Female

Ethnic Classification
1 ☐ American Indian/ Alaskan native
2 ☐ Caucasian(white)
3 ☐ Black
4 ☐ Asian/Pacific Islander/Indian Subcontinent
5 ☐ Hispanic (Spanish origin)

Handicapped
1 ☐ No
2 ☐ Yes*

Vietnam Era Veteran
1 ☐ No
2 ☐ Yes

Disabled Veteran
1 ☐ No
2 ☐ Yes

* IF YES, INDICATE THE DISABILITY AND ANY ACCOMODATION REQUIRED TO PERFORM THE JOB YOU ARE APPLYING FOR

FOR COMPANY USE ONLY
ORGANIZATION/BUSINESS AND EEO-1 JOB CODES

FACILITY CODE

Organization/ Business   EEO-1

NOTE:
1. See pamphlet 4619 for instructions. (EEO Dept., Tacoma.)

U.S. MILITARY BACKGROUND

BRANCH OF SERVICE	DATE IN	DATE OUT	HIGHEST GRADE HELD

INDICATE SPECIALIZATION, TRAINING OR WORK EXPERIENCE OBTAINED

REFERENCES (BUSINESS/CHARACTER)

NAME	POSITION	COMPANY	ADDRESS
1			
2			
3			

I have previously ☐ applied for employment ☐ been employed by the Weyerhaeuser Company

LOCATION   POSITION   DATE

FROM WHOM DO YOU RECEIVE THIS APPLICATION?

MEDICAL REPORT

Do you have any handicaps or health problems which may affect performance on the positions for which you are applying? (Information may help in suitable job placement)

Have you had any past injuries or health restrictions that may be aggravated by performing the position(s) for which you are applying? EXPLAIN.

Are you able and willing to wear safety equipment required by the Company?
☐ Yes ☐ No

I certify that the information shown on this application is true and correct to the best of my knowledge. I authorize previous employers and references to furnish Weyerhaeuser Company such information as it considers necessary to evaluate my qualifications for employment unless so indicated. I understand that completing a medical history form and taking a physical examination at Company expense may be required before final acceptance as an employee. I further agree that the falsification or withholding of pertinent information will be grounds for discharge from employment.

Weyerhaeuser Company offers employment under the legal terms of the doctrine of employment at will - which means that either the employee or the company is free to end the employment relationship at any time with or without cause. Only the officers of the company may authorize contracts of employment other than at will.

SIGNATURE   DATE

FIGURE 9.4 *(Cont'd)*

validity of application forms in fields ranging from sales work to health care and military careers. The **weighted application form,** in which some items judged important are given more predictive weight than others, has proved especially useful.[21] Few organizations, however, have conducted validation studies for their own application forms.

The questions asked on an application form — or with any selection device — should be clearly job related. Federal and state laws, administrative rulings, and court decisions have drastically modified the kinds of preemployment questions that may be asked through such devices as application blanks, reference checks, and interviews. Various laws prohibit or curtail questions pertaining to race, color, religion, national origin, age, marital status, and disablility status. Questions about arrests, spouses, child care arrangements, military discharge, membership in organizations, pregnancy, and whether the applicant owns or rents a home are generally prohibited or circumscribed. The requirement that a photograph accompany an application can be considered evidence of discrimination.

To illustrate, in the state of Washington, with some exceptions, an employer

- may not make any inquiry about race, color of skin, color of hair, eyes, and so on.
- may not make any inquiry that implies a preference for persons under forty years of age.
- may not request the applicant to submit a photograph, even on an optional basis.
- may not inquire about height and weight, unless the employer can show that no employee with the ineligible height or weight could do the work.
- may not inquire into applicant's national origin, ancestry, birthplace, or mother tongue, but may make inquiries into applicant's ability to read, write, and speak foreign languages, when such inquiries are based on job requirements.
- may not inquire whether applicant is a citizen, but may inquire as to whether applicant is prevented from becoming lawfully employed because of visa or immigration status.
- may not inquire about marital status.
- may not inquire about the sex of the applicant.
- may not make any inquiry about religious affiliations or religious holidays observed.
- may not make inquiries about a spouse, spouse's employment or salary, children, child care arrangements, or dependents, but may inquire as to the applicant's ability to meet specified work schedules.
- may not inquire as to type or condition of military discharge, but may inquire as to training or work experience in the armed forces of the United States.
- may not make overly general inquiries about disabilities, but may inquire about handicaps or health problems which might affect work performance or which should be taken into account in job placement.
- may not make inquiries relating to arrests, but may, under some circumstances, make inquiries about convictions.

Although this is not an exhaustive list, it does indicate the extent to which the use of application forms and other preemployment devices is constrained by law.[22]

These constraints present a dilemma for many organizations. Employers covered by Title VII of the Civil Rights Act and having one hundred or more employees must maintain records and file an annual report not later than March 31 indicating the impact of their selection procedures on the work force regarding such dimensions as sex, race, or ethnic background. How, then, does an employer keep such records if these questions cannot be asked on an application blank or in the interview? One method is to request, but not require, the applicant to fill out a separate part of the application blank that is detached and left with the receptionist prior to any review of the applicant's qualifications.

Reference Checks

Reference checks involve communicating with previous employers and others who can provide information about the applicant. The checks serve two purposes: they verify (or contradict) what the applicant has told the organization, and they produce supplemental information that can be very useful in a hiring decision. Reference checks are commonly conducted over the telephone; less often they are accomplished through an exchange of letters, and in rare cases they involve a personal visit.

Most employers check references. One study found that 96 percent of the companies surveyed checked the dates of the most recent job and the reasons for leaving the job, and 90 percent checked the salary and position in the most recent job. Three-fourths of the firms surveyed checked the professional references listed by the applicant.[23]

However, many firms have found it increasingly difficult to obtain information about applicants beyond simple factual data. The main reason is that, increasingly, applicants have sued their former employers on the grounds of defamation in references, dismissal interviews, or press releases. Although employers have a right to share factual data, they become vulnerable to expensive lawsuits when they provide negative opinions.[24] For example, the District of Columbia Court of Appeals upheld an award of $250,000 to a man who claimed that his former employer had defamed him with a poor job reference. The court found that the reference was based on secondhand knowledge and gossip.[25] As a result of such cases, some organizations are restricting the information they will give out to simply verifying dates of employment and job title. Some will provide information on a former employee only after they have obtained written consent from that employee.[26] On the recruiting side, obtaining a written release from a candidate prior to checking references would appear to be a wise practice. In general, it is important to remember that the EEOC has established strict standards for the job relatedness of information obtained during a reference check.

Paradoxically, as organizations become more cautious about providing information about former employees, this lack of information has exposed employers to lawsuits, including suits over **negligent hiring** or retention. It appears that the terminating organization can be sued for negligence if someone responding to reference checks fails to disclose data indicating that the terminated employee might commit some injurious act; and the new organization can be sued if the employer fails in "its common law duty to hire persons who are not likely to injure others."[27] Because of this dilemma and the other problems cited above, the human resources department would be wise to develop policies both for obtaining references on candidates and for providing reference information on former employees, and to clear the policy statements with legal counsel. (For more on the dilemmas in reference checking, see *Contemporary Issues* on page 230.)

Contemporary Issues

The Truth Can Hurt

As long as reference checks are requested, employers will continue to face legal questions surrounding the release of information contained in employee records.

Many companies have adopted a "name, rank and serial number" approach when responding to reference checks, giving only date of hire, date of termination and final salary. Such strict policies — the safest from a legal standpoint — arise largely out of fear. While employers might want to freely exchange information to help them make better hiring decisions, they fear the danger of being sued by a former employee for defamation if incorrect or inappropriate information is released.

Many employers have sought to establish policies that allow for the release of information in a controlled manner to protect themselves from law suits. When developing such policies, there are some important decisions that employers must make. These include deciding:

- Whether to respond to verbal requests over the telephone or require all inquiries to be in writing.

- How much and what type of information to provide.

- Whether to require signed releases before information is required.

- Who should be given authority within the company to provide reference information.

- Whether any exceptions should be allowed to company policy in the face of unusual or extenuating circumstances.

Regardless of the policy ultimately adopted, care should be taken to avoid tying the company's hands by specifying that "information regarding current/former employees is strictly confidential and will only be released with the written consent of the current/former employee" or that "individuals will be advised of all requests by third parties for information and their permission secured before information is released." Such "privacy" provisions, while perhaps admirable, could lead to difficulties.

Take, for example, a company that included a privacy statement in its policy manual. The company found itself unable to cooperate fully in a law enforcement investigation (which the employer itself had initiated) into a theft at its own plant for fear that it would violate its own privacy policy if it provided information on several employees who were "suspects." Thus, while it is important to be cautious, it is just as important not to place restrictions on the company's ability to release information as necessary.

Care also must be taken when responding to telephone inquiries to ensure that they are bona fide. Indeed, one employer recently discovered (too late) that an alleged representative of an employment agency, who indicated that he was calling to check a reference, was actually an attorney calling to ascertain how the company would respond to a reference inquiry regarding his client. The fact that he was told by the employee's former supervisor to "stay away from him with a 10-foot pole" did not enhance the company's chances of avoiding litigation. This company could likely have avoided this problem had it required that all reference inquiries be channelled to one central source, say the human resources department, and politely informed the caller that the reference request must be made in writing pursuant to company policy.

Importantly, limiting the type of reference information you provide will further insulate your company against litigation. This might include, for example, verifying only that the information provided by the current/former employee is either correct or incorrect.

Requiring a signed release from the current/former employee will provide yet an additional defense should litigation be brought against the company. However, because there may be times when you may want to provide information without a release — such as when you believe you have a legal duty to do so — you should ensure that your policy statement on references provides you with that flexibility.

This leads to the final and perhaps most difficult issue confronting employers faced with reference requests. Does an employer have an affirmative duty to provide more than just "name, rank and serial number" to a prospective employer? While the answer is generally no, situations may arise when such a duty may in fact exist. When? When the hospital that terminated a physician for malpractice receives a reference request from another hospital considering hiring the physician. Or when the school district that

fired a teacher for child abuse receives a request from another school district that is considering hiring the teacher.

In such critical, safety-sensitive situations, it would not be difficult to imagine a jury holding that the terminating employer had a duty to exercise due care and advise the prospective employer — in response to a reference inquiry — of the specific reason for the employee's termination.

Otherwise, the company could find itself liable for being negligent.

Source: Robert J. Nobile. Reprinted by permission of publisher, from *Personnel Journal*, Costa Mesa, CA 92626. All rights reserved.

Physical Examinations

As one of the final steps before the hiring decision, a physical examination may be conducted by a physician or nurse appointed by the organization. In some firms, the candidate fills out a health questionnaire, and only those with apparent health problems are referred to a physician.

Physical exams serve several purposes. They help an organization place its employees in suitable jobs; someone with a back ailment, for instance, would not be assigned to lift heavy objects. The exams also permit firms to screen out applicants whose health problems may result in a high rate of absenteeism. Further, by establishing a record of the employee's health at the time of hiring, physical exams forestall possible claims for workers' compensation for preexisting conditions. In most states, the firm's liability is reduced if a new injury is shown to be related to a preexisting one.[28]

As part of the examination, a company may have the doctor measure various dimensions of the applicant's strength, reflexes, coordination, or other physical skills. These attributes can then be used to judge the individual's qualifications for a job involving physical effort. For example, for a job that involves walking along a narrow catwalk, measures of balance might be useful. The legal and ethical requirements that apply to other phases of the selection process apply to physical exams as well. Questionnaire items and physical standards may be challenged if they are not clearly job related.

Under the Americans with Disabilities Act, a job offer may be made conditional on the results of a medical examination. However, such an examination must be "required for all entering employees in the same job category regardless of disability."[29] Under the ADA, a physical examination will become even more of a placement tool than in the past, in contrast to being used as a screening device.

Selection Tests

Tests are generally administered and evaluated before the final stage of interviewing. Managers can then use the test results as guidelines in asking candidates about their abilities, experience, and interests. The testing of applicants offers two apparent advantages: test results seem to be objective, free from personal bias; and they are usually expressed numerically, so that they lend themselves to statistical analysis and thus can be validated. Nevertheless, testing has been the most controversial part of the selection process. As a result of court cases and government challenges, the use of tests declined in the 1970s and through the mid-1980s, but it has increased again in recent years as firms have adjusted to the legal restrictions. Part of the resurgence in testing has been due to the positive results of the validity testing program of the U.S. Employment Service.[30]

The employment of professionals to interpret and administer tests, the training of human resources staff in test use, and the provision of space and time for testing can involve considerable expense. Given these costs, human resources managers should restrict the use of tests to areas where they will do the most good. Above all, tests should be only one factor in the hiring decision. In the past, some managers — impressed by the statistical success and the scientific aura of tests — have given the results too much weight. Small differences in test scores are unlikely to indicate important differences in the candidates.

Types of Tests

The tests used in the selection process generally fall into one of several broad categories:

- *Measures of proficiency, achievement, or knowledge.* A wide range of skills and information can be measured. In a test of manual dexterity, for example, an applicant might be asked to place small pegs into tight holes using a pair of tweezers. A test of clerical skills might involve spelling, reading comprehension, and arithmetic.

- *Measures of aptitude or potential ability.* These differ from proficiency tests in that they assess the candidate's ability to learn new skills rather than the amount he or she has already learned. Common types of aptitude tests include measures of short-term memory, spatial perception, number discrimination, and motor abilities. The U.S. Employment Service has developed a General Aptitude Test Battery (GATB) that can be administered, at a firm's request, by the state Job Service. Specific Aptitude Test Batteries (SATBs) are also available. (The GATB was "put on hold" in mid-1991 pending a decision as to whether it was creating an adverse impact on minority groups. Late in the year, the Civil Rights Act of 1991 outlawed any "race norming" of tests or test batteries such as the GATB.)[31]

- *Measures of mental ability or intelligence.* These could be seen as a subcategory of aptitude tests. Generally, they concentrate on a person's abilities with words, numbers, logical reasoning, and spatial relationships.

- *Measures of personality.* Personality inventories attempt to construct a profile of a person's attitudes, behavior, and habits. "Friendliness," "confidence," "conventionality," and "dominance" are examples of what such a test might measure.[32] A popular personality test, the Myers-Briggs Type Indicator test, attempts to measure such dimensions as the degree of extroversion, introversion, intuition, thinking, feeling, judging, and the like.[33] A subset of personality measurement is the use of the polygraph and honesty tests, which attempt to measure truthfulness. (These are discussed in the next section.)

- *Measures of interest.* Tests in this category attempt to discover a person's likes and dislikes. They may ask such seemingly irrelevant questions as whether the candidate enjoys golf, likes babies, or prefers math to history. The responses are built into an interest profile that may help predict a person's satisfaction in a particular job.

- *Measures of physical ability.* As the preceding section noted, during the physical exam a doctor may test for strength, balance, reaction time, or other bodily traits considered necessary for the job.

- *Measures of substance abuse.* In recent years more and more organizations have required applicants to be tested for substance abuse, usually by urinalysis. A 1988 survey found 26 percent of 245 responding firms administering drug tests to applicants.[34] (See Figure 9.5.) A larger 1990 survey found 54 percent of firms using drug tests in screening job applicants. (See Chapter 20 under "Drug Testing.")

Legal and Ethical Challenges   Of all selection devices, tests have probably faced the most intense legal and ethical challenges. Validity is more difficult to establish for interviews than for tests, yet tests have been subjected to greater criticism and legal scrutiny.

In an early court case challenging testing procedures, *Myart* v. *Motorola* (1964), compensation awarded to a black applicant who had been rejected on the basis of a brief intelligence test.[35] In *Griggs* v. *Duke Power Company* (1971), an intelligence test

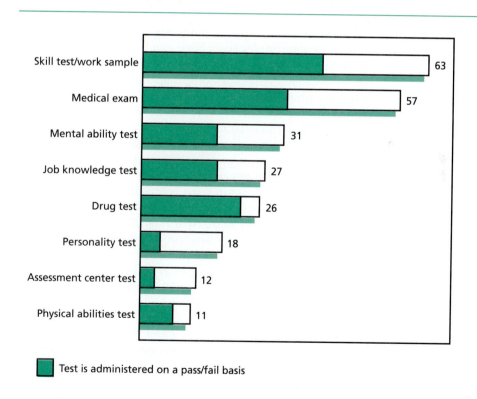

Skill test/work sample — 63
Medical exam — 57
Mental ability test — 31
Job knowledge test — 27
Drug test — 26
Personality test — 18
Assessment center test — 12
Physical abilities test — 11

■ Test is administered on a pass/fail basis

FIGURE 9.5 Most common tests and examinations (Percent of companies using tests for any job category)

Source: Reprinted with permission from *Recruiting and Selection Procedures*, PPF Survey No. 146, p. 19 (May 1988). Copyright 1988 by The Bureau of National Affairs, Inc. (800-372-1033)

was again found discriminatory because the firm could not establish "a demonstrable relationship to successful performance."[36] More recently, in a case before a U.S. district court, Albermarle Paper Company agreed to pay back wages to a group of black employees who had been refused promotion because of scores on job qualification tests.[37] Many other court cases and EEOC rulings have prohibited tests that were not fully validated.

Although the early legal cases focused on intelligence tests, personality testing has received even more criticism. Some critics believe it is morally wrong to administer any such test; others feel that measures of personality characteristics are sometimes used as a basis for rash decisions. There is also a question of privacy. According to one line of argument, applicants who think a test is improper can simply refuse to take it. But an applicant may presume that not taking the test means not getting the job; hence there may be no true choice. A firm can perhaps reduce the applicant's fear of a personality test by explaining its nature and purpose beforehand and by guaranteeing that the results will be kept confidential.

As indicated in Chapter 3, the use of **polygraph tests** (in which certain physiological changes are recorded when the applicant gives an answer) is outlawed for most private employers under the Employee Polygraph Protection Act of 1988. Exceptions can be made when there is a reasonable suspicion of theft or other incident resulting in an economic loss to the firm. Private security organizations and drug firms, as well as government agencies, are exempt from the federal law. The first state legislation restricting the use of polygraph testing was enacted in Hawaii in 1968.[38]

Honesty tests — pencil and paper questionnaires — essentially inquire into a job applicant's attitudes about theft and have been developed largely as an alternative to the polygraph. In 1991 the American Psychological Association released a report on honesty tests concluding that "for the few tests for which validity information is available, the preponderance of the evidence is supportive of their predictive validity."[39] However, the report cautions employers not to use forms of honesty tests that lack such documentation.[40]

Substance abuse testing is very controversial, and the law on this matter is only emerging. In general, it would appear that courts will look more favorably on the use of drug testing in screening applicants than in testing present employees. Testing of present employees in state agencies, in particular, comes into conflict with claims about federal and state constitutional rights to privacy.[41] Under U.S. Department of Transportation rules, civilian employees in safety-sensitive positions in six transportation industries — aviation, trucking, rail, mass transit, pipeline and the Coast Guard — are subject to random drug tests. In addition, they are subject to testing if there is reasonable suspicion of use, during routine physical examinations or after an accident.[42] (See Chapter 20 for more on substance abuse testing.) Testing for AIDS or HIV infections is illegal under the Americans with Disabilities Act.[43] (For more on AIDS, see Chapter 20.)

In general, every firm should assess the full implications of its overall testing program and reassess the program periodically. Tests can be very helpful devices if used carefully, selectively, and with due consideration for the person being tested. Useful guidelines for evaluating selection tests are shown in Table 9.1. It should be added that, under the Civil Rights Act of 1991, in using tests in employment and promotion decisions, it is unlawful to establish separate cutoff scores on the basis of race, color, religion, sex, or national origin. (See Figure 9.3, Section 106.)

The Selection Interview

Interviews can be used at several stages of the selection process. Screening interviews take place early in the process. Often short — perhaps ten to fifteen minutes — they focus on the applicant's basic qualifications for the job, with the goal of screening out candidates who are not qualified. Sometimes the final stage in the process is a job-offer interview, at which the best candidate is offered the position. In between these two stages fall one or more detailed selection interviews, which may be conducted by human resources staff, the supervisor, and the department head, and sometimes members of the work team.

The interview offers a chance for the manager to fill in gaps in the information provided by application forms and tests. It may lead to entirely new types of information as well. In particular, interviews are used to assess intangible factors such as motivation and enthusiasm that cannot be shown on an application form.

TABLE 9.1   Evaluation selection tests: a checklist

1. Compare the tests and the jobs for which they are designed. Are the tests specifically related to the appropriate qualifications for the job?
2. Who designed the tests — a professional test-publishing company or someone in-house at the organization?
3. If designed in-house, were the tests validated by a professional on the basis of specific job-related criteria?
4. If the test designer was in-house, what were his or her qualifications?
5. For what settings were the tests first designed? Have the tests been updated? What changes were incorporated?
6. Who administers the tests? The personnel director? An outside consultant?
7. What are the qualifications of that administrator? And who has responsibility for overseeing his or her efforts?
8. Did the population used in validating the tests include a representative sample of minorities?
9. Is there a continuous program of revalidation?
10. Have passing scores been reevaluated and updated? When?
11. Have any applicants who failed a test been hired? Is there information on why and when it happened?
12. Can failed applicants be retested? How and why?
13. Have the tests been applied to current employees as well? What is the standard reaction if they fail?
14. Do all applicants take the same test? If not, why?
15. Are all tests administered uniformly? Are they graded consistently?
16. What are the organization's practices on retaining the results of the tests?

Source: From the book, *Hiring the Right Person for the Right Job* by Cecilia Dobrish, Rick Wolff and Brian Zevnik. Copyright © 1984 by Alexander Hamilton Institute. Reprinted with permission of the publisher, Franklin Watts Inc., and the Alexander Hamilton Institute.

Although interviews can be the least objective part of the process, they are generally considered the most valuable. Interviews are also likely to have the greatest impact on the applicant, contributing more than any other element to his or her view of the firm and attitude toward the job. Thus, it should be remembered that any interview preceding a job offer is an extension of the recruitment process, as well as part of the selection process.

Interview Scenarios

Interviews can follow several scenarios. In the **group interview,** a number of candidates are interviewed at once. Generally, they are allowed to discuss job-related matters among themselves while one or more observers rate their performance. This type of interview is usually considered most appropriate in the selection of managers; it can also be used with groups of current employees to evaluate their potential for supervisory roles.

In the **panel interview,** one candidate meets with a panel of two or more representatives of the firm. One of the panelists may act as a chairperson, but each of the firm's representatives takes part in the questioning and discussion. This format allows the interviewers to coordinate their efforts and follow up on each other's questions.

The most common scenario is the **one-on-one interview**, in which the candidate meets privately with a single interviewer. Often a well-qualified candidate will pass through a series of such interviews, first with a member of the human resources department, then with the manager in whose unit there is a job opening, and finally perhaps with the manager's superior. The rest of this section focuses primarily on the one-on-one scenario.

Through the use of **videotape interviewing,** in which one-on-one interviews are videotaped, managers are able to play back interviews to refresh memories or to look for new data. Storing the interview on videotape has the additional advantages of making it possible for others to see the interview and of altering the sequence of interviews. Disadvantages include the possibility of interviewees' resistance to being videotaped or intimidation by the technology.[44]

In the **computer-assisted interview,** the applicant is presented with a series of questions on a video screen to which he or she responds by pressing the appropriate key on a keyboard. Preliminary experience suggests that the procedure is faster than face-to-face interviewing, that applicants are more candid, and that it overcomes the problem of lack of consistency between interviewers.[45] Obviously, this approach cannot assess emotional responses or interpersonal skills, but it has promise as a helpful additional tool in the selection process. Because of programming and development costs, it appears to be the most practical choice when fairly large numbers of candidates are to be interviewed for a given job.

Interview Techniques

The three basic scenarios lend themselves to a variety of specific interviewing techniques. The most common are the structured interview, the nondirective interview, and the situational-problem interview.

In the **structured** or **patterned interview,** the interviewer follows a standard list of questions to be asked of all applicants. This method produces uniformity of data from one interview to the next; it ensures that no important questions will be forgotten; and it helps to guarantee that all the applicants have been treated in the same way. If the interview is too rigidly structured, however, the interviewer may neglect chances for follow-up questions, and the candidate is unlikely to provide any information spontaneously.

The **nondirective interview**, as its name implies, takes the opposite approach. The interviewer's questions are held to a minimum, and they are open-ended. Rather than asking about specific details of the candidate's last job, the interviewer may say, "Tell me about your work in this field." The aim is to follow the applicant's own lead, to let him or her express thoughts and feelings that might be relevant to the job. Instead of filling silences with new questions, the interviewer may simply nod to encourage the applicant to continue.

The nondirective technique can reveal information that would never have come up in a structured interview. It requires substantial time, however, and it may fail to touch on important aspects of the candidate's qualifications. For these reasons, few organizations use it in its pure form. Typically, the interviewer tries to mix the nondirective technique with a structured approach, encouraging the applicant to expand on his or her ideas, but making certain that standard topics are covered.

In the **situational-problem interview,** the candidate is given a specific problem to solve or a project to complete. Often this technique is used in the group interview scenario; while the group discusses a problem and works out an answer, the interviewers rate each candidate on, for example, quality of ideas, leadership capacity, and ability to work with others.

Problems in Interviewing

Whatever their format, interviews must overcome a number of typical problems. One is the personal bias of the interviewer. What if the interviewer likes blondes, or dislikes large people, or thinks that anyone older than forty is "over the hill"? Those who conduct interviews must learn to ignore their personal preferences. In some cases, however, a belief about a certain category of people may be so deeply ingrained that the interviewer is unaware of its existence. Such stereotypes are a principal factor in discrimination against minorities, women, older workers, and persons with disabilities, and they can influence attitudes toward other groups as well.

If an applicant looks very impressive in one particular area, the interviewer may concentrate on that to the exclusion of other matters. Weaknesses in the candidate's background may be overlooked, or their significance may be discounted. This tendency is known as the **halo effect**. The opposite tendency, known as the **horn effect**, is to turn one negative characteristic into a conclusion that the candidate is weak on all fronts.

The proper phrasing and timing of questions is often a difficult problem to solve. In a structured or semistructured interview, questions should be specific enough to draw out the necessary information, but they should not prematurely reveal what answer the interviewer would like to hear. For instance, the question "I suppose you've had experience running a Model 20B?" suggests that the operation of a 20B is a job requirement, and the candidate may be tempted to inflate his or her experience. A better initial question might be "What kind of machinery have you handled?" Then a later question could zero in on the 20B.

Effective Interviewing

Although the needs of different organizations will vary, it is possible to suggest the elements that an effective interview generally includes. The interviewer begins by studying all the materials already available on the candidate. Planning every session in advance, the interviewer knows which topics are critical for each individual applicant.

The candidate is shown to a quiet room, free from distractions. No phones are ringing; no one interrupts with messages for the interviewer. To begin, the interviewer engages in general talk about neutral subjects to put the applicant at ease and establish rapport. Soon, however, the interviewer turns the discussion to the matter at hand.

Whether the format is structured or nondirective, the interviewer listens closely to everything the applicant has to say, avoiding snap judgments and categorizations. One goal is to understand the applicant's own outlook. If the format allows, the interviewer pursues hints and follows up important leads but remains careful not to turn the session into an interrogation. Encouraged to ask questions, the applicant understands that his or her needs are being considered. The interviewer avoids not only verbal threats but also gestures and other nonverbal signals — such as glancing impatiently at the clock — that might increase the applicant's nervousness. If the applicant tends to be aggressive or abrupt, the interviewer remains unruffled.

Throughout the discussion the interviewer focuses on both technical qualifications for the job and intangible qualifications, such as motivation, energy, and enthusiasm. In evaluating the intangibles, the interviewer considers not just the particular job opening but also the entire staff of that department, the characteristics of the coworkers and superiors, and the organizational climate and culture. The interviewer takes notes on the candidate's answers but does so discreetly, so as not to hinder the discussion.

Before the session ends, the interviewer makes certain that the applicant understands the exact nature of the job. It is important for both the company and the candidate that any misconceptions be dispelled. Sometimes an interviewer will need to "sell" the firm — that is, emphasize its attractiveness in order to persuade a good candidate to accept the job — but the persuasion should not encourage unreasonable expectations.

The applicant is given a date by which he or she will learn the firm's decision; or, if a next step is already planned, the candidate is told exactly what it will entail. When the interview is over, the interviewer personally conducts the candidate back to the reception area.

Finally, the interviewer writes up the notes from the interview, often on a standardized form. In evaluating the candidate, the interviewer tries to allow for subjective factors that might influence his or her judgment. Was there anything personally objectionable about the applicant? If so, is it related to the job requirements? Do the judgments entered on the interview report have a rational basis?

When the interview follows these guidelines, the firm should have a solid body of information on which to base the last phase of the selection process, the selection decision.[46]

The Selection Decision

When all the candidates have been tested and interviewed and their references checked, the final decision generally rests with the supervisor or head of the department in which the job opening exists, who will select the one candidate most qualified for the job. The human resources department, however, regularly must approve the salary and benefit package to ensure consistency of pay scales throughout the firm.

The job offer itself can be made by a supervisor, or manager, but in large firms it is frequently handled by the human resources staff. The offer is sometimes extended by phone or in a letter; in other cases, the candidate is called in for a final interview and the offer is made in person. At this time the salary and benefits are stated precisely; the prospective employee is told of any further conditions that must be met, such as passing a physical examination; a starting time is established; and, if the candidate needs time to think the matter over, a date should be set for notifying the firm of acceptance or rejection. Aspects of the position such as salary and benefits should have been discussed earlier in general terms so that the candidate is not surprised by any of the particulars. Unrealistic promises by the company representative should be avoided; these can lead to low morale or litigation later on.[47]

In the satisfaction of filling a job opening, the human resources staff should not forget the applicants who failed to get the job. All those who participated in tests or interviews should be quickly notified of the firm's decision, and those who went furthest in the selection process should receive personal letters. Consideration for these people is important for the organization's reputation. Moreover, the "near misses" may be candidates for future job openings.

The success of a selection decision depends on all of the previous steps in the staffing process: the initial planning, the recruitment of qualified candidates, and the various selection techniques used to find the best candidate for the job. Only by careful attention to all these stages can an organization assure itself of hiring capable people.

Employment Eligibility

There is one additional component in the employment process that both precedes and follows the employment decision — the verification of **employment eligibility.** The **Immigration Reform and Control Act** requires employers of four or more workers to hire only American citizens and aliens authorized to work in the United States. Eligibility for employment must be verified for *each* new employee, including U.S. citizens, within three days after he or she starts to work. Both the employee and the employer must complete and sign form I-9, with the employer noting which documents were presented for eligibility and attesting that the documents appear to be genuine. Form I-9 must be retained by the employer for at least three years.[48] (The problem of illegal employment of aliens is a worldwide problem. See *International Perspective* on page 240.)

Since Title VII of the Civil Rights Act prohibits discrimination against any person on the basis of national origin in hiring, discharge, recruitment, compensation, and other terms and conditions of employment, employers must be careful to avoid violating the Civil Rights Act in the process of verifying employment eligibility. A procedure that many firms have used is to include an item on the application blank that inquires into the applicant's eligibility to work in the United States. Citizenship status is then checked after employment.[49] For example, the application form used by the Erie Insurance Group has this item: "Do you have a legal right to accept a job in the United States?"[50]

International Perspective

The Short Cut

They are called the "new wetbacks". But there is a big difference between the Africans and Asians who try to slip across the Straits of Gibraltar and the Mexicans who swim or wade across the Rio Grande. Europe's "wetbacks" prefer not to enter the water.

They do not always manage to avoid it. Most of them are shipped across in open, flat-bottomed boats, equipped with a single outboard motor, designed for inshore fishing. They are meant to hold seven people at most, yet they often take on more than 20. The Moroccan skippers of these frail craft often force their passengers over the side when they come within swimming distance of the Spanish coast. This brutal practice adds yet another danger to an already perilous enterprise. With its swirling currents and roaring winds, the mouth of the Mediterranean is one of the world's most hazardous stretches of water.

In the past three years, 36 bodies have been found by the Spaniards in the main entry zone on either side of Tarifa, a windswept town 14 kilometres (nine miles) from the Moroccan coast. How many more corpses have been washed out into the Atlantic or back on to the coast of Morocco is anybody's guess.

Yet there is no shortage of hopefuls ready to part with the $600 it costs on average for the one-way ride. By the end of August the Civil Guard unit headquartered at nearby Algeciras had made 1,208 arrests this year, compared with 842 in the whole of the last year and 263 in 1990. This suggests a spectacular rise in the number of attempted crossings.

The police claim to pick up two-thirds of the total. Even half that proportion would be remarkable, given how little effort the Spanish government has put into catching these people. The Civil Guards have no patrol boats, though they have been promised five in October. They have to rely on land-based watchers and tip-offs from fishing boats, merchant ships and a recently started helicopter patrol. The closer you get to this bit of "Fortress Europe", the more you find its anti-immigrant walls are made of cardboard.

About half the would-be immigrants are Moroccans, whom the Spanish can easily identify and send back home. A virtually insoluble problem arises with the other half, most of them black Africans. These generally arrive without papers, and lie about their origins in the expectation that Spain will thus be unable to deport them. Usually they are right. The Spaniards occasionally persuade consular officials from countries which they suspect people come from to identify their nationals; but many of the countries have no representation in Spain. Morocco refuses to take illegals back unless it can be proved they set off from the Moroccan coast.

So most of those picked up are simply served with an expulsion order, in the implausible hope that this will persuade them to go home. Instead, some make for France. Others stay in Spain, working illegally in jobs more prosperous Spaniards now disdain. Without papers, it is a precarious existence — but a lot better than the one they left behind.

Source: *The Economist*, September 12, 1992, p. 56. © 1992 The Economist Newspaper Group, Inc. Reprinted with permission.

Summary   Recruitment and selection, the processes by which a firm finds and chooses its employees, are perhaps the most critical tasks any organization faces. Without the right people, no firm can function effectively. For a recruitment program to be successful, managers should cooperate with the human resources staff to define needs and predict vacancies.

Depending on its particular needs, an organization may recruit either from its current staff or from outside the firm, or both. For internal recruiting, the principal methods are job posting, the use of computerized skills inventories, and referrals from other departments. For external recruiting, organizations rely on advertisements, public or private placement agencies, field recruiting, including campus recruiting, and internships. Groups that have experienced discrimination in the past (women, minorities, older workers, and those with disabilities) are special targets of contemporary recruiting.

Selection standards should be chosen carefully to predict a candidate's success on the job. For many organizations these standards must also comply with legal requirements. The critical criteria in this regard are job relatedness, reliability, and validity, as suggested by the Uniform Guidelines issued by the federal government. Care must be exercised in the use of all selection devices and procedures to avoid unfair and illegal discrimination.

The usual sources of information about applicants include application forms, reference checks, physical examinations, tests, and interviews. Each of these provides important pieces of information. Testing seems perhaps the most objective way of rating candidates on dimensions that may be vital to job performance, but the tests a firm administers should show high levels of validity and job relatedness to avoid charges of discrimination. It is unlawful to use different cutoff scores on the basis of race, color, religion, sex, or national origin.

Interviewing may be the most subjective phase of the selection process, but many firms consider it the most valuable. In an effective interview, the candidate's own ideas and attitudes will be explored more fully than at any other stage of the selection process. Both the candidate and the firm will then be well prepared for the job offer, the point at which the best applicant is notified of his or her success. Lastly, the employer must verify the applicant's employment eligibility. Without violating the Civil Rights Acts, each organization is required, under federal immigration laws, to verify each candidate's legal right to accept employment in the United States.

Ethical Dilemma

John Samuelson, employment interviewer, believes that many women are not up to the pressures of supervisory and managerial roles in business. Therefore, in interviewing female candidates for supervisory jobs, he tenaciously interrogates them in an attempt to create a high level of stress. Those who become visibly upset or tearful he rejects.

Discuss the ethics of John's interviewing practices.

Key Terms

recruitment	bottom-line principle
selection	adverse impact
job posting	biodata
bid	weighted application form
employee referral	reference checks
skills inventory	negligent hiring
Job Service	polygraph test
executive search firm	honesty test
field recruiting	group interview
glass ceiling	panel interview
glass wall	one-on-one interview
reasonable accommodation	videotape interviewing
screening	computer-assisted interview
reliability	structured or patterned interview
validity	nondirective interview
criterion-related validity	situational-problem interview
content validity	halo effect
construct validity	horn effect
job relatedness	employment eligibility
Uniform Guidelines on	Immigration Reform and Control
Employee Selection Procedures	Act

Review Questions

1. Describe the recruitment process and discuss the organizational and environmental factors that influence it.
2. What are the basic methods of recruitment? What roles are played by the various managers and professionals, including human resources professionals, in the use of these methods?
3. Discuss how and why organizations attempt to recruit specific groups such as women, minorities, and the handicapped.
4. Describe the selection process and discuss its implications for both the applicant and the organization.
5. What roles do different managers and professionals play in the selection process? Discuss.
6. Explain the concepts of job relatedness, reliability, and validity and their relation to selection standards.
7. Discuss the impact of the legal environment on selection procedures.
8. Discuss the use of application forms, reference checks, and physical examinations in employee selection, including any advantages and difficulties with these procedures.
9. What are some of the advantages and problems associated with testing programs?
10. Describe the different types of interviews, some problems encountered in interviewing, and the characteristics of an effective interview.

Opening Case Questions

Case 9.1 New Components in the Electronics Business

1. What basic projections need to be made before Beth Ann and the company start a major recruiting effort?

2. If you were Beth Ann, what sources would you probably use in your recruiting efforts and what problems would you need to anticipate?
3. Who should do the recruiting and selecting that is facing this company?

Case 9.2   It's Only Common Sense, Isn't It?

1. What assumptions was Mitch making? To what extent were these realistic? To the extent that Mitch's concerns had some basis in reality, what organizational solutions might be considered?
2. Discuss male candidates, including single fathers, relative to this case.

Comprehensive Case

The New Codes of Discriminatory Hiring

"Have them talk to Maria," the recruiting agency's job order from the employer said. "She's in room 20–30."

This detail of the transaction between a California employment agency and one of its clients sounds innocent, but in fact it is one of the latest ways companies have used to circumvent equal opportunity hiring laws. The instructions seem to indicate simply who the job candidate should see and where. But the use of "Maria" lets the agency know that the employer wants Hispanic workers, and the room number tells the agency that the employer only wants applicants who are in their twenties. If the company had wanted only Caucasian applicants, the contact person would have been "Mary"; if the name used had been "Adam," the company would have wanted only male applicants.

Before the days of nondiscriminatory hiring laws and the Equal Employment Opportunity Commission (EEOC), an employer could have simply told an employment agency, "We want a young Hispanic woman." But when the EEOC found out about the codes used by Interplace, a Los Angeles employment agency, it filed a lawsuit which resulted in a $2 million judgment. The money will be divided among some thirty-nine hundred people whose employment opportunities were affected by the discriminatory practice. Interplace was also ordered to conduct its own affirmative-action recruiting, encouraging applicants who are Hispanic, African-American, and non-Japanese Asian.

The lawsuit settlement is the largest ever against an employment agency, but the EEOC is currently investigating complaints against other agencies nationwide. It has received reports that insurance companies, Wall Street firms, and manufacturers have used similar codes to screen potential employees. Some agencies apparently use even more direct codes, having customers say, for instance, "no accents," when they don't want minorities of any kind.

This isn't the first time Interplace has been affected by scandal. It used to be owned by Japan's Recruit Company. Recruit's practice of giving Japanese legislators free or bargain-priced stock was an important element in a Japanese scandal, which grew so large that it resulted in the fall of the government of former Prime Minister Noboru Takeshita.

Whether or not Interplace's code was related to its parent company's other illegal activities, Interplace may have developed the code in part because it specializes in finding people who speak both Japanese and English. The EEOC alleges that if job seekers were over forty but not of Japanese ancestry, they were potential candidates to be illegally screened out by Interplace. Some of the blame for the illegal scheme may belong to the companies using Interplace. American hiring laws are much stricter than those in other countries; a number of Americans have won discrimination lawsuits against foreign companies, and agencies dealing with such companies often find themselves in a position of teaching the companies about American laws.

One agency executive recounts sending one well-qualified applicant after another to fill an administrative secretary position at a Japanese company. All were turned down. Finally, a receptionist told the executive the root of the problem: the Japanese boss wanted a blonde.

While catering to such personal biases is clearly unfair, the recruiting agencies often find themselves trying to satisfy more legitimate employer needs. For instance, Tadaki Endo, an American citizen born in Japan, wanted to hire a salesperson specifically to handle Japanese customers of his San Francisco Fleet & Leasing. Asking for someone who speaks Japanese to fill such a position simply makes good business sense.

But is it fair to ask that the applicant understand the Japanese culture? Peter Fernandez got the job precisely for that reason. Growing up with a Japanese mother, he not only spoke the language but knew something of Japanese customs. Fernandez feels that his knowledge pays off. When, in the slow process of getting to know a Japanese customer, most American salespeople would get impatient and give up, Fernandez knows to wait, accept another invitation to lunch, let the client bring up the subject of business.

Experts on Japanese business have long chided American companies trying to sell to Japan for their reluctance to hire employees who understand such nuances of Japanese business culture. The need for such people will clearly continue to grow. More and more American companies are trying zto break into the Japanese market. And the number of Japanese-owned manufacturing plants built in California alone more than doubled between 1985 and 1990. Although few would defend Interplace's use of the discriminatory code, the legitimate need to hire employees with partic-

ular linguistic or cultural expertise means that recruiting agencies and government watchdogs will probably continue, in and out of court, to define the line between acceptable and unacceptable hiring practices.

Sources: "Deciphering a Racist Business Code," *Time*, October 19, 1992, pp. 21–22; Hal Foster, "Pacific Report," *Los Angeles Times*, July 1, 1991, p. D1; Kathleen Pender, "Employment Agency Faces Contempt Proceeding," *San Francisco Chronicle*, May 16, 1990, p. C1; and Stacy Wong, "Placement Agency to Pay $2-million Settlement," *Los Angeles Times*, October 7, 1992, p. D2.

Discussion Questions

1. Why not use a coding system and send an employer candidates with the racial, ethnic, sex, age, or national origin qualifications the employer wants?
2. Under what circumstances would it be appropriate for an employment agency to screen people for their understanding of a particular culture or their capabilities in the use of a particular language?

CHAPTER 10

Career Transitions

LEARNING OBJECTIVES

- Explain why the effective management of career transitions is important both to individual employees and to the organization as a whole.
- Characterize an effective orientation program.
- Describe the procedures commonly used for making promotion decisions.
- Give examples of how the labor agreement governs staffing decisions and policies in the organization.
- Outline some of the options organizations have for avoiding layoffs.
- Identify some actions management can take to ensure that employee terminations are nondiscriminatory.
- List the phases of a career crisis and identify ways organizations can minimize crises and offer support.

CASE 10.1   The Transfer

Mike O'Connor and his wife, Margaret, had been fighting recently. Nothing serious, but a lot of arguments about little things. It was probably the transfer.

Mike's transfer was anything but a simple move from one department to another or one office to another. It was a whole change of lifestyle. Or so it seemed to him and Margaret. In a huge "restructuring," the company had offered Mike the choice of a layoff from the Boston plant or a transfer to the Los Angeles plant. He had looked at other jobs in the Boston area, but nothing seemed to come close to the responsibility and salary he would have in L.A. He and Margaret had flown out there at company expense, and both had agreed that accepting the transfer was the best thing to do.

But now the kids were homesick for Boston. They were having a tough time making friends in their new neighborhood, and their classes in school were out of phase with what they had been studying. Margaret didn't like the nearby supermarket as well as the neighborhood stores she was used to back east. Driving to work took Mike longer, and it seemed as if the traffic was heavier. They were both worried about how they were going to come out in terms of taxes.

The new job was O.K. but Mike was having trouble sorting out the office politics. He was becoming aware of some kind of conflict between two of the higher managers, and that subordinates were taking sides in subtle ways, such as not sharing information and not socializing much across department lines. He was catching on quickly to the customer-contact part of his job, and that was going well. Generally, he liked his new boss, but he didn't have a clear sense that his manager thought he was doing a good job, although he had no signals that anything was amiss. Yesterday his boss had asked him how the transfer was going, and he had tried to respond with a cheerful "O.K." But what he had really wanted to tell his boss was about the difficulties he and his family were encountering. ◀

CASE 10.2   The Promotion Decision

The position of sales manager in the industrial accounts department of Enterprise Insurance was vacant. The previous department manager, Steve Tanaka, had been very successful and had just been promoted to vice president of sales. He and the company president, Nancy Finley, thought Al Thompson might be Steve's logical successor. As a sales representative, Al had shown that he was bright, aggressive, and ambitious.

Nancy and Steve wanted some confirmation that Al was the right candidate for the job, so they hired a psychologist to provide some additional information about Al's qualifications. The psychologist, who had done a good deal of work with the firm over the years, gave Al a battery of tests, interviewed him at length, and wrote a report evaluating his potential as a manager.

Al did well on the tests. He scored very high on the intelligence test, and according to the interest survey, his interests were clearly compatible with the role for which he was being considered. Moreover, his academic credentials were outstanding; they included an advanced degree with honors from the best business school in the region. The psychologist saw no reason not to recommend Al for the managerial position, and she found plenty of evidence for predicting that Al would be successful. She wrote her report accordingly, and Al was offered the job, which he promptly accepted.

Al was very pleased with the job offer, viewing it as a desirable career move, as well as an opportunity to earn considerably more money. As a sales representative he had been paid on a salary-plus-commission basis. Now he would receive commissions based on a percentage of all of the insurance sold by his subordinates, as well as a substantial increase in salary.

Shortly after Al accepted the new position, a memo was circulated announcing his promotion to manager, effective the following Monday. Right after lunch on the day this announcement was made, a delegation of Al's new subordinates came to Nancy's office requesting a meeting. To Nancy, it seemed more like a demand than a request. What the delegation wanted to talk about was widespread dissatisfaction with the decision to promote Al to manager.

Nancy immediately called a meeting of all of the industrial salespeople. Steve was included in the meeting, but Al was not invited. It was immediately apparent when the meeting convened that the salespeople were angry about the promotion and that some were ready to leave the company. What bothered them most, they said, was that Al had a reputation for promoting his own interests at the expense of others. He had a long history of taking customers from his peers in ways they perceived as unethical. One sales representative stated it this way: "Al's not a team player; he's out for himself. I don't trust him and I won't work for him." It was clear to Steve and Nancy that they had a serious problem on their hands.   ◀

*A*nyone who has been transferred can probably identify to some extent with Mike O'Connor's experience in Case 10.1. Transfers or promotions, as well as the first days on a new job, can be exciting but anxiety-producing transitions. When a change of cities is involved and a family is uprooted, the transition can be much more complex and traumatic. Others, including coworkers, supervisors, and managers, are also affected.

Case 10.2 dramatizes how another significant career event, a promotion, can be perceived positively or negatively by various people close to the situation. In a promotion, an employee leaves one career role and takes on another; what this really means is that the individual's relationship with a number of other people will change. Everyone who has some connection with the promoted employee — both before and after the promotion — will have some perceptions and feelings about the transition and what it means to him or her individually. If there are to be productive outcomes for all concerned and minimal negative effects on job performance and satisfaction, those involved in the promotion decision must be concerned not only with the qualifications of the promotion candidate; they must also consider the consequences of the decision for all affected employees and for the organization itself.

This chapter is about several of the most significant transitions that can occur in people's working lives and that also have major implications for organizations: coming into an organization as a new employee; transferring to another job; being promoted; experiencing a demotion, layoff, or discharge; resigning from an organization; and retiring. Fortunately, many people do not have to face *all* of these career changes, but most will probably experience some of them. Whether or not one experiences these changes personally, it is important to understand what they mean to people and, better yet, to be able to help manage these transitions as constructively and effectively as possible.

Orientation

On the first few days at a new job, employees are faced with an unfamiliar situation to which they must somehow adjust. New surroundings, new coworkers, and new job procedures can make even the calmest and most competent workers feel anxious and insecure. Therefore, most organizations offer some kind of **orientation**: a program designed to help new employees get acquainted with the company and make a productive beginning on the job.

Even in organizations without formal orientation programs, probably a high proportion of supervisors and peers are sufficiently sensitive to the plight of the newcomer to informally provide at least a modicum of assistance. For example, someone shows the new employee the location of his or her workstation, the location of the restrooms and cafeteria, and perhaps the location of elevators and exits and takes the newcomer around the work area. Some people will go to considerable lengths to help a new person feel welcome and to adjust to the new situation.

It should be recognized, however, that orientation procedures vary widely in their usefulness to the new employee. Their usefulness depends on whether the program is haphazardly or systematically designed and on the extent to which the orientation has been captured by dysfunctional norms. (A dysfunctional norm might be "We always see if the new person 'can take it.'") Without planning and without soliciting cooperation of the work group, present employees will sometimes engage in dysfunctional behaviors.

Consider the case of a new employee who is assigned by peers to sweeping the warehouse three times a day when once would have sufficed, or the new worker who is sent on foolish errands by other employees. This behavior is known as **hazing**, or harassing with unnecessary tasks or practical jokes. Hazing is damaging to the newcomer's morale and lengthens the time it takes for the new employee to be productive. At the other extreme, just ignoring a new employee can also prevent the employee and the unit from getting off to a good start.

Characteristics of Orientation Programs

Formal orientation procedures for new employees usually include introductions to coworkers and a tour of the facilities. More comprehensive orientation programs also provide information about the daily routine, employee benefits and services, work rules, safety rules and programs, training and promotion practices, company organization and operations, company products or services, and company history. The general outline of a thorough orientation program at the Erie Insurance Group is shown in Figure 10.1.

A systematic orientation program may last only a few hours or may extend over several weeks. Information may be given through interviews, group meetings and discussion, handbooks, videotapes, tours, or combinations of these and other methods. Checklists are often used to ensure thoroughness. (See Item 4 of the orientation schedule shown in Figure 10.1.) Many programs include follow-up interviews at the end of three or six months' employment to determine how well the new employee is getting along.

ORIENTATION SCHEDULE

Welcome to the ERIE. The purpose of employee Orientation for you, your supervisor and the ERIE to get acquainted. Orientation is designed to help you learn a new job and adjust to a new working environment.

The folowing schedule has been designed to help make your Orientation Program as smooth as possible.

1.   NEW EMPLOYEE SIGN UP (Thirty to Forty Minutes)
     You will reprt to the Employment Department, Human Resources Division, at the start of your first working dayto complete the necessary paperwork and receive an Employee Handbook. You will also receive a brief explanation and outline of the Orientation Program

2.   COMPLIMENTARY LUNCH (One Hour)
     Your supervisor will accompany you to lunch on your first working day. A lunch ticket will be provided for you, compliments of the ERIE.

3.   PHYSICAL EXAMINATION (Forty-Five Minutes)
     Within the first week of employment, you will be scheduled to report to the Health Services Section for a routine physical examination. Physicals are normally scheduled for your first working Wednesday

4.   EMPLOYEE ORIENTATION CHECKLIST
     Your supervisor should discuss with you your position responsibilities, department rules, and company policies and procedures during your first two weeks of employment. An Orientation Checklist (Form HR B-31) has been provided to assist your supervisor. He or she will complete it with you and return it to the Employment Department, Human Resources Division.

5.   ORIENTATION INFORMATION SESSION (One and One-Half Hours)
     You will also be scheduled to attend an orientation information session in the Development Center during your first month of employment. During this session, you will see a videotape about the ERIE and a slide presentation which will aquaint you with company policies and procedures as outlined in the Employee Handbook. You will also learn about the services available to you as an ERIE employee.

6.   FOLLOW-UP CONTACT
     the Employment Department will contact your supervisor after approximately one month to ckeck that your orientation is progressing smoothly. You are also encouraged to contact your supervisor or the Employment Department if you have any questions or problems.

7.   HOME OFFICE TOUR (One and One-Half Hours)
     You will be scheduled for a tour of the Home Office complex within your first month of employment to help you become familiar with your new workplace.

8.   PERFORMANCE ASSESSMENT
     Your supervisor will conduct a Performance Assessment with you after your first 60 days on the job to let you know how you are doing. This is a good time for you to discuss any concerns or suggestions with your supervisor.

9.   ORIENTATION INTERVIEW
     An Orientation Interview is scheduled after apprximately 60 days of employment. This interview gives you a chance to discuss your thoughts about working at the ERIE and verifies that you have been given information you need as a new ERIE employee.

FIGURE 10.1   Orientation schedule of the Erie Insurance Group

Source: Courtesy of the Erie Insurance Group.

A number of potential problems are associated with the orientation procedure for new employees. For example, giving too much information in an orientation session can be almost as much of a problem as providing too little. If a great deal of information is given to employees all at once, they may feel overwhelmed and may not retain much. Those who design the orientation program should be sensitive to such matters as how much information to supply at a given session, how to sequence the various parts of the program, and how well the new employees are assimilating the information. Providing plenty of opportunity for questions and discussion is an effective way to clarify the presentation.

The new employee's immediate supervisor also plays an important role in the orientation process. First, the supervisor must cooperate in releasing the new employee from the job to attend orientation sessions. At a minimum, supervisors should also be responsible for introducing the new employee to fellow workers and to his or her assigned tasks. Ideally, supervisors work closely with the human resources department in designing the orientation program, and selected supervisors are invited to give presentations. As an example of organization-wide cooperation in developing an orientation program, at the Metropolitan Life Insurance Company, employees, supervisors, and managers from all segments of the business collaborated in designing a program, which included a series of videotapes.[1]

Employee handbooks are typically given to new employees during the orientation process. Handbooks are useful for providing information about such matters as benefits and work rules and are handy reference guides when employees have questions during the ensuing weeks and months.

In recent years a number of lawsuits have grown out of improperly or ambiguously worded statements in the employee handbooks of some organizations. In particular, terminated employees have challenged dismissals on the grounds that the employee handbook gave them contractual rights to employment or to procedural protections. Legal opinion suggests that employers who wish to set some limitations on job rights should "set forth clear, conspicuous disclaimers of contractual intent and must include statements reaffirming the at-will nature of employment in all employee materials."[2] It is also recommended that supervisors refrain from making statements implying that employees are entitled to permanent employment.[3] (For more on the "employment-at-will" rule, see Chapter 19.)

Reducing Anxiety

An orientation program should have as one of its chief objectives a reduction in the new employee's anxiety. At Texas Instruments Incorporated, a large electronics manufacturing firm, a research study was undertaken to determine the effectiveness of the standard orientation program. The usual procedures called for a two-hour orientation seminar, after which the employee was sent to the supervisor for job instructions and then on to the workstation. Interviews investigating how new assemblers felt about their first day on the job revealed the following:

- The first few days on the job were anxious and disturbing ones for new employees.
- Hazing practices by peers intensified anxiety.
- Anxiety interfered with the training process.
- Turnover of newly hired employees was caused primarily by anxiety.
- New employees were reluctant to discuss problems with their supervisors.

Additional interviews with supervisors and middle managers about their feelings in working with new employees uncovered these insights:

- Supervisors and middle managers experienced as much anxiety as the new employees.
- They felt inadequate with seasoned, competent subordinates.
- They cut off downward communication to conceal ignorance.
- Supervisory defensiveness discouraged upward communication.[4]

The results of these interviews prompted the company to experiment with a different orientation procedure. In this experiment, a group of assemblers who were new to the company first attended the usual two-hour orientation session and then participated in an "anxiety-reduction seminar" for the rest of the day. This seminar focused on presenting new employees with information about the job environment and about the personalities and practices of their new supervisors. The new employees were given statistics indicating the high probability of their success, were told what to expect in the way of hazing and rumors from other employees, and were urged to take the initiative in asking questions of their supervisors. The seminar also allowed considerable opportunity for questions and answers.

The experiment both reduced anxiety and produced other positive results. By the end of four weeks, the experimental group was performing significantly better than a control group in assembling, welding, and inspection. Attendance was also better.[5]

Improving Orientation Programs

Other research suggests ways of increasing the effectiveness of orientation programs. For example, a study in one company found that supervisors frequently lacked the skills to bring new employees aboard (for example, introducing the new employee to fellow workers); there was usually little feedback about early performance; and new employees had many questions and concerns about the reward system, transfer policies, the career development process, and other matters. As a result, a number of corrective measures were taken, including three days of supervisory training in orientation methods and the establishment of procedures to follow the progress of each new employee for six months. In addition, a one-day workshop involving a facilitator working with supervisors and their new employees was designed to encourage feedback and to iron out misunderstandings. The overall results included increased productivity and job satisfaction among new employees, with substantial annual savings stemming from improved performance.[6]

In general, research and experience indicate that orientation procedures should be thoroughly planned and that those conducting the programs should address specific problems faced by new employees. No one orientation system will be best in all circumstances, but it is clear that participative approaches and genuine human warmth and concern for each individual are vital. The human resources department should play a key role in planning and coordinating the orientation program in collaboration with line managers and supervisors.

Internal Staffing Process

The movement of human resources within an organization is as important as the recruitment and selection of people from outside and calls for the same careful planning and use of fair and systematic procedures. Employees may be reassigned to new positions at the initiative of the organization to fill staff vacancies, to reduce labor costs, or to place workers in jobs that are more appropriate to their interests and abilities. Employees also seek reassignments as their interests and abilities develop through experience. Matching individual needs for growth and development with the needs of the organization is a major goal of the internal staffing process. Inadequate or shortsighted attention to internal staffing changes can have negative effects on morale and productivity, which in turn can seriously impair the organization's ability to attain its objectives.

Most often, supervisors or managers are responsible for initiating employee reassignment. Because the human resources department has an overall view of the organization's staffing needs and goals, that department is typically given the authority to coordinate and review plans for internal staffing changes and to ensure that decisions comply with company policy. In unionized organizations, the labor contract spells out the rules and procedures governing transfer, promotion, and other internal staffing changes pertaining to those employees covered by the contract.

Transfer   Employees may be reassigned, or asked to **transfer**, from one job to another, one department to another, one shift to another, or one geographic location to another. These reassignments may be initiated by the organization (called **involuntary transfer**) or by the employee with the approval of the organization.

Most organizations have specific transfer policies and procedures that have been developed mainly in response to three problem situations. The first is that of the employee with a history of poor performance or problem behavior whom the department head does not want to keep on staff. Without definite rules about transfers, such employees tend to be reassigned from one department to another in a kind of organizational game of musical chairs. Consequently, many firms put constraints on the transfer of problem employees and require that some other solution be reached. In instances where another supervisor or department head is willing to accept the employee, careful evaluation is necessary to make sure that the transfer is fair to everyone involved and that the move is in the interests of the total organization.

The second problem is the need to ensure a close match between an employee's qualifications and the new position. Careful appraisal of an employee's performance and potential should precede any transfer to make certain that his or her qualifications suit the new job. It does not make sense to be careful about initial hiring and then to be casual about a transfer later on. The human resources department can play an important role in this appraisal process by helping to develop thorough procedures and then monitoring transfers to make certain that supervisors are using those procedures appropriately.

The third problem, which can be particularly delicate, is that of relating the employee's present wage or salary to the compensation offered in the new position. It is neither financially sound nor fair to other employees to transfer a worker from a job paying $4,000 per month to one paying $2,000 per month and to continue to pay the higher salary, unless there are extraordinary circumstances, such as a pending retirement or ill health that is assumed to be temporary. Ordinarily, such a transfer would be unwise and would suggest that there are issues not being dealt with, such as inadequacies in the employee's performance or in the salary structure.

Relocation, or the transfer of an employee from one location to another, presents additional problems. Cost is a major factor. In 1991 it was estimated that it cost an average of $37,600 to relocate an employee within the United States.[7] Distant moves for a GTE mid-level manager was budgeted at $70,000 in 1992.[8]

Employees transferred at company request are typically reimbursed for moving costs and other expenses. Some examples of relocation costs often absorbed by the organization include assistance in the sale of the present home, a house-hunting trip, subsidized mortgage payments so the employee can afford a new home, travel to the new location, and costs of temporary living arrangements. Obviously, such costs should not be incurred lightly, and organizations must give careful consideration to the merits and drawbacks involved in each transfer decision.

There are human costs as well as financial considerations involved in the relocation of human resources, and these are particularly significant in the case of involuntary transfers. According to one source, the relocation of more than half of the 40 million Americans who move each year is due to company transfer. With so many people moving, it is little wonder that greater attention is being paid to the impact of relocation on employees and their families. Research indicates that the impact is greatest on families with school-age children, particularly teenagers. Spouses seem to carry the heaviest burden of the family's adjustment to the new community.[9]

The **dual-career couple** (both spouses are employed) must make difficult choices when one partner faces the possibility of relocation; this also creates a challenge to the organization wishing to transfer one of the partners. This problem is arising more frequently as more and more women are moving into professional roles. Sometimes the employee accepts the transfer (or promotion) and the spouse finds employment in the new community; sometimes the employee turns down the transfer; and sometimes the employer also hires the spouse. Each situation is unique and requires a careful analysis by the affected couple, including an analysis of housing costs. The matter becomes even more complicated in the case of international transfers. (See *International Perspective* on page 255.)

More and more common is the **commuter marriage,** in which each spouse may work three to five days a week in a different location. Even when only one spouse is employed, a commuter marriage can result when a plant or office closes and the employee accepts a position with the company in a different city. Obviously, commuter marriages can create stresses and strains in marriage and family relationships.[10] This is even more likely in the case of international commuter marriages.[11]

In the light of these financial and human costs, it is becoming more common for firms to be less insistent that employees accept transfers or promotions to different geographic areas. Further, with rising relocation costs, organizations are more likely to analyze carefully the costs and benefits of shifting human resources from one area to another.

Promotion

A **promotion** is a type of transfer involving the reassignment of an employee to a position that is likely to offer higher pay and greater responsibilities, privileges, and potential opportunities. In general, the purpose of a promotion is to staff a vacant position that is worth more to the organization than the employee's present position. This additional worth is usually reflected in the pay range for the position, although in some instances the organization relies on additional prestige. (An example, in the case of some academic institutions, is the professor who moves into the role of department chair for a term of three or four years. There is prestige attached to the position but frequently no additional pay. This may be why colleagues

International Perspective

Solving the Dual International Career Dilemma

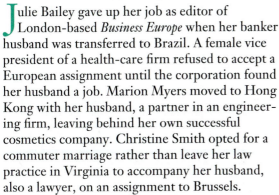

Julie Bailey gave up her job as editor of London-based *Business Europe* when her banker husband was transferred to Brazil. A female vice president of a health-care firm refused to accept a European assignment until the corporation found her husband a job. Marion Myers moved to Hong Kong with her husband, a partner in an engineering firm, leaving behind her own successful cosmetics company. Christine Smith opted for a commuter marriage rather than leave her law practice in Virginia to accompany her husband, also a lawyer, on an assignment to Brussels.

The increasing number of dual career couples has added greatly to the complexity of international transfers. In an international relocation the "trailing spouse" faces legal and linguistic barriers, local employment and union regulations, differing professional and licensing requirements.

All of these make it difficult to find employment overseas, much less to continue a career. In each case, the couple must decide how to accommodate the overseas assignment and their careers simultaneously. Facing the career challenges of an international posting requires couples to be creative, optimistic, flexible and determined.

On the other side of the equation, international human resource managers struggle to support such complex family situations. The need for consistent, cost-effective, equitable and administratively simple HR policies does not lend itself to satisfying the infinite variables involved in transferring career couples overseas. Distance increases administrative headaches; case-by-case assistance increases costs. Human resource managers must face the demand to develop dual career assignment policies using the same flexibility, sensitivity and creativity so valued in expatriates.

Currently, 70 percent of all marriages in the United States are dual-earner partnerships, according to a report from the Conference Board. Surveys offer conflicting data about whether the dual career issue increases the number of early returns, the number of expatriate divorces and the number of refusals to accept the overseas relocation. According to a just-published survey from The National Foreign Trade Council and Windham International, "Most companies feel that spouse careers have a major impact on the rejection of international assignments."

There is also a perception, among human resource managers, that "invisible failures" in dual career assignments — defined as less-than-optimum employee performance — may be common. Most agree that the issue is already of significant importance and will only become more acute. According to ORC's research, international HR managers believe that dual career overseas assignments will be one of the top five major challenges they must face in this decade.

In recent years, a number of organizations have evolved to counsel and support expatriate spouses about their career options while living abroad. FOCUS Career Services in Brussels and London, for example, provides advice on work permits, the local job market, educational opportunities and networking.

The Women on the Move conference held regularly in Europe brings together women who have successfully combined a career and an expatriate lifestyle with those in search of mentors. With the number of women assignees increasing rapidly (currently over 5 percent), the conference intends to target "male trailing spouses" for its November 1993 London gathering.

Until the late 1980s, corporations either dealt with the issue on a case-by-case basis, selected employees without career spouses or assumed that the household had only one primary breadwinner. As one international personnel director in Paris said when discussing an unemployed, unhappy career spouse, "All she needs is a cup of coffee and a good cry and she'll get over it."

Confronted with spouses who realize coffee and a cry are not viable solutions to career disruption, companies such as 3M, Motorola, Colgate-Palmolive and Monsanto have begun to design programs to help the accompanying spouse.

Based on the preliminary results of Bennett Associates' survey of accompanying career spouses worldwide, active involvement in the career of the accompanying spouse is the type of assistance preferred above all other interventions. This type of involvement can include sourcing potential employers and arranging interviews. Although this may be an expensive, risky and time-consuming activity, it is one companies may need to address in the near future.

International dual career couples and human resource managers alike are pioneers in uncharted territories. Although progress has been made, definitive approaches to dealing effectively with the dual career dilemma are still beyond the horizon. Some of the answers may lie in better candidate/spouse assessment and selection, open communication between international assignee and HR, further research and very creative problem solving on all levels.

Source: Rita Bennett, "Solving the International Career Dilemma." Reprinted with the permission of *HR News* (formerly Resource) published by the Society for Human Resource Management, Alexandria, VA.

approach the newly promoted person and cheerfully inquire whether congratulations or condolences are in order.) Sometimes an employee is promoted into a newly created, higher-paying position to take advantage of the employee's unique talents.

What constitutes a promotion, as opposed to a transfer or demotion, depends on one's point of view. Sometimes a promotion is offered to a person who considers it a demotion or a step backward in his or her career. An example is the research scientist who is offered the directorship of a research laboratory, but who has no wish to be involved in administration. (There can be a way out of this dilemma — the "dual ladder" concept, discussed a little further in this section.)

In unionized organizations, the labor contract typically requires that **seniority**, or an employee's length of service with the department or organization, be a consideration in promotion decisions. In some contracts, seniority is the only deciding factor; other contracts allow consideration of both seniority and ability. Because management tends to argue for ability and unions tend to emphasize seniority in selecting promotion candidates, labor contracts often reflect a compromise. For example, a contract may call for the use of a formula for making promotion decisions, such as promoting the employee with the greatest seniority if ability and experience are equal. Many contracts permit promotion of any candidate who is "head and shoulders" above others in ability. Practices vary a great deal, however, from firm to firm.

One problem with any promotion decision is that the organization must continue a productive relationship with those employees who are by-passed. Fair and consistent implementation procedures for making promotion decisions will help reduce negative feelings on the part of employees who are not promoted. Some of the procedures or devices used in making promotion decisions are career progression ladders, interviews, tests, peer ratings, assessment centers, and fallback positions.

Career Progression Ladders

Career progression ladders (also called career paths, job ladders, or promotion ladders) are charts that illustrate the horizontal and vertical movement of employees from one job to another within an organization. A sample career ladder is shown in

Figure 10.2; a more detailed version might include the salary for each job and the experience and training required.

The strong orientation of many scientists, engineers, and other professionals toward continued technical work rather than supervisory or administrative assignments has led a number of firms to establish parallel promotional opportunities, sometimes called **dual ladders** or **parallel ladders.** In other words, the professional-technical employee can advance to such positions as "senior research scientist," as well as to more managerial positions such as "director of inorganic research."[12]

Career progression ladders are used to help employees visualize potential advancement within the organization and to plan the sequence of training and work experience necessary to reach particular career objectives. The device is also useful in the human resources planning process. For example, charting and examining existing patterns of career progression can be useful in eliminating dead-end paths, in developing training programs, and in advising on staffing decisions. Finally, when available to all employees in the organization, career progression ladders can help create a healthy perspective on the part of supervisors and employees alike: such charts symbolize that there is high mobility in the organization and that change is normal and to be expected. These charts can also enlighten those supervisors and managers who have a tendency to hold on to capable employees long after they have outgrown their jobs and are ready to move on.

Interviewing and Testing Interviews are widely used to allow potential candidates to express interest in higher-level job opportunities and to evaluate candidates for promotion. As in the selection process (see Chapter 9), a wide variety of interview approaches is used to make promotion decisions.

The extent to which tests are used in the promotion process varies widely by type of job and by industry. For example, one survey found that 17 percent of manufacturing firms use proficiency or aptitude tests in evaluating office-clerical candidates for promotion. In nonmanufacturing, the percentage was 28, and in non-business organizations (government, education, hospitals) the percentage was 40. The same study found that tests are used for promotion considerably more often in plant or service jobs than in professional or technical jobs.[13] Assessment centers typically use tests as part of the assessment process (see pages 258 and 259).

Like all selection devices, interview and test results are subject to legal challenge if discrimination or adverse impact is alleged. For example, as a result of an EEOC class-action suit, the CF&I Steel Corp. agreed to pay awards of $500,000 to 331 Hispanics of both sexes who alleged they had been discriminated against in the selection of supervisors.[14]

Peer Ratings **Peer ratings** are the evaluation of an employee's performance or potential for advancement by those of equal rank. Research has shown that peer ratings tend to be fairly accurate predictors of supervisory or managerial success.[15] They do not appear to be used very extensively, however, for making promotion decisions.

In Case 10.2 at the beginning of the chapter, the crisis involving the promotion of Al Thompson might have been avoided if information from peers about nominees for sales manager had been solicited. The important information about Al Thompson that the psychologist and top management did not have was that Al was not trusted by his peers. The psychologist could have found this out by interviewing

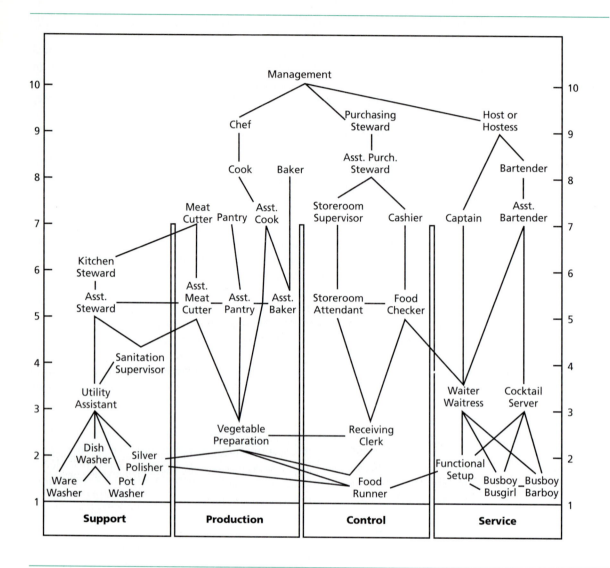

FIGURE 10.2 Career progression ladder for a food service facility

Source: William P. Fisher and Paul Gaurner, *Career Ladders in the Food Service Industry* (Chicago: National Restaurant Association, 1971), p. 25. Reprinted by permission.

each member of the department or by devising some kind of rating sheet that department members could fill out on a confidential basis.

Assessment Centers

In an **assessment center**, information about an employee's promotability and career development is gathered systematically and analyzed as the candidate participates in a series of tests, interviews, and exercises. The assessment center concept appears to be an effective, although expensive, approach to supervisory and managerial selection. Assessment centers are becoming increasingly popular in a variety of organizations in this country and abroad. It has been estimated that more than two thousand organizations are using this approach.[16]

The devices used in assessment centers include extensive interviews; tests of mental ability, skill in reasoning, and knowledge of current affairs; the leaderless group discussion; presentations by each member of the group; and simulation exercises. One popular simulation is the "in-basket" exercise, in which each candidate decides how to handle a series of memos that he or she finds in an in-basket. Other examples are business games in which teams of six candidates manage a toy company; mock interviews; and an exercise called the "Irate Customer Phone Call" (used at J. C. Penney). Staff members observe and score participants' performance on these exercises.[17]

An important component of an effective assessment center program is the feedback session, in which a member of the assessment staff explains the scores and ratings to each participant. These sessions are useful in minimizing participant frustration stemming from lack of information about results, and studies indicate that such feedback contributes to employee learning and development. Studies at Michigan Bell, for example, found that most employees who had participated in the assessment center and feedback process had a good understanding of their ratings and felt that the information given them would be helpful in their careers.[18]

Numerous studies of both men and women managers have found that assessment results are useful predictors of managerial success, which indicates that assessment centers can increase the proportion of successful to unsuccessful managers.[19] In addition, the assessment center is particularly useful in identifying managerial potential among women and minority-group employees. Finally, such centers can help identify lower-level managers who are promotable to higher positions. Here, the center can be a vehicle for upward mobility across department or division lines.

Fallback Positions

Establishing **fallback positions** is sometimes part of the promotion process. In this procedure, one or more positions that have the same status and pay as the promoted employee's original job are identified ahead of time. Should the promotion prove unsuccessful, the employee is transferred to the fallback position. This procedure "lets everyone know that (1) there is some risk in the promotion or transfer, (2) the company is willing to accept some of the responsibility for it, and (3) moving into the fallback position does not constitute failure."[20]

Demotion

A **demotion**, sometimes called a "downward transfer," is a type of transfer involving a cut in pay, status, privilege, or opportunity. Demotions may result from organizational staff reductions or disciplinary penalties. With an employee who is unable to perform adequately in a particular job, the purpose of a demotion is to remedy a previous mistake in staffing.

In some instances, demotions are mutually satisfactory arrangements stemming from an employee's health problems or changing interests. A demotion may simply be a return to a fallback position. On the other hand, demotions are frequently a shock to the affected employee and bring about the kinds of reactions associated with a career crisis, which is discussed later in this chapter.

To some extent the impact of a demotion depends on the organization's particular culture. If there is a great deal of movement up, down, and sideways in the organization and general acceptance that most employees have a zigzag pattern of career progression, a downward assignment may be accepted as simply another transfer. Such acceptance probably depends, however, on a high degree of job security and considerable trust in higher management's intentions.

Employee Separations

Other significant career transitions are those involving the separation of employees from the organization. Employees may leave the organization involuntarily, through layoff or discharge, or voluntarily, through resignation or retirement. Although the reasons for separation vary, each instance should be analyzed and understood in terms of its impact on the individual employee and on the organization as a whole. Sudden or unexpected removal from the organization can be particularly difficult for the affected employee and can damage the morale of coworkers and the organization's general climate. Even when the employee initiates the separation, the organization must be able to continue functioning until the vacancy is filled. Thus, the effective management of employee separations is vital to the healthy and continued functioning of the organization.

Layoff   A **layoff** — frequently called **downsizing** — is the temporary or indefinite removal of employees from the payroll. Generally, the purpose of the layoff is to reduce the organization's burden of excess labor costs when human resources cannot be used effectively. Layoffs may affect relatively small groups of employees, but when a large organization runs into serious financial problems, large numbers of workers may be laid off. In some instances, management is too quick to lay off employees because of financial downturn, thus depleting the organization's valuable human resources for the long term and damaging the morale and security of retained employees.[21] Furthermore, contrary to the views of many investors, layoffs (usually under the label "restructuring") frequently do not lead to improved profits and stock prices over a subsequent three-year period.[22] In some instances, however, layoffs may be the only option remaining for an organization facing possible bankruptcy.

Although there have been many instances of white-collar and supervisory employee layoffs in recent years, hourly paid production workers are typically the first to be affected by production cutbacks. Some organizations provide accrued vacation pay, **supplemental unemployment benefits (SUB)**, and continued health and life insurance to employees affected by a layoff, especially if the layoff is expected to be temporary. SUB clauses in labor contracts, which provide for company payments to laid-off workers, are designed to extend or enlarge the unemployment benefit payments provided under state law. **Severance pay**, usually a lump-sum payment at the time of permanent separation, is more common for nonunionized salaried workers than for unionized production and maintenance workers. (At the top executive level, severance pay has been labeled the **golden parachute**. Severance arrangements for some CEOs displaced by acquisition or merger have, indeed, been golden. For example, the CEO of Revlon, Inc., was paid $34 million when the cosmetics and health care company was acquired by Pantry Pride.)[23]

In a unionized organization, the labor contract governs the order of layoff and method of **recall**, or rehiring of laid-off employees. Seniority is usually the controlling factor: often the most senior employee is laid off last and is the first to be recalled. In such cases, the layoff is based on **reverse seniority**. In addition, the contract typically establishes the maximum period during which a laid-off employee has recall and other rights. **Bumping** provisions permit employees with greater seniority to accept a demotion and to replace less senior employees who are laid off. Bumping can work effectively only when the more senior employee is qualified and able to perform the work of the less senior employee.

When a large organization runs into serious financial problems, large numbers of workers may be laid off.

Federal law affects layoffs through both the Worker Adjustment and Retraining Notification Act of 1988 (Plant Closings Bill) (see Chapter 3) and EEOC requirements. For example, the long-established practice of basing layoff decisions on seniority alone has come squarely into conflict with EEOC requirements that organizations increase the numbers of female and minority employees in their work forces. Court rulings on this issue have been contradictory. In one case, involving the Jersey Central Power & Light Co., a court of appeals ruled that a conciliation agreement to establish an affirmative action program to hire more blacks and women could exist side by side with the collective-bargaining agreement that provided for laying off the least senior people first. Blacks and women would probably be laid off first because they would be apt to have the least seniority. But in *Watkins* v. *United Steelworkers*, a federal district court ordered the employer to apply seniority to white and black workers separately and to allocate future layoffs between black and white workers in proportion to their representation in the work force at the time of the layoffs.[24] Yet in *Firefighters Local 1784* v. *Stotts*, the Supreme Court ruled that a seniority system cannot be overridden to protect an affirmative action program in a layoff situation.[25]

The use of **inverse seniority** in layoff situations is gaining some support as a way out of the dilemma between reverse seniority and affirmative action. Under the concept of inverse seniority, the most senior workers are given the first opportunity to elect layoff. Volunteers may be motivated by such interests as traveling, remodeling the house, or simply desire for a change of pace. Those who volunteer are provided with unemployment compensation plus supplemental unemployment benefits. The success of inverse seniority plans depends on the company's SUB program and on the particular state concurring in the legality of paying unemployment compensation to such workers.

Discharge   **Discharge** (also called dismissal, termination, or firing) is management action in which an employee is separated from the organization for violation of company rules or inadequate performance. Because discharge is a traumatic experience for the affected employee, and usually for others as well, most managers are extremely reluctant to dismiss an employee unless there are substantial and well-documented reasons for such action. In many cases, timely warnings and effective supervisory involvement in correcting problems can eliminate the need for employee termination. The policy of many organizations is that each discharge case be reviewed by a higher authority before a final decision is reached. Federal civil service regulations, as well as most state and local civil service regulations, require that all dismissals be reviewed.

Termination policies are also affected by laws, EEOC rulings, and court decisions that seek to protect the worker from discrimination and to uphold fair employment practices. Although the right to discharge an employee is well established in the United States, management must be careful that discharge practices do not discriminate against women, minorities, the disabled, and older workers. An analysis of court cases led to the following conclusions about management's rights to terminate employees:

> First, it is clearly apparent that an employer does have the right to fire or lay off employees for legitimate business reasons, regardless of whether they are members of protected classes. Thus all employees can, justifiably, be fired for the following reasons: unsatisfactory work records (including poor productivity and/or quality of work), poor safety records, refusal of work orders, unexcused absences, inability to perform work, and violation of clearly stated company policies.[26]

To preclude courts from ruling that discharges are a pretext for discrimination, however, management should do the following:

1. Document unsatisfactory performance
2. Keep all employees informed about the quality of their performance
3. Give all deficient performers reasonable opportunities to improve
4. Inform all employees about company policies and rules governing employee behavior and about the contents of their job descriptions
5. Be consistent in the application of punishment and administer the same punishment to all employees who violate rules[27]

Discharge will be discussed further in Chapter 19 under the topic "Protection Against Arbitrary Dismissal."

Resignation   **Resignation** is the voluntary separation of an employee from the organization. Resignations should be analyzed for their implications for the particular organization. Although some resignations may permit an organization to correct a mistake in staffing or to bring in "new blood," excessive turnover can be very costly: with each departure, the organization loses the investment it has made in recruiting, selecting, and training the departing employee. (For an innovative "up and out" planned resignation program featuring university tuition benefits, see the following *Contemporary Issues* on page 263.)

Many companies systematically analyze their rate of **turnover**, which is usually calculated as the ratio of separations to total work force for some period, and attempt to maintain it within reasonable proportions. This analysis is sometimes made for particular departments, divisions, or classes of employees to identify areas where turnover is excessive. Obtaining this information is an important first step in under-

Contemporary Issues

Nice Degree — Go Away and Use It

A leading employer here is financing higher education for its workers. But instead of welcoming them back once they've earned their degrees, it tells them it never wants to see them again.

The novel plan, developed by Canadian Tire stores in the Vancouver area, is in contrast to programs of many large companies, which typically strive to retain employees after paying for their advanced degrees and fret if they decide to quit.

One reason that Canadian Tire has taken another tack is that 80 percent of the 1,000 employees in its 21 stores are in their late teens or early 20's and have entry-level jobs as stock or retail clerks, cashiers, shippers and receivers. The jobs are relatively easy to learn — and monotonous.

"We're not a Boeing needing long-term, skilled employees," said Vernon Forster of Pacific Associate Stores Ltd., the partnership that owns the Vancouver franchise. Mr. Forster said he and his partners, Donald Graham and Peter Lige, both alumni of the International Business Machines Corporation, wanted to help employees reach beyond jobs of limited challenge, prospects and pay.

"We think we're doing a terrible disservice by keeping somebody who has more potential than we can fulfill," Mr. Lige said.

Added Mr. Forster, himself an alumnus of Scott Paper and Procter & Gamble: "We want to avoid having a seething mass of malcontents who are bored."

There are clear benefits for Canadian Tire. The partners say that under the three-years-and-out program, productivity rises, and greater turnover at peak wage levels lowers the company's overall wage costs. In fact, the savings on wages more than compensate for the extra costs for tuition. (Wages start at $6 (Canadian) an hour, rise to $7.50 the second year and hit a $9 ceiling the third year.)

Founded as a tire repair shop 65 years ago, Canadian Tire sells automotive products, hardware, sporting goods and housewares in 414 stores throughout Canada. Most stores are individually owned and have 30 or 40 employees. The Vancouver partnership has annual volume of $100 million (about $86 million in United States currency), a $10 million payroll and what are described as healthy, though undisclosed, profits. Under a profit-sharing plan, every worker got at least a $2,000 bonus in 1991.

Mr. Forster said the idea for the program came from newspaper accounts of philanthropists who promised to pay for the college education of disadvantaged school children if they completed high school. To implement it, in 1988, the company began requiring that new employees pass tests showing they can complete a university education and sign a contract limiting the total number of hours they can work to 6,240 hours (three years, full time). At that point, employees must leave.

But to sweeten the blow, the company, which is not unionized, agrees to pay up to $3,000 toward any course of study the employee chooses — and to give him or her part-time work in any of the Canadian Tire stores at the top scale of $9 an hour.

More than 100 employees, or about 10 percent of the work force, have signed the so-called Ignition Initiative contract, and about 60 are now enrolled in classes. Employees hired before the program began can remain at the company as long as they want, but they are limited to earning $9 an hour.

In the few management slots in the Vancouver operation, turnover is also encouraged. "It's like a graduate school," said Mr. Forster. "They move up and out." Some have turned their Vancouver experience into a graduate school for running Canadian Tire franchises. "Six of our managers are now managers of larger Canadian Tire stores elsewhere in the country," he said.

Management specialists here and in Toronto describe the concept as both innovative and intriguing.

"What's intriguing," said Peter J. Frost, associate dean of the faculty of commerce and business administration at the University of British Columbia, "is that they have combined cost saving with developing people. This has become an important investment in the community."

Roger N. Wolff, dean of the faculty of management at the University of Toronto, added that it's "a really good program for kids who drop out of school early and are trying to sort things out." He said it could probably be applied to other large retailers like McDonald's or Hudson's Bay.

"It really looks like a win-win situation," added Mr. Wolff.

Source: *New York Times*, January 5, 1992, p. 23. Copyright © 1992 by The New York Times Company. Reprinted by permission.

standing and controlling turnover.

Exit interviews are used by most organizations to obtain information about the causes of turnover.[28] Usually, the interview is conducted by a representative of the personnel department, who tries to determine why the employee is leaving the organization. These interviews are also used to make certain that company property has been checked in and that the employee understands the disposition of various benefit programs. (See Figure 10.3 for the exit interview form used by the Erie Insurance Group.)

Postemployment surveys that ask separated employees to supply reasons for their resignations are sometimes used in place of exit interviews, on the assumption that data obtained a few weeks later are more valid than those obtained at the time of departure. In either case, supervisors are likely to be defensive about any criticism of their performance, and human resources specialists will need to use the data in a constructive, nonpunitive way if supervisors are to learn from the experience. The resignation of an employee to take a job with greater responsibilities can reflect positively on a supervisor's training and development skills, although it can also be a signal that the organization needs to increase the opportunities for advancement.

Retirement

Retirement is the separation of older workers from the organization; it allows them to pursue interests outside of work while opening up positions and career opportunities for other employees. With the 1986 amendments to the Age Discrimination in Employment Act, most employers can no longer impose retirement on the basis of age. (See Chapter 6.)

While a majority of workers are retired with a guarantee of a regularly paid retirement income, or **pension,** in addition to their government social security payments, coverage varies a great deal by occupation or industry. For example, Table 10.1 shows that in 1987 about 79 percent of employees in public administration and about 57 percent in manufacturing were covered by pensions. In contrast, only about 20 percent in retail trade and 11 percent in personal services were covered.[29] (Presumably, these statistics include part-time workers and employees of very small organizations. These categories are the least likely to have pension benefits. A survey of 957 firms, cited in Chapter 16, found 89 percent of the firms offering some sort of pension plan.)

Retirement can be a difficult transition, since it involves a radical change in lifestyle and can mean the end of a number of meaningful relationships and experi-

ERIE
INSURANCE
GROUP

An Equal Oppurtunity Employer

EXIT INTERVIEW

EMPLOYEE DATA

EMPLOYEE'S NAME	POSITION TITLE
☐ DIVISION (LIST) ☐ BRANCH OFFICE ☐ DISTRICT CLAIMS OFFICE	IMMEDIATE SUPERVISOR
☐ DEPARTMENT (LIST) ☐ SECTION ☐ UNIT	FINAL DAY/DATE OF EMPLOYMENT / AGE / ☐ MALE ☐ FEMALE

REASON FOR TERMINATION

WHAT IS YOUR REASON FOR LEAVING?

DO YOU HAVE ANOTHER POSITION? ☐ YES ☐ NO	IF YES, HOW DOES IT COMPARE WITH OURS? (I.E. SALARY, BENEFITS, HOURS, WORKING CONDITIONS, ETC.)

HOW DOES YOUR NEW SALARY COMPARE WITH OURS? ☐ LOWER ☐ EQUAL ☐ HIGHER ☐ MUCH HIGHER	HOW DO YOUR NEW BENEFITS COMPARE WITH OURS?

WHAT COULD WE HAVE DONE TO PREVENT YOUR LEAVING?

DATA REGARDING YOUR POSITION WITH THE ERIE

HOW LONG WERE YOU IN YOUR PRESENT POSITION? YEARS MONTHS	HOW LONG HAVE YOU BEEN EMPLOYED BY THE ERIE? YEARS MONTHS	WERE YOU GIVEN A COPY OF YOUR POSITION DESCRIPTION? ☐ YES ☐ NO	WAS YOUR POSITION FULLY EXPLAINED TO YOU? ☐ YES ☐ NO	(IF "No," please explain under comments)

COMMENTS

WERE THE CONDITIONS OF WORK, SALARY, HOURS OF WORK, ETC. CLEARLY EXPLAINED TO YOU? ☐ YES ☐ NO   COMMENTS ▶

WHAT ASPECTS OF YOUR POSITION DID YOU LIKE BEST?

WHAT ASPECTS OF YOUR POSITION DID YOU LEAST LIKE?

HOW DO YOU FEEL ABOUT YOUR PROGRESS HERE?

HR B-11 4/85 (R)   (PLEASE TURN TO OTHER SIDE)

FIGURE 10.3 Exit interview form, Erie Insurance Group

Source: Courtesy of The Erie Insurance Group.

DATA REGARDING YOUR SUPERVISOR	
	WHO IS YOUR IMMEDIATE SUPERVISOR?
	HOW WOULD YOU RATE YOUR SUPERVISOR'S ABILITY TO PERFORM HIS/HER POSITION? ☐ EXCEPTIONAL ☐ SUPERIOR ☐ ACCEPTABLE ☐ NEEDS IMPROVEMENT ☐ UNACCEPTABLE
	DO YOU LIKE YOUR SUPERVISOR? ☐ YES ☐ NO COMMENTS ▶
	WHEN YOU NEEDED INFORMATION, WERE YOU ABLE TO GET IT EASILY FROM YOUR SUPERVISOR? ☐ YES ☐ NO COMMENTS ▶
	HAVE YOU HAD ANY DIFFICULTIES WITH YOUR SUPERVISOR? ☐ YES ☐ NO COMMENTS ▶
	WHEN YOU HAD A SUGGESTION ABOUT YOUR WORK, COULD YOU EASILY DISCUSS IT WITH YOUR SUPERVISOR? ☐ YES ☐ NO COMMENTS ▶
	DID YOUR SUPERVISOR HANDLE YOUR COMPLAINTS AS WELL AS HE/SHE COULD HAVE? ☐ YES ☐ NO COMMENTS ▶

DATA REGARDING YOUR WORK ENVIRONMENT	
	DID YOU LIKE YOUR WORK ENVIRONMENT? (I.E. CLEAN REST ROOMS, CLEAN LUNCH AREA, CLEAN WORK AREA, ADEQUATE LIGHTING, ETC.) ☐ YES ☐ NO COMMENTS ▶
	WHAT SUGGESTIONS DO YOU HAVE TO HELP MAKE THE ERIE A BETTER PLACE TO WORK?

EMPLOYEE'S SIGNATURE

FOR HUMAN RESOURCES USE ONLY	
	COMMENTS
	INTERVIEWER'S SIGNATURE INTERVIEW DATE

FIGURE 10.3 Exit interview form (continued)

TABLE 10.1 Pension plan coverage by occupation

Workers covered by pension plans by percent of U.S. workers in each industry in 1987.	
Public administration	78.8%
Transportation, public utilities	63.3
Mining	58.3
Manufacturing	56.7
Professional	50.7
Finance, insurance, real estate	48.2
Wholesale trade	41.8
Construction	32.0
Business services	25.9
Retail trade	19.7
Entertainment, recreation	19.4
Personal services	11.1
Agriculture, forestry, fisheries	9.5

Source: U.S. Bureau of the Census — 1988

Source: Working Age, AARP Newsletter Vol 6, No 2. Sept/Oct. 1990. © 1990, American Association of Retired Persons. Reprinted with permission.

ences. Many organizations have responded to this reality by introducing a number of programs to help the older employee prepare for retirement. Activities such as preretirement seminars to discuss retirement problems and opportunities, individual and group counseling, and newsletters or magazines written especially for those of preretirement age are frequently included in such programs. Counseling and information sessions frequently include spouses. In addition, some firms make an effort to continue a relationship with retirees by inviting them to social events, having special days for retirees to visit the company, retaining the names of retired employees on mailing lists for the company's newspaper or magazine, and sponsoring clubs for retired employees. Other organizations, such as churches, universities, unions, and libraries, also sponsor pre- and postretirement programs for their members or the general public. Some companies pay tuition for courses that will be helpful in postretirement careers or hobbies.[30]

Phased retirement is becoming increasingly popular in the United States and abroad. Many organizations have developed part-time work or job-sharing approaches that allow employees nearing retirement to reduce gradually the number of hours they work per day, per week, or per year. Among the various versions of phased retirement programs are a gradual reduction of the workweek, progressively longer vacations with pay, or progressively longer leaves without pay. These approaches appear successful when they are voluntary and when the employee's salary, combined with retirement benefits, comes fairly close to the regular salary.[31] The Polaroid Corp. provides leaves of absence of three months without pay for employees who want to participate in a "retirement rehearsal" program. They can then return to work if they decide they are not ready to make the transition into retirement. The program includes financial and personal counseling.[32]

Managing Career Changes

A career change such as demotion, transfer to an undesirable job or location, layoff, discharge, or unemployment for any length of time is typically a traumatic event, or **career crisis,** for the individual directly involved. The crisis is apt to be particularly severe when the change is unexpected. Much of the trauma is also experienced by persons close to the situation — coworkers, supervisors, the family, and close friends. Mike and Margaret O'Connor, in Case 10.1, are experiencing a career crisis. We can assume that they will cope with their situation and that it will turn out positively. However, a crisis such as a discharge or layoff, in a small percentage of cases, can result in a suicide, homicide, or both, particularly if the crisis is associated with alcohol or drug abuse or mental illness and if there is no support system.

All too often, a financial emergency or some other organizational crisis becomes a career crisis for a number of individuals. For example, a general announcement to a company's employees that 10 percent of the work force will be laid off or that a plant is going to close means negative career changes — and personal crises — for a significant number of workers. Just the worry about losing a job — even though the loss does not occur — creates a kind of crisis for many employees. Less negative career changes, such as a person choosing early retirement with substantial financial benefits, may take on crisis proportions if the individual is dissatisfied or unable to cope with the new situation.

One theory suggests that people tend to go through a series of predictable phases when faced with a negative career change or crisis:

- *Shock.* The person experiences a threat to preservation, is unable to handle the reality, and experiences helplessness, intense anxiety, confusion, and perhaps panic.
- *Defensive retreat.* The person clings to the past, reassures himself or herself that he or she is still the same person and things have not changed, indulges in wishful thinking, and becomes angry with any threat to this equilibrium. Thinking becomes rigid, and the person refuses to consider any changes in goals, values, or lifestyle.
- *Acknowledgement.* Defenses break down because others do not support the unrealistic beliefs and because things do not return to their former state. There is a renewed encounter with reality and perhaps renewed stress. There may be depression and bitterness. The person begins to reorganize thinking and attitudes.
- *Adaptation and change.* The person begins to explore internal resources, thinking and planning are reorganized around new realities and resources, new satisfactions are experienced, anxiety and depression decline, and the person develops a renewed sense of self-worth. The individual is now coping successfully and is no longer in a state of crisis.[33]

This theory has three major implications for human resources management. First, people in a state of shock or defensive retreat because of a career crisis are likely to be substantially less effective in their jobs and in interpersonal and group relationships than formerly. The second implication logically follows: management should do whatever it can to avoid creating unnecessary crises. The costs to the organization and to individuals can be very high. The third implication is that changes and transitions that must occur should be managed as carefully and humanely as possible to prevent or minimize crises.

*Minimizing
Crises*

Numerous companies have responded to an organizational crisis by laying off or terminating employees without looking at other options open to them and without much apparent concern for the individuals affected. On the other hand, many organizations have managed crises in humane and imaginative ways that have minimized the trauma for individuals. For example, when the Ford Motor Co. decided that it was necessary to close the assembly plant in San Jose, California, it became a joint labor-management effort. This joint effort included assistance to dislocated workers in the form of orientation meetings, assessment and testing, adult basic education, vocational exploration courses, in-plant seminars, vocational training, tuition assistance, on-the-job training, job search training and job placement, and preferential placement in other plants.[34] (Such an approach to relocating employees is frequently called *outplacement.*)

When the management of Hewlett-Packard decided to close out its fabrication business at its Loveland, Colorado, Division, a major effort was made to place the four hundred employees affected. The company wanted to maintain its policy of avoiding layoffs if at all possible, and implemented a variety of short- and long-term programs. For example, the employees viewed as surplus were given priority consideration for openings both within the area and outside the region, such as in California, with the company paying the relocation expenses. Some employees who volunteered were loaned to other divisions to meet short-term hiring needs. A voluntary severance package was offered to those who were at least fifty-five years of age and had been with the company for at least fifteen years.[35]

IBM, in keeping with a no-layoff policy which the company successfully maintained until 1993, went to great lengths to protect the interests of employees when the company found that it was necessary to close its Greencastle, Indiana, plant. All employees were offered jobs at other IBM locations, with IBM paying the costs of relocation. The company also offered to purchase the homes of all employees who chose to relocate, but since it was anticipated that the announcement of the plant closing would depress real estate prices, the offer was based on preannouncement appraised values. For those who chose to leave the company, IBM offered double the regular separation pay, plus retraining assistance up to $5,000, plus help in finding another job, plus pay for increased commuting costs to a new job for two years. The same benefits were made available to those who chose early retirement.[36] In 1993, faced with a massive cost-cutting program in which twenty-five thousand jobs would be eliminated worldwide, IBM announced that some layoffs would be likely. However, the company hoped to eliminate most of the targeted jobs by offering early-retirement incentives, severance pay, relocation, and retraining.[37]

**Outplacement
Programs**

Outplacement programs, like those conducted by Ford, can assist employees in coping with the personal crisis associated with a layoff or other type of termination. Outplacement programs typically include the following components:

1. Information to affected employees about the planned action, such as termination payments and extension of benefits and outplacement services
2. Counseling with affected employees concerning job-seeking methods
3. Announcements to other organizations and to employment agencies about the availability of qualified employees
4. Newspaper ads urging employers to contact the firm faced with the separations
5. Development of a résumé for each affected employee to be sent to potential employers

Figure 10.4 diagrams the components of a thorough outplacement and counseling program. Authors Brammer and Humberger identify four phases of counseling that can help a terminated employee develop renewed self-esteem and to conduct a successful job search. These are orientation, job evaluation, job targeting, and job campaign.

The first phase, orientation, includes planning and negotiating for services with the outplacement counselors, termination of the employee, immediate counseling with the affected employee, additional counseling, and life and career planning. In phase 2, the terminated employee is engaged in a process of self-examination through dialogue with the counselor and through a battery of tests. Phase 3 helps the person focus on what types of jobs to pursue and in what areas — geographic location, industry, and so on — those jobs might be found, and on developing résumés. Phase 4 includes the job campaign and, it is hoped, a new position. The outplacement counselor works with the individual throughout the process.[38]

Assistance to Remaining Employees

Attention to the morale and psychological needs of the employees who remain during and after a layoff or other crisis situation is also important. Remaining employees need ongoing information about company plans and intentions, and they need ongoing listening to — and sometimes counseling — about their fears, or stress, or even guilt. (Like the battlefield soldier who survives fallen comrades, the survivor of a layoff may feel guilty as well as relieved to have survived: "Why should they have to go and I don't?") Further, to protect both morale and productivity during a layoff situation, supervisors and managers at all levels must give a great deal of attention to working with the remaining employees on the realignment of job responsibilities. (See also the Comprehensive Case on page 277.)

Retraining Workers

Some organizations that have enjoyed continuous growth have adopted a policy of retraining workers whose present skills are no longer needed rather than laying them off. Crown Zellerbach, for example, paid workers full wages to learn new skills when the company modernized a Louisiana pulp mill. The Boeing Co. enrolled laid-off electronic technicians in college, where they learned microprocessing skills.[39] Hallmark maintains a continuous retraining program in order to retain its human resources and to avoid layoffs.[40] When the assembly line of the General Motors Corp.'s Saturn plant was shut down for four days due to a strike at the Lordtown parts plant, Saturn's management did not lay off employees. Instead, management and the union implemented a massive training program. Classes were presented in such areas as quality control, computers, and health and safety — all part of the company's goal of ninety-two hours of training per employee for the year.[41]

Contingency Plans

Should an organizational crisis arise, the very survival of the company may be at stake. Therefore, management is wise to give careful, advance thought to those options or **contingency plans** that can be implemented to minimize negative effects on the company's human resources. A company faced with a severe cash-flow problem, for example, might consider the options shown in Figure 10.5. First, management might impose a hiring freeze. If this action does not achieve the necessary savings, a voluntary retirement program that might include financial incentives for retiring early can be introduced. If savings targets are still not met, management has the option of freezing all wages, salaries, and employee benefits for several months.

Next, the organization might move to voluntary layoffs or quits. (Under a voluntary layoff program, employees might be offered a layoff featuring continuation

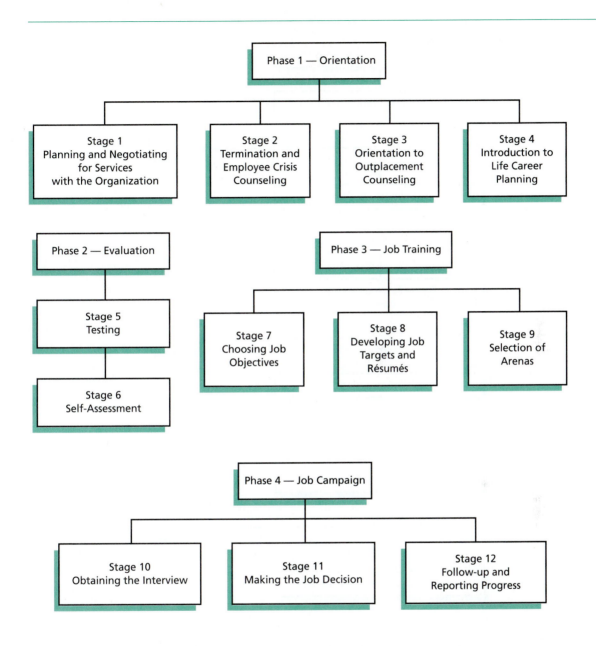

FIGURE 10.4 The outplacement counseling process

Source: Lawrence M. Brammer/Frank E. Humberger, *Outplacement & Inplacement Counseling*, © 1984, p. 8. Adapted by permission of Prentice-Hall, Englewood Cliffs, New Jersey.

of benefits and a guarantee of a job at the end of a year. The voluntary quit program would include severance pay based on some formula that included length of service.) If labor costs are still too high, the next step is to reduce the pay of all employees in proportion to salary. An alternative might be to reduce temporarily the hours of employees paid by the hour.

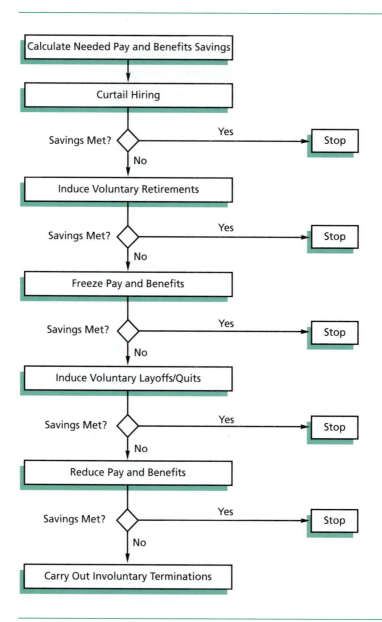

FIGURE 10.5 Options during a cash-flow crisis

Source: Bruce R. Ellig, "Pay Policies while Downsizing the Organization." Reprinted, by permission of publisher, from *Personnel*, May-June 1983, © 1983. American Management Association, New York. All rights reserved.

Only after all these procedures have failed to produce the required cost reductions will the organization initiate a program of involuntary terminations or layoffs. These terminations will probably affect the employees with least seniority first and might be made on a departmental, plantwide, or organization-wide basis. Of course, the program will need to comply with antidiscrimination laws and with any existing union-management contract.[42]

Crisis Management Teams   Numerous organizations have crisis management teams that are prepared to act in emergencies and to assist with problems that persist after the immediate crisis. While we have been emphasizing the crises of layoff and discharge, there are other major crises that can deeply affect employees and their families and the ability of the organization to function. Many crises, while perhaps rare for individual companies, are quite evident from a nationwide or international perspective — for example, earthquakes, floods, fires, explosions, ice storms, hurricanes, tornadoes, the shooting of fellow employees by a disgruntled, unstable former employee, riots such as those that occurred in Los Angeles in 1992, and terrorist activities affecting employees abroad. All of these have human resources implications. (See also Chapter 20, "Safety and Health Management.")[43]

Career Counseling and Planning

Career counseling programs and career planning techniques can help individuals cope with career transitions of various kinds. Career counseling and planning can also be of help to people suddenly confronted by a crisis.

Career counseling is available from personnel department specialists in large organizations or through private agencies or educational institutions. Frequently, line managers do a great deal of informal career counseling. Effective career counseling, according to author Edgar Schein, requires "(1) counseling skill; (2) information about the person being counseled — aptitudes, motives, experience, specific strengths and weaknesses; and (3) information about the career options and paths available within and outside the organization." Schein goes on to say that "no one person may be in a position to do the whole job" and that a combination of performance appraisal, personal assessment, and information seeking may be required before an individual is ready to make good judgments about career alternatives.[44]

Life- and career-planning workshops have been used by many individuals to understand more fully their career goals and aspirations and to cope with major changes in their careers such as the loss of a job. (Life or career planning is frequently used in conjunction with outplacement counseling programs; see Figure 10.4.) These workshops, which may be offered within or outside the organization, can last from a few hours to two or three days. Participants are usually strangers or, if from the same organization, are ordinarily assigned to different discussion groups so that openness and confidentiality can be maintained. Under the direction of a qualified trainer, participants become involved in a series of writing and discussion exercises designed to increase their awareness of their own needs and feelings. The results of each person's explorations are usually shared and discussed in a small, supportive group under the direction of the trainer. The following assignment is typical:

Prepare a life inventory of important "happenings" for you, including the following:
a. Any peak experiences you have had
b. Things which you do well
c. Things which you do poorly
d. Things which you would like to stop doing
e. Things which you would like to learn to do well
f. Peak experiences you would like to have
g. Values (e.g., power, money, etc.) you want to achieve
h. Things you would like to start doing now[45]

Herbert Shepard, who is generally credited with developing the life- and career-planning approach, sees life planning as making plans for "life-worth-living" — a process of self-confrontation so that one can make more effective life and career choices.[46]

Much useful career counseling takes place when individuals seek assistance from a counseling psychologist, social worker, clinical psychologist, or psychiatrist. Issues about career crises or career directions frequently come up in these sessions. Such counseling can be of great assistance in making career plans, particularly when an individual is experiencing a negative career change.

Summary

Effective management of career transitions is important both to the individuals involved and to the organization. How internal staffing changes and employee separations are planned and managed has significant consequences for organizational effectiveness and employee morale and development. Group orientation methods and attention to individual needs and concerns show promise of reducing turnover and enhancing performance. Employee handbooks are valuable orientation and training devices. However, to avoid lawsuits from employees who have been terminated, organizations need to set forth appropriate limitations on job rights in clear and unambiguous language in handbooks and other documents.

Transfers are significant matters for both individuals and the organization. The impact of involuntary geographic moves on employees is coming under increased scrutiny by organizations and employees alike.

A variety of procedures is used in making promotion decisions, including interviews, tests, peer ratings, assessment centers, and career progression ladders. Assessment centers, although expensive to operate, are being used extensively to identify managerial talent and have proven useful for increasing the movement of women and minorities into management ranks. Career progression ladders and the concept of the fallback position can also be very useful devices.

Traditional seniority rights and affirmative action programs are frequently in direct conflict in many layoff situations, and court decisions are beginning to probe the dilemma. The concept of inverse seniority is being used in some organizations as a partial solution.

The right to discharge nonproductive employees is essential in maintaining standards of performance, but discharge should be for just cause, only after the employee has had a reasonable opportunity to improve, and only after careful review. This approach makes sense as an effective management practice; it is also important in avoiding court rulings that discriminatory practices have occurred.

A variety of practices can assist in managing the transition of employees into retirement, including seminars, counseling, and phased retirement. The exit interview is widely used to obtain data from employees who resign.

Theory and experience suggest that people go through various phases when there is an organizational crisis that creates a personal career crisis, such as being confronted with the possibility of a demotion or being laid off. The more employees and managers alike understand these phases, the more constructive plans can be made to manage crises. Outplacement programs have been used successfully by many firms in layoff situations. Management would be wise to have contingency plans ready for use in a financial crisis, so that a series of steps can be taken that will minimize the impact on the human resources of the organization. Crisis management teams can be invaluable in a wide variety of crises, including natural disasters.

Counseling and life- and career-planning workshops can be very useful in managing the various transitions that individuals face in their work lives. Empathetic and understanding supervisors can be very helpful with these transitions.

Ethical Dilemma

Horst Arndt, new president of Z Electronics, and Barbara Ko, new vice president of human resources, believe that employee layoffs are the best way to reduce costs quickly in a business downturn. The company employs about eighteen hundred people and is located in a town with a population of about sixteen thousand. Business has been good for a decade, and the last layoff was some twelve years ago, when the company was much smaller. A high proportion of employees have been hired since then, and many believe the management-inspired slogan that "we're like a big family." The announcement that 20 percent of the employees would be laid off and the subsequent separations came as a shock to the work force and to the town. During the ensuing weeks, the few physicians, counselors, ministers, and financial advisers were swamped by appointments with both laid-off employees and those remaining on the payroll. House and automobile repossessions began to increase. The small social services agency reported that substance abuse, and child, spouse, and parent abuse had increased markedly. The big shocker was the suicide of a fifty-two-year-old supervisor, who was one of those laid off.

What are the ethics of the company's actions? Who benefited and who got hurt, both in the short term and the long term?

Key Terms

orientation	supplemental unemployment benefits (SUB)
hazing	severance pay
transfer	golden parachute
involuntary transfer	recall
relocation	reverse seniority
dual-career couple	bumping
commuter marriage	inverse seniority
promotion	discharge
seniority	resignation
career progression ladder	turnover
dual ladders	exit interview
parallel ladders	postemployment survey
peer rating	retirement
assessment center	pension
fallback position	phased retirement
demotion	career crisis
layoff	outplacement
downsizing	contingency plans

Review Questions

1. Why is the effective management of career transitions important to individual employees and to the organization?
2. What would be the characteristics of an effective orientation process?
3. Discuss several procedures used in making promotion decisions, including assessment centers, and discuss any problems with each.
4. Describe how the labor agreement governs staffing decisions in the organization.
5. Discuss some procedures that management can use to ensure that employee terminations are nondiscriminatory.
6. Outline some of the options organizations have for avoiding layoffs.
7. What are some of the career crises that employees may face, what happens to people in a crisis situation, and what can the organization do to help alleviate some of the adverse consequences of crisis situations?

Opening Case Questions

Case 10.1   The Transfer

1. What had changed in Mike's life? In Margaret's life? What additional complexities would there be if Margaret were also employed?
2. What do we know about what the company has done to assist Mike and his family with this transition? What more might the company do or have done?

Case 10.2   The Promotion Decision

1. Was the psychologist at fault for recommending Al for the promotion, based on the data she had?
2. What other steps could Steve and Nancy have taken to ensure they were doing everything to fill the position with the correct employee?
3. Now what can Steve and Nancy do?

Comprehensive Case

Downsizing Without Layoffs

During the 1980s, many companies having difficulty making a profit decided to "downsize"; they tried to become smaller, usually by laying off workers, without reducing corporate profits. The logic seemed simple enough: if a company could make the same number of products or provide the same services with fewer people on the payroll, the smaller company would be "leaner," "meaner," and more profitable.

Like most simple quick fixes to economic problems, downsizing often does not work. Chrysler Corp. is one of the number of companies that had to go through the process time after time, as the lean, downsized company seemed to start expanding as soon as one round of layoffs was finished. Other companies discovered to their distress that cutting employees also cut profit, and they ended up smaller in every way. Even companies that seemed initially successful at doing the same work with fewer people didn't seem prepared for the human side of downsizing.

Most such companies assumed that the employees who weren't let go would be grateful to retain their jobs and would soon forget about the pain caused to their newly fired friends. But such assumptions proved unfounded. Layoffs frequently leave the survivors feeling guilty and worried that they might be next. Morale very often gets battered, and the remaining employees may feel angry or bitter toward the company and become less productive as a result. Rumors multiply about the company's new goals and next cuts, and employees end up spending much of their time worrying about and preparing for the scenarios that they've heard about through the grapevine.

Because of such negative consequences, many companies are looking for different ways to become more efficient. Those that lay off employees are now more likely to do so while paying careful attention to the attitudes of both those losing their jobs and the survivors. Such companies announce the downsizing in advance to avoid creating the "we" versus "they" mentality and to allow employees who were thinking about leaving or retiring to do so and thus reduce the number of people actually laid off. They also put a good deal of effort into informing survivors about the nature of the new company and retraining and reorienting them to the new corporate structure. Corporate openness and honesty seems crucial for companies that want to cut payroll, not profits.

Other organizations have learned a different lesson from the recent history of downsizing. They recognize that laying off employees may not only have severe human consequences, but also make the company unable to become profitable again if the economic situation improves. Revenue growth generally depends on doing more, not less, and so a number of progressive companies have experimented successfully with a variety of ways to shrink the payroll without permanently losing employees or frightening survivors.

One successful strategy, especially for large corporations, has become known as human resources balancing, which uses a combination of approaches to balance out the personnel needs in various areas of the company. In the late 1980s, the Loveland, Colorado, division of Hewlett-Packard Co. used such balancing to deal with a surplus of four hundred employees. A first step was to look for job openings at other Hewlett-Packard plants in the area and around the country. This approach allows the company to move its human resources where they are needed most, and though it may require employees to relocate, it enables them to keep their jobs and their seniority. Hewlett-Packard also joined the list of companies making voluntary terminations more attractive; fully 40 percent of the excess personnel chose to accept severance packages and leave the company. It also reclassified employees and transferred them to other jobs. Sometimes these transfers involved demotions, but for most people the loss of some pay or prestige is easier to bear than the loss of a job.

Household International Inc. of Prospect Heights, Illinois, dealt with its economic hard times in a similar way, setting up a "displaced employee committee." The company froze outside hiring at all locations, and once a month committee members would meet and trade details of openings in their division and of employees who were being displaced. The company found that it could internally transfer almost all employees who were willing to relocate or to broaden their job focus. The committee was so successful that it eventually changed its name to the "career-development committee."

Many other approaches to downsizing seem to be applications of simple common sense. Companies find ways to do work in-house rather than give it to subcontractors. Or they ask some or all employees to take a few days of unpaid leave each month, equitably spreading the burden of the work slowdown. They rearrange schedules to eliminate overtime and the use of temporary workers. Occasionally, they even "loan" employ-

ees to competitors or put them on temporary leave with benefits.

All of these strategies rest on one assumption: the employee is a valuable resource, not a commodity to be bought or sold at every change in the business climate. The results so far seem to indicate that companies that value their people and treat them humanely in difficult times are more likely to survive financially than are companies that can't see beyond the bottom line.

Sources: Bernard Baumohl, "When Downsizing Becomes Dumbsizing," *Time*, March 15, 1993, p. 55. G. James Francis, John Mohr and Kelly Andersen, "HR Balancing: Alternative Downsizing," *Personnel Journal* 71 (January 1992):71–78; Elizabeth Lesly and Larry Light, "When Layoffs Alone Don't Turn the Tide," *Business Week*, December 7, 1992, pp. 100–101; William J. Morin, "Help for the Post-Layoff 'Survivors,'" *New York Times*, January 15, 1992, p. F13; Peggy Stuart, "New Internal Jobs Found for Displaced Employees," *Personnel Journal* 71 (August 1992):50–56; and Curt M. Thompson, "Reorientation Eases the Pain and Loss of Downsizing," *HRfocus* 69 (January 1992):11.

Discussion Questions

1. Based on this selection, what are some of the negative aspects of using layoffs to reduce costs?
2. What were some of the approaches used to avoid or mitigate the negative aspects of layoffs?

CHAPTER 11

Skills Training

LEARNING OBJECTIVES

- Define training and distinguish among skills training, skills retraining, and management / career development programs.
- Outline the steps involved in determining the organization's need for a skills training program.
- Describe the considerations that underlie the selection of individuals for a training program.
- List the advantages and disadvantages associated with particular training methods.
- Identify the basic principles of learning underlying an effective training program.
- Describe the roles of human resources directors and other managers in the development of training programs.

CASE 11.1   High-Tech Terror

Penny

Penny was beginning to dread coming to work. Her boss had bought a computer and printer, as well as a word-processing program and several other programs. He claimed the system would cut Penny's typing and calculating workload in half.

But Penny had little hope for that happy prospect, since it was taking her so long to learn how to use the new equipment. The salesperson who had installed the computer had been patient with her but had left after about half an hour with a casual, "The instruction manual is very thorough. Just refer to it if you have any other questions."

Well, she sure had plenty of those! Things were always going wrong, and looking up all the answers in the manual took forever. Often she couldn't find the solution to a particular problem, and one time she lost almost three hours of work because she hadn't known how to save her work on a storage disk. Twice she had gathered her courage and phoned the salesperson for help, but the second time he had been rather curt, referring her once again to the manual. Clearly, she was on her own in learning this new skill.

Penny couldn't remember when her confidence had been so low. Her work, far from being reduced, was piling up at an alarming rate, and she had the feeling that her boss was beginning to be irritated with her slow progress. She stared wistfully at her old reliable Olivetti typewriter and wished that the world hadn't become so high-tech.

Amy

Amy switched on her computer and inserted the word-processing disk. Within a few seconds, the rough draft she had been working on before lunch was on the screen and ready for further revision. Half an hour later, Amy turned on the printer, which began printing the completed article while she made some telephone calls about her next project.

The new computer and printer had proven to be invaluable in Amy's job as writer and editor for Quality Health Care's monthly newsletter. Amy's assistant, Nick, had previously spent most of his time typing and retyping drafts of Amy's articles. The word processor, however, which enabled Amy to compose and revise right on the computer screen, had eliminated this burden. Nick was now free to do most of the research and legwork connected with the newsletter.

Amy had been a bit apprehensive about the new equipment in the beginning, but before it was installed, her boss had arranged for her and Nick to take a computer and word-processing class at the local community college. That, plus a one-day workshop offered by the computer firm after the equipment was installed, had given Amy and Nick the "hands-on" experience necessary to operate the computer with confidence.

Thanks to the new word processor, much of the time pressure Amy had felt about getting out the newsletter was gone, and she found herself enjoying her job more than ever. ◀

CASE 11.2

The Apprenticeship Program

Miriam Klein, director of training for SuperStrong Aluminum Products, North America, was tired. Burned out would be more accurate. She had been doing a lot of communications and team skills training lately, and reorganizing the orientation programs in the plants had been almost a full-time job in itself. And just a week ago, she and her staff had finished interviewing a representative sample of supervisors from all of the plants to determine current employee training needs. She had kept her boss, the HR vice president, informed on a regular basis.

Miriam's assistant had just finished a summary of the interview results, and Miriam had gone to lunch at a quiet little restaurant to read the report. The good news was that the implications were clear. There wasn't going to be much room for confusion or debate. The bad news was that a lot of work was going to be required. "Guess who?" she said to herself. "Tired ol' yours truly, Miriam Klein. I'm going to have to get a machinist apprenticeship program going. It's clear as a bell that we can't hire enough skilled machinists, and we're going to have to get involved in training them. And that won't happen overnight."

As she thought about it, she started jotting down some categories of people she would need to approach. Here is what she wrote on her napkin:

> Vocational school (city and county)
> Machinist union (others?)
> My boss (start here)
> Manufacturing vp (next?)
> Maintenance vp
> State dept. of labor & industries
> U.S. Labor Dept. regional office
> Other training directors (soon)

Miriam's internal monologue began to take on a more positive tone. "I'm just going to be persuasive with my boss and make a case for another assistant. I've got to delegate a lot more if I'm going to try to pull a coalition of people together. Fortunately, I know a lot of other training people through American Society for Training and Development, and I know several of the government people. I've been on the advisory board for the local vocational high school and community college, and those contacts will help. And I know some of the union leaders, at least in this region."

Miriam folded the napkin, put it in her purse, and took her time finishing lunch. She treated herself to a piece of cheesecake with strawberry glaze. "This I deserve," she said to herself. ◀

The cases at the beginning of this chapter dramatize the importance of training. Whereas Penny in Case 11.1 was terrified by the prospect of having to use the computer, Amy found her job greatly eased by the word processor. The main element contributing to these different experiences was training. Case 11.2 illustrates not only the importance of training, but the complexity of developing long-term, technical-skill training in a community or region. In this case, the

Contemporary Issues

What Are the Effects of Job-Related Learning?

Job-related learning has two important economic uses: it leverages individual choices and earnings, and it improves institutional performance. The effect of job-related learning on opportunity, individual earnings, and choice is powerful. On average, about half of one's lifetime earnings are driven by learning in school and on the job. The other half is affected by career and locational choices and by dumb luck. A person with skill can trade earnings for a preferred occupation or employer. People with low skills have less to bargain with; thus their choices are limited and their earnings are low.

Source: Anthony Carnevale and Harold Goldstein, "Schooling and Training for Work in America: An Overview," in Louis A. Ferman and others, eds, *New Developments in Worker Training: A Legacy for the 1990s* (Madison, WI, Industrial Relations Research Association, 1990), p. 28.

---

form of machinist training would probably be an apprenticeship program. The powerful effects of the job-related learning is stressed in *Contemporary Issues* above.

The money annually paid for training by business and industry also demonstrates the importance of training. It has been estimated that American business firms with 100 or more employees invested $45 billion in 1991[1]. The national figures include the costs of running company-owned training centers like Hamburger University at Oak Brook, Illinois, run by McDonald's Corp.; General Electric Co.'s training center in Croton-on-Hudson, New York; and the Aetna Institute for Corporate Education at Hartford, Connecticut, run by Aetna Life and Casualty Co.[2] Another indication of the importance business and industrial firms attach to training is the estimate, made a few years ago, that some forty-five thousand employees across the United States were assigned full-time to training and development activities.[3] Since then the figures have no doubt grown substantially. In the aggregate, however, the training of workers by American industrial firms is not as thorough or as widespread as in Germany or Japan (see Table 11.1). Besides, training budgets seem to be particularly vulnerable to reduction when companies are cutting costs or downsizing.

In the organizational context, **training** can be defined as *organizationally directed experiences designed to further the learning of specific job behaviors that will contribute to organizational goals.*[4] In the ideal situation, training helps to further both the goals of the organization and the individual's goals.

Broadly speaking, we are using the term *training* to mean the same as "skills training." Skills training can vary all the way from learning how to use a particular tool to learning a new procedure or even to learning skills in running meetings, if the job requires such skills. The concept of training usually implies fairly direct or immediate applicability.

In practice, however, the terms *training* and *skills training* frequently overlap with the concepts of "development" and "management development" or "career development." In general, we will use the latter terms to connote learning experiences

TABLE 11.1 Worker training compared

	UNITED STATES	**GERMANY**	**JAPAN**
School-to-work transition	Left mostly to chance; some employers have ties with local schools	Apprenticeship for most non-college-bound youth	Personal relationships between employers and local schools
Vocational education **Extent**	Available in most urban areas	Universally available	Limited; mostly assumed by employers
Quality	Wide range: poor to excellent	Uniformly good	Fair to good
Employer-provided training **Extent**	Largely limited to managers and technicians	Widespread at entry level and to qualify for promotion	Widespread
Quality	Wide range; some excellent, but more often weak or unstructured	Very good	Very good
Public policies	Federal role very limited; State aid to employers growing	Govern apprenticeship; encourage continuing training	Subsidies encourage training by small firms

Source: U.S. Congress, Office of Technology Assessment, *Worker Training: Competing in the New International Economy* OTA-ITE-457 (Washington, D.C.: Government Printing Office, September 1990), p. 16.

that are above and beyond the immediate technical requirements of the job. These terms have a stronger connotation of future or potential use than does the term *training*. Further, management and career development usually has a larger conceptual component than skills training and tend to focus on organizational issues. Skills training tends to focus more on specific tasks.[5] This chapter concentrates on skills training; management and career development is discussed in Chapter 12.

As shown in Figure 11.1, there are seven major steps that need to be managed in developing a skills training program. These usually involve a considerable amount of dialogue between human resources professionals and other supervisors and managers. *Ordinarily, the flow is approximately as shown, but the various steps are interdependent and in some instances may be conducted simultaneously:*

1. Determining the need for skills training
2. Translating skills needs into training objectives
3. Selecting trainees
4. Determining the curriculum and choosing training methods

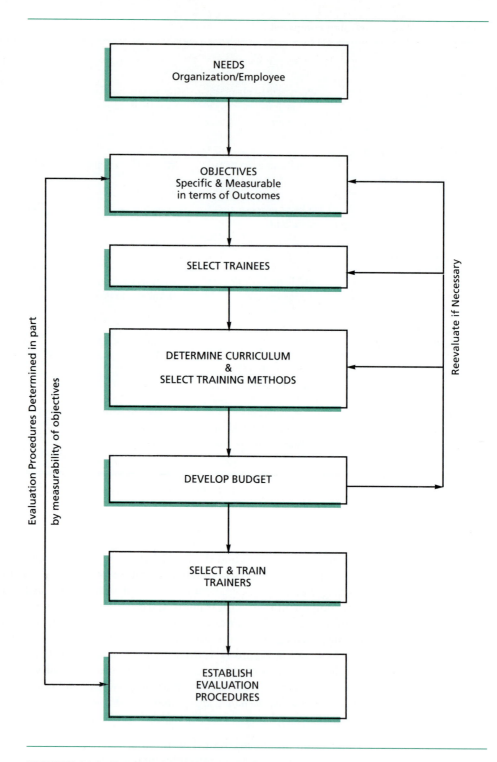

FIGURE 11.1   Developing a training program

Source: Developed by Richard Alan Engdahl, Cameron School of Business Administration, University of North Carolina, Wilmington. Reprinted by permission.

5. Formulating the budget
6. Selecting and training trainers
7. Establishing evaluation procedures

As indicated in Figure 11.1, the decisions made in each step in the development of a skills training program may need to be reexamined in the light of new information. For example, after the overall objectives and general curriculum have been planned, interaction with potential trainees or participation of the trainers selected may lead to revisions in training objectives and the curriculum. Extensive involvement by the trainers and trainees in the evolution of a skills training program is extremely important. As another example, the training methods and the size of the trainee group may need to be changed if a recommended budget is not approved.

Determining the Need for Skills Training

The first major step in developing a skills training program is to determine the organization's *need* for such a program. There are at least two basic reasons for first determining the need for skills training.

First, training can be expensive. Good training justifies its expense, but improper training increases cost with no corresponding benefits.

Second, training that is not of sufficient quality to meet the needs of the organization and its members can actually be damaging. Workers who go through a skills training program and remain undertrained for the tasks their jobs require can become discouraged, discontented, and perhaps ex-employees.

Management and the human resources staff should be alert to any indications that employees need additional training. Excessive customer complaints about service could indicate a need for training. Similarly, excessive waste material could indicate that machine operators need more training. High employee turnover in a department could indicate that supervisors need additional training in leadership skills. Excessive mistakes by employees might indicate a need for remedial reading, mathematics, or other basic training. The U.S. Department of Education estimates that 30 percent of unskilled workers, 29 percent of semiskilled workers, and 11 percent of all managers, professionals, and technicians are **functionally illiterate**: that is, they "are unable to read, write, calculate or solve problems at a level that enables them to cope with even the simplest tasks."[6] In the area of reading alone, when these statistics are contrasted with the estimate that the average American worker is required to spend up to one-fourth of each working day reading such material as manuals, forms, charts, and electronic display screens,[7] there must be a tremendous amount of inefficiency and unused human potential in American organizations.

Although these nationwide deficiencies suggest a widespread need for additional training in basic skills, a systematic approach is required to properly assess training needs in individual organizations. In each organization, management should analyze (1) organizational needs, (2) job specifications, and (3) the present skill levels of employees.

Organizational Needs

The analysis of organizational needs should focus on the number of employees with various combinations of skills needed at each level and in every part of the firm for specified periods. One portion of the organizational analysis, for example, might zero in on determining which departments need how many qualified welders, and when they will be needed.

The human resources staff should also decide how much should be presented about company policies during skills training. Although not always considered part of skills training, orientation regarding company policy and practices can be particularly important, especially for new employees. For example, some new employees may have acquired their basic skills in a training or vocational program not operated by the hiring organization and may still need instruction in how their new employer does things.

Job Specifications

Many organizations have written job specifications that define the skills needed for each job in the firm. By carefully examining these specifications, the human resources staff can obtain a clear idea of the nature of skills needed for each job. A secretarial position, for example, might require skills such as telephone answering, typing, word processing, transcription, and bookkeeping.

The human resources staff must also ensure that the specifications are up-to-date, accurate, and complete. (The written job description for a secretarial position in a firm, for example, may still include skills involving taking dictation and filing, which the firm's secretaries are no longer required to do.) Periodic discussions with supervisors responsible for each job can often be quite helpful in accomplishing this task. The human resources staff can compare the written job specifications with the supervisors' perceptions of the skills they believe workers should have for each job.

The supervisor can also indicate any specific skills that recent employees still lack after completing various training programs. Telephone etiquette and listening skills, for example, may have been omitted. The supervisor's responses can therefore serve as a way to evaluate existing training programs and to improve future ones.

Present Skill Levels of Employees

An analysis of worker skills and qualifications as shown by personnel files — assuming they are up-to-date and accurate — can assist in determining training needs. For example, in cooperation with the human resources staff, supervisors can analyze performance appraisal results to identify skill deficiencies. This analysis can then be used to design the specific skills training programs needed to close the gap between the organization's needs and the present qualifications of its employees. Obviously, this means that the appraisal system must be designed to identify skill deficiencies.

Translating Needs into Objectives

Once training needs have been determined, the human resources staff is ready to translate the skills needed into specific **training objectives,** or desired outcomes of training activities. These objectives are then used to determine the specific courses that will be offered. (In discussing program objectives, it should be noted that there is a cascading of objectives from the broad objectives of the overall program down to the objectives of a specific course within the curriculum or even the objectives of a particular unit within a course.)

Ideally, training objectives should include such matters as the specific skills to be taught, the number of people to be trained and from which units, and the period within which such training should take place. For example, part of a firm's quality improvement training program could be based on the following objectives:

To have 80 employees complete the training program in statistical quality-control techniques by December 1, 1994. The 80 who complete this program should consist of 60 inspectors and 20 supervisors, each of whom should be able to provide statistical quality control for any company production line.

Objectives for the training program that do not relate directly to specific job skills should also be considered. Examples of these kinds of objectives include employee health and safety guidelines, promotion opportunities, and self-study opportunities.[8]

Training objectives include the general content of the training to be given. An extensive survey of companies with a hundred or more employees inquired into the types of training given, and the responses are shown in Table 11.2. The most frequently reported training subjects were new-employee orientation, performance appraisals, leadership, hiring/selection process, interpersonal skills, word processing, new equipment operation, team building, delegation skills, and listening skills. It should be noted that some of the training, such as word processing and new equipment operation, is skills training. Other training, such as leadership and motivation, is more in the nature of employee or management development. Some of the training, such as team building, is often categorized as "organization development," as will be discussed in Chapter 21.

Selecting Trainees

Selecting individuals for training is a very important decision for both the organization and the individuals chosen. From the organization's perspective, providing the right training to the right people can help create and maintain a well-trained and stable work force. Conversely, mistakes can be costly. Providing training for individuals with limited performance potential or lack of interest is simply a waste of time, effort, and money. Overlooking individuals with ambition and potential represents a lost opportunity and can contribute to higher employee turnover. It should be assumed that ambition and potential are widespread in the organization and exist at all age levels.

From the individual's perspective, those selected for additional training are likely to receive higher pay, additional prestige, and greater opportunities for promotion. Those not selected can suffer a loss of prestige among fellow workers and can be effectively blocked from promotion.

There are at least four considerations important in selecting trainees: (1) federal regulations and other legal guidelines, (2) employee needs and motivation, (3) skills obsolescence and retraining, and (4) multi-skilling.

Federal Regulations and Other Legal Guidelines

Federal regulations and other legal guidelines have a significant impact on trainee selection. These guidelines have a twofold purpose. First, some guidelines encourage the selection of economically disadvantaged individuals for training programs as a way of reducing the number of economically disadvantaged persons in the society. Second, other guidelines focus on preventing discrimination in the selection of trainees because of race, sex, age, disability status, and the like.

Ideally, managements of organizations should be interested in getting the best people into their training programs without regard to any factors other than their qualifications. A firm may pursue an affirmative action program, however, either

learn all of the jobs of the team, and employees are usually paid according to the number of skills that they have developed. (This is called "skills-based pay" — see Chapter 14.) Some of the companies using this approach are Motorola, Inc., AT&T, and Hoechst Celanese Corporation.[13] Multi-skilling is also relevant in firms where self-managed teams are not being used, but where the company wants greater flexibility in the case of absences due to illness or family emergency, or when there is a sudden shift in production requirements. Graphic Controls is an example of such a firm.[14]

Determining the Curriculum and Choosing Training Methods

After the training objectives have been determined and translated into specific course areas and the trainees have been identified and evaluated, management will be in a position to decide the overall curriculum, that is, the array of courses to be offered. In a sense, the curriculum is a sort of grand plan of what training is to be presented and with what frequency.

But part of what must be added to the grand plan is the matter of training methods. Will the training be on the job, off the job, prior to employment, or prior to a formal assignment? Will it be done by lecture, computer assisted, or carried out by some other method? Will it be long term or short term? Some of the various options open to the human resources staff are described in the following discussion.

On-the-Job Training   Many firms use **on-the-job training (OJT)** as their primary skills training approach. Although OJT can be quite effective, some firms mistakenly view it as putting employees to work and hoping they pick up enough information and experience to survive and perform acceptably. This approach is not true OJT. True OJT includes specific procedures for delivering actual training to the employee. One method for doing this is known as **job instruction training (JIT)**.*

The JIT system was developed originally by the War Manpower Commission during World War II. Figure 11.2 shows the essential steps of the JIT system as presented on pocket cards for supervisors during the war. Although some of the terminology is outdated — today the card would read "new person" or "new worker" rather than "new man," and "he or she" rather than "he" — the fundamental approach is sound. The approach clearly goes far beyond just telling, and includes preparation, interaction, showing, illustrating, trying the new skill, asking questions, observations, and follow-up. The JIT system includes the major characteristics of any effective training program: determination of training needs, recognition of the needs of the trainee, feedback to and from the trainee, frequent appraisal, and correction.

JIT is an effective method of training for several reasons. First, it can yield effective training results at a relatively low cost. Second, it is relatively easy to teach to supervisors responsible for providing OJT to their subordinates. Third, different specific training techniques can be used in conjunction with JIT, such as classroom

*Another way the initials JIT are used is to convey the notion of "just-in-time" production. See Chapter 3 and Alex Taylor III, "Why Toyota Keeps Getting Better and Better and Better," *Fortune*, November 19, 1990, p. 72.

Practical methods to guide you in instructing a new man on a job, or a present worker on a new job or a new skill

FIRST, here's what *you must* do to get *ready* to teach a job:
1. Decide what the learner must be taught in order to do the job efficiently, safely, economically and intelligently.
2. Have the right tools, equipment, supplies and material ready.
3. Have the work place properly arranged, just as the worker will be expected to keep it.

THEN, you should *instruct* the learner by the following *four basic steps*:

STEP I—PREPERATION(of the learner)
1. Put the learner at *ease*.
2. Find out what he already knows about the job.
3. Get him interested and desirous of learning the job.

STEP II—PRESENTATION (of the operations and knowledge)
1. *Tell*, *Show*, *Illustrate*, and *Question* in order to put over the new knowledge and operations.
2. Instruct slowly, clearly, completely and patiently, one point at a time.
3. Check, question and repeat.
4. Make sure the learner really knows.

STEP III—PERFORMANCE TRY-OUT
1. Test learner by having him perform the job.
2. Ask questions beginning with *why, how, when* or *where*.
3. Observe performance, correct errors, and repeat instructions if necessary.
4. Continue until you *know he knows*.

STEP IV—FOLLOW-UP
1. Put him "on his own."
2. Check frequently to be sure he follows instructions.
3. Taper off extra supervision and close follow- up until he is qualified to work with normal supervision.

REMEMBER—If the learner hasn't learned, the teacher hasn't taught.

FIGURE 11.2   Job Instruction Training (JIT) card used by supervisors in manufacturing plants during World War II

Source: War Manpower Commission, *The Training Within Industry Report* (Washington, D.C.: Bureau of Training, Training Within Industry Service, War Manpower Commission, 1945), p. 195.

training, simulation, and others discussed below. Fourth, since much of the training is provided by an individual's supervisor or coworkers, there is assurance that the training relates directly to the specific work situation.[15]

Apprenticeship Training

Apprenticeship programs, in which employees learn by working with those already skilled in their jobs, are a major means of entering approximately eight hundred skilled trades in the United States, such as welder, pipefitter, cabinetmaker, cosmetologist, electrician, machinist, and medical laboratory technician.[16] Most apprenticeship programs begin with classroom training that focuses on theory and on auxiliary skills needed to perform the job. Trainees then go on the job, where at first they are allowed to perform only limited tasks. The performance of more elaborate or sophisticated tasks is allowed and encouraged as the trainees' skill and experience increase. Eventually, they should be able to perform all of the job-related tasks of a skilled craft worker.

The typical apprenticeship program lasts approximately four years and is generally operated by an employer, an employer association, or jointly by management

Vestibule training does have certain potential benefits for some organizations, however, such as those that employ a number of disadvantaged individuals (who may not meet minimum job qualifications) and those that need employees with hard-to-find specialized skills (such as firms in various high-technology fields). Organizations such as these may have no alternative but to provide training in basic skills.

Off-the-Job Training

Many of the training techniques discussed thus far are either OJT approaches or are a major component of an OJT program. A variety of off-the-job training methods can also be effective.

Lectures and Conferences

Many firms use lectures and conferences as vehicles for delivering training in many types of skills. In fact, most training programs, including OJT, use lectures and/or conferences as part of their overall approach. Most training programs, for example, actually begin with a lecture or a conference.

Depending on several factors, lectures and conferences can be held on-site or at facilities away from the firm. Organizations typically conduct these meetings on-site if qualified trainers are available in-house or if trainers can be brought in temporarily and if no special facilities are required. If required training facilities are not available on-site, the training program must be conducted elsewhere. Organizations sometimes hold conferences off-site in order to provide a more relaxed environment and to minimize the usual workplace distractions such as telephone calls.

Programmed, Computer-assisted Instruction

Programmed, **computer-assisted instruction** is one of the fastest growing training techniques. Although rudimentary teaching machines were used as early as 1924, the widespread availability of computers has greatly furthered the use of programmed training. Computerized training systems are available for a wide range of jobs, including those of serving person, mechanic, repair person, and jet pilot.[21]

Computer simulation of job situations is of particular importance. Many tasks can be simulated with the aid of a computer to allow the trainee to gain the practical equivalent of on-the-job experience.

The computer permits training in which the trainee interacts directly with the computer program.[22] For example, the trainee can read questions directly from the computer screen, supply the answer via the keyboard, and immediately receive a grade or a corrected answer. This immediate feedback can be quite beneficial, especially if the trainee must master one unit of material before proceeding to new material.

Audio-visual Aids

Audio-visual materials, such as videodiscs, videocassettes, and films, are also used in skills training programs. They can be used with other approaches, such as lectures and conferences, or alone for initial skills training or brush-up training.

The wide availability of videocassette recording (VCR) equipment has encouraged greater use of audio-visual training. A potentially valuable use of VCR materials involves taping training sessions conducted by the best in-house trainers and distributing these tapes throughout the company as instructional cassettes. This approach can yield the benefits of quality training without the expense of sending the best trainers to remote sites. The most serious disadvantage of this approach is the lack of interaction between the trainer and the trainee. However, the value of such tapes can be augmented by the use of classroom or group discussions of the tapes.

Two-way satellite transmission of training sessions, or **videoconferencing,** is another advance in audio-visual technology that can be used in skills training. Although still relatively expensive, this form of transmitting training material may become much more affordable in the future. Its primary advantage is that it allows interaction between trainees and trainers at remote sites. To illustrate, AMP Inc., a large manufacturer of electrical and electronics connection devices, presents interactive training programs worldwide to its engineers and technicians through satellite transmission. This has been accomplished through a cost-effective partnership with a Public Broadcasting Service (PBS) affiliate in Harrisburg, Pennsylvania.[23]

Interactive Video   The development of **interactive video (IAV)** further overcomes some of the lack of interaction in the use of audio-visual materials. This approach combines a computer and keyboard, a video screen, material stored on a videodisc, and a video camera and tape. To illustrate, sales representatives at Pfizer Inc.'s international division practice sales calls on physicians by watching and interacting with several simulated sales calls that have been stored on a videodisc. At intervals, the "doctor" who appears on the video screen asks pointed questions and the trainee selects a response from one of several options. The computer then calls up the corresponding segment from the disc and displays the doctor's response. Meanwhile, the trainee's performance is being taped and combined with the images selected from the videodisc. The trainee can repeat the exercise until he or she is satisfied, and can show the final tape to a supervisor or instructor for a coaching session.[24] IBM uses a similar approach to train sales personnel,[25] and Federal Express Corp. combines interactive video and job knowledge testing in training its thirty-five thousand customer-contact employees.[26]

Formulating the Budget

Formulating a training budget will be an interactive process with the other steps in developing a skills training program. Budget constraints may limit the human resources manager's alternatives and must therefore be considered during all phases of the development process.

Costs that must be included in the training budget include staff planning time, trainee wages, trainer wages, and direct expenses such as the cost of training materials, travel, accommodations, and meals. If the desired training program does not fit within budget constraints, the human resources manager must consider modifications, such as fewer trainees, different trainers, different training techniques, and a different training location.

Selecting and Training Trainers

An effective training program cannot be developed if effective trainers are not available. Organizations have the option of using staff trainers or of seeking contract trainers outside, or of doing both.

Staff Trainers   When available, **staff trainers** — full-time specialists on the organization payroll or members selected to do part-time training — can be less expensive than trainers who are independent contractors, depending on the total training load. Internal training can also be totally designed and executed by the organization. The key to success, however, is selecting the right individuals and providing them with the tools they need to be effective.

Selecting good trainers is often not easy. Many firms, for example, tend to select their best workers or supervisors as trainers. Although this can work well, two potential problems must be considered. First, the most productive people are taken away from their production tasks. Second, high productivity does not necessarily mean that a worker or supervisor will be a good trainer. In addition to possessing expertise, a good trainer must be able to explain and teach.

Once selected, trainers must be educated in the overall process of training and in the specific training program in which they will be involved. For example, they must understand the program's objectives so they can develop appropriate presentations. Further, they may need to learn more about how people learn (see the section headed "Principles of Learning" later in this chapter). The human resources director, or training director in larger firms, can be particularly helpful in supporting and coordinating training for trainers.[27]

A positive by-product of using company supervisors and managers as trainers is that their involvement tends to increase their support of the training program. Further, their participation gives them a chance to test new ideas in a safe environment. Consequently, their involvement becomes a developmental opportunity with value in its own right.

Contract Trainers   If staff trainers are not available because of inadequate qualifications or for reasons such as production pressures, the firm can turn to **contract trainers**. When such trainers are sought, both the individual trainers and the training organization must be evaluated carefully to ensure quality training. If external facilities are also to be used, they must, of course, be inspected. Before such training begins, at least one conference should be held with members of the outside training organization to discuss issues such as training objectives and to provide any other information the trainers might need.

The use of outside trainers has several advantages. First, productive employees are not taken off the job. Second, firms can be hired that specialize in training and have experienced trainers who understand the process of training and how it should be done. Third, the time, effort, and cost of arranging specialized outside training can sometimes be less than for internal development of a similar training program. Fourth, the organization needing training has a wider choice from which to select training programs, which is particularly important when the training involves skills not currently being used in the firm. Fifth, the firm may have more control because it is generally easier to dismiss an external trainer than to redirect and improve an internal training program.

Determining Evaluation Procedures

The results of all training programs should be evaluated. The five key purposes of conducting this evaluation are as follows:

1. Determine whether a program meets its objectives
2. Identify strengths and weaknesses in the training process
3. Calculate the cost/benefit ratio of a program
4. Determine who benefited the most from a program and why
5. Establish a data base for future decisions about the program[28]

Training programs can be evaluated with a variety of methods. The most popular method involves analyzing questionnaires filled out by the trainees either at the end of the training session or within a few weeks.[29] Although in some situations employees can accurately evaluate the quality of the training program, in other situations their subsequent performance or degree of improvement is a more valid measure.

If specific performance factors can be measured, the trainees' performance after the training can be compared with the objectives for the training program.[30] If the training objectives have been met, then the training has been successful. For example, a training objective could be to train ten people to type a minimum of fifty words per minute with an error rate of less than 1 percent. In this case evaluating the success of the training program would involve testing the typing skills of all trainees both before and after the training. If the objective was found to have been met, the program would be evaluated as having been successful.

Principles of Learning

Several principles of learning are especially relevant to a discussion of skills training. Among these principles are trainee readiness, training relevance, and reinforcement.

Trainee Readiness

People who are not ready to learn will not learn. Consequently, an effective training program must comprise individuals who are ready to learn the skills at hand. Determining trainee readiness involves examining two important issues.

First, the trainee must possess the skills and qualifications that are considered prerequisites for the present training. For example, individuals undergoing training to be accounts-receivable or accounts-payable clerks must be fairly adept at arithmetic. Similarly, many trainers are finding that the greatest drawback in teaching people to use personal computers is that many people do not know how to type.

Depending on the situation, when trainees lack the prerequisites, management must either seek other trainee candidates or provide the trainees with the additional background needed to prepare them for the desired training. Such pretraining is often particularly important when the trainees are educationally disadvantaged.

Management has a vested interest in trainees possessing minimum initial qualifications. Trainees who begin a training program without the prerequisites may become frustrated and discouraged. Their confidence in their ability to do the work can be destroyed. When this occurs, trainees are likely to drop out of the training program and, perhaps, leave the organization.

A second aspect of readiness that must be examined is whether the trainee candidates possess the desire to upgrade old skills or gain new skills. Although individuals can sometimes request or otherwise indicate their interest in training, in other situations their interest can sometimes be quite difficult to ascertain. Problems can arise, for example, when training is mandatory, such as when the training is related to a new process or approach the organization is undertaking. Employees often feel threatened by change because they are comfortable with the old ways of doing things. In situations such as these, the training program must be designed so that the trainees learn and understand early the need for the training and why they should participate. Essentially, the trainer must nurture the trainees' desire to be trained.

*Training
Relevance*

Most trainees quickly develop perceptions about whether training is relevant. If trainees perceive that the instruction will actually help them on the job, they are much more likely to be receptive to the training. If they do not perceive relevance, they are more likely to demonstrate active or passive resistance to the training. For example, if automotive mechanics and their supervisors do not perceive the importance of training in customer relations, they will resist it. They must first be made aware that their relationship with customers can help minimize customer dissatisfaction and gain repeat business for the firm, which, in turn, will result in continued employment and opportunities for advancement. (Management may have to stimulate this awareness with positive financial incentives.)

Reinforcement

Reinforcement is another critical principle of learning. It involves the process of providing financial rewards or nonfinancial incentives (such as praise or recognition) when the trainee reaches a higher level of skill. Training programs should be divided into segments or phases so the trainees can show improvement and achievement periodically and frequently. The trainer can then provide reinforcement incentives as the trainee reaches each progressive skill level. **Skills-based pay**, through which employees are paid according to the number of skills they have mastered, is a powerful way of reinforcing the learning of new skills (see Chapter 14).

Reinforcement can often encourage trainees to become more interested and involved in the training, thereby improving the quality and rate of learning. All training programs should contain a plan for reinforcement.

Role of Human Resources Directors and Other Managers

Both human resources directors and other managers play critical roles in the development of training programs. Human resources directors must assume leadership in developing such programs. They (or a deputy such as the training director) are responsible for assessing training needs; determining training objectives and the curriculum; selecting trainees; choosing the training method; planning, coordinating, and evaluating the training sessions; selecting and educating trainers; and formulating the training budget. Even when contract trainers are used, the human resources staff is still responsible for all of these tasks, but its direct involvement may be much less than when the training is done in-house. Another major responsibility of the human resources staff is coordinating the training program with managers and supervisors across the organization and getting them involved in the overall effort.

Managers and supervisors throughout the organization play a major role in providing information for the human resources department to use in developing and evaluating training programs. If properly involved, they can supply valuable information regarding training needs, trainee qualifications, training methods, and training evaluation. They can also participate directly in the training program as trainers. In fact, some managers feel that training to increase subordinates' performance capabilities is one of their most productive tasks.

The use of highly respected managers and professionals also provides instant credibility to a well-planned training program. At General Dynamics' Convair plant in San Diego, fifty-two such veterans were chosen to instruct in a voluntary training program held after normal working hours for managers and technical leaders.[31]

Summary

Skills training involves experiences directed by the organization to help employees learn information and behavior that contribute to organizational and individual goals. Organizations in the United States spend billions of dollars each year on training programs. Developing a training program consists of seven basic steps. These steps are interdependent and ideally involve a considerable amount of dialogue between human resources professionals and other managers.

First, the need for skills training must be determined. To determine the need, management must analyze organizational needs, job specifications, and employees' skill levels.

Second, the skills needs must be translated into specific training objectives. The training objectives should state the specific number of people to be trained, the specific skills on which the training should focus, and the time for completing the training. The specific content of the training to be given will then stem from the objectives.

Third, the trainees must be selected. When selecting trainees, management must consider relevant federal and other legal guidelines, employee needs and motivation for training, and skills obsolescence and retraining needs.

Fourth, the curriculum must be designed and the training method chosen. On-the-job alternatives include job instruction training, apprenticeship training, and vestibule and preemployment training. Off-the-job training alternatives include lectures and conferences; programmed, computer-assisted instruction; audio-visual aids; videoconferencing; and the use of interactive video systems.

Fifth, the budget for the training program must be formulated. Both the total training budget and the benefits of the specific training program must be considered. At this point, adjustments may need to be made in steps three and four to be compatible with the resources the organization is willing to commit.

Sixth, trainers must be selected and educated. Both staff trainers and outside contract training specialists can be considered.

Seventh, evaluation procedures for the training program must be determined. The purposes of conducting this evaluation are to determine whether a program meets its objectives, to identify the strengths and weaknesses of the program, to calculate the cost/benefit ratio, to determine who benefited the most from the program and why, and to establish a data base for future decisions.

Two other key matters must also be recognized. First, training programs must be compatible with the principles of learning, particularly trainee readiness, training relevance, and reinforcement. Second, both human resources directors and other managers play critical roles in the development and implementation of effective training programs.

Ethical Dilemma

Ernest is an American supervisor working in an American plant in Mexico. His conversational Spanish is fair, but most of his subordinates cannot speak English. When Ernest talks with other supervisors, both Mexican and American, in the presence of Mexican subordinates, he speaks only English. He has been known to say, "I don't think they should be involved in what our plans are. And, besides what they don't know won't hurt them."

To what extent is Ernest's behavior ethical or unethical? Is there a training issue in this situation?

Key Terms

training
functionally illiterate
training objectives
retraining
Job Training Partnership Act (JTPA)
on-the-job training (OJT)
job instruction training (JIT)
apprenticeship program
Joint Apprenticeship Committees

preemployment training
vestibule training
computer-assisted instruction
videoconferencing
interactive video (IAV)
staff trainers
contract trainers
skills-based pay

Review Questions

1. Discuss the importance of skills training. List and discuss the major factors that should be analyzed to assess needs properly.
2. List several dimensions that should be considered in setting objectives for skills training.
3. Discuss the major factors that should be considered in selecting trainees.
4. List and discuss the major on-the-job and off-the-job training methods.
5. Discuss the major issues regarding using staff and contract trainers.
6. Why should training programs be evaluated?
7. Discuss the key principles of learning as they pertain to skills training.
8. Discuss the role of human resources managers and line managers in skills training.

Opening Case Questions

Case 11.1   High-Tech Terror

1. Why do Penny and Amy have such different opinions of their word processors? Did Penny get on-the-job training?
2. If you were Penny's boss, what would you do now? How might you recognize that there is a problem?

Case 11.2   The Apprenticeship Program

1. What is the nature of the task facing Miriam Klein?
2. Why is the apprenticeship program likely to involve vocational schools?

Comprehensive Case

Are Apprenticeships the Answer?

Most discussions about government support of higher education focus on what the government should do for the minority — only about 25 percent of the total population — of young people who complete four-year college programs. Businesses, too, tend to concentrate their in-house training efforts on managers rather than line workers. The United States has, it seems, a bias towards educating only those at the top of the scholastic and occupational ladder.

According to many leaders in both business and education, that bias must change, for the good of the entire country, as well as the individuals who will never call themselves college graduates. A 1986 study by Northeastern University's Center for Labor Market Studies demonstrated how hard the last two decades have been on less-educated workers. The gap between the earnings of college graduates and high school graduates has been widening. Between 1973 and 1986, earnings for men under twenty-five with a high school diploma fell 28 percent, adjusted for inflation. During the same time period, high school dropouts fared even worse, with real earnings falling 42 percent. As the high-pay manufacturing jobs of the past move overseas, the future continues to look bleaker for less-educated workers.

The plight of such workers concerns not just the individuals themselves but the nation as a whole. One of the reasons frequently cited for America's deteriorating position in the global economy is the shortage of trained, skilled workers. Countries with higher educational standards for all their citizens make better long-term use of their entire human resource pool.

In the eyes of many people, including, apparently, President Clinton, apprenticeship programs hold the greatest hope of solving the problems of what is being called the "forgotten half" of the country's young people. Typically, these programs require some investment from businesses,

government, schools, and the individuals involved and they include both classroom work and on-the-job training. The programs often begin in high school and continue as the student goes on to a two-year technical or community college program. The results are young people who have a marketable skill, some experience in the workplace, and the confidence that such experience brings.

Most apprenticeship programs look to Europe, particularly Germany, for models. Some 70 percent of Germany's current workers entered the work force through its apprenticeship program; the country currently has about 1.8 million apprentices. Beginning in the seventh grade, German students learn about the occupations available to them. Over the next few years, they choose between a college preparatory or vocational program, and by the time they turn eighteen, most of the vocational students have signed contracts with employers that detail the training and pay they will receive.

Although few in the United States envision such a large-scale American apprenticeship program anytime soon, most American programs emulate the German cooperation among government, schools, and unions. One American program often cited as a successful model is Boston's Project ProTech. Students in the program hold part-time hospital jobs during their last two years of high school and two years of junior college. In the hospitals, they get experience in radiology, hematology, or histology (the study of tissues), and at the end of the process they should have a certifiable medical skill. The program focuses on health care in part because health care workers are already in short supply, and the number of jobs in the field is expected to increase.

For the 120 students in Project ProTech, the program clearly works. Some of the students see the program as a way to avoid a lifetime of low-paying, dead-end jobs, which are all their older siblings have to look forward to. And the businesses for which they work can usually count on hiring skilled, well-trained workers who may already feel a sense of loyalty to the business.

While such pilot programs have been succeeding around the country, serious barriers stand in the way of translating isolated, small successes into significant national policy. One is cost. In Germany, employers pick up the bulk of the tab for apprenticeship programs, but few American companies are likely to make such an investment. ProTech uses almost $1 million from a federal grant to help only 120 students out of a total Boston high school population of 15,000.

Another problem is reaching the people who most need the help. Most American apprenticeship programs begin in the last years of high school, after many students have already made the decision to drop out. They also tend to be highly selective therefore end up with only the most motivated students, some of whom, after gaining confidence in the program, decide they want to go on to four-year colleges after all. For a national apprenticeship program to succeed, it must reach a majority of the nation's schoolchildren early in their school careers.

But perhaps the most significant hurdle apprenticeship programs must overcome is the historical sense of distrust between educators and businesspeople, a distrust that results from significant philosophical differences. Business leaders often complain that schools don't teach students the skills they can use on the job after they graduate. Educators counter that schools should be educating students in ways that will open them to many possibilities, not training them in one particular skill that may become obsolete overnight. They point to studies that show that fewer than one-third of the graduates of traditional vocational programs end up working in the field that they are trained for.

If apprenticeship programs are to succeed, government must also be involved, and not just financially. The country needs a system of skills certification so that a student can come out of the program with credentials that will be nationally recognized.

There are no quick solutions to these problems, but that does not deter advocates of apprenticeships. For now, anyway, it seems as though the country has no other choice.

Sources: Jason DeParle, "Trying to Make Teen-Agers Tomorrow's Skilled Workers," *New York Times*, November 26, 1992, A1, A12; Karen Matthes, "Apprenticeships Can Support the 'Forgotten Youth,'" *HRfocus* 68 (December 1991):19; Karen Matthes, "Germany's Model Program," *HRfocus* 68 (December 1991):19; and Rick Wartzman, "Apprenticeship Plans Spring Up for Students Not Headed to College," *Wall Street Journal*, May 19, 1992, A1, A5.

Discussion Questions

1. What are the differences between the United States and Germany in terms of skills training?
2. What are the features of Boston's Project Pro-Tech?

CHAPTER 12

Management and Career Development

CASE 12.1   Where Have All the Managers Gone?

Louise Smith, the human resources manager for Stores, Inc., had a difficult problem. She needed to recommend four store managers for the four new stores the firm was planning to open during the next three months. A close examination of the company's human resources revealed that there were no assistant managers with more than three years' experience, which was far less than the experience necessary for the store manager's position.

Ten years earlier, Stores, Inc., had adopted a fast-growth strategy of opening four to eight new stores each year. At that time, store managers were required to have had at least ten years of experience in positions of increasing responsibility. That requirement had been relaxed considerably to help the organization meet its growing need for managers. The company had also begun to hire experienced managers from competitors at inflated salaries. This was causing considerable discontent among the managers who had been promoted from within the company.

Louise dreaded facing her boss, the founder of Stores, Inc., with her problem. She knew that she and the HR department were not going to look very good when she presented her recommendations and tried to explain. She was probably going to get an angry question like "How did we get into this situation, anyway?"   ◄

CASE 12.2   Which Is More Important, Inspiration or Skill?

Molly Forrester, vice president of marketing, had just come back with new insights from a one-week group dynamics workshop. Most of the training took place in ten-person groups of executives — all strangers in the beginning — and was highly unstructured in that the trainer did not set the agenda. One device used by the trainer was to ask participants communicating with each other to focus on what each was saying and the feelings each one had. Molly came away with the idea that improved communications and teamwork on the job probably depend on the ability of two or more people — jointly — to learn and practice effective communications.

"It takes two to tango," Molly commented to the CEO and the human resources vice president shortly after returning from the group dynamics laboratory. "I'm beginning to wonder about those one-day inspirational workshops we've been sending people to. Most of them come back all pumped up about what a great workshop it was, and perhaps more enthusiastic and even a bit more assertive, but I don't see much improvement in working together in meetings. I think the key is the mutual practicing of the skills they've learned, and I don't see that happening as the result of a one-day self-image-enhancing course."

"Well," the HR vice president responded, "I thought the one-day thing was pretty good. Maybe we ought to send several people to both kinds of workshops. I think we could stretch the budget that far. And you could take in the next one-day session, while I go to that one-week group dynamics workshop. Then we can compare the two and maybe integrate what we learn." "Great idea," Molly responded. "Let's do it."   ◄

Management and career development programs represent efforts to increase the organization's present and future ability to meet its goals by providing educational and developmental experiences for managers and all employees above and beyond the immediate technical requirements of their jobs. In today's highly competitive and rapidly changing business world, managerial development is particularly important. In addition to competence in their own areas of specialization, managers must be prepared to handle new assignments and meet the complex demands of accelerating changes in the external environment.

Formal programs specifically designed to prepare employees for managerial positions are widespread and can be considered part of the overall management and career development effort in organizations. Without managers capable of directing and motivating employees and performing other managerial tasks, high employee skill levels will not be enough to make a firm successful. This chapter focuses on planning and executing effective management and career development programs. Some of the topics included in these programs can be seen in Table 11.2 in the last chapter. Frequently found courses are leadership, team building, delegation, time management, goal setting, stress management, quality improvement, conducting meetings, and managing change.

Planning Effective Development Programs

The development of appropriate and effective management and career development programs requires consideration of both organizational and employee needs. Six common themes appear to underlie many training needs in today's organizations.[1] These themes tend to match prevailing organizational and environmental characteristics. The six themes are as follows:

1. Managerial careers are in a state of flux as new jobs are opening up and traditional, stable jobs are disappearing.
2. People want to know more about their immediate jobs, about other jobs in their organization, and about their organization as a whole.
3. As more emphasis is placed on teams and teamwork, supervisors and managers need to acquire additional skills in interpersonal communications, group decision making, and chairing meetings.
4. Employees need their organization's help to help themselves.
5. Basic skills (for example, mathematics, grammar) are still important and cannot be overlooked.
6. Many career transitions represent ideal training opportunities, such as when employees start a new job, experience technological or other changes on their present jobs, or anticipate organizational changes.

Organizational Considerations

An effective management and career development program obviously must meet the needs of the organization. Management must determine these needs and convert them into objectives to guide the formulation of the program. Although each organization may possess a unique combination of needs, a careful analysis of the following four aspects of organizations will usually begin to reveal some significant management and career development needs: (1) human resources planning,

(2) organization adaptation and improvement, (3) organizational culture and climate, and (4) organizational effectiveness.[2]

Human Resources Planning

Human resources planning is a primary component of the management development program. Since firms that run out of promotable managers face serious consequences, as Louise Smith recognized in Case 12.1, the human resources director must ensure that there are enough managers with appropriate technical and human skills to fill all anticipated positions. Failure to do so typically results in emergency "crash" development programs, the hiring of competent managers away from competitors, or promotion of someone who is simply not ready to handle the job. None of these alternatives is particularly attractive, and all can be more expensive than a well-planned development program.

To ensure continuous availability of managerial talent, the human resources director should carefully analyze the firm's current human resources chart to determine how many managers will be needed in the future and when. This analysis involves two major components. First, management turnover rates must be forecast, such as by tracking managers' ages in relation to retirement and examining normal attrition due to voluntary departures and dismissals. Second, changes in the organization's human resources chart must be analyzed. For example, does the firm anticipate new managerial positions as a result of growth or expansion or fewer managerial positions because of contraction? Stores, Inc., in Case 12.1 had apparently failed to complete this second step adequately, or, if it had, it had not followed through on the implications.

The results of this phase of human resources planning should indicate the number of managers and qualifications needed. Since some individuals may not progress as desired, more prospective candidates should begin the development program than will actually be needed. This means, of course, that candidates should understand that participation in a development program does not guarantee promotion. (See Chapter 6 for more on human resources planning.)

Organization Adaptation and Improvement

Another major area of management and career development involves organization adaptation and improvement. Successful organizations tend to match or fit the environments in which they operate. Further, they continuously strive to improve their internal processes so that they can adapt more quickly and effectively. Essentially, the management development program should provide the organization with the ability to adapt to changing environmental conditions.

To help ensure environmental fit, the human resources manager must understand the overall goals and strategies of the organization and the character of managerial expertise needed to achieve these goals and strategies. For example, if the organization intends to grow rapidly by developing new products internally, it will need managers who are able to create and nurture an innovative and entrepreneurial spirit. Conversely, if an organization intends to focus on cost control as the key to success, the management development program should be oriented toward developing managers who are cost conscious and adept at cost control. If an organization is growing internationally, the program should have a strong cross-cultural component. (For a discussion of cross-cultural training, see Chapter 22).

Organizational Culture and Climate

The management development program can also focus on maintaining and nurturing the desired organizational culture and climate. When the top management of an organization considers its culture and climate to be of major importance, the management development program, or at least portions of it, must focus on fostering appropriate managerial skills and attitudes. The top managements of many successful firms, for example, believe that everyone in the organization must be oriented toward delivering customer satisfaction. In these firms, enhancement of customer-oriented attitudes is a priority in all training and development programs. Procter & Gamble is an example. The firm's P & G College, attended by new employees, new supervisors, and higher managers, places strong emphasis "on the marketplace, on the consumer, on the customer, on the competition."[3]

Organizational Effectiveness

The overriding concern in virtually all management development programs is that they make the organization more effective. Organizational effectiveness is influenced by a variety of factors (see Chapter 4), many of which can be incorporated into management development programs. For example, a clear understanding of available managerial career paths can result in higher job satisfaction, lower management turnover rates, and greater loyalty to the organization. In general, if employees understand the nature of other jobs and managerial positions in the firm, communication throughout the organization can be enhanced, which increases organizational effectiveness.

The four organizational considerations — particularly organization adaptation and improvement, organizational culture and climate, and organizational effectiveness — are very evident in the concerns expressed by trainers. The most critical training and development challenges faced by trainers in firms of a hundred or more employees are shown in Figure 12.1. Quality improvement, technological change, customer service, and corporate culture top the list.

Employee Considerations

An effective management and career development program can increase employee satisfaction and motivation. If this objective is to be met, employee needs must be considered when the development program is being planned. In addition to employee needs, management must consider union attitudes.

Need Fulfillment

If designed properly, management development programs can help fulfill higher-order needs of the participants. Many managers, and those who aspire to be managers, have a strong need for achievement. Being selected for a management development program can sometimes be an achievement in itself. It can also be a vehicle for subsequent achievement, such as promotion and other career goals. It is therefore important that those responsible for designing management development programs have a clear understanding of participants' needs and provide a clear understanding to the participants of how the program can help them fulfill their needs.

Another need that management development programs can help fulfill is the need to belong. This can be particularly important in supervisory training programs. The program may provide supervisors with the chance to meet others in similar positions and to discuss problems of mutual interest. Since supervisors are in the awkward position of being directly between management and the nonsupervisory work force (and often recently part of that work force), they may enter the training with

Quality Improvement — 20

Technological Change — 15

Customer Service — 12

Corporate Culture — 10

New Market Strategies/Organizational Missions — 9

Centralization — 8

Productivity Improvement — 6

Staffing — 4

Decentralization — 4

Other — 3

Succession Planning — 3

Mergers/Aquisitions — 2

Remedial/Basic Education — 2

International Competition — 1

* Percent of respondents selecting this challenge.

FIGURE 12.1 Training and development challenges

Source: Reprinted with permission from the Oct. 1991 issue of *Training* Magazine. Lakewood Publications, Minneapolis, MN. All rights reserved.

feelings of frustration regarding their transition to management. In addition to fulfilling needs to belong, the development program may also show the supervisors that higher-level management does care about them.

There is some evidence that such factors may be more important than the actual content of training.[4] For example, after interviewing participants of an Outdoor Management Training (OMT) program, researchers reported that "Several of our program participants said that being sent to the OMT was one of the few signs they had ever received that the organization cared about them."[5] Thus, the symbolic value of being chosen to participate in special programs should not be discounted.

Union Attitudes

Attitudes held by union leaders can have a tremendous impact on the effectiveness of development programs, particularly those involving members of the labor force who are moving into supervisory management positions. It is important that union leaders be supportive of the supervisory training programs so that they do not convey negative or cynical opinions to trainees. One way to secure this support is to involve the union leaders from the very beginning in developing the programs.

In actual practice, the degree of the union leaders' involvement in training and development programs varies greatly from organization to organization. Generally, organizations with good labor-management relationships have more union involvement. Union leaders are normally very interested in training and development programs for their members and may, in fact, sponsor their own training programs. By allowing union leaders to participate in the firm's training programs, management puts itself in a better position to become involved in the union's training programs.

Role of the Human Resources Department

Human resources staff members typically have a leadership role in determining training and development needs, recommending programs, developing seminars and teaching aids, scheduling classes, obtaining feedback on program effectiveness, and perhaps serving occasionally as trainers or conference leaders. The actual degree of participation in each of these activities often depends on whether the organization is large enough to have a separate training department.

In any organization, the human resources director must involve other managers in the training and development effort. Supervisors must understand and approve of the goals of the development program and help persuade potential participants that the program is relevant and beneficial. Supervisors can also be especially useful in helping to determine who will attend development programs. The enthusiastic support of management often leads to greater interest and enthusiasm among participants.

In less formal training situations, the human resources department may serve as an information source. It can provide information to employees about training opportunities that are not part of the organization's formal training program. It may also provide information about the firm's training policies, such as a tuition refund program. In one study of 617 firms, 97 percent provided tuition reimbursement programs of some kind for managerial and professional employees. (Hourly employees were included in these programs in 78 percent of the firms.)[6]

Successful Programs and Curricula

Many factors can influence the success of a management development program. Six specific keys to success have been formulated for internal development programs.[7]

1. Secure top management support, and make it visible. When top management believes something is important, their beliefs are transmitted to other members of the organization. Therefore, efforts must be made by the human resources department to educate senior executives about the program, to involve them at every stage, and to frequently publicize program successes and positive results.

2. Carefully blend new ways of doing things with organizational norms. Successful programs must sometimes challenge certain organizational norms while respecting others. For example, some firms have found that training programs

involving changes tend to be more successful when the traditional chain of command is respected and the program has a look that is polished and professional rather than experimental.

3. Ensure compatibility between individual training and organization structure and systems. Some programs fail because the individual managers are given training that is wasted in an "overstructured" organizational environment, such as one with too many forms and rigid systems (for example, performance appraisal systems and job-grading schemes). Others fail because of inadequate follow-up. Merrill Lynch & Co., Inc., for example, supplements formal courses by having top management discuss high-potential management candidates on a quarterly basis, by providing mentors and advisory councils, and by other activities.

4. Use existing resources, including training programs, information systems, and people. This helps control costs and builds a supportive climate.

5. Create multiple feedback loops. Since people learn and gauge the extent of their learning by obtaining feedback from their environment (that is, from friends, supervisors, spouses, technology, meetings, presentations, and the like), training programs should also have built-in feedback. Examples of feedback loops include written evaluations, peer evaluations, discussions with mentors and supervisors, and advisory councils.

6. Promote volunteerism and choice. Since development tends to be a self-initiated activity, firms must provide employees with encouragement and opportunities both to volunteer for programs and to choose among various offerings and career paths.

A well-planned curriculum is also critical to a successful program. The needs and abilities of program participants and the specific content of the programs will vary widely. Planners should therefore be aware of the basic approaches for planning a specific curriculum.[8]

Developing Managerial and Supervisory Abilities

There are many techniques and approaches in use today for furthering managerial and supervisory abilities and for meeting the developmental needs of employees. Some organizations have a narrow, limited approach. Others, such as Marion Laboratories, Inc., have a broad, multiple-faceted approach to management and career development. Figure 12.2, the Marion development wheel, shows the many different methods by which employees at Marion can acquire the skills and experiences needed for advancement — and demonstrates a positive, creative approach to career development.

We will turn now to some specific training and development techniques in widespread use today. For convenience, these techniques can be divided into two categories, on-the-job and off-the-job training methods. (As shown in Figure 12.2, Marion Laboratories has two off-the-job categories: "inside Marion — off the job" and "outside Marion.")

On-the-Job Training Methods

Although on-the-job training (OJT) methods are considered more useful for skills training (as discussed in Chapter 11), OJT also forms an important part of managerial and supervisory development. Even if an organization has a well-developed off-

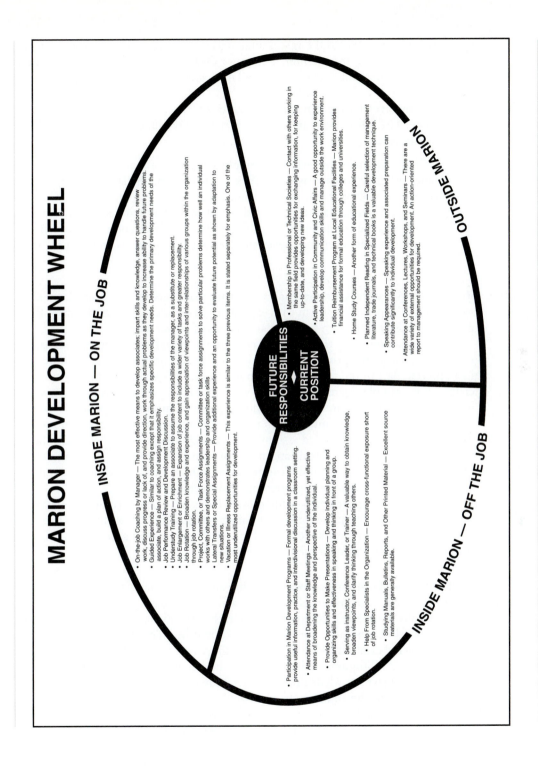

FIGURE 12.2   Marion development wheel

Source: Marion Laboratories, Inc. Reprinted by permission.

Note: In a 1989 merger, Marion Laboratories, Inc. became Marion Merrell Dow Inc. As a result, the information in this figure is not current.

311

the-job training program, OJT is still often necessary, particularly to provide an element of practicality to the training. The major OJT methods are coaching, rotations and transfers, understudy assignments, and mentoring.[9]

Coaching

Coaching involves frequent helping activities on the part of a superior toward a subordinate. The following is an excellent statement of what the superior should do in the role as coach:

> *Coaches* are managers who help employees grow and improve their job competence on a day-to-day basis. Coaches set challenging goals, inform employees what is expected of them, and evaluate progress toward those goals. Coaches also appraise performance in a regular and objective manner. Improved performance change is supported by using positive feedback and reinforcement. In addition, coaches train employees to fill in during absences and prepare them for promotion.[10]

Rotations and Transfers

Rotations and transfers are designed to prepare managers to take on additional responsibilities by providing them with experience in different areas of the firm. Rotations and transfers are often based on an analysis of career paths.

Many rotations and transfers are considered lateral promotions: that is, the manager is placed in a position that carries similar authority and responsibility, but in a different part of the firm. The new position can be outside the manager's "specialty." For example, managers hired to work in the human resources or personnel department may be required to serve stints as production supervisors or salespeople. Such assignments are not intended to prepare the manager for a career in production or sales. Rather, the varied assignments can help the personnel specialist better understand the unique problems and needs of managers in other operating departments. These experiences should lead to better human resources decisions and recommendations, such as in hiring, training, and discipline.

A contrasting approach is McDonnell Douglas Corp.'s rotational program within a particular discipline for recent college graduates. For example, in the fiscal area, high-potential recruits are rotated into such subareas as accounting, financial planning, contract administration, and overhead budgeting.[11]

Understudy Assignments

Understudy assignments involve assigning an inexperienced manager to work for a more experienced manager, often on an "assistant to" basis. The understudy manager normally progresses from performing rather mundane, detailed tasks to more advanced work. Eventually, the understudy should be able to perform at about the same level as the experienced manager. The effectiveness of understudy assignments depends on the willingness and ability of the higher-level manager to share experience and to transfer knowledge to the understudy manager.

A variation of the understudy approach involves placing novice managers on certain committees. The best committees for such assignments include a mixture of experienced and inexperienced managers, whose interaction results in a coaching type of situation. Sequencing these assignments so that the inexperienced manager is faced with progressively larger responsibilities can result in effective training. However, creating artificial committees or limiting assignments to low-level committees can be counterproductive, particularly when the manager perceives the activity as a waste of time and effort.

Mentoring   According to the *American Heritage Dictionary*, a **mentor** is "a wise and trusted counselor or teacher."* In contrast to the coaching function performed by an employee's immediate superior, mentoring is a role filled by someone other than the immediate superior.

Although informal mentoring occurs daily in all types of organizations, more and more firms are establishing formal mentoring programs. In such programs, managers who wish to be mentors indicate their interest in this additional activity and are given a specific assignment. At Merrill Lynch, for example, mentors are department heads or higher executives who volunteer to coach four individuals over a six-month period. The four people are all from outside the mentor's department.[12]

Mentors can play several valuable roles:

1. *Sponsor:* to widen opportunities for special assignments
2. *Teacher:* to help solve real problems, to create learning situations with hypothetical problems, and to transmit organizational culture
3. *Devil's advocate:* to provide challenges and to give the trainee practice in asserting ideas and being influential
4. *Coach:* to support trainees in finding out what is important to them, what skills they possess, and what interests and long-term aspirations they have[13]

Several guidelines can help ensure a successful mentoring program:

1. Make sure that mentor participation is voluntary and that potential mentors have a realistic picture of the time involved and problems that might emerge.
2. Provide mentors with information about the mentoring role, but encourage them to develop their own style and approach.
3. Encourage mentors and trainees to negotiate realistic expectations, and urge mentors to make clear what they can and cannot do.
4. Give mentors recognition and visibility.
5. Keep the trainee's supervisor informed.[14]
6. Avoid pairing up people who seem to be clones of each other. There will be more growth for both parties if they can look at different ways of doing things.

These guidelines can help organizations avoid potential problems and can increase the possibility that the mentoring program will be rewarding for the trainee, the mentor, and the organization.

Off-the-Job Training Methods   The general nature of managerial and supervisory development requires that much of the training be performed off the job. All the off-the-job training methods discussed in this section can be conducted in-house (but off the job) or by outside firms that specialize in training. In-house training is most often conducted by larger firms that need a large and ongoing supply of managers and supervisors. Smaller firms typically cannot justify the cost of doing much of this kind of training themselves.

Figure 12.3, based on an extensive survey of firms of a hundred employees or more, shows the most common methods used in training supervisors and middle managers. Most supervisory and management development programs use more than one method, of course, and frequently use several.

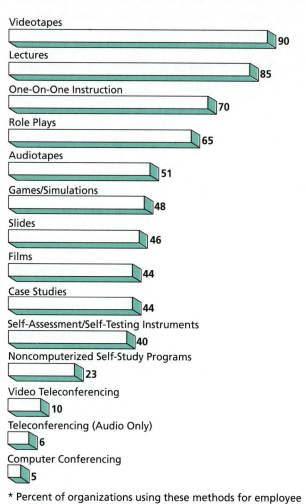

Videotapes **90**
Lectures **85**
One-On-One Instruction **70**
Role Plays **65**
Audiotapes **51**
Games/Simulations **48**
Slides **46**
Films **44**
Case Studies **44**
Self-Assessment/Self-Testing Instruments **40**
Noncomputerized Self-Study Programs **23**
Video Teleconferencing **10**
Teleconferencing (Audio Only) **6**
Computer Conferencing **5**

* Percent of organizations using these methods for employee training.

FIGURE 12.3 Instructional methods used

Source: Reprinted with permission from the Oct. 1991 issue of *Training* Magazine. Lakewood Publications, Minneapolis, MN. All rights reserved.

Seminars and Lectures

Most management and supervisory training programs include seminars and/or lectures, particularly at the beginning. Both seminars and lectures involve assembling a group of trainees and a group leader, although seminar groups tend to be smaller than lecture audiences. In seminars, the group leader generally focuses on coordinating and motivating discussion among the group members. The content, for example, may be based on assigned readings. In lectures, the leader presents material in a classroom-lecture manner, and the group members tend to focus on the acquisition of knowledge. As indicated, however, most training and development programs use a variety of methods, and a two-hour "lecture" session might include a lecture followed by discussion, a videotape followed by small group discussion, and group reports.

Laboratory Training

Laboratory training can be described as experience-based learning workshops that utilize one or more approaches, such as case discussions, role plays, computer simulations, management games or problem-solving exercises, and/or relatively unstructured group discussions. In some forms of training, the main objective is to provide an opportunity to derive insights from the dynamics of the sessions. In other forms of laboratory training, the major objective is to apply specific managerial and supervisory techniques to making decisions and taking action in simulated work situations. Trainees typically receive feedback about their decisions or actions. The knowledge and insight from such training is often supplemented by lectures.

Four approaches can provide the trainees with practice in making managerial decisions. First, **computer simulation models** can be developed to simulate or approximate various business situations. The simulation program generally provides the trainee with information about a specific type of decision, such as forecasting the price of key raw materials. The trainee then analyzes the situation and makes a decision. After receiving the trainee's decision, the simulation program can calculate the outcome and provide feedback to the trainee. Although no computer model can completely simulate an actual business situation, models can provide participants with sufficient realism to allow practice applications without undue risk that the organization's operations will be disrupted or that the firm will lose money.[15]

Second, **gaming simulations** (or **management games**) can be used. These are management development exercises in which participants are given background information, instructions about rules and conditions, and perhaps roles to play.[16] One example would be a complex computerized game in which competing groups make a series of management decisions such as product price, sale of stock, wage rates, and inventory size, and are given scores as they progress through a series of changes in the economic environment. Another example — not computerized — is a consensus exercise in which members of groups make individual decisions and then attempt to improve their individual scores through effective group interaction. Such an exercise is used to highlight the advantages of and problems with consensus decision making and to provide a laboratory in which participants can examine group dynamics.

Third, **case studies** involve providing the trainees with written or videotaped descriptions of decision-making situations. The participants are required to analyze each case and make appropriate decisions. The case is subsequently discussed, with emphasis normally on the trainees' analyses, decisions, implications of those decisions, and probable decision outcomes. Executive MBA programs, for example, are often based on this method. The **incident process** is a specialized form of case method in which the leader presents a problem or dilemma — some critical incident that actually happened in an organization — and the participants have the task of drawing out the relevant facts by questioning the leader. A decision is made after the participants believe they have the essential facts.[17]

Fourth, **role playing** tends to be more appropriate for problems and decisions having to do with human relations. Participants are typically provided with a specific situation that they must analyze, and then each assumes and acts out the role of a specific person. Since each role player brings his or her own personality to a given role, all participants experience the realistic variability that managers actually encounter in real job situations.[18]

T-Groups

T-groups (derived from the term *training groups*), a form of laboratory training, usually involve small groups, of approximately ten to twelve participants, meeting

Seminars and lectures are frequently a part of management training programs such as this one, where American middle-management executives learn Japanese-style management.

under the guidance of a trainer. The groups are largely unstructured in the sense that there is a very flexible agenda and a minimum of formal leadership. The discussions are essentially unguided by the trainer, except that there is a strong emphasis on learning about effective group development and processes, developing more effective interpersonal skills, learning how to communicate feelings and perceptions clearly and in constructive ways, and learning from the perceptions and reactions of others.[19] (See *Contemporary Issues* on page 317, where the importance of skills in interpersonal relations negotiations, and teamwork is emphasized.) The training Molly Forrester had just experienced in Case 12.2 was a T-group experience. (One of the issues she was wrestling with when coming back to work was whether company dollars were better spent on this kind of training or on inspirational programs using more traditional lecture methods.)

Because of the self-disclosure and potential stress involved, it is very important that T-groups be conducted by highly qualified professionals, and that participation be voluntary. Further, it is recommended that these groups consist of "strangers," that is, people who are neither working in the same unit of an organization nor have a reporting relationship. "Team building," discussed in Chapter 21, which focuses on intact teams, has some similarities to T-group dynamics but is much more task- and issue-oriented.

Transactional Analysis

Transactional analysis (TA) is another training technique requiring a high level of trainee participation. The focus of TA is on viewing the interactions between individuals and between groups as transactions. TA is based on the concept that each person has a three-dimensional behavior pattern based on three ego states — parent, child, and adult.[20]

The primary use of TA in business and industrial settings appears to be in helping employees become more sensitive to the nature of their interactions with others. For example, TA can be used to help salespeople improve their relationships with customers. Managers can use TA to help them deal with subordinates by trying to

Contemporary Issues

Group Effectiveness: Interpersonal Skills, Negotiation, and Teamwork

In the past two decades, there has been a tremendous increase in the use of teams in the workplace. The team approach has been linked conclusively to higher productivity and product quality, as well as to increased quality of worklife. Change strategies are usually dependent upon the ability of employees to pull together and refocus on the new common goal.

Whenever people work together, successful interaction depends upon effective interpersonal skills, focused negotiation, and a sense of group purpose. The quality of these three factors defines and controls working relationships.

Interpersonal skills training is directed toward assisting the employee to recognize and improve the ability to judge and balance appropriate behavior, cope with undesirable behavior in others, absorb stress, deal with ambiguity, listen, inspire confidence in others, structure social interaction, share responsibility, and interact easily with others.

Such skills are essential to successful **negotiation.** Conflicts, both major and minor, are a fact of worklife. They can sap productivity and short-circuit strategic plans.

The key to diffusing potential conflict situations is to enhance employee negotiating skills at all levels.

Training in this skill includes techniques for separating people from the problem, focusing on interests not positions, inventing options for mutual gain, and insisting on the use of objective criteria. It also relies on a sound base of interpersonal skills and a clear understanding of the approach demanded by the circumstance.

Interpersonal and negotiation skills are the cornerstones of successful **teamwork.** Teams are organized in the workplace so that appropriate talents and skills can be directed through group effort to accomplish vital tasks and goals. This pooling of resources, however, frequently requires team members to have an array of skills that individual or routine jobs do not demand.

Quality teamwork results when team members know how to recognize and cope with various and unique personalities and when each has a sense of the cultures and approaches that other team members represent. Team members also need an understanding of group dynamics, which evolve and change as the team approaches its goal. Lastly, team members must be aware of the technical skills that fellow members have and how those skills can be applied.

Teamwork can only occur when team members provide and receive feedback in a focused manner. Individuals gather and process information in personalized ways; good teamwork calls for the recognition and use of certain valuable differences between members of the team.

Training in teamwork is crafted to capture the essential elements of building team relationships. The major objective is to develop an inventory of skills and attitudes that can be applied successfully in the workplace to resolve problems and foster innovation.

The strategic relevance of interpersonal, negotiation, and teamwork skills is evident. They are basic tools for achieving the flexibility and adaptability that America's workforce must have in order to remain competitive.

Source: Excerpted from Anthony P. Carnevale, Lila Gainer, and Ann S. Meltzel, *Workplace Basics: The Skills Employees Want* (Washington, D.C.: U.S. Government Printing Office, 1988), pp. 14–15.

ensure that the adult ego state is used by both parties to a transaction. In general, TA can help improve the quality of communication between individuals and groups.

Behavioral Modeling

Behavioral modeling (sometimes called interaction modeling) consists of presenting or showing participants a particular behavior or way of doing something, such as handling employee complaints, and then having the participants practice the behavior through role playing. This approach may consist of six to twelve modules for small groups in a series of two- or three-hour sessions spread over a few weeks or months.

Behavioral modeling emphasizes positive reinforcement for participants demonstrating appropriate behaviors during the role playing. Whereas other training approaches often address both effective and ineffective management techniques, behavioral modeling usually addresses only useful and effective practices.[21]

In-basket Training

In-basket training consists of giving trainees a set of memos, letters, and other items that a manager might find in the in-basket upon arriving at work. The trainee is required to respond by (1) delaying a decision about the issue, (2) referring the issue to someone else in the organization, or (3) making a decision about the issue. The trainer and the group then analyze the responses to see whether any improvements can be made.

The objective of in-basket training is to help trainees determine which decisions can be made quickly, which must or should be delayed, and which should be referred to others. This training emphasizes a critical characteristic of effective management. In-basket training is also useful for teaching good time management, which is important enough in most managerial jobs to justify the cost of the training. (As discussed in Chapter 10, in-basket exercises are also used in many assessment centers.)[22]

Outdoor-based and Wilderness Programs

In recent years, a significant number of companies have involved executives in outdoor-based and wilderness programs that have such objectives as fostering individual growth and development, increasing self-confidence and risk taking, and building leadership and teamwork skills. In **outdoor-based programs,** a permanent conference center is used for both indoor and outdoor learning. For example, participants may undertake some challenging physical, team-oriented task outdoors and then return indoors to debrief the experience. In most **wilderness programs,** the learning takes place in a wilderness area involving such activities as river rafting, mountain climbing, or scaling obstacles, with debriefing occurring at the campsite. Group discussions and short lectures are usually included in both types of programs.[23]

Some outdoor-based programs are part of a broader program that includes several phases. For example, the General Foods Executive Leadership Program includes five phases that take a total of about twenty-five days spread over an eighteen-month period. The five phases include theater and the humanities; outdoor types of team development activities; self-assessment; peer teaching; and a team project of importance to the company.[24]

Although outdoor and wilderness programs enjoy considerable popularity, their contribution needs to be studied carefully. In particular, the extent to which participants can translate these outdoor experiences to their relationships and performance back on the job is a crucial matter. As in perhaps all experiential and laboratory learning, much depends on the skill of the trainers, the voluntary nature of the program, and the efforts made to modify the culture of organizations to accommodate the learnings. In addition, there have been some accidents — for example, five executives of an advertising agency drowned when a raft overturned in rapids — but most programs appear to have avoided any serious accidents.[25] Clearly, this is a dimension that must be considered.

Developing Employee Potential

Although the development of employee potential is the major objective of all training programs, there are several special cases that should be addressed individually. These special cases include career development for nonsupervisors in professional and technical positions, women, minorities, older workers, and the disabled. Managing diversity and employee counseling are also important topics.

Professional-Technical Employees

All employees of an organization need some attention to their career development. In addition, there are employees in certain nonsupervisory positions — such as in engineering, accounting, and legal work — that perhaps warrant a wider range of developmental opportunities.

Career development for most nonsupervisory employees may involve only such activities as a standard introduction or orientation, ongoing coaching, and periodic meetings at which executives explain new challenges and opportunities facing the organization. These aspects of career development can be extremely valuable to the organization because of their desirable influence on performance and their potential for creating loyalty and identification with the organization.

Career development for technical-professional positions, such as those in engineering, accounting, and law, is typically similar to that for other employees, but additional aspects are needed. These people must keep up with rapid technological, legal, and other changes that are affecting or can affect their jobs and the direction of the organization. Thus, additional development opportunities are required, such as special seminars and attendance at professional conferences.[26]

Women

While the proportion of women in managerial and management-related jobs has grown rapidly to 43 percent, the proportion of women in top executive positions is very low — at only 5.1 percent in *Fortune* 500 companies, according to one report.[27] The "glass ceiling" in many organizations is real in the United States and worldwide. (See *International Perspective* on page 320 and the excerpts from the Glass Ceiling Act of 1991 in Figure 12.4.) Yet some firms have an outstanding record in promoting women compared with most companies. For example, in 1990 about 25 percent of the upper-management ranks at CBS were women, and at U S West, women made up 21 percent of the 1 percent of the work force earning salaries of $68,000 or more.[28]

The imbalance in the proportion of women in top management positions indicates the ongoing need for special career development programs for women. Federal agencies and the court system have recognized this imbalance and have placed many firms under court order to move more women into managerial positions. The Labor Department is planning to be even more aggressive in this matter, and the Glass Ceiling Act will add an important stimulus.

SEC. 202. FINDINGS AND PURPOSE.

(a) Findings. — Congress finds that —

(1) despite a dramatically growing presence in the workplace, women and minorities remain underrepresented in management and decisionmaking positions in business;

(2) artificial barriers exist to the advancement of women and minorities in the workplace;

(3) United States corporations are increasingly relying on women and minorities to meet employment requirements and are increasingly aware of the advantages derived from a diverse work force;

(4) the "Glass Ceiling Initiative" undertaken by the Department of Labor, including the release of the report entitled "Report on the Glass Ceiling Initiative", has been instrumental in raising public awareness of —

(A) the underrepresentation of women and minorities at the management and decisionmaking levels in the United States work force;

(B) the underrepresentation of women and minorities in line functions in the United States work force;

(C) the lack of access for qualified women and minorities to credential-building developmental opportunities; and

(D) the desirability of eliminating artificial barriers to the advancement of women and minorities to such levels;

(5) the establishment of a commission to examine issues raised by the Glass Ceiling Initiative would help —

(A) focus greater attention on the importance of eliminating artificial barriers to the advancement of women and minorities to management and decisionmaking positions in business; and

(B) promote work force diversity;

(6) a comprehensive study that includes analysis of the manner in which management and decisionmaking positions are filled, the developmental and skill-enhancing practices used to foster the necessary qualifications for advancement, and the compensation programs and reward structures utilized in the corporate sector would assist in the establishment of practices and policies promoting opportunities for, and eliminating artificial barriers to, the advancement of women and minorities to management and decisionmaking positions; and

(7) a national award recognizing employers whose practices and policies promote opportunities for, and eliminate artificial barriers to, the advancement of women and minorities will foster the advancement of women and minorities into higher level positions by —

(A) helping to encourage United States companies to modify practices and policies to promote opportunities for, and eliminate artificial barriers to, the upward mobility of women and minorities; and

(B) providing specific guidance for other United States employers that wish to learn how to revise practices and policies to improve the access and employment opportunities of women and minorities; and

(b) Purpose. — The purpose of this title is to establish —

(1) a Glass Ceiling Commission to study —

(A) the manner in which business fills management and decisionmaking positions;

(B) the developmental and skill-enhancing practices used to foster the necessary qualifications for advancement into such positions; and

(C) the compensation programs and reward structures currently utilized in the workplace; and

(2) an annual award for excellence in promoting a more diverse skilled work force at the management and decisionmaking levels in business.

FIGURE 12.4   The Glass Ceiling Act of 1991

Source: Civil Rights Act of 1991 Section 202.

International Perspective

The EC's Glass Ceiling

Little research has been done in the area of women's career advancement in Europe. With that in mind, The Conference Board Europe recently contacted 30 companies with reputations for successfully recruiting, promoting, and retaining women. Some of the findings were quite revealing: European employment for these 30 firms totals more than half a million. Of that, only a third are women.

And from there, the numbers get smaller and smaller. Only 5 percent of the women rank as managers, a mere 0.5 percent have reached the top 10 percent salary bracket, and only .01 percent sit on a board.

A primary barrier to advancement, we found, has been the persistence of traditional notions about women's roles and abilities. This may be due, at least in part, to the fact that Europe has many more old family companies than the United States. Another factor may be that many European companies continue to hide behind supposed cultural differences to avoid offering women equal work opportunities.

Occupational segregation is also a barrier to advancement. In Luxembourg in 1983, women accounted for one third of all workers but for 80 percent of all service employees. Figures provided by the Organization for Economic Cooperation and Development (OECD) show that as of 1985, 63 percent of women working in Austria were in just six (of 75) occupational categories.

Some strides have been made in occupational segregation, though. In the past, legislation governing how many hours women could work and at what times of day served to crowd women into a few job sectors. But this legislation has gradually been repealed. The result: Occupational segregation has declined throughout Europe, with the notable exceptions of Germany, Belgium, and Sweden.

In Sweden, where the labor force of 4.4 million is almost equally split between men and women, a 1988 Government labor report showed few women in stereotypically male jobs. Most Swedish working women can be found in the public sector or in traditionally female jobs, such as teaching, nursing, and secretarial work.

And even in those sectors in which women are well represented as employees, they are underrepresented in management. In Britain, more than 90 percent of nurses are women, but almost half the chief officers — the most senior post in each health district — are men. Nearly half of all civil servants are women, but only 8 percent are at principal level — the gateway to senior posts — and only 4 percent are above that. And even though the majority of new lawyers are women, men achieve partnerships at twice the rate.

One problem in the pipeline to senior positions is the bottleneck at the end. Not only are there fewer and fewer slots as you go up the ladder, but, at present, most of the top jobs are held by men. "Like promotes like," says Rosalind Miles, head of the Center for Women's Studies at Coventry Polytechnic. "Men tend to promote men."

Not surprisingly, women's wages continue to lag far behind those of their male counterparts. Women's earnings range between 50 and 90 percent of men's throughout Europe. Even when hours worked, occupation, industry, tenure, and age are taken into account, the pay gap still exists. Women in manufacturing earn less than men in every EC state. Wages in the service sector, where most women are employed, are lower in most member states than those for agricultural workers.

Still, there are signs that a more equitable workplace is on the horizon. Affirmative action, an American term with heated connotations for some, is gradually gaining acceptance in Europe. One out of every three firms in our survey is actively searching for female managerial candidates. Another sign: Britain recently clarified legislation on equal pay. This promoted a spate of claims from women — so many, in fact, that the Federation of British Industries, a nonprofit employers' group, urged companies to review their wage structures in order to avoid further waves of demand.

As in America, the assumption in Europe in the early 1970s was that inevitably women would attain equity in the workplace and the same level of success and responsibility as men. That this hasn't happened yet led the OECD to conclude in a recent study: "The slow pace of change in opportunities for women suggests that gender parity will not happen solely as a result of economic expansion but only if it is identified as a public policy goal." For now, however, social change continues to advance at a crawl, and women remain concentrated in the lowest-paying sectors of the European labor market.

Source: Rebecca Rolfes, "The EC's Glass Ceiling," *Across the Board* 29 (April 1992):58. Reprinted by permission.

Systematic on-the-job approaches discussed earlier, such as coaching, rotations and transfers, understudy assignments, and mentoring, can be particularly helpful. Research has shown that challenging, successfully completed projects like troubleshooting, startups, and international assignments are especially important to the career progression of executives, yet women are less likely to be assigned to these projects.[29] Therefore, careful attention must be paid to human resources planning and decisions about assignments to ensure that women have equal opportunities.

Training programs should also stress the special problems often faced by women in managerial positions. These problems include potential lack of acceptance by their male counterparts and by subordinates and lack of support from family for career aspirations.

Minorities

Problems encountered by minorities are often similar to those faced by women managers. One of the greatest problems is likely to be the limited number of role models in higher-level managerial positions. Prejudicial attitudes held by other employees and managers can also be a serious constraint.

Career development for minorities must stress that minorities can in fact achieve managerial positions, and, of course, this must be demonstrated through the actual promotion and reward processes of the organization. Training must also focus on coping with resistant attitudes at all levels in the organization. "Managing diversity" (or "valuing diversity") programs, to be discussed later in the chapter, are an important way to address the problem of attitudes. Support groups formed by minorities and women can also be immensely helpful for career guidance and psychological support. For example, Security Pacific National Bank helped create a program called Black Officers Support System (BOSS) to assist in recruiting blacks and in reducing their turnover once they were hired.[30]

Older Workers

Amendments to the Age Discrimination in Employment Act removing ceilings on retirement make it even more important that organizations pay attention to the long-term career development of all employees, including the older worker. There are at least four myths about older workers that tend to make them vulnerable to discrimination in training and advancement opportunities.

One myth is that older workers are less motivated, less efficient, and less productive than younger workers. Research shows that, in most jobs, productivity remains constant until employees are well past traditional retirement ages. A second myth is that older workers are resistant to change and less flexible than younger workers. Research indicates that these characteristics are not related to age and that most older workers want to stay up-to-date with their skills and knowledge. A third myth is that older workers tend to have poor attendance records. Labor force studies show that workers between the ages of fifty and sixty have attendance rates equal to or better than those of most other age groups. A fourth myth is that older workers have more accidents. Workers fifty-five and older make up 13.6 percent of the work force, but have only 9.7 percent of on-the-job injuries.[31] (Risks of accidents stay fairly even from ages twenty-five to sixty-four. However, permanent disabilities tend to rise slightly for workers aged sixty-five and older.)[32]

Subtle discrimination stemming from such myths can, of course, affect the self-confidence and risk taking of older workers, and might discourage them from pursuing training opportunities. But there are additional problems that training and development programs need to take into account. For example, visual displays need to accommodate to changes in visual ability; conference rooms need to accommodate to those whose hearing may be slightly impaired; and trainers need to be alert to feelings of isolation that older trainees may have when placed in training situations with younger workers.[33]

The Disabled

While the Americans with Disabilities Act (ADA) now outlaws discrimination against qualified disabled persons who can perform the essential functions of the position (see Chapter 6), numerous organizations have been employing and training the disabled for many years. For example, in cooperation with state departments of vocational rehabilitation, McDonald's has trained some nine thousand disabled persons over the past decade, and 87 percent of them have been employed in its restaurants. Much of the training is basic skill training, but there is considerable one-on-one coaching involved during the first few weeks of employment. All employees and supervisors where the disabled are to be employed participate in seminars to help them understand and appreciate the challenges and frustrations the disabled will face.[34]

Another example is Kreonite, a small photographic and graphic arts film manufacturer in Wichita, Kansas. It has recruited and trained persons with disabilities since 1973. All kinds of positions are held by the disabled — for example, electronic assembler, injection mold machine operator, and fiberglass trimmer. As one part of the company's broad program for the disabled, volunteers from the company were trained in signing by the Kansas Elks Training Center in order to communicate with employees who were deaf.[35]

Managing Diversity

Managing diversity programs sponsored by many companies feature seminars on cultural awareness and appreciation. To one author, the term *managing diversity* means "having an acute awareness of characteristics common to a culture, race, gender, age, or sexual preference, while at the same time managing employees with these characteristics as individuals."[36] Since the ADA became law, undoubtedly this definition would also include the disabled.

U S West has promoted the concept of valuing diversity—using the term "pluralism" — by adopting the following corporate philosophy statement:

Pluralism: A culture that promotes mutual respect, acceptance, teamwork and productivity among people who are diverse in work background, experience, education, age, gender, race, ethnic origin, physical abilities, religious belief, sexual affectional orientation and other perceived differences.

U S WEST recognizes that diversity is strength — that diversity is an issue of fairness — diversity is an employee representation that mirrors the communities in which we work and the customers we serve.[37]

This philosophy statement, in turn, has become the basis for a number of programs. For example, by April 1993, all 65,000 U S West employees were to have attended a one-day program called "The Value of Human Diversity." Similarly, the company's managers, plus union stewards, have all been required to attend a three-day program called "Managing a Diverse Workforce." The performance of the top 125 corporate officers is appraised relative to how well they actually support diversity. This evaluation is based on the criteria set forth in a document called a "Pluralism Performance Menu."[38]

Employee Counseling Firms should also consider providing individualized counseling beyond formal training programs for all employees, particularly managers. The anxiety and stress associated with family, legal, financial, and other off-the-job problems can prevent managers from performing up to their ability, regardless of their potential and the excellence of the organization's formal training programs. The training programs can and should be used to inform trainees about the availability of individualized counseling and other assistance.[39]

Evaluating Career Development Programs

Career development programs are much more difficult to evaluate than skills training programs. One of the primary difficulties involves establishing specific objectives. General objectives, such as to create better managers and improve managers' human relations abilities, provide little guidance for evaluation purposes. Even when good objectives are established, it is difficult to design a single training program that can fulfill all of them. Management training tends to be an ongoing process, thereby involving a number of specific training programs over time. These problems compound the difficulties of evaluating career development efforts.

One systematic approach to evaluating programs consists of five steps:

1. Determine the history and rationale of the program.
2. Determine the degree to which the program places primary emphasis on its most important goals.
3. Analyze change occurring in trainees, that is, program effectiveness, comparing the outcomes of the program with its stated objectives.
4. Examine the general adaptability of the program.
5. Introduce modifications as required.[40]

Feedback is one of the most critical elements of the evaluation process. The results of the analysis must be presented to the appropriate decision makers in a clear and understandable manner.

Summary   Management and career development programs are aimed at developing managers and educating all employees above and beyond the immediate technical requirements of their jobs. These programs are becoming more popular because organizations are more aware of the need for competent and adaptable employees and managers at all levels. In addition, new jobs are opening up and traditional jobs are disappearing, people want to know more about their jobs, and employees need their organizations' help in order to help themselves. A good management and career development program therefore meets the needs of both the organization and its employees.

A wide variety of development techniques is available. On-the-job methods include coaching, rotations and transfers, understudy assignments, and mentoring. Off-the-job techniques, which can be conducted by the firm or by external trainers, include seminars and lectures; laboratory training, such as computer simulations, case studies, and role playing; T-groups; transactional analysis; behavioral modeling; in-basket training; and outdoor-based and wilderness programs.

Several categories of employees often need special attention from the organization to develop their potential. These include nonsupervisors in technical and professional positions, women, minorities, older workers, and the disabled. Managing diversity programs can be invaluable in changing attitudes toward various groups. Employee counseling should be made available for all employees.

Career development programs must be evaluated in order to keep them relevant and serving organizational objectives. Although evaluation is difficult, primarily because management development is a complex and ongoing process, a productive evaluation of the program's contributions to managerial performance can be made through a systematic, step-by-step process.

Ethical Dilemma

With the support of CEO Eloise Kelley, the HR director of High Altitude Airways, Tony Nathan, has hired an outside trainer who has a reputation of being inspirational and highly effective in using participative methods. A series of one-day workshops is planned, each workshop involving about fifteen managers from across the company. Eventually, some three hundred managers will have participated in the one-day seminar. The training department is being careful to avoid assigning any boss-subordinate pairs to these sessions. Generally, the workshops are well received, but a few managers are beginning to be concerned that they may have revealed leadership or technical deficiencies that may, in some way, hurt their careers. As one participant said, "You say something in a short session that you really don't have time to explain or talk over with people, and it may come back to haunt you."

To what extent is it ethical to ask participants in a one-day workshop and from the same company to be candid in divulging self-perceived leadership or technical deficiencies? What are the pros and cons? If you were Tony Nathan, what would you do if you began to hear of these concerns?

Key Terms

management and career
   development
coaching
understudy assignments
mentor
laboratory training
computer simulation model
gaming simulation
management game

case studies
incident process
role playing
T-group
transactional analysis (TA)
behavioral modeling
in-basket training
outdoor-based programs
wilderness programs

Review Questions

1. What is "management and career development"?
2. Discuss the major categories of needs that must be considered in developing management training programs.
3. Discuss the keys to success for internal development programs.
4. What is "mentoring"? Discuss successful mentoring programs.
5. List and discuss *on-the-job* methods for management development.
6. List and discuss *off-the-job* methods for management development.
7. What are some unique challenges in the development of professional-technical employees? Women? Minorities? Older workers? The disabled?
8. What seems to be the central thrust of "managing diversity" programs?
9. How can management development programs be evaluated?

Opening Case Questions

Case 12.1   Where Have All the Managers Gone?

1. What can Louise Smith do at this point to overcome the problem?
2. How could the problem have been avoided?

Case 12.2   Which Is More Important, Inspiration or Skill?

1. Which do you believe is more important in management and supervisory development programs, inspirational programs or workshops that focus on the development of interpersonal and team skills? Explain.
2. If the vice president of marketing and the human resources vice president decided it would be desirable, how might the two approaches be integrated?

Comprehensive Case

Still Fighting the Glass Ceiling

Since the resurgence of the women's movement in the 1960s, most forms of direct discrimination against women have disappeared. A company cannot refuse to promote a woman simply because of her sex. Yet women continue to hold only a tiny number of positions at the top of America's corporate ladders. Millions of women have been entering the work force, and many make it to middle management positions, but few wind up as CEOs. The often invisible but very effective barriers to women's progress in the business world have been called "the glass ceiling." You may not be able to see it, but if you are female, you will probably feel it.

Business leaders and analysts constantly look at the employment numbers to gauge whether the situation is improving. Optimists point out that during the decade of the 1980s the number of women earning MBAs and law degrees increased substantially, as did the earnings of women employed full-time. Half of entry-level managers are now women, compared with about 15 percent fifteen years ago.

But the higher up the corporate ladder you look, the more discouraging the numbers become. Yes, there are two or three times as many women in senior management as there were twenty years ago, but still 97 percent of senior managers are men. And there is only one woman at the top of a *Business Week* 1000 company. A recent poll showed that more women perceive the male corporate culture to be a barrier to their progress now than was the case just a few years ago. And female enrollment at executive training seminars — an important element in almost any top executive's résumé — has actually been dropping.

Why do women still have such difficulty getting to the top? Some try to pin the blame on women themselves, arguing that women do not try hard enough, give up their careers to have families, or do not amass the training and experience necessary to run corporations. A recent study by three researchers in Chicago focused on the careers of a thousand men and women with comparable education and career orientation. The researchers examined and ultimately rejected a number of different hypotheses to explain why, after five years, the women in the study were making 11 percent less than the men and getting fewer transfers. The study concludes, "Corporate America has run out of explanations that attribute women's career patterns to women's own behavior."[1]

This conclusion comes as no surprise to those who study the subtle workings of corporate promotions. It is relatively easy to implement a recruiting program to hire women for entry-level positions. But then the problems begin. Because of the general stereotype that women are supportive and better with people than with numbers, many companies place female managers in communications and human resources positions, not in the line jobs that more often lead to the executive suite. This trend develops into what has been called the "glass wall": women are given fewer chances than men for lateral movements and therefore have trouble gaining the kind of varied job experiences that are becoming a prerequisite for corporate leaders.

Many women have a difficult time learning how to improve their on-the-job behavior because male managers give women employees much less feedback than they give other men and few are willing or able to act as mentors to young women managers. Further, despite their good intentions, many men have difficulty breaking out of the "white male model." When searching for a new vice president, they tend to look for someone very much like themselves.

Improvement in the status of women in the workplace will probably come about through a combination of many varied pressures. Time favors women, though by itself it leads only to very slow change. One analyst calculated that, at the

[1]Linda K. Stroh, Jeanne M. Brett, and Anne H. Reilly, "All the Right Stuff: A Comparison of Female and Male Managers' Career Progression," *Journal of Applied Psychology*, 77 (June 1992): 258.

current rate of change, women will fill half of all corporate senior management positions by the year 2466. More optimistic observers note that the baby boomers, who are beginning to take over top corporate spots, have grown up in a more feminist world than did their parents and will be less blind to the effects of gender bias.

Pressures for change are also mounting in the courts and government. Women have won significant damages in discrimination lawsuits, and during the Bush administration, Labor Secretary Lynn Martin released a "Status Report on the Glass Ceiling," which called attention to the slow progress in overcoming the problems women face in corporations. Companies that have lost discrimination lawsuits or been chided by the government are often among the first to create special career tracks and mentoring programs to offset biases.

The marketplace creates its own pressures, and these may eventually be most telling in destroying the glass ceiling. Companies are gradually waking up to the monetary losses they incur by not maximizing their use of female talent. One study found that companies lose up to 1 percent of their total operating expenses because of gender bias. Part of this loss comes from turnover. More and more women who are frustrated with their

progress in large corporations are leaving to join or form smaller companies. It is probably not just coincidence that most observers see small, agile companies as being the hope for America's economic future, while larger, more traditional, more heavily male-dominated corporations sag under their own weight. Women account for half of America's human resources. It seems inevitable that America's corporations will come to recognize that not making full use of that half will mean economic suicide.

Sources: Anne B. Fisher, "When Will Women Get to the Top?" *Fortune*, September 21, 1992, pp. 44–56; Julie Amparano Lopez, "Study Says Women Face Glass Walls as Well as Ceilings," *Wall Street Journal*, March 3, 1992, pp. B1, B2; Nancy J. Perry, "If You Can't Join 'Em, Beat 'Em," *Fortune*, September 21, 1992, 58–59; Linda K. Stroh, Jeanne M. Brett, and Anne H. Reilly, "All the Right Stuff: A Comparison of Female and Male Managers' Career Progression," *Journal of Applied Psychology* 77 (June 1992): 251–260; Larry Reynolds, "Women's Groups Vow to Crack the Glass Ceiling," *HRfocus* 68 (December 1991): 1, 9; Amanda Troy Segal, "Corporate Women," *Business Week*, June 8, 1992, pp. 74–78; and Peggy Stuart, "What Does the Glass Ceiling Cost You?" *Personnel Journal* 71 (November 1992): 70–80.

Discussion Questions

1. According to this case, what appear to be the forces that create "the glass ceiling"?
2. What are the arguments for breaking down these barriers?

CHAPTER 13

Performance Appraisal and Review

LEARNING OBJECTIVES

- Describe the major purposes of performance appraisal.
- Explain how the performance appraisal process can affect employee morale either positively or negatively.
- Discuss the major considerations involved in developing an appraisal program.
- Identify common appraisal errors.
- Describe several performance appraisal methods.
- Cite the advantages and disadvantages of MBO and team MBO.
- Describe several procedures for conducting effective appraisal interviews.
- Cite some findings from research on the appraisal interview.
- Identify several factors that can affect the choice of an appraisal method.

| CASE 13.1 | **Three Appraisals** |

A: Keep Them in the Dark

Alex Nord and Mike Greene were having coffee and pie after their victory in the Monday night bowling league. They were good friends and often shared their work experiences even though they worked for different employers. Alex noticed a worried look on Mike's face and commented, "What are you frowning about? We won three straight games tonight."

"Well," said Mike, "tomorrow's my annual performance review and I'm kind of uptight about it. I think I've had a good year, but I'm not sure. Sometimes in the past the boss has really unloaded on me during the appraisal. It's almost like he's saved things up all year long. He's praised me a couple of times this past month, though, so maybe this will be a good session. Anyway, I'll sure be glad when it's over."

"At least you have an appraisal to look forward to," lamented Alex. "I don't think my boss knows what they are. I'm not sure what he expects of me, but I do know that when I goof up, I'll hear about it. Otherwise, he says nothing. We all operate on the principle of 'no news is good news.'"

B: Let's Compare Notes

It was a dreary, rainy afternoon as Mark's car moved along the freeway toward Leavittville. Mark and his four companions had formed the "Leavittville car-pool" about a year before. Tonight's trip home was like most others — the group shared "war stories" about life at the Apex Insurance Company. As driver, Mark got to choose the topic for discussion during the twenty-minute ride. He selected performance appraisal, since he had just had his first annual review that morning.

"I think performance appraisals are a joke," said Bill. "My boss rates us all excellent so he doesn't have to explain poor ratings to anyone. Why should I work harder than others when we are all rated the same?"

"You know," responded Sue, "my boss is just the opposite. He gives us all low ratings. I bet he thinks that motivates us to work harder. Ha!"

"Well," advised Jane, "you just don't know how to use the system. All I do is put on my best behavior for about two to three weeks before my annual review and I always get good marks."

"Yeah, it's even easier for me," said Joe. "My boss and I are fraternity brothers. As long as I cooperate with him during the year, I get excellent ratings."

"Whew," thought Mark, "at least my boss doesn't do those things. He told me this morning that my performance has been average, just like all the rest of the people in the department."

C: The Painless Interview

Hal knocked on Joan's office door and entered when she responded, "Come in." "Ah, Hal, you're early, but sit down and let's go over this appraisal material." "Fine," said Hal. "I'm early because I'm concerned about this past year. I don't think my performance has been up to par."

"Well," commented Joan, "let's go over the last year systematically. First, as we look at this appraisal form, where do you think you performed at an above-average or better level?" Hal identified five areas and Joan agreed with him. "Now," she asked, "where was your performance below average, and what factors contributed to that performance?" Again, she and Hal were pretty much in agreement, although Joan indicated that she thought Hal's communication skills also could be improved.

After this discussion, Joan and Hal spent twenty minutes discussing what Hal could do to improve in the areas where he was weak. They concluded by setting some specific performance goals for him during the next year.

"Gee," thought Hal as he walked back to his office, "that Joan is an A-OK boss, and she sure made this interview easy. I'm going to work much harder next year." ◄

CASE 13.2   The Upward Appraisal

Jan Carpenter, director of nursing for Great Lakes Hospital, was apprehensive. Her boss, the president of the hospital, had pushed hard for an upward appraisal system involving all supervisory and management personnel, including all top management. The system had been tried once, a year ago, and as far as Jan was concerned, it was a mixed bag.

Anonymous ratings from subordinates were collected and delivered to each manager after being reviewed by each manager's superior. There were eight dimensions on the rating form, each with scales from a high of "outstanding" to a low of "very unsatisfactory." It seemed to Jan that she had come out fairly well. All the nursing supervisors had rated her "very good," "excellent," or "outstanding" on each item. However, two of her subordinates had written what Jan interpreted to be sarcastic comments in the comments section of the forms. These comments were very upsetting to Jan, even though she wasn't totally sure what they meant. She hadn't raised the matter with her boss, nor had he discussed the ratings with her, other than to say, "Well, the ratings looked pretty good — better than mine." He then changed the subject.

"So here we go again," Jan thought. "I'm not sure this system is helping me any. All it does is give me something else to worry about, plus make me a little bit paranoid." ◄

Performance appraisal and review is the formal, systematic assessment of how well employees are performing their jobs in relation to established standards and the communication of that assessment to employees. As the opening cases indicate, this process is of great importance to the employees involved. How appraisal systems are used and how appraisal results are communicated affects morale and organizational climate in significant ways. Moreover, the results of performance appraisal also have a significant impact on other human resources processes, such as training and development, compensation, and promotion decisions. This chapter discusses these effects in some detail and provides an overview of commonly used appraisal methods, including the appraisal interview.

Informal appraisals tend to take place on an ongoing basis within the organization as supervisors evaluate their subordinates' work and as subordinates appraise each other and their supervisors on a daily basis. But systematic, formal appraisal of an individual employee is likely to occur at certain intervals throughout that person's history of employment. For example, a person may be appraised when he or she is considered for employment, during the first few days on the job, at the end of six months and each six months thereafter to review the person's salary and to determine any needs for improvement, and at the end of a few years to assess suitability for promotion. In a sense, then, the appraisal process as it applies to an individual employee is cyclical, in that it tends to be repeated again and again.

It is important to recognize that performance appraisal, in addition to being periodic, should be an ongoing process. Regularly scheduled formal appraisals should not keep supervisors from appraising or coaching their subordinates whenever necessary. Saving up performance evaluation data — especially negative data — and "dumping" them on the employee once or twice a year is ineffective. To the extent that the climate is supportive, employees desire performance **feedback,** or information on how well they are doing their jobs, and this feedback should be provided to them when it is timely and relevant.

Importance of Performance Appraisal

Performance appraisal is important in organizations because of the numerous purposes for which it is employed and its impact on individuals as well as the organization.

Extent of Use   Most industrial organizations use systematic performance appraisal procedures for both nonsupervisory and managerial employees. For example, one study involving 324 companies in southern California found that 94 percent had formal appraisal systems.[1] Nonindustrial organizations — such as military services, government agencies, hospitals, and universities — also use such procedures extensively. Performance appraisal has been mandatory in most federal agencies since Congress passed the Civil Service Reform Act of 1978.[2]

Purposes   Performance appraisals are used for a variety of essential purposes. Table 13.1 shows the eleven most common uses in the 324 California industrial organizations — Los Angeles and surrounding counties — cited above. Determining compensation is by far the most frequent use of appraisals, but performance improvement and feedback to employees are also major uses. Documentation of personnel decisions, partly as a defense against potential charges of unfair employment practices, is also a major use of appraisals.[3]

Generally speaking, the many purposes of performance appraisal can be grouped into two main categories: evaluation goals and coaching and development goals. According to author Michael Beer, **evaluation goals** include the following:

1. Giving feedback to employees so they know where they stand
2. Developing valid data for pay (salary and bonus pay) and promotion decisions and providing a means for communicating these decisions
3. Helping the manager make retention and discharge decisions and providing a means for warning employees about unsatisfactory performance

Coaching and development goals include the following:

1. Counseling and coaching employees in order to improve their performance and develop future potential
2. Developing commitment to the organization through discussion of career opportunities and career planning

TABLE 13.1 Primary use of appraisals in 324 southern California organizations

	SMALL ORGANIZATIONS %	LARGE ORGANIZATIONS %	TOTAL %
Compensation	80.2	66.7	74.9
Performance improvement	46.3	53.3	48.4
Feedback	40.3	40.6	40.4
Documentation	29.0	32.2	30.2
Promotion	26.1	22.8	24.8
Training	5.1	9.4	7.3
Transfer	8.1	6.1	7.3
Discharge	4.9	6.7	5.6
Layoff	2.1	2.8	2.4
Personnel research	1.8	2.8	2.2
Manpower planning	0.7	2.8	1.5

Source: "Appraisal Trends" by Alan H. Locher and Kenneth S. Teel reprinted with permission from *Personnel Journal,* Costa Mesa, California. Copyright September, 1988. All rights reserved.

3. Motivating employees through recognition and support
4. Strengthening superior-subordinate relations
5. Diagnosing individual and organizational problems[4]

Impact on the Individual

Because of the importance of performance appraisals to employees, the appraisal methods used and the manner in which results are communicated can have positive or negative effects on employees' morale. When appraisals are used for discipline, pay increases, promotions, discharges, or layoffs, they are likely to be regarded with apprehension by those employees who tend to underestimate themselves, by the less productive members of the organization, or by those who feel appraisals will be arbitrary or unjust. Similar feelings result when employees don't know or understand the criteria being used to assess them, or when they see the appraisal as overly critical rather than helpful. (For specific complaints of employees about the appraisal system in one company, see *Contemporary Issues* on page 335.)

The more employees understand about the appraisal process, and the more appraisals are used as developmental opportunities rather than occasions for criticism, the more the need for self-actualization will be satisfied. As will be discussed later, leadership style and organizational climate have a profound effect on the motivational and satisfaction outcomes of the appraisal process.

Impact on the Organization

The performance appraisal system, to a large extent, is an extension of job design (see Figure 13.1) and has major effects on the organization generally. In addition to assisting in such matters as making compensation and promotion decisions and in providing feedback on performance, the results of the appraisal process can supply useful data about the success of other personnel activities such as recruiting, selection, orientation, and training. If, for example, the appraisal process reveals that significant numbers of employees are deficient in some area of skill or knowledge,

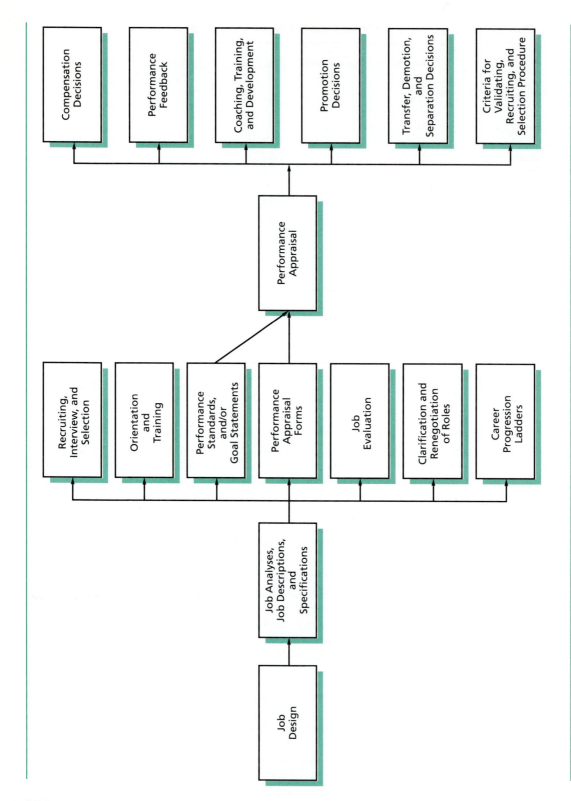

FIGURE 13.1 The performance appraisal system as an extension of job design (see also Figure 7.6)

Contemporary Issues

Employee Focus Groups Assess the Appraisal System at Metropolitan Property and Casualty Insurance Company

Employee focus groups, facilitated by a team from the corporate human resources staff, were held in a cross section of offices to determine employee perceptions of the current performance appraisal program. The participants' responses were frequently quite emotional and occasionally vitriolic as they described a system that they saw as not only deficient but a key roadblock to employee-management communications. There were some supporters of the process, but the overwhelming consensus was that it needed to be changed.

While there were differences between the management and nonmanagement views of the current program, both groups agreed on the basics: Each year the manager completed a performance evaluation form, rating the employee's performance on a scale from one to six. The manager and the employee then met to discuss the rating.

Not unexpectedly, many of the concerns of the focus groups were about the manner in which the program was being administered. Although very important, these concerns were overshadowed by the more substantive comments that questioned the core values and goals underlying performance evaluation at Metropolitan P&C. Areas of employee discontent included:

- Doer/receiver — employees abhor the fact that the appraisal is something that is *done* to them by the manager

- Accuracy — few believe that managers can make the fine distinctions in performance that are required by a large number of ratings

- Timing — assessing performance that occurred from six to 12 months previously makes no sense and probably is inaccurate

- Tone — the evaluative nature of the appraisal makes it an uncomfortable process for the manager and the employee and often results in either a quick, superficial meeting or a lengthy confrontation

- Perspective — the appraisal concentrates on the past rather than providing direction for the future

- Personal development — rarely discussed, this is a secondary consideration and never part of the primary agenda.

Although concerns about the performance appraisal program had led to the decision to review the system, the extent of dissatisfaction was considerably greater than expected. Rather than supporting the strategies of the organization and the achievement of the staff, there was a tangible link between performance appraisal and demotivation.

Once the problems were identified, the focus group identified elements of the ideal program. Highlights of their recommendations were to:

- Provide a system that has a developmental focus rather than an evaluative emphasis

- Make the process prospective so that it emphasizes future achievement, rather than merely reviewing history

- Include the mutual establishment of work goals as a clear performance target

- Provide a partnership role for the employee so that the system no longer has a *doer* and a *receiver*

- Have a structure that opens the avenues for ongoing communication between manager and employee so the focal point isn't an annual discussion

- Relate compensation decisions to an individual's achievement.

Source: Joseph P. McCarthy, "A New Focus on Achievement," *Personnel Journal* 70 (February 1991):74. Reprinted by permission.

modifications can be made in these other personnel areas. In large organizations, the results of appraisals are often used as criteria to study the validity of selection procedures.

Developing an Appraisal Program

In designing an appraisal program, attention should be given to relevant laws and court decisions, the choice of appraisers, the role of the human resources department, and the validity and reliability of the appraisal methods.

Legal Requirements

Increasingly, courts have applied equal employment opportunity legislation and guidelines to performance appraisals, whether used for test validation, promotion, transfer, layoffs, or other decisions. Three court cases are particularly significant.

In *Rowe* v. *General Motors Corporation*, the Fifth Circuit Court of Appeals found that supervisors' subjective evaluations of the "ability, merit, and capacity" of hourly employees used in promotion decisions had had an adverse impact on black employees. Thus, the company had violated Title VII of the Civil Rights Act.[5]

In *Brito* v. *Zia Company*, performance appraisals were used as the basis for deciding whom to lay off. The court determined that a disproportionate number of Spanish-surnamed workers had been laid off, and it ordered the company to suspend performance ratings because the evaluators were not all in a position to observe performance on a daily basis, and the appraisals were not administered and scored under standardized and controlled conditions.[6]

In *Albermarle Paper Company* v. *Moody*, the U.S. Supreme Court confirmed the Equal Employment Opportunity Commission's interpretation that performance ratings were "tests" and criticized the paper company's test-validation procedures in which ratings were used as criteria. The rating procedures were found to be too vague and subject to each supervisor's interpretation.[7]

Overall, these court decisions have carried over into the more recent 1978 Uniform Guidelines on Employee Selection Procedures, which clearly include performance appraisal in their coverage. This means that performance appraisal procedures are subject to similar standards of reliability, validity, and job relatedness as all other selection techniques. Practically speaking, however, since 1978 the courts have tended to allow fairly unsophisticated techniques of appraisal — for example, the use of graphic rating scales instead of BARS (see discussion later in the chapter) — as long as conditions such as the following are present:

1. A job analysis has been conducted to determine characteristics necessary for successful job performance.
2. These characteristics are incorporated into the rating instrument, which provides written standards for the rater.
3. Supervisors are trained in the use of the instrument, and standards are applied uniformly to majority and minority employees.
4. There is a formal appeal mechanism and/or review of ratings by upper management.
5. Evaluations and termination decisions are backed up with documentation of substandard performance.
6. Performance counseling is used to help below-standard performers improve their performance.[8]

Choosing Appraisers   Determining who will evaluate employees is critical in designing the appraisal program. It is generally conceded that appraisal by the immediate supervisor is necessary and the most effective method. However, other persons are sometimes involved in the appraisal process and in various combinations.

Supervisor Appraisals   Appraisals by the immediate supervisor are the most common. The supervisor has the formal authority to conduct appraisals and usually controls the rewards for performance. In addition, this person is typically in the best position to observe the subordinate's performance and to judge how well that performance serves the goals of the unit and the organization.

Self-appraisals   In some organizations, subordinates appraise their own performance. There are pros (in terms of morale) and cons (ratings tend to be less reliable) to this approach. Research suggests that self-appraisal has limited usefulness as an evaluative tool but has much more promise as a developmental tool.[9]

Self-appraisals can be combined with supervisor appraisals to yield more useful results. In this system, the supervisor and the employee independently prepare evaluations and then meet to discuss their assessments. They then focus on future responsibilities, improvement plans, developmental activities, career objectives, and a performance summary. One advantage of the combined approach is that the two independently prepared evaluations provide a formal basis for a discussion to clarify supervisors' and subordinates' expectations and perceptions. (See Figure 13.2 for an

---

☆✿�֍✦✷☆✹☆✿✦✧✤ ✿✦✷☆✦✷✚ ✿✦✧✿✤✿✦✤✳✳✳☆☆ ✷✷✳✳✷✦✷✤✳

☆✿✦✧✤＿＿＿＿＿＿＿＿＿＿＿＿＿＿＿＿＿＿＿＿＿＿＿

Please review/comment on the following areas:

- –Goals set for the Review period, together with your performance against these.

- –Ability to meet your position responsibilities, as you understand them.

- –Perceived strengths and areas you need to work on.

- –Training requirements related to your job, and career or job family progression if applicable.

FIGURE 13.2   Example of performance review forms independently prepared by the employee and supervisor

Source: Courtesy of Analog Devices Human Resources Department.

   **SALARY EXEMPT**

PERFORMANCE REVIEW

FROM_____ TO_____

NAME _____ JOB TITLE _____

GRADE _____ DEPT _____ SUPERVISOR_____ DATE DUE _____

<u>INSTRUCTIONS</u>

A.   Please attach a narrative to this form, summarizing the Performance Review in a manner that covers the following areas:

   1.   Performance related to any expectations set for the Review period, plus the rationale for the chosen Performance Rating.

   2.   The Employee's overall ability to do the job, with particular reference to the levels of competency demonstrated and/or required.

   3.   Any other Performance factors, such as those related to ADI and Division value.

   4.   Any job-focused training and development activities that the employee has been involved in, or are planned for in the future.

   5.   Career development aspects, such as the employees career goals. Your views on these plus any agreed career-focused T&D activities.

B.   Please also attach the Pre-Discussion Worksheet.

C.   Please circle the appropriate Performance Rating description.

Marginal   Needs   Fully Met   Commendable   Distinguished
             Improvement Expectations

D.   Please list any agreed goals for the next Review period on the back of this form and provide the emloyee with a copy

E.   Comments by Employee on overall Review and discussion.
    (For optional completion by Employee)

F.   Employee Signature_____ Date _____

    Supervisor Signature_____ Date _____

    Approval_____ Date _____

    H.R. Dept _____ Date _____

FIGURE 13.2   (continued)

example of independently prepared review forms. These are used as part of a broader goal-setting and review process — see the discussion of management by objectives later in the chapter.)

Peer Appraisals   Peer appraisals were used in only 5 percent of 3,052 organizations surveyed in 1989.[10] However, they do have the advantage of being relatively reliable, partly because peers interact with each other on a daily basis and partly because the use of peer raters presents a number of independent judgments.[11] Some firms, such as Schreiber Foods, have found employees to be generally satisfied with peer appraisal systems — particularly when used for developmental purposes — as long as the ratings are kept confidential and used in conjunction with performance feedback from supervisors. Peer ratings can have undesirable consequences, however. One study found that negative peer ratings led to significantly lower performance, group cohesion, and satisfaction among those receiving the negative ratings.[12] On a positive note, members of self-managed teams at Digital Equipment Corporation evaluate other team members' performance using participatory performance appraisal processes. Results in terms of commitment and productivity appear to be positive.[13]

Subordinate Appraisals

Appraisals by subordinates, like peer ratings, are not widely used. Some businesses, however, have used subordinates' ratings of their supervisors to help the supervisors improve their own performance. Examples of organizations that do use such a procedure are Cigna, Du Pont, Amoco, Johnson & Johnson, and Chrysler Corp.[14] (Case 13.2 is about one manager's experience with subordinate appraisals.) In some colleges and universities, students' ratings are used to help professors improve lectures and course content, and in some cases they are used in compensation and promotion decisions as well.

Customer/ Outside Appraisals

Appraisals from informed outsiders are sometimes used. For example, some universities solicit appraisals of the scholarship of candidates for academic promotion from scholars at other universities. Appraisals from customers will probably grow in importance with the spread of Total Quality Management (TQM) programs, discussed in Chapter 21.

Group or Committee Appraisals

Although the person who typically performs the appraisal is the immediate supervisor, another approach involves that person plus a group from the next higher level of supervision. This group or committee procedure (sometimes called "multiple rater performance appraisal") has been supported on the grounds that several people who know the subject of the rating can provide more data than the supervisor alone.[15] This procedure is used frequently in colleges and universities, with higher-ranking professors evaluating those of lower rank. A version of this procedure, applicable to any type of organization, is to use a committee of four to eight raters selected by the employee. One of the raters is the immediate supervisor, but others could be peers, subordinates, or higher management.[16]

Role of the Human Resources Department

The basic accountability for scheduling and conducting performance appraisals rests with the immediate supervisor or whoever else is designated to conduct the formal review. The human resources department, however, can play a critical role in the design and implementation of the program. Determining who evaluates and what method will be used are design issues that must be coordinated by the human resources director in cooperation with other managers. In addition, that department can provide organization members with training in how to use the system and how to conduct appraisal interviews. Finally, the human resources department is the logical group to conduct research on the equity of appraisals throughout departments and on the reliability and validity of whatever systems are established.

Reliability and Validity

The concepts of reliability and validity, discussed in detail in Chapter 9, are also relevant to performance appraisal. In performance appraisal, **reliability** refers to the consistency with which a supervisor rates a subordinate in successive ratings (assuming consistent performance) or the consistency with which two or more supervisors rate performance when they have comparable information. The reliability of appraisal methods can be increased by improving the training of raters and by using more descriptive standards in appraisal systems.

The **validity** of performance appraisal is the extent to which appraisal procedures measure real differences in performance. Logic suggests that the more the supervisor uses data on actual performance, the more valid the ratings become. Thus, the most valid ratings are those in which actual performance corresponds to rated performance.

Appraisal Errors

The reliability and validity of the appraisal program are especially important in view of equal employment opportunity legislation and guidelines. Unfortunately, supervisors can make several kinds of errors when conducting appraisals that make the process less reliable or less valid than it might otherwise be.

The **halo error** represents the situation in which the rater generalizes from one aspect of a person's job performance to all aspects of performance. For example, the supervisor may rate the "quantity of work" for a person as "excellent" and then inappropriately rate all other dimensions as "excellent" when they actually are only "average" or "good." The halo error can also work in reverse. (See the discussion of the "horn effect" in Chapter 9.) A form of the halo error is illustrated in Joe's experience in Case 13.1B.

The **error of central tendency** occurs when the rater tends to rate the performance of all or most of the persons being appraised around the center of the rating scale (perhaps in the "average" category). The central tendency error also occurs on an individual basis if the supervisor is to rate an employee on numerous performance dimensions and rates all of the dimensions in the middle of the scale. Mark's treatment in Case 13.1B represents this error.

The **leniency error** is made by the appraiser who gives employees higher ratings than they deserve. As illustrated by Bill's situation in Case 13.1B, this usually results in a distribution of employee ratings that is concentrated toward the high end of the rating scale. Employees expect consistently high ratings to be accompanied by rewards such as merit pay increases and promotion. If such rewards are seldom forthcoming, the entire appraisal system may fail. The opposite kind of error can also occur. Supervisors who pride themselves on being strict or "tough" may rate everyone severely.

Another source of error is simply that supervisors read different meanings into the words and the scales on performance appraisal forms. This source of error, and the other sources, underscore the necessity for training appraisers in the use of appraisal systems.

Performance Appraisal Methods

Many approaches are used in appraising performance. This section examines some of the more commonly used methods.

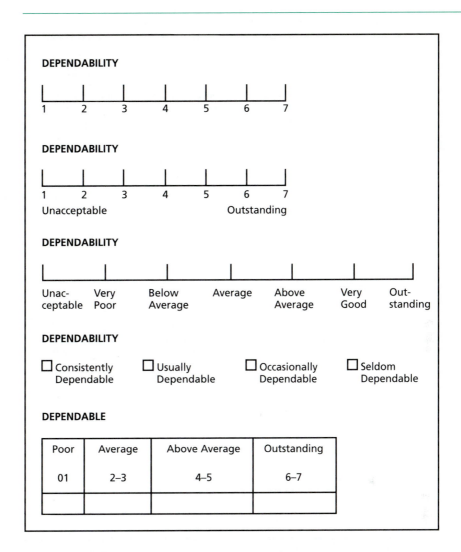

FIGURE 13.3   Examples of rating scales

Source: From *Performance Appraisal and Review Systems* by Stephen J. Carroll and Craig E. Schneier. Copyright © 1982 by Scott, Foresman and Company. Reprinted by permission.

Graphic Rating Scale

The **graphic rating scale method**, also called the conventional rating method,[17] is used most often. There are many versions of graphic rating scales, but all concentrate on specific employee behaviors or characteristics as they relate to work performance. In early versions of this method, the rater placed a check mark on a form under the word or phrase best describing the degree to which an employee demonstrated each behavior or characteristic.

Among the many types of rating scales in use in organizations, some are numerically based and others present raters with a choice of adjectives with which to describe employee behavior. Figure 13.3 provides some examples of these rating scales.

INSTRUCTIONS

This Performance Assessment form is designed to meet the requirements of a broad range of Department Manager's and Supervisor's positions. Each assessor must relate those aspects of assessment that are indicative of the employee's performance in the position. The key performance factors are identified in the left hand column. The statements below describe specific dimensions of the performance factor that should be considerd in assessssment of that factor, (i.e. "quality"). Performance factor weightings have been developed for

PERFORMANCE FACTORS TO BE ASSESSED

RATING LEVEL

	NOT ACCEPTABLE	NEEDS IMPROVEMENT
▶▶▶▶▶▶▶	KEY: weak in work performance, does not carry share of work. If performance does not improve can result in disciplinary action up to and including dismissal.	KEY: not completely up to expectations or standards in all aspects; will have to show improvement to reach satisfactory level.

QUALITY PERFORMANCE

1. Thoroughness, accuracy, and timeliness as compared with standards, established principles, policies, procedures, plans, objectives, and safety requirements.
2. Cost performance effectiveness of results.
3. Decision making effectiveness.

NOT ACCEPTABLE	NEEDS IMPROVEMENT
• often has to do work over • requires too much instruction • others time is too often lost because of errors or protecting against errors • normal reviews are too often found to be insufficient • judgement exercised too often results in adverse consequences • quality of department or section's performance is significantly below standards or expectations.	• on occasion produces work that has to be done over • requires more than normal amount of instruction • is somewhat prone to making errors unless work is reviewed frequently • on occasion judgement is incorrect or improper • quality of department or section's performance occasionally below standards or expectations.

Briefly eplain basis for rating on factor of QUALITY:

QUALITY PERFORMANCE

1. Progress toward or completion of objectives, projects or assignments.
2. Volume of production.
3. Ability to get work completed on schedule.

EXCEPTIONAL / DISTINGUISHED	SUPERIOR
• applies unusually effective effort • seeks and does additional work beyond that required • gets work out in less time than most others • extremely energetic worker, few exceed level of achievment • quantity of department or section's perfprmance is recognized by other departments, etc., as being exceptionally high	• generally exceeds work output requirements • on occasion beats schedule • carries more than normal share of the workload • can usually be relied upon to get work completed under critical time constraints.

Briefly eplain basis for rating on factor of QUANTITY:

UTILIZATION OF RESOURCES

1. Efficient allocation, coordination and use of funds, equipment, facilities, and materials.
2. Efficient and effective utilization of personnel.
3. Savings through control of costs.
4. Profitable expenditures.
5. Quickness to grasp, interpret and adjust to instructions, new situations, methods and procediures.

NOT ACCEPTABLE	ACCEPTABLE / GOOD
• often fails to properly utilize personnel, equipment, services, or other resources • is unwilling to adapt to changing Company needs • shows little interest in improving the job and/or the job enviroment • unable to assign work to others in a fair and equitable manner, plays favorites.	• makes effective use of most resources under normal range of conditions • willingly conforms to changing company policy and departmental procedures • takes on required job responsibilities • has shown average interest in improving the job and/or the job environment • ascigns work to others in a fair and equitable manner.

Briefly explain basis for rating on factor of RESOURCE UTILIZITION:

FIGURE 13.4   Graphic rating scale for assessing department managers and supervisors, Erie Insurance Group

Source: Courtesy Erie Insurance Group (from form entitled "Performance Assessment for Department Managers and Supervisors")

use with this form and must be used in compiling each assessed Employee's summary performance. The statements in the boxes below are descriptive of performance that is representative of a given level. Their purpose is to characterize the nature of performance at a given level. **They are not inclusive and it is not necessary that every statement be descriptive of the Employee's performance in order to assess performance at that level.**

EMPLOYEE'S NAME_____

ACCEPTABLE / GOOD	SUPERIOR	EXCEPTIONAL / DISTINGUISHED
KEY: does a completely satisfactoy job, meets expectations or standards for performance.	KEY: is excellent in the job, performance is noticeably and usually well above standards or acceptable level.	KEY: an unusually effective employee who is excited in performance by few others.
• regularly produces work of specified quality • work is rarely below standards or expectations • can be relied upon to use proper judgement when required • normal reviews are sufficient • carries out instructions and and incorporates suggestions as inspected • quality of department or section's performance meets standards or expectations.	• frequently produces work that exceeds standards or expectations • can be relied upon to almost always use proper judgement where required in work • accuracy, completeness and correctness of work is very high quality • quality of department or section's performance meets standards or expectations.	• quality of work is exceptionally high on a continuous basis • displays excellent judgement where required in work • accuracy, completeness and correctness of work is almost never doubted such that normal reviews can be bypassed in "crises" situations • quality of department or section's performance is recognized by other departments, etc., as being exceptionally high.

ACCEPTABLE / GOOD	NEEDS IMPROVEMENT	NOT ACCEPTABLE
• meets normal work output expected of satisfactory manager or supervisor • carries share of divisions workload as expected • is a good steady manager or supervisor • gets work done on time when reasonable time is provided.	• work output on occasion (not a rare exception) is below normal or standard • needs somewhat more than occasional supervision • at times needs to be told what to do next • at times does not carry fair share of division's workload.	• work output is below normal or standards • wastes time unless continually supervised • wants to be told what to do next • does as little as possible • is a "clock watcher" and the like.

NEEDS IMPROVEMENT	SUPERIOR	EXCEPTIONAL / DISTINGUISHED
• on occasion has been reluctant to adapt to changing organizational needs • cannot consistently be depended on to make effective use of resources even under normal conditions • has shown only minimal interest in improving the job and/or the job enviroment • on occasion has failed to assign work to others in a fair and equitable manner.	• makes effective use of resources under varying operating conditions • always plans ahead to maintain individual and group effectiveness and efficiency • is highly adaptive to new situations • looks for more efficient and effective ways of getting the job done, is an innovator and the like • very effective in assigning work to others in department or section.	• consistently makes effective and economical use of all resources given under difficult operating conditions • seeks additional job responsibilities for self and others • is exceptionally adaptive to new situations • is highly creative and continually looks for ways in which to improve the job and/or the job enviroment • consistently is able to manage department or section in a cost effective manner.

FIGURE 13.4   (continued)

PERFORMANCE FACTORS TO BE ASSESSED (CONT.)

LEADERSHIP	NOT ACCEPTABLE	NEEDS IMPROVEMENT
1. Ability to set objectives, maintain communication, and instill in others the desire to accomplish objectives. 2. Ability to size up a problem, get and evaluate the facts, reach sound conclusions and present them effectively. 3. Willingneess to make decisions and the degree to which decisions or actions are sound. 4. Recognition and development of the aptitiudes, abilitites, and capabilities of others. 5. Temperament and emotional control.	• fails to motivate people to accept his/her leadership • does not possess maturity of viewpoint and stability for the job • unable to effectively control feelings and emotions at critical times • fails to develop personnel. Does not delegate authority • absence periodically or at critical times causes serious problems for others • department or section lacks cohesiveness and commitment because of his/her ineffectiveness.	• sometimes fails to exercise effective leadership guidance of others • inclined to be unable to control emotions under unusual or pressure situations • rarely shows initiative • often unsuccessful in developing personnel Delegates authority reluctantly • does supervision of department or section needed in his/her absence.

Briefly explain basis for rating of factor of LEADERSHIP PERFORMANCE:

INTERPERSONAL RELATIONS	SUPERIOR	EXCEPTIONAL / DISTINGUISHED
1. Verbal communication skills both face to face and on the telephone. 2. Writing skills in communicating instructions, thoughts and feelings to others. 3. Ability to get along with "peers" and executive management. 4. Attitude toward work. 5. Ability not to let personal activities adversely affect work relationships and work activities. 6. Willingness to do fair share of unpleasant tasks.	• relations with others are very good and frequently enhances group cooperation • is enthusiastic about work • often takes on unpleasant tasks to help get the job done • is better than most others in communication skills • personal activities do not interfere with work of others.	• relations with others are exceptionally good and always enhances organizational effectiveness and efficiency • extends self frequently to help others • is very enthusiastic about work • is willing to do more than share of the unpleasant tasks • is an exceptionally effective communicator.

Briefly explain basis for rating of factor of INTERPERSONAL RELATIONS:

APPLIED JOB KNOWLEDGE	ACCEPTABLE / GOOD	NOT ACCEPTABLE
1. Understanding of all phases of his/her work and related matters. 2. Company and work unit policies and procedures. 3. Product or process knowledge. 4. Technical and non-technical skills required for the position. 5. Initiative.	• is well informed of the job requirements and related work • knows well and uses effectively the necessary methods, procedures, equipment, etc. • handles newly assigned work and changed methods with normal instruction • requires normal supervision of regular responsibilities.	• needs abnormal amount of help from others • has often demonstrated inadequate knowledge of the details of the job • is slow to grasp instructions • depends overly on others • is slow in learning new or changed methods or procedures • shows little if any initiative to keep abreast of latest changes in professional knowledge and developments.

Briefly explain basis for rating on factor of APPLIED JOB KNOWLEDGE:

WORK HABITS / JUDGEMENT	EXCEPTIONAL / DISTINGUISHED	ACCEPTABLE / GOOD
1. Care in handling confidential or sensitive matters or material. 2. Scheduling and laying out of work for self and others. 3. Initiative. 4. Attitude. 5. Judgement on work related and personnel matters. 6. Use ot time.	• is a very enthusiastic worker • makes job a key interest in life • completes assignments accurately in the shortest time possible • under any circumstances can be relied upon to never violate confidences • very sound and unbiased reasoning and decisions • accomplishes significantly more than others by effective use of time.	• schedules operations, activities or tasks for self and others as expected • has a positive attitude about company and job • uses proper judgement in handling confidential and sensitive matters • reasons out own conclusions–sometimes uses incorrect sense of values and/or priorities • uses time reasonably effectively.

Briefly explain basis for rating on factor of WORK HABITS/JUDGEMENT:

FIGURE 13.4   (continued)

ACCEPTABLE /GOOD	SUPERIOR	EXCEPTIONAL / DISTINGUISHED
• provides leadership, motivation, and direction under ordinary conditions • reasonably well-balanced and self-possessed under ordinary job conditions • occasionally shows initiative. Sometimes makes suggestions • often encourages people to assume responsibilities • delegates authority to others • moderate supervision needed in his/her absence • adequately controls feelings toward and about others.	• generally wins confidence and loyal support for his/her leadership • usually maintains effectiveness under pressure, influences other personnel to maintain composure • is progressive, has creative imagination • encourages people to take authority. Delegates responsibility prudently. Department or section runs smoothly in his/her absence. • effectively utilizes the skills and contributions of personnel • recognizes and develops the skills of others in department or section.	• consistently lead his/her people. Wins and holds support for his/her leadership and company policies • confident and inspires confidence. Self-reliant, realistic, dependable in effective control of methods and people • initiative and creativeness results in increased efficiency • develops full potential of his/her people. Operations run smothly, even in his/her absence. • extremely effective in develping personnel • has unusual ability to control feelings toward and about others.

NOT ACCEPTABLE	NEEDS IMPROVEMENT	ACCEPTABLE / GOOD
• relations with others are often a liability and diminish organizational effectiveness and efficiency • is clearly ineffective in communication both oral and/or written • is unwilling or unable to carry fair share of unpleasant tasks • personal activities frequently interfere with work or the work of others • negative attitude adversely affects department or section's climate.	• on occasion has been unable to get along with other people or personnel in department or section • has difficulty handling both oral and/or written communication with others • on occasion is unwilling or unable to do fair share of unpleasant tasks • on occasion personal activities interfere with work or the work of others • on occasion attitude toward or about others has adversely affected working relationships.	• willingly conforms to established rules and regulations • personal activities do not interfere with work or the work of others • is an effective communicator • approaches work and relations with others with a positive attitude • gets along with others.

SUPERIOR	NEEDS IMPROVEMENT	EXCEPTIONAL / DISTINGUISHED
• knows job requirements better than most others doing similar type of work • is very effective in using the necessary methods, procedures, equipment, etc. • has taken initiative to keep up to date on latest techniques and approaches to job.	• needs more than occasional help from others • at times does not demonstrate required knowledge of company policies, procedures, etc. • tends not to grasp instructions well • needs additional training in technical and/or non-technical aspects of job to meet expectations or standards.	• knows job "up and down" • puts considerable time and effort in keeping abreast of latest changes in professional knowlege and developments • exceptionally knowledgeable on all work of the department and related areas • has exceptional knowledge of requirement of job and role in the company.

NEEDS IMPROVEMENT	SUPERIOR	NOT ACCEPTABLE
• on occasion looks for "easy work" • has on occasion violated confidences • at times does not properly plan to the degree such that performance of self and others suffers • at times work area, equipment, and the like are not properly maintained • jumps to conclusions or uses poor reasoning • not allocating time properly occasionally causes bottlenecks, missed deadlines, etc.	• tends to exceed standards of expectations in completing work • very postive attitude about company and job • effectively uses time • shows interest in learning more about the job and department or section functions • good sense of values, level headed • very effective in handling confidential and sensitive matters.	• generally looks for "easy work" • violates confidences on sensitive matters and/or in handling material • seldom plans work for self and others to the degree necessary • tends to disregard rules and regulations • has shown unacceptable judgement on a number of occasions • has not demonstrated proper application of technical and non-technical skill for position.

FIGURE 13.4 (continued)

Contemporary versions of the graphic rating scale are more likely to use only characteristics that are closely related to actual job performance and to exclude such characteristics as "loyalty." In addition, contemporary versions are more likely to use scales that include descriptive statements of different performance levels for each characteristic. Figure 13.4 shows an example of a graphic rating scale used to assess managers and supervisors at the Erie Insurance Group. (Not shown are two pages at the end used for summary statements.)

Check List   Another relatively straightforward appraisal approach uses the **check list method**. Under this approach, the rater is presented with a list of positive or negative adjectives or descriptive behavioral statements and is asked to check off all those that apply to the person being rated. A score can be developed by tallying the positive checks. The following are illustrative check list statements:

_____ Cooperates with coworkers
_____ Keeps workstation neat and clean
_____ Can be expected to complete work on time
_____ Maintains detailed records
_____ Reluctant to ever work overtime
_____ Cannot accept constructive criticism

In a basic check list approach, all items are considered to be of equal value. Greater sophistication occurs with the use of a **weighted check list,** in which each item receives a weighted value based on its perceived importance to successful job performance. Weighted values are determined by those highly familiar with the job.

Check lists are easy to use and are not subject to such rating errors as central tendency or leniency. They are not problem free, however. Because it is important that items in the list be relevant to the job, it may be necessary to develop different lists for different job categories. The process of weighting is difficult and requires professional assistance. Supervisors often complain about "being in the dark" with this approach. They are not sure what the items measure, and they have difficulty interpreting the results. This, of course, hinders the developmental counseling aspect of the appraisal process.

Essay   In the **essay method**, the appraiser writes a free-form essay describing the subordinate's performance in a number of broad categories. Some categories that can be included in these forms are (1) overall appraisal of the employee's performance, (2) the employee's promotability, (3) jobs the employee can currently perform, (4) the employee's strengths and limitations, and (5) additional training needs.[18] Sometimes essay appraisals supplement other appraisal methods rather than substituting for them.

This approach gives the appraiser flexibility by not requiring attention to a specific set of factors. On the other hand, because of the method's open-endedness, it is difficult to compare essay appraisals made by different supervisors. The method is also dependent on the writing skills of the supervisor and is a time-consuming procedure.

Critical Incidents   The **critical-incidents technique** requires the appraiser to keep a record of unusually favorable or unfavorable occurrences in an employee's work. An example of a positive critical incident would be the following:

3/15 Employee stayed late to correct machine malfunctions that were causing high number of product rejects for poor quality. Correction of problem enabled completion of special project on time.

An example of a negative critical incident would be the following:

9/12 After repeated warnings to follow all safety procedures, employee failed to close shut-off valve, thereby flooding entire work area.

The positive aspects of this approach are that it provides a factual record for subsequent discussions and decision making and that it provides data directly related to job performance.[19] On the negative side, the approach requires close and continuous observation by the appraiser. This is time-consuming and costly, and workers may become very apprehensive when they know their supervisor is keeping a "log" on them.

Ranking

Ranking methods are used less frequently than the other methods discussed. There are a variety of ranking procedures, but basically the supervisor ranks all employees from best to poorest on one or more scales. If groups differ in size, statistical corrections need to be made to compare the relative standing of individuals across groups. Another difficulty in ranking methods is that the distance in performance between two people tends to be obscured.

One of the most serious problems with ranking methods is that rank order can be misinterpreted, leading to morale and motivation problems. For example, an employee may be ranked the lowest in his or her group, but may be a member of an outstanding group and performing at a very acceptable level. In another group, the lowest-ranked person may indeed be performing at a substandard level. Thus, much depends on how a ranking is interpreted.

Behavioral Rating Scales

An outgrowth of the critical-incidents technique is the development of **behaviorally anchored rating scales (BARS),** which focus on specific job behaviors rather than traits or characteristics. These scales reduce the amount of judgment or subjectivity required of the rater and rely mostly on the rater's powers of observation.[20] The job relatedness of BARS can also be more readily demonstrated, which makes them less vulnerable to charges of contributing to discriminatory practices.

Figure 13.5 shows an example of a BARS for one performance dimension ("organizational ability") for check stand work in a grocery store. Similar scales would be developed for other relevant behaviors in this job. The main advantage of this method over less rigorously developed graphic rating scales appears to be that the scales and terminology are clear and demonstrably job related, and thus presumably increase both reliability and validity.[21]

Behavioral observation scales (BOS) are developed through a process similar to that used for BARS. The major difference is that several behaviors are listed individually for each performance dimension, and the rater is required to assess the individual on each behavior.

Behaviorally anchored rating scales and behavioral observation scales are costly to develop. They take considerable time to formulate, and scales must be developed for each individual job or for clusters of similar jobs. Because BARS and BOS are based on careful job analysis, however, they are likely to be particularly acceptable to government enforcement agencies, courts, and lawyers. Lawyers, for example, tend

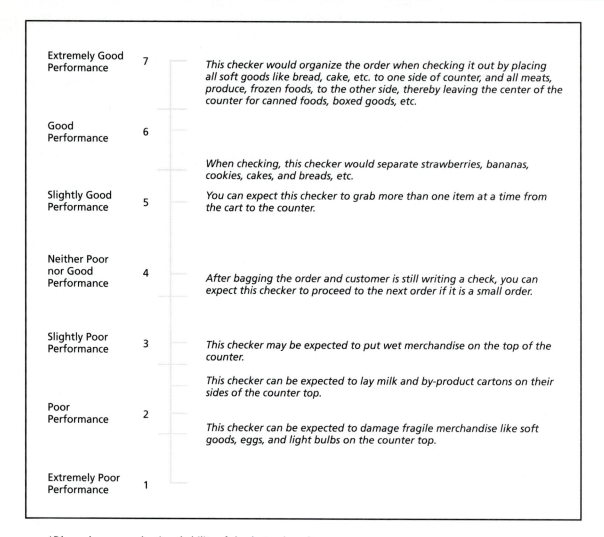

Extremely Good Performance	7	*This checker would organize the order when checking it out by placing all soft goods like bread, cake, etc. to one side of counter, and all meats, produce, frozen foods, to the other side, thereby leaving the center of the counter for canned foods, boxed goods, etc.*
Good Performance	6	
		When checking, this checker would separate strawberries, bananas, cookies, cakes, and breads, etc.
Slightly Good Performance	5	*You can expect this checker to grab more than one item at a time from the cart to the counter.*
Neither Poor nor Good Performance	4	*After bagging the order and customer is still writing a check, you can expect this checker to proceed to the next order if it is a small order.*
Slightly Poor Performance	3	*This checker may be expected to put wet merchandise on the top of the counter.*
		This checker can be expected to lay milk and by-product cartons on their sides of the counter top.
Poor Performance	2	
		This checker can be expected to damage fragile merchandise like soft goods, eggs, and light bulbs on the counter top.
Extremely Poor Performance	1	

*Dimension: organizational ability of check stand work

FIGURE 13.5   Appraising check stand work using a behaviorally anchored rating scale*

Source: Lawrence Fogli, Charles Hulin, and Milton R. Blood, "Development of First-Level Behavioral Job Criteria," *Journal of Applied Psychology* 55 (February 1971): 7. Copyright 1971 by the American Psychological Association. Reprinted by permission.

to find BOS scales more defensible in court than graphic rating scales. However, as indicated earlier in the chapter, less sophisticated techniques, such as the use of graphic rating scales, tend to be acceptable to the courts as long as a number of conditions are present, including job analysis, supervisory training in the use of the scales, appeal procedures, and the like.[22]

Management by Objectives (MBO)

Management by objectives (MBO) is a system that features an agreement by a superior and a subordinate on the subordinate's objectives for a particular period and a periodic review of how well the subordinate achieved those objectives. An attempt is usually made to write objectives in quantitative terms, although some experts believe that certain objectives or targets can and should be stated in qualitative terms.

The MBO system generally includes the following steps:

1. The supervisor and the subordinate mutually agree on the primary elements of the subordinate's job.
2. The supervisor and the subordinate mutually agree on the subordinate's specific objectives for the specified period (usually six months or a year).
3. The subordinate establishes a plan of action necessary to meet each objective.
4. During the specified period, the subordinate periodically reviews progress toward objectives, perhaps jointly with the supervisor. Progress checks may indicate the need to change action plans or modify objectives.
5. At the end of the specified period, the supervisor and subordinate meet to jointly evaluate the subordinate's performance on objectives.

Figure 13.6 shows two pages from Weyerhaeuser Co.'s "Performance Planning and Appraisal Report" form. (The letters S,E,F,A, and BA refer to Superior, Excellent, Full, Adequate, and Below Adequate.) Although these two pages include graphic rating scales, the form is consistent with an MBO approach because it focuses on goals to be achieved during the coming period and calls for interaction between supervisor and subordinate in goal setting and in the review of the subordinate's performance.

Advantages

Perhaps the greatest benefit of MBO is that it provides an objective, performance-based method of appraisal. At the individual level, MBO can give individual employees greater direction and self-control, build their self-confidence, motivate them, improve their performance, further their growth and development, and provide them with full knowledge of the criteria on which they will be evaluated. In an interpersonal sense, MBO can enhance superior-subordinate relationships, improve communications, and provide a better coaching framework. Possible organizational benefits include better overall performance, identification of management advancement potential and developmental needs, better coordination of objectives, and less duplication and overlap of duties and activities.

Analysis of the research shows that when top-management commitment has been high, the average gain in productivity under MBO programs has been 56 percent. Productivity gains were shown in sixty-eight out of the seventy research studies.[23]

Disadvantages

The MBO approach should not be viewed as a perfect system. When effectively used, MBO programs are systems of joint target setting and performance review. When a superior's directives are unreasonable, however, the MBO program can become a one-sided, autocratic, and time-consuming mechanism. Other potential problems include the following:

1. Too much emphasis on measurable quantitative objectives can lead to neglect of other important responsibilities.
2. Emphasis on measurement and quantification may result in sacrifice of quality.

Performance Planning
and Appraisal Report

Weyerhaeuser

CONFIDENTIAL

EMPLOYEE NAME (LAST, FIRST, AND INITIAL)	GROUP OR DEPARTMENT	LOCATION
POSITION TITLE	APPRAISAL PERIOD	
	FROM / / TO / /	

I. PERFORMANCE OBJECTIVES
Please Print or Write Legibly - Form Designed for Handwritten Entry

PLANS: At the beginning of the appraisal period, list the most significant results, objectives, projects and standards expected of the individual.

RESULTS: At the end of the appraisal period, indicate results achieved.

High   Low
S   E   F   A   BA

S   E   F   A   BA

S   E   F   A   BA

S   E   F   A   BA

S   E   F   A   BA

S   E   F   A   BA

FORM4168 1/88 Printing Services TP-1 Tacoma

FIGURE 13.6.   Sample pages from Weyerhaeuser's performance appraisal form
Source: Courtesy of Weyerhaeuser Corporation.

Evaluate the performance of this employee for the appraisal period just completed by describing his or her job behavior on each of the following factors. It is extremely important that the ratings you provide indicate how effective the employee's behavior was in meeting specific job duties and responsibilities related to each factor. After carefully considering each description you should circle the rating which most closely describes your assesment of the employee's performance on this factor. It is critical that you justify your rating by listing a few specific examples of relevant job behaviors.

Where a person has no job objectives or responsibilities relating to a particular factor, or where the factor has already been covered in the job objectives section, simply leave blank or write 'see objectives section'.

	High				Low
	S	E	F	A	BA

QUALITY OF WORK

Provides adequate documentation where expected. Goes beyond stated requirements as appropriate, to produce a better product or result. Accuracy, thoroughness, clarity and usefulness evident in completed assignments. Caliber of work produced or accomplished.

JUSTIFICATION (state specific examples) _____

_____

_____

	High				Low
	S	E	F	A	BA

QUANTITY OF WORK

Accomplishes job objectives by the following assignments and self initiated projects through to completion. Acceptable volume of work compared with what may reasonably be expected under existing circumstances. Meets reasonable deadlines for work completion.

JUSTIFICATION (state specific examples) _____

_____

_____

_____

	High				Low
	S	E	F	A	BA

JOB KNOWLEDGE

Understands principles, concepts, techniques, requirements, etc. necessary to accomplsh job duties. Keeps abreast of trends, developments, markets, product innovations and/or new concepts in the field which may improve ability to perform job function.

JUSTIFICATION (state specific examples) _____

_____

_____

_____

	High				Low
	S	E	F	A	BA

INITIATIVE

Takes action without being told. Effective in coping with unusual situations and problems. Has new ideas, starts action and uses originality to meet and handle work situations. Can work independently.

JUSTIFICATION (state specific examples) _____

_____

_____

_____

	High				Low
	S	E	F	A	BA

PLANNING

Schedule work assignments in order to meet deadlines and uses subordinates and resources most efficiently. Can set goals and priorize assignments appropriately. Can cooperate effectively with others in designing work schedules or assignments. Anticipates future needs and problems.

JUSTIFICATION (state specific examples) _____

_____

_____

_____

	High				Low
	S	E	F	A	BA

COST CONTROL

Controls cost and meets budgetary and profit objectives through such methods as returning surplus materials to stock, eliminating unnecessary operations, prudent use of resources, meeting cost objectives, etc.

JUSTIFICATION (state specific examples) _____

_____

_____

_____

FIGURE 13.6   (continued)

3. If evaluation is based on goal attainment, subordinates may be inclined to set low goals so as to ensure their attainment.
4. There may be a tendency to set and enthusiastically adopt only those objectives that are important to one's superior.
5. Superiors using MBO can falsely assume there is no need for periodic coaching and counseling of subordinates.[24]

Team MBO   Most MBO programs are conducted on a one-on-one superior-subordinate basis. In many instances, one-on-one MBO does not account adequately for the interdependent nature of most jobs, particularly at the managerial and supervisory levels, nor does it ensure optimal coordination of objectives between various organizational groups. Accordingly, it may be useful to take a team approach to reviewing targets and achievements.

Essentially, **team MBO** involves the application of the basic MBO process to work groups. First, overlapping units work with "higher" and "lower" units on overall organizational objectives, as well as set unit objectives. Then individuals work with their peers and superiors to define roles and to develop individual objectives.[25] This approach can lead to greater participation by subordinates in setting objectives and can improve relationships within teams and between superiors and subordinates. However, the success of a team approach greatly depends on the overall leadership style, climate, and culture of the organization. In particular, there needs to be a high trust level, a participative, supportive leadership style, and strong norms of openness and cooperation.

The Appraisal Interview

Most performance appraisal systems include an **appraisal interview.** Traditionally, the interview has been a verbal communication of the results of the appraisal to the employee concerned. These interviews are conducted with varying degrees of participation on the part of the person being appraised.

Purposes   The overall purpose of the appraisal interview is to let employees know where they stand or how they are doing. Other purposes include, but are not limited to, the following:

1. Encouraging present behavior
2. Explaining what is expected of employees
3. Communicating results of salary or promotion decisions
4. Planning for future performance improvement
5. Improving supervisor-subordinate relationships

Procedures   Because appraisal interviews often have the conflicting purposes of evaluating the employee's past performance and helping develop future performance, it is often recommended that the interview have two distinct parts. Authors H. Kent Baker and Philip Morgan suggest that the interview be conducted in two stages, each consisting of specific steps. The first is the *evaluation stage*, which provides information for administrative uses, such as pay-increase decisions, and presents base-line data for establishing future goals. There are six steps in this stage:

1. Schedule the interview in advance and prepare for it. Both the supervisor and the subordinate should review the subordinate's performance ahead of time.
2. Create an atmosphere that facilitates two-way communication. Put the subordinate at ease and minimize interruptions.
3. Begin with a statement of the purpose of the interview.
4. Encourage the employee to participate. One way is to ask the employee to appraise his or her own performance verbally.
5. Discuss total performance. Do not focus just on weaknesses; cover strengths as well.
6. Summarize and document the interview. Ask the employee to summarize the key aspects of the session, record the primary conclusions, and have both parties sign the document.

The second stage is the *development stage*, and here the supervisor's role shifts to that of a counselor. The supervisor and the subordinate work together toward performance improvement. There are seven steps in this stage:

1. Repeat steps 1–4 in the evaluation stage.
5. Set future performance goals. This involves establishing specific goals and plans for achieving them.
6. Formulate a development plan. Here the focus is on specific personal growth and development goals, such as acquiring new skills.
7. Prepare a working document. Goals and development plans are put in writing.[26]

A somewhat similar set of steps has been developed by authors Craig Schneier and Richard Beatty as shown in Figure 13.7. One of the differences is that Baker and Morgan recommend deferring discussion of future performance goals to a second major stage of the process.

Research   Research shows that leadership style and organizational climate have a large influence on the outcome of the performance appraisal interview. In an early study, research at General Electric Co. found that leadership style in the form of criticism by supervisors in appraisal interviews led to defensive behavior on the part of subordinates. On the other hand, more participation in planning goals improved the supervisor-subordinate relationship.[27]

In a follow-up study many years later, GE found that organizational climate had a significant impact on its appraisal program. Subordinates and appraisers alike felt that appraisals went better when the climate was perceived as promoting trust, support, and openness. In this type of climate, the appraisals placed greater emphasis on subordinate development. In addition, subordinates participated more in the appraisals; and appraisal interviews, conducted in an atmosphere of trust, were more open and instructive.[28]

Choosing the Appraisal Method

With a wide range of appraisal methods currently available, an organization is faced with a difficult task in selecting the best approach to meet its needs. Before making recommendations, human resources professionals should examine two areas with special care: (1) various factors that can help or hinder the implementation of a

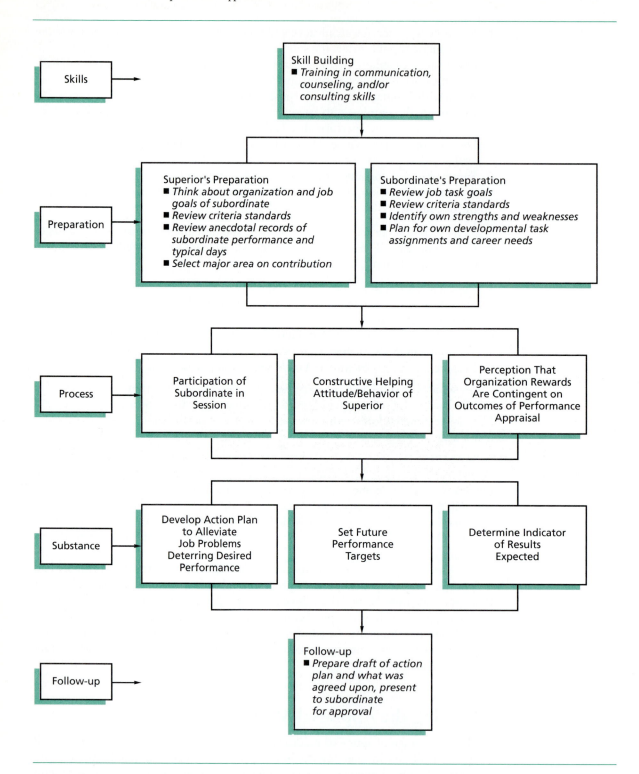

FIGURE 13.7   Factors contributing to the effectiveness of performance appraisal review sessions

Source: Craig E. Schneier and Richard W. Beatty, "Combining BARS and MBO: Using an Appraisal System to Diagnose Performance Problems," *Personnel Administrator* 24 (September 1979):57. Reprinted by permission.

particular appraisal program, and (2) the appropriateness of the appraisal method for the specific jobs to which the appraisal system will apply. (In the large, international firms in Japan, it would appear that performance appraisal is relatively unimportant in promotion decisions because of the emphasis on seniority. See *International Perspective* on page 356.)

Organizational Considerations

Many factors have an impact on the appraisal system. Three factors that are especially important are leadership style, organizational climate, and training in appraisal procedures. We have indicated that leadership style, in terms of the amount of criticism that is used, greatly impacts the outcomes of the appraisal interview. Leadership style goes beyond this: skills in participative leadership are required in many aspects of the appraisal system if the organization wants a collaborative, problem-solving, future-oriented system. For example, such skills are needed at the outset in developing the system in a cooperative way with employees and supervisors. As another example, participative leadership skills are needed in working with individuals and groups in establishing goals where real agreement is reached.

Similarly, as the research has shown, the broader organizational climate affects the outcomes of appraisal interviews. If the organization wants fairly high employee satisfaction with the appraisal system, the overall company climate must move toward such elusive goals as increased trust, openness, and support and toward a developmental approach to dealing with organizational members.

Training in appraisal is also important to the success of any appraisal system. Regardless of which appraisal method is used, appraisers must be coached in how to use it properly. There is no substitute for this training, which can minimize the occurrence of rating errors and improve reliability and validity. For example, one study of training in the use of behavioral-observation and trait-based scales found that when individuals received four hours of training in their use, there was a significant reduction in rating errors in each method.[29]

Appropriateness to the Job

In many respects, the choice of an appraisal method boils down to a selection between one that is trait based or one that is behavior based, or some combination of the two. Appraisal methods that focus on employee traits or characteristics have been used for years. These methods can be developed quickly and easily, and they can be used for many jobs. Their advantages are offset by major shortcomings, however. The primary limitation of trait-based appraisal, especially when applied across jobs, is that it is unlikely to be highly job related. Personal traits or characteristics (such as a sense of humor, neatness, or shyness) may or may not have a bearing on job performance. The issue is basically one of validity, and as pointed out earlier, the validity of an appraisal method is critical in today's legal environment.

Partly because the courts have generally favored behavior-based methods, organizations are moving toward increased use of behavior-based performance appraisals developed through job analysis, which contributes to the validity of the process. Behavior-based methods include behaviorally anchored rating scales, behavioral observation scales, and management-by-objectives approaches. As discussed earlier, however, more traditional rating methods can still be used as long as

International Perspective

Employee Loyalty in Japan

When it comes to employee loyalty, it's the Japanese who usually come to mind. Japan, after all, is home to the concept of company as family, where decisions are made by consensus and a workday includes drinks after five with co-workers.

To perpetuate this vision, internationally competitive corporations in the country engage in a practice called the Lifetime Employment System. At these companies, it's understood that an employee will work there until reaching age 55. Then, the employee will work for a supplier until he or she decides to retire.

Although only about 25% of the work force is protected by the guarantee of lifelong employment, it serves as a national ideal.

Lance Heiko, management professor at Bryant College in Smithfield, Rhode Island, who is an expert in Japanese manufacturing and management, cites the following reasons for the existence of such a system in Japan. For one thing, he explains, Japanese companies make a tremendous investment in terms of training their employees to their own proprietary ways of thinking. To lose an employee is to lose a major investment in the company.

He also says that despite the over-population of the island of Japan, the country has too few workers. "Because Japanese culture is fundamentally sexist in nature, the companies don't capitalize on half of the potential human talent and that's all of the women in the country," says Heiko. The result is that the companies have to hang on to every worker because there simply aren't enough people to go around.

The Lifetime Employment System has advantages, primarily a virtual lack of turnover. According to Michael Marquardt, vice president of the World Group in Bethesda, Maryland, having a guarantee of employment allows for promotions to be based on the length of time an employee has been with the company rather than on individual accomplishments. Employees know that the longer they stay with the company, the more responsibility they will acquire.

Another advantage of this system is a willingness of upper-level managers and technicians to train and develop their subordinates because they don't have to worry about being replaced.

This approach to employment differs greatly than in the U.S., where the fear of losing a job is used as motivation for productivity. Despite the prevailing national attitude of "at will" employment in the U.S., Heiko says that until recently, some companies, such as Detroit-based General Motors Co., have had similar kinds of systems for white-collar workers and managers. Generally, the businesses that make these long-term commitments to employees have loyal workers. "When you don't see individuals being loyal to a company," says Heiko, "there's usually been a history in which the company has proven that it can't be trusted."

Of course, the promise of long-term employment in exchange for loyalty has its disadvantages. In Japan, it often means the sacrifice of time with the personal family for the corporate family. For some people, such as Sam Okamoto, a former Tokyo Disneyland employee, it's just not worth it.

"Life involves almost all working," Okamoto says of his former life in Japan. "I couldn't accept that kind of environment. That's the biggest reason I relocated my family from Japan to here," he says.

Okamoto currently is vice president at Long Beach, California-based The Works, a company that designs theme parks and restaurants, and he says he's very happy to be working here.

Source: Dawn Gunsch, "Employee Loyalty in Japan," *Personnel Journal* 71 (September 1992):54. Reprinted by permission.

organizations take the time and care to develop them around performance-based dimensions that are clearly job related.

Summary

Performance appraisal is the formal, systematic assessment of how well employees are performing their jobs in relation to established standards and the communication of that assessment to employees. How performance appraisal is conducted can have an impact on employees' needs for security, belonging, esteem, and self-actualization.

Appraisals can be conducted by the immediate supervisor(s), the employee, the employee's peers, customers or other outside appraisers, committees, or the employee's subordinates, or combinations of these. A committee of higher managers or a committee selected by the employees is sometimes used to conduct appraisals in addition to the immediate supervisor. The most common approach is to have the immediate supervisor conduct the appraisal on a semiannual or annual basis.

Laws and court cases affect the appraisal process. Performance appraisals are treated like employment tests under the EEOC guidelines and must therefore be reliable and valid. Reliability and validity can be reduced by appraisal errors such as the halo error, central tendency, or leniency. The use of job analysis, written standards for rating scales, supervisory training in the use of appraisal instruments, appeal or review procedures, and documentation and counseling relative to substandard performance will tend to strengthen management's position in the event of legal challenges to management decisions — for example, in discharge cases. Courts have tended to allow fairly unsophisticated methods of appraisal, providing such conditions are present.

Numerous approaches are used in appraising performance, including the graphic rating scale, the check list, the essay, the critical-incidents method, behaviorally anchored rating scales, ranking methods, and behavioral observation scales.

In addition, management by objectives (MBO) is a widely used performance-based approach that focuses on the results achieved by the subordinate. In this method, the superior and subordinate agree on the subordinate's objectives for a specified period, and the subordinate is responsible for monitoring progress toward objectives. Performance reviews are then based on the extent to which objectives have been attained. A team approach to MBO can be used to enhance the interdependence between jobs and work units, but special conditions are needed for success. Research studies on MBO programs have generally found substantial increases in productivity as a result of the programs.

Contemporary practice tends to emphasize job behaviors or performance and to deemphasize personal traits or characteristics. Most performance appraisal systems include an appraisal interview. Appraisal interviews meet a variety of employee needs. Some experts feel, however, that the two main purposes of appraisal — evaluation and development — are incompatible and cannot be achieved simultaneously. These individuals recommend a two-stage interview, with the first stage focusing on evaluation and the second on employee development. Research shows that leadership style and organizational climate affect the outcome of appraisal interviews. The training of supervisors and managers in the use of an appraisal system is very important for the system to be effective.

Ethical Dilemma

Some of the middle level managers at SpeedTransport & Shipping, in anonymous interviews with a compensation consultant, acknowledged that they set MBO targets low enough to ensure the receipt of substantial bonuses at the end of the year.

What ethical or other kinds of problems exist in this situation? What, if anything, should be done? Under what circumstances would it be ethical for the consultant to inform the CEO of this situation?

Key Terms

performance appraisal and review	check list method
feedback	weighted check list
evaluation goals	essay method
coaching and development goals	critical-incidents technique
reliability	behaviorally anchored rating scales (BARS)
validity	behavioral observation scales (BOS)
halo error	management by objectives (MBO)
error of central tendency	team MBO
leniency error	appraisal interview
graphic rating scale method	

Review Questions

1. What are the two major purposes of performance appraisals? Describe each.
2. Discuss the circumstances in which appraisals can have negative effects on employee morale, and circumstances in which appraisals can have positive effects on morale.
3. In what ways are appraisals affected by the Civil Rights Act?
4. Describe halo and horn errors, error of central tendency, and leniency error in the use of appraisals.
5. What is the difference between graphic rating scales, the critical-incidents method, and behaviorally anchored rating scales?
6. What are the main features of MBO? Team MBO?
7. List and describe the steps that would be taken in a sound appraisal interview process.
8. What have been some central findings from GE's research on the appraisal interview?

Opening Case Questions

Case 13.1   Three Appraisals

1. What mistakes are being made by Mike's and Alex's supervisors relative to performance appraisal? (Part A)
2. What mistakes are being made by the supervisors of the people in the car-pool, and what are the consequences? (Part B)
3. Why, in your opinion, did the interview seem easy to Hal? (Part C)

Case 13.2   The Upward Appraisal

1. What was bothering Jan about appraisals by her subordinates?
2. What could be done to make the appraisal system more helpful to Jan?

Comprehensive Case

Appraising the Boss

Appraisals of subordinates, especially those below management level, are an almost universally accepted part of organizational life. Managers appraise the people who report to them for a number of reasons: to make sure everyone is working toward the same goals, to help employees improve and adjust their actions and styles, and to provide a basis for recommending merit bonuses or remedial training. In many organizations, appraisals are a key part of the planning and goal-setting process without which organizations might drift or employees might work at cross purposes.

Yet despite all the benefits of employee appraisals, most organizations make use of fewer than half of the available appraisers; their appraisal systems work only from the top down. For a number of reasons, organizations have not traditionally asked employees to evaluate their supervisors. But as the roles of managers evolve and the need to get the best possible work out of everyone becomes even more pressing, many organizations are discovering the value of bottom-up appraisals.

Much of the resistance to appraising the boss stems from conceptions of what it means to be a manager or an executive and how responsibilities and accountability change as people move up the organizational hierarchy. Some see the lack of appraisals as one of the perquisites of managerial life and feel that it would demean executives to be evaluated by those who work for them. Managers' jobs require autonomy, creativity, and flexibility, and they cannot be held accountable to the strict performance standards against which their employees' conduct is measured. After all, this reasoning goes, the organization can judge managers on the basis of the quality and productivity of their units. If the unit is performing well, why waste time to find out what the members of the unit think of their boss? Anyway, subordinates would never do honest appraisals for fear of retribution.

Such attitudes ignore some of the fundamental truths of current organizational life. For one thing, the lack of clear guidelines for managerial behavior makes feedback ever more important the higher one goes on the organizational ladder. A worker on the factory floor can count — in terms of products completed or errors made — the quantity and the quality of a day's work. Most managers, and especially top executives, have no equivalent way of judging how effective they have been. If they have any interest in making the next day's work more productive, they need to get feedback from those around them.

Not surprisingly, surveys show that many managers and executives are frustrated by the lack of such feedback, especially from subordinates. Most managers can count on hearing from the boss if something in their department goes especially well or badly, but subordinates are much less likely to drop by the office and say, "that was a big mistake." Yet such a comment may be the only way that the manager can avoid making the same mistake again. Many managers are promoted to their positions as a result of some technical expertise, not necessarily because of their abilities to deal with people. Therefore, feedback from their subordinates may be the best managerial training they can hope for.

The changing role of the manager in many American organizations makes appraisals by subordinates ever more crucial. In the past, many managers saw their jobs in almost military terms — they would hand out orders, and their subordinates would follow the orders, perform the required tasks, and report back. In such a system, it would not always make sense to ask the subordinate, "How did you like your order?" Increasingly, however, managers are asked to act not as generals but as coaches — supporting, motivating, and facilitating the work of the people under them. It seems eminently logical for a coach to ask, "How can I support you better?"

Organizations that use bottom-up appraisals find that they are valuable not only for improving supervisors' managerial skills but also for empowering subordinates and making them feel that they have a stake and a say in the direction the organization takes. To the extent that such appraisals result in more effective managers and more content employees, they clearly also have a long-term effect on the organization's overall performance and competitiveness.

Chrysler Corp. began using reverse-appraisals in 1988. It instituted the program gradually. Each level of management evaluated the level above, then was in turn evaluated by the next level below, giving almost everyone a chance to be an appraiser before being appraised. To reduce the fears and tensions associated with the appraisals, subordinates' appraisals were carefully kept anonymous, and they did not become part of the managers' annual performance appraisals.

The whole concept of supervisor appraisals is so new that effective appraisal instruments and techniques are still being perfected. A popular method of conducting the appraisal is to devise a questionnaire specifically geared to a particular department, covering aspects of the job that subordinates can reasonably assess.

In at least one organization, First Investment Company, upward appraisals have succeeded in significantly lowering turnover, improving subordinates' perceptions of management, and bolstering morale. After three years of the system, most managers actually find that they like the appraisals because the feedback gives them an opportunity to correct mistakes and misperceptions and to focus on the blind spots in their own managerial approaches. As such results become better known, bottom-up appraisals may become a fixture of organizational life.

Sources: Clinton O. Longenecker and Dennis A. Gioia, "The Executive Appraisal Paradox," *Academy of Management EXECUTIVE* 6 (May 1992): 18–28; George P. Nicholas, "Upward Trend Continues in Appraisal Process," *HRfocus* 69 (September 1992): 17; Joyce E. Santora, "Rating the Boss at Chrysler," *Personnel Journal* 71 (May 1992): 38–45; Scott Warrick, "Supervisor Review Sheds Light on Blind Spots," *HRMagazine* 37 (June 1992): 111–120.

Discussion Questions

1. What are the potential benefits of upward appraisals?
2. What, in your opinion, may be some of the pitfalls of such appraisals? (Include Case 13.2 in your discussion.)

CHAPTER 14

Wage and Salary Administration

LEARNING OBJECTIVES

- Identify the goals of an equitable wage and salary program.
- Outline three methods of job evaluation.
- Describe how wage and salary surveys are used to make pay decisions.
- Describe a procedure for developing a pay structure using a graph.
- Describe the features of a merit-pay plan.
- Explain why specific rules and policies are needed to administer the wage and salary program and to handle pay adjustments.
- Explain how government regulation affects wage and salary administration.
- Define comparable worth and explain its impact on wage and salary administration.

CASE 14.1   Circle O Hamburgers

Bill Stevens had just been promoted to personnel director of Circle O, a small fast-food chain specializing in hamburgers and French fries. Circle O now employed about 120 full-time people, mostly supervisors, cooks, and maintenance people, and another 340 or so part-time workers. Most of the part-timers were high school or college students working at or near the minimum wage, but some were in supervisory or craft jobs. The best electrician in the company, for example, was a college senior majoring in physics. Some of the sharpest supervisors were also college students working part-time. They came from all kinds of majors — liberal arts, business administration, health sciences, engineering, and others.

Bill was pleased and excited about his new position. He had started working at the counter in one of the restaurants while in college and had quickly worked up to a part-time supervisory job. When he graduated, he was immediately promoted into a full-time supervisory job, and within two years he was managing one of the restaurants. He was soon making useful suggestions to top management about management practices, including personnel matters. Early on he had caught the eye of the president and founder of Circle O, and before another two years went by he was promoted into the newly created personnel director's job.

That evening, while having dinner with his fiancée, Peg, Bill mused aloud about his new position. "One of the advantages of my having so much experience with Circle O is that I can see a lot of problems that need working on. The trouble is, I'm not too sure I'll be able to solve some of them. There's going to be a lot more to this job than being concerned about making and selling good hamburgers."

"Say more," Peg responded.

"Well, for one thing," Bill replied, "I've got to get a handle on why there is so much turnover among our full-time supervisors. I suspect it's partly because the pay structure doesn't make any sense. I'm not even sure there is a pay structure. A really good supervisor with a year's full-time experience will get 30 percent more pay in one of our suburban restaurants than if he or she is working downtown. Some of our best full-time supervisors make less on an hourly basis than some of our part-time supervisors. I wonder if that makes sense. Some managers give pay increases twice a year, others only once. Some seem to give pay increases for length of service, some for having a congenial personality, and some for real performance. Some new supervisors are making less than their more experienced subordinates. Some of these things didn't seem fair to me when I was a supervisor. I wonder, too, whether Circle O is really competitive with other growing chains. I know of several of our people who recently went with competitors. You know Karlyn and Jeff — they've both gone with competitors. Maybe I should call them up and ask them why.

"What do you think, Peg? Any reactions to what I'm saying? Sounds like a mess, doesn't it? You've taken a course in personnel management. Maybe you could give me some advice."

"Wow," said Peg. "That sounds like chaos. You're going to earn your pay. I have several reactions — let's start with the frequency of salary review. . . ." ◄

CASE 14.2   Pay Scales in the Laboratory

Dr. Beverly Scott was the head of a large applied research organization staffed mostly with engineers and scientists, many with advanced degrees. For two years in a row, she had been faced with very unpleasant dilemmas regarding pay increases for employees. Two years ago profits had been down and she could afford to give increases averaging only 3 percent. But inflation was at about 8 percent that year, so there seemed to be no way to make anyone happy. A year ago the company had been losing money, and Beverly had had to tell her employees that their salaries were going to be reduced 5 percent. That certainly had not been pleasant news, but people had accepted it.

This year the dilemma was a happier one. Profits were up, so Beverly could afford increases averaging 9 percent. At the same time, inflation was down to only about 5 percent. The dilemma was whether to help everyone regain lost ground in a substantial way or whether to give very large increases to a few of the "superstars" and only modest increases to the other employees. Beverly wanted to ensure that none of the best performers left. On the other hand, everyone in the organization was performing well in spite of what had happened to salaries two years in a row, and there was a real sense of team spirit. She did not want to erode this.

"I'd better do two things first," she thought. "First, I ought to analyze what we have given each person over the last three years. Second, I should think through what our philosophy about rewards really is — or ought to be. Come to think of it, I'd better ask for opinions from the entire top management group to be sure we are all in agreement." ◀

These cases involve a critical aspect of human resources management: the compensation of employees through wages and salaries. An adequate and fair pay system is important in satisfying workers, retaining valuable employees, and remaining competitive with other organizations that provide similar goods and services.

At Circle O Company, Bill Stevens senses that a haphazardly designed and inconsistent pay system is at least partly responsible for the high turnover among supervisory employees. He senses, too, that there may be morale problems in this group. He is also aware of some of the complexities in the situation, such as part-time supervisors working along with full-time supervisors, and downtown versus suburban locations. Bill is aware that high turnover and low morale are costly to Circle O and are harming overall performance. One can infer that a more carefully designed and consistently applied pay system might alleviate some of the turnover, thereby improving the overall effectiveness of the organization.

Case 14.2 suggests the complexity involved in making pay-increase decisions. These decisions must take into account external realities (such as rates of inflation) and internal realities (such as the organization's ability to pay). As Beverly Scott realized, there must also be agreement about the basis for making increases. Pay increases can reward **merit** (quality of performance), length of service, or both. But to be fair, the basis for increases should be standardized for all employees doing similar jobs throughout the organization.

The issues Bill Stevens and Beverly Scott face are only some of the typical problems in wage and salary administration. Among the considerations involved in designing an adequate pay system are the following:

- Equity or fairness of pay in comparison with the pay of others in the organization
- Competitiveness of the wages or salaries with those paid by other organizations in the same industry or locality
- The organization's ability to pay
- Whether to give pay increases on the basis of performance, length of service, or both
- What kind of wage or salary differentials there should be between satisfactory and outstanding performers, and between supervisors and their subordinates
- Rules of administration — for example, how frequently the pay structure and the pay of individuals should be reviewed, and how fast someone can move through a rate range (the lower and upper dollar limits assigned to a pay grade)
- What time perspective to have in mind — for example, whether pay decisions should be based strictly on performance over the last year, or whether performance and the organization's ability to pay over the past several years should be taken into account

This chapter addresses these considerations by outlining procedures and methods for determining fair and adequate compensation, describing rules for administering the pay system, and exploring current issues surrounding pay decisions. Government regulation of wage and salary programs is also discussed.

The Wage and Salary Program

Wages and salaries — the payment received for performing work — are a major component of the compensation and reward process, which is aimed at reimbursing employees for their work and motivating them to perform to the best of their abilities. In addition to pay, most employees receive benefits such as health insurance and paid holidays; and they receive nonfinancial rewards such as security, recognition, and privileges. Although individual employees vary in the extent to which they value pay in relation to other work rewards, for most people the pay received for work is a necessity. Thus, the wage and salary program of any organization is a vital concern to the employees within it.

Definition of Terms   In popular usage, the words *wage* and *salary* are sometimes considered synonymous; strictly speaking, however, they have slightly different meanings. **Wage** (or **hourly pay**) refers to an hourly rate of pay and is the pay basis used most frequently for production and maintenance employees (blue-collar workers). **Salary** refers to a weekly, monthly, or yearly rate of pay. Clerical, professional, sales, and management employees (white-collar workers) are usually salaried.

Generally, wage-earning (hourly) employees are paid only for the actual hours worked, whereas salaried employees, if paid by the month, are paid the same amount each month regardless of the slight differences in total working hours from month to month. If paid weekly or every two weeks, however, salaried employees are essentially paid the same hourly rate across the year. Under the Fair Labor Standards Act (FLSA), a weekly pay equivalent must be computed in order to arrive at an hourly rate for salaries paid monthly or twice per month.

The real differences between wage and salaried status, then, do not include whether or not there is an hourly rate, because an hourly rate can always be computed. The differences exist in the benefits and conditions associated with each status in particular organizations. As shown in Table 14.1, salaried workers typically have certain benefits or privileges that wage employees do not, such as fewer work rules, and less chance of having their pay docked for absences. However, wage employees are more likely to receive daily overtime and call-in pay. (Call-in pay typically is a guaranteed number of paid hours for being called back to work. For example, a company might telephone an electrician to come back to work after his or her normal workday and pay that person a minimum of an extra four hours' pay even if the job only requires one hour of work. Labor contracts usually include call-in pay provisions.)

Nonexempt employees are the workers covered by the overtime provisions of the Fair Labor Standards Act and the Walsh-Healey Act. These employees must be paid time and one-half the regular rate of pay for any time worked beyond forty hours in one week. **Exempt employees** are workers not covered by the overtime provisions of these laws. There are several categories of exempt employees, including those in bona fide executive, administrative, and professional positions, outside sales jobs, the more highly paid computer jobs, and certain other categories as defined by the Wage and Hour Division of the U.S. Department of Labor.

TABLE 14.1 Typical features of hourly and salaried work

HOURLY	SALARIED
Time clocks	No time clocks, except in unusual situations — for example, organizations using flex-time.
Pay docking	Pay docking rare. Normally, gross offenders of the company's attendance policy will be warned and, if there is no improvement, terminated.
Daily overtime	No daily overtime. Nonexempt employees will get weekly overtime for hours worked beyond 40.
Call-in pay	No call-in pay.
Piece rates (sometimes)	No piece rates; bonuses sometimes paid.
Wash-up time	No wash-up time.
Formal paid rest periods	Paid rest periods common but not guaranteed.
Layoffs	Layoffs rare.
Sick days	Except in government, a limit on paid sick days is rare. If employee is sick, he gets paid.
Cumbersome work rules	Few work rules. Certainly, none of the inflexibility associated with hourly status.
Formal discipline program for lateness and absence	Formal program may exist, but more probably it is within supervisor's or department head's discretion to determine what steps to take.

Source: Edward J. Mandt, "The Time-Clock Anachronism," *Across the Board* 23 (December 1986): 7. Reprinted by permission of The Conference Board.

Management is not required by federal law to pay overtime to these employees, but may do so in some cases. (See also Chapter 8 on overtime work.)

It should be noted that a classification of "exempt" must be made on the basis of comparing actual job duties with criteria established by the Department of Labor. A job title, for example, is not sufficient data for a human resources department or a manager to claim that the job should be exempt from overtime status.

Goals

Determining wage and salary payments is one of the most critical aspects of human resources management because (1) the organization's reward system has such a profound effect on the recruitment, satisfaction, and motivation of employees and (2) wages and salaries represent a considerable cost to the employer. A carefully designed wage and salary program that is administered according to sound policies and consistently applied rules is essential if human resources are to be used effectively to achieve organizational objectives. In essence, a wage and salary program should be designed with the following goals in mind:

- To meet the needs of employees, including desires for security and self-esteem
- To motivate workers to achieve desired levels of performance
- To be cost effective or based on what an organization can afford to pay
- To be competitive with other organizations in order to attract and retain human resources
- To comply with wage and salary provisions in the labor contract and with federal and state laws and regulations
- To be fair and consistently applied throughout the organization

Important Considerations

The goals of the wage and salary program suggest that intricate and interrelated factors affect the pay structure of an organization and the pay scale for given jobs. Each employer has the difficult task of weighing these factors and making numerous decisions that ultimately determine how much a specific employee will be paid.

Worth of the Job and the Employee

Most people would probably agree that some jobs are worth more to an employer than others. For example, negotiating multimillion-dollar contracts with the government is considered to be worth more than emptying wastepaper baskets. One employee may be worth more than another in the same job. Sales Manager A consistently sells twice as much as Sales Manager B and is considered of more worth than B to the firm.

Prevailing Wages and Salaries

It is important that the organization know the typical wages or salaries being paid in the labor market for the various jobs represented in the organization. If a company pays its computer programmers only two-thirds as much as other companies in the community or region, for example, it is likely to lose most of its programmers and find it impossible to recruit competent replacements. If programmers are in very short supply, competition will probably drive up the salaries paid to these specialists. The decision to pay average, below-average, or above-average wages in relation to the external labor market is a major strategic decision in human resources management.

Collective Bargaining

Collective bargaining has a major impact on the pay system within given firms and within industries. In a unionized organization, collective bargaining determines the wages for jobs covered by the contract, rules of wage administration for these jobs, and methods for determining the relative worth of jobs. Nonunionized firms are ultimately affected by collective-bargaining agreements made elsewhere, since those firms compete with unionized firms for the services and loyalties of human resources. In addition, there are strong pressures within a unionized organization to pass along any wage or benefit gains made through contract negotiations to the nonunion segment of the work force.

Economic Realities

The wage and salary structure and pay decisions affecting individual employees will also be directly influenced by economic realities. Two of these realities are the organization's ability to pay and inflation. If a firm has been highly profitable for several years in a row, it is much more likely to pay significantly above-average wages and to grant liberal pay increases than if it is losing money. If an organization is losing money, there is a strong possibility that a reduction in wages and salaries will be one of the options examined.

If inflation is driving up wages and salaries in the external labor market, many organizations may find it difficult to maintain appropriate balances within their wage and salary structures, particularly if beginning wages and salaries are going up faster than a company can adjust its wage and salary structure. This creates **salary compression** — a narrowing of the differentials between job levels — and reduces the organization's ability to grant merit increases because so much money is required to adjust the overall structure.

Perceptions of Equity

As has been discussed in Chapter 5, perceptions of equity are important to job satisfaction and performance. To feel fairly treated, a person must feel that personal contributions (such as education and training, skill, seniority, effort, and job performance) correspond to personal outcomes (such as pay, recognition, privileges, and job satisfaction). In addition, these personal contributions and outcomes must be in line with those of other people, particularly coworkers and employees in the same organization. If they are out of line, job performance and satisfaction will suffer. No one is immune from having feelings about equitable or inequitable treatment in matters of compensation. Equity with the U.S. House of Representatives was the justification used by the U.S. Senate to raise the salaries of its members by $23,000 in 1991.[1]

Job Evaluation

Job evaluation is the systematic determination of the relative worth of jobs in a particular organization. This procedure is used to answer such questions as the following: Will technicians be paid more than researchers? If so, how much more? Will word processors be paid more than secretaries, or should both groups receive the same pay? On what basis can these decisions be justified?

Basically, job evaluation involves gathering information about jobs and then comparing them, using specially constructed scales. The result of this comparison is a hierarchy of jobs based on the extent to which each job presumably contributes to organizational effectiveness. The hierarchy is used to establish and justify different levels of pay for the various positions within the organization.

There is no easy, precise way to determine the exact contribution each job makes to overall effectiveness. A key concern in job evaluation, then, is to identify **job factors** that are considered to be of value and to determine systematically the degree to which each is present in each job. Responsibility, skill, effort, and working conditions are examples of factors that are commonly considered appropriate dimensions for determining relative **job worth,** or value to the organization. The choice of job factors — and the use of job evaluation itself — reflects basic assumptions consistent with equity theory: (1) it is logical to pay more for jobs requiring greater skill and training and demanding more from employees in effort, responsibility, and training, and (2) people feel more fairly treated if pay differentials reflect a hierarchy of jobs based on relative worth. Job factors and their relative weights are typically identified by a close study of job descriptions, which are based on job analysis. (Figure 14.1 shows how job analysis is related to job evaluation.)

Methods   Most organizations that pay wages use job evaluation. For example, if the owner of an insurance brokerage simply decides that the receptionist should be paid more than a typist, an informal job evaluation procedure has been used. Although this procedure may have been too subjective and too quickly applied, nevertheless a rudimentary form of job evaluation has occurred. Unless the decision has been made to pay the same wage to everyone in the organization, the question becomes what job evaluation procedure should be used and how systematically should it be applied. At the Circle O Company in Case 14.1, it appears that the job evaluation procedures are subjective and vary a great deal from restaurant to restaurant.

Formal job evaluation procedures are used in a high proportion of all but the smallest organizations. One study of 197 organizations found 75 percent of the firms using one or more formal job evaluation plans. Close to half of the firms relying on formal plans used two or more plans covering different categories of employees.[2] This practice reflects the common assumption that factors and scales that are adequate for production and maintenance jobs may not be appropriate for clerical, professional-technical, or executive positions. The use of different job evaluation methods for different groups is currently being challenged, however; see the discussion of comparable worth later in this chapter.

Three types of formal job evaluation methods have been particularly conspicuous in the last twenty or thirty years. In order of popularity, they are (1) the point-

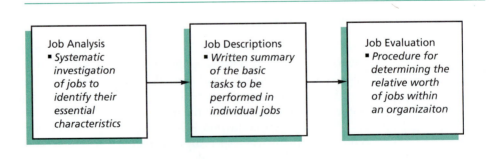

FIGURE 14.1   Relationship of job analysis, job descriptions, and job evaluation

factor method, by far the most widely used; (2) the classification method; and (3) the ranking method.[3] A fourth method, factor-comparison, is much more complicated than the others; since it is rarely used, we will not deal with it here.

The Point-Factor Method

The **point-factor method** of job evaluation uses several factors common to the jobs being evaluated. Scales divided into point distances are used to determine the degree to which these factors are present in a given job. Once all the scales have been applied to each job being studied, the points chosen for each scale are added to provide a total for each job. The point total designates the relative worth of the job. It is important to recognize that these scales are used to measure the job — not the job incumbent.

Figure 14.2 shows the scale used for the factor called "latitude of responsibility" in a point-factor system of job evaluation that encompasses three major categories or areas. These areas are further divided into six job factors. As shown in Figure 14.3, the three areas are "responsibility," "know-how," and "relationships." "Responsibility" is divided into the factors of "latitude" and "authority." "Know-how" is divided into the factors of "diversity," "degree," and "application." "Relationships" is not divided into factors and is simply called "human relations skill" in the pie chart. This particular system provides a maximum total of 2,000 points, of which 800 are allocated to "responsibility," 800 to "know-how," and 400 to "relationships." For an illustration of how points were allocated for the job of accounting clerk in one organization, see Figure 14.4.

Many versions of the point-factor method of job evaluation are in use today. Although most include responsibility, skill, effort, and working conditions, any one version may have its own unique set of factors. As few as three or as many as twenty-five or more factors may be used, with the average probably about ten. Other factors might be "job complexity," "education and experience required," "mental requirements," "supervisory responsibility," "responsibility for

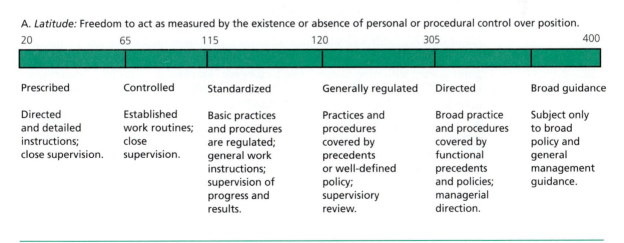

A. *Latitude:* Freedom to act as measured by the existence or absence of personal or procedural control over position.

20	65	115	120	305	400
Prescribed	Controlled	Standardized	Generally regulated	Directed	Broad guidance
Directed and detailed instructions; close supervision.	Established work routines; close supervision.	Basic practices and procedures are regulated; general work instructions; supervision of progress and results.	Practices and procedures covered by precedents or well-defined policy; supervisiory review.	Broad practice and procedures covered by functional precedents and policies; managerial direction.	Subject only to broad policy and general management guidance.

FIGURE 14.2 "Latitude of responsibility" scale of a point-factor method of job evaluation
Used with permission.

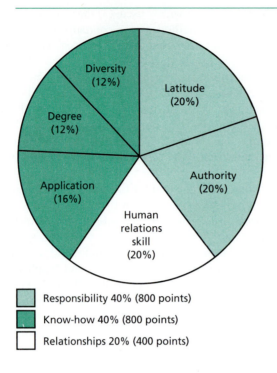

FIGURE 14.3   System total — 2,000 points

Used with permission.

equipment," "outside contacts," and so forth. "Job complexity" is often associated with jobs involving some hazard, such as dealing with toxic substances or radioactive materials. This factor can be used to acknowledge the required safety practices and equipment that increase the complexity and relative worth of the job.

The widely used Hay Guide Chart-Profile Method of job evaluation includes three major factors: "know-how," "problem solving," and "accountability." Each major factor is further divided into subfactors.[4] A system used in the federal government in recent years, called the Factor Evaluation System (FES), is essentially a point system with nine factors. The factors are "knowledge required," "supervisory controls," "guidelines," "complexity," "scope and effect," "personal contacts," "purpose of contacts," "physical demands," and "work environment."[5]

Another version of the point-factor method is called the *job component method* of job evaluation. This method uses a questionnaire such as the Position Analysis Questionnaire (PAQ), described briefly in Chapter 7. The PAQ uses 194 items to measure job behaviors required on forty-five job dimensions. These scores are then combined to yield a "job value." Although the procedure appears complicated, it has been used by some organizations to develop wage structures considered equitable by the courts.[6]

The Classification Method

The **classification method** of job evaluation starts with one-paragraph descriptions of a predetermined number of levels, grades, or "classes" of jobs, each of which corresponds to a **pay grade;** for example, Grade I, Grade II, Grade III, and so on.

Responsibility	
Latitude	120
Authority	83
Know-how	
Diversity	97
Degree	126
Application	120
Relationship	
Human relations skill	100
TOTAL SCORE	646
SALARY GRADE	7
DATE SCORED _____	BY: _____
	CHECKED _____

FIGURE 14.4   Points allocated to an accounting clerk position

Used with permission.

These descriptions of each grade feature gradations of job responsibility, skill and education required, and the like. Job descriptions for other jobs in the organization are then examined, and these jobs are classified into grades or levels that seem most appropriate. This method requires a decision at the outset on the number of pay grades to be included in the wage and salary plan. Actual amounts to be assigned to pay grades, of course, may be made after the job evaluation is completed. Called the General Schedule (GS) classification system in the federal government, this method has been used for years by the U.S. Civil Service Commission. In the GS system, federal jobs are assigned to one of eighteen pay grades.

The Ranking Method

In the **ranking method** of job evaluation, the raters simply rank the various jobs examined. No attempt is made to determine the critical factors in each job. Instead, an overall judgment is made of the relative worth of each job, and the job is ranked accordingly. Because of the difficulties in ranking a large number of jobs at one time, the paired comparison technique of ranking is sometimes used. With this technique, decisions are made about the relative worth of only two jobs at a time. Since each job is compared with every other job, however, the number of comparisons to be made increases rapidly with the addition of each job to the list.

The chief disadvantage of the ranking method is that there are usually no agreed-upon guidelines as to what elements or factors the organization considers valuable. Thus, there are no "yardsticks" for measuring job value, and the underlying assumptions of those doing the ranking may never be brought into the open. There is the obvious danger that the rankings will be done in very subjective fashion and will be based on impressions rather than objective information. This method, then, contrasts with the other two methods, in which job factors can be examined, discussed, and modified as part of the evaluation process.

Problems   A number of potential problems can arise no matter which job evaluation method is used. Among these are inaccurate or incomplete job data; negative reactions from unions; and the need for employee understanding, acceptance, and support of the evaluation procedure.

Inaccurate Job Descriptions   If the information recorded in the job description is inaccurate or incomplete, the job evaluation will be inaccurate. For example, a job description may present an inflated picture of the actual job or, conversely, may not do justice to some of the important activities performed. In addition, if employees or supervisors do not believe that job descriptions reflect accurately the jobs actually performed, they will perceive the job evaluation procedures and the resulting wage and salary structure as unfair.

Careful and systematic job-data collection that attempts to secure agreement among employees and supervisors about the accuracy of descriptions can minimize these problems. In addition, job analysis should be repeated when there is reason to believe that the job has changed significantly. Then the job evaluation procedure can be applied to the revised job description to determine whether the job should be paid at a different rate.

Union Reactions   The attitudes of union leaders toward job evaluation have been mixed over the years but have usually not been supportive. Two officers of the Communications Workers of America (CWA) said this:

> Unions have traditionally approached job evaluation with apprehension and skepticism, if not open condemnation. The Communications Workers of America . . . has been no exception. Until just a few years ago, our union rejected job evaluation on the grounds that it was a management tool to manipulate wages outside of the collective bargaining process.[7]

An example of long-standing support, however, is the industry-wide job evaluation plan adopted by the United Steelworkers and the steel companies that covers all production and maintenance jobs.[8]

In the context of a joint agreement with AT&T to explore new participative approaches to solving problems, prior to the divestiture of the seven regional companies, the Communications Workers and the company established a joint national Occupational Job Evaluation Committee. The committee then developed a job evaluation plan that included the following objectives and principles:

- All employees would have the right to appeal the job description, scoring, and relative worth of their jobs.
- Information about the job evaluation plan would be made available to all employees and union representatives.
- No wages would be reduced as a result of the plan.
- The plan would consider the changing technological nature of work as well as the accompanying emotional and psychological effects of technological change.
- Employees would be provided with opportunities to maintain and improve their skills through training, job design, and transfer.[9]

Supervisory and Employee Participation and Acceptance

Supervisors and higher management, as well as other employees, will need to understand, accept, and support the job evaluation system if it is to work. The challenge lies in selecting supervisors and other managers to participate in job evaluation committees and in obtaining their commitment of time and attention to the process. Broad participation is necessary for informed decisions and acceptance in the organization; on the other hand, large committees are expensive and sometimes unwieldy.

Wage and Salary Surveys

Because the wage and salary program affects the recruitment and retention of qualified employees, whether the organization should pay wages and salaries above, below, or equal to the averages for similar jobs in the community or industry deserves serious consideration. To establish a competitive wage and salary structure, an organization typically relies on data obtained from **wage and salary surveys**, which collect information on wages and salaries paid in other organizations. Wages paid in the surrounding metropolitan area or region tend to be the most important factor in determining general wage levels for most nonmanagement and first-line supervisory jobs. In establishing salary rates for professional and managerial employees, most medium-sized and large organizations examine national and industry-wide patterns as well.

Most firms either conduct their own wage and salary surveys or participate in surveys conducted by other organizations, including consulting firms. These surveys may be carried out by mail, telephone, or interview. In addition, surveys are published periodically by the American Management Association, the Society for Human Resource Management, the U.S. Bureau of Labor Statistics, the Administrative Management Society, the Federal Reserve System, and various employer and professional associations.

A major problem in using data from wage and salary surveys is the need to make accurate comparisons between companies. Careful inquiry needs to be made about the actual scope and responsibilities of the jobs surveyed, since job titles alone or even brief descriptions can be misleading. Appropriate statistical methods need to be used, too, in collecting and analyzing the survey data. A simple average of the wages paid by firms for a certain job does not take into account the numbers of employees involved or the size of the firms. For example, the average salary paid to computer programmers who are long-time employees of a small company may not be typical of the industry as a whole. On the other hand, averages weighted with the numbers of employees may be distorted by inclusion of large, well-paying firms in the sample along with a few small firms that have recently entered the industry. There may also be significant differences between urban and suburban rates of pay, which will affect survey data.

Another important consideration is whether benefits are included in the wage and salary survey. Some firms pay only average wages but offer unusually expensive benefits. Other organizations pay high wages, but are very conservative with employee benefits such as pensions, holidays, and sick leave.

An area of uncertainty about wage and salary surveys is the extent to which there will be future court challenges. Antitrust laws have been used to attack salary survey practices in at least two cases; in these instances, the matter was settled out of court. In one of these cases, salary survey practices of the Boston Survey Group, comprising thirty-four employer members, were challenged by a women's political action group, "9 to 5." The women's group asserted that the annual survey of this association was used to hold down salaries in various clerical jobs filled primarily by women. The Boston Survey Group entered into a consent decree with the state attorney general and agreed to alter its survey practices. One change agreed upon was that no individuals would be identified and that only aggregate data would be used.[10]

Determining Pay Rates

Once the relative worth of jobs has been established by job evaluation, the actual rates to be paid for particular jobs need to be determined. Although no precise science governs this determination, one procedure commonly used is the two-dimensional graph. In this procedure, job evaluation points for **key jobs** are plotted against actual amounts paid or against desired pay rates as suggested by wage and salary surveys. (Key jobs are jobs that are found in many organizations and that have relatively stable content.) A line drawn through the key jobs plotted on the graph suggests the approximate contour the other jobs should follow. Plotting the remaining jobs then reveals which jobs seem to be improperly paid with respect to the key jobs and to each other. Any clustering of jobs can also be observed, and this clustering will suggest which jobs may be grouped in different pay grades.

Figure 14.5 shows the pay grades of a hypothetical pay plan for the administrative-clerical employees of a small organization. The figure also shows how all of the jobs under this pay plan may be plotted on a graph. The horizontal axis represents the points obtained through a point-factor system of job evaluation; the vertical axis represents salary levels. Tentative pay grades, or ranges I–V, have been identified on the vertical axis to suggest the structure of this particular plan. The line drawn through the jobs, which leaves approximately the same number of jobs above and below the line, indicates the relationship of pay rates to points. (In this figure, the line has been drawn simply by inspection. A "least squares" or regression line is sometimes computed to establish a more accurate relationship between points and pay.) In this example, two jobs above the line have been tentatively identified as overpaid, and three jobs below the line may be underpaid. (Jobs above the line that are considered excessively overpaid are called **red-circle jobs** and those below the line that are considered excessively underpaid are called **green-circle jobs.**)[11]

A majority of organizations surveyed in one study used **rate ranges** (or pay ranges) for the various pay grades for both hourly and salaried employees.[12] (For example, the jobs in Grade III shown in Figure 14.5 are paid from $1,350 to $1,750 per month.) While this practice is very prevalent for salaried positions, the use of ranges for hourly production and maintenance employees has grown rapidly. (For example, a firm might pay jobs in a grade from $8.50 to $12.50 per hour, in contrast to having a single rate for the grade.) A rate-range plan allows the employee to receive pay increases for the same job on the basis of individual merit, seniority, or both. Typically, the rate range is defined in terms of a minimum, average (or midpoint), or maximum amount.

The number of pay grades assigned to a pay plan is not at all standardized across companies; it may vary from as few as five to as many as thirty. Similarly, there is no typical dollar spread associated with rate ranges or grades. For production and office-clerical jobs, the spread of the pay grade may vary from 10 to 20 percent on

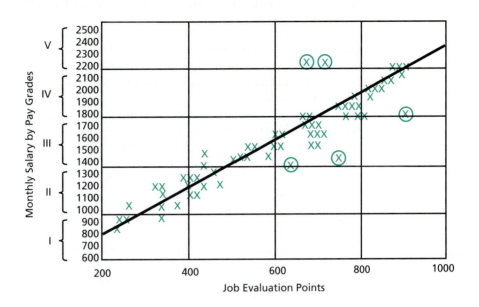

⊗ Underpaid or overpaid

FIGURE 14.5 Job evaluation points plotted against pay, showing "overpaid" and "underpaid" jobs

either side of the midpoint. For professional, technical, or managerial jobs, the range spread may vary from 30 to 50 percent on either side of the midpoint.[13] In addition, rate ranges may or may not overlap, although the typical practice is to have some overlap to allow a very experienced employee to earn as much as another employee with less experience in the next higher pay grade.

Adjusting the Pay Structure

As the widespread use of wage and salary surveys indicates, prevailing patterns in wages and salaries have an important impact on pay. Even firms that do not consider wage and salary survey data when designing a pay structure are bound to be affected sooner or later by outside pressures. For example, it would be impossible to staff an organization in a period of high inflation unless wages and salaries were adjusted to accommodate the upward movement of wages and costs of living in the area. In other instances, the need to reduce costs may mean that wages and salaries must be revised downward.

Wage and salary adjustments — whether upward or downward — must be made with great care so that unwanted distortions do not occur within the pay structure. Of chief concern is maintaining adequate pay differentials between jobs at different levels in the organizational hierarchy. Supervisors will understandably feel unfairly treated if there is little or no differential between their pay and that of their subordinates. Studies report that differentials between rank-and-file jobs and supervisory jobs typically range from 15 to 25 percent.[14]

Appropriate differentials must also be maintained between exempt and nonexempt groups to reflect differences in skills and training and to prevent perceptions of unfairness. Since nonexempt groups are eligible for overtime payments, whereas exempt employees may or may not be paid for overtime, management must be sensitive to any problems created by overtime payments to the former group. While some firms pay straight-time overtime to professional-technical and sales employees and first-level supervisors, a big majority of companies surveyed avoid inequities by paying time-and-one-half pay for overtime work to these groups. An exception is the case of middle managers, who are more likely to be given compensatory time off or paid straight time.[15] (Figure 14.6 outlines the steps that are usually taken in developing or revising a wage and salary plan.)

Competition and Inflation

The general upward rise in wage and salary levels in this country has meant that all organizations have needed to consider how to handle upward changes in their pay structures. Some firms give general percentage or **across-the-board pay increases** to accommodate pressures from inflation or competition. Across-the-board increases are also frequently used to adjust the wages of the nonunionized part of the work force to reflect increases granted to unionized employees. Other organizations include a general adjustment factor in merit or length-of-service raises, although the organization may not label that portion of the increase as such.

Wage Cuts

The necessity for wage cuts can also be a serious problem. Under pressure from a variety of forces, including government deregulation and a general economic downturn in a number of industries, a significant number of organizations have had to lower wage and salary levels in recent years. Such pay reductions had to be negotiated if there was a contract with unionized employees, of course. In some instances, certain benefits such as profit sharing were extracted by the union as the price of making wage concessions. In instances where top management took significant cuts in pay, rank-and-file employees accepted pay reductions with less resentment than when management did not bear a comparable burden. For example, after the executives of Delta Air Lines, Inc., took pay cuts in the summer of 1983, a pay freeze for nonunion employees later in the year was more palatable than it might have been otherwise.[16] (Again in 1992, senior Delta executives agreed to a pay reduction — an average of 5 percent — when the company reported a quarterly loss.)[17] In 1991, John Sculley, CEO of Apple Computer, announced that the top executives of Apple would take 5 to 10 percent cuts in their base pay. This occurred after Apple workers protested sizable layoffs from Apple's work force.[18]

In some cases management has successfully pressed unions for wage reductions, only to raise its own salaries or the salaries of nonunion employees subsequently. For example, early in 1981, union employees at Braniff Inc., agreed to a 10 percent pay cut. A few weeks later, management approved a pay increase of 11.4 percent for lower and middle managers and secretaries.[19] As one might expect, such actions were promptly branded as unfair by the union. The other side of this coin is that management may have been trying to prevent serious turnover, particularly in the managerial ranks. A company in economic difficulty is subject to talent raids by other organizations.[20]

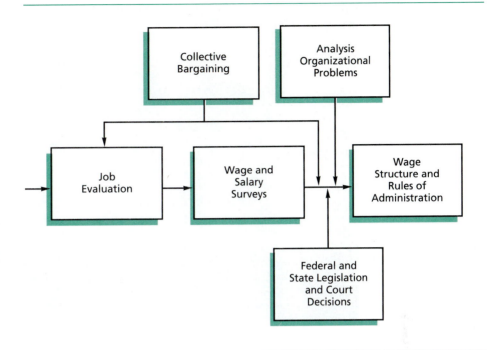

FIGURE 14.6   Steps in developing or revising a wage and salary plan

Rules of Administration

In addition to guidelines about handling such matters as general adjustments, over-paid or underpaid jobs, and differentials between supervisors and their subordinates, various other rules need to be developed to administer the wage and salary program effectively. For example, it must be determined to what extent salary advancement will be based on length of service and to what extent on merit, how often salaries will be reviewed and adjusted, what controls over total wage and salary costs will be used, and what rules will govern reclassification of a job into a higher grade.

Merit-Pay
Plans

Under a **merit-pay plan,** pay raises known as merit increases are determined by job performance: that is, employees who achieve a certain level of performance relative to established standards or relative to the performance of others "earn" an increase in their regular rate of pay. Typically, merit-pay decisions are based on a perform-ance appraisal system that translates performance ratings into pay increases.

On the whole, merit increases represent the most commonly used form of pay progression. A survey of nearly two hundred organizations of various types — man-ufacturing, nonmanufacturing business, and nonbusiness — revealed that 92 percent of the respondents offered merit increases.[21] As shown in Table 14.2, merit pay was used in more than 80 percent of the organizations in the case of middle managers, first-level supervisors, and professional-technical and office-clerical employees. Slightly fewer organizations used merit pay with sales employees (75 percent). Pro-duction-service employees were the least likely to be offered merit pay (58 percent of organizations).

The usefulness of merit pay is especially apparent in the retail industry where wages are directly related to performance.

Despite their relative popularity, merit-pay plans sometimes prove to be ineffective motivators of performance. If, for example, the organization's performance appraisal system does not adequately distinguish between levels of performance, pay-increase decisions are likely to be influenced by non-performance-related variables. (These variables are identified in Figure 14.7.) Or, if the merit system is not carefully controlled, increases tend to be granted automatically at regular intervals, and employees may perceive that increases are based on length of service as much as on actual performance. Under these circumstances, the merit-pay plan may have no impact on performance or satisfaction.

TABLE 14.2 Prevalence of Base Pay Increases, by Employee Group

| | **Percent of Companies** | | | | | |
	PRODUCTION/ SERVICE	**OFFICE/ CLERICAL**	**PROFESSIONAL/ TECHNICAL**	**SALES**	**FIRST-LEVEL SUPERVISORS**	**MIDDLE MANAGERS**
(Number of Companies)	**(172)**	**(197)**	**(196)**	**(126)**	**(195)**	**(195)**
Merit increases	58%	82%	84%	75%	85%	86%
General increases	44	31	30	17	28	26
Skill- or knowledge-based increases	19	17	21	12	15	15
Length-of-service increases	23	14	12	5	11	8

Source: Reprinted with permission from *Wage and Salary Administration*, Personnel Policies Forum Survey No. 147, p. 19 (June 1990) Copyright 1990 by The Bureau of National Affairs, Inc. (800-372-1033).

What the organization communicates about pay increases may also diminish the motivating effects of merit-pay plans. For example, in some organizations merit increases are not clearly distinguished from across-the-board increases made to adjust the entire pay structure in response to inflation or labor-market competition. And even when merit pay is clearly labeled as such, the rising cost of living often minimizes the incentive power of the pay increase.[22]

Deciding on the general philosophy and rules about rewarding length of service versus merit and measuring merit are particularly complex matters. Some organizations reward both length of service and quality of performance; that is, employees who are performing satisfactorily receive pay increases on the basis of length of service. Outstanding performers are moved through the range faster, but below-standard performers receive no pay increases. Instead, they are given warnings and some coaching about their performance.

Because of the complexities of doing research on the effectiveness of merit pay plans, such as the wide variation in the plans and how they are administered, few rig-

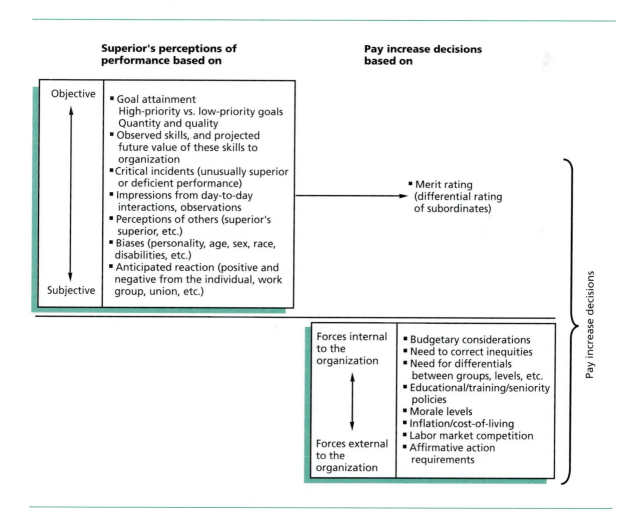

FIGURE 14.7   Probable variables affecting pay increase decisions

orous studies have been conducted. However, one recent study of 398 stores of a large retail chain found strong evidence of the usefulness of merit pay. Simply put, profitability was higher in stores where it could be shown that performance was correlated with pay.[23]

Skill-based Pay

Many organizations, particularly those using self-managed teams, have adopted **skill-based** (or **knowledge-based**) **pay** plans. Workers at the Corning Incorporated ceramics plant, for example, are paid in accordance with the number of skills they have mastered.[24] Skill-based pay is entirely compatible with merit rating plans because pay ranges can be established for each skill level.[25] Surveys of firms using skill-based pay suggest that a large majority experience productivity improvements and lower operating costs despite the additional training costs.[26] (For more on skill-based pay, see the Comprehensive Case on page 390.)

Controlling Wage and Salary Expenditures

Rules are needed to maintain some control over wage and salary expenditures by the various units within the organization and by the organization as a whole. One mechanism used successfully is the **compa ratio**, a calculation that tells to what degree the jobs within a pay grade will average out near the midpoint of the range. If the midpoint value is 100, a compa ratio of 105 means that the average salary for the jobs in that pay grade is 5 percent above the midpoint. Organizations use compa ratios as controls by requiring managers to stay within certain percentage limits for each job grade or for all job grades combined.[27] Other indices that can be used in wage and salary control are budgets, comparisons among departments or divisions, total payroll, and unit labor costs.

Pay Increases

Additional rules are needed to handle promotions from one pay grade to another or from one pay plan to another. Since managers will be inclined to try to obtain more money for people who have reached the top of a range — particularly long-service employees or outstanding employees for whom no genuine promotion is available — control must be maintained to resist such pressures. Otherwise, people will be moved into higher pay brackets when there has been no genuine promotion. Another pressure that is sometimes exerted is a request that the job be reevaluated, with the idea of using an inflated job description to justify reclassification into a higher pay grade. Such practices tend to subvert the meaning and usefulness of job evaluation and introduce inequities in compensation administration.

There are usually more variables operating in pay-increase decisions than most employees — and even many employers — realize. As shown in Figure 14.7, some of the variables that affect pay-increase decisions have little or nothing to do with individual performance or the supervisor's perception of performance. Some variables that affect merit ratings, such as the superior's perception of the quantity and quality of the work performed, are related directly to individual performance. But other variables may be much more subjective. For example, the supervisor making a decision about a subordinate's pay increase may be influenced by his or her superior's impressions of that subordinate. Or the supervisor may give a larger increase than is warranted just to avoid unpleasantness. Other subjective factors may be biases about personality, age, sex, race, or disabled status. Discrimination based on the latter four, of course, is illegal.[28]

The Pay-for-
Performance
Concept

The many variables shown in Figure 14.7 suggest why the concept of **pay for per-formance,** which is written about so much in business publications, is difficult to implement. Basically, "pay for performance" could involve any number of pay or incentive plans that attempt to create a direct link between the employee's per-formance and compensation. For example, the concept could include merit pay tied to some rating scale, pay or bonuses tied to results achieved under an MBO program, or commissions or incentive pay distributed under some kind of incen-tive system. (Incentive systems will be discussed in the next chapter.) Practically, many organizations have moved toward minimizing automatic increases based on seniority and have moved toward emphasizing merit pay and/or incentive systems. However, variables like labor market competition and inflation are part of the re-ality in which any compensation system exists, and must be accommodated in some way.[29]

Government Regulation

Federal and state legislation have an impact on basic wage payments, particularly through minimum-wage laws and overtime regulations. Especially the Equal Pay Act of 1963, which aimed to correct imbalances between the pay of men and women for equal work, is having far-reaching consequences.

Minimum and
Overtime Wage
Laws

Under recent amendments to the Fair Labor Standards Act (FLSA), employees must be paid a minimum of $4.25 per hour. A lower "training wage" for newly employed teenagers was also established; it was to expire on March 31, 1993.[30] The law contin-ues to provide for even higher minimum wages in certain industries as set by the De-partment of Labor. Most states also have minimum wage laws.

Further, as indicated earlier, overtime payments must be paid to nonexempt employees but are not required for exempt employees. Thus, it is important for or-ganizations to be aware of the current criteria used by the Labor Department to de-termine which employees fit the exempt and nonexempt categories.

A case involving Howard Johnson's restaurant and motel chain illustrates the significance of these laws. To settle proceedings brought by the U.S. Department of Labor, the company agreed to pay some $5 million in overtime wages to five thou-sand current and former employees whom top management had treated as exempt. Among these employees were salaried manager trainees and assistant managers earning less than $250 per week, as well as hourly managers and manager trainees. Howard Johnson contended that these employees were exempt from overtime pay because they were part of "management." The Department of Labor insisted this was not correct because investigation showed that the employees were spending more than 40 percent of their time in "routine, non-management" work and that they earned less than $250 per week.[31]

In a later case involving Nordstrom, Inc., Washington State's Department of Labor and Industries ordered the retailer to pay back wages to employees for over-time duties for which they had not been paid, including delivering merchandise to customers. The union estimated the back wages at $30 to $40 million, although the company set aside only $15 million to pay back-wage claims.[32]

Equal Pay Act   The Equal Pay Act of 1963, which amends the Fair Labor Standards Act, prohibits discrimination in wage payments for equal work on the basis of sex. According to this law, male and female employees are to receive the same pay "for equal work on jobs the performance of which requires equal skill, effort, and responsibility, and which are performed under similar working conditions...."[33] (Note the four major job evaluation factors explicit in the law.)

As a consequence of the Equal Pay Act, many corporations have been faced with lawsuits on behalf of female employees. In a large number of instances, companies have been required to pay sizable sums in back pay and to increase wage scales for female employees. In the Corning Glass Works case, the first to reach the Supreme Court, the Court held that the Corning Glass Works had discriminated against women by paying a higher base wage rate to male night-shift operators than to female operators on the day shift.[34] In *Schultz* v. *Wheaton Glass Company*, a U.S. circuit court ruled against the employer, who was charged with discrimination against female inspector-packers. These employees were awarded nearly $1 million in back pay. The Supreme Court refused to hear the case on appeal, thus confirming the decision. The case is significant because the decision supports the notion that the jobs must be "substantially equal" and not "identical" to warrant equal pay.[35]

In another case, Northwest Airlines was ordered to pay nearly $60 million in back pay to female flight attendants. In this suit, the female attendants charged that male attendants doing similar work were paid more, that women were required to share double rooms on layovers while men were given single rooms, that the company paid cleaning allowances for uniforms only to the men, and that only women were required to meet weight restrictions. A federal district court ruled in favor of the female flight attendants, and the decision was upheld by a federal appeals court.[36]

Current Issues

A number of issues surrounding pay decisions affect wage and salary practices in organizations today. Chief among them is the issue of comparable worth, a highly sensitive, complicated, and still unresolved question that continues to stimulate much debate and legal action. Other important issues concern the desirability of placing all workers on salaried status and the need for secrecy about pay decisions. (Another issue, to be discussed in Chapter 18, is whether the long-term effects of "two-tier" wage scales are beneficial or detrimental in employee relations.)

Comparable   In essence, **comparable worth** is the concept that women should be paid in the
Worth   same rate range as men for work of *comparable* worth, as well as for equal work. Factors that could lead to differences within a pay grade include seniority, quality or quantity of work, or certification or licensing. The fact that jobs held predominantly by women generally pay less than those held predominantly by men has focused attention on the question of whether pay differences among occupations are based on real job worth, or whether they simply reflect a long tradition of sex discrimination. Debate on this question is far from over. It appears that court cases and legislation on this issue are likely to extend the debate through the 1990s. Comparable worth has also become an issue in collective bargaining. For example, in one dispute,

fifteen hundred city workers in San Jose, California, walked off their jobs over the issue.[37] It also motivated a walkout by sixteen hundred technical and clerical employees at Yale University, led by the newly organized Local 34 of the Federation of University Employees.[38]

The comparable worth issue stems in part from the fact that, on average, women are paid less than men. It is estimated that women earn seventy-two cents for each dollar earned by men.[39] Differences in years of labor-force experience and vocational and occupational training can explain close to half the disparity, but a sizable proportion appears to stem from other factors.[40] (See also *Contemporary Issues* on page 000.)

Many explanations for the persistent earnings gap have been put forward. One study found that men and women view the reasons for the disparity very differently. Women are much more likely to attribute the earnings gap to organizational practices, whereas men are much more likely to place the responsibility for the gap on the women themselves.[41] Geraldine Ferraro's explanation is as follows:

> Women's earnings hover at just 60% of men's despite decades of social, legislative, and demographic change.... Women are first channeled into certain sectors of the economy, then they are clustered into the lowest paying occupations within those sectors, and finally they are confined to jobs that, by virtue of being female-dominated, are undervalued and underpaid.[42]

Comparable worth is seen by some as a way of overcoming this gap in earnings. Those who support the concept assert that (1) women have historically been "crowded" into certain occupations through discriminatory practices in society; (2) the labor market reflects this crowding and thus the employment discrimination that caused the crowding; and (3) if the labor market is discriminatory, so too are the pay systems based on it.[43]

Bringing the argument closer to the organization, Helen Remick states:

> The practice of setting wages according to job families (occupation) is a sure way of producing sex-biased results. It is clear that the market place is biased against women; therefore to use the market place as a basis for paying clerical workers less than maintenance workers, for example, is to perpetuate discrimination.[44]

Remick would minimize market effects by relying largely on a single job evaluation system within a given organization. In fact, she defines comparable worth in this way: *"the application of a single bias-free point factor evaluation system within a given establishment, across job families, both to rank-order jobs and to set salaries."*[45] Fairness, according to Remick, would be enhanced by looking for bias in the following areas:

1. *Factors chosen for analysis.* Does the job evaluation system include factors usually associated with women's work (for example, responsibility for people rather than things, literacy, the noise of office machines, or the poor working conditions created by many word processors)?
2. *Factor weights.* Are factors usually associated with women's work always given less weight? Can such differences be justified on bases other than sex?
3. *Application.* The best system in the world can be undone with a biased application. Are your job descriptions bias free, or do men manage and women supervise, men interpret and women use? Are the evaluators sensitive to the full scope of women's jobs?

Contemporary Issues

Wage Gap Closes

The gap between men's and women's salaries is not what it is generally believed to be, says an article in *The American Enterprise* written by economist June O'Neill of the City University of New York's Baruch College. In fact, she says, the difference between the salaries of childless white women and their male counterparts is actually less than 10 percent when such factors as schooling, industry, skill level and work experience are taken into account.

O'Neill says that the gap is larger when the sampling is inclusive of all working women because women entering the workforce before the 1980s tended to have less education and to have delayed working full-time until they were in their 30s. The wage gap, which held even at around 58 percent for more than 30 years — from 1950 to 1981 — has narrowed dramatically in the last decade. O'Neill credits better education, more work experience and less turnover among women with children for narrowing the wage gap in the 1980s. The gap should become even smaller as increasing numbers of well-educated women who began their careers in their 20s — and who have acquired skills and work experience — make up more of the workforce in years ahead.

Source: Reprinted by permission of publisher from *Personnel*, March 1991, © 1991 American Management Association, New York. All rights reserved.

4. *Salary setting*. Is a single salary scale used? If not, do the scales for women's jobs give consistently less return (lower salary) for worth (points)?[46]

Opponents of the comparable worth concept argue that job evaluation does provide a procedure for determining relative job worth, but that there are circumstances in which jobs and their contexts are too dissimilar to use one job evaluation scheme to cover all jobs. In addition, relating labor-market rates to key jobs is a fundamental aspect of using job evaluation to determine wages.[47] According to George Hildebrand,

> Certain jobs are standardized, usually due to technology across many firms in a given local labor market; in fact, they reach across several industries as well. For example, on the blue collar side, there are machinists and millwrights, or computer programmers, secretaries, and accountants on the clerical side. These jobs provide the basis upon which the wage curve can be built, precisely because they tie the external and internal markets together. For these reasons, they are called key jobs.[48]

Donald Treiman emphasizes that the recruitment and retention of employees with different technical or professional skills require attention to quite different labor markets, some local and some national.[49] Further, the argument continues, the way to reduce differences in the pay of men and women is to increase the upward mobility of women into the professional and managerial ranks.

It is uncertain where the arguments will lead; however, federal government action and court decisions have generally rejected the concept of comparable worth. For example, the Equal Employment Opportunity Commission rejected the concept and ruled it would not litigate comparable worth claims,[50] and the U.S. Civil

Service Commission voted five to two to reject the concept as a remedy for pay differentials between men and women.[51] A U.S. circuit court of appeals overturned a district court decision that had previously found the state of Washington discriminating against women by paying them less than men performing jobs of comparable worth.[52] However, the state subsequently agreed to a $482 million settlement with the Washington Federation of State Employees to provide for equity adjustments and to end the prolonged litigation.[53]

The comparable worth concept appears to have more support at the municipal government level. Public unions have succeeded in negotiating settlements in Los Angeles and San Francisco, and pay equity adjustments have been made in Seattle, Chicago, West Hartford, Ann Arbor, Virginia Beach, Sioux City, and elsewhere. Overall, however, the debate appears to be far from over.[54] (See *International Perspective* on page 386 regarding comparable worth in Portugal.)

Wage Versus Salaried Status

In recent years, some firms have placed all employees on salaried status. The change has usually been made because differences between the salaried and wage payroll in such benefit areas as sick-pay eligibility and time off with pay for personal reasons were not great, were irritating to wage employees, and were difficult to justify. Other reasons include the perception by many employees that salaried status carries more prestige and may provide more job security. In many instances management has concluded that the costs of placing workers on salaried status would not be large and that there might be gains in good will and employee relations.

Salaried status does not guarantee job security, however. And although salaried status may carry more prestige, it does not necessarily mean more pay, because many blue-collar workers are paid higher hourly rates than many white-collar workers.

The major problems involved in shifting large groups of employees from wage to salaried status usually relate to changes in employee benefits, as suggested by Table 14.1. Generally, the shift to salaried status means an increase in benefits such as sick leave, major medical insurance, severance pay, group life insurance, time off for personal business, and so forth. Therefore, management must agree on the purposes of such a move and examine the true cost implications carefully. The reaction of those employees already on the salaried payroll must also be considered. If part of their "income" has been higher status and more liberal privileges and benefits than those of the hourly employees, they may react by pressing for higher wages, either individually or through unionization.

Secrecy

The extent to which employees are informed of the details of wage and salary programs varies widely. Most unionized workers are informed through the wage contract about details of their respective wage programs, particularly if single rates are paid for given categories of jobs. In other words, they know exactly how much each fellow employee is being paid. Probably a small percentage of nonunion employees has very accurate knowledge of the specific salaries being paid individuals. About one-third of the companies in one survey, however, provided copies of wage schedules and progression plans pertaining to employees' own job categories, and the other two-thirds made this information available. More than half of the firms provided access to information about wage schedules for job categories other than the employees' own.[55]

International Perspective

Comparable Worth in Portugal

According to the Portuguese Constitution of 1976, "all workers without any distinction of sex are entitled to retribution of labour, according to quantity, nature, and quality, thus observing the principle of equal pay for equal work, in order to ensure a decent living." In 1979, Legislative Decree No. 392/79 extended those constitutional principles by requiring that "equal pay for working men and women for equal work or work of equal value done for the same employer, is ensured." The legislation provides that job descriptions and job evaluations shall be based on objective criteria common to the two sexes. It does not cover work at home and domestic service, the state services, and local authorities.

However, Legislative Decree No. 426/88 deals with the implementation of equal pay and equal treatment in central, regional, and local administration.

Under the Decree, provisions in individual or collective agreements that are contrary to the principle of equal pay are deemed to be null and void. The legislation further provides that a lower (female) rate of remuneration prescribed in a contract or agreement shall be replaced automatically by the higher (male) rate. Penalties are prescribed for breach of Equal Remuneration Provisions.

Source: "Comparable Worth in Industrialized Countries," *Monthly Labor Review* 115 (November 1992):41.

Whether to make the actual salaries paid individuals common knowledge is a controversial matter. An argument against making salary information available is that such information tends to create considerable friction in the organization. Although management may be prepared to defend the overall program, supervisors often have great difficulty justifying the legitimacy of minor differentials between people. Since people are likely to compare their own performance with that of their peers and these judgments can easily differ from those made by supervisors and higher managers, disagreements over relative ranking are bound to occur. Most managers try to minimize this problem — and the time and effort spent dealing with complaints — by maintaining secrecy about salary data. A policy of secrecy also may assume that employees are thus spared unnecessary stress and the behind-the-scenes commiseration that would otherwise occur.

Some research suggests that secrecy about average salaries and salary ranges (not necessarily salaries of individuals) may create dissatisfaction rather than prevent it. One researcher surveyed 563 middle and lower managers in seven organizations and found that they tended (1) to underestimate the salaries of their superiors, (2) to overestimate the salaries of subordinates, and (3) to overestimate the salaries of their peers. Associated with these inaccuracies in perception was dissatisfaction with the differentials among themselves and between themselves and both superiors and subordinates.[56] Other researchers, however, queried 575 professional employees in an organization and found that only about half were willing to have their salaries known to others. This held true by occupational group, by self-assessed performance level, and by age. There was also some tendency for the more highly paid persons to prefer to have salaries kept confidential.[57]

Role of the Human Resources Department

In most organizations, the human resources department plays a major role in wage and salary administration. A survey of 590 responding organizations found that the human resources department in 80 percent of the organizations had sole responsibility for wage and salary administration, and had joint responsibility in most of the other 20 percent.[58]

The human resources department is likely to develop the job evaluation system, perhaps with the help of an outside consultant, and will coordinate and manage the system. This includes making certain that accurate job descriptions are written and having one or more representatives on a job evaluation committee.

As a rule, the human resources department conducts surveys of wages and salaries or participates in surveys the department uses in revising the pay structure. Once top management has approved modification of the overall pay structure, the human resources department typically monitors compliance with that structure and with the rules that have been established. Generally, individual managers make decisions about the pay of subordinates within the framework of wage and salary plans, and the human resources department ensures that the limits are not exceeded and that the spirit and intent of the plans are adhered to.

Summary

Determining wages and salaries is one of the most critical aspects of human resources management, since it has such a profound effect on the recruitment, retention, satisfaction, and motivation of employees. Careful job analysis, job evaluation, and design of the wage and salary structure and rules of administration are crucial to the effective management of organizations.

Job evaluation is the process of determining the relative worth of jobs to the organization. Basically, job evaluation includes gathering information about jobs and then using some kind of scale or scales to develop a hierarchy based on value to the organization. The point-factor method of job evaluation is the most widely used.

Wage and salary surveys are used to establish pay grades, and job evaluation is used to allocate jobs to the different grades. In conducting surveys, care must be taken to assess accurately the scope and responsibilities of the jobs surveyed, since job titles or brief descriptions can be misleading.

Many questions need to be answered in determining the wage structure. Judgments and perceptions about equity, competition in the region or industry, and ability to pay provide partial answers to these questions.

To carry out the philosophy of the compensation system, maintain the integrity of the pay plans, and control costs, it is necessary to develop rules about progression within salary ranges and the movement of jobs into higher pay grades. Merit increases represent the most commonly used form of pay progression. Developing a philosophy about how merit and length of service relate to salary progression and developing procedures for determining relative merit are particularly important matters. One useful cost-control tool is the compa ratio. Some organizations, particularly those that have developed and encouraged self-managed teams, have used the concept of skill-based pay.

Collective bargaining has a major impact on wage structures within organizations and industries. Union leaders have generally been resistant to job evaluation, but there have been notable instances of cooperation in the establishment of job evaluation systems.

At any one time, many variables affect pay-increase decisions. Even if measures of performance are entirely objective, numerous additional forces, both inside and outside the organization, affect these decisions.

Minimum wage legislation and laws that control overtime payments — the Fair Labor Standards Act and the Walsh-Healey Act in particular — need to be adhered to if an organization is to avoid serious penalties. The Equal Pay Act prohibits discrimination in pay for equal work based on sex and is having far-reaching effects. The concept of comparable worth goes beyond the concept of equal pay for equal work and extends to payment within the same rate range for comparable work. How widely this controversial concept should be applied is likely to be a subject of debate, lawsuits and court decisions, and proposed legislation well through the 1990s.

Other issues include whether to place all employees on salaried status and the extent to which wage and salary information should be open or secret.

The human resources department plays a major role in wage and salary administration in most organizations. That department is heavily involved in the job evaluation program, in salary and benefits surveys, in recommending changes in the structure and rules of the compensation program, and in coordinating and monitoring the overall program.

Ethical Dilemma

Mort's interactions with a lot of people, including his boss, are somewhat abrasive. He is a hard worker and an exceptionally high producer, but frequently irritates those around him. The company's merit-rating form suggests that the area of interpersonal relations is only one of six general performance factors that the company considers the most important. Mort's boss rates him low on interpersonal relations and skews his other ratings downward so that Mort is consistently given minimal merit raises. Mort has loudly complained about these raises to both his boss and fellow workers.

Are the ratings Mort receives justified? To what extent is this an ethical problem?

Key Terms

merit	merit pay
wage or hourly pay	wage and salary survey
salary	key job
nonexempt employee	red-circle job
exempt employee	green-circle job
salary compression	rate ranges
job evaluation	across-the-board pay
job factors	increases
job worth	merit-pay plan
point-factor method	skill-based or knowledge-based pay
classification method	compa ratio
pay grade	pay for performance
ranking method	comparable worth

Review Questions

1. What are the goals of an equitable wage and salary program?
2. Discuss the forces influencing the pay structure and pay decisions.
3. Briefly describe methods of job evaluation.
4. Describe how wage and salary surveys are used to affect the compensation structure and pay decisions.
5. Describe what is meant by a merit-pay plan.
6. Discuss the kinds of rules and procedures that are needed to administer a wage and salary program and the reasons for these procedures.
7. Explain how governmental regulation affects wage and salary administration.
8. Define comparable worth and discuss its impact on wage and salary administration.
9. Discuss the pros and cons of secrecy in wage and salary matters.
10. Discuss the role of the human resources department in wage and salary administration.

Opening Case Questions

Case 14.1   Circle O Hamburgers

1. What are some of the questions Bill should ask in determining the extent to which the wage structure is equitable and serving the needs of the organization?
2. What can Bill do about different managers giving widely different pay increases?
3. What can Bill do about the turnover rate?

Case 14.2   Pay Scales in the Laboratory

1. What additional factors besides inflation and performance should Beverly consider in determining pay increases?
2. Should Beverly reward a few "superstars" with large increases and give only modest increases to others?

Comprehensive Case

Models for Skill-based Pay Plans

Skill-based pay schemes can be found in a number of U.S. industries. A recent (1990) study by the American Compensation Association of alternative pay practices showed 33 percent of their study group to have skill-based pay programs. Proctor and Gamble has implemented such plans in some 30 plants, and Polaroid is attempting to become the first corporation to pay virtually all employees through skill-based pay plans. Most companies that implement the programs see the promise of an organization that can better perform its mission with highly trained, flexible, thinking employees rather than a "hired pair of hands."

As an organization works through the strategic and financial implications of skill-based pay, it will inevitably need to come to grips with what the skill-based pay plan will actually look like: How will the variety of jobs be organized into a plan that is fair and workable and meets both employee and organizational needs? This article examines several models for skill-based pay plans and suggests situations in which each might best be implemented.

What Isn't Skill-Based Pay

Most larger organizations already have a job hierarchy that rates level of job responsibility within a job family. The most common example is the movement from apprentice to journeyman in many of the trades. Other examples might be ratings of positions such as secretarial/clerical, chemist, maintenance and support services.

Strictly speaking, such hierarchies are not skill-based pay programs, although they may have much the same purpose. Rather, they address the scope of a single job and compensate the employee accordingly, often as a promotion as they grow within the job. This model assumes one fairly complex job requiring substantial training or experience and a continuum of levels of proficiency that are definable. For example:

- Chemist I — Can do basic setup of standard test procedures and conduct basic tests accurately and efficiently.
- Chemist II — In addition to above, can calibrate equipment and conduct all advanced tests.
- Chemist III — In addition to above, can design and evaluate new testing procedures, provide training for new staff and diagnose and repair equipment.

Skill-based pay programs, by contrast, usually include a number of less complex, more discrete jobs. Some additive formula for mastering a number of different jobs is what constitutes the individual's pay grade. In other words, pay is based on the employee's knowledge of how to do different jobs rather than on the scope of a defined job or even how well the employee performs a job. (Merit pay plans, however, are quite compatible with skill-based pay plans because pay ranges or matrixes can be established for each skill level.)

Here are some models for skill-based pay programs:

The Stair-Step Model

This model is helpful when a small number of significantly different full-time jobs exist. The jobs may vary in terms of skill or complexity, and a fairly logical learning progression can be defined from entry level to more complex jobs, which make the "steps."

The jobs constituting each step are clearly defined. Each step may be similar in relative difficulty, or each step may become increasingly difficult. If difficulty among steps varies, so, proportionally, will the percentage of increase in compensation. The highest paid employee will typically have mastered all of the jobs and be available to perform any of them as needed. A five-step example is as follows:

TABLE C.1 Relative-point rating system

JOB EXAMPLE: LENS TECH

1 point	Image system, optics, cleaning, final cleaning, lap mounting, dismounting.	
2 points	Calculation, base curve hogging.	
4 points	Flange polish, base curve polish, surface inspection, radioscope, front curve blocking, cutdown.	
5 points	Base curve fine cut, OZ polish, auto edger, dry thickness Rx, loupe and candle.	
7 points	Beveling, front curve fine cut.	
8 points	Hand polish, power change, hand beveling, hand edging.	

The Job Levels Might Then Become:

Lens Tech I	0 to 5 points
Lens Tech II	6 to 12 points
Lens Tech III	13 to 22 points
Lens Tech IV	23 to 35 points

- Assembly Tech I — Functions in one or more of the following jobs: pallet breakdown, line restocking, burr removal and line jockey.

- Assembly Tech II — Has mastered all of the above jobs.

- Assembly Tech III — Has additionally mastered the jobs of major assembly, soldering, acid bath and final inspection.

- Assembly Tech IV — Has additionally mastered the jobs of government spec., soldering, component assembly, setup and preventive maintenance.

- Assembly Tech V — Has additionally mastered the jobs of test equipment calibration, acid bath setup, MIS input, auditing and training.

Applications for this model are manufacturing operations, especially cells, and complex distribution or receiving functions, among others.

The Skill Blocks Model

Similar to the stair-step model, this model also groups jobs. However, job progression need not be linear. An employee would usually begin in an entry-level grouping or "skill block" of jobs, but further progression to mastering other blocks might be determined by the needs of the organization as well as the employee's interests and abilities.

In the following example, after mastering the A block, an employee could then begin learning any of the B blocks. After mastering a B block, the employee could then move to other B blocks or the C block. An employee's compensation would be greater for mastering a C block because it is more difficult than the B blocks.

- A block (entry level) — Molding: operates molding machine and performs molding machine set up function.

- B blocks (more difficult) — Finishing: operates finishing machine and performs finishing machine setup function.
  Inspection: operates both inspection machines and makes rework/scrap decisions.
  Packaging: operates packaging equipment and performs inventory and shipping functions.

- C block (most difficult) — Quality control: performs quality control functions and operates MIS input.

Because of the variable ways in which employees may progress, job levels may not be feasible, as they are in the stair-step model. Rather, percentage increases are usually more easily administered. For example, from an entry-level wage, an employee might earn a 3 percent increase

TABLE C.2 Skill/performance pay matrix

	PERFORMANCE RATING			
SKILL LEVEL	Needs to improve	Solid performer	Exceeds standards	Always superior
1	$4.40	$4.62	$4.85	$5.09
2	$4.62	$4.85	$5.09	$5.35
3	$4.85	$5.09	$5.35	$5.61
4	$5.09	$5.35	$5.61	$5.90
5	$5.35	$5.61	$5.90	$6.19

for each B block and an 8 percent increase for mastering the C block.

The Job-Point Accrual Model

In some organizations, a wide variety of jobs exists, too many for most employees to master fully. In addition, the jobs may vary widely in difficulty and importance to the organization's goals. In such a situation, the job-point accrual model is quite useful. The varied jobs are given a relative-point rating based on organizational criteria such as value added to the product, learning difficulty, performance difficulty, impact on quality, physical demand, use of judgment and so on. The sum of the points for each job that is mastered then places the employee in his or her pay grade. For example, jobs might be rated as shown in Table C.1.

Learning all jobs is simply not feasible, especially if the employee is to retain enough skill in each of the learned jobs to function near standard.

The School-Curriculum Model

This model is somewhat like the stair-step model except that each step has some set and some varied requirements. For efficient functioning of the operation, some jobs will be "key," for most employees to master, while other "elective" jobs may only need to be mastered by a few employees. Therefore, each step has some required jobs and some elective jobs. A simplified example might be:

- Tech I — Training on key jobs A and B and an elective job.
- Tech II — Mastery of key jobs A and B and one elective job.

- Tech III — Mastery of key jobs A, B and C and three elective jobs.
- Tech IV — Mastery of key jobs, A, B, C, D and E and five elective jobs.
- Tech V — Mastery of key jobs A, B, C, D and E and seven elective jobs; trains new employees.

The Cross-Departmental Model

Often a small organization — perhaps at a remote site — has several small departments that function independently and have substantially different jobs. In this case, it can be helpful if employees from one department are able to "float out" and assist for extended periods of time in other departments because of work flow or unexpected staffing shortages. The following example might be for a small or remote site that has four departments: production, quality assurance, customer service and shipping/receiving.

- Grades 1, 2 and 3 — Can perform jobs within a department, according to a skill-based pay model.
- Grade 4 — Has mastered jobs in own department and can float to one other department.
- Grade 5 — Has mastered jobs in own department and can float to two other departments.
- Grade 6 — Has mastered jobs in own department and can float to any other department.

Skill Level/Performance Matrix

This model combines one of the above skill level models with the employee's performance rating to designate salary level. It requires, in addition to the skill-based pay system, a fairly objective performance rating system that can be summarized as a single rating. Table C.2 is an example of the matrix.

Interestingly, pay could actually go down from time to time if an employee's skill level stayed the same but his or her performance rating declined.

Issues to Be Addressed

A number of issues will need to be thoughtfully addressed as the specific model is developed. These include:

- How long it will take an employee to move between steps?
- Will the steps be large or small or even vary?
- How do you certify that an employee has actually achieved a step?
- What will the costs be over time?
- Will the organization provide the time and resources for increased cross training.

Any skill-based pay plan will need to be custom designed for the particular organization, taking into account such variables as culture, past pay practices, union contracts and so on. It is also

quite feasible that different models may be used in the same organization. Perhaps none of these models will exactly fit an organization's needs, but thoughtful planning and participative management can effectively modify one or more of these models.

Successful programs rely upon the individuals who are actually doing the work to contribute to the program's development. Based on the experience of an increasing number of companies, however, a well-designed skill-based pay plan will improve employee satisfaction and motivation, and, in effect, compensate employees more effectively for their contributions to the organization.

Source: "Models for Skill-based Pay Plans" by Richard L. Bunning, *HR Magazine* February 1992 vol. 37. Reprinted with the permission of HRMagazine (formerly Personnel Administrator) published by the Society for Human Resource Management, Alexandria, VA.

Discussion Questions

1. What is skills-based pay?
2. What is the difference between the job-point accrual model of skills-based pay and the point-factor method of job evaluation?

CHAPTER 15

Incentive Plans

LEARNING OBJECTIVES

- Outline various incentive plans used to motivate production workers, sales personnel, and professional and managerial employees on an individual basis.
- Discuss the problems associated with individual incentive plans.
- Describe the conditions under which group incentive plans are particularly effective.
- List the objectives of productivity gainsharing and profit-sharing plans.
- Describe the suggestion plan system and indicate some of the problems involved in implementing such plans.
- Identify the incentives that may be used in a positive reinforcement program.

CASE 15.1   Do We Need Incentives?

George Sims, production manager at HiQuality Furniture Manufacturing, had just come back from his quarterly meeting with the production department employees. There had been seventy-two people there, including George's assistant, the six supervisors, and the three clerical assistants. At the meeting, George had given his usual pep talk about the importance of maintaining quality, decreasing the number of rejected parts, and working more efficiently to raise production. He had also told the group that the company wasn't in bad shape, but profits and HiQuality's share of the market were slipping some. His remarks had prompted a few questions, but no one had offered any concrete suggestions for improving the department's performance. By and large, apathy had characterized the meeting, and that apathy was disturbing.

George believed that the employees generally liked and trusted him, but he could also sense their lack of enthusiasm for really getting down to work and improving things. "I wonder whether we need an incentive system of some kind," he thought. "Maybe we should give people a bonus for turning out components at a rate above some standard. As it is, everyone in the same job classification gets the same pay, and there's no real incentive to do an outstanding job. I think I'll get the supervisors in here and toss around the idea of an incentive plan with them."

When George met with the supervisors, he found general agreement that people were not working up to capacity but no suspicions that they were deliberately goldbricking. A lively discussion followed his proposal to introduce an incentive plan that would reward highly productive workers with extra pay. Several supervisors felt an incentive plan would be a good idea, but one commented, "We'll have nothing but bickering with the union if we go that route. They'll argue about every standard, and getting them ever to raise a standard will be like pulling teeth." Another supervisor remarked, "When I worked for Mountain View Furniture, workers played incredible games to beat the system. They even constructed a bin under the floor where they hid finished pieces to pull out when someone got behind. No one ever figured out how they built that bin and the trap door without being seen."

But another supervisor said, "Yes, but at Furniture Tech they've got a plantwide incentive system, and everyone is making at least 50 percent more than we're making here, including the supervisors. I understand they spend a lot of their time in meetings, though."

Those remarks prompted discussion and joking about whether supervisors should be included in the incentive system and comments like, "Who needs more meetings?" One of the young, new supervisors then said, "Yeah, but if people go to meetings to figure out how to work smarter, maybe that's not so dumb. . . ."

The meeting concluded with George saying, "Thanks for your ideas. We'd better get more information on incentive plans and then talk some more. I can see this is a more complicated issue than I thought." ◀

CASE 15.2   The Bonus Is Coming out of Our Hides

The administrator of Vistaview Hospital, a proprietary hospital in the foothills of the Rockies, had recently started a bonus system for department heads, providing them with quarterly bonuses based on cost savings within individual departments.

The administrator was thinking of extending the system to all employees if it worked well with department heads, but he had kept the idea to himself, not wanting to raise expectations and then disappoint people if the system didn't work out.

Sue and Al, members of the surgical nursing staff, were eating lunch in the hospital cafeteria with three other members of the surgical unit. Sue was usually cheerful and positive, but today it was clear that she was unhappy. Considerable resentment showed in her tone.

"What do you think of the department-head bonus system, Al?" she inquired. She didn't wait for an answer but went on to say, with some heat, "I think the department-head bonuses are coming out of our hides. We work harder and save money for the hospital, and then the department head gets a bonus. To top it all off, now they're going to lay off one of the new nurses in a cost-cutting move. It'll be whoever has the least seniority."

Al sighed, "It doesn't sit very well with me, either. I can see why we have to get costs down. But it seems to me we're all in the same boat. I felt better about cooperating in cost reduction before the administrator started the bonus system. Now it seems as if it's the department heads' cost-reduction program, not ours. Makes me feel like a lackey. My wife says I should bring it up at the next department meeting. But that puts me in the position of appearing greedy."

"So it's okay for the department heads to be greedy, but not us, eh?" Sue responded. "I'll tell you what it makes me feel like doing — I just won't mention some ideas I have for reducing costs. It looks as if all we'll get for our efforts is more work and some folks losing their jobs."

"I agree," said Al. "Maybe we should check around, and if others feel the same way, we should bring the matter up when the administrator meets with the staff next week. He's a good sort, and probably we should give him a chance to extend the program to everyone before we try to kill it. How do the rest of you see it?" ◀

Incentive plans provide financial or nonfinancial rewards to employees who make substantial contributions to organizational effectiveness. There are many kinds of incentive plans, offering various rewards on different bases. Some plans tie rewards to the output of individual employees; others reward the productivity of groups; still others are based on the overall profitability of the organization. But the common purpose of all incentive plans is to encourage employees to achieve specific organizational goals, such as increasing profits, lowering costs, raising productivity, improving product quality, and so on. Some organizations have two or more incentive plans operating simultaneously, such as an individual bonus scheme plus an organization-wide profit-sharing plan.

The opening cases illustrate some of the challenges and problems associated with the use of incentive plans. On the one hand, it seems reasonable to try to motivate workers by offering rewards for exceptional performance, as George Sims suggested in Case 15.1 and the hospital administrator attempted in Case 15.2. On the other hand, there are real difficulties in implementing this idea in an equitable and manageable fashion. Among the considerations involved are these:

- What incentives should be offered to encourage higher productivity and performance? That is, to what extent does higher pay guarantee greater output?

- Can nonfinancial rewards encourage desired performance? If leadership style shifts toward praise and recognition for superior performance, will the rewards be adequate in the long run if profits increase?

- How will productivity and quality be measured?

- Will cooperation and productive relationships among workers and groups be threatened by the reward system? (In Case 15.2, the bonus system for department heads was beginning to lessen cooperation between the nursing staff and the department head.)

- How will traditional pay differentials between supervisors and employees be affected if employees can earn extra pay for producing more? (In Case 15.1, there was some joking among the supervisors about what would happen to their compensation; that joking was probably masking a real issue.)

- Is there sufficient trust between management and workers to implement an incentive system? Will the plan be viewed positively by employees, or will they perceive it as pressure to work harder without a corresponding increase in compensation?

The motivation-performance-satisfaction relationship shown in Figure 5.3 (Chapter 5) provides a convenient way of thinking about the potential value of incentive systems as well as some potential drawbacks. If, under an incentive plan, more pay is desired (positive valence) and there is a high expectancy that extra effort will lead to higher performance and, in turn, to higher reward, motivation is likely to be high. Satisfaction is a likely outcome.

If, on the other hand, employees mistrust management and fear a work speedup, in which there is pressure to work harder to meet ever-rising standards without a corresponding increase in compensation, motivation under an incentive plan and employee satisfaction are likely to be low. Similarly, if employees fear that increased productivity will reduce the number of employees needed and thus result in layoffs (an outcome with a negative valence) or that management will reap most of the benefits (lack of perceived equity), motivation and satisfaction will be low. Under these circumstances, incentive plans do not meet individual needs and goals, and group norms will develop in opposition to such plans. Resistance may be overt, as through a union, or it may take covert and subtle forms, such as the withholding of cooperation.

These and other issues will be explored in this chapter, which focuses on the purposes, limitations, and benefits of a variety of incentive plans found in organizations today. The chapter begins with an overview of commonly used incentive systems, examines the rapidly growing use of productivity gainsharing plans, explores profit sharing, and then offers a look at suggestion plans and positive reinforcement programs. The chapter also discusses external influences on incentive plans, various factors that affect the choice of an incentive system for a particular organization, and the role of the human resources department in managing the system selected.

The four major types of incentive plans considered in this chapter are individual incentive plans, group incentive plans, productivity gainsharing plans, and profit-sharing plans (see Figure 15.1). All are variable pay systems. **Variable pay** is defined as "compensation, other than base wages or salaries, in which payment fluctuates according to some standard."[1] Merit pay (discussed in Chapter 14) is not variable in the sense that merit increases are simply added to an employee's base pay and remain a permanent part of the person's regular compensation. An exception is when base pay is reduced, but this is not common.

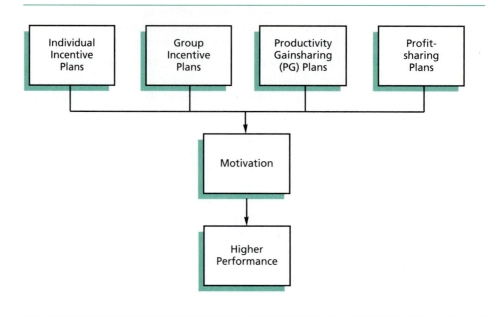

FIGURE 15.1   Four major types of incentive plans tie financial rewards to performance

Individual Incentive Plans

Reward systems tied to the performance of individual employees are known as **individual incentive plans**. These plans take several forms, depending on the category of workers for which they are designed. In most cases, a certain pay rate is guaranteed, and the rewards represent additional compensation.

Incentives for Production Workers   Individual incentive plans for production workers typically offer additional financial compensation to those employees who produce work over and above a specified quantity and/or quality. When properly designed, these plans can contribute to organizational efficiency by raising worker productivity and lowering the production cost of each unit. Such plans are intended to *assist* in increasing efficiency, however, not to accomplish it alone. In manufacturing, for example, incentive plans are often designed in conjunction with acceptable changes in work methods to sustain efficiencies gained through time-and-motion studies or through work simplification. In other words, some job-design strategies can be used to organize tasks more efficiently or to simplify them, and the incentive system is designed to motivate the worker to use the more efficient methods. (Some job-design strategies, as we discussed in Chapter 7, are aimed at creating more meaningful and challenging jobs and to be intrinsically more motivating.)

One incentive system traditionally used with production workers is the **piece-rate plan** (or piecework plan), in which compensation is based on the number of units produced. In most piece-rate plans, the worker is guaranteed a *base rate*, or minimum hourly wage that assumes a certain rate of production, and is paid extra for production above that rate. Under straight piece-rate plans, the worker is paid an additional set amount for each unit produced above the standard. Under **differential piece-rate plans,** the worker who exceeds standard production is compensated at a higher rate for all work than workers who satisfy only the minimum standard. For either type of plan, base rates are often determined through job evaluation and wage surveys, whereas production standards are frequently established by time-and-motion studies.

Under **production-bonus** incentive systems, workers who surpass minimum production standards are given a bonus payment based on cost savings associated with higher productivity. An example is the **standard-hour plan,** under which "standard time" for completing a particular job or task is established. The worker is paid the standard rate even when he or she completes the job in less than standard time. For example, if the standard time for a particular job is nine hours, and an employee completes it in six hours, the employee's earnings are still nine times the hourly rate.[2]

Another type of individual incentive plan is the **measured day-rate plan**. Under this plan, employees are rated every two or three months on several factors, such as productivity, quality of work, dependability, and versatility. If rated high, they may make as much as 20 percent above the current pay rate. This merit rating fixes the wage until the next merit rating, when the individual's pay may be raised or lowered. This plan differs from typical merit-rating plans in that it gives significantly greater weight to productivity, and wages can be reduced if the rating falls.[3]

Overall, individual incentive plans for production workers are declining in use.[4] Some of the reasons are considered under "Problems" further in this section. An additional reason is that productivity gainsharing (PG) plans, also discussed in this chapter, are gaining in popularity.

Incentives for Sales Personnel

Sales-pay plans featuring **commissions,** or bonuses based on the number of items or dollar volume sold, can also be considered individual incentive plans. One study of nearly sixteen hundred firms found that 70 percent paid sales personnel some combination of salary and commission.[5] Most stockbrokers and many real estate agents are paid solely on a commission basis.[6]

One of the advantages of commission payments is that they tend to be tied to revenues and profits. Presumably, they stimulate both, but when a firm is faced with a recession, a commission system automatically allows it to lower its costs. The main disadvantage to employees on a straight commission, of course, is that their standard of living is less secure than if they were paid a base salary.

Incentives for Managerial and Professional Employees

Performance bonuses of some kind are the most frequently used incentive plans for management and exempt employees. The details vary greatly from company to company. For example, bonuses may be allocated on the basis of an overall judgment about a manager's or a professional's contribution, or end-of-year bonuses may be allocated on the basis of the extent to which the person attains the objectives agreed on at the beginning of the year under an MBO plan.

Spot bonuses are cash awards for extraordinary achievement or performance. They are given on a more spontaneous basis and are usually intended to award individual performance that is not regularly recognized in other ways. In one study of 191 companies, 26 percent used spot bonuses. Unlike more traditional bonus plans that focus on managerial and professional employees, workers in most categories tend to be eligible for awards under spot-bonus plans. Sales employees are somewhat less likely to be included, presumably because they are already being paid on a commission basis.[7]

Bonuses as one-time payments rather than as additions to the base salary are gradually gaining acceptance. One advantage of such bonuses is that they do not further inflate a salary structure if it is decided that the structure is too high. A disadvantage, quickly seen by employees, is that bonuses do not increase benefits such as pensions and insurance, which are usually tied to salary level.[8]

Another form of incentive is the **stock option.** Under such a plan, the executive, manager, or professional is granted the right to buy a certain number of shares of the company's stock at a given price and by a specified date. The number of shares allocated is determined by an appraisal of the person's performance. If the value of the stock goes up substantially over the predetermined price, the person can make a significant profit when the option is exercised. If the stock price goes down, the option is not exercised.

Breaking with the tradition of reserving stock options for executives, in 1991 Merck & Co., Inc., gave each of its 37,000 employees a one-time option to purchase a hundred shares of Merck's common stock at $127.25 a share. The stock can be purchased after September 6, 1996. Other companies that have extended stock options to all employees are PepsiCo, Inc., which gave the options in 1989 and says it was the first company to do so; Wendy's International; Du Pont; and Waste Management.[9]

One version of the stock option takes the form of **stock appreciation rights (SARs).** Under an SAR plan, an executive can relinquish the right to purchase the stock and receive an amount equal to the increased value of the stock from the date the stock option was granted.[10]

In recent years, there has been substantial criticism of executive incentive plans on the grounds that most focus on short-term rather than long-term results. For example, one study found 85 percent of the responding firms rewarding executives on the basis of growth in earnings per share of the company's stock. Earnings-per-share growth, however, does not necessarily correlate with stock-price growth.[11] Earnings per share can easily be manipulated in the short term — for example, by cutting back on research and development or by selling assets — in ways that do not contribute to the long-term success of the organization.[12] As a result, many corporations have established incentive systems that reward executives on the basis of return on equity and growth.

Employee Recognition Programs

Many organizations have programs to honor outstanding achievement that tend to place more emphasis on recognition than on financial awards. Many, however, include cash awards or other prizes, including travel. To illustrate, the Science & Technology Division of Unocal Corporation holds an annual Creativity Week in which the division recognizes those scientists who have been unusually creative. Creativity Week features award ceremonies, panel discussions, seminars, and placing the names of those recognized on an "Inventors Wall of Fame." Recipients of awards receive a plaque and a cash award.[13]

Not all recognition programs have totally positive aspects. For example, "Employee of the Month" programs that feature a placard and picture of the current "winner" may simultaneously be creating a number of "losers," according to author Aubrey Daniels. Furthermore, even the "winner" may be uncomfortable about this particular form of recognition. Instead, Daniels argues, organizations should seek to find ways to create "many winners instead of just one."[14]

Problems   Problems in the use of individual incentive plans are numerous. Several have already been mentioned: the financial insecurity associated with straight commissions; the fact that executive bonuses frequently reward short-term rather than long-term performance; and employee resistance based on fear of a work speedup or of layoffs stemming from higher productivity. (In Case 15.2, nursing staff members were concerned about layoffs being an outcome of the department head bonus plan.) Employees will resist the incentive plan unless they are convinced that the system works for them and not against them. This means the system must be explained as carefully as it is designed.

Dissension can occur if workers' take-home pay under an incentive plan exceeds that of their supervisors. This can happen if the supervisors are not included in the incentive plan, or if an adequate differential is not provided between the employee incentive plan and the supervisory pay plan.

Establishing Reward Standards   One of the most difficult problems is establishing standards to determine what amount of productivity or what level of performance should be rewarded. No matter how skilled and fair the person or committee establishing the standards may be, standards always involve value judgments. In setting standards for production jobs, for instance, opinions will differ on what rate of output should be considered average or normal, and results of time-and-motion studies cannot be considered 100 percent reliable. The problem of establishing standards is even more complex for professional and managerial jobs, in which output is less easily measured and evaluations of individual performance tend to be more subjective.

Electronic Monitoring   A growing number of firms are measuring productivity with computer or other work monitoring, which is much faster and more accurate than time-and-motion studies using a stopwatch. One such firm is Equitable Life Assurance Society of the United States, where the standard for processing a simple claim has been 6.5 minutes.[15] To date, computer or other electronic monitoring is not commonly used in connection with most incentive systems, but some organizations use it to provide objective measures for merit-pay decisions. The danger is that monitoring may be perceived as a repressive and overly controlling system; in turn, this can damage morale and lower performance, especially if production standards are unreasonable. Further, computer or other electronic monitoring can result in emphasizing speed or quantity over quality. Bell Canada, Federal Express Corp., and Northwest Airlines are among a number of companies that have ceased electronic monitoring of performance for this reason.[16]

There are also some legal risks in monitoring performance by electronic means, particularly if the surveillance is hidden. Video cameras, microphones, and computer programs can measure productivity without detection, but the employer runs the risk of both civil suits and criminal charges for this invasion of privacy. Such risks are in addition to those of decreased trust and morale levels in the organization.[17] (See also Chapter 19.) Besides, there is some evidence that employees who work on computer terminals and whose performance is electronically monitored may have a higher incidence of both physical and psychological ailments than non-monitored employees.[18]

Nonperformance Variables   Other problems with individual incentive plans may arise when forces over which the employee has no control affect productivity or performance. For example, production workers will resent pay reductions for lower output caused by machine breakdown, defective raw materials, and so forth. Salespeople will resent low commissions when sales decline because of ineffective advertising, inferior manufacturing, or a downturn in the economy. Productivity on some jobs is so much a function of variables other than individual performance that individual incentive systems may not be applicable at all.

Beating or Manipulating the System   Other problems arise from the understandable tendency of the worker to try to "beat the system" — that is, to get the system to pay off in the rewards the worker wants. For example, unless standards of cooperation and quality are built into the system, some employees may attempt to maximize earnings at the expense of quality or service, or at the expense of other workers' production. A salesclerk may "push" easy-to-sell items that may not be the most profitable ones. Moreover, incentives tied directly to output do not guarantee consistently high production rates. Workers may, for instance, perform rapidly at times and then hide surplus production to cover periods when they wish to slow down or when machines are being set up or repaired. (See Case 15.1, where the example of workers hiding finished pieces of furniture illustrates this situation.) Or, while engineers are studying the job, a worker may deliberately slow down in order to obtain a low standard that will later yield a large bonus when it is exceeded. Reducing output because of group pressures and fears that standards will be raised has been extensively documented over the years.[19] In still another scenario, employees may postpone handling difficult customer complaints until a day comes along when they are ahead of their assigned quota, thus reducing the quality of customer service.[20]

Damage to customer relations — at least temporarily — occurred at Sears, Roebuck and Co.'s auto center apparently because of the way an incentive system was being misused by employees. According to media accounts, a commission system for auto center employees and pressure on center managers to increase sales led to extensive selling of unneeded parts to customers. Investigations in several states, including California, Illinois, and New York, led to Sears agreeing to pay some $15 million to settle charges.[21] In an "Open Letter to Sears Customers" published in various newspapers, Sears announced that "We have eliminated incentive compensation and goal-setting systems for automotive service advisors.... We have replaced these practices with a non-commission program.... Rewards will now be based on customer satisfaction."[22]

Managerial and professional employees have devised their own ways of beating or manipulating the system. For example, when bonuses are tied to the achievement of specific objectives like those in an MBO system, there may be a tendency to set one's objective fairly low in order to obtain a large bonus rather easily. The type of bonus system can also affect the accounting procedures executives use. If the bonus plan is related to profits and has an upper limit, executives are inclined to choose accounting procedures that carry over profits until the executive needs them to sustain his or her income.[23]

Another example of an incentive bonus system for professionals that produced unintended results comes from a large bank. To maximize their bonuses, employees in the loan department at Chase Manhattan Bank built up a huge portfolio with a high-risk borrower that subsequently defaulted on interest payments.[24] This problem could have been avoided if the incentive system had been designed to reward employees for the *quality* of the loans they made, not just their dollar value.

It is natural for workers at all levels to want to maximize personal outcomes under an incentive system — in a sense, that is why incentives are offered in the first place. But an effectively designed incentive system will protect organizational interests by providing safeguards against potential abuse.

Group Incentive Plans

Most **group incentive plans** for production workers are individual plans applied to small groups of workers. Piece-rate compensation is the most prevalent group incentive, but commissions and production bonuses can also be applied to groups. In general, the purpose of group incentive plans is to encourage the teamwork and cooperation needed to attain high productivity or performance. Group plans are particularly appropriate where several employees must work together to perform a single task and where the contributions of particular individuals are difficult to measure. (Group plans are frequently used in total quality management programs — see Chapter 21 — and have advantages over individual merit pay, as shown in *Contemporary Issues* on page 404.)

An example of a successful group incentive plan is that agreed on by Crown Zellerbach Corp. and the International Woodworkers of America to compensate loggers in Washington and Oregon. Under the plan, logging crews have been compensated as a group on a piece-rate basis. Pay has been based on how much wood the crew cuts and hauls to the mill each day, measured in cubic feet. The new incentive system was accompanied by certain changes in work methods and greater worker

Viking freight's incentive compensation program utilizes production bonuses to reward employees for superior performance and achievement of corporate objectives.

Contemporary Issues

Why Group Variable Pay Is the Best Way to Link Pay to Quality

Group Variable Pay

- Rewards teamwork and collaboration.
- Encourages communication.
- Encourages group to improve systems.

- Makes meaningful quality outcome measures the group measures.
- Encourages focus on "bigger picture."
- Increases flexibility; ability to respond to changing needs.
- Requires re-earning each performance period.

Individual Merit Pay

- Can create internal competition for pay raises.
- Can encourage withholding of information.
- Encourages individuals to try to improve systems on their own, which is very difficult to accomplish.
- Uses individual quality outcome measures, which are difficult to develop meaningfully.
- Encourages micro focus.
- Decreases flexibility.
- Becomes an annuity.

Source: Patricia K. Zingheim and Jay R. Schuster, "Linking Quality and Pay," *HRMagazine* 37 (December 1992):56. Reprinted with permission of *HRMagazine* published by teh Society for Human Resource Management, Alexandria, VA.

---

participation in decision making and problem solving. Each crew was given the freedom to set its own hours and allocate tasks to maximize productivity. (For example, older workers could be assigned to less strenuous tasks.) A few months after the incentive system was implemented, management reported that many employees were making more money and that some fifty jobs had been saved as a result of increased productivity. Moreover, workers participated in local labor-management committees that tackled issues of safety and quality. A strong emphasis on safety is particularly important for both the company and the union when an incentive system is used in a hazardous industry.[25]

Group incentive plans — and individual incentive plans, too — tend to be practical for production workers when some or all of the following conditions are present:

1. Units of production are readily measured.
2. Handling or processing by workers is a major determinant of productivity.
3. Time-and-motion study or work simplification can increase job efficiency, and the company employs experts in these specialties.
4. Technological changes affecting jobs are relatively infrequent.
5. Competition requires better predictability of unit labor costs.
6. Close supervision is impractical.
7. Employees trust management not to change standards arbitrarily.

Many successful high-tech firms use some form of group incentive system for research and development teams. For example, such incentives might be provided to a team that makes a scientific breakthrough, obtains a new patent, or reaches an important milestone. To illustrate, one Silicon Valley firm provides division managers with a pool of money that can be allocated to various research and development teams, depending on their relative contribution to the company, and based partly on confidential peer ratings.[26]

Productivity Gainsharing Plans

More and more companies are offering incentives based on the productivity of the organization or a plant as a whole. These incentives, frequently called **productivity gainsharing (PG) plans,** attempt to stimulate production efficiency by allowing employees to share in overall labor- and production-cost savings through periodic bonus payments. Broad employee participation is a feature of many PG plans. Typically, workers participate in committees that develop and process suggestions about various production matters, such as work methods, equipment and materials, scrap reduction, plant layout, and so on.

PG plans are applicable to a wide variety of industries in addition to manufacturing. For example, PG plans have been developed in the transportation and restaurant industries and in the federal government.[27]

The type of PG plan most frequently found is a hybrid version of one or more of the plans described below. A study of 223 goods-producing and service firms using gainsharing plans found 43 percent using a customized plan, 22 percent using Improshare, and 15 percent using the Scanlon Plan.[28]

Improshare   One of the newest and most popular PG plans is **Improshare.** It was developed by Mitchell Fein, who incorporated into the plan certain refinements of more traditional individual and plantwide incentive systems. Improshare focuses on the number of hours saved for a given number of units produced by subtracting from the hours allotted for those units the hours it actually took to produce them. The savings realized by producing the units in a shorter than expected time are then shared by the firm and the worker. The plan has been adopted by such firms as Firestone Tire & Rubber Co., Rockwell International Corp., Stanley Home Products, and McGraw-Edison.[29]

Improshare differs from most PG plans in that participative procedures such as production committees and consideration of employee suggestions for improving efficiency are optional. For this reason, executives and union officials who place less value on employee participation but are nevertheless interested in increasing efficiency may find Improshare an appropriate incentive system. For the plan to succeed in a unionized firm, however, some minimum level of trust and cooperation must exist between management and labor.

The Scanlon   The **Scanlon plan** is a well-known gainsharing plan that not only allows but also re-
Plan   quires extensive participation. The plan is based on a ratio of labor costs to productivity. When labor costs decline in relation to productivity, the employees are entitled to a share of the savings through bonus payments. When labor costs do not

go down, of course, there are no savings to share. Ordinarily, all employees benefit from cost savings, including production, clerical, sales, and supervisory personnel.

The Scanlon plan is distinguished by its emphasis on union-management cooperation and committee participation by employees at all levels. (In fact, the originator of the plan, Joseph Scanlon, would not institute the plan without union consent and participation.) A production committee in each department, whose members include union-elected or appointed representatives and supervisors, meets regularly to discuss ways of increasing production and to evaluate suggestions from employees for improving efficiency. These suggestions are referred for further consideration to a company-wide screening committee consisting of union officials and top management.[30]

Other PG Plans   Other group incentive and participation systems paying bonuses for cost savings are the Rucker Share-of-Production Plan and the Kaiser-Steel Union Sharing Plan. The Rucker plan is similar to the Scanlon plan, but its bonus payments are based on a more complex analysis, including an "economic engineering audit" of operations for several preceding years. Under the Kaiser plan, savings in labor, supplies, or materials stemming from increased efficiency are shared with employees.[31]

The Lincoln Incentive Compensation Plan of the Lincoln Electric Company combines the features of plant-wide productivity plans, group incentive plans, and individual piece-rate plans. At Lincoln Electric, individual workers are compensated on a piece-rate basis, but employees work together on productivity committees to explore ways to lower costs and increase profitability. Each employee is rated by superiors on quality and quantity of production, and a bonus is calculated accordingly. The typical worker's take-home pay is about double that for similar jobs in competitive firms. This plan is coupled with other benefits, including guaranteed lifetime employment and an employee stock ownership program.[32]

Spot gainsharing (SGS) plans are productivity gainsharing plans with a fixed time frame and adapted to solving specific problems. SGS plans have been used, for example, to solve serious backlog problems without adding employees. Once the backlog problem has been solved, or the expiration data reached, the plan is terminated.[33]

Problems   Workers' lack of understanding or willingness to focus on production problems can cause serious difficulties under participative PG plans. Effective communication by both management and the union and the involvement of middle management in participative procedures are also essential to the success of these plans. A particularly sensitive problem with the administration of these plans is the opportunity given workers or union officials to criticize management in any area. Unless criticism is given and accepted in a constructive manner, relationships between workers and management may deteriorate seriously.[34]

In general, the success of most PG plans seems to depend on the following factors:

1. Top management and top union-leadership support
2. Mutual trust among management, union, and employees
3. Careful planning and installation to ensure both understanding and acceptance
4. Sincere and diligent efforts by all parties to make the plan work
5. Extensive and real participation by employees, union officials, supervisors, and other managers at all levels, and assumption by all parties of the responsibilities that accompany constructive and cooperative problem solving

6. An emphasis on teamwork and sharing of information at all levels

7. Workers who try to work smarter, not faster, and who press for better planning and more efficient management[35]

Profit-Sharing Plans

A **profit-sharing plan** is an incentive system in which some portion of the organization's earnings is distributed to employees to supplement their usual wages or salaries. Generally, the purpose of these plans is to motivate employees to contribute to organizational profitability. Profit-sharing plans may also be used to encourage cooperation, boost morale, and increase employees' financial security. The profit-sharing plans of a particular organization may include all employees or may cover only a selected group of top executives and managerial personnel.

Types of Plans   There are three types of profit-sharing plans: (1) current-distribution, or cash, plans, (2) deferred-distribution plans, and (3) combined plans that involve both current and deferred distribution. Under current-distribution plans, some percentage of profits — for example, 25 percent of net profits — is distributed in cash at intervals of one year or less. Under deferred-distribution plans, some percentage of profits is deposited in an irrevocable trust and credited to the accounts of individual employees, with the money made available at retirement or termination. Some plans permit employees to contribute additional amounts to their accounts. Various methods are used to allocate the pool of profit-sharing money to individual employees. For example, the amount an employee receives may be based on the individual's base salary, on seniority, on merit rating, or on some combination of these factors.

The Bureau of Labor Statistics reports that, in 1989, there were 442,771 profit-sharing plans in the United States that were qualified under the Employment Retirement Income Security Act (ERISA). Most were deferred-distribution plans. One in five participants could borrow money from his or her account, and one in ten could draw out funds for any purpose.[36]

While most profit-sharing plans are of the deferred-distribution type, some companies have moved to cash plans in order to tie the profit sharing more closely to productivity. For example, some automobile manufacturing companies, faced with intense foreign competition and declining profits, have negotiated cash profit-sharing plans with the United Auto Workers. In 1987, payments averaging about $3,700 — equaling about 11 percent of paychecks — were made to Ford Motor Co. employees covered by profit sharing. Aluminum Company of America (Alcoa) started a cash profit-sharing plan for salaried employees in 1988. Two major unions representing hourly workers at Alcoa rejected the plan, however.[37] Some airlines, including American Airlines, Inc., and Western, have offered cash profit-sharing plans as a way of motivating employees to focus on productivity and efficiency.[38]

Problems   The most difficult problem in profit-sharing plans is determining the formula for distributing profits to employees. Such critical matters as payments to stockholders, taxes, and investment capital must be taken into account. Whether to allocate profit shares on the basis of rank, length of service, merit, or plant or departmental performance must be dealt with.

Under deferred-distribution plans, a problem can be the lack of an immediate relationship between the employer's efforts and rewards. Rewards that are payable upon retirement may seem a long way off and may prove to be ineffective motivators of present performance. Another problem with any profit-sharing plan is the effect on employee morale when profits are down or nonexistent because of factors outside the employees' control, and there are no profit distributions to share. When profit-sharing funds are invested in stocks, employees can become very unhappy when the stock market declines.[39]

Suggestion Plans

A **suggestion plan** is an incentive system under which employees are rewarded if they offer useful ideas for improving organizational effectiveness. The usual reward is a cash payment, although a number of firms offer merchandise or travel. (Both cash and merchandise awards are considered taxable income to the employee.) Suggestion plans are commonly used to obtain employees' ideas on reducing costs, increasing safety, or improving product quality. Some companies, however, promote suggestion plans to give employees more opportunity to participate in company matters. In other words, suggestion plans can be useful devices for improving communication with management. Supervisory and professional employees are often excluded from these plans, however, on the assumption that cost control is a regular part of their jobs.

The typical suggestion plan features boxes placed at convenient locations throughout the workplace, with appropriate forms available. Employees use the forms to write out their suggestions and deposit them in the box for subsequent evaluation, usually by a special committee. (Squibb Corporation uses electronic terminals, where employees can type in their suggestions.)[40] If a suggestion is accepted, a cash award is usually paid, based on some percentage of the first year's savings resulting from the suggestion. A flat fee or standard amount is paid when cost savings are difficult to measure or for nonrevenue-producing suggestions such as safety improvements. If a suggestion is rejected, the contributor is usually given an explanation of why. (See Figure 15.2 for an example of a suggestion comment form used by the Erie Insurance Group.) The Japanese practice is to reward every suggestion. (See *International Perspective* on page 410.)

Plans soliciting suggestions from individuals have been around for a long time. For example, in 1954 Congress approved the Government Employees' Incentive Awards Act, which provided not only for cash awards for accepted suggestions but also for substantial cash awards for "superior accomplishments" or "special acts or services."

Team approaches to suggestion plans, however, are of more recent origin. For example, the Ford Motor Co. permits groups of hourly workers to win its top suggestion award of $6,000.[41] Black & Decker's Household Products Division has established a team approach in which volunteers are grouped into teams across departmental lines. In this program, called "Everyone Counts," teams are expected to thoroughly research their ideas, including identifying any hidden costs and demonstrating how to bring the ideas to fruition.[42] The Employee Involvement Association (formerly the National Association of Suggestion Systems, or NASS)

PIPELINE 620

POLICY STATEMENT:

The Pipeline program is designed to facilitate communication between employees and management. Through Pipelines, employees can communicate in writing suggestions, inquiries, opinions or complaints about company operations, policies and practices. Pipelines adopted for use by the company will be considered for cash awards.

PROCEDURES:

SUBMISSION:

1. Pipeline forms are located in racks adjacent to bulletin boards in all offices.
2. On the Pipeline form, all comments should by typed or written in ink for legibility.
3. Completed Pipelines should be submitted directly to the Division Officer, Human Resources Division. Self-addressed envelopes are provided in the racks for employee convenience. All submitted Pipelines become the property of the ERIE.
4. Pipelines will be handled in confidence. Copies of submitted Pipelines, with the employee's name omitted, will be forwarded to the appropriate members of management for review and comment.
5. Employees submitting Pipelines may elect to discuss their Pipelines with a representative from the Human Resources Division or another member of management by marking the appropriate box on the form.
6. Employees whose Pipleines are determined by the appropriate members of management to merit an award will receive a congratulatory letter and a fifty ($50.00) dollar award. If a number of employees jointly complete a Pipeline, the award will be evenly divided. Pipeline authors who are no longer employed by the ERIE at the time the Pipeline Review Committee approves awards are ineligible to receive Pipeline awards.
7. Each January , the Pipeline Review Committee will reevaluate all Pipelines adopted during the previous year. The best Pipelines will be nominated for the top Pipeline award. If there is a Pipeline judged to be worthy of the award, the top Pipeline will be awarded one thousand ($1,000) dollars. The remaining best Pipelines will receive two hundred and fifty ($250.00) dollar awards.

ELIGIBILITY FOR CASH AWARDS: All submitted Pipelines are eligible to be considered for cash awards with the following exceptions:

1. Division officers and branch managers are not eligible to receive Pipeline awards.
2. Other management employees are eligible to receive awards only if their Pipeline idea is not considered to be part of their normal position responsibilities.
3. Pipelines about the Activities Association, Cafeteria, Credit Union and other independent groups not governed by the ERIE are not eligible to receive awards.
4. Pipelines are valid for one year from the date they are submitted.

IMPLEMENTATION: Implementation of Pipeline ideas shall be the responsibility of the division officer in whose division the Pipeline is applicable.

FIGURE 15.2   The Erie Insurance Group "Pipeline" form

Source: Erie Insurance Group.

International Perspective

Employee Suggestion Systems in Japan

Implementation Before Submission and All Suggestions Accepted

Although not all suggestions are actually implemented, all of them are accepted. In other words, when all three phases of the creative process are completed (problem found, problem solved, solution shown to be implementable) by the employees themselves, a suggestion has been created and is accepted. About ninety-six percent of the suggestions end up being put into practice.

An "idea" is not a "suggestion" until it has gone through all three stages of the creative process. Every suggestion receives a monetary award. The vast majority of the suggestions are small $5 (500 yen) ideas. These are accepted and assigned the award by the supervisor on the spot. The suggestions that are more creative and significant are evaluated by a committee against multiple criteria including creativity and contribution to goals; they receive bigger awards of up to $10,000 and more.

The main objective is to accept all ideas and encourage the little ones as well as the big ones. It is the *process* of getting involved in one's work that counts, not the quality of any single idea. The goal is to have thinking workers and a spirit of never-ending improvement. Of the small ratio (about four percent) of accepted suggestions that do not get implemented right away, most are the kind that require skills beyond the scope of the

suggestors. The team leader or the supervisor can get additional help from other departments for these ideas. Also, it may be found that the implementation of a suggestion is not timely or is inappropriate in the bigger picture. In this case, the idea is not implemented, but is given credit anyway. This is the way the system is supposed to operate and works very well in actual practice.

Employees are told they are expected to create new ideas. Some companies even establish informal goals per person per month. Each formal work group has a team leader who ensures that daily production is met and new ideas keep flowing at the same time. The team leader communicates, coordinates, and gets help across the organization as needed. This prevents the work group from worrying unduly about maintaining daily production and saying "we don't have time to work on new ideas." Workers are given overtime as needed to complete their suggestions. The overtime is usually aimed at implementation work. Much of the problem finding and problem solving work is done continuously in people's minds off the job as well as on the job. When people are creatively involved in their work, ideas about new problems and solutions can occur to them at any time.

Source: Min Basadur, "Managing Creativity: A Japanese Model," *Academy of Management EXECUTIVE* 6 (May 1992):33–34. Reprinted by permission.

sponsors a Team Idea Plan through which small groups of employees are encouraged to develop and submit ideas and are rewarded as teams.

Successes   Reports on cost savings from suggestion systems have generally been favorable. According to the Employee Involvement Association, in 1991 its one thousand members saved more than $2 billion through suggestion plans. This translated into "an average net savings of $6,405 per suggestion adopted."[43]

Examples of cost savings from earlier years include Southern California Edison's suggestion plan producing $100 million in savings over a five-year period,[44] and American Airlines, "Ideas in Action" program saving $41 million in one year.[45] At Black & Decker, savings of $580,000 were recorded in the first three months of a team suggestion program.[46]

In many instances, a suggestion can result in huge cost savings for the employer, yielding a substantial reward to the contributor. Here are some examples:

- At Eli Lilly, senior operator Gerald (John) Niehaus, Jr., discovered a way to increase the recovery of a solvent, thus making larger amounts available for recycling. The amount awarded — $177,197 — was 25 percent of the first year's savings.[47]

- An airline flight officer suggested that air cargo be shifted slightly to the rear of the aircraft, thereby altering the center of gravity and reducing the fuel required for takeoff. The suggestion saved the airline $458,500 the first year and earned the employee $45,850.[48]

- Rhonda Pease, an inspector for Pratt & Whitney's Aircraft Group, suggested a procedure that allowed inspectors to avoid writing identical headings on each page of the multipage forms they used daily. Her suggestion saved the company 12,500 hours per year, and Pease won the company's maximum award of $7,500, plus a $1,000 bonus.[49]

- The highest award reported to the Employee Involvement Association in 1981 — $193,260 — was presented to a team of employees at Martin Marietta–Astronautics Group in Denver.[50]

Problems In spite of many successes, suggestion plans have a number of inherent problems. Evaluating suggestions is a challenging task that requires an analysis of the possible ramifications of implementing a particular idea. Cost-saving suggestions that involve the elimination of jobs must be carefully weighed in terms of their effects on other workers and on the overall climate of the organization. Another problem relates to the origin of the idea. Since many ideas originate as fragments of ideas supplied by others, a claim for an award by one worker may be resented by others who believe they had a hand in formulating the suggestion. Conversely, many ideas probably do not mature because of fears that someone will steal them. Team approaches to suggestion systems may have an advantage in enhancing cooperation and avoiding disputes over the origin of ideas.

Another problem is making the rejection of an idea acceptable to the contributor. In particular, it can be difficult to convince the suggester that the idea had already been put forward by someone else or that it is already being worked on. Lawsuits can and do occur because of these problems. For example, two United Air Lines, Inc. employees sued the company on the grounds that it had rejected their idea and later adopted it independently. In court, the company argued that it had been studying the idea long before the employees made their suggestion. Subsequently, the company made $1,000 "incentive awards" to the two employees. United then dropped its suggestion plan, indicating there had been a large number of disagreements about the size of awards. IBM, on the other hand, describes its plan as "extremely worthwhile" and points out that, with 250,000 suggestions each year and yearly awards totaling $12 million, "a lawsuit now and again is not surprising."[51]

A particularly serious issue is that many suggestion systems by-pass the supervisor. Supervisors may interpret suggestions as a reflection on their competence and may retaliate in some way, or else workers may simply fear such retaliation. Some of these problems are minimized or avoided under participative gainsharing plans such as the Scanlon plan. Although this plan gives recognition to individuals for suggestions, all employees, including supervisors, stand to gain from accepted suggestions because bonuses are distributed to all.

The high mortality rate of suggestion systems indicates that these plans need to be managed carefully. The Employee Involvement Association offers several guidelines for administering suggestion plans, recommending that

- what is a suggestion be defined carefully.
- strict eligibility standards be developed.
- the system be explained clearly to all employees and the most important points of the policy be printed on the suggestion form.
- suggestions be acted on quickly.
- a "fair and reasonable" award be made for every adopted suggestion.
- an employee be told in writing why a suggestion is rejected.
- there be an appeals procedure available to employees who want a suggestion reconsidered.[52]

As with any incentive program, full and continuing support by top management is essential. Timely response to constructive suggestions and tactful explanations for rejected ideas are ways of demonstrating such support and can help ensure broad participation in the plan. A suggestion system that is installed and then ignored will very quickly be viewed as useless.

Positive Reinforcement Programs

Positive reinforcement programs, in which the principles of behavior modification and operant conditioning are used to influence worker behavior, are found in a number of companies today. (See Chapter 5 for a review of reinforcement theory.) Unlike incentive plans that rely on financial rewards to reinforce desired behaviors (productivity, cooperation, and so on), many positive reinforcement programs rely primarily on nonfinancial incentives. These incentives or reinforcers include praise, recognition, and avoidance of punishment.

Successes   One of the first companies to use a positive reinforcement program was Emery Air Freight Corporation. Emery's program involved four key steps: (1) defining the behavioral aspects of performance and conducting a performance audit; (2) establishing specific goals for each worker, ideally through participative approaches; (3) allowing employees to keep records of their own work; and (4) praising the positive aspects of employees' performance and withholding praise for substandard work.[53] These steps are summarized in Figure 15.3. Other organizations that have used this approach are Michigan Bell (to improve operator and maintenance services), General Electric Co. (in training programs for supervisors of minority female employees), and the B. F. Goodrich Chemical Group.[54] The results of these programs include cost savings at Emery Air Freight; improved cost efficiency, safety, and service at Michigan Bell; cost savings and increased productivity at GE; and substantially increased productivity at B. F. Goodrich Chemical.[55]

Positive reinforcement programs, like other incentive programs, typically involve attention to many variables in the work situation. For example, increased attention is usually paid to training, to communications, and to union-management relations under these programs. Therefore, reported gains and improvements may not always be the direct result of nonfinancial incentives.

Problems   In many instances, employee compensation is not changed when an organization institutes a positive reinforcement program. There are indications, however, that money ultimately becomes a consideration for those involved in the program, especially if increased productivity leads to higher profits. It is not stretching equity theory (see Chapter 5) too far to speculate that increased profitability stemming from employee performance will create considerable tension among workers if they do not share in the organization's financial gains. In other words, although the avoidance of layoffs or bankruptcy may be perceived by employees as a fair exchange for improved productivity, higher and higher profits without a return to employees will ultimately be perceived as inequitable. Indeed, in the Michigan Bell positive reinforcement program, it was found that satisfaction with pay decreased; as equity theory would explain it, the employees began to perceive their outcomes as inadequate relative to their contributions.

External Influences

Federal and state laws have some impact on incentive systems in that they put a floor under such plans through minimum-wage provisions. Further, laws set forth rules for computing base and overtime pay and specify the records that must be kept. Bonuses or commissions measured by production, efficiency, or hours worked must be included in the regular rate of pay in computing overtime payments. Excluded from this requirement are gifts; Christmas and special occasion bonuses; payments made to profit-sharing, thrift, and savings plans; and irrevocable contributions to a bona fide trust.[56]

In addition, profit-sharing plans must be approved by the U.S. Treasury Department to comply with federal income tax laws. Also, reports to the government on deferred-distribution profit-sharing plans are required under the Employee Retirement Income Security Act (ERISA).

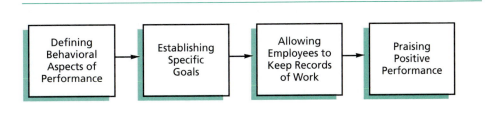

FIGURE 15.3   Steps in establishing a positive reinforcement program

Labor leaders share no universal policy on incentive systems; in fact, union attitudes vary from opposition to enthusiasm. Some incentive plans have been established at the insistence of unions; others have been discontinued at their insistence. Historically, union attitudes have shifted from unqualified opposition to a desire to bargain over the details of such plans and to monitor their administration. Notably, the United Auto Workers (UAW) have been pressing for profit sharing for almost a quarter of a century, but it was not until 1982 that profit-sharing plans were successfully negotiated with Ford and General Motors.[57] The UAW's position on profit sharing is not unqualified, however; the union believes profit sharing and productivity sharing should be supplemental to a base wage structure that protects workers' purchasing power.[58]

Internal Influences

Several important variables affect the selection and administration of incentive plans in a particular setting. A major consideration is the *technology* being used by the organization. For example, piece-rate systems are seldom used where the pace of work is governed largely by machines, such as on an automobile assembly line.[59] Another important variable is the *size of the unit for which performance gains are measured*: that is, whether the incentive plan focuses on individuals, groups, a total plant or organization, or a combination of these. Another variable is *participation*: how much those affected are involved in the selection, design, and administration of the plan itself; and to what extent employees are encouraged to cooperate with peers and supervisors in improving unit-wide and plant-wide productivity.

Other important variables include management philosophy and organizational culture and climate. If it is management's stated philosophy, for example, that all employees should benefit directly from significant organizational gains, the organization might well move toward a plant-wide or organization-wide incentive plan that will allow employees to "share the wealth." If the culture of the organization includes the notions that top management is omniscient, that the employees' role is to do as they are told, and that people who ask questions or make suggestions are troublemakers, a participative incentive system can never work and will probably not be attempted. If the organizational climate includes a great deal of mistrust, an incentive system, to succeed, would need to be very simply designed, with little chance for either management or employees to distort the results.

Contemporary thought about incentive systems suggests that variables such as these are important in determining the "fit" between a given incentive system and a particular organization. Further, as organizational culture and climate change, incentive systems can be modified accordingly. For example, as trust levels and skills in cooperation increase in the organization, a firm might move from an individual incentive plan to a highly participative plant-wide plan that includes extensive committee and task force work.[60]

Role of the Human Resources Department

A survey of about six hundred responding organizations found that the human resources department had all or some responsibility for the following activities in 81 percent or more of the organizations in which the activity was found:

- Award or recognition programs (95 percent of firms)
- Incentive pay plans (86 percent)
- Profit-sharing plan administration (89 percent)
- Stock plan administration (81 percent)[61]

Thus, in organizations having incentive systems, the human resources department is likely to be heavily involved in their management. Further, the human resources department is extensively involved in wage and salary administration matters, including job evaluation, that serve as the foundation for most incentive plans. In addition, the department will be actively involved in negotiating any incentive plans pertaining to unionized employees.

Like most other human resources activities, incentive systems require the active collaboration of the entire management team. The controller or chief financial officer, in particular, must be extensively involved because of his or her expertise in accounting and financial matters. Individual and group piece-rate systems need the expertise of industrial engineers, and gainsharing plans require the assistance of both accountants and industrial engineers. Production managers, of course, are key people in the management of any incentive systems that have to do with the quantity and quality of production.

An area of human resources department responsibility that should be emphasized in the management of incentive plans is training. Ongoing training of various kinds is important to the success of almost any incentive plan: skills training so that employees can successfully earn bonuses; supervisory training so that supervisors will have the technical and leadership skills to assist their subordinates (this is particularly important for group incentive or gainsharing plans that have a strong participative component); training in work simplification and work methods; and so on. The human resources department also has a major role in communicating with employees about the purposes and philosophy underlying any incentive programs.

It should be emphasized, too, that the human resources director and department have a major role in weaving an incentive plan into the fabric of the basic compensation plans and other human resources practices. Moreover, in many organizations, there are several incentive systems operating simultaneously. For example, like Lincoln Electric employees, Wal-Mart Stores, Inc., employees (called "associates") participate in several incentive plans. At Wal-Mart, these include bonuses, stock purchase plans, and profit sharing.[62] Such plans must be compatible and mutually reinforcing, and human resources professionals play a major role in formulating and administering them.

Summary

Properly planned, installed, and administered incentive plans can increase efficiency and productivity, decrease costs, and increase the pay of employees, supervisors, and managers. Effective incentive plans, however, require attention to a wide range of organizational variables.

Four major categories of incentive plans are tied directly to performance. These are individual plans, group plans, plant-wide productivity plans (or productivity gainsharing [PG] plans), and profit-sharing plans. The use of individual incentive systems, such as piece-rate plans, appears to be declining. The transformation of individual incentive schemes into group incentive plans is probably increasing, since some firms have switched from individual to group plans in recent years. The number of plant-wide productivity plans (or productivity gainsharing plans) appears to be rapidly increasing.

Individual and group plans tend to be practical when worker handling or processing is a major determinant of productivity, units of production are readily measured, and employees can trust management not to change standards arbitrarily. Piece-rate plans tend not to be used when the pace of work is governed largely by machines. Group plans are particularly appropriate when workers' jobs are highly interdependent and cooperation is essential. Productivity gainsharing plans appear to have the most promise for promoting collaboration between employees, supervisors, and management to achieve organization-wide or plant-wide cost savings and productivity improvements. Important variables in the applicability and long-term success of various kinds of incentive plans are management philosophy and organizational culture and climate. Scanlon plans, for example, require a commitment to extensive participation and considerable mutual support and trust.

Extensive use of suggestion systems and widespread reports of significant cost savings attest to the value of these programs. To be successful, however, these plans need such features as clear rules, fair and reasonable awards, prompt administration, and appeal procedures. Team approaches to suggestion plans, a recent innovation, would appear to have promise in enhancing cooperation and in avoiding disputes about the origin of ideas.

Positive reinforcement programs, based on operant conditioning and behavior modification principles, have met with some success. Employee compensation is ordinarily not changed when these plans are instituted, but there are indications that money ultimately becomes a concern if increased productivity leads to higher profits.

Environmental influences on incentive systems include collective bargaining and the impact of federal and state laws. Laws establish minimum wages and rules for the calculation of basic rates and overtime. They also stipulate what records must be kept. Profit-sharing plans must be approved by the U.S. Treasury Department, and reports must be made to the federal government on deferred-distribution plans. Recently, unions have won profit-sharing plans from management in return for wage concessions, particularly in the automobile industry.

The human resources department is likely to be extensively involved in the management of incentive systems. Many organizations will have several plans operating simultaneously. The management of these plans will be collaborative, involving production managers, industrial engineers, accounting and finance professionals, and supervisors. In particular, the human resources department plays key roles in the compensation aspects of incentive programs and in the training and the communications necessary for the long-term success of these plans.

Ethical Dilemma

The regional managers of Tankfill Petroleum have been pressured by company headquarters in Texas to increase sales of extra products like windshield wipers, fan belts, tires, and antifreeze. In cooperation with the human resources department, a committee of regional managers has devised an incentive scheme for service station employees that awards 20 percent of the net profits on such sales to the individual employee at the end of each quarter. Sales have increased dramatically, but some customers and some service station operators are beginning to grumble that unnecessary sales are being made, particularly to inexperienced drivers.

What are the ethical issues, if any, in this situation? If you are a regional HR director, what would you recommend to the corporate HR director at headquarters?

Key Terms

incentive plan
variable pay
individual incentive plan
piece-rate plan
differential piece-rate plan
production bonus
standard-hour plan
measured day-rate plan
commission
spot bonus

stock option
stock appreciation rights (SARs)
group incentive plan
productivity gainsharing (PG) plan
Improshare
Scanlon plan
spot gainsharing (SGS) plans
profit-sharing plan
suggestion plan
positive reinforcement program

Review Questions

1. Briefly describe various individual incentive plans used for production workers, sales personnel, and professional and managerial employees. What are some of the problems associated with using these plans?
2. Under what conditions are group incentive plans particularly effective?
3. Discuss some of the features of productivity gainsharing plans and some of the problems associated with these plans.
4. What are profit-sharing plans and what are some of the problems connected with them?
5. Discuss the advantages and disadvantages of suggestion plans.
6. What are the basic features of positive reinforcement programs, and what are some potential problems with these programs?

Opening Case Questions

Case 15.1   Do We Need Incentives?

1. What is the purpose of an incentive plan, and would it address HiQuality Furniture Manufacturing's immediate problem and needs?
2. What kinds of questions regarding an incentive plan should George and the supervisors ask?

Case 15.2   The Bonus Is Coming out of Our Hides

1. What could the hospital administrator have done to prevent unhappy employees?
2. What does this situation suggest about the secrecy factor in wage, salary, and bonus systems?

Comprehensive Case

The Big Payoff from Suggestion Systems

In 1898 an employee at Eastman Kodak Company made the first use of a formal suggestion system in the United States: the employee suggested that someone should wash the windows. Such a start may bring to mind outmoded images of dusty, unused suggestion boxes or of the cartoonist's drawing of a bottomless suggestion box placed directly over a trash can. But in fact many companies are finding that this old and often overlooked method of involving employees in improving their company can pay off in a big way.

In 1991, for instance, employees' suggestions saved their companies over $2 billion for the fifth year in a row. (The Employee Involvement Association — formerly the National Association of Suggestion Systems — representing over 1,000 organizations, keeps track of such things.) Of the more than 1.1 million suggestions made, 321,089, or 37 percent, were adopted; the average adopted suggestion resulted in a net saving of $6,405. In the same year, companies spent about $164 million to reward suggesters. That companies saved more than ten times as much as they invested in awards demonstrates why suggestion systems have suddenly become so popular.

Of course, setting up a suggestion system requires more than simply establishing a suggestion box. The company must be committed to the system, encourage involvement in a number of ways, and ensure that the system does not falter after the initial enthusiasm wears off.

Although the goal of suggestion systems is to prompt employees on every level to come up with ideas, support from the system must start at the top of the organization. Executives must make the system's objectives clear, create an environment in which management genuinely welcomes new ideas, and develop a well-publicized process by which suggestions are gathered, evaluated, and rewarded. If at all possible, the organization should involve employees in setting up and implementing the system, and it should explain the process in writing to everyone.

Promotion is key to the long-term viability of a suggestion system. The organization initially needs to let employees know how seriously it will take the system, how suggestions will be handled, and what the benefits for the organization and for suggesters will be. Although cash is the most widely used award for good suggestions, recognition by their organization and their peers may be the most important factor in motivating employees to make suggestions. Therefore, a certain amount of hoopla, hype, and humor seems justified.

Cotton States insurance company introduced its "Profit From Ideas" system with a meeting in which managers threw cash in the air every time the speaker said the word "cash,' and each employee left the meeting with a promotional T-shirt, an informational brochure, and lots of suggestion forms. Other companies make a big deal of the regular meetings at which suggestions are recognized, and, in addition to cash awards, hand out humorous gifts that often end up as office trophies, proudly displayed by the winners. Companies have found that it is a good idea to make some mention even of those people who made suggestions that were not adopted so that suggesters would not feel that they had "lost" or "failed."

The organization should keep track of where the suggestions are coming from, and if there is a lull in the activity from one particular group, management should target that group with a special promotion. Similarly, the entire system can be reinvigorated by a campaign to produce suggestions about a particular issue, such as quality or safety. Experts suggest that at first an organization may want to emphasize the simple quantity of suggestions; later it would focus on improving the quality of suggestions, perhaps even offering writing help for employees who do not feel that they can express themselves adequately on the suggestion forms.

The details of the system need to be well thought out so that awards will have the desired motivational effect and employees will not undermine the system by taking it too casually. Cotton States, for instance, requires that employees support their suggestion with specifics — how it will work, what it might save and cost, what drawbacks it might have. Evaluators do not accept suggestions that employees should make and carry out as part of their normal job duties, nor do they reward complaints about a situation that make no attempt to solve a problem.

A major question for organizations instituting suggestion systems is whether rewards should be tied to the potential savings from the suggestion. Some organizations promise suggesters an award that equals 10 to 25 percent of the first year's savings produced by their suggestion. Others simply give a standard cash award to the best suggestion each month. In either case, the organization must also find a way to show its appreciation for suggestions that have value even though they may not directly save money.

In many organizations, suggestion systems are just a part of a much larger effort to involve employees in making their organizations better, more profitable places to work. Suggestion systems may be the ideal means for starting such employee involvement. They spur employees to think about how their ideas contribute to the larger goals of the organization, and they demonstrate to everyone that good ideas from even the lowest-paid or the beginning workers can pay off.

Sources: Wendy Chamblee, "Suggestion Programs Empower Employees, Reap Profits," *HRNews,* December 1991, p. A9; Beth Enslow, "Making Employee Involvement Work," *Across the Board* 28 (November 1991):27; Dawn Gunsch, "Employee Suggestions and Resulting Savings Continue to Increase," *Personnel Journal* 71 (August 1992):17; Karen Matthes, "What's the Big Idea? Empower Employees Through Suggestion," *HRfocus* 69 (October 1992):17; Rosalie A. Steele, "Awards Energize a Suggestion Program," *Personnel Journal* 71 (October 1992):96–100.

Discussion Questions

1. What ingredients appear to be necessary for a successful suggestion system?
2. In light of this case and the content of the chapter, what should constitute a "suggestion"?

CHAPTER 16

Employee Benefits

LEARNING OBJECTIVES

- Identify the factors involved in determining benefits for a particular organization.
- Describe the major types of benefits that require significant financial contributions from employers.
- Explain the impact of ERISA on private pension plans.
- List the advantages of flexible benefit plans.
- Explain the importance of controlling benefit expenditures and identify some cost-control measures.
- Outline the role of the human resources department in administrating benefits.

CASE 16.1   Which Goes? Health Care Benefits or Part-Time Student Employment?

Sales at High Efficiency Generators were down. The market for equipment to generate electricity from wind was correlated with the price of oil. When oil prices were high, interest in HEG's products by utilities and entrepreneurs tended to increase substantially. When oil prices dropped, demand for HEG generators dropped.

Stephanie Jackson and Barry Campbell, founders and major stockholders of HEG, and president and technical director, respectively, had succeeded in keeping HEG profitable during most of the previous downturns in the market. Part of this success was due to the extensive use of temporary, part-time technicians recruited from the college student population in the area. Most were physics and engineering students, but some business and liberal arts students were used in purchasing, accounting, and personnel. Some of the students were keenly interested in the environmental aspects of HEG's products. The company paid well, but the college students understood that HEG might need to lay them off at the end of any semester if there was a business downturn. The company furnished few benefits to these employees other than paying the substantial social security, workers' compensation, and unemployment compensation taxes.

Stephanie, Barry, and the human resources director, Pete Thompson, were having a preliminary meeting to plan strategy relative to the new business downturn. "I hate to do it, but it looks as though we'll have to lay off some of our college students at the end of the semester," Stephanie said. "Well, I assume that at least we won't need to lay off any of our full-time regulars," Barry added. "Boy, I hate to see some of those students go. They are really smart, and they are terrific workers."

"I hesitate to say this," Pete interjected, "but I'm wondering if we don't need to reduce costs in some additional ways this time. Some of the benefits for regular employees are killing us. Medical insurance, in particular, has gone through the ceiling. I think we've got to negotiate a new contract with our health care provider, and probably require our employees to pick up part of the cost."

"Maybe if we cut back on health care costs, we could hang on to a few more of the college students we think might be candidates for permanent jobs when they graduate," Stephanie ventured. "But we've got to consider the impact on the regular work force in whatever we do. They're the ongoing core of this company." ◄

CASE 16.2   The Holiday Turkeys

"And a happy New Year to you, too," muttered Len Colfax, human resources director for Nutritional Foods, as John Andrews walked away from Len's office. John was the best supervisor of shipping the company had ever had. But he was almost belligerent in his insistence on equitable treatment for the people in his department.

This morning, John had blustered in to complain about the turkeys the company had given each employee the day before the holidays. "The idea of giving holiday turkeys is fine," John had grumbled. "But they all ought to weigh the same. Several people in my group weighed their birds and found discrepancies of as much as two pounds. They joked about it, but I could see that a couple of people were irritated. Someone said they suspected that the sales department people got turkeys as much as five pounds larger. I don't know about that, but the company ought to do a better job of being fair about these things." With that, John stalked out.

Len groaned. Talk about looking a gift horse in the mouth! Still, one lesson he'd learned in his years as human resources director was that employees can be very sensitive to what they perceive as unfair treatment. There was no reason why the supplier couldn't have provided turkeys closer to the same weight. Next year Len would insist on that. Also, next year it might be a good idea to explain that, even though the company had done everything possible to provide turkeys of equal size, there might be differences of a few ounces but that it would probably even out over the years.

Len made some notes for his file and smiled ruefully. "Live and learn," he thought. ◄

I n addition to compensation in the form of wages and salaries, organizations provide workers with various services and programs known as **employee benefits**. In the past, these programs and services were often called fringe benefits, but now they make up such a large part of the total compensation package that the term *fringe* is no longer appropriate. The term *supplementary benefits*, however, is still commonly used to refer to this aspect of employee compensation.

The chapter-opening cases give only a few examples of the many kinds of benefits a particular organization may offer. These range from legally required benefits (such as social security payments) to time off with pay (for holidays, personal business, vacation, and so on) and optional "give-away" items such as free coffee or gifts at certain holidays. Although these benefits may be offered at no expense to the employee, they certainly are not "free." Benefits represent a significant cost to the organization, as the human resource director in Case 16.1 was reminding the company founders. And, as Case 16.2 suggests, the allocation of benefits is as sensitive a matter as wage and salary administration in that perceived fairness and determining what is equitable treatment are crucial considerations in designing a successful benefit program.

Current Practices and Problems

Although equity considerations affect the design of a benefit program just as they affect the organization's wage and salary program, the process of determining benefit payments is somewhat less complicated than establishing pay rates. Figure 16.1 shows the factors involved in determining benefits for a particular organization. Job analysis, job evaluation, and merit ratings are not directly involved in this process. But because many benefit payments (sick leave, vacations, and holiday pay) stem from the actual wages and salaries paid to employees, determining base pay is the first step in establishing the benefits program. Probably the most critical and time-consuming step is the analysis of relevant data, including benefit surveys (to ascertain benefit practices in competing firms); cost analysis of various benefits and the organization's ability to finance them; and identification of employee preferences

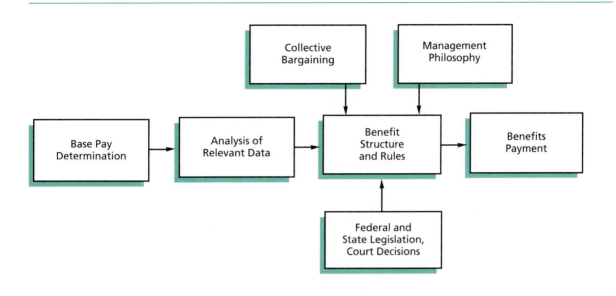

FIGURE 16.1   Process of determining employee benefits

for particular programs and services. Federal and state legislation will have a bearing on benefit decisions, as will collective bargaining in the unionized organization. In fact, many benefits are required by law or are specified by the labor agreement. In any organization, too, management philosophy will have some impact on benefit decisions. Many employee benefits are initiated by management's desire to enhance morale, to avoid unionization, or to compete with other organizations in recruiting and retaining qualified workers.

The Importance of Employee Benefits In addition to basic wages and salaries, the benefits supplied by the organization are very important to the well-being and security of its employees. Consider the tragic situation of an employee who declines to participate in a permanent disability program and who later suffers an injury and becomes permanently disabled. Benefit programs can be crucial to maintaining an employee's standard of living when health problems occur.

Employee benefits are also important to the organization in some positive ways. If carefully selected and properly managed, they can be helpful in recruiting and retaining qualified employees. For example, the generous benefits provided by the Marion Laboratories (see Figure 16.2) undoubtedly are a factor in the company's success in attracting applicants and in retaining talented people. In addition, some benefits can reduce costs in other areas. For example, Bechtel Group, Inc., found that its commuter vans and other ride-sharing programs at its southern California facility made it unnecessary to build a previously planned $3.5 million parking garage.[1] As another example, some organizations have found that the costs of exercise and fitness programs have been partly offset by reduced health care claims from those employees who work out regularly.[2]

Employee benefits are significant in a negative sense because they have grown increasingly expensive, and if a company is not careful, it may "give away the store."

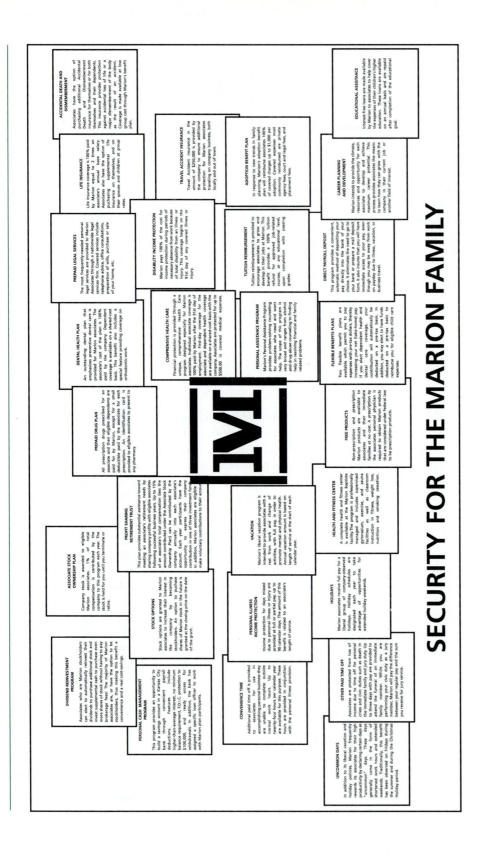

FIGURE 16.2 Comprehensive benefits plans available from Marion Laboratories

Source: Courtesy of Marion Laboratories, Inc.

Note: In a 1989 merger, Marion Laboratories, Inc. became Marion Merrell Dow Inc. As a result, the information in this figure is not current.

Case 16.1 illustrates how benefit costs can be a major concern to top management. In fact, as a percentage of pay, employee benefits have increased faster than basic wages and salaries in most years for several decades. Table 16.1 shows the growth in employee benefits as a percentage of wages and salaries since 1929. Between 1965 and 1991, employee benefits grew from 21.5 to 38.2 percent of wages and salaries. In recent years, the managements of some organizations have literally taken back some employee benefits to prevent losses or serious cash-flow problems, thus to some extent slowing down the overall rise in benefits across the nation.

Types of Benefits   There are many employee benefits from which to choose. Some, such as social security, are **mandatory benefits;** that is, organizations are required by law to provide them. Many organizations offer other, nonmandatory benefits that are attractive to both the employer and the employee. Among these are insurance plans; pensions; payment for time not worked; and any number of optional payments and services such as tuition refunds, van pools, and a variety of discount programs. It would be impossible to describe *all* the benefits found in contemporary organizations, but it is

TABLE 16.1 Growth of Employee Benefits, 1929 to 1991

Type of payment	1929	1955	1965	1975	1986	1991
			(Percent of wages and salaries)			
1. Legally required	0.8	3.3	5.3	8.4	11.1	12.2
Old-Age, Survivors, Disability, and Health Insurance (FICA taxes)	0.0	1.4	2.3	4.6	5.9	6.3
Unemployment Compensation	0.0	0.7	1.0	0.8	1.2	0.7
Workers compensation	0.6	0.5	0.7	1.0	1.0	1.7
Government employees retirement	0.2	0.5	1.0	1.7	2.8	3.2
Other	0.0	0.2	0.3	0.3	0.2	0.3
2. Agreed-upon	0.4	3.6	4.6	7.4	9.7	12.7
Pensions	0.2	2.2	2.3	3.6	2.8	5.1
Insurance	0.1	1.1	2.0	3.4	5.6	6.7
Other	0.1	0.3	0.3	0.4	1.3	0.9
3. Rest Periods	1.0	3.0	3.1	3.7	3.3	2.5
4. Time not Worked	0.7	5.9	7.3	9.4	10.2	9.9
Vacations	0.3	3.0	3.8	4.8	5.2	5.2
Holidays	0.3	2.0	2.5	3.2	3.1	3.1
Sick leave	0.1	0.8	0.8	1.2	1.4	1.2
Other	0.0	0.1	0.2	0.2	0.5	0.4
5. Bonuses profit-sharing, etc.	0.1	1.2	1.2	1.1	1.2	0.9
Total benefit payments	3.0%	17.0%	21.5%	30.0%	35.5%	38.2%
Wages and Salaries (Billions $)	$50.50	$212.10	$363.70	$814.70	$2,093.00	$2,812.60
Total benefit payments (Billions $)	$1.50	$36.10	$78.20	$244.40	$743.00	$1,074.40

Source: Estimated by U.S. Chamber of Commerce from U.S. Department of Commerce data and U.S. Chamber of Commerce Survey

useful to be familiar with the major types to which organizations make substantial financial contributions.

Mandatory Benefits

Federal and state laws require most organizations to provide certain benefits that protect workers in the event of illness or accidents and during periods of unemployment and retirement. These benefits are provided through the Old-Age, Survivors, Disability, and Health Insurance program, more commonly known as **social security**. The Social Security Act of 1935, as amended, makes mandatory the provision of pension payments, unemployment compensation, and workers' compensation. The pension benefits are paid for through the Federal Insurance Contributions Act (FICA) deductions from employee paychecks, matched by employers' contributions. The employer is responsible for withholding social security taxes and for making contributions to the federal government on a quarterly basis.

As the number of people eligible to receive social security benefits grows, social security taxes are rising dramatically. In 1974, employees were required to contribute 5.85 percent of the first $13,200 earned and employers had to match that amount. By 1993 the percentage had risen to 7.65 on the first $57,600 earned.[3]

Unemployment compensation is administered under a dual system of state and federal laws. The purpose of these laws is to provide emergency income to people when they are unemployed and to encourage employers to provide stable employment. The Federal Unemployment Tax Act of 1935, as amended, requires employers of four or more employees performing types of work covered by the act to pay an unemployment insurance tax to the federal government. The federal government then makes refunds to the various states. Typically, unemployment compensation benefits are available from state governments for a period of up to twenty-six weeks. Individual states are free to authorize or prohibit the payment of unemployment compensation to workers who are on strike.[4]

Workers' compensation provides payments to workers or dependents in the event of job-incurred injuries, illnesses, or death. Medical and rehabilitation services are also provided. These benefit programs are administered by the state. The total cost is borne by employers, although the method of insuring may vary from state to state and may involve a state fund, approved insurance companies, or special funds set up by employers. In 1990, total workers' compensation payments made in the United States amounted to $53 billion.[5] Escalating medical costs and multimillion-dollar lawsuits by injured employees increased the cost of workers' compensation 83 percent between 1985 and 1991.[6]

Pensions

In many cases, social security payments provide only a minimum income for retirement and must be supplemented with other funds. Therefore, many organizations offer pension benefits beyond those available under the Social Security Act; these represent a significant cost in the typical benefit program. A 1992 study of 1,008 firms found 84 percent providing some form of pension plan; however, small firms are less likely to provide pensions than larger firms.[7] (There are also wide variations in pension coverage by type of occupation. (See the section on retirement in Chapter 10.)

There are many kinds of pension plans. Under *contributory plans*, both employees and employers are required to contribute to the pension fund. Under *noncontributory plans*, pension funding is the sole responsibility of the employer. In noncontributory plans where contributions are based on company profits (*deferred profit-sharing plans*), accumulated funds are usually allocated on the basis of salary (and the size of the pension fund depends on profit size).

Defined *benefit* **pension plans** specify the amount of the pension that will be received by the retiree. Typically, the amount is based on a fixed formula including such variables as salary and length of time the participant is in the plan. A common practice is to guarantee a certain proportion of the employee's average salary during the last few years of employment, given a certain number of years of service. For example, the plan might guarantee a pension of 50 percent of the average monthly salary earned during the last three years of employment if the employee has accumulated twenty-five years of service. The formula might provide for larger amounts beyond twenty-five years.[8]

Although defined benefit plans are widely used in the United States, they are declining in popularity, partly because of the increase in 401(k) plans (to be discussed below). According to a U.S. Bureau of Labor Statistics study, 63 percent of full-time employees in medium and large private organizations participated in defined benefit plans in 1989.[9] But the number of organizations — including small organizations — offering defined plans appears to be going down. A study of 957 firms by the U.S. Chamber of Commerce found 44 percent offering defined plans in 1989, down from 48 percent two years earlier.[10]

Defined *contribution* **pension plans** feature specified formulas for contributions going into the plans, but do not specify the amount to be received by the retiree. Defined contribution plans are typically a mixture of 401(k) plans and profit sharing.[11]

A pension benefit program adopted by many organizations in recent years is the **salary reduction plan,** also known as the "401(k) plan." Under Section 401(k) of

401(k) Pension Plans are one of the many benefit options that employers provide. Frequently, companies match employees' contributions.

YOUR EMPLOYEES MAY NOT BE ACCUSTOMED TO THE 401(K) SERVICE WE PROVIDE. BUT THEY COULD GET USED TO IT.

For complete information about our full range of 401(k) services, call Paul Allen, Dreyfus Group Retirement Plans, at (800) 762-9523, ext. 803.

Dreyfus
Group Retirement Plans

the Internal Revenue Code, an employer may establish a retirement savings plan to which employees can contribute through payroll deductions. The employee's contributions reduce the employee's taxable income, and no income taxes are paid until the employee starts drawing from the fund after retirement. Frequently, companies match employees' contributions, and employees can choose which of several investments they wish to participate in, such as money market funds or company stock purchase plans. Under the Internal Revenue Code, such plans are required to have broad employee participation, including significant participation by lower-paid employees.[12]

Employees can also save for retirement and pay reduced taxes by participating in an **employee stock ownership plan (ESOP)**. Under these plans, employees may purchase company stock through payroll-deduction or installment plans, usually below market price. Generally, employees are eligible to sell the stock or withdraw dividends only on retirement or termination of employment, when they must pay taxes on those assets. Advocates of ESOPs point out the potential morale and incentive value of employees owning stock; conversely, however, the effect on morale if the value of the stock declines needs to be considered. ESOPs were given a boost by favorable clauses in the Employee Retirement Income Security Act (ERISA) of 1974, as amended, which was passed to help ensure that pension plans are adequately funded and protected against failure.[13] It was estimated that more than ten thousand companies had enrolled 11.5 million workers in ESOPs by 1989.[14]

There are some potential abuses of ESOPs. Critics point out, for example, that employees are often represented only by an ESOP trustee, and frequently that person is a company official. This gives workers little say in major decisions, such as what course of action to take in the event of a hostile takeover attempt by another company. Advocates point out that companies sharing ownership with most or all employees have been growing two to four times as fast as companies in which employees do not own stock.[15]

All private pensions are now regulated under ERISA. Although the act does not *require* a company to establish a pension plan, it does benefit workers in a number of significant ways. First, the law creates a tax incentive for employers to set aside certain funds for pension plans and establishes an insurance program to protect those funds. Second, the law broadens employee participation in pension plans by prohibiting overly strict eligibility rules. A pension plan must now include all employees who are at least twenty-five years of age and who have worked in the organization for at least one year. Third, the law establishes minimum **vesting** standards, under which an employee who has worked a certain length of time or reached a certain age is entitled to receive the employer's contributions to the pension fund even if the employee leaves the job before retirement. However, **portability,** or an employee's ability to transfer vested benefits to another employer (to maintain all retirement moneys in one account) or to an individual retirement account requires the agreement of the employer.[16]

Insurance   Companies typically provide health, life, and disability insurance and frequently dental and accident insurance. Such insurance contributes to the financial security of employees or their families in the event of illness, death, or accident. A U.S. Chamber of Commerce study indicates that 90 percent of 1,008 responding firms made payments to life insurance plans for employees; 98 percent made payments to employee health insurance plans.[17] These benefits may be based partly on employee contributions (contributory) or may be furnished entirely by the employer (noncontributory).

Company-sponsored insurance plans are typically group plans that provide benefits at lower cost than if coverage were purchased for individuals. Because all or most employees are included, the employer can negotiate favorable rates with the insurance company or health care provider.

One of the fastest-growing forms of medical insurance is health care coverage through a **health maintenance organization (HMO).** Health maintenance organizations function as both insurers and providers of health care. For a monthly fee, these organizations offer total health care, including physical examinations, laboratory tests, surgical and hospital services, consulting-nurse and emergency-room services, and prescriptions filled at the HMO pharmacy. Small charges may be made for prescriptions, and limits may be set on some kinds of services — for example, the number of consultations at a mental health clinic. Examples of such organizations are the Kaiser-Permanente Medical Program (California), Group Health Cooperative of Puget Sound (Washington), Community Health Care Center Plan (Connecticut), and Harvard Community Health Plan (Massachusetts; not connected with Harvard University).[18]

Another rapidly growing form of health care coverage is the **preferred provider organization (PPO),** which overlaps or can resemble so-called managed-care networks. Preferred provider organizations are networks of doctors and hospitals who have agreed to provide health care at discount rates and to practice according to a set of guidelines. The system is usually managed by a contract manager such as an insurance firm. One of the typical features is that the employee goes first to a primary-care physician, who regulates access to specialists and hospitals.[19]

Some insurance plans offered build on a basic foundation of other plans. For example, a company might pay for a basic hospital and surgical plan but provide a major medical plan and a salary-continuation plan on a contributory basis. The major medical plan picks up coverage where the basic plan leaves off and helps employees meet hospital and medical expenses associated with catastrophic situations such as long-term illnesses. Salary-continuation insurance provides a designated level of income for a stated period after an employee's sick-leave eligibility runs out.

Child Care Because of the large numbers of mothers who are in the work force and who have young children (see Chapter 3), as well as the significant number of working men with sole responsibility for young children, child-care services are becoming increasingly important. (See *Contemporary Issues* on page 430.) Child-care programs are of several kinds, and sometimes have a combination of features. Information and referrals are the most frequently found services, followed by counseling assistance, help with child-care expenses, and employer-sponsored day-care centers. Other programs that support child care are job sharing, voluntary part-time work, flextime, and flexible leave programs.

In 1988 it was estimated that about 114,000 companies were providing child-care benefits of some kind. Of these, some 18,000 sponsored day-care programs.[20] Other types of organizations — thirty state governments, for example — provide child-care support for their employees.[21]

Contemporary Issues

FYI — Single-Father Households Are Fastest Growing Group

Between 1985 and 1989, single-father households became the fastest growing family group in the United States, according to new data released by the Bureau of the Census.

The number of single fathers caring for their children rose 33.1% in the late '80s. By 1991, there were 1.4 million single-father families in the U.S.

This number is still small compared to the 8.7 million single-mother families, but just as the rapid growth of single-mother households in the early 1970s signaled long-term changes in family structure (including the rise in no-fault divorce), so the current growth of single-father households reflects long-term social trends, including changes in custody laws and a growing number of never-married fathers caring for their children.

Employers who have tended to think of single-parent families as a women's issue may want to revisit their assumptions. Single fathers have many of the same workplace needs as single mothers but also often have to contend with unequal leave policies, for example, and the attitudes of co-workers or supervisors who think men taking advantage of family-friendly policies aren't serious about their careers.

The rapid rise in single-father families will likely spur demand for gender-neutral family policies and changes in corporate attitudes about men and work.

Source: Issues in HR, July–August 1992, p. 4. Reprinted with the permission of *Issues In HR*, published by the Society for Human Resource Management, Alexandria, VA.

Family Leave   Organizations are paying more and more attention to their practices regarding **family leave,** or leave of absence for taking care of infants and family members and relatives who are ill. The reasons are several, including a federal law passed in 1993, EEOC rulings, the rapidly growing number of women in the work force, and the growing number of the elderly. (In Europe, some forms of family leave are heavily subsidized by employers, as required by law. See *International Perspective* on page 439.)

In early 1993 the federal government passed a Family and Medical Leave Act requiring larger employers to provide workers with unpaid leave for family or medical emergencies. Some of the features of the law are as follows:

- Employers with fifty or more employees (about half of all employees and 5 percent of U.S. companies) within a seventy-five-mile radius are covered. Employers include businesses, nonprofit, and governmental organizations.

- Workers are to be offered as much as twelve weeks of unpaid leave after childbirth or adoption, to care for a seriously ill child, spouse, or parent, or in the event of the employee's own serious illness.

- Employers are required to continue health care coverage during the leave.

- Employers are required to guarantee that employees can return to the same or comparable position.

■ Employers can exempt "key" employees — defined as their highest-paid 10 percent of the work force and whose leave would cause economic harm to the employer.[22]

Elder Care

Assistance in the care of elderly relatives — **elder care** — is another area of employee benefits that is gaining more attention. One reason is the new Family and Medical Leave Act mentioned earlier. Another is that demographics are changing dramatically. For example, the U.S. Senate Special Committee on Aging predicts that by the year 2010 there will be twenty-two elderly persons per hundred working-age persons — in contrast with nineteen per hundred today — and that by the year 2050 the ratio will be thirty-eight per hundred.[23] Besides the economic implications, concern about elderly relatives can have a major impact on employee peace of mind, attendance, and productivity.

Most of the elder-care assistance provided by organizations thus far is in the form of employee counseling and information about elder-care resources in the community. Some organizations provide liberal leaves for the purpose of taking care of elderly relatives, and some are supporting day-care centers for both children and the elderly. As in the case of child care, personnel practices such as flextime, job sharing, and voluntary part-time work can be of assistance to employees with elder-care responsibilities.[24]

Payment for Time Not Worked

Payments for vacations, holidays, and sick leave averaged 10.4 percent of payroll in 1991, based on a survey of 1,008 firms. Paid rest periods, coffee breaks, lunch periods, wash-up time, clothes-changing time, travel time, and so forth, constituted another 2.2 percent of payroll, for a total of 12.6 percent.[25] (See Table 16.2.)

These benefits are obviously important to employees but are a significant cost to employers. Unless there are adequate controls, the firm can easily subsidize a great deal of employee time that is not devoted to organizational purposes. In addition, managers and supervisors must spend considerable time making certain that time-off benefits are administered equitably.

An example of how pay-for-time-not-worked benefits can be excessive and lead to lower productivity comes from Sweden. Alarmed by the high numbers of employees who were calling in sick, the government reduced sickness benefits from 90 percent of employees' wages to 65 percent during the first three days of illness. Immediately, short-term absenteeism dropped by one-fifth in Electrolux's Swedish factories.[26]

On the other hand, pay-for-time-not-worked benefits are important in keeping the organization competitive in recruiting and retaining employees. Further, it is clearly in the interests of the organization to have employees who remain healthy and who have opportunities to renew both energy and perspective.

Other Benefits and Services

Many other benefits are found in American organizations. Some are common; others are unusual. Here are some examples (in some cases, with the names of organizations that offer them):

■ Personal "floating" holidays — holidays taken at the employee's discretion — in 36 percent of the firms surveyed[27]
■ Prepaid legal services[28]

- Physical fitness programs (Chrysler, PepsiCo, Inc., Xerox Corp., Kimberly-Clark Corporation, Campbell Soup Company, and Fluor Corporation)[29]
- Bicycle parking (required by law in Palo Alto, California)[30]
- Discounts of nearly 50 percent of the typical closing costs in the purchase of a new home (TRW Space & Defense Sector)[31]
- Free coffee and popcorn on work breaks (AMC Theatres, Saint Petersburg, Florida)[32]
- College tuition loans to employees' children[33]
- Van-pool programs and free or subsidized mass-transit passes (A common practice with commuter van pools is to assign a ten-passenger van to one employee who drives several other employees, all of whom pay a fee that is less than the actual costs of commuting.)[34]
- Paid sabbaticals of several weeks to several months (Tandem Computers, Inc., Rolm Corp., McDonald's, Du Pont, and Intel Corp.)[35]
- Free turkeys to all employees at Christmas (Russell Stover Candies)[36]
- Sick-leave "banks" (pooling of compensated-leave days in a common fund to cover extensive illness)[37]
- Movies in factory cafeteria during lunch[38]
- Payments of up to $2,500 to assist employees in adopting children[39]
- Special medical plans for disabled children of employees[40]
- Tuition reimbursement prior to and after retirement[41]
- Mental health insurance for services of psychologists and psychiatrists[42]
- Child development center on company premises[43]
- Financial planning for employees[44]
- Maid service to clean homes of nurses (Callaway Community Hospital, Fulton, Missouri)[45]
- Five-dollar haircuts for members of the U.S. Congress[46]
- Accrual of $2,000 worth of college tuition credits in two years, starting after three months of employment (Burger King)[47]

And, in the realm of the highly unusual, and from overseas:

- An Australian judge reinstating a deceased worker for two months so that the family would receive higher death benefits (Western Mining Corporation)[48]

Some of these benefits, such as movies during lunch in the company cafeteria, are relatively inexpensive. Others, such as paid leaves of absence, are very expensive and ordinarily are feasible only in very large organizations or in circumstances where ongoing professional development is critical in meeting organizational goals.

Costs of Benefits Employee benefits are now receiving more attention than in the past because they have become a major part of the cost of being in business. Further, the general trend is for benefits to continue to increase as a percentage of wages and salaries. The costs of health care, in particular, have escalated dramatically in recent years.

Relative costs of various employee benefits across business and industry in 1991 are shown in Table 16.2, which is based on a survey of companies of all sizes and includes both hourly and salaried employees. According to this survey, employee benefit payments for all companies averaged 39.2 percent of payroll. The biggest costs in the typical benefit program are legally required payments (largely social security taxes), medical and medically related benefit payments, and retirement and savings plan payments. Payment for time not worked represents another substantial cost. As indicated above, if costs of rest periods, lunch periods, and so on are added, compensation for nonwork time totals 12.6 percent of payroll.

It should be noted, however, that there are wide variations in the mix and level of employee benefits among companies and industries. For example, the level of benefits in the primary metal industries (41.7 percent of payroll) is much higher than in banks, finance companies, and trust companies (30.9 percent).[49]

Flexible Benefit Plans

Flexible benefit plans (or **"cafeteria" benefit plans**) are gradually being adopted by more and more organizations. Under these plans, employees can choose a particular mix of benefits adding up to a certain dollar amount. Two of the recent additions to the list of firms with such plans are American Airlines, Inc., and United Hospitals, Inc.[50] A survey at the end of 1989 concluded that more than one-third of all firms in the United States with more than a thousand employees had flexible benefit plans.[51]

There are four basic approaches to flexible benefit plans: core, module, flexible spending account, and combined.[52] The *core* approach provides a basic "core" of benefits that the company considers important. This core represents a reduction in total benefits from previous levels, and employees can then use the dollar difference to select from a "menu" the benefits that fit their particular circumstances. The *module* approach provides several packages of equivalent value from which the employee can select his or her benefit program. For example, an employee burdened with poor health might choose a package that provides a large amount of disability insurance and extensive medical coverage with low deductibles. The *flexible spending account* approach provides each employee with a certain dollar total from which to select benefits. *Combined* approaches feature various mixtures of the other three approaches.[53]

Flexible benefit plans are likely to be adopted by more and more organizations in the future. One factor supporting this trend is the availability of the microcomputer, which makes it easier to develop and administer such programs and to provide information to employees. In addition, the flexible benefit approach gives some organizations a better way to control benefit costs. A particularly important factor, of course, is employee acceptance, and employees have generally been enthusiastic about such plans.[54] Unions, too, are gradually endorsing flexible benefit plans. For example, a recent contract between Alcoa and the Aluminum, Brick and Glass Workers included such a plan.[55]

Impact of the Environment

Numerous forces in the environment influence the level and type of benefits paid for or provided by employers. Among these forces are laws, court decisions, collective bargaining, economic conditions, and changes in the work force.

TABLE 16.2 Employee benefits, by type of benefit: All employees, 1991

Type of benefit	TOTAL, ALL COMPANIES	TOTAL, ALL MANUFACTURING	TOTAL, ALL NON- MANUFACTURING
Total employees benefits as percent of payroll	39.2	38.8	39.4
1. Legally required payments (employers' share only)	8.9	9.2	8.8
a. Old-Age, Survivors, Disability, and Health Insurance (employer FICA taxes) and Railroad Retirement Tax	7.1	7.1	7.1
b. Unemployment compensation	0.5	0.6	0.5
c. Workers' compensation (including estimated cost of self-insured)	1.3	1.5	1.1
d. State sickness benefit insurance	0.1	0.1	0.0
2. Retirement and saving plan and other payments (employers' share only)	6.0	5.3	6.2
a. Defined benefit pension plan contributions	2.7	2.1	2.9
b. Defined contribution plan payments (401 k type)	1.4	1.0	1.5
c. Profit sharing	0.5	0.9	0.4
d. Stock bonus and employee stock ownership plans (ESOP)	0.4	0.6	0.3
e. Pension plan premiums (net) under insurance and annuity contracts (insured and trusted)	0.4	0.1	0.5
f. Administrative and other costs	0.6	0.6	0.6
3. Life insurance and death benefits (employer's share only)	0.5	0.5	0.5
4. Medical and medically-related benefit payments (employers' share only)	10.4	10.4	10.4
a. Hospital, surgical, medical, and major medical insurance premiums (net)	7.8	7.8	7.8
b. Retiree (payments for retired employees) hospital, surgical, medical, and major medical insurance premiums (net)	1.0	1.0	1.0
c. Short-term disability, sickness or accident insurance (company plan or insured plan)	0.3	0.3	0.3
d. Long-term disability or wage continuation (insured, self-administered, or trust)	0.2	0.2	0.3
e. Dental insurance premiums	0.6	0.6	0.6
f. Other (vision care, physical and mental fitness, benefits for former employees)	0.4	0.5	0.3
5. Paid rest periods, coffee breaks, lunch periods, wash-up time, travel time, clothes-change time, get ready time, etc.	2.2	2.0	2.3

TABLE 16.2 Employee benefits, by type of benefit: All employees, 1991 (*Cont.*)

Type of benefit	TOTAL, ALL COMPANIES	TOTAL, ALL MANUFACTURING	TOTAL, ALL NON-MANUFACTURING
6. Payments for time not worked	10.4	10.8	10.2
a. Payment for or in lieu of vacations	5.6	5.5	5.6
b. Payment for or in lieu of holidays	3.2	3.5	3.1
c. Sick leave pay	1.2	1.2	1.2
d. Parental leave (maternity and paternity leave payments)	0.0	0.0	0.0
e. Other	0.4	0.6	0.3
7. Miscellaneous benefit payments	0.9	0.6	1.1
a. Discounts on goods and services purchased from company by employees	0.3	0.1	0.3
b. Employee meals furnished by company	0.1	0.0	0.1
c. Employee education expenditures	0.2	0.2	0.2
d. Child care	0.0	0.0	0.0
e. Other	0.4	0.3	0.5
Total employee benefits as cents per hour	635.7	683.7	620.8
Total employee benefits as dollars per year per employee	$13,126	$14,317	$12,761

Source: U.S. Chamber of Commerce, *Employee Benefits, 1992 Edition*, p. 13.

Laws and Court Decisions

As evident in regard to the Family and Medical Leave Act of 1993, discussed earlier, federal laws, as well as state laws and court decisions, have a significant effect on benefit policies and practices in organizations. The mandatory benefits prescribed by the Social Security Act and the impact of ERISA on pension benefits have already been noted. But other important laws regulating benefits also directly influence the design and administration of benefit programs.

The Welfare and Pension Plans Disclosure Act of 1958, with subsequent amendments, placed a record-keeping and report-submitting burden on employers and unions that administer pension and welfare plans. Under this law, organizations administering welfare and pension funds are required to submit reports to the secretary of labor, must have bonded officials to handle such funds, and are subject to legal action if they misuse such funds.[56]

The Retirement Equity Act of 1984 amended ERISA in a number of significant ways, particularly with respect to the rights of spouses. For example, pension and profit-sharing plans must now pay survivor's benefits to the spouse if the employee dies before retirement. After retirement, if the participant in the pension plan dies first, the spouse must continue to receive a monthly benefit of at least 50 percent of what was being paid the retiree, unless the spouse has cosigned a benefit election form choosing some other option. Further, the law prevents workers from losing their vested benefits when they stop working temporarily, a provision that will help women who wish to stay home with their children for a few years.[57]

Amendments in 1978 to the Age Discrimination in Employment Act raised the permissible upper limit on private-sector employees' retirement age from sixty-five to seventy; amendments effective in 1987 removed the limit entirely. Two years after the 1978 amendments raised the limit to seventy, a survey of 267 firms found that 86 percent of the firms had experienced little or no impact on benefit plans. The most frequent changes were the improvement of medical insurance benefits for early retirees and the initiation of preretirement counseling or planning programs.[58] Several more years may be needed before the impact of the amendments effective in 1987 can be fully assessed. At a minimum, organizations must restructure their benefit plans to accommodate employees who work beyond what was previously considered normal retirement age. For example, the Omnibus Budget Reconciliation Act of 1986 (OBRA) restricts defined benefit plans — plans that specify the amount of the retirement benefit — from suspending or reducing contributions to the accounts of employees when they reach normal retirement age and requires these plans to continue accruals at unreduced rates.[59]

The Equal Pay Act of 1963 has also had a major influence on benefits. Under this law, it is "an unlawful employment practice for an employer to discriminate between men and women with regard to fringes." In particular, benefits designed to assist the "head of the household" or "principal wage earner" are considered discriminatory when the effect is to favor male employees. Similarly, it is unlawful to have pension or retirement plans that provide for different benefits or that set different compulsory or optional retirement ages based on sex.[60]

In the landmark *Arizona* v. *Norris* decision, the Supreme Court ruled in 1983 that women and men must be paid equal pension benefits for equal contributions. The case was brought by Nathalie Norris, an employee of the state of Arizona, who had joined an annuity plan offered by the state through a commercial insurance company. Her contribution per month was $199, the same as for male employees, but her monthly benefit beginning at age sixty-five was scheduled to be $33.96 less than for male employees. Norris claimed that this was sex discrimination under Title VII of the Civil Rights Act. The Supreme Court agreed with her, thus overturning the traditional practice of insurance companies and pension plans of paying women smaller benefits because women generally live longer than men and draw benefits longer.[61]

Under the Pregnancy Discrimination Act of 1978, an amendment of Title VII, employers must give pregnant workers the same group health insurance or disability benefits they give other workers suffering medical problems or disabilities. EEOC guidelines on this law included a controversial provision that wives of employees were also entitled to insurance coverage for pregnancy when the employer's insurance program covered spouses for other disabilities.[62] In a related case but with implications beyond pregnancy care, the Supreme Court, in *Newport News Shipbuilding and Dry Dock* v. *EEOC* (1983), ruled that employers must treat female and male employees equally in providing health insurance for their spouses.[63]

Federal laws pertaining to holidays for government employees have had a major effect on holiday practices throughout the country. Federal employees observe the following holidays on Monday: Martin Luther King Day, President's Day, Memorial Day, Labor Day, and Columbus Day. As a result, most states adopted similar laws pertaining to state employees, and a large proportion of private employers subsequently moved the observance of these holidays to Mondays.

The Consolidated Omnibus Budget Reconciliation Act of 1985 (COBRA) required employers to provide certain employees and members of their families with continued health insurance at group rates under some circumstances, including termination of employment (except for gross misconduct), reduction of hours, death, or divorce.[64] The Tax Reform Act of 1986 — and consequently Section 89 of the Internal Revenue Code — added requirements for employers to a number of benefit areas. In general, benefit plans — including health, accident, group term, qualified group legal, dependent care, and educational assistance programs — must ensure that a wide spectrum of employees can participate so that the plans do not discriminate in favor of highly paid employees.[65]

Collective Bargaining and Economic Conditions

Over the years, collective bargaining has had a major impact on the benefits provided to unionized employees. Furthermore, when benefits are negotiated between management and unions, similar benefits are often extended to nonunionized employees in the same organization. In addition, unions typically call attention to benefits negotiated elsewhere to support arguments for increasing benefits in a particular firm.

Union efforts to increase benefits are sometimes motivated by factors other than the enhancement of benefits for workers. For example, assuming that premium pay on Sundays or holidays is a supplementary benefit, double or triple time for work on those days may be sought by the union to discourage supervisors from scheduling such work. Additional holidays or vacation time may be sought to reduce unemployment, since more time off with pay requires additional workers to operate plants.

Labor-market conditions also affect the benefits paid by organizations. Shortages of certain skills and competition for those skills tend to be factors in increasing benefits. For example, if competition for engineers is keen, a company may endeavor to attract employees by initiating a tuition-payment and time-off program that permits engineers to work on advanced degrees at nearby universities.

The organization's ability to finance supplementary programs and services will directly affect the size and scope of its benefit package. A young, struggling firm will not be able to afford an extensive benefit program, nor will a firm in a profit slump want to expand its employee benefits. On the other hand, if a company is experiencing high profits and rapid growth, management may be inclined to be generous in expanding the employee benefit package.

Canceling benefits when times are less favorable is difficult because employees have come to expect them. Nevertheless, during recent recessions, many companies have been forced to reduce benefits. For example, in 1982, International Harvester Co. (now Navistar) and the United Auto Workers agreed to subtract a week of paid vacation and three paid personal holidays. This concession by the union saved the company $200 million over two years. The benefits were then restored in 1985.[66] In some instances, unions have traded wage cuts for benefits such as stock ownership plans. For example, Republic Airlines, facing heavy losses, reached an agreement with the Airline Employees Association to extend a 15 percent pay cut for a year and a half in exchange for an employee stock ownership plan and profit sharing.[67]

Work Force Changes

Changes in the composition of the work force also affect employee benefits. For example, as indicated earlier, the growing number of single-parent families and of employed women with children has increased the pressure for day-care centers, as well as for more flexible work schedules. These factors can partially account for heightened employee interest in flexible benefit packages.

If an organization's work force consists of a high percentage of young people just out of school who remain with the firm an average of two years, there may be little demand for a pension plan and little interest on the part of top management in establishing one. On the other hand, there may be need for careful attention to good cafeteria services, carefully managed rest periods, and liberal vacation and unpaid leave policies. If the work force includes a high percentage of employees with families, both employees and management may be greatly interested in group medical and life insurance programs and other benefits designed to increase family security.

Managing Employee Benefits

The management of employee benefits is a critical concern in any organization. In the first place, benefits are expensive. At the same time, an organization is likely to be at a severe disadvantage in recruiting and keeping qualified employees if management does not try to maintain a reasonably attractive benefit package. Moreover, employee benefits cannot be managed capriciously without adverse consequences. In Case 16.2 at the beginning of the chapter, Len Colfax, the human resources director, was reminded that even small, unexplained differences in employee benefits can lead to perceptions of unfair treatment and, in turn, irritation or anger. For these reasons, careful attention must be paid to the design and administration of the benefit program.

Benefit Surveys

Because of rapidly rising costs, managers have been paying more attention to **benefit surveys** — surveys of the benefits offered by other firms. Benefits for unionized firms are usually surveyed by both management and the union prior to contract negotiations.

Because employee benefits are part of the total compensation package, benefit surveys should be made simultaneously with wage and salary surveys to obtain the most complete and useful data. To establish or revise either aspect of the total package without giving attention to the other is to ignore a significant component of the overall compensation strategy.

Employee Preferences

Management can obtain important guidance in modifying benefit programs by periodically identifying employee preferences. Firms often make incorrect assumptions when they do not make inquiries.[68] Some of the methods used to identify these preferences are personal interviews with a cross section of employees, meetings with small groups of employees, and questionnaires accompanied by computer printouts of current benefits so that employees can readily visualize the present package.[69]

More sophisticated methods of measuring employee preferences are also available. For example, an organization might ask a random sample of employees to rank various combinations of benefits and services. Various pairs of benefits at different levels of cost and coverage are printed on separate cards so that employees can make a series of choices between various pairings. A statistical analysis of the rankings and of the costs of each pair can help management make decisions among various options.[70]

International Perspective

Maternity Leave in the European Community

Country	Maternity Leave	Pay
Belgium	14 weeks (6 before birth)	100% for 1–4 weeks, thereafter 80%
Denmark	28 weeks (4 before birth)	90% of salary
FRG (Germany)	14 weeks (6 before birth)	100% of salary or fixed sum
Greece	15 weeks (6 before birth)	100% of salary
Spain	16 weeks	75% of salary
France	16 weeks (6 before birth)	84% of salary
Ireland	14 weeks (6 before birth)	70% of salary
Italy	20 weeks (8 before birth)	80% of salary
Luxembourg	16 weeks (8 before birth)	100% of salary
Netherlands	12 weeks (6 before birth)	100% of salary
Portugal	90 days (6 weeks before birth)	100% of salary
UK	40 weeks	6 weeks at 90% of salary and 12 weeks at a fixed reduced sum.

Source: National Women's Health Network, Washington, DC. *The Network News*, July/August. "Protection at Work of Pregnant Women and Women Who Have Recently Given Birth — a Proposal for a Directive from The European Commission, Annex 1 Maternity Leave." Reprinted by permission.

Benefit Structure and Rules

Detailed administration rules are usually developed before benefit programs are implemented. For example, for sick-leave benefits, rules must be established on the length of time that salaries or wages will be continued, when benefits will start, the relationship between benefits and length of service, the maximum sick leave that will be granted in any one year, and whether a physician's statement will be required as proof of illness.

If careful attention is not given to the development of benefit rules, policy must be decided quickly the first time the occasion arises, which means making a hasty decision that may later be regretted. Such spur-of-the-moment decision making can result in inconsistent or costly practices. Suppose a company has not considered what sick-leave benefits are to be given to newly hired employees. A new person joins the firm, calls in sick on the third day of employment, reporting that he or she has mononucleosis, and, on the basis of a supervisor's "top-of-the-head" decision, draws full pay for six months. From the organization's point of view, this is a costly decision offering little or no return. Thus, without detailed rules of administration there will be no controls on benefit costs. In addition, there can be no realistic cost forecasts because there will be too many unanticipated variables affecting expenditures.

Equitable, explainable rules are also necessary to ensure that benefit policies are fair and applied consistently to all employees. For example, using the above illustration of the six-month paid leave for the new employee, assume that an employee with three years' service in a different department becomes ill and is told that, under company policy, the maximum sick leave that can be drawn is two months' pay. Almost certainly, the employee will perceive this treatment as inequitable and react angrily. According to equity theory, contributions (hard work, three years' service) and outcomes (two months' sick leave) will be perceived as grossly out of line as compared with the new employee's contributions (two days of getting oriented to the job) and outcomes (six months' leave with pay). Typically, the longer a person has been an employee, the longer the allowable sick leave.

In the interest of fairness and to safeguard morale, management must examine benefits and privileges within and across major categories of employees carefully and develop policies and practices that are perceived as equitable by everyone in the organization. No one is immune to negative feelings that stem from perceptions of inequitable treatment. For example, federal bankruptcy judges are excluded from many of the privileges enjoyed by U.S. district court and appeals judges, including use of the judges' dining room, use of a special elevator, and use of the judges' parking lot. One former federal bankruptcy judge reported that the system made him feel "like a second-class citizen."[71]

Managing Costs

Carefully developed rules are important in managing the costs of employee benefits. It is also important that organizations periodically conduct detailed cost analyses of expenditures in each benefit area. These analyses can provide guidance for cost containment.

General Motors Corp., for example, found that less than 2 percent of its workers accounted for 20 percent of the absenteeism. In other words, a high percentage of the costs associated with absenteeism (sick pay, training time, inefficiencies, and so on) were generated by just a very few people. Working with the United Auto Workers, the company and union negotiated a contract in 1985 to trim the vacation, sickness, and accident pay of workers who were chronically absent during a six-month period. Benefits are cut by the percentage of absent days. In addition, the company and union agreed to pay workers bonuses of up to $500 for perfect attendance during the year.[72]

Health care costs have risen so rapidly that many organizations are working hard to control and reduce them. Of all human resources areas, the cost of health care benefits is the area of greatest concern to personnel executives, as well as to other executives.[73] According to surveys, some of the most popular cost-containment techniques or approaches are the following:

- Careful internal administration of claims submitted by employees
- Offering health care coverage through a health maintenance organization (HMO) or preferred provider organization (PPO)
- Self-insuring under the company's own plans[74]
- Creating "fitness" or "wellness" programs (Tenneco Corporation's main reason for building an exercise facility for its employee fitness program was to gain an advantage in recruiting high-talent employees, but the company found that about 40 percent of the cost was returned through reduced medical claims.)[75]
- Increasing or introducing copayments or deductibles (For example, employees might be required to pay the first $250 of medical care during a one-year period instead of the first $100.)

- Joining with other companies to form a coalition to work with local health service providers to keep costs down
- Conducting an analysis of the extent to which various benefits are used (GM's analysis of the proportion of workers using sick leave is an example.)
- Mandatory second opinions regarding surgery
- Incentives for outpatient testing and surgery
- Workplace screening programs to identify serious problems early[76]

Other methods of reducing benefit costs include paying bonuses to employees who have no absences for a certain number of weeks.[77] Some organizations offer end-of-the-year bonuses to employees who have not used up money set aside for health coverage,[78] and bonuses may also be paid to employees who quit smoking for a full year. (Smokers are reported to cost more in terms of fire insurance, workers' compensation, and life and health insurance premiums).[79] In addition, flexible benefit plans can be used to control the costs of employee benefits. Because of the urgency and complexity of managing health care costs, some organizations are employing specialists with titles such as manager of health care costs or, as at PepsiCo, manager of cost containment and flexible benefits."[80]

Role of the Human Resources Department

Human resources departments typically have a major role in the development and management of employee benefit programs. A survey of organizations of all kinds reported the proportion of organizations in which human resources departments have total or some responsibility for the following programs. The first figure is the percentage of firms having the activity; the second is the percentage of those having the activity that assign the activity to the personnel or human resources department:

- 99% Vacation leave processing, 98%
- 99% Insurance benefits processing, 97%
- 99% Workers' compensation administration, 89%
- 98% Unemployment compensation, 95%
- 94% Pension and retirement planning administration, 93%
- 82% Tuition aid and scholarships, 96%
- 66% Food service and cafeteria, 44%
- 51% Medical services, 75%
- 51% Flexible benefits plan administration, 96%
- 8% Child-care center, 60%*

A number of these benefit programs are based on accounting, financial, and statistical information. Therefore, the organization's interests are best served if the human resources department works closely with other professionals in accounting, finance, and insurance, as well as with legal counsel, in administering these programs. In addition, the expertise of these departments will be invaluable in analyzing

*Reprinted with permission from *Bulletin to Management* (BNA Policy and Practice Series), BNA Survey No. 57, pp. 2–3 (June 25, 1992). Copyright 1992 by The Bureau of National Affairs, Inc. (800-372-1033)

costs and cost trends. Finally, changes in employee benefit programs should be based on broad consultation with managers across the organization, and new programs will require top management approval before implementation.

Assessing Alternatives and Employee Reactions

A major contribution the human resources department can make to organizational efficiency is to examine various benefit alternatives carefully. The first steps are to establish specific objectives for the entire benefit program and to determine the purpose of offering benefits in particular areas. The human resources department is often responsible for exploring various benefit options and determining which ones are the most cost-effective. For example, faced with a higher proportion of women employees, including women managers, and a higher proportion of single parents, many companies are looking at ways to provide day-care service to families with young children. A company-run day-care facility is only one possible solution, and the human resources department might explore the advantages and disadvantages of a number of other options. The alternatives include establishing a service that refers employees to day-care centers already available in the community; contracting with quality day-care centers for a certain number of spaces and then providing these spaces for employees' children at a discount to the employees; or establishing a voucher system through which the organization pays some fraction of the day-care services selected by the employee.[81]

Periodically assessing employee and supervisory reaction to the usefulness of various benefit programs will assist the human resources department in planning revisions in those programs. Questionnaires and interviews are probably the most useful devices for making this assessment. When extensive modifications in benefits are being considered and when choices must be made about where benefit dollars are to be spent, inquiry into employee preferences can provide the organization with important guidance.

Communicating Information

The human resources department plays a major role in determining how effectively information about benefit programs is provided to employees. Studies over the years have shown that many employees are unaware of some of the benefits that are provided, and many tend to underestimate substantially the costs of those benefits of which they are aware. Lack of awareness, of course, reduces the motivational value employee benefits may have and may lead to lack of uniformity in employee use. Lack of awareness can also contribute to inadequate planning by the employee. For example, if an employee does not understand the savings and tax advantages of a salary reduction plan, the employee may not take advantage of it, and may lose eventual retirement income.

The human resources department, therefore, has a major challenge to provide information and counseling about employee benefits. Information can be presented on benefit statements[82] or on video display terminals. At the Westchester County, New York, locations of General Foods Corporation, employees can use touch-screen retrieval devices to obtain information on their benefits and to ask "what if" questions in order to analyze various benefit options.[83] At Levi Strauss, employees can view and analyze their total compensation packages using their personal computers (PCs) to log on to an interactive computer network.[84]

The human resources department also has some information obligations under the law. Under ERISA, an employee participating in a retirement plan must be furnished information such as an understandable summary of the plan and an annual report on its financial status. Employees are entitled to certain information upon request, including their total accrued benefits.[85]

Sensitivity to Equity Issues

Finally, human resources specialists can make a major contribution to the management of benefit programs by being sensitive to issues of equity. As benefit programs are developed and proposed, it is particularly important that differences in benefits among groups of employees be justifiable and readily explained. For example, production and maintenance employees may accept the notion of special parking privileges for top management if executives must leave the plant with some frequency during workdays, but it is more difficult to accept special parking privileges for supervisors who are on the same work schedule as other employees. A decreasing scale of benefits and privileges down through the managerial and supervisory ranks is usually more defensible than a system in which only a few top managers have extraordinary benefits and department heads just below them have very few.

Because it is difficult to anticipate every circumstance that might arise in the administration of a given benefit program, human resources specialists are wise to keep a log of decisions made in order to treat people consistently and to clarify policies when necessary. Such recording can help the human resources department identify practices that need to be curtailed.

Summary

Employee benefits are important to the well-being and security of employees and important to organizations for the purpose of attracting and retaining qualified personnel.

Employee benefits have grown increasingly costly to employers. Payments required by law have accounted for about one-third of this amount. Health care costs are of particular concern to employers and human resources executives.

The level and type of benefit programs available to employees vary widely among firms and industries. Flexible benefit plans (or "cafeteria benefit plans") are gradually being adopted by organizations across the country. Many federal and state laws and court decisions influence the type and level of employee benefits provided by employers. By law, most employers are required to pay into social security, unemployment compensation, and workers' compensation funds. Other laws regulate voluntary benefits, ensure nondiscriminatory benefit practices, or establish taxable status. The Family and Medical Leave Act of 1993 requires employers with fifty or more workers to provide unpaid leave for up to twelve weeks in the case of a family or medical emergency.

Collective bargaining that increases the benefits of unionized employees tends to result in increased benefits for nonunionized employees. Competition in recruiting qualified talent tends to increase employee benefits, whereas lack of financial resources will obviously restrict an organization's ability to offer generous programs. The changing nature of the work force has also influenced employee benefits. For example, the rapid increase in the number of women employed has added to the pressure for child-care assistance and family leaves. Management philosophy is also a major factor in the type and level of employee benefits.

Benefits must be managed carefully to enhance recruitment and retention efforts and morale, to avoid excessive costs, and to avoid problems of perceived inequity. Tools in the management of benefit programs are benefit surveys, other assessments of employee preferences, carefully planned rules of administration, and careful cost analysis. Many techniques can be used for controlling costs, including establishing deductibles and ceilings on benefits and even providing rewards for not using a benefit.

The human resources department has a major role in the development and management of benefit programs. It is in everyone's interests for that department to draw on the expertise of specialists in accounting, finance, and insurance in administering these programs and in analyzing costs and cost trends. Changes in benefit programs should be based on consultation with managers across the organization and will require top management approval before implementation. Ideally, employees' ideas and support will be solicited in making changes in benefit programs.

Ethical Dilemma

Nonexempt employees at Gourmet Restaurant Supply are entitled to four hours off with pay per month for personal business when necessary. Supervisor Jeff Gilbert permits his niece to take off double or triple this amount when she pleads a special problem.

What are the ethics of this situation?

Key Terms

employee benefits
mandatory benefits
social security
unemployment compensation
workers' compensation
defined benefit pension plan
defined contribution pension plan
salary reduction plan
employee stock ownership plan (ESOP)

vesting
portability
health maintenance organization (HMO)
preferred provider organization (PPO)
family leave
elder care
flexible ("cafeteria") benefit plan
benefit survey

Review Questions

1. Discuss the significance of employee benefits to the employee and to the organization.
2. What are the major factors in determining employee benefits in a particular organization?
3. Explain the impact of ERISA on private pension plans.
4. What is the difference between an HMO and a PPO?
5. Discuss the advantages of flexible benefit plans and some of the problems associated with such plans.
6. Explain the importance of controlling the costs of benefits and identify some cost-control measures.
7. Outline the role of the human resources department in benefits administration.

*Opening Case
Questions*

**Case 16.1   Which Goes? Health Care Benefits or Part-Time Student
Employment?**

1. What are the pros and cons of Stephanie's idea of cutting back on health care costs in order to keep a few more part-time students?
2. Is the HEG Company exploiting college students?

Case 16.2   The Holiday Turkeys

1. What does this case demonstrate about employee attitudes regarding benefits?
2. Why do you think there is so much concern in the work force about equitable treatment?

Comprehensive Case

Benefits for the Whole Family

In many organizations, the organization's doors used to separate two very different worlds. When employees walked through the door, they ceased being mothers and fathers, sons and daughters, and became simply workers. Any attention these workers paid to life on the other side of the door was viewed as an illegitimate distraction. Employees sneaked to pay phones at lunch hour to call the school nurse and see if Suzie was feeling better, or they spent hours in the evenings and on the weekends arranging for an array of baby sitters and home-care providers.

Changing social patterns and economic pressures are rapidly destroying that sense of separation. To cite just one example, a study showed that the percentage of organizations offering child-care service almost tripled between 1988 and 1992, from 10 percent to 29 percent. (Ironically, the movement to integrate work and family issues has not been led by those who prescribed a "return to family values": former President George Bush vetoed the Family and Medical Leave Act, which many saw as the federal government's first major step toward speeding that integration. President Bill Clinton, however, signed the bill into law in 1993, in the first few weeks of his administration.) Such changes did not stem primarily from altruism on the part of organizations. Instead, many companies have realized that workers will be content and productive on the job only if they are not constantly worrying about what is happening on the other side of the company's door.

A number of demographic factors have influenced these changes. More children are living with single parents — in 1991 there were about 8.7 million single-mother families in the United States and about 1.4 million single-father families. In fact, single father households are the fastest growing American family group. At the same time, about one-third of the work force cares for older relatives. Further, in most two-parent families, both parents work.

The Family and Medical Leave Act of 1993 focused on one particular family-and-work issue: employees being able to take a significant period of time off from work in order to take care of family matters without losing their jobs. Most of the other leading industrialized nations have such policies; indeed, many offer much longer leaves, and with more pay, than have been proposed in the United States. Such policies recognize that neither employees nor their employers can realistically ignore such events as the birth or adoption of a child or the major illness of a close family member.

To help fill the void left by federal inaction on family-and-work issues, in 1992 one hundred small companies joined with eleven of the nation's largest organizations to raise over $25 million to finance three hundred programs in forty-four cities caring for employees' children and aging relatives. In the joint statement that announced the project, the companies declared, "Dependent care is a primary concern of American business."[1]

The details of one organization's approach to family-and-work issues illustrate why such issues are "a primary concern" and demonstrate how a creative and sympathetic organization can meet employees' needs at relatively low cost. The Los Angeles Department of Water & Power (DWP) is the nation's largest public utility, employing about eleven thousand workers, three-quarters of them male. In another era, an organization with such a heavily male work force probably would not have paid much attention to family issues, stereotyping them as concerns for their employees' wives. Ironically, the DWP Work Family Services program got its start in 1983 when a number of DWP's male employees expressed their anger at not being included in a United Way child-care survey, which had contacted DWP's female employees.

---

1. Quoted in Tamar Lewin, "11 Companies Join on Family Project," *New York Times*, September 11, 1992, A10.

Prompted by the men's outrage, the company studied the issue and calculated that it was losing $1 million in productivity per year as a result of absenteeism related to child-care problems — and that figure did not measure the effect of such problems on morale, and employee retention, and the part they played in tardiness and stress.

Soon DWP was responding to its employees' child-care needs, offering reduced-cost child care at local centers, care for mildly sick children, and a host of parental resources. Some of the more unusual aspects of the developing program give the best sense of how the company met its goals in creative ways. DWP now offers a lactation program for women returning to work after having a baby. For example, nursing mothers can use the company's breast pumps in two specially constructed lactation rooms, portable pumps are provided for traveling employees, and ice-pack kits are provided to keep the milk cold until it can be refrigerated.

While this program might seem to be a luxury offered to a small group of employees, the company says that its goal is to reduce absenteeism. Babies fed their mother's milk tend to be healthier than formula-fed babies; healthier babies mean more content parents who are absent less and get more work done. So the company may, in effect, be paying for breast pumps rather than for replacement workers.

DWP has also set up a number of classes and support groups focusing on such issues as caring for newborns, single-parenting, and dealing with hyperactive children. Recent fathers who have attended the groups act as mentors to new and expectant fathers, and fathers and their children participate in quarterly "Daddy-and-Me" activities. DWP also provides employees who work outside the office with beepers when a family emergency is imminent. The program began as a response to the desire of expectant fathers to know when their wives were going into labor. Recognizing the productivity loss when field employees tried to stay near a telephone all day, the company expanded the program, giving beepers to parents of sick children and people with elderly parents.

Of the many ways to measure the success of such programs, one of the most basic is to look at turnover, since the cost of finding, training, and retaining a new employee can be so high. At DWP, the results are clear: the turnover rate of employees not involved in work-and-family programs is 5 percent; for those who are involved, it drops to 2 percent. At companies like DWP, it seems that the door between work and family is always open, and everyone is benefiting.

Sources: Tamar Lewin, "11 Companies Join on Family Project," *New York Times,* September 11, 1992, A10; Sue Shellenbarger, "Firms Put Resources Behind Elder Care," *Wall Street Journal,* March 6, 1992, B1; "Single-Father Households Are Fastest Growing Group," *Issues in HR,* July/August 1992, 4; Charlene Marmer Solomon, "Work/Family Ideas That Break Boundaries," *Personnel Journal,* October 1992, 112–117; "Work & Family Survey Report 1992," Society for Human Resource Management, 606 N. Washington St, Alexandria, VA 22314; and Timothy L. O'Brien, Vdayan Gupta, and Barbara Marsh, *New York Times,* February 8, 1993, p. B1.

Discussion Questions

1. What are some of the economic and organizational arguments for providing more assistance to employees in managing home-related problems?
2. Why would DWP's male employees become outraged when a United Way survey on child care did not include them?

CHAPTER 17

Labor Organizations and Unionization

LEARNING OBJECTIVES

- Explain why workers join unions.
- Describe the major types of labor organizations.
- Identify the legal constraints on management and on labor during the unionization process.
- Outline the steps in the unionization process.
- Discuss current issues in the labor movement, including changing trends in union membership and relevant economic and social issues.

CASE 17.1   For or Against the Union

Candice Larscheid and her good friend and coworker Mary Butler had just finished their shift at the Millersburg textile mill, where they had been employed for more than fifteen years. Candice and Mary were both hourly employees and earned $9.25 per hour. The mill had never been organized, but the union had finally obtained enough support to force an election to decide whether the employees would have representation for the purpose of collective bargaining. The election was to be held the next day and neither woman had quite made up her mind whether to vote for or against the union. As they walked toward the parking lot, Candice said to Mary:

"Well, tomorrow is the day. I still don't know what I'm going to do. I went to the meeting last night and I listened to what the union guy had to say. He says we don't make enough money and that the places they've organized all make more than we do. I could use more money."

"Look, Candice, I didn't go to that meeting but I know what management thinks about all this. They are really upset and some of them are talking like they might just shut the mill down if we go ahead and vote for a union. I know we don't make much money but it is better than nothing."

"It isn't just the money. I get hassled all the time in there. Some jerk is always trying to get me to have a beer with him after work and the supervisor keeps suggesting we get together. I don't think I would have so much trouble if we had a union and I could complain about things to someone we select instead of someone the company tells us we have to deal with."

"Well, you know, Candice, it might not be so great with the union either. Everything around here will end up being based on seniority. Now we can talk with management and not have to go through some union officer who could care less whether you or I are better qualified than some guy who has been here longer. Plus, we would have to pay union dues." ◄

CASE 17.2   The Engine That Couldn't

Art Jones was an abrasive, technically effective employee who tended to taunt his supervisors. He was a mechanic in a small company that sold and repaired marine engines for both fishing vessels and pleasure craft. He had been with the firm for more than twenty years. The shop supervisor, Dan Gulbrandson, did not like him, but his fellow workers were generally tolerant and took some pleasure in Art's baiting of the supervisory staff.

One day Dan received a call from the general manager saying there had been a complaint that a part had been installed incorrectly in the engine of a large sailboat: the engine was cutting out, and the owner was furious. Art Jones was the mechanic who had been assigned to repair the engine.

Dan summoned Art to his office and used some strong language in accusing Art of installing the part upside down. Art vehemently denied that he had installed the part incorrectly and used some strong language of his own. He went on to indicate that the management staff was too busy drinking coffee and talking about their social lives to know what was going on. Dan ended the interview by saying, "Get the hell out of here. We'll see . . ." Art went back to his workstation. Dan went down to the general manager's office.

The next day, Art was handed a discharge slip by his foreman, who said, "I'm sorry about this, but that's the way it's got to be." Art locked up his tools, went home, telephoned the representative of the international union, and filed a grievance.

Over the next few days a good deal of time was spent by the mechanics in the shop discussing Art's discharge and commiserating with each other about a wide range of things they didn't like about their working conditions. By the end of the week, Art's grievance had become a cause célèbre.

As the grievance went through several steps, the company insisted that Art had been properly discharged for unsatisfactory work and a bad attitude and, furthermore, that he probably should have been discharged long before. The union was equally insistent that the discharge was improper. The case went to arbitration.

The arbitrator held that there had been no progressive discipline, such as warnings in the file, that Art was not aware that the meeting in Dan's office could lead to discharge, and that discharge was too severe a penalty under the circumstances. The arbitrator ordered Art reinstated, but without back pay and with an implied admonition to him to shape up. ◄

A labor union is an organization that bargains for employees over wages, hours, and other terms and conditions of employment. The right of workers to organize unions and bargain collectively with employers has been well established in the United States since the passage of the Wagner Act (or National Labor Relations Act) in 1935. National and local unions, as well as professional associations and associations of government employees that have become bargaining agents, are major participants in the determination of wages, hours, and conditions of work.

Through union membership, employees play a part in creating rules governing the workplace, in contrast to the frequently found (but not necessarily) one-sided decision making by the employers. To deal effectively with organized labor and even to manage relations with nonunionized employees, all managers and human resources professionals need to understand how unions operate, why they are formed, and the laws and regulations that govern them. This chapter addresses these issues; Chapter 18 is devoted to the topic of labor contract negotiations and administering the agreement, including the use of grievance-arbitration procedures.

Why Workers Join Unions

Much has been written about why workers join unions. It is generally agreed that not only economic but also sociological and psychological factors are involved. In an essay written in 1945, and that remains remarkably relevant, E. Wight Bakke described unionization as a result of workers' beliefs that union membership would help them achieve the following conditions or goals:

1. Companionship and respect of others
2. Degree of economic comfort and security enjoyed by those with whom they associate
3. Control over their own affairs
4. Understanding of the forces and factors at work in the world around them
5. Fair treatment for themselves and others and respect for personal integrity[1]

Basically, if workers are sufficiently unhappy with one or more of these conditions and believe that a union can make the situation better, they are likely to vote for the union.

The above list suggests that the desire to improve wages and benefits, although important, is only one of the reasons that workers join unions. Indeed, a study of white-collar employees found that dissatisfaction with leadership and supervision actually provided a stronger push toward unionization than that supplied by dissatisfaction with financial rewards.[2] (In Case 17.1, Candice wants a union for several reasons, including the expectation that the union would assist employees with their grievances. In Case 17.2, Art telephones a representative of his union to ask for help with a grievance.)

Forming a union or joining one may be an attempt to increase personal job satisfaction, but it is more often a reaction against what is seen to be unfair treatment. Unionization, in other words, is frequently the result of workers' efforts to bring about justice and order in the workplace. This was indeed one of the main intents of Congress when it passed the Wagner Act. The director of the AFL-CIO Department of Legislation states, "We're organizing where individuals feel they're not being fairly treated."[3]

Unionization, therefore, is an attempt to fulfill a variety of human needs — including those for security, community, esteem, and a sense of fair treatment — that

The UAW is an international union and belongs to the AFL-CIO, the largest and most powerful labor organization in the United States.

have not been otherwise satisfied in the workplace. At least in part, membership in a union has met these needs for the great majority of union members. If this were not true, unions would never have been able to organize successfully even with the protections provided by the Wagner Act; and the incidence of decertification of bargaining units, the procedure by which workers renounce a union, would be much higher than it is. (For some of the contemporary themes in union organizing, see *Contemporary Issues* on page 453.)

For some workers, however, union membership may not be a matter of choice. Under the union-shop provisions of some labor contracts, employees are required to join the union as a condition of employment. But once a union has been certified as the bargaining agent, the majority of union members tend to favor retention of the union to other alternatives.

Types of Labor Organizations

The union is the most prevalent type of labor organization through which employees bargain collectively. But unions are not the only agents representing organized labor. A number of professional associations, such as the National Education Association (NEA), which were originally created to advance the professional interests of their members, now engage in collective bargaining with employers. In this chapter, the term **employee association** includes these organizations, as well as associations of state and local government employees that bargain with employers but do not refer to themselves as unions.

Although labor organizations have come to include a growing number of white-collar workers, unionization began with blue-collar workers, who still supply the majority of union members in the United States. Unions of blue-collar workers tend to be categorized as either craft or industrial unions.

Craft Unions   **Craft unions** are composed of workers who possess the same skill or perform essentially the same task or function. Among the earliest craft unions were shoemakers, cigar wrappers, and printers. Among present craft unions, the carpenters and machinists are two of the largest. A craft union attempts to organize all the practitioners of that craft who are employed by the same employer or located within a particular area.

Craft unions seek not only to represent all those who engage in the craft, but also to restrict the number who can enter the craft. Apprentice programs requiring as much as several years of instruction, as well as state licensing requirements, limit the supply of craft workers and enhance the union's ability to demand higher wages.

Because the members of craft unions may work for more than one employer during any given year, contracts frequently cover an entire geographic region rather than a single employer. The building trades union, in particular, tries to negotiate an agreement with all the construction companies within a given area. Members such as plumbers and electricians can then move among construction sites without having to enter into a separate round of bargaining with each company.

A craft union often employs a **business agent** to negotiate and administer the labor contract and to handle the union's day-to-day business affairs. The **steward** is usually an employee of the particular company and a member of the union; his or

Contemporary Issues

The Union Pitch Has Changed

With membership at a post–World War II low, organized labor is focusing on attracting members. Using slick marketing techniques, unions are getting involved in everything from the credit-card business to community relations.

James D. Morgan, a director with the New Orleans law firm McGlinchey, Stafford, Cellini & Lang, says unions are transforming their image to stay in tune with the changing workforce. Morgan advises employers on how to counter organizing campaigns.

According to Lilli Segre Tossani, a legal assistant for the firm's Labor Resource Center, it's evident that labor is doing its homework, because the results are showing up in its professional organizing efforts.

She says that unions are carefully targeting markets with individually orchestrated campaigns that address specific worker concerns — adequate health insurance, VDT emission, sexual harassment, job security, worker safety and working conditions.

Some unions are concentrating on community-based organizing attempts. The Amalgamated Clothing and Textile Workers Union (ACTWU) and the International Ladies Garment Workers Union (ILGWU), for example, have targeted immigrants by appealing to them at the community level.

The unions are trying to "think social," says Nick Unger, ACTWU's New York political director. That means offering English classes and counseling people on subjects such as unemployment insurance and immigration problems.

Although attention is being paid to this approach, it is not really new, according to Morgan. It has been used before when there is a relatively large employer that makes an attractive target.

"The union has to have the prospect of a good return," he says, "they're businesses too."

The United Foods and Commercial Workers International Union (UFCW) also has used the community approach to organize catfish plants in Alabama and Mississippi. The UFCW is now using the same style of organizing in North Carolina poultry plants after a fire in a poultry plant there cost 25 workers their lives.

Morgan, who has been involved in fighting some of the catfish plant organization efforts, says that the labor organizers turned to local religious and black community leaders.

"It takes on the flavor of the civil rights movement with themes like self-respect and 'get rid of the plantation mentality,' " he says.

"If well done it can be extremely effective," according to Morgan. Although the election results were mixed, "a well-planned campaign of this sort is a very effective tool."

Just because a human resource person is not in a blue-collar, factory environment doesn't mean that the person won't face a union campaign.

Unions are making at least a few inroads into white-collar areas such as insurance and hospital workers, Morgan says, and since that's where more and more jobs are, that's where he expects to see more union attention.

Source: Excerpted from Stephenie Overman, "The Union Pitch Has Changed," *HRMagazine*, 36 (December 1991):44–45. Reprinted with the permission of *HRMagazine* (formerly Personnel Administrator) published by the Society for Human Resource Management, Alexandria, VA.

her union assignment is to make sure that the labor contract is being followed. Frequently, stewards are required to "punch out" on the time clock when conducting union business. (See also "shop stewards" below.) The steward is a major source of the information from which the business agent determines whether the employer is in compliance with all the terms of the labor agreement. The steward represents the workers only for the duration of a particular job at the site where the craft union is providing workers. When the job is finished, the steward is once again simply another member of the union.

Industrial Unions

Whereas the members of craft unions tend to be skilled trades workers, **industrial unions** include many semiskilled or unskilled workers. Craft unions, as we have seen, organize all the practitioners of a particular craft, for example, electricians; industrial unions attempt to organize all the workers in a given industry, no matter what jobs these workers perform. Thus, all the workers engaged in the production of automobiles in unionized plants are members of the United Auto Workers of America, and all the workers employed in the different stages of steel production in unionized steel plants are members of the United Steelworkers. Besides autoworkers and steelworkers, industrial unions include organizations of rubber workers, miners, textile workers, truck drivers, and others.

Local industrial unions are usually administered by union officers, who are not only elected from among the workers but very often continue to be full-time workers. In addition to its local officers, the membership elects **shop stewards.** Operating at the department or line level, the stewards serve as links between the union members and the officers. They forward the complaints and the desires of the membership to union officials and pass information back to the members. They participate in the adjustment of **grievances** (formal complaints by union workers) and are active in the negotiation of the collective-bargaining agreement.[4]

The typical industrial union has less bargaining power than the typical craft union. This is because it is easier to replace semiskilled workers than skilled craft workers. This relative ease of replacement may have been a factor in the United Auto Workers going back to work after a five-month strike against Caterpillar Inc., in 1992. The strike ended when Caterpillar threatened to fill strikers' jobs with permanent replacements.[5]

White-Collar Organizations

The reluctance of white-collar employees to organize has diminished considerably as the nature of white-collar work has changed. An increasing movement toward large organizations and the requirements of technical efficiency in the computer age have dramatically reduced the differences between assembly-line workers and many clerks and technicians.

White-Collar Membership

As white-collar work has become more routine and bureaucratized and white-collar workers have become easier to replace, they have also become more willing to consider a union to protect their jobs and advance their interests. This is in contrast to overall union membership, which has been declining as a proportion of the total work force. Whereas there were only 4.9 million white-collar union members in 1970, a figure that represented 21.8 percent of total union or association membership, there were 7.1 million white-collar members in 1990, or 42.6 percent of the total union or association membership.[6]

In addition to the sheer increase in membership, unions were established in white-collar occupations that had not previously been organized. Insurance workers, government inspectors, school administrators, and even professionals at the National Labor Relations Board were for the first time organized into unions.

Public Employee Unions   The Wagner Act, which granted employees the right to organize and to engage in collective bargaining, specifically excluded public employees. Eventually, however, changes in federal and state law permitted and thereby encouraged the transformation of public-employee associations from organizations that could only engage in informal negotiations with government employers to ones that could bargain collectively. In the past twenty years, the proportion of government workers belonging to unions has increased from 11 to more than 36 percent.[7]

Though many public employees can now bargain collectively, the process is usually not totally the same as that available to organized employees in the private sector. Federal employees, in particular, do not have the right to strike. To illustrate, over eleven thousand federal air controllers, members of the Professional Air Traffic Controllers Organization (PATCO), defied the law in 1981 by going out on strike and were promptly fired by President Reagan.[8] (In 1993, fired controllers were allowed by President Clinton to reapply for jobs.) In addition, federal employees are permitted to bargain only on working conditions and on grievance procedures; they may not bargain over wages, hours, or other matters excluded by law.

Teachers in the public schools constitute nearly one-third of all the public employees in the United States, and they have organized themselves in numbers and at a rate that the most powerful industrial unions can only envy. By 1987 the NEA, with 1.7 million members, had become the largest among the many employee associations and unions; it even exceeded the Teamster membership of 1.6 million. By 1991 NEA membership had reached 2.1 million, while Teamster membership had dropped to 1.5 million.[9]

Moreover, public school teachers have been quite willing to strike, even though it is against the law in nearly every state. Nor is this simply the result of local organizations deciding the matter for themselves. At its 1967 convention, the NEA reversed its long-standing opposition to strikes and declared its readiness to supply its affiliated state and local associations with legal services and financial support when they struck school systems.[10]

Structure of Union Organizations

Most unions in the United States are organized on four levels: local; intermediate; national or, in the case of those with members in both the United States and Canada, international; and as a federation of unions. The United Auto Workers (UAW), for example, is an international union with headquarters in Detroit, Michigan, and is headed by an elected president. The UAW is divided, however, into ten intermediate bodies, or regions, each of which has an elected regional director. Each region, in turn, is made up of dozens of local unions, whose members elect their own local officers. Finally, the UAW is a member of the American Federation of Labor–Congress of Industrial Organizations (AFL-CIO). To put this in perspective, a worker at the Ford Motor Co.'s River Rouge plant, just outside Dearborn, Michigan, the company's world headquarters, would be a member of Ford Local 600, of UAW Region 1-A, of the UAW, and of the AFL-CIO.

Local Union   The local is the basic unit of union organization. In a craft union, the local may include all the unionized practitioners of that craft in a city. In an industrial union, the local is ordinarily made up of all the union members in a single plant or mill. The local union negotiates at least part of the collective-bargaining agreement with the company, manages the routine operations of the agreement, handles most of the grievances brought by workers, supervises the conduct of strikes, and, when necessary, disciplines union members.

Most local unions are run according to democratic principles. Officers are elected by the dues-paying members, usually for a one-year term. Under the election rules of most unions, advance notice must be given that an election is to be held, nominations must be open to any member, and the election itself must be by secret ballot. When the officers — typically a president, a secretary-treasurer, and an executive board — have been elected, they run the affairs of the local and preside over its monthly meetings.

National Union

Although the local union elects its own officers and plays an important role in representing its members' interests, it is not necessarily autonomous. Most local unions are chartered by a national union and must comply with the provisions of the national organization's constitution. Moreover, the national union often has the ultimate authority to approve settlements negotiated at the local level, to decide whether a strike is legitimate, to supervise local elections, and to determine financial procedures and practices. It also has the authority to decide whether national rules have been ignored, and if it finds that they have, to determine whether to remove the local officers and administer the affairs of the local directly through the imposition of a trusteeship.

The national union is governed by periodic conventions of local-union representatives. National conventions are held by most unions either every year or every other year. The convention may amend the constitution, establish union policy, and elect the officers who will lead the union. Between conventions, the national union is governed by the elected officers, usually a president and an executive board.

The national union provides a wide range of services to its locals. In many cases, the national union attempts to organize the unorganized workers within the jurisdiction of a local and provides assistance with grievance and arbitration administration and with strike activities. It also may represent the interest of locals and their membership in political activities at both the state and national levels. Some national unions, of which the UAW is one of the best examples, have even become heavily involved in the internal affairs of political parties.[11]

AFL-CIO

The majority of national and international unions belong to the AFL-CIO. In fact, the AFL-CIO is perhaps better known to the American public than any of the ninety national and international unions that make it up. With more than fifty-five thousand local unions and 14 million members, the AFL-CIO is the largest and most powerful labor organization in the United States.[12] (Figure 17.1 is an organizational chart of the AFL-CIO.)

The basic policies of the AFL-CIO are determined by a convention that meets every two years. The convention is composed of delegates sent by each affiliated national and international union in proportion to the size of its membership. Between conventions, the AFL-CIO is governed by an executive council made up of the federation's president, secretary-treasurer, and thirty-four vice presidents — all elected by majority vote of the convention.

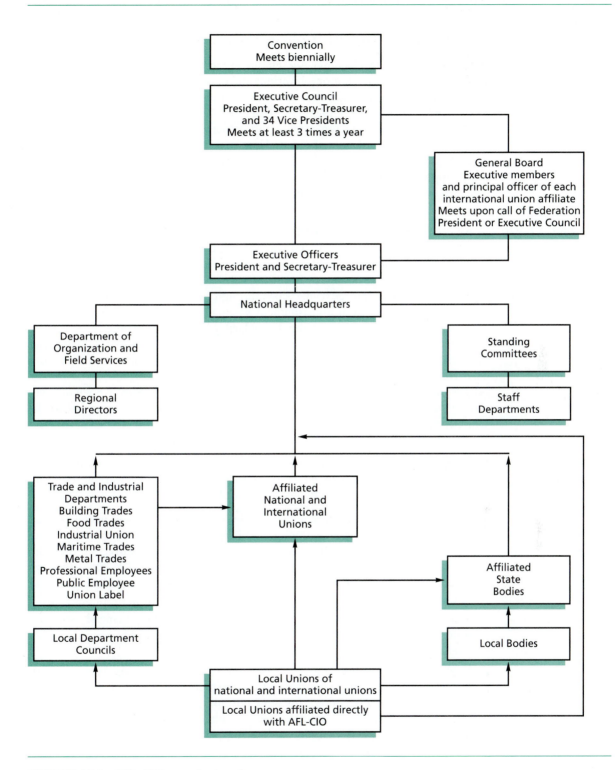

FIGURE 17.1 AFL-CIO organization chart

Source: Reprinted with permission. "Chart 1, Structure of the AFL-CIO, p.2, from *Directory of U.S. Labor Organizations* 1992–93 Edition, by Courtney D. Gifford. Copyright © 1992 by The Bureau of National Affairs, Inc., Washington, D.C. 20037.

Legal Impact on the Labor Movement

Under Section 7 of the Wagner Act, employees were guaranteed the right to form and organize their own labor organizations and to become members of labor unions. The act allowed union employees to choose representatives who exercise exclusive bargaining rights for all employees in that union.

The process of organizing a union and inducing workers to join it is subject to numerous provisions of both the Taft-Hartley Act, passed in 1947, and the Landrum-Griffin Act of 1959. Some of the regulations pertaining to organizing campaigns apply to the union, and some apply to management. All these regulations are enforced by the National Labor Relations Board (NLRB).

The NLRB   As we saw in Chapter 2, the NLRB was created under the Wagner Act. The board has five members, each of them nominated by the president of the United States and confirmed by the Senate to serve a six-year term. The board determines policy and also serves as the judge in appeals to the NLRB.

The NLRB may enforce its decisions through court order and injunctions or, in some cases, by fine or even imprisonment when a court order has been disobeyed. More specifically, Section 10 of the Taft-Hartley Act empowers the NLRB to require persons to "cease and desist" from unfair labor practices, to reinstate employees with or without back pay, to require reports showing the extent to which parties have complied with orders, and to petition federal courts to enforce its orders. NLRB orders, however, like the orders of any federal administrative agency, are subject to review by the courts. Decisions of the NLRB may be appealed to the United States Circuit Court of Appeals and, ultimately, to the Supreme Court.

Constraints on Management   During an organizing drive, management is not free to do whatever it wishes to oppose the formation of a union. Most of the following restrictions were written into the Wagner Act and subsequently became part of the Taft-Hartley Act:

- Employers may not "interfere with, restrain, or coerce employees in the exercise of [their] rights" to organize a union and bargain collectively or to refrain from union activity. This prohibits direct or implied threats to fire workers if they join a union or to close the plant if a union is organized. (In Case 17.1, if management threats to shut down the mill actually occurred, this would be an illegal act.)

- Employers may not "dominate or interfere with the formation or administration of any labor organization. . . ." Thus, a union that receives financial assistance from the company is illegal. The union is supposed to be, and is required by law to be, the sole creation and agent of the workers.

- Employers may not discriminate against any employee in hiring, tenure of employment, or terms and conditions of employment either to encourage or discourage union membership. This does not apply, however, to the situation in which a labor agreement requires union membership as a condition of employment. In that case, if the employee does not pay the required initiation fee and membership dues, he or she may be discharged.

- Employers may not discriminate against workers for filing charges or giving testimony in an NLRB proceeding.

■ Payments of money or the provision of other things of value by management or its representatives to an official of a union that is attempting to organize a company's employees is illegal, as is the acceptance of such payments or demands for them.[13]

Constraints on Labor   Just as there are major prohibitions on the conduct of management, labor must operate in the face of several important constraints imposed by the Taft-Hartley Act:

■ Unions may not restrain or coerce workers in their right to refrain from union activity. Mass picketing, for example, that prevents entrance into a plant by non-striking employees or the refusal to process a grievance because the employee has been critical of the union are violations of the prohibition.

■ A union may not cause an employer to discriminate against an employee with regard to wages, hours, and conditions of employment or for the purpose of influencing the decision whether or not to join a union. Under this prohibition, it would be illegal to compel the employer to discharge employees who criticize a union practice or speak out against a contract proposal.

■ A union may not strike against an employer to compel the employer to recognize or bargain with that union when another union has already been certified as the representative of the employees of that employer.

The Landrum-Griffin Act placed several major limitations on the use of picketing by unions. Within one month of beginning to picket a firm for organization purposes, the union must file for an election. If the election goes against the union, picketing must stop for at least twelve months. Picketing to inform the public that a company is nonunion is legal unless the picketing stops deliveries to and from the company or causes other employees to withhold their services.

The Process of Unionization

The sequence of events in unionization is described in Figure 17.2. The first phase begins with an organizing effort of some kind. The initiative for organizing workers may come from the employees themselves, from a union that already represents some of the employees of the firm, or from a union that represents workers elsewhere. Typically, an organization drive starts with an aggressive campaign by a union that already represents part of a company's work force or with a campaign conducted by an outside union.

The first phases of a drive for organization are likely to be quiet. Workers may be contacted at their homes or in restaurants or other places near work, and a good deal of soliciting and campaigning may take place between fellow workers on the job. Sometimes an outside union will contact workers on the job — as is often the case, for example, in retail stores. Management's first indication that a unionization drive is under way may be nothing more tangible than rumor or nothing more threatening than a simple handbill. (See Figure 17.3 for an example of an actual handbill used in an organizing drive. Only names and location have been changed.)

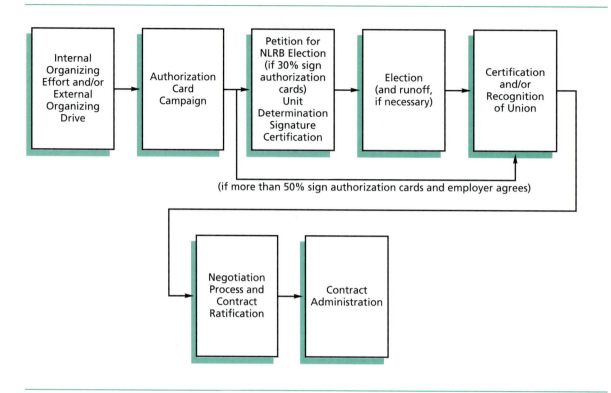

FIGURE 17.2   Unionization process

Role of the Human Resources Department

Once management realizes that an organizing drive has begun, it must itself become organized. The emotional, legal, and power aspects of the unionization drive require that management responses be coordinated by one individual and one department within the company. If there is a centralized human resources or industrial relations department, this assignment will ordinarily be given to the human resources or labor relations director.

The human resources department helps protect the interests of the company by watching for unfair labor practices by union organizers and for unlawful infringements on the company's property rights. That department also advises first-line supervisors and other managers about what they can and cannot do during the unionization campaign.

The drive for unionization is almost always filled with emotion, and, for this reason, efforts by the human resources department to minimize the defensive behavior of both supervisors and employees may, if the union is recognized, be especially beneficial during the early stages of the collective-bargaining relationship. The sooner hostile feelings diminish, the sooner both parties can move to establish a constructive working relationship.

Petition for NLRB Election

Before the Wagner Act, a union could usually obtain recognition only by demonstrating employee support through the use of the strike. Labor relations were often

ATTENTION! ALL OFFICE AND LABORATORY PERSONNEL OF THE XYZ COMPANY

Recently a large number of non-union employees in the labs and offices have contacted the Local 1 of the Plant Workers in regard to representation for wages, hours and working conditions. They are interested in representation which provides the know-how in dealing with the Company for working conditions and other Contract provisions as they affect monthly salaried office and laboratory employees.

This Union has been the bargaining agent for the wage personnel at XYZ Company for almost 20 years, and has been very successful in meeting all the situations peculiar to the XYZ Company, and has obtained for its members a broader range of benefits than has been obtained by other unions in this area.

Why stake YOUR job-security, YOUR opportunity for advancement, on the whims of your boss or supervisor? Make your boss follow the rules for advancement, wage progression, and job-security as set forth by a Labor Organization of your own choosing.

Why should your rates, rate ranges, and wage pro-

gressions be controlled solely by the vagaries of a capricious boss? Why not have a definite rate range, with automatic progression, as set forth in a bona-fide Union Contract? It is a protection you do not have now, but which you *will* have if you fill in and sign the attached card and drop it in the mail TODAY! Signing this card does not obligate you in any way. It merely indicates your desire to be represented by a progressive Union of your own choosing — Local 1 of the Plant Workers.

All Names Will Be Held In the Strictest Confidence! Sign it — and mail it — Today!

NOTICE ....NOTICE

In order to acquaint you more fully with the benefits obtainable with your organization, there will be a MASS MEETING of all eligible personnel, to be held in the ballroom of the Johnson Hotel, Monday evening, March 3rd, at 8:00 P.M.

FIGURE 17.3 Handbill used in unionization drive

conducted as though there were a quasi war. The Wagner Act and the NLRB have changed what was once an all too frequently violent confrontation between management and labor into a peaceful and closely regulated process in which the employees are left to choose for themselves whether or not to become members of a union for the purpose of collective bargaining.

This process usually begins when an organization wishing to become the bargaining representative for employees files a petition with the appropriate regional office of the NLRB. The petition will ask that the NLRB supervise an election of the employees to determine whether a majority of them favor this organization as their bargaining representative. The petition, in most cases, is filed only after the union has asked for recognition from management and the request has been refused. The petition must be supported by evidence that a substantial interest in union representation exists among the employees. This evidence is usually supplied through authorization cards signed by more than 30 percent of the employees in the bargaining unit.

Once a petition has been filed and the NLRB has determined that it has jurisdiction, the board will hold a conference with both the union and the company to see whether there is agreement on the appropriate bargaining unit, voter eligibility, and the form of ballot, as well as the date, time, and place for the election. If the parties agree on all these items, a **consent election** will be held. If there is disagreement on even one of these items, the NLRB has authority to determine the employees' choice of a bargaining representative and the appropriateness of a bargaining unit in industries engaged in interstate commerce (with the exception of railroads, airlines, agriculture, and government agencies).

Determining the Bargaining Unit

An **appropriate bargaining unit** is a group of employees who share common employment conditions and interests and who may reasonably act together for purposes of collective bargaining. The NLRB is empowered to decide the appropriate bargaining unit subject to certain provisions of the Taft-Hartley Act.

The board will consider, for example, the extent to which the proposed unit reflects a distinct community of interest among the employees to be represented with respect to wages, working conditions, skill, and the like. It will examine the history of collective bargaining at that location or at other facilities owned and operated by the organization. It will seek to discover whether distinct crafts are involved. It will analyze the relationship of the proposed unit to the organization structure of the company, the scope of the required unit, and the scope of the employer's bargaining practices (that is, whether the employer bargains as part of an employers' association). If this examination leads to no clear conclusion on the appropriateness of the bargaining unit, the NLRB may hold an election to determine the interest of the employees.

Representation Election

Once the bargaining unit has been determined, the level of interest in representation has been deemed substantial, and no barrier has been found to exist, the representation election is conducted by officials of the NLRB. The election is conducted at the employer's location during working hours. A secret ballot is used that carries the appropriate company and union designations. The NLRB, however, may choose to conduct the election by mail ballot if it believes that a regular election would not be fair because, for example, adverse weather is expected or excessive travel is required to get to a central voting location.

The purpose of the election is to determine whether a majority of the employees in the bargaining unit wish to have representation. The NLRB defines a majority as a simple majority of those who actually participate in the election. If there are more than two choices on the ballot — if, for example, employees are asked whether they favor unionization and, if so, which of several competing labor organizations they wish to join — a **run-off election** will be held if no single choice receives a majority on the first ballot. Once the employees have voted to be represented by a union, the NLRB formally certifies that union as the recognized bargaining agent for those workers.

Decertification

Just as employees in a bargaining unit have the right to decide whether they wish to form or join a union, they have the right to decide whether to end their affiliation with the union. To petition for what is called a **decertification election,** an employee or employee representative files a petition supported by at least 30 percent of the employees in the bargaining unit. The petition may be filed, however, only at least twelve months after the union has been certified as the recognized bargaining agent of the employees or when the labor contract that has been negotiated between the union and management expires.

Although only the employees can petition for a decertification election, the employer may achieve the same effect by raising a question about whether the union continues to enjoy the support of a majority of the employees and petitioning the NLRB for a representation election. Even when a petition is filed, the employer remains obligated to bargain with the union until the representation issue has been resolved.[14] Whether the employee files a petition for a decertification election or the employer files a petition for a representation election, if the employees vote to decertify their union, twelve months must pass before another representation election can be held.

Management, including supervisors, is constrained by the NLRB and the courts as to what it can and cannot do during the decertification process. Of the three phases in the process — initiation, petition, and election — management actions are the most severely limited in the initiation phase. For example, management may not suggest that employees would be better off without a union, may not recommend to employees that a decertification petition be circulated, and may not volunteer information about the decertification process. During the next two phases, management actions continue to be limited but some activity is permissible; for example, management may respond to employee requests for the names and addresses of employees.[15]

Current Issues

Labor unions have become an established part of American life, and the great majority of their members continue to believe that unions make a difference in their lives. Unions, however, like other institutions, have undergone substantial changes and face significant challenges. Organized labor must deal with several very difficult economic and social issues. In particular, the national debt and foreign competition threaten the whole American economy and the ability of organized labor to retain and attract members by providing increased economic benefits. Moreover, the changing characteristics of union members will greatly affect the way in which unions seek to deal with the substantive problems they face.

Changing Trends in Union Membership

Membership in unions and employee associations dropped from 20.1 million in 1980 to 16.7 million in 1990. As a proportion of all wage and salary employees, union membership declined from a high of 34.7 percent of workers in 1954 to 16.1 percent in 1990, and then to 15.8 percent in 1992. However, as we have seen, unionization of the white-collar segment of the work force has been increasing.[16]

Declines in union membership have been reflected in the statistics on the number of representation elections won by unions in recent years. In 1990, for example, manufacturing sector unions won only 40 percent of 1,066 elections, in contrast to winning 54 percent of 4,361 elections in 1970. Results were even less favorable for the unions in the mining industry.[17]

Decertification elections are also an indication of declining union membership. For example, in the state of Washington, one of the most heavily unionized states in the United States, unions lost about three-fourths of 200 decertification elections in a recent five-year period.[18]

This decline has gone hand-in-hand with decreases in employment in goods-producing industries — the segment of the economy traditionally most heavily unionized — and increases in employment in service-producing industries, where traditionally there has been less unionization.

In response to this declining rate of union membership, unions in the future are likely to recruit new members from those segments of the work force that are growing most rapidly. Efforts to unionize professional and white-collar employees and to increase the levels of female and minority membership are also likely to continue.[19]

Technological Change and Competition

Perhaps the most serious problems faced by the American labor movement are the result of rapid technological change. Management, confronted with high labor costs, high taxes, and the high cost of energy, and facing competition from abroad that sometimes has at least the advantage of significantly lower labor costs, is constantly seeking new machinery and new methods to increase efficiency. The requirements for both the number of workers and their specific skills are changing almost continually, and temporary layoffs are seemingly becoming inevitable. (Productivity is also an issue south of the U.S. border. See *International Perspective* on page 465.)

When businesses fail or find it necessary to engage in massive reorganizations to avoid financial losses, as has happened in automobile, steel, coal, air transportation, and other industries, facilities are closed and layoff situations become much more serious. The response of a union may vary from (1) resistance to all changes, to (2) support for changes combined with efforts to minimize layoffs and other adverse effects on employees, to (3) cooperation with management in the solution of cost, production, and quality-of-work-life problems.

The reactions of unions to technological change and the introduction of new work methods have been anything but uniform. In general, craft unions tend to resist change more than industrial unions because, with membership based on a particular craft, efficiencies that result in layoffs are likely to reduce the number of dues-paying members. On the other hand, competition may also stimulate change in situations where it is obvious that without new equipment and methods a particular craft may be unable to survive. For industrial unions, the situation is somewhat different. Technological changes often create new occupations that may remain in the bargaining unit; consequently, resistance to change is likely to be lower.

From the perspective of its power to affect the nation's standard of living, its ability to meet foreign competition, and its capacity to assist underdeveloped countries, the labor movement needs to adopt a policy of support for technological change while working with management and government to minimize the adverse effects of change on individual workers. Training programs, moving allowances, severance pay, supplemental unemployment benefits, extended unemployment compensation, and aggressive counseling and placement are only some of the methods that require the cooperation of labor, business, and government.

Right-to-Work Laws and Union Security

Right-to-work laws have now been passed in twenty-one states. These laws prohibit both (1) the **closed shop,** in which the employer may hire only union members, a practice declared illegal under the Taft-Hartley Act (although the Landrum-Griffin Act modified the Taft-Hartley Act to permit what is almost a closed shop in the building and construction industry), and (2) **union shop provisions** in contracts, which make union membership a necessary condition for continued employment. Right-to-work laws also outlaw **maintenance of membership requirements** — clauses that require workers who belong to a union at the beginning of a con-

International Perspective
Workers in Mexico Strike Over Measures to Boost Productivity

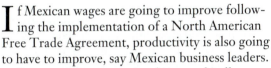

If Mexican wages are going to improve following the implementation of a North American Free Trade Agreement, productivity is also going to have to improve, say Mexican business leaders.

Some employees aren't taking too kindly, though, to new work rules proposed by management to improve efficiency and worker productivity. (A favorite response of Mexican workers to complaints about productivity has been "If you pretend to pay me, I'll pretend to work.")

Since August, tens of thousands of auto, oil and textile workers have gone on strike to protest efforts to trim payrolls and make pay contingent on productivity instead of seniority. More walk offs are anticipated.

Volkswagen's giant production facility in Puebla, Mexico, for example, was shut for nearly four weeks during a wildcat strike protesting an agreement the leader of the Independent Auto Industry Workers Union signed, reportedly without informing the rank and file, that would institute Japanese-style production teams and base pay on productivity rather than seniority. The Puebla

plant is the last place in the world Volkswagen still builds Beetles, Mexico's most popular car, and the strike is estimated to have cost the company more than $10 million in lost sales.

Similarly, 20,000 textile workers went on strike to protest a new contract that would reduce the required number of workers per loom. Under the old contract, Mexican textile companies were required to have two workers per loom, but as trade barriers come down, Mexican textile firms are having to compete with foreign producers that operate with as many as 34 times fewer workers per loom.

If these and the recent strikes plaguing General Motors' U.S. operations are any indication, workers on both sides of the U.S.-Mexico border can be expected to vigorously resist any attempts to change work rules and eliminate jobs that will likely follow the enactment of the proposed North America Free Trade Agreement now waiting ratification by both countries and Canada.

Source: *Issues in HR*, November–December 1992 p. 6. Reprinted with the permission of *Issues in HR* published by the Society for Human Resource Management, Alexandria, VA.

contract's term to remain members throughout the period covered by the contract except for a specified interval near the contract's expiration date when withdrawal is permitted).

Not surprisingly, unions object to right-to-work laws, in part for economic reasons. In general, unions feel that those who are represented should be required to assume the financial and other responsibilities of membership; they feel that allowing anyone to enjoy the benefits without paying the costs of collective bargaining will ultimately destroy labor organizations. The financial problems occasioned by right-to-work laws may be minimized by **agency shop provisions,** by which nonunion members of the bargaining unit must contribute to the union an amount usually equivalent to the regular dues. Agency-shop provisions, however, are seldom found in union contracts and have been declared illegal in some right-to-work states.

Though state right-to-work laws are a threat to union security and a constant ir-ritant to organized labor, 98 to 100 percent of all union contracts, depending on ge-ographical region, contain union security provisions, with 83 percent providing for one or more of the principal forms of union security: the union shop, modified union shop, maintenance of membership, or agency shop.[20]

Changing Image of Labor

The public's impression of organized labor has changed over the years, and govern-ment policy has frequently been altered in accordance with those changes. In gen-eral, public opinion has tended to be in favor of unions but also in favor of government regulation of union-management relations. In 1988 a Gallup poll found that 61 percent of those Americans surveyed approved of unions.[21]

Among workers there has been considerable ambivalence in recent years about the effect of unionization on economic benefits. A poll conducted by the AFL-CIO found the following:

> Over 75 percent of all workers — and over 75 percent of non-union workers — state that they agree that unions in general improve the wages and working con-ditions of workers. Over 80 percent of all workers agree that unions are needed so that the legitimate complaints of workers can be heard. Yet when asked to as-sess the effect of organization on their present employer, 53 percent of non-union workers state that wages and fringe benefits would not improve and 74 percent state that job security would not improve.[22]

Perhaps most disconcerting of all from the point of view of organized labor was the discovery that

> non-union workers do not perceive unions as pursuing an institutional agenda drawn from the needs and desires of their members. Sixty-five percent of such workers express agreement with the statement that "unions force members to go along with decisions they don't like." Sixty-three percent state that they be-lieve that union leaders — as distinguished from union members — decide whether to go on strike. . . . And, among the population as a whole . . . 50 per-cent state that they believe that most union leaders no longer represent the workers in their unions.[23]

Overcoming this negative image is essential if the labor movement is to reverse its declining rate of growth.

Summary

Employees join unions and other labor organizations for a number of reasons. Typ-ically, these reasons include the seeking of fair treatment and better wages, benefits, and working conditions.

The different types of labor organizations through which employees bargain with management include craft unions, industrial unions, and employee associa-tions. Craft unions comprise workers with the same trade or skill, such as carpentry or printing. Industrial unions tend to consist of as many workers in a particular industry as the union can organize, regardless of craft — for instance, in the automobile or steel industries. The term "employee association" is frequently used to denote organizations of professional or white-collar employees that have a bargaining relationship with employers. The National Education Association and various associations of government employees are examples.

Large unions may have several levels of governance, including local, regional, and national levels. Shop stewards, found in both craft and industrial unions, typically are full-time workers and play key roles in processing grievances and in serving as links to union officers at the local level. Business agents are frequently employed by craft unions to negotiate and administer the labor contract.

The National Labor Relations Board (NLRB) of five members enforces the regulations of the Wagner, Taft-Hartley, and Landrum-Griffin Acts. Some of the board's activities include determining bargaining units, holding representation elections, certifying and decertifying unions as bargaining agents, and requiring employers and unions to cease and desist from unfair labor practices.

The process of unionization is regulated by federal law, and both unions and employers are restricted in what they can do during an organizing campaign. The process of decertification is also regulated by law, and management must essentially stay aloof from the process, particularly in its early phases.

The employer's response to the drive for unionization is usually coordinated by the human resources department. That department is in a position to minimize conflict and tension, which, if not kept in control, could seriously interfere with the early stages of collective bargaining following union recognition.

The American trade union movement is still strong in numbers and well established in law and public policy. However, it faces increasing difficulties. The membership is declining in proportion to the total work force as larger percentages of that work force are employed in service, trade, and professional occupations. Unions are attempting to deal with this problem by redoubling their efforts to organize white-collar workers, including those employed by government.

Managerial pressure for rapid technological change and improved productivity has also presented a major challenge. Unions have had to choose between resisting change to protect the immediate interests of some workers and encouraging change while minimizing the effects of worker displacement in order to acquire long-term advantages for the majority of American workers.

Ethical Dilemma

Union member Maury Stone has sometimes been openly critical of the union. Labor relations director Jennifer Turner has approached Maury "off the record" and has sounded him out about starting a union decertification campaign. "We could make it worth your while but, of course, this conversation never happened."

Discuss the ethical aspects of this situation. What should Maury do?

Key Terms

labor union
employee association
craft union
business agent
steward
industrial union
shop steward
grievance
consent election

appropriate bargaining unit
run-off election
decertification election
right-to-work laws
closed shop
union shop provisions
maintenance of membership
   requirements
agency shop provisions

Review Questions

1. Why do workers join unions?
2. Describe the difference between craft unions and industrial unions.
3. Discuss the role of the shop steward.
4. List at least three constraints on management and two on the unions relative to a unionization drive.
5. Describe the steps that usually occur in the formation and recognition of a union as a bargaining agent for employees.
6. What steps occur in the decertification of a union? What are some of the constraints on management?
7. Discuss several issues facing the labor union movement.

Opening Case Questions

Case 17.1 For or Against the Union

1. Why is Candice leaning toward voting for the union?
2. Why is Mary resisting the notion of a union?

Case 17.2 The Engine That Couldn't

1. What should Dan have done regarding Art's past behavior?
2. How could Dan have handled this situation with Art regarding the upset customer?
3. If you were Art, what would be your reasons for filing the grievance?

Comprehensive Case

Fighting to Stay Relevant

The best news for unions in recent years was that they did not lose any more ground. Between 1990 and 1991, the percentage of the entire work force represented by unions remained constant, at 16.1 percent. The absolute number of union members actually dropped in that period by about 172,000, but at the same time the total number of people employed fell by over 1 million.

That may not seem like much to cheer about. However, for most of the past thirty years, American unions have had to seize upon any small sign of hope in an otherwise gloomy picture. Since the early 1960s, the percentage of the overall work force in unions has been dropping, and since 1979, the overall number of union members has been falling as well. With unions now representing fewer than one out of every six American workers, many wonder if unions as we know them will soon cease to be a force to reckon with in American labor.

Several factors have added to unions' problems in recent years. Perhaps the largest — and one that seems irreversible — is the globalization of the economy and the increasing ability of companies to move plants anywhere in the world in search of inexpensive labor. In their heyday, unions could strike a plant in the hope that if they could prevent local people from crossing the picket line they could keep the company shut down until it agreed to union demands. Now, depending on the context, if the company has legitimate economic reasons, it can say to the union, "Stop striking or we'll move the work to another plant." Many companies have followed through on such threats.

While plant relocations were gaining national attention in the 1980s, a combination of political factors added to unions' woes. The Reagan and Bush administrations portrayed unions as special interest groups out of touch with American work-

ers. When federal air traffic controllers held an illegal strike early during his presidency, Ronald Reagan simply replaced them, effectively breaking the union and demonstrating that even a powerful union of skilled and crucial workers could no longer be counted on to help its members. Since then, with more conservative Reagan and Bush appointees in place, judges have tended to rule more often against unions, while the National Labor Relations Board (NLRB), the government's main body for handling unions' grievances, has not been quick to jump to unions' defense. On the average, the NLRB has been taking eighteen months to reach decisions on the legitimacy of particular firings of union supporters.

The combined impact of these political and economic forces has helped to undermine what was once unions' strongest social weapon — the stigma of being a "strike-breaker," or "scab." Around the country, workers — many of them current or former union members themselves — have shown their readiness to cross unions' picket lines and replace striking workers. Companies clearly have a psychological edge, since many workers now seem to believe that if they do not cross the picket line someone else will, and few people seem ready to make a purely symbolic personal sacrifice.

In many cases, unions have added to their own image problems. Many workers see unions as no better than the companies they are fighting: slow-moving, bureaucratic, controlled by old white males out of touch with the increasingly non-white, female work force. The frequent stories about corruption pervading unions like the Teamsters have added to this image, as have several recent battles among various unions pitted against each other to represent a particular group of workers. When the United Auto Workers caved in after a five months' strike at Caterpillar in 1992 without winning any concessions, disgruntled union members felt that the union was abandoning workers to save itself.

In desperation, unions have recently developed two strategies for regaining some of the lost ground. One is to target health care, which is the single largest industry in the United States that cannot relocate to another country. A recent NLRB decision has made unionizing various groups of hospital workers easier, and union organizing at hospitals has picked up around the country, particularly at larger hospitals. Even unions that have traditionally had nothing to do with health care, like the United Automobile Workers and the United Steelworkers of America, have gotten into the act.

The other union strategy that has led to some successes is to use companies' legal and environmental violations as bargaining leverage. The United Food and Commercial Workers, for instance, gave regulatory agencies and the press videotapes of alleged violations of safety and child-labor laws at a chain of stores they were trying to organize. The union has not won the battle against that particular chain. However, during the height of the publicity over the alleged violations, another chain, Smith's Food & Drug Centers, voluntarily agreed to recognize the union, perhaps in part to avoid similar scrutiny. Union undercover investigations have led to fines against a New York pharmaceutical chain and proposed Federal Highway Administration penalties against Greyhound Lines. Unions hope that such victories will not just enable unions to get a foothold in new companies but will also help convince the public that unions are necessary to keep workplaces safe.

The most optimistic way to view the decline of unions' popularity is to see it as a sign that workers have in fact won many of the rights that they traditionally needed unions to help them gain. The bitter antagonism between owners and employees that helped drive many workers into unions is disappearing. Most of the nation's largest companies now have worker-involvement programs, and most modern managerial theory encourages cooperation and teamwork rather than the maximum exploitation of workers. Nonunion groups, such as the Black Caucus at Xerox Corp., have taken on many of the roles that unions used to play, but rather than strike to make their voice heard, they are more likely to find that management has an open ear. The future of labor unions in the United States may well depend on the willingness and ability of American management to continue this trend toward the ideal organization, in which everyone works together for the benefit of all.

Sources: Dana Milbank, "Unions' Woes Suggest How the Labor Force in U.S. Is Shifting," *Wall Street Journal*, May 5, 1992, A1, A6; Linda Thornburg, "Large U.S. Hospitals Report Organizing Activity," *HRNews*, July 1992, A30; Robert Tomsho, "Unions Search for Regulatory Violations to Pressure Firms and Win New Members," *Wall Street Journal*, February 28, 1992, B1; "Unions Laboring to Attract a New Generation," *Seattle Times*, September 16, 1992, D12; and "Union Membership, 1991," *Monthly Labor Review* 115 (March 1992): 2.

Discussion Questions

1. What seem to be the factors in the drop in union membership?
2. Describe two strategies that unions have been recently using to increase membership.

CHAPTER 18

Negotiating and Administering the Labor Agreement

LEARNING OBJECTIVES

- Define collective bargaining and identify its major purposes.
- Identify activities and tactics that are signs of good-faith bargaining.
- Describe the major types of bargaining relationships.
- Indicate what is involved in preparing, analyzing, and resolving bargaining proposals from the points of view of both labor and management.
- Explain how negotiating impasses may be resolved.
- Describe the role of strikes and lockouts in the collective-bargaining process.
- Describe the grievance-arbitration procedure and its purposes.
- Describe the role of the arbitrator, including how it differs from the role of the mediator.
- Contrast interest, final-offer, and expedited arbitration.

CASE 18.1   The Management Negotiating Team

Jack Warren and Peter Jacobs were both members of the negotiating team for the Jupiter Automobile Company and had been in intensive negotiations with the union for over a week. The strike deadline was only forty-eight hours away. Utterly exhausted, Jack remarked: "I'm fed up. Let them strike. We can take a strike and probably ride it out. At least if it doesn't go more than sixty days. I don't think the union can go that long. We might even break the union if we take them on. They have been completely unreasonable and have made the most outrageous demands I have ever heard. Don't they know we barely made a profit last year?"

Peter looked across the table where they had just finished lunch and said to Jack, "You must be out of your mind. The union wants you to think like that. They would love to have you decide that a strike is all right. Then they can throw the whole blame for it on us. They want a strike. Their new president wants to show he is tougher than the guy he beat in the last election. If they want to have a strike, let's make sure it is because they want it and not because we appeared to force them to do it. Forget what they have put out on the table. All we do is react to what they demand. Why don't we put together a complete proposal of our own and tell them, and the public, that we are ready to negotiate around the clock to avoid a strike?" ◄

CASE 18.2   The Union Negotiating Team

Kathy Baroni and Mike Walsh, the two top labor negotiators, were having lunch at a coffee shop just down the block from the headquarters of Jupiter Automobile Company. With only forty-eight hours to go before the strike deadline, they were both irritable. Mike, who had been through every contract negotiation with Jupiter for the last thirty years, had a look of complete disgust. "This guy Warren is the worst ever. Where do they get these guys? He has about as much idea of what it takes to feed a family or what it is like to work on the line as you could expect from someone who was born rich, lived rich, and if we are lucky, will die rich real soon. I asked him why he thought a 10 percent wage increase was too much and he said any wage increase was too much. I asked him whether he thought we were entitled to at least recover the wage concessions we made during the last three years and he said we were lucky to have jobs. He's got some nerve. I felt like clobbering him. What are we going to do? Charlie got elected president of the union because all the guys believed he could get a good contract and avoid a strike."

Kathy, who seldom said anything, had listened patiently while Mike complained about everything the management team had done or said. But now, as Mike seemed on the verge of beating his head against the table, she smiled slightly and said: "It doesn't matter. Jacobs isn't terribly bright, and the other guy, Warren, is nothing. They don't decide anything. Jupiter isn't going to permit a strike and we don't want one. Charlie has a private meeting with Jupiter's president late tonight. This thing will be over tomorrow and those two guys in there will never have any idea what happened." ◄

Once a union has been certified as the exclusive bargaining agent for a group of employees, management and the union are both required by the Taft-Hartley Act to bargain collectively with each other over wages, hours, and conditions of employment. **Collective bargaining,** the process by which a formal agreement is established between workers and management regarding wages, hours, working conditions, and similar matters, is a key aspect of labor-management relations. This bargaining normally proceeds through discussion and debate over proposed provisions in the contract. The provisions proposed may be based on contracts already in existence in similar plants or industries or on alterations one side or the other would like to have made in the practice followed in the past. After the initial labor contract has been agreed upon, signed, and implemented, subsequent negotiations will be concerned with how the existing contract is to be changed.

The end of the collective-bargaining process is signified by the signing of the labor-management contract. A contract is a means by which the parties establish the rules that will govern their relationship, and, as former solicitor general Archibald Cox once described it, the labor contract is "the basic legislation governing the lives of workers in the plant."[1] In other words, the purpose of collective bargaining is to reach agreement on the specific ways labor and management will conduct themselves until the expiration of the contract.

Collective bargaining, which may on the surface appear to resemble the give-and-take that goes on between a buyer and a seller in an open-air market or on a used-car lot, is in reality much more complex. Labor and management conduct their negotiations within a web of government regulations that both limit their strength and protect their rights. Both sides also come to the bargaining table with considerably more power than any two individuals are ever likely to have. The union may elect to strike rather than agree to less than what labor demands, and management may decide to lock out the employees (or close down operations) rather than continue to operate without a contract it finds satisfactory. The process becomes even more complicated when the government or a neutral third party intervenes to resolve bargaining disputes.

Government Rules and Regulations

Federal labor laws impose a wide range of legal constraints on both labor and management during the negotiating process. In particular, there are legal guidelines pertaining to good-faith bargaining, issues that are negotiable, and the power that can be exercised by both labor and management.

Obligation to Bargain in Good Faith

The Taft-Hartley Act requires that labor and management "meet at reasonable times and confer in good faith with respect to wages, hours, and other terms and conditions of employment . . . but such obligation does not compel either party to agree to a proposal or require the making of a concession."[2]

Precisely what constitutes bargaining in good faith is a problem with which both the National Labor Relations Board (NLRB) and the courts have struggled for years. The NLRB and the courts have, however, developed general guidelines under which certain activities or tactics are taken as indicative of either an intent to bargain in good faith or a refusal to do so. Thus, an intent to reach an agreement, active participation, and the making of counterproposals are all signs of good-faith bargaining. Stalling tactics, sudden shifts in position when agreement seems close, rejection of provisions that are a routine part of almost any labor contract, and refusal to sign the contract after agreement has apparently been reached are clear indications of bargaining in bad faith.[3]

Moreover, the refusal to furnish data necessary for bargaining is an unfair labor practice. This means that the company is legally required to supply information about individual earnings, job rates and classifications, pensions, operations and earnings of the incentive system if there is one, merit increases, time-study data, and piece rates. Furthermore, when a company attempts to justify a refusal to grant a wage increase on economic grounds, the obligation to bargain in good faith requires the company to furnish enough data to the union to permit it to bargain in an informed fashion.

Even where no single action constitutes a failure to bargain in good faith, a combination of actions, sometimes referred to as **totality of conduct,** may violate the duty to bargain in good faith. Perhaps the most famous example of this is a tactic employed by General Electric Co., which came to be called *Boulwarism*, after company vice president Lemuel Boulware. GE formulated a contract proposal based on management interpretation of a survey it had conducted of employee attitudes and wants. This proposal was then offered to the union as the company's final position. Although some, including GE, considered this a realistic approach that eliminated the exchange of initial offers that are unlikely to be acceptable, the NLRB concluded that the company's totality of conduct did not meet the standards of good-faith bargaining.

The obligation to bargain in good faith, although something each side has a right to expect of the other, may nonetheless be violated without serious legal consequences. Other than issuing an order directing the violator to stop bargaining in bad faith, there is very little the NLRB can do. In addition, the Supreme Court upheld the Taft-Hartley provision that the obligation to bargain in good faith "does not compel either party to agree to a proposal or require the making of a concession."[4]

In other words, a contract cannot be imposed on the parties; both labor and management must agree to it. Fortunately for labor-management relations, this kind of determined bad-faith bargaining is seldom seen.

What Is Negotiable

Determining the subjects that can be negotiated through collective bargaining is an extension of the good-faith problem. The NLRB has established three categories of bargaining issues: illegal, mandatory, and voluntary. **Illegal bargaining issues** are those that would conflict with the law and may therefore not be made a part of the labor contract even if both sides agree to do so. For example, an agreement not to pay employees overtime for time worked beyond forty hours in a week would be illegal because it violates the Fair Labor Standards Act, which requires overtime pay. A refusal to bargain over demands that are contrary to the law, the NLRB has ruled, is not an unfair labor practice. Another example of an illegal agreement is a "hot cargo" or "hot goods" arrangement, under which the union and the company agree to cease handling the products of, or cease doing business with, other firms or persons. (Certain exceptions are allowed in the construction and garment industries.)

Mandatory bargaining issues include wages, hours, and conditions of work, and **voluntary bargaining issues** include all those that are lawful but not mandatory. Refusal to bargain all the way to a genuine **impasse** (or deadlock in negotiations) over mandatory issues is an unfair labor practice, and so is insistence on negotiating to an impasse over voluntary issues.[5]

It has sometimes been difficult to determine precisely the distinction between mandatory and voluntary issues. But it is reasonably certain that the NLRB and the courts consider at least the following matters to be mandatory subjects of collective bargaining: subcontracting, profit-sharing plans, stock-purchase plans, pension and employee welfare plans, workloads, production standards, plant rules, and successorship clauses requiring a new owner to assume the contractual obligation of the employer.[6] Table 18.1 lists examples of typical items in union-management agreements, most or all of which are probably mandatory items.

Legal Constraints on Labor and Management

When negotiations are not successful and the union decides to strike or the company decides to lock out the employees, federal law imposes several major obligations on both management and labor. (A **strike** is a work stoppage by employees. A **lockout** is a situation where management literally keeps employees away from their jobs by locking the doors.) The party that desires to terminate or modify a contract must give written notice at least sixty days before the effective date of the termination or modification. A strike or lockout during this period constitutes an unfair labor practice.

TABLE 18.1 Examples of typical items in union-management agreements

Absenteeism	Leave of absence	Strikes, lockouts
Apprenticeship and training	Management rights	Subcontracting
Arbitration	Meal periods	Supplemental unemployment compensation
Call-in pay	Merit rating	
Contract length	Overtime pay	Supplementary benefits
Discipline, discharge	Overtime rules	Tardiness
Discrimination	Pensions	Tests
Dues checkoff	Premium pay (Saturday)	Time off for union business
Grievances	Premium pay (Sunday)	Tools
Holidays	Premium pay (holidays)	Transfers
Hours (daily)	Promotions	Travel allowances
Hours (weekly)	Recall	Union literature, distribution of
Incentive rates or standards	Rest periods	Union security
Insurance, health	Retirement	Vacations
Insurance, life	Safety	Wages
Job posting and bidding	Seniority	Work clothes
Labor-management committees	Severance pay	Workload
Layoffs	Shift differentials	Work rules
	Sick leave	

Once a strike actually takes place, management may not refuse to deal with the union but must instead continue to bargain in good faith. Moreover, management can replace strikers with new employees only during an **economic strike,** or a strike over wages, hours, or conditions of work. If the strike is in response to an unfair labor practice by management, the company may be required to release the replacements and reinstate and provide back pay to the workers. Even when an economic strike is over, management must rehire the strikers, providing there are openings for which they qualify. As a practical matter, the union will frequently insist on the reinstatement of all striking employees as a condition of bringing the strike to an end.

The union is also limited by the law in what it can do during a strike. Unions or their agents may not threaten employees with loss of their jobs or with bodily injury for failing to support the union's activities. Unions may not engage in what are called **coercive secondary boycotts.** For example, if a union picketed a retail store that handled the products of a manufacturer with which the union had a dispute, that would be a secondary boycott and therefore illegal. (However, the Supreme Court has held that giving out handbills urging a consumer boycott is not illegal.)[7] It is also illegal to engage in **jurisdictional strikes,** or strikes to force an employer to assign work to one union, trade, or craft instead of some other, unless the employer is refusing to comply with an NLRB order regarding such work.

National Emergency Disputes

When a strike occurs that could threaten the economic well-being of the nation or imperil the national defense, it is called a **national emergency dispute,** and the president of the United States is empowered by the Taft-Hartley Act to take steps to avoid it. The president may direct the attorney general to petition the appropriate federal district court to forbid a strike or lockout for a period of eighty days. If the dispute has not been settled after sixty days, the NLRB will conduct an election to determine whether the employees will accept management's last offer. If the employees vote to turn this offer down, the union may legally strike at the end of the eighty-day period. As a last resort, the president is authorized to report on the situation to the Congress, with a recommendation for action appropriate to protect the national interest.

Types of Bargaining Relationships

Collective bargaining is often regarded as a struggle between management and labor in which management attempts to give as little as possible while labor seeks to get everything it can. From this perspective, collective bargaining is mainly a battle over the division of wealth and power. This type of bargaining is called **distributive bargaining** because it involves the distribution of things that exist in limited quantity. The gain that one side makes is necessarily at the expense of the other. (Cases 18.1 and 18.2 provide examples of distributive bargaining.)

Distributive bargaining is of course not the only form of collective bargaining. The second major type, called **integrative bargaining,** describes the situation in which both sides clearly benefit from an agreement because both labor and management share common goals and concerns. There are several forms of integrative bargaining, and these are discussed after a more detailed look at the distributive approach.[8]

Distributive Bargaining

Distributive bargaining is the most common strategy used in the United States. Before negotiations begin, the union presents in writing its initial demands for changes in the contract. At least some of these demands are beyond what the union reasonably expects to obtain and may form part of the agenda the union will pursue in years to come. By mentioning them at the outset, the union provides itself with something it can afford to give up as part of the bargaining that will take place and, in addition, begins the process of making the proposals credible by bringing them before both management and the public.

Management may or may not present a list of its own demands, but if it does, the list will typically be shorter than the union's. Management may also have in mind some contractual changes but, in the belief that the union will also be in favor of them, will let them be suggested by the other side.

In the initial bargaining sessions, the union explains and defends its demands for nonwage and nonfringe benefits, while management explains its position. Many of these early sessions may be slow moving and frustrating to the participants, and much haggling may occur over procedural matters.

Typically, the parties eventually proceed to earnest bargaining over noneconomic issues, with the understanding that any agreement reached will remain tentative until the entire contract has been negotiated. Management will concede certain items, but only if the union drops some other demands or agrees to several of the contract changes management has proposed.

Once items that carry no economic cost have been agreed on, negotiations become considerably more tedious and intense as the bargaining shifts to wages and employee benefits. Each side attempts to get the other to move toward its position, and each seeks to discover the other's final position without disclosing its own. Gradually, the union's wage demands begin to be lowered and the company's wage offer begins to rise.

If the positions are reasonably close, the parties will more than likely split the difference and sign a new contract. If the positions are too far apart, each side will try to convince the other that it views the prospect of a work stoppage with perfect equanimity. Management or labor, or both, may even seek to widen the arena within which the conflict takes place by publicizing their positions through the print and electronic media.

When agreement is finally reached on a new contract, the mood almost always shifts from the somber and sometimes belligerent tone taken during collective bargaining to a festive atmosphere. The labor and management representatives joke, shake hands, and make statements to the press that the settlement is fair and just to employees, management, and shareholders alike. This ritual relaxes the tensions that have built up and eases the way for the mutual cooperation that will be necessary for proper administration of the contract during the period it is in force. (For a description of bargaining in Japan, see *International Perspective* on page 478.)

Integrative Bargaining

Though far less prevalent than distributive bargaining, examples of integrative bargaining have been appearing with increasing frequency. The integrative strategies require that both management and the union drop combative attitudes and adopt a genuine interest in the joint exploration of solutions to common problems. To work effectively, integrative bargaining must become a way of life for the two parties that includes continual efforts to improve relationships through regular discussions of

International Perspective

Bargaining in Japan

It is a Kabuki drama — a highly stylized, exaggerated performance — and even companyism gives way to its logic. Every Japanese knows this, although it's not written down anywhere. When Japanese negotiators go into a bargaining session, they cannot agree to terms right away. They have to go back for a second session and then a third session. Finally, red-eyed and fatigued after many sleepless nights, they can accept at last what they rationally were prepared to accept at the outset. Only when it is clear that they have fought valiantly to the end, when all agree that they could not really have done anything else, can they do what they must.

If management goes into a wage negotiation with a union and comes out a few minutes later with an agreement for a 5 percent increase, the deal cannot possibly last. Everyone will say the settlement was either too high or too low and will fight against it. But if the negotiators lock the door and sit in the room until morning and then stagger out, to announce, grudgingly, that 5 percent was the absolute best they could do under impossible circumstances, then the deal will fly. It's the sheer agony of the struggle that makes the result acceptable. Companyism gets much of its strength from this consensus-building mechanism. Before corrective action is possible, all must suffer visibly.

Source: Excerpted from Kenichi Ohmae, "The Fallacy of Doing More Better." Reprinted from *Across the Board*, March 1991; The Conference Board, New York City.

---

problems at all levels and a willingness to attempt to settle these problems without third-party intervention. Solutions to the most difficult problems can be approached by establishing special committees, whose members are drawn from both management and labor, to study the issues and determine the facts.

There are three major forms of integrative bargaining: **concessionary bargaining,** in which there is considerable joint problem solving but through which labor actually gives up something it had earlier won; **productivity bargaining,** in which wage increases are tied to the union's acceptance of work practices that will increase efficiency; and **quality-of-worklife (QWL) projects,** which, as the phrase suggests, are collaborative attempts by labor and management to improve the working lives of employees to enhance their ability to produce.

Concessionary Bargaining

In recent years the serious economic difficulties faced by many American organizations have led a number of them to seek concessions from the unions that represent their employees. One of the most interesting examples of this took place in the automobile industry in 1981, when General Motors Corp. negotiated a contract with the United Auto Workers (UAW) in which the union agreed to several major concessions.

The UAW, which for more than a generation had extracted significant wage increases for its members in every new contract, agreed to a wage freeze. It also agreed to give back nine paid holidays it had won in previous negotiations and to defer three cost-of-living adjustments for a year and a half. In exchange for these and other concessions, General Motors promised to keep open four of seven plants that had been scheduled for closing, began a profit-sharing plan for employees, guaranteed that workers with ten years or more of seniority would have an income should they be laid off, and stipulated that in the future supervisory personnel would be laid off in proportion to hourly workers.[9]

As this example demonstrates, concessionary bargaining presupposes a willingness by both sides to seek a solution to a common problem in a spirit of tolerance and trust. Had the UAW sought to hold on to everything it could, or had General Motors demanded sacrifices from the union without making any of its own, the ultimate result might very well have been disastrous for the automobile industry. In recent years concessionary bargaining has occurred in numerous other industries — steel, airlines, communications, electronics, and many more. To illustrate, Northwest Airlines negotiated wage cutbacks of up to 15 percent with its pilots and machinists in return for three board seats and more than one-third of the company's equity.[10] (When the union makes concessions for only a short time — say, one or two years — the term *snap-back bargaining* is often used.)

One of the most significant kinds of adjustments that have been negotiated in concessionary bargaining is the two-tier, or "B," wage scale. A **two-tier wage scale** features a wage scale for new hires that is significantly lower than that for employees already on the payroll. Although two-tier wage scales have aided companies in remaining competitive, such systems have led to dissension and conflict within unions and between companies and unions, including a strike by the pilots of United Air Lines. For these reasons, two-tier pay scales are declining.[11] (Equity theory would suggest that such plans are not likely to be successful in the long run. See Chapter 5.)

Productivity Bargaining

Under the productivity bargaining approach, management offers wage increases or other incentives on the condition that the union agrees to changes in work rules and practices that will increase productivity and/or quality. In the United States, one of the most interesting examples of productivity bargaining again involved the United Auto Workers. The UAW and the Harmon International Company, which manufactures automobile mirrors, agreed to what they called a Work Improvement Program. After an attitude survey was conducted to identify major problems, a labor-management committee was set up to review the results and, on the basis of its findings, to design experiments to improve the ways in which the work was done.

Small groups of workers and supervisors were given the authority to change their methods of work with the aim of improving both productivity and their own satisfaction with their jobs. One project used a system of rewards in which workers who exceeded the production standard for eight hours in less time could choose either to take the balance of the time off or to earn more money by working the full eight-hour shift. Productivity increased, and the workers requested more in-plant training with which to take advantage of the new opportunity.[12]

In some instances, when it has become apparent that a plant or a product line is no longer competitive and that layoffs might result, the union has taken the initiative to work jointly with management to reduce costs. For example, the Amalgamated Clothing and Textile Workers Union (ACTWU) requested the management of Xerox Corp. to establish a joint labor-management **study action team** to find ways to reduce costs in the components manufacturing operations plant. The study action team, including engineers, hourly employees, and managers, found ways to increase productivity and quality that exceeded everyone's expectations and helped keep the plant competitive. Such study action teams have been used extensively at Xerox.[13]

Quality-of-Work-Life Projects

Many collaborative efforts to improve productivity, as well as the working life of employees — frequently called quality-of-work-life (QWL) projects — both result from and illustrate integrative bargaining. Although QWL projects are not limited to unionized settings, most of them have in fact involved union-management cooperation. QWL projects typically have many components, including agreement with the union on job security, skills training, the use of self-managed teams, and the use of quality circles. Some of these projects are being merged with total quality management (TQM) efforts. (Quality circles, QWL, and TQM are discussed in some detail in Chapter 21.)

Conducting Negotiations

Negotiators of the labor agreement are chosen representatives of labor and management. Generally, both sides develop a plan to carry out their bargaining strategies. Figure 18.1 shows typical compositions of both the management and union negotiating teams. This section describes how these negotiators are selected and their responsibilities in the negotiation process.

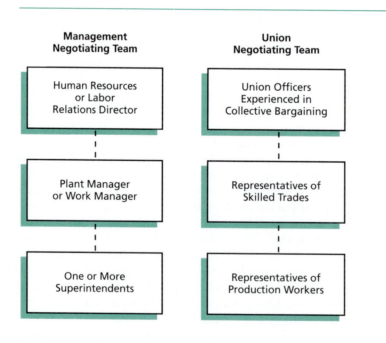

FIGURE 18.1   Membership of bargaining teams

Contract negotiations are conducted by chosen representatives of labor and management. If negotiations reach an impasse a third party may be called upon to help resolve the dispute.

The Management Team

Management is usually represented in collective bargaining by the top-ranking human resources professional, who calls on operating managers for advice and assistance during the negotiations and who may join with one or more operating managers to form a bargaining team. In some large corporations, each plant manager is expected to take charge of labor relations and to either conduct negotiations personally or delegate that responsibility to a staff specialist. The negotiations may be followed closely by corporate headquarters, or they may be evaluated only in the context of the overall performance of the plant.

Most corporations, however, do not withdraw so completely from the conduct of negotiations. If each plant is left on its own, the union that represents the employees in all of the company's plants will be able to insist that an advantage gained at one plant should be applied to all the others, a tactic known as **whipsawing**. To prevent the union from exploiting this possibility, nearly all large corporations have a centralized labor relations department to monitor negotiations at each of their operating facilities.[14]

The management team that is assembled to conduct negotiations normally ranges in size from two to six people, with an average of three or four. Besides the human resources or labor relations director, who is almost always a member and is usually the chief spokesperson, the management team commonly includes the plant manager or works manager and superintendents. Many firms use lawyers for legal advice during negotiations, but few have included them as active members of the negotiating team.

The authority of management's negotiating team is usually limited by guidelines established by the top management of the company. The negotiating team is expected to keep the chief executive officer of the company informed of the progress of negotiations. If the union demands anything that requires either a major financial commitment or major changes in plant operations, no decision can be made and no concessions granted without the CEO's prior approval.

The imposition of these limitations is quite logical, since contract negotiations affect the entire enterprise, sometimes decisively. The limitations are also necessary to protect the negotiators from the consequences of their own impulsive behavior. But because the CEO of the company has the power to change the guidelines at any time, the CEO could, if he or she were a member of the negotiating team, ignore them at will. For this reason, company CEOs seldom participate directly in negotiations as members of negotiating teams. (In Case 18.2, if Kathy Baroni is right, Jupiter's president and the union president are about to reach an agreement outside of the formal bargaining session in order to avert a strike. It appears fortunate that the company president has not been caught up in the rancor of the bargaining session. However, this outside action may undermine future negotiations.)

The Labor Team

Just as the composition of management's negotiating team may depend on the degree to which the plant manager is permitted to operate independently of corporate headquarters, membership on labor's team will be influenced by the relationship between the local and the national union. The four basic union structures that determine the role of the local union in collective-bargaining negotiations are as follows:

1. National negotiations. The national union negotiates wages and employee benefits with the employer as, for example, takes place in the steel and automobile industries.

2. Pattern bargaining. The local unions in a single company or industry negotiate and sign individual collective-bargaining agreements but as part of an effort coordinated or controlled by the national union. Union insistence on pattern bargaining was partially at the root of Caterpillar Inc.'s willingness to take a strike by the UAW in 1992. The union pressed for a settlement similar to the one negotiated with Deere & Company the previous year.[15] (The five-month strike ended when Caterpillar's management threatened to hire permanent replacements for strikers who would not return to work.)

3. Council bargaining. Several local unions negotiate through a council structure in which the officers of each local select a bargaining team to represent them all.

4. Independent bargaining by locals. A local union negotiates all the terms of the agreement directly with the employer.

No matter which of the four structures a local union finds itself operating under, it must select a committee to represent it in negotiations. The local usually selects the bargaining committee at a meeting of its membership. Although the committee is occasionally composed of the local's officers, more frequently it consists of a combination of officers and ordinary members selected by the membership for the express purpose of serving on the union's negotiating team. (See Figure 18.1.)

The selection of bargaining representatives in the local union often involves political considerations as well as the issue of competence. For example, a union member elected to the bargaining committee can use the position to enhance his or her popularity. Selection of the bargaining committee, then, is a part of the political process that is a constant characteristic of life in a local union.[16]

Preparing, Analyzing, and Resolving Proposals

When a company or industry is having serious difficulties, management is likely to come to the bargaining table with proposals to cut costs. In a period when wage levels tend to rise each year, however, many employers do not develop bargaining proposals of their own. They prefer to react to the demands put forward by the union rather than risk revealing too much of what they are actually prepared to concede by to do so only after analyzing the existing labor contract carefully to see how changes can be made to reduce the cost of labor and increase the control and discretion of management.[17]

Management's major concern, as well as the principal question it must ask about every proposal put forward by the union, is what it will cost the company. Negotiators for management will attempt to calculate costs on the basis of prior experience. For example, statistical summaries of employees categorized by age, seniority, and job classification supply information from which it is possible to establish the cost of union proposals that would change such things as vacation time, pensions, and health insurance. Management can also quickly determine the total cost of a wage increase by using a formula that multiplies the increase by the number of affected employees and adds the consequent increases in premiums paid for holidays and overtime and in outlays for such benefits as social security. These extra costs are frequently called "roll-up costs."

The proposals that are made by the union and analyzed by management may be divided into five major categories:

1. Wages and benefits. Among the most important issues to be resolved during negotiations are increases in the base wage rate, changes in incentive-rate formulas, differences in wages between shifts, compensation for overtime, and the cost-of-living allowance (COLA). These proposals have an obvious effect on the direct cost of labor, as do employee benefits.

2. Working conditions. Health and safety standards, work schedules, shift assignments, and work rules are the principal issues in this category.

3. Job security. Proposals regarding promotions, transfers, layoffs, unemployment compensation, and severance pay policies fall into this category.

4. Management rights. Management almost always reserves the right to control the type and pace of production and to discipline employees within the limits established by the contract. Moreover, management frequently insists on a provision that clearly states that anything not mentioned in the contract continues to be within the range of management's authority.

5. Individual rights: Labor contracts usually establish a procedure under which employees can obtain a remedy for grievances or alleged violations of the contract by management. (The grievance-arbitration procedure is discussed in detail later in this chapter.)

Resolving Negotiating Impasses

When negotiations reach an impasse, several options are available. A third party may be called upon to help resolve the dispute, or the government may intervene and try to pressure both sides to do what is necessary to reach an agreement. In some cases, the union and management will exercise their considerable power by engaging in pressure tactics such as a strike or lockout. (A strike by players in the National

Football League in 1987 and a bargaining impasse with the owners caused most of the disputed matters to be thrown into the courts or before federal agencies for several years. See *Contemporary Issues* on page 485.)

Mediation and Conciliation

Mediation and conciliation is a system under which a third party helps labor and management to come to an agreement. **Conciliation** means helping the parties develop and adhere to an agenda, as well as giving them encouragement to address as objectively as possible the issues on which they are divided. **Mediation,** on the other hand, suggests a rather more active approach, in which the third party suggests specific alternatives for the two sides to consider. Unlike **arbitration,** in which the third party hands down a decision that is final and binding, neither mediation nor conciliation empowers the third party to make decisions that labor and management must then accept. Mediation and conciliation depend entirely on the ability of the third party to assist the union and management teams to reach an agreement voluntarily. Obviously, the mediator must win the trust of both parties.

The great majority of mediators are supplied by the state and federal governments. Because mediators must be trusted by both labor and management to be effective, the Federal Mediation and Conciliation Service (FMCS), which was created by the Taft-Hartley Act in 1947, is an independent agency. The FMCS is notified automatically of a potential dispute because the Taft-Hartley Act requires that a party that wants to terminate or modify a labor contract must notify the other party sixty days, and the agency at least thirty days, before the date on which the contract expires.

Med-arb

Med-arb (pronounced "meed-arb") is a combination of mediation and arbitration, in which the union and management agree that the issues that cannot be settled by mediation will be decided by the third party. As in normal arbitration, what the third party decides becomes final and binding.[18]

Fact-finding

In **fact-finding,** a neutral party, either an individual or a panel, is appointed to determine the facts in a dispute. The fact-finder then makes a report that, it is hoped, will provide the parties with a more accurate understanding of the situation and thus increase the likelihood that an agreement can be reached. Even if the parties themselves are not persuaded by the facts to alter their bargaining positions, the public, when fully informed of the real basis of the disagreement, often brings pressure to bear on the parties to end the conflict. Fact-finders, however, have even less power than mediators; they may not even make recommendations to the parties unless this authority has been expressly given.

Strikes, Lockouts, and Slowdowns

Strikes and lockouts, or the threat of them, are an integral part of the collective-bargaining process. Both the strike and the lockout are methods by which one side attempts to obtain concessions from the other through the application of economic pressure. In the lockout, management literally locks out the employees in the hope that they, or the union that represents them, will be more eager to reach agreement when they no longer have an income.

Though the lockout puts pressure on the employees, it also curtails or stops production. Management sometimes keeps operating with supervisors and temporary

Contemporary Issues

NFL: Labor Talks End in Agreement, Peace

New York — After five years, the NFL has apparently reached the brink of labor peace, a peace that will include the league's first unrestricted free agency.

After 12 hours of meetings Monday and yesterday, the players and owners announced they had reached agreement in principle on the first agreement since the 24-day strike in 1987 that threw almost all labor matters into the courts or before federal agencies.

Neither side would give details, but it is believed the agreement is very close to the "framework" agreed upon two weeks ago, which would bring free agency for the first time, impose a salary cap and cut the draft from 12 rounds to seven.

Details from the meetings of the last two days were sparse, indicating two things:

- That there was indeed progress close to a settlement — when things are close, the rhetoric stops.

- Participants indicated that the agreement was still a bit shaky and that the league negotiators must still do a selling job through Christmas and over the final weekend of the regular season.

"It's got to be a fair deal or we'll have to take our chances in court," said Cleveland owner Art Modell, one of the owners who prefers negotiated settlement to court action. He said there were still some points unresolved.

The agreement follows a period in which the league's labor relations were shifted from collective bargaining to court.

Last September, a jury in Minneapolis handed down a verdict throwing out Plan B, the league's limited free agency plan. Judge David Doty, who presided at that trial, subsequently let nine unsigned veterans become free agents this season, including All-Pro tight end Keith Jackson, who left Philadelphia and signed with Miami.

Doty, who must approve this settlement, also had a behind-the-scenes role in the talks, urging the two sides to reach agreement on their own. He told both sides that neither might like any settlement he imposed.

Last week, the owners met in Dallas to consider the plan put forth in the agreement between commissioner Paul Tagliabue and Jim Quinn, lawyer for the players in the Minnesota suit and chief negotiator for them in the contract talks.

But Tagliabue could get only three members of the seven-member negotiating committee to agree on the settlement and after a long session involving all 28 teams went back to work with Quinn.

One source familiar with the framework agreed upon two weeks ago said that he had spoken Monday night with negotiators, who told him the tentative agreement didn't differ much.

That would mean free agency for players with five years' experience and a salary cap kicking in when player costs reach 67 percent of gross revenue. It would include a seven-round draft with $2 million per team allocated for draft choices — less than some high firstrounders get now.

In general, that would allow most teams to keep stars.

One sticking point, on which the union won't compromise, is allowing all plaintiffs in the various lawsuits to be set free.

There are currently 16, three of whom comprise the heart of the Philadelphia Eagles' defense — Reggie White, who will be a free agent this year, and Clyde Simmons and Seth Joyner, whose contracts expire next year.

Philadelphia owner Norman Braman has objected that his team would be gutted, but the players have declined to budge on that issue.

Source: Associated Press as reprinted in the *Honolulu Star-Bulletin*, December 23, 1992, p. D6. Reprinted by permission of the Associated Press.

nonunion employees during a lockout, usually at a reduced level. Workers lose wages, but management loses profits. By and large, the lockout is used only when a union strikes against one member of an employers' association and all the members of the association retaliate by locking out their employees.

The strike is labor's ultimate weapon. Through the strike, economic pressure is brought to bear on the employer. Workers withhold their services and, unless management is both willing and able to replace the strikers with other, nonunion workers, the company's operations are interrupted. The strike, however, is a two-edged sword; it hurts the business by stopping work, but when work stops so do wages.

However, the union does not always need to put all its members on strike to cause the company economic hardship. **Selective strikes,** or strikes against only some of a large employer's plants, are sometimes used to reduce the number of employees taken off the organization's payroll. This in turn decreases the burden placed on the fund the union has created to provide financial assistance to striking union members.

Strikes involve considerable preparation by both labor and management. They also involve, paradoxically, a certain amount of cooperation between them. Unions, for example, have usually cooperated with management to minimize damage to equipment during a shutdown and have almost always allowed maintenance crews to maintain and repair equipment during a strike. The union fully expects the strike to end eventually and wants to protect the company's capacity to employ its members.

Confronted with the possibility of a strike, management needs to make plans in a number of areas. Relations with customers and suppliers, protection of the plant, the decision whether to operate with nonstriking or new employees, and the continuation or suspension of employee benefits are all matters that have to be considered before the strike actually takes place. To ensure that the proper plans are made, usually establish strike committees organizations that have had experience with strikes. Among the executives of a company, the human resources director is almost always on the strike committee. The other members typically include vice presidents in charge of such functions as sales, manufacturing, purchasing, and engineering.

Among the most important and difficult questions the strike committee must address are how to treat any nonunionized segment of the work force during a strike and whether to replace the striking employees with other workers. If the strike is not likely to last very long, most companies keep nonunion workers, including supervisors, on the job. These employees have a legal right to ignore the strike by union members and to cross any picket line that may be put up. Although occasional outbreaks of violence still occur, most strikes and picket lines are relatively free from physical danger.

The second issue, whether to replace strikers, is more difficult to deal with. Although it is legal to replace strikers in a strike over wages and benefits, it is not legal to do so when the strike concerns an alleged unfair labor practice by management. But replacing strikers with other workers can transform a work stoppage into a bitter struggle for the survival of the union and may create problems once the strike is over. What, for example, is to be the status of replacements in relation to returning strikers? Moreover, employee morale may be seriously harmed, perhaps permanently, and harmony in the workplace may become an impossibility.

The **slowdown,** in which workers find ways to reduce productivity, is a tactic particularly troublesome for management. In a typical slowdown, workers find ways to use the company's own rules and procedures to restrict production. For example, at the McDonnell Douglas Corp. plant in Long Beach, California, a United Auto Workers local orchestrated a slowdown in which workers refused to install parts without blueprints, quit sharing tools, and worked up to just the minimum level of their job requirements. At Boston's City Hospital, instead of striking, seven hundred nurses followed contract rules to the letter. They declined to work overtime, and refused to move beds or answer telephones or do other work outside their job classifications.[19] Although management may discharge workers for not working up to performance standards, it becomes much more difficult to discharge employees who are following management's own rules and working up to minimum standards. Slowdowns, like strikes, have typically found resolution at the bargaining table.

Grievance-Arbitration Procedures in Unionized Organizations

Both management and the union have crucial roles in administering the collective-bargaining agreement. Besides monitoring compliance with the terms of the contract, both parties are major actors in the administration of the grievance-arbitration procedure. In unionized organizations, employee grievances (complaints) are usually handled through **grievance-arbitration procedures** specified by the labor contract. These procedures involve systematic, union-management deliberation of a complaint at successively higher organizational levels. If the problem is not settled at any of these internal levels, the complaint is submitted to an outside, impartial party, or *arbitrator*, whose decision is final and binding. Most grievances are brought by employees, although management may use this procedure to process a complaint about the union. Almost all labor contracts contain grievance procedures, and about 98 percent contain provisions for arbitration as a final step.[20]

The grievance-arbitration procedure is shown in Figure 18.2. Typically, the grievance procedure is set in motion when an employee, or a union officer on behalf of the employee, brings a verbal or written complaint to the employee's immediate supervisor. About 51 percent of labor contracts require that the grievance be presented in writing at the first step.[21]

If the problem is not handled to the satisfaction of the employee at this first step, he or she may then take the grievance to the next higher managerial level designated in the contract, through a total of three, four, or five steps. The most common practice is for the contract to provide for three steps, exclusive of arbitration.[22]

At these later stages, the grievance is always presented in writing, and the employee is almost always represented by a union official or committee that meets with management representatives. (Figure 18.3 is an example of a form used for making a grievance statement.) Management is often represented by a grievance committee that includes a member of the personnel or industrial relations department. In fact, the human resources department is usually involved in all internal deliberations on the grievance. Sometimes a contract specifies that the general manager or company president will participate in the last stage of internal deliberations. However, the vast majority of grievances are settled at or before this step.[23]

Finally, a grievance that cannot be settled between the union and management is submitted to an arbitrator. The arbitrator conducts a hearing and hands down a

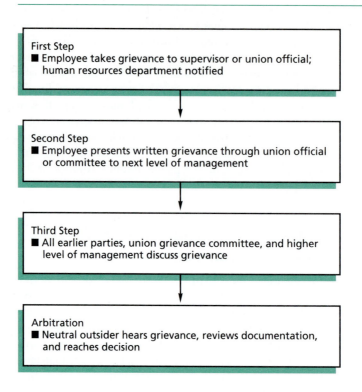

FIGURE 18.2   Typical grievance procedure under a union contract

decision that both parties have agreed in advance to accept as final and binding. (Case 17.2 in the previous chapter is an example of a grievance that ultimately was settled by an arbitrator.)

Selection of Arbitrators   The procedure for selecting arbitrators (who are sometimes called *umpires*) is spelled out in the labor contract. In most cases, decisions are made by a single arbitrator. Some contracts, however, call for three-member arbitration boards that consist of union and company representatives plus an impartial chairperson. (This practice has been criticized, however, because of the natural tendency for union and management to sympathize with their respective board members, which means that only the chairperson is truly a neutral decision maker.) The majority of contracts state that the parties will try to agree on an arbitrator; if they cannot agree, they must turn to an impartial agency for the selection.[24]

The agencies used most widely in selecting arbitrators are the Federal Mediation and Conciliation Service, mentioned earlier, and the American Arbitration Association. Both maintain up-to-date rosters of qualified arbitrators and will supply lists from which an arbitrator can be chosen. If desired, these agencies will select the arbitrator. Many arbitrators, however, are selected directly by the parties without going through an intermediary. According to FMCS statistics, discharge and disciplinary problems tend to reach arbitration with the most frequency.[25]

```
┌─────────────────────────────────────────────────────────────────┐
│                      GRIEVANCE STATEMENT                          │
│                                                                   │
│  EMPLOYEE: _____ CLOCK NO.: _____ SHIFT: _____     │
│                                                                   │
│  JOB CLASSIFICATION: _____ PLANT: _____ DEPT.: _____   │
│                                                                   │
│  DEPT. SUPERVISOR: _____                   │
│                                                                   │
│  STATEMENT OF SUPERVISOR: _____  │
│  _____ │
│  _____ │
│  _____ │
│  _____ │
│  _____ │
│  _____ │
│  _____ │
│  _____ │
│  _____ │
│  _____ │
│  _____ │
│  _____ │
│  _____ │
│                                                                   │
│  EMPLOYEE: _____ DEPT. STEWARD: _____     │
│                 Signature                       Signature         │
│                                                                   │
│  RECEIVED BY: _____ TIME: _____ DATE: _____   │
│               Supervisor                                          │
│                                                                   │
│  Prepare in quadruplicate for distribution                        │
│                                                                   │
│  1. Original and one copy (Labor Relations)  UNION FILE NO. ____ │
│  2. Department                                                    │
│  3. Chief Steward            LABOR RELATIONS NO. _____     │
└─────────────────────────────────────────────────────────────────┘
```

FIGURE 18.3 Example of a form used for submitting a grievance

Under **ad hoc arbitration,** an arbitrator is appointed for each case. Less common is the permanent umpire system, under which the parties agree to use a particular arbitrator, or several arbitrators in rotation, for the life of the contract. The advantage of permanent arbitration is that the arbitrator can develop an understanding of the particular characteristics and unique problems of the parties involved.

Labor arbitrators come from many walks of life, but generally they are highly knowledgeable and experienced in labor-management relations. Professors and lawyers constitute a large proportion of arbitrators, but ministers, judges, accountants, economists, public officeholders, and others are often found in the arbitrator role.[26]

Role of the Arbitrator

The arbitrator's role is generally considered **quasi-judicial,** that is, analogous to or approaching the role of a judge. The arbitrator is expected to listen to evidence, weigh it impartially and objectively, and make a decision based on the labor contract.

There are some important differences between the role of an arbitrator and that of a judge, however. First, arbitration hearings tend to be much more informal than courtroom proceedings. The parties may or may not have legal counsel present at the hearings, and the proceedings are not bound by the rules of evidence, as they are in a court of law. Nevertheless, the proceedings are expected to be conducted with dignity and fairness, and they are likely to include cross-examination and the submission of documents as evidence.[27]

In addition, arbitrators are not bound by precedent to the extent that judges are expected to adhere to legal precedents in the judicial process.[28] Although an arbitrator may study other arbitrators' decisions to sharpen his or her understanding of the issues and although both parties may cite arbitration decisions in support of their positions, the arbitrator's decision is not limited or constrained by the decisions of arbitrators in other cases.

Although both labor and management ordinarily expect the arbitrator to assume a quasi-judicial role, other expectations and the arbitrator's own convictions about his or her role do come into play, which can create dilemmas for the arbitrator in the decision-making process. According to author Harold Davey, the arbitrator may be expected to play the role of "mutual friend," a "father confessor," or a "labor-relations psychiatrist" and is sometimes expected to use a "split-the-difference" approach.[29] In general, however, the decision-making authority of the arbitrator is limited by the **submission agreement,** which is signed by both labor and management representatives. This agreement, sometimes called a "stipulation" or an "agreement to arbitrate," describes the dispute and the authority the arbitrator can exercise.

Legal Support for Arbitration Decisions

In general, federal and state courts have tended to uphold decisions reached through arbitration. This is not surprising given the fact that, under the labor contract, union and management have agreed in writing to abide by the decision of an impartial third party; in effect, both parties have agreed in advance not to appeal the decision. Ordinarily, arbitration decisions are subject to legal challenge only when the courts find evidence of fraud, corruption, incorrect calculations, or misconduct on the part of the arbitrator (such as refusal to hear evidence or lack of impartiality in relation to one of the parties).[30] In the *Trilogy* cases, as they have come to be called, the Supreme Court held that an award must be enforced if the arbitrator based the decision on an interpretation of the labor contract.[31]

However, two later Supreme Court cases have slightly modified legal support for the arbitration process. In the 1974 *Alexander* v. *Gardner-Denver* case, the Court held that an arbitrator's decision is not final and binding if the decision violates Title VII of the Civil Rights Act. In this case, an arbitrator upheld a company's discharge of a black employee, but the employee took the matter to court. The lower courts upheld the arbitrator's decision, but the Supreme Court sent the case back to the federal district court to determine whether the employee's civil rights had been violated in the discharge.[32]

In *Hines* v. *Anchor Motor Freight* (1976), the Court established the principle that courts can negate arbitration awards when the union has not adequately represented employees. In the *Hines* case, three truck drivers were discharged for allegedly falsifying expense sheets pertaining to a certain motel. They insisted to the union that they were innocent, but the union representatives ignored their assertions and simply pleaded for mercy at the subsequent arbitration hearing. The arbitrator upheld the discharges. Several months later, the motel clerk admitted that he had embezzled the money, and the truck drivers sued both the union and the company. The Supreme Court maintained that the union's misconduct had "seriously undermined" the arbitration process and that the employees were entitled to relief from both the union and the employer.[33]

Overall, very few arbitration awards are appealed. It is estimated that less than 1 percent of arbitration awards in the private sector are appealed to the courts.[34]

Other Kinds of Arbitration

Arbitration is most often used during contract administration: that is, once the labor contract has been successfully negotiated and put into effect, arbitration is used to resolve differing interpretations of the agreement that arise during day-to-day operations of the organization. Occasionally, however, arbitration is used to resolve impasses in the negotiation of the contract itself.

Interest arbitration involves submitting to an arbitrator any point the parties cannot agree on in negotiating a contract. For example, under the Experimental Negotiation Agreement between the United Steelworkers and ten steel companies, points of dispute in bargaining are submitted to an arbitrator, and both sides agree not to resort to a strike or lockout.[35] Interest arbitration is mandatory under some state laws, particularly in collective-bargaining situations involving police and firefighters.

In interest arbitration, the arbitrator is no longer in a quasi-judicial role. His or her role is now legislative, meaning that the arbitrator is "expected to fashion a wage and benefit package for the parties based on his [or her] judgment of what is fair, reasonable and appropriate."[36] The procedure has been argued against because of this dilemma: if the arbitrator is wise, skillful, and imaginative in making decisions, the parties will tend to rely too heavily on arbitration, thus undermining the system of free collective bargaining. On the other hand, if the arbitrator is unwise, blundering, and unimaginative, the parties will try to avoid "the scourge of compulsory arbitration."[37] In either case, the legislative role can be an extremely uncomfortable one for the arbitrator.

Final-offer arbitration, sometimes called "last-offer ballot" or "forced-choice arbitration," may also be used to resolve bargaining impasses. Under this procedure, each party submits a package of contract provisions to an arbitrator, who must make a choice. The usual procedure is for the arbitrator to choose one complete package or the other, but some contracts permit the arbitrator to make choices item by item.[38] An advantage of final-offer arbitration is that both sides must bargain reasonably to obtain the arbitrator's approval of the package; a disadvantage is that the final award may be very one-sided.

One other type of arbitration procedure should be mentioned. In an effort to minimize the financial costs and time delays associated with grievance arbitration, the American Arbitration Association has initiated an accelerated procedure known as **expedited arbitration**. The rules for this procedure are that the two parties in the dispute do not file prehearing or posthearing briefs, no stenographic record is taken, awards are made within five days of the end of the hearing, and the arbitrator's opinions, when required, are kept very short. Since this alternative approach was introduced in 1972, experience has shown that expedited arbitration can increase the efficiency and cost-effectiveness of the grievance procedure.

Implications for Human Resources Managers

With unionization, and the collective bargaining that goes with it, decisions about the organization of work and about staffing, appraisal, and compensation are no longer made by management alone. A labor contract now governs much of the work situation, and management faces serious limitations even in the areas where it can still make decisions about human resources independently of the union. Provisions of the union contract are usually quite extensive in their reach. One of the most stringent limitations on management discretion and power results from the insistence by many unions that seniority alone determine most staffing and pay decisions.

The coming of the union also alters the structure of authority within the organization. Typically, there is a tendency to centralize direct contact with the union in a single official, usually the human resources director or industrial relations manager. Moreover, management can no longer deal unilaterally with employees as a group nor as individuals with respect to wages, hours, and working conditions, and this loss of flexibility is often seen as a major disadvantage.

One consequence may be a greater emphasis on both human resources planning and on the selection and hiring of employees. Human resources planning becomes more important because, for example, a contract that provides for supplementary unemployment benefits (as do the contracts negotiated in the auto industry by the UAW) dramatically increases the cost attached to laying off employees. The importance of employee recruitment, selection, and hiring increases because this is one of the few major human resources policy areas in which the employer retains broad latitude for independent decision making.

Typically, the human resources department is heavily involved in the handling of complaints through formal grievance procedures. Ordinarily, that department (or the industrial relations section) will be consulted at various steps of the grievance procedure. (Figure 18.4 is an example of a check list the human resources department might use or hand out to supervisors to ensure the constructive handling of grievances.) Depending on the particular organization, top operating officials or the human resources director, or both, will decide the organization's position on whether a case will go to arbitration. Usually, the human resources department is at least consulted in this decision.

When a case goes to arbitration, the immediate supervisor involved in the case and other members of management are likely to participate in planning the arbitration presentation, and they may be used as witnesses. The human resources or personnel director, however, is likely to be the chief strategist for the organization unless the organization is represented by an attorney.

Summary   Collective bargaining is the process by which a formal agreement is established between workers and management regarding wages, hours, working conditions, and grievance procedures. Collective bargaining presents opportunities for enhancing cooperative and productive relations between labor and management. It also permits the possibility of conflict and the pursuit of narrow and immediate economic self-interest and/or power aggrandizement. Strikes and lockouts, powerful bargaining tools of labor and management, respectively, are subject to various laws and regulations that limit the exercise of power by either side.

I. Background Information   Yes   No

A. Do you have a current copy of the labor contract?
B. Have you carefully read the contract?
C. Have you attended supervisory training sessions on contract administration?
D. Have you clarified ambiguous clauses with upper management?
E. Do you know the steps in the grievance procedure and your responsibilities under each step?
F. Are you aware of the interpersonal relations in your area and sensitive to potential grievance issues?
G. Are you familiar with job responsibilities and job decisions in your area?
H. Have you reviewed past grievance decisions and all relevant company policies?
I. Do you know the union representative in your area?

II. Initial Interaction with Employees

A. Do you take time to deal with an employee's problem immediately or within a reasonable time?
B. Are you an active listener?
C. Do you let employees express their points of view without interrupting?
D. Do you remain objective during the dialogue with an employee?
E. Are you sensitive to the needs of employees as well as the strict rules of the organization?
F. Do you deal with employees as individuals?
G. Do you initiate immediate action relative to the issue?
H. Do you follow through with your decision?

III. First Step in Grievance Procedure (Investigation)

A. Do you take complete and accurate notes during discussions with the employee?
B. Do you ask questions and seek clarification on certain issues to improve your understanding of the issues?
C. Do you remain objective and not give the appearance of having prejudged the outcome?
D. Have you attempted to determine the causes of the grievance as well as the grievance itself?
E. Are specific answers given to questions involving the who, what, where, when, and why of the grievance?

(Evaluation)

A. Have you discussed the issue with other supervisors or members of upper management?
B. If the problem involves a major issue, have you consulted with the industrial relations department or appropriate legal counsel?
C. Are you aware of the intent of the contract as well as the literal interpretation?
D. Is the incident a clear violation of contract, law, or precedent?
E. Have you analyzed the grievance with respect to its effect on subsequent management decisions and its effect on the employee?

(Implementation)

A. Are you sensitive in communicating decisions to employees?
B. Do you use the grievance procedure as an opportunity to improve your own effectiveness as a supervisor?
C. Do you explain the reasoning behind your decisions and encourage employees to discuss issues with you?
D. Do you follow through with your decisions and attempt to prevent subsequent grievances?
E. Do you create an environment of active communications?

The above items are designed to direct the supervisor in constructive grievance handling. If you answer no to any of the questions, you may be losing the opportunity to improve your effectiveness in handling employee grievances.

FIGURE 18.4   Check list for constructive grievance handling

Source: Reprinted by permission from pages 272–274 of *Supervisory Management: Tools and Techniques* edited by M. Gene Newport; Copyright © 1976 by West Publishing Company. All rights reserved.

Both unions and management have much to gain by sending to the bargaining table negotiators who are mature, intelligent, well trained, and well prepared, and much to lose if they do not. Precisely these same qualities of maturity, intelligence, and diligent application to the task at hand are required of government officials or other third parties who become involved in the collective-bargaining process as fact-finders, mediators, or arbitrators.

Although distributive bargaining continues to be the most frequently used method of collective bargaining, the integrative approach offers the possibility of solving problems to the mutual benefit of the parties, especially with respect to the issues of quality, productivity, job interest, and employee participation in workplace decisions. Concessionary bargaining, productivity bargaining, and joint efforts to improve the quality of working life are different forms of integrative bargaining. Concessionary bargaining has been prevalent in recent years as companies have sought to obtain concessions from unions in order to remain competitive.

Contract negotiations are usually conducted by a team of negotiators from each side. The human resources director or labor relations director is usually the chief spokesperson on the management team.

Mediation and conciliation — usually involving specialists supplied by state or federal governments — are frequently employed to avoid strikes. Med-arb, a combination of mediation and arbitration, is sometimes used. Fact-finding involves a neutral party determining the facts of a dispute and making a report of those facts to the two parties.

Almost all labor contracts provide for grievance-arbitration procedures. The typical procedure involves joint union-management deliberation of the problem, starting at the supervisory level and then moving to successively higher managerial levels. Binding arbitration is typically the last step of the process if the parties cannot settle the dispute at earlier steps.

Discipline and discharge cases are the most likely to be heard by an arbitrator. Labor contracts typically call for a single ad hoc arbitrator who is selected jointly by the union and management.

The arbitrator's role is quasi-judicial. Arbitration hearings are more informal than courtroom proceedings and are not bound by the rules of evidence, nor is the arbitrator bound by precedent.

Collective bargaining has major implications for human resources professionals since many aspects of human resources utilization are affected.

Ethical Dilemma

After several weeks of more or less unproductive bargaining with management, the union negotiating committee conspires to start a rumor that the company is planning to subcontract out most maintenance work. This is not true, but it angers enough union members so that they vote favorably on giving the union committee the right to call a strike.

What are the ethics of this situation?

Key Terms

collective bargaining
totality of conduct
illegal bargaining issue
mandatory bargaining issue
voluntary bargaining issue
impasse
strike
lockout
economic strike
coercive secondary boycott
jurisdictional strike
national emergency dispute
distributive bargaining
integrative bargaining
concessionary bargaining
productivity bargaining
quality-of-work-life (QWL)
   project

two-tier wage scale
study action team
whipsawing
conciliation
mediation
arbitration
med-arb
fact-finding
selective strike
slowdown
grievance-arbitration procedures
ad hoc arbitration
quasi-judicial
submission agreement
interest arbitration
final-offer arbitration
expedited arbitration

Review Questions

1. What is collective bargaining, and what are its purposes?
2. What is good-faith bargaining?
3. Describe the differences between distributive and integrative bargaining.
4. What is meant by "concessionary bargaining"? Give examples.
5. What is meant by "productivity bargaining"? Give examples.
6. What are some typical steps involved in both the management and the union preparing for and conducting negotiations?
7. What is the role of the mediator?
8. What is "fact-finding" in labor relations?
9. What are some of the problems a company strike committee needs to address in the event of a strike? Discuss.
10. Describe the grievance-arbitration process.
11. What is the role of the arbitrator?
12. How do interest arbitration, final-offer arbitration, and expedited arbitration differ from the more conventional form of arbitration? Explain.

Opening Case Questions

Case 18.1   The Management Negotiating Team

1. What are some of the factors behind the perceptions of the company negotiators?
2. What might be some pros and cons of "negotiating around the clock"?

Case 18.2   The Union Negotiating Team

1. What are some of the factors behind the perceptions of the union negotiators?
2. What type of relationship exists between the union and the Jupiter Automobile Company?

Comprehensive Case

Who Really Won at Caterpillar?

At first glance, there was a clear winner of the five-month strike against Caterpillar Inc., which ended in April 1992. The union — the United Auto Workers (UAW) — backed down on all of its major demands, accepting terms that it had earlier labeled "inadequate" and "regressive." When the company threatened to replace permanently the 12,600 strikers, the union caved in. Around the country, observers declared another victory for management and another big defeat for unions.

But though few would dispute that the strike further weakened the already frail position of American labor unions, the damage may turn out to be just as great for the company. The end of the strike marked not just the end of workers' hopes for higher pay, but also the death knell for a model employee-involvement program. By saving money through facing down the union, Caterpillar may have set itself — and to some extent, American industry as a whole — back several years in its drive to become an efficient, innovative company capable of keeping its position as the world's top maker of construction equipment.

Until the mid-1980s Caterpillar had a history of long, destructive strikes, a poorly motivated work force, and bitter labor-management relations. After the particularly rancorous 1982 strike ended, both sides agreed to try to form a new kind of relationship. This agreement resulted in the creation, in 1986, of the Employee Satisfaction Process (ESP), soon implemented in all of Caterpillar's plants.

ESP became a model of how Japanese-style teamwork and worker-management cooperation could succeed in America's heartland. Management began listening to employees' suggestions, the suggestions began paying off, and workers became committed to the company that now seemed to value them.

At Caterpillar's Aurora, Illinois, plant, teams sprang up with names like the What Ifs, The Cat Scanners, and Wheel Do It. The What Ifs redesigned the parking lot to reduce accidents, and the company followed their advice. Teams in the paint department visited dealers, listened to gripes about the dull finish on the company's tractors, and ended up changing both paint and paint guns, pleasing everyone. Traditional barriers between workers and management began to disappear. Workers felt a new sense of self-worth, and some who became expert team facilitators traveled to other Caterpillar plants and even gave talks to other companies.

In a two-month period in 1989, 241 employee ideas resulted in almost $5 million worth of savings at the Aurora plant. By the end of 1991, five years of employee involvement had boosted Caterpillar's overall productivity by 30 percent. Caterpillar was using its ESP program as a marketing tool, bragging to customers about its improved quality and productivity. Workers proudly showed customers through the plant, treating them as "our customers."

The late-1991 strike was the result of a clash between the UAW and Donald Fites, who became Caterpillar's chairman in 1990. Although Fites's two predecessors had worked to improve relations with the UAW, Fites saw the union as threatening to keep the company from competing successfully with its Japanese rivals. In particular, he objected to the UAW's insistence on pattern bargaining, the practice of all companies within an industry agreeing to the same union contracts. The union wanted Caterpillar to sign a contract similar to one agreed to by its competitor, Deere & Company, in 1991. Fites argued that accepting the wage increases in such a contract would make Caterpillar unable to compete worldwide. The union was also asking for more control of plant decisions — a logical outgrowth of the employee-involvement programs, perhaps, but a request that Fites saw as challenging the company's "right to manage."

The strike was in essence the result of a clash between two different philosophies. While the union saw success as a matter of everyone working together for the benefit of all, Fites was a believer in the "lean and mean" approach and a more traditional distance between management and worker, cutting jobs wherever he could.

Although most Caterpillar workers came back when the strike ended, new ESP buttons read "Employees Stop Participating." Workers who had overcome their distrust of management to participate in the employee-involvement programs concluded that their earlier distrust had been confirmed. Many employees felt betrayed: they had committed themselves to the company, saving it millions of dollars with their ideas, and in return the company had locked them out and threatened to replace them with "scabs."

In publicizing its victory, Caterpillar pointed out that by avoiding a pattern contract, it would save $80 million in just three years. But it is difficult to put a dollar figure on the kind of trust that takes years to build and the kind of teamwork that had been paying off so well for Caterpillar. Caterpillar seems to have won the battle by facing down the union, but it will not be clear for years whether it has really won the war to become a more productive and competitive company.

Sources: Jonathan P. Hicks, "Still Bitter at Company and Union, Caterpillar Strikers Return to Their Jobs," *New York Times*, April 21, 1992, p. A11; Kevin Kelly, "Caterpillar's Don Fites: Why He Didn't Blink," *Business Week*, August 10, 1992, pp. 56–57; Robert L. Rose and Alex Kotlowitz, "Strife Between UAW and Caterpillar Blights Promising Labor Idea," *Wall Street Journal*, November 23, 1992, pp. A1, A8; and Louis Uchitelle, "Ousting Strikers a Costly Tactic," *New York Times*, April 21, 1992, C2.

Discussion Questions

1. Why did the UAW call off the strike at Caterpillar?
2. Describe the ESP program at Caterpillar before the strike. What is the near-term future of the ESP program?

CHAPTER 19

Rights, Responsibilities, and Justice

LEARNING OBJECTIVES

- Outline the employer's legal obligations in relation to sexual and other harassment.
- Describe the extent to which employees in private organizations enjoy freedom of speech.
- Describe the type and extent of privacy protection typically experienced by employees.
- Cite instances in which the employment-at-will doctrine is legally invalid.
- Define organizational due process and describe formal and informal procedures for handling grievances in the nonunionized organization.
- Explain the role of the human resources department in protecting employee rights and in protecting the organization from legal action.

CASE 19.1   The Open-Door Policy

Plastic Products, Inc. was proud of its "open-door" policy, which encouraged employees to communicate their problems and concerns to management. When Al Tompkins, a student at Western University, was hired on a part-time basis, he was informed that this policy was the organization's way of responding to employees' suggestions and complaints and maintaining good relations throughout the firm. Al's supervisor, Maria Lopez, explained it this way: "We have an open-door policy around here. That means if you have a complaint or a disagreement with me we can't settle, you're free to go to my boss with the problem. And you won't suffer any repercussions, either." Al was also told by both the personnel recruiter and his supervisor that he could approach the personnel department for advice about any matter pertaining to his employment at Plastic Products. Al's private opinion was that the open-door policy was probably fluff, and that anybody who took a complaint beyond his or her immediate supervisor would probably be in deep trouble as a result.

Al had no occasion to test the policy until his second year with the company. He had been working four days a week from 5:00 until 9:00 p.m., but during spring quarter of his senior year the university offered a management seminar that met twice a week from 3:30 until 7:00 p.m. Al very much wanted to enroll in the seminar, so he talked with Maria about the possibility of changing his work schedule. Maria listened to everything Al had to say and then said, "Well, let me think about it. I've got to consider the reaction of other people in the department, how we would cover your work, and so on. But frankly, I'm doubtful at this point — I'm just not sure the department can accommodate a change like that."

The next day Maria walked over to Al's workstation and said, "I'm afraid I've got bad news. I don't see how we can arrange a different schedule for you. We're too short on people, and we don't have much flexibility. I'm sorry. Is there some other class you could take instead?"

Al was disappointed and irritated. He saw himself as a hard worker and a valuable employee, and it seemed to him that the company should be able to handle this request. "Well," Al said, "that's a real disappointment. But thanks for considering the matter."

But the matter didn't go away for Al. He worried about it for a couple of days, and then he went to Maria's office. "Maria, about my wanting to change my working hours around for a few months — if you don't mind, let me take the case to Gary Schuler. When I was hired, you told me it was OK to appeal things beyond you to your boss."

"That's perfectly all right," Maria responded. "I'm truly sorry my decision was so unsatisfactory to you, but you know I had to think of the department as a whole. Maybe Gary can figure out a way to cover your job that I haven't considered. I have a suggestion. Let's the two of us meet with him and lay out both sides of the matter, and we'll see where it goes from there."

The meeting with Gary Schuler was very cordial. Al was struck by how carefully Gary listened to both sides of the problem. At no time did Al feel he was doing something that was inappropriate or unappreciated. It was also clear that Gary had great respect for Maria and the job she was doing for the company. The best part was that, in the end, Gary and Maria figured out a way to accommodate Al's request, and everyone was satisfied with the arrangements that were made.

A few weeks later, the subject of open-door policies was discussed in the senior seminar. Al was eager to speak up. "Let me tell you about an experience I had that proves some companies are serious about responding to what their employees have to say," he said. "I was skeptical, but now I'm convinced that an open-door policy is one way an employee can be heard and understood. Believe me, Plastic Products is a great place to work. Here's what happened." ◀

CASE 19.2   Sexual Harassment?

Mimi Burke was one of two women who had been recently assigned to a Great Plains Power & Light field crew. The utility had been aggressively recruiting women, and Mimi, like her coworker, Marvella Fredericks, had successfully completed the rigorous training program. They had been placed on their first assignment in a unit with seven men and three large vehicles.

At first, the men in the crew were prone to make remarks like "We've got to be careful, the women are taking over the world," or "Wait 'til we have an ice storm — then you'll wish you were back in the kitchen." This type of comment tended to disappear as the women absorbed their full share of the workload, including the dangerous assignments.

But Mimi and Marvella were growing increasingly uncomfortable around the supervisor, Al Hensen, who would come out in his panel truck to review progress and to bring additional supplies. For one thing, he had several calendar pictures of nude women prominently displayed in the truck, and had no reluctance in calling Mimi's and Marvella's attention to new pictures he would add. On one occasion, when Mimi was getting some supplies from his truck, he said, "Maybe you and I ought to get together for a photography session — of course, I probably couldn't put your picture up here." Mimi said, "Are you kidding?" and turned away. In relating the incident to Marvella, Mimi found out that Marvella had experienced similar remarks from Al.

"I wonder if we've got a sex harassment thing going on here," Mimi said. "I don't know, but I can handle that guy," Marvella responded. "I'm not worried about it. I just try to avoid him." "But we shouldn't have to put up with his pictures and his comments," Mimi said. "If this continues, I'm going to see the people in personnel and get some advice." ◀

A rapidly evolving area in human resources management is employee rights and organizational justice. Outside the work situation, the United States Constitution guarantees many rights, such as freedom of speech, freedom of the press, freedom of assembly, and the right to due process of law. (**Due process** refers to legal proceedings carried out in accordance with established rules and principles that acknowledge the rights of individual citizens.) But what rights, if any, does an employee have on the job? What organizational due process rights exist?

The chapter-opening cases give partial answer to these questions. In Case 19.1, Al Tompkins had the right to appeal beyond his immediate supervisor, a right granted through company policy and supported by the behavior of Al's superiors. (Had management not supported the open-door policy, Al would undoubtedly have received clear signals that going over the boss's head was not a wise thing to do.) In Case 19.2, Mimi Burke understood that she could bring a complaint to the personnel department, or at least ask them for advice, without being afraid of the consequences. We do not know what procedures Great Plains Power & Light provided beyond access to the personnel department, but Mimi does have recourse to the legal system, as will be discussed later in the chapter.

Fair treatment of employees and a concern for individual rights represent a challenge to every organization because the possibility of injustice exists over a wide range of managerial decision areas. Compounding this challenge is the tendency of employees to evaluate the fairness or equity of decisions and actions that affect them either directly or indirectly. Minimizing perceptions of inequity and determining what is just treatment are major concerns in human resources management, and they are problems every manager confronts daily.

This chapter discusses the rights of employees, the responsibilities these rights imply for both employers and employees, and the problem of justice in the workplace. In particular, the chapter explores the various ways organizations accommodate the wants, needs, and rights of individuals in an effort to ensure just and fair treatment of all employees. There is a growing body of law and an emerging pattern of personnel practice pertaining to organizational justice. Because of these laws and practices, many organizations conscientiously follow fair and orderly procedures in making decisions that affect employees' lives. The extent to which a particular organization actually "tunes in" to employee perceptions of equity and adheres to a concern for employee rights is affected by many variables, such as management philosophy, organizational culture, and prevailing leadership style. But in the ideal situation, organizational justice remains an overriding goal in all management decision making, and procedures are adopted to guarantee substantial responsiveness to the rights of individual workers.

Employee Rights

Historically, there has been little constitutional or legal protection of the rights of workers on the job. Author William Kaplin states the matter directly: "Because the Constitution was designed to limit only the exercise of government power, it does not prohibit private individuals or corporations from impinging on such freedoms as free speech, equal protection, and due process."[1]

This condition is gradually changing, however. Some rights of employees are now specifically identified and protected through government policy, federal and state laws, and various court decisions. At the same time, rising levels of education and other social changes have affected the attitudes and expectations of many workers, who are now more likely to expect fair treatment in the workplace. The employee rights protected by law, the responsibilities and obligations these rights imply, and the impact of rights protection on management and human resources practices is the focus of this section.

As discussed in several preceding chapters, laws, court decisions, and administrative rulings have created major protections for job applicants and employees against discrimination based on race, color, religion, national origin, sex, age, or disability status. Veterans have certain protections under government contracts, in federal employment, and in some state employment situations. Nondiscriminatory treatment in the workplace is a basic employee right, and laws prohibiting discrimination affect all areas of human resources management.

Prohibitions Against Sexual, Age, Ethnic, and Disability Harassment

A major aspect of discrimination that has not yet been discussed is **sexual harassment,** which is now illegal under federal law. Sexual harassment was defined by the Third Circuit Court of Appeals in *Tompkins* v. *Public Service Electric & Gas Company:*

> Title VII of the Civil Rights Act is violated when a supervisor, with the actual or constructive knowledge of the employer, makes sexual advances or demands toward a subordinate employee and conditions that employee's job status — evaluation, continued employment, promotion, or other aspects of career development — on a favorable response to those advances or demands, and the employer does not take prompt action and appropriate remedial action after acquiring such knowledge.[2]

Under the law, an employer may be held liable for not investigating and taking appropriate action should a problem of sexual harassment develop between two employees. Although employees of either sex may be subject to sexual harassment, probably most of the victims are women; certainly the plaintiffs in most of the suits filed under Title VII are women.

One of the earliest suits that brought an employer to court involved a male vice president of Johns-Manville Corp., who discharged a woman project coordinator who refused to have an affair with him. Subsequently, a district court in Denver found the corporation guilty of sexual discrimination under the Civil Rights Act and liable for damages. An out-of-court settlement was made for a reported $100,000.[3]

The Equal Employment Opportunity Commission issued guidelines in 1980 clarifying the illegal aspects of sexual harassment. One provision states that an employer may be held liable for unlawful sexual discrimination against employees who were qualified for, but denied, employment opportunities and benefits secured by a fellow employee who submitted to the employer's sexual advances.[4] In 1986 the U.S. Supreme Court broadened the definition of sexual harassment in the case of *Meritor Savings Bank* v. *Vinson.* In this case, the Court held that under Title VII of the Civil Rights Act sexual harassment exists when a hostile, abusive, or intimidating environment is created as well as when salary, benefits, or opportunities are affected.[5] Thus, there are at least two kinds of sexual harassment: (1) **quid pro quo sexual harassment,** when there is a quid pro quo (something for something) aspect to a supervisor's advances; and (2) **hostile environment sexual harassment,** when an unwelcome or hostile environment is created by a supervisor's or other employee's actions.[6] (This second type of harassment is probably what is occurring in Case 19.2.)

The liability of employers in instances of sexual harassment means that organizations are legally responsible for safeguarding their employees from such treatment. To protect the rights of individual employees and the interests of the organization, top management should issue a strong policy statement prohibiting sexual harassment and stating the disciplinary steps that will be taken if this policy is violated. In addition, management must make certain that there will be no retaliation against an employee for bringing complaints of policy violation and that all complaints will receive a fair hearing. Further, training and management development programs should include sexual harassment awareness training. A large pro-

In spite of the reality of disabilities discrimination, Don Wardlow has found his niche as the first full-time blind professional baseball announcer.

portion of companies, particularly those with a hundred or more employees, now provide such training.[7] (Attitudes regarding what constitutes sexual harassment differ from country to country. See *International Perspective* on page 504.)

There are also other forms of harassment that are illegal. For example, **age harassment** violates the Age Discrimination in Employment Act of 1967, as well as the Civil Rights Act of 1964. Thus, when an older worker is subjected to derogatory remarks like "He is more accident prone than younger workers" or "You can't teach an old dog new tricks" and is denied the opportunity to learn new tasks, these may be evidence of age harassment and discrimination. Harassment on the basis of national origin, religion, color, race, or disability status is similarly illegal. To illustrate, an employer may face national origin harassment claims for tolerating slurs regarding an employee's manner of speaking.[8]

Prior to the Civil Rights Act of 1991, victims of intentional discrimination based on racial or ethnic bias — which could include harassment — could obtain compensatory and punitive damages. The Civil Rights Act of 1991 extends such damages, as well as jury trials, to victims of international sex, religious, and disability discrimination. (Damages can range up to $300,000, depending on the size of the employer's work force.) Consequently, it is likely that there will be an increasing number of lawsuits, particularly suits from women alleging deliberate sexual harassment.[9]

Freedom to Organize and Contract Rights

The right of nonsupervisory employees in business and industry to organize and bargain collectively with an employer has long been recognized in the United States. This right is not absolute because many procedural rules must be followed, but it is extensive and includes the right to engage in union-organizing activities without reprisal from the employer. Moreover, as discussed in the previous chapter, the right to organize and bargain collectively is gradually being extended into new

International Perspective

France Outlaws Sexual Harassment

The French Parliament has approved legislation that makes sexual harassment punishable by a jail sentence of up to one year and a fine of up to 100,000 francs ($18,000).

According to observers, the new law is a direct result of the Clarence Thomas-Anita Hill hearings in the U.S. last fall which, for the first time, provoked serious discussion in France about the nature of sexual pressure in the workplace.

To be sure, "sexual harassment" is perceived differently in France than it is in the United States. A poll in the magazine *Le Point*, for example, indicates that 45% of French women would not consider it harassment if a male manager asked a woman to spend a weekend with him to discuss her request for promotion, and 20%

would not consider it harassment if a woman were asked to undress during a job interview. What *does* constitute sexual harassment is not yet well defined by either popular sentiment or the law.

The new law applies only to relationships between a supervisor and his or her subordinates — it does not address harassment by clients or co-workers — and, in addition to the fines and jail sentence, requires work committees in companies with more than 50 employees to conduct information campaigns on the issue and gives unions and civil rights groups the right to assist employees complaining of harassment.

Source: Issues in HR, July–August 1992 p. 6. Reprinted with the permission of *Issues in HR* published by the Society for Human Resource Management, Alexandria, VA.

---

domains through state and federal laws and rulings. For example, union organizing and collective bargaining are now protected in not-for-profit hospitals, nursing homes, and federal and state government agencies.

Under collective-bargaining agreements, the right to organize and bargain collectively is reinforced by **contract rights:** that is, employees are guaranteed the rights for which they have contracted with management for the duration of the agreement. These rights are enforceable through arbitration procedures and the courts. Rights negotiated into the agreement typically include the right to file grievances and to take individual cases to arbitration, and employees are usually protected against dismissal without **just cause.** In essence, dismissal for just cause means that employment can be terminated only for valid, job-related reasons, such as poor performance and violation of company rules. Employees' rights to procedural or legal due process are implied or specified in most collective-bargaining agreements and underlie employment conditions in state agencies and other institutions in which personnel decisions are considered state actions.[10]

Individual employees in nonunionized organizations can also enter into contracts with their employers. An example is a salary and benefits contract between a company and an executive or between a professional football player and a club owner. Contracts like these provide rights for the duration of the agreement and are enforceable through the court system.[11]

Speech Rights and Obligations

Freedom of speech is a right many American citizens take for granted. But under prevailing court decisions and currently accepted standards, employees do not have complete freedom in what they can say about superiors and the employing organization Author David Ewing explains the limitations of free speech in the workplace this way:

> First, no employee should have a right to divulge information about legal and ethical plans, practices, operations, inventions, and other matters that the organization must keep confidential in order to do its job in an efficient manner.
>
> Second, no employee should have a right to make personal accusations or slurs which are irrelevant to questions about policies and actions that seem illegal or irresponsible.
>
> Third, no employee should be entitled to disrupt an organization or hurt its morale by making speeches and accusations that do not reflect a conviction that wrong is being done.
>
> Fourth, no employee should be entitled to rail against the competence of a supervisor or senior manager to make everyday work decisions that have nothing to do with the legality, morality, or responsibility of management actions.
>
> In addition, no employee is entitled to object to discharge, transfer, or demotion if management can demonstrate that unsatisfactory performance or violation of a code of conduct was the reason for its action.[12]

These statements imply that employees have the right to speak out or "blow the whistle" if the organization is engaging in illegal, immoral, or irresponsible practices but that they must act in a responsible manner. The courts have tended to support these limited speech rights. However, consistent with Ewing's conclusions, the Supreme Court has ruled that there are limits to how far an employee in public employment can go in complaining about working conditions and supervisors and that employees who exceed those limits can be fired.[13]

Numerous court decisions and some state laws are enforcing the right of employees to "blow the whistle," particularly in public employment. Here are two examples:

- In 1973, in *Rafferty* v. *Philadelphia Psychiatric Center*, the Court reinstated a psychiatric nurse who had been fired for being critical of patient care and staff behavior at the hospital where she worked.[14]

- In a 1979 Supreme Court case, *Girhan* v. *Western Line Consolidated School District*, a schoolteacher was reinstated after her contract had not been renewed because of "insulting," "hostile," "arrogant," and "loud" comments she made to her principal during a private conversation. The Court ruled that the First Amendment protected public employees' conversations with a superior.[15]

Whether these protections will be extended very far into the private sector remains to be seen. However, some court cases and legislation suggest a gradual extension of protection. This has been particularly true in situations where an incident internal to the organization overlaps with the activities of a public agency or is contrary to public policy, as the following examples illustrate.

- In 1959, in *Petermann* v. *International Brotherhood of Teamsters*, a California appeals court reinstated a union business agent who had been fired for refusing to commit perjury on the orders of his boss.[16]

- In 1980 the Connecticut Supreme Court ruled that an employee of a frozen foods plant could not be fired for protesting to his superiors that the company was putting less meat into the entrées than the label indicated.[17]

- The Occupational Safety and Health Act, the Coal Mine Safety Act, and the Water Pollution Control Act protect employees who report violations of these laws.[18]

- In 1984 a New Jersey jury found that the Mobil Corporation had unfairly fired a research biologist who had tried to get the company to report two toxic chemical accidents that she believed should have been reported under the law. The company claimed the employee was fired for being incompetent but settled by paying $425,000 in compensatory and punitive damages.[19]

- In 1991 Northrop Corp. agreed to pay almost $9 million to settle a suit brought under the federal False Claims Act by two former employees who had alleged that the company falsified tests on the air-launched cruise missile being built by the company.[20]

By 1987 more than half of the states had passed "whistle-blower" protection laws. These statutes often apply to both private- and public-sector employees, and prohibit discharge, threats, or other kinds of retaliation for **whistle blowing**.[21] Organizations, in turn, have developed whistle-blowing policies, that is, policies and procedures that allow employees to voice concerns about legal, ethical and/or moral issues. In one sample, 60 percent of manufacturing companies and 78 to 81 percent of other types of firms had formal procedures for processing such concerns. Of the companies having a formal procedure, 77 percent designated the human resources department as one outlet for expressing concern about unethical or illegal behavior.[22]

Privacy Protection

Under the Privacy Act of 1974, federal employees have considerable protection against misuse of personnel records. This law establishes strict requirements for the collection and distribution of personnel data. In most employment situations, however, employee privacy is not guaranteed by law: that is, establishing a policy of confidentiality and controlled access to personnel records is the option of the employer, and there have been many instances in which personnel information has been managed irresponsibly.

Some organizations routinely divulge medical, salary, appraisal, and disciplinary information without employee permission to outside sources such as government agencies, credit bureaus, insurance companies, law firms, or unions.[23] This problem is made more acute by the computerization of personnel records, which makes access to data much easier. In other cases, access to information is so restricted that employees themselves are not allowed to inspect their own files and correct inaccurate data.

Current debate centers on whether privacy safeguards should be legislated by the government or established voluntarily by organizational policy. On the one hand, several states and the District of Columbia have passed laws requiring that employees be granted access to their personnel files. (These states include California, Connecticut, North Carolina, Wisconsin, Arkansas, Oregon, Maine, Illinois, New Hampshire, Michigan, and Pennsylvania.)[24] On the other hand, the Federal Privacy Protection Study Commission has urged that organizations voluntarily adopt practices that ensure confidentiality and responsible control of personnel records. The commission's recommendations are as follows:

1. Limit the collection of information on employees and applicants to what is relevant to specific personnel decisions.

2. Give employees access to, and the right to copy, their personnel records upon request.

3. Inform employees and applicants about the uses to which their records are (or will be) put.

4. Designate and separate those records not available to an employee (the commission expressed a strong preference for there to be very few records not available). The commission specifically suggested that individual employment performance, medical, and insurance records be available to employees.

5. Correct records the employee identifies as inaccurate or explain why corrections were not made.

6. Curb the release of information to third parties without the employee's consent, except for routine directory information concerning position held, employment dates, and salary.

7. Limit the internal use of records maintained on employees and applicants.[25]

Presumably, salary information would be released only to confirm the salary already reported by an employee to an outside party.

Another area of concern and debate that relates to privacy is the matter of surveillance of employees in the workplace. As indicated in Chapter 15, there are both threats to morale and legal risks in using video cameras, microphones, computers, or other devices to monitor performance. Stress can increase, morale and trust levels can go down, and the employer may face civil suits and criminal charges.[26]

A Supreme Court decision protects government employees to some extent from secret monitoring. In *O'Connor* v. *Ortega*, the court held that government employees are entitled to a "reasonable expectation of privacy" in the workplace.[27]

In the private sector, judges have held that to win damages, employees must prove that their "reasonable expectations of privacy" outweigh the company's reasons for the surveillance.[28] An example of grounds for a suit might be a company's persistent monitoring of employee telephone calls without a compelling business reason to do so.[29] Some states have privacy guarantees in their constitutions that can create liability for employers who use surveillance in the workplace.[30] However, employers can partially protect themselves from suits by informing workers of surveillance policies. Some companies ask job applicants to sign privacy waivers as a condition of employment.[31]

Protection Against Arbitrary Dismissal

The extent to which employers are free to dismiss workers and the rights of workers facing dismissal have not been established in any final or absolute sense by the legal system. Traditionally, federal and state courts have supported an **employment-at-will rule** (sometimes called a *termination-at-will* rule or the *absolute right to discharge*), which specifies that an employer in a private institution may dismiss an employee, with or without specific cause, in the absence of a written employment agreement. The rule is based on the assumption that the employee may also quit at any time, without notice, and for any reason. This rule is gradually being modified, however, by Congress and by state and federal courts.

There are now specific situations in which at-will dismissal is illegal, and various court decisions have upheld the rights of workers who have been dismissed unfairly. For example, the employment-at-will rule does not apply when dismissal of an employee constitutes discrimination or any violation of civil rights laws. Moreover, the concept of "just cause" overrides the at-will doctrine under many collective-bargaining agreements; it is, in other words, a breach of contract to dismiss an employee for anything but legitimate business reasons. As discussed, dismissal that violates a significant public policy is also forbidden by law — largely through the weight of court decisions.

Several other exceptions to employment at will should be mentioned. The first pertains mostly to public employment; the others apply more generally.

The Job as a Property Right

Through a series of decisions, the Supreme Court has established that employees of state and public institutions have a right to a fair hearing whenever personnel decisions deprive them of a "property interest" or "liberty interest" under the Fourteenth Amendment to the Constitution. This clause reads, "Nor shall any state deprive any person of life, liberty, or property, without due process of law." In general, the principle is not that state and public employees have an absolute right to their jobs, but that dismissal cannot occur without procedural due process.

For example, in *Board of Regents* v. *Roth* (1972), the Court maintained that faculty members of a state university have property rights to their jobs and are therefore safeguarded by due process. The due-process principle means that the employee is to be given fair notice of charges, as well as an opportunity to speak in his or her own defense.

Even in the private sector, legislation and court actions have sometimes indicated that employees have a property interest in their jobs. In one case, for example, employees of a bankrupt company were allowed to file claims against the employer for accrued vacation benefits.[32] In the event of bankruptcy or liquidation of a company, employee pension claims take legal precedence over all other claims (except taxes) up to 30 percent of the net worth of the firm.[33]

Good Faith and Fair Dealing

Court decisions in at least three states indicate that employers must deal fairly and in good faith with employees, even in organizations operating under the employment-at-will rule. The Massachusetts Appellate Court held that a jury could decide whether an employer had discharged a long-term employee in order to avoid paying him large sales commissions. The court ignored a written contract reserving the employer's right to discharge an employee for any reason and ruled that if the jury found the employer's motives suspect, the discharge was improper because the law imposes a covenant of good faith and fair dealing on all contracts. The Montana Supreme Court upheld a $50,000 award to a cashier who claimed she was discharged without warning and had been forced to sign a resignation letter. The court found that the jury had sufficient evidence to find fraud, oppression, or malice on the part of the employer. In California, a court found that an employee could sue for wrongful discharge when the company violated its own procedures for handling employee disputes.[34]

The Implied Contract

Finally, the employment-at-will rule may be deemed invalid in situations governed by an **implied contract,** or an inferred understanding of the conditions of continued employment. Court decisions in several states have ruled against companies that violate promises of job tenure implied in employee handbooks, personnel policy manuals, or in statements made in employment interviews.[35] As a result, many organizations are including disclaimers about job security in handbooks and manuals. Further, managers and human resources department staff members are being cautioned to avoid any implied promises of job security in interviews pertaining to such personnel actions as hiring, transfer, relocation, and promotion.[36] (See the discussion later in the chapter on avoiding legal action.)

Grievance Procedures and Due Process in Nonunionized Organizations

Most of the employee rights described in the previous section are protected by legislation and court decisions. As discussed in Chapter 18, in unionized firms, the collective-bargaining agreement specifies the contract rights of workers, which are also enforceable through the courts. But management, too, can take steps to protect the rights of employees by adhering to what is called **organizational due process.** Organizational due process consists of established procedures for handling employee complaints and grievances, protection against punitive action for using these procedures, and systematic and thorough review of complaints and grievances by unbiased or neutral parties. In employment situations governed by a sincere commitment to organizational due process, employees have the right to object to management action and to be heard without fear of management retaliation.

The systems and procedures for carrying out organizational due process vary from informal methods (such as the open-door policy described in Case 19.1) to formal systems (such as the grievance-arbitration procedure used in Case 17.2 in Chapter 17. Appeal procedures in military, civil service, and some business and industrial organizations reflect a commitment to organizational due process, as do tenure policies and procedures in colleges and universities. In general, all these methods share one major purpose: to provide a means for reviewing (and possibly modifying) management actions in cases where employees believe they have been treated unfairly.

Informal Procedures

One way of handling grievances is through an **open-door policy,** which gives employees access to their superiors so that problems can be brought into the open and resolved in a mutually satisfying way. Many complaints of unjust treatment can be handled through informal discussion of the problem by the employee and his or her supervisor. If the supervisor is an effective listener and genuinely interested in seeing justice done, problems can often be solved and inequities minimized with little time and cost.

If such a discussion does not resolve the issue, employees in some organizations are encouraged to take the problem to the human resources department or to higher management so that the merit of the grievance can be evaluated objectively. An effective resolution of the grievance at this level requires a fair assessment of all sides of the case. The human resources or management representative may need to confer with the supervisor, consider the needs of other employees, and take into account perceptions of equity in order to determine the validity of the complaint and to decide what further action should be taken.

Formal Grievance and Appeal Procedures

Employee complaints of unjust treatment can also be handled through formal grievance procedures, which allow employees to present their complaints to designated parties and which generally specify who is ultimately responsible for settling the issue. The most common formal system for handling grievances is the grievance-arbitration procedure found under collective-bargaining agreements. (See Chapter 18.)

POLICY NUMBER	780
EFFECTIVE DATE	7/15/85
PAGE	1 OF 2

OPEN DOOR POLICY

I. PURPOSE

To afford all regular full and part time employees the opportunity to resolve job-related complaints and problems.

II. SCOPE

This policy applies to all U.S. facilities except those of subsidiaries and those located in Puerto Rico.

III. POLICY

It is the policy of the Company that all regular and part time employees be treated fairly and equitably. An employee who has a job-related problem, question, or complaint, or has been disciplined or discharged may utilize the procedures set forth in this policy. The Company will not tolerate any recrimination against employees who avail themselves of this policy.

All procedures set forth in this policy are guidelines only.

IV. PROCEDURES

Step One—Most job-related problems can and should be resolved directly between the employee and immediate supervisor. Employees are encouraged to discuss such problems with their immediate supervisor who should be constructive and objective in efforts to resolve the matter.

In those cases where the immediate supervisor is the subject of the complaint, the employee will be permitted to begin the procedure with step two.

Step Two—If the problem cannot be resolved with the supervisor, the employee should discuss the problem with the department head or submit the complaint in writing to the department head. If the complaint is submitted in writing it should (1) clearly identify the problem, (2) describe the outcome of step one, if appropriate, and (3) state the specific relief requested. The department head will consider the facts, conduct an investigation, as appropriate, and make a decision which will be communicated to the employee within a reasonable time-frame after receipt of the complaint.

Step Three—If the employee is not in agreement with the decision of the department head, the employee should pursue the problem further by requesting that the complaint be presented to the Personnel Director/Manager/Representative for review and decision. If the Personnel Director/Manager/Representative believes the decision of the department head should be modified and agreement cannot be reached, or, if the Personnel Director/Manager/Representative concurs with the decision, the employee should refer the complaint, in writing, to the Division or Plant Manager as the next step. The written complaint should be submitted no later than five (5) working days after receipt of the decision from the Personnel Director/Manager/Representative.

Step Four—Upon receipt of the written request, the Division/Plant Manager will review the decision made at step three and take whatever steps are necessary to uphold or modify the decision. The Division/Plant Manager's decision will be communicated to the employee within a reasonable time-frame.

FIGURE 19.1 Motorola's "Open-Door Policy"
Source: Courtesy of Motorola, Inc.

<table>
<tr><td>**POLICY NUMBER**</td><td>780</td></tr>
<tr><td>**EFFECTIVE DATE**</td><td>7/15/85</td></tr>
<tr><td>**PAGE**</td><td>2 **OF** 2</td></tr>
</table>

Step Five—If the employee is not in agreement with the Division/Plant Manager's decision, he/she may request that the complaint be reviewed by the Chairman of the Company. The Chairman or member of the Chief Executive Office will conduct a full examination of the facts and a decision shall be communicated to the employee and shall be final.

V. EXCEPTIONS

Exceptions to this policy must be approved by the Chief Executive's Office.

CROSS REFERENCES

Performance Review Policy (#207)
Rules of Conduct and Corrective Discipline (#1005)

FIGURE 19.1   (Continued)

A large proportion of American workers, however, are not covered by collective-bargaining agreements. Of these nonunion employees, among those who work in medium-sized to large organizations, probably a majority have access to some kind of formal grievance procedure. (See Figure 19.1 for Motorola's grievance procedure, called an "Open Door Policy.")

A survey involving 218 responding organizations found established grievance procedures for nonunionized employees in 71 percent of the organizations. However, only 5 organizations — 2 percent — specified arbitration, or outside appeal to a neutral party, as the final step in the procedure. (All 5 were nonbusiness organizations.) Nonbusiness organizations, such as government agencies, were more likely to have a formal grievance procedure than business organizations.[37]

Review Boards and Tribunals   **Disciplinary review boards** are sometimes used in business and industrial firms to review instances of disciplinary action and to correct or amend a penalty that an employee considers unfair or too harsh. These boards usually consist of a committee of three or more managers and, in a small number of companies, a psychiatrist or psychologist. By emphasizing a corrective, problem-solving approach, disciplinary review boards can successfully counteract any punitive tendencies in supervisors' dealings with subordinates.

Internal tribunals, as distinguished from external tribunals such as arbitration proceedings and courts of law, are frequently found in leading nonunion companies. The task of these tribunals is to hand down a binding decision consistent with company-published policies and procedures. Although these tribunals — sometimes called **peer review panels** — vary in their memberships, most of them include one or more of the fellow workers of the person filing the complaint or grievance in addition to management representatives. These tribunals also typically include a representative of the personnel or human resources department, who can interpret company policies and procedures to other members of the panel.[38]

The Corporate Ombudsman

A unique institution in the administration of organizational justice, the **ombudsman,** has appeared on the American scene in recent years. *Ombudsman* is a Swedish word meaning representative or attorney.[39] Originally, the ombudsman was typically an eminent attorney appointed by a legislative body to investigate citizens' complaints against administrative officials and to report on the findings. More recently, some corporations and other types of institutions have begun to use this role for internal investigation and resolution of employees' complaints. A complaint is brought by the employee, the ombudsman investigates, and then uses his or her influence to resolve the matter.

Though a few American organizations such as Xerox Corp., Control Data Corp., General Electric Co., Boeing Vertol Company, Massachusetts Institute of Technology, and the University of Washington have had some experience with a corporate or institutional ombudsman, little of this experience has been reported in the literature.[40] (For an exception, see *Comtemporary Issues* on page 513.) What reports have emerged have suggested that an ombudsman can be very effective in combating subtle abuses of subordinates.[41] In some organizations, an executive with other responsibilities is assigned the ombudsman role. For example, one company has used the director of communications to handle complaints, and another designates a "where-to-turn" person, who reports directly to the president of the company.[42]

There is a risk that an ombudsman will be more loyal to management than to employees. This will depend in large part, however, on how the ombudsman is chosen and the degree to which management truly wishes to be responsive to complaints and grievances. One author has recommended that ombudsmen be picked from lists of state-licensed specialists and that they be chosen jointly by management and employee representatives.[43]

Access to the Courts and Government Agencies

Although all citizens have access to the courts, judges will usually not become involved in an alleged injustice in the employment relationship unless laws have been violated. An exception is the increasing involvement of the courts in reviewing whether due process has occurred, usually in cases of state employment (or state-related employment) and under the Fourteenth Amendment.

The government involves itself in organizational justice through the action of administrative agencies responsible for enforcing laws pertaining to minimum wages, child labor, overtime, fair employment, and unfair labor practices. Decisions handed down by these agencies are usually enforced by court action upon proper judicial review. Appeals of such decisions are also normally handled by the courts. For the most part, however, courts have held that the aggrieved employee must exhaust all of the organization's internal procedures before seeking a judicial remedy.

Contemporary Issues

A Day in the Life of an Ombudsman

David T. Nassef was a vice president of personnel for business systems and had been with Pitney Bowes Inc. for 20 years when the company decided to establish an ombudsman in 1988. He stepped into the job. And now he's a "one-man band," the sole ombudsman responsible for Pitney Bowes's 30,000 employees worldwide. Actually, he does have a little help — a secretary, as well as a psychiatrist, psychologist, attorney, and organizational designer on retainer.

Employees drop by Nassef's office daily with their questions, problems, and complaints. Or they may give him a call or send him a letter. Those employees who want to be especially discrete meet him at McDonald's, churches, and airports. "Airports are big," says Nassef. "I'm always flying into Dallas or Chicago and meeting someone in the airport."

What follows are some of the issues Nassef faces on a day-to-day basis, and how he goes about resolving them:

Environmental hazards. "A production worker comes forward and says she thinks we're polluting the air at her work station. She's angry and says, 'If the company doesn't do something about it, I'm going to do something about it.' I go to the unit head of manufacturing and our private conversation reveals that he doesn't know whether there's any truth to the employee's claim or not. So we call in the safety engineers and test the air. It turns out the air is polluted. So now we have to start looking for solutions. We might be able to reconfigure the machines in the production area to cut down on the pollution."

Benefits. "The wife of a business manager in rural Wisconsin has recently become an invalid. The prognosis is that her disability will be long term. So I visit the community to try to determine what's available in the way of care. In such situations, I'm always careful to find out from the employee what options are favorable.

"In this case, it turns out that what's needed is nonmedical custodial care. There's no need for someone in a white uniform and hat. Then we work out a way for the business manager to pay for the custodial care. Maybe an annuity plan; there are lots of different variables to consider when it comes to health care."

Sexual harassment. "An employee comes by my office. She reports that her supervisor has been making off-color comments. She is extremely uncomfortable with him and feels demeaned in social situations when he starts in with his locker-room talk. She is a wife and a mother. So I tell her to stop him the moment he starts in again and to say, 'As a wife and mother, when you say these things it makes me feel . . .' This approach is very effective at putting things in perspective. It should make the supervisor stop and think, 'Hey, wait a minute, I wouldn't want someone talking this way around my wife or mother.'"

Restructuring. "A line manager calls me and says that the need to focus on quality has forced him to restructure his division. 'But if I use such and such approach,' he says, 'it's going to have a negative impact on the older workforce. And if I take care of the senior workforce, it's going to be at the expense of women. Maybe I should just offer early retirement.'

"Line managers can get real narrow. They typically think they have only one or two options. Most times they have more, but they're so close to their operations that they can't see them. I usually have a good knowledge of a manager's organization. So I might suggest thinking about peak and valley employment. On certain weeks designated employees can work a 40-hour week, while on others they can work 20 hours. Or I might suggest that he consider the timing of the restructuring. Does it have to all be done in January? Perhaps it can be spread over six months. That opens up a whole new set of variables."

Fraud. "One of our production people comes to me and says, 'Look what they're asking me to do. They want me to lie about the production figures!' So I go and check it out. On the surface, it does look like someone is playing with the numbers. But it turns out that the cost accounting system put in place 10 years ago was changed four years ago. Only no one communicated this to the production group. So they were having to force fit their numbers, when all they really had to do was change their tabulation forms."

Source: Justin Martin, "New Tricks for an Old Trade," *Across the Board* 29 (June 1992):43. Reprinted by permission of The Conference Board.

Implications for the Human Resources Department

The human resources department plays a major role in protecting employee rights and developing procedures for carrying out organizational due process. The importance of this role continues to grow as laws, practice, and theory pertaining to organizational justice evolve. Human resources specialists, as well as all managers, face a special challenge in determining what is fair and equitable treatment and in following procedures for correcting unfair decisions and remedying injustice. Moreover, the human resources department is in a unique position to influence organizational climate and culture so that management and employees are sensitive to their respective rights and responsibilities. At the same time, the human resources department can monitor organizational policy and management practices to ensure consistency, fairness, and cost-effectiveness in resolving grievances and handling disciplinary problems.

Protecting Employee Rights

As one of its most important responsibilities, the human resources department can play an active role in helping the organization avoid discrimination and unjust practices at the policy level. The department can take the lead in developing strong policy statements against all forms of discrimination and harassment and can secure top management support in monitoring and enforcing these policies. Providing information on and training in nondiscriminatory decision making and the legal rights of employees is another way the human resources department can promote organizational justice. Moreover, the human resources staff needs to be knowledgeable about what the organization legally may or may not do if employees attempt to unionize, and it should be prepared to advise supervisors and managers accordingly.

One of the main things the human resources department can do in the area of speech rights and obligations is to help the organization develop multiple avenues for employees to be heard and understood. This may mean providing training programs for supervisors that include sessions on active listening and participative approaches to running meetings. The department may also recommend that small-group discussion sessions be held to allow employees to communicate with members of top management on a regular basis. In addition, a human resources specialist can act as a mediator between an employee and supervisor in cases of misunderstanding or disagreement so that a constructive relationship can be restored and maintained. And because rights imply responsibilities, the human resources staff can play a major role in counseling employees about the limits of free speech in the workplace.

To protect employee privacy, the human resources director is wise to promote the adoption of safeguards to ensure confidentiality of personnel data as recommended by the Federal Privacy Study Commission. In addition, the human resources staff should protect privacy on a day-to-day basis by ensuring confidentiality of staffing decisions, compensation and benefits administration, grievance resolutions, and so on. Privacy protection by the human resources department "establishes the basic pattern for handling employee privacy within the organization, since managers will likely follow the tone of the 'examples' on this issue set by their personnel administrators."[44]

Avoiding Legal Action

To avoid possible litigation, as well as to enhance employees' motivation and commitment, the human resources department should be an advocate of organizational due process. In particular, the department should insist on progressive discipline procedures (see Chapter 8), including careful documentation of unsatisfactory performance, and thorough review procedures in potential discharge cases.

Company handbooks and personnel policy manuals present a special dilemma for human resources departments. On the one hand, it is reasonable to acknowledge that due process, reasonable job security, and discharge for just cause are basic components of the organization's personnel policy. On the other, if handbooks and manuals state or imply that the employee's job is guaranteed in the absence of just and sufficient cause for discharge, dismissed employees may be able to sue the employer on the basis of implied contract violation. Legal action seems particularly likely when employment procedures and policy statements have helped create expectations of job permanence in the mind of the employee and when his or her record of pay increases and promotions suggests a pattern of satisfactory performance. Statements of policy and conditions of employment, then, must be carefully worded and qualified so that management is not unnecessarily restricted in the dismissal actions it can take. A team of lawyers makes the following suggestions:

> Although many employers may not yet have adopted detailed "just cause" disciplinary procedures in their employee manuals, thereby avoiding difficulties confronted by employers who fail to follow their own procedures, it is a good idea in any event to state in writing the fact that discharge is solely at the employer's discretion. If grounds for dismissal are stated in a manual, the employer should also state that the list is not exhaustive and is subject to unilateral change. In addition, an employer may want to state that progressive disciplinary measures or grievance steps may be dispensed with at the employer's discretion, depending upon the nature of the discharge.[45]

A survey of 222 firms of all types found that 78 percent had taken specific measures to avoid legal problems in the event of employee dismissals. Of those that had taken measures, more than 6 out of 10 changed or removed wording in company manuals or handbooks to avoid any suggestion of an employment contract. About half of these firms added wording to handbooks and application forms specifying that employment could be terminated for any reason. An example is the following statement found in the employee handbook of a small manufacturing company: "Neither this handbook nor any other communication by employer representatives, written or oral, is intended in any way to create an employment contract binding on either party."[46] Typically, the human resources department plays a major role in the development of such statements, which attempt to keep the organization out of legal entanglements but at the same time try to enhance the motivation and commitment of the work force.

Summary   Employees in the United States have a significant number of rights based on law, court decisions, and administrative rulings. Among these rights are prohibitions against discrimination based on race, color, religion, national origin, sex, age, or disabled status. Sexual harassment is now illegal under federal law. Age harassment is also illegal, as is harassment based on color, religion, or national origin.

Nonsupervisory workers have the right to organize and bargain collectively. This right is reinforced by contract rights stemming from labor-management agreements. Individual employees can also enter into contracts with the employer in nonunionized situations.

Employees do not have complete freedom in what they can say about their supervisors and the employing organization. In a number of states, however, public employees appear to have the right to "blow the whistle" on illegal, immoral, or irresponsible acts.

Employees in the private sector thus far have few legal protections from invasions of privacy stemming from misuse of personnel records. A federal commission, however, has urged business firms to adopt safeguards voluntarily.

The "employment-at-will" doctrine is gradually being modified by courts. Some court decisions indicate that employers must deal fairly and in good faith with an employee in the case of a dismissal.

Organizations vary in the degree to which organizational due process is followed for complaints or grievances. Informal processes, such as effective listening and problem solving by supervisors, often solve many problems. Formal grievance procedures for nonunion employees are frequently found in mid-sized to large organizations, but arbitration is infrequently used in the nonunion setting. Internal tribunals, sometimes involving peers of the person filing the grievance, are used in some firms. Aggrieved employees also have access to government agencies and the courts, although courts have traditionally avoided getting involved in alleged injustices unless laws have been violated.

The human resources department plays a major role in ensuring that employees at all levels are heard and understood and that they are treated equitably. That department should ensure that there are adequate safeguards against misuse of the information in personnel records, that progressive discipline procedures are followed, and that any potential discharge cases are reviewed thoroughly. The human resources department usually also is involved in monitoring grievance procedures, advising supervisors and managers at the various stages of grievance hearings, setting strategy, and making the decision about whether a case will go to arbitration. The human resources department has a major challenge in developing statements in company handbooks and personnel policy manuals that set forth policy but also protect the organization from unnecessary restrictions in dismissal cases.

Ethical Dilemma

Arnie is sixty-three, a grandfather seven times, white-haired, and a skilled machinist. He emigrated from Scandinavia when he was in his thirties and retains a pronounced accent. There are no other Scandinavians in the machine shop. Through a series of coincidences, all of the other machinists in the shop are young men, mostly single and given to horseplay. Arnie has openly disapproved of some of the horseplay, particularly when materials have been damaged.

Lately, the other machinists have begun to mimic Arnie's accent in front of him, and to comment on his age with statements like "How are you going to run a machine when you can no longer stand up?" Arnie has been getting increasingly upset and dejected and almost every evening has been talking with his wife about the situation.

Discuss the ethics of Arnie's treatment by (1) the younger employees and (2) the company. What are the likely consequences? Is this illegal age harassment? Ethnic or national origin harassment?

Key Terms

due process	employment-at-will rule
sexual harassment	implied contract
quid pro quo sexual harassment	organizational due process
hostile environment sexual harassment	open-door policy
age harassment	disciplinary review board
contract rights	internal tribunals
just cause	peer review panels
whistle blowing	ombudsman

Review Questions

1. List some employee rights protected by law.
2. Outline the employer's legal obligations in relation to sexual harassment.
3. Discuss the extent to which employees in private enterprise have the right of free speech.
4. What privacy rights do employees have, if any?
5. What is the employment-at-will doctrine? Cite instances in which the doctrine is invalid.
6. Define organizational due process and describe formal and informal procedures for carrying out justice in the nonunion organization.
7. What is the role of the human resources department in protecting employee rights?

Opening Case Questions

Case 19.1   The Open-Door Policy

1. Discuss work situations you have encountered that are similar to Al's. In what ways could your experience have been improved?

2. If you worked with Al, how would you feel about taking on an increased workload so Al could attend his class?

Case 19.2   Sexual Harassment?

1. Is this a case of sexual harassment? If so, what type? What might the legal penalties be?
2. What do you think Mimi should do?

Comprehensive Case

Sexual Harassment in the Workplace

The confirmation hearings of Supreme Court Justice Clarence Thomas forced many Americans to admit, belatedly, that sexual harassment is a major issue in the American workplace. Although the all-male Senate Judiciary Committee, and ultimately the entire Senate, voted to confirm Thomas, the hearings may prove to have been a watershed in the public perception of harassment. For some victims of harassment, the outcome of the hearings and the abuse heaped on Thomas's accuser, Anita Hill, confirmed the futility of bringing sexual harassment charges: no one believes the victim, even if she is a law professor. But others turned their rage at the treatment of Hill into personal action. During the year after the hearings, the Equal Employment Opportunity Commission reported that harassment claims jumped 50 percent.

Companies can no longer afford to assert that "it doesn't happen here." Surveys consistently show that a majority of female American workers feel they have been sexually harassed on the job. The problem is not just an American one — over 80 percent of the women surveyed in Japan and Spain reported sexually harassing behaviors. And besides sapping morale and poisoning interpersonal relations in the work force, harassment costs money. The combined cost of harassment-related lawsuits and turnover can total millions of dollars yearly for even moderately sized companies.

Human resources managers need to know what harassment is, the best ways of preventing it, and how to handle it when it does occur. Sexual harassment is not limited to physical contact or sexual propositions. To a large extent, harassment is in the eye of the beholder: if a woman feels she has been harassed, her company has a problem. Increasingly, courts have been willing to listen to her problem and to hold her employer responsible.

In a Miami case, a former general manager of a hotel won a $1 million suit against the hotel chain's owner because her boss forced her to have sex with him in order to keep her job. The infamous Tailhook scandal, involving the systematic sexual abuse of dozens of women by naval aviators, led to the resignation of the secretary of the navy, public condemnation of the navy's cover-up, and the filing of million-dollar lawsuits by the victims. In 1992 the U.S. Court of Appeals ruled that warning a sexual harasser and providing counseling for him were not enough; the employer must take action that contributes to eliminating the problem.

Perhaps even more important have been decisions broadening the scope of harassment suits. In 1991 a judge approved the first class action suit for sexual harassment, ruling that large groups of women can sue if they are subjected to a "hostile work environment" created, in that particular case, by the public posting of nude photographs, sexual cartoons, and graffiti, even in supervisors' offices. And the courts have begun acknowledging that men and women often think and react differently. One standard for judging whether an act constitutes harassment is if it would offend a "reasonable woman."

To reduce the actual incidents of sexual harassment and therefore their organizations' liability, human resources managers need to take a proactive stance, doing all they can to eliminate such harassment and setting up a grievance procedure specifically to handle harassment cases. The organization must begin by releasing clear public statements and written policies about its refusal to tolerate sexual harassment. Such policies must be more specific than those included in general nondiscrimination pledges, and they must make employees aware that sexual harassment includes a "hostile work environment," not just more direct "sex or you're fired" threats.

Organizations should train all employees about sexual harassment. Many are finding that having employees attend lectures or read brochures is not enough. More effective are techniques that involve participants in role-playing and serious discussions with their colleagues of both sexes. Many men need to be told that the intent of their actions is not as important as the effect those actions have on their recipients. Many women need to be assured that they do not have to put up with behavior that makes them uncomfortable; it is not "just part of the job."

The procedures for handling sexual harassment grievances need to be clearly spelled out and designed to ensure privacy and anonymity. The policy should provide someone for the victim to first appeal to other than the victim's supervisor, since the supervisor may be the harasser. Because of the "reasonable woman" standard and because most victims of harassment are female, women should play important roles in the grievance procedures whenever possible. The organization needs to train people to determine whether a particular act constitutes sexual harassment, and these "judges" need to rely on the organization's clear definition of harassment. Most organizations set up review or appeal panels so that if a grievance goes full course, a variety of women and men will have a chance to assess the situation.

Organizations can go beyond simply dealing with individual cases and take surveys of employees to get a sense whether unreported sexual harassment is widespread. As part of their sensi-tivity to the whole issue, human resources managers need to ensure that the accused harassers' rights are not violated, and they may need to deal with men whose reaction to the issue is "I just won't work with women any more." Management teams truly determined to create a supportive, nonthreatening workplace should probably listen to groups of women discuss the Hill-Thomas hearings. The hearings left many women saying in frustration, "Men just don't get it." Organizations need to make clear to all their employees that they "get it."

Sources: Albert R. Karr, "Issue of Sex Harassment at Workplace Is Gaining More Attention World-Wide," *Wall Street Journal*, December 1, 1992, p. A4; Mark L. Lengnick-Hall, "Checking Out Sexual Harassment Claims," *HRMagazine* 37 (March 1992):77–81; Betty Southard Murphy, Wayne E. Barlow, and D. Diane Hatch, "Employers Warned to Take Disciplinary Steps to Stop Harassment," *Personnel Journal* 71 (November 1992):22–24; "$1 Million Award In Harassment of Hotel Manager," *Seattle Times*, October 11, 1992, p. A5; Ellen Joan Pollock, "Judge Approves First Sex-Bias Class Action," *Wall Street Journal*, December 18, 1991, p. B1; Jonathan A. Segal, "Seven Ways to Reduce Harassment Claims," *HRMagazine* 37 (January 1992):84–86; Troy Segal, "Getting Serious About Sexual Harassment," *Business Week*, November 9, 1992, pp. 78–82; Peggy Stuart, "Prevent Sexual Harassment in Your Work Force," *Personnel Journal* 70 (December 1991):33.

Discussion Questions

1. Using this case and the chapter discussion, describe the two kinds of sexual harassment.
2. What is the organization's responsibility in regard to sexual harassment?

CHAPTER 20

Safety and Health Management

LEARNING OBJECTIVES

- Give several reasons why organizations are actively involved in safety and health management.
- Explain the major provisions of the Occupational Safety and Health Act (OSH Act) and describe the impact this law has had.
- Describe some common accident-prevention methods.
- List some physical and environmental hazards commonly associated with occupational disease.
- Describe the purpose of an employee assistance program.
- Characterize an effectively managed safety and health program.

CASE 20.1   Can We Afford a High-Quality Safety Program?

Stan Ishikawa, president of a small chemical company, Magic Compounds, was meeting with the human resources director, Jeff Albers, and the vice president of manufacturing, Gina Terrel. There were two main items on the agenda: (1) the expansion of plant facilities and hiring to accommodate increased business and (2) the safety and health program.

"Let's start with the second item," Stan said. "Changes we need to make in ventilation and recycling and disposal will affect plant construction and the kind of equipment we need to buy. And besides, we're going to be spending months planning the expansion, and we won't get very far today."

"I'd just as soon start there, too," said Gina. "There have been some disturbing things in the newspapers and on television lately that make me think we ought to audit our present safety program, as well as be very careful about what kinds of things we do relative to any expansion."

"What kinds of things are you referring to?" asked Jeff.

"The deaths at that chicken processing plant in North Carolina where the fire door was padlocked, for one," Gina said. "And the cyanide poisoning case in Illinois a while back. There were criminal charges brought in those cases. And there have been other scary incidents — whole towns evacuated because of chemical leaks, and so on. We passed an OSHA inspection a while back, and I think we are in good shape, but we've been so busy hiring people lately and getting production out that we could be getting sloppy."

"I agree," said Jeff. "I think it would be wise to do our own audit. We can get the safety committees involved in making inspections, and we can get them involved in reviewing our planned equipment additions. By the way, Stan, we have a chemical engineer on every committee. That was Gina's idea — and very smart."

"We're in 100 percent agreement," Stan responded. "We want the safest possible work situation for our employees. And I'm sure that's what they want. However, we've got to watch costs — we can't afford to do just cosmetic things. Let's make sure we're contributing to safety when we make changes. On the other hand, let's not be stingy. The president in that cyanide case went to jail for murder, I believe, and I think the chicken company guy went to prison for manslaughter. And I doubt if a chemical leak in the atmosphere makes one popular at the Rotary Club. So for a lot of reasons I'm glad you two want to get on top of the safety matter. It's got to be as high a priority as anything we do."   ◄

CASE 20.2   Just Whom Am I Protecting?

Jill Meyer, head of the data-processing department, was troubled. One of her long-term employees, Jerry Hawkins, had come to work late, and he appeared to be slightly tipsy. His speech was a little slurred, and he was bubbling over with friendliness. Ordinarily, Jill didn't have close contact with Jerry, because Jerry reported to one of the supervisors, Bob Scott. But today Jill had come into Bob's area when Jerry arrived, and both had seen Jerry's condition.

Jill went back to her office and within a minute Bob joined her. Bob was obviously upset. "We've got to do something about Jerry," Bob blurted out. "We've talked about him before — he's come in half drunk or hung over from time to time for years — but now it's happening more frequently. I've confronted Jerry several times and he always denies he's had anything to drink, or he claims he's been to a wedding breakfast, or something. Trouble is, he's such a nice guy and does such a good job when he's sober that it's hard to confront him. I'm not sleeping well at night these days, worrying about what to do."

"You're absolutely right," Jill responded. "We've got to do something. What do the other members of your group say about it?"

Bob's reply was immediate. "They're demoralized. They're tired of covering for Jerry and tired of correcting his mistakes. I think one of my best people is going to quit if we don't take action. The trouble is, I'm not sure what to do."

"Have you documented any of this — his condition, his mistakes, or any other ways his performance is affected?" Jill asked.

"Unfortunately, no," Bob replied.

"Here's a suggestion, then," said Jill. "Go right back to your unit and give Jerry some short work assignment that ordinarily he could do accurately — like making some computer entries and doing a printout — and see what you get. I think you're going to find that he makes a lot of mistakes. If so, sit down with him in the conference room, confront him with the data, and give him an ultimatum. And let's put it in writing."

"I'll do it," said Bob. "But I may want to come back and check signals with you before I have my session with him. We need to decide whether our ultimatum means a warning, a layoff, or a discharge."

"Yes, we should," Jill replied. "I'll call up the personnel department to see what advice they have for us. I should have faced up to this a long time ago."

Before Jill placed her call, she sat thinking for a minute. "Wow," she thought, "I wonder if Bob and I have been protecting Jerry because he's such a nice guy and usually such a good worker, or whether we've been protecting ourselves from the pain of facing up to something very unpleasant. When I hear Bob say he can't sleep at night and that his people are demoralized, it's easy to see that protecting one person is making life miserable for a bunch of other folks."

Jill picked up the telephone and dialed personnel. ◀

C ase 20.1 is a reminder of how vital it is that organizations have effective health and safety practices, not only for the welfare of employees but also because of consequences to families and the broader community. So far, Magic Compounds has had a successful record in health and safety, and clearly top management wants to keep it that way. But the case also shows that the historical evolution of excellent practices in one organization may not necessarily be duplicated in another plant, or in a different industry, or in a different country. Unsafe practices and the potential for death, disease, and disability are still with us. Clearly, those American organizations with the best safety records should not become complacent, and those with substandard records must improve. And it may be that developing countries have a lot of catching up to do. This also suggests that governments may play an important role in effective health and safety management. Governments may undercontrol and thus allow serious conditions to exist. Or governments can overcontrol and get in the way of the effective management of the health and safety program of a plant.

Case 20.2 is about alcohol abuse and the difficult problems it creates for the person, fellow workers, and management. A serious and costly problem, substance abuse is often met with a kind of conspiracy of silence, but it must be confronted for the good of the person and the organization. In this case, the department head, Jill Meyer, has begun to realize that protecting one person from a confrontation may be doing great harm to others and to the organization.

This chapter is about the important matter of safety and health in the workplace. It discusses why managers and employees alike must be concerned about this issue and describes federal regulations pertaining to safety and health, variables related to accidents, and problems associated with the prevention of occupational disease. Also discussed are alcohol and drug abuse, excessive stress, and emotional illness — all health problems that can be very costly to organizations and to the individuals involved, as well as to families and communities. The chapter ends with some principles about how to manage safety and health programs.

The Concern for Employee Safety and Health

Ensuring the physical well-being of employees in the workplace is the primary goal of the safety and health management process. In recent years the human resources department has taken on greater and greater responsibility in this area, but in fact, organizations began shouldering some of this responsibility even before the modern personnel department came into existence. Once the Supreme Court upheld the constitutionality of state workers' compensation laws in 1911, safety specialists were commonly employed in industrial firms. Naturally, these organizations wanted to hold down the costs of insurance and reduce the number of claims filed by their employees, so they depended on safety specialists to help establish and maintain safer working conditions in their plants.

Today, safety and health management is a complex activity requiring the expertise of specialists from many disciplines, such as industrial hygiene, occupational medicine, ecology, psychology, and safety engineering, to name only a few. Moreover, concerns in safety and health management now reach beyond physical conditions in the workplace to embrace a regard for workers' mental and emotional well-being and a commitment to protecting the surrounding community from pollution and exposure to toxic substances.

Involvement in safety and health management represents an organization's response to a number of compelling influences, the most basic of which is a sense of social and humanitarian responsibility. Government intervention, pressure from labor unions, and the general public consciousness account for much of the progress in this area. Finally, experience and knowledge of issues in worker protection have led to a greater appreciation of how safety and health management is directly related to organizational effectiveness. To protect the well-being of employees is to protect the organization's most valuable resource and to avoid the staggering costs and negative public image associated with safety neglect.

Social and Humanitarian Responsibility

A sense of social responsibility grows out of the recognition that business and industrial organizations do more than seek profits. Organizational activities affect workers as people and society as a whole, and these effects should be considered in the planning and management of all day-to-day operations. The establishment of safe, healthful, and environmentally sound working conditions is a priority in any socially responsible organization.

Safety and health practices in many firms go far beyond the standards required by law, which suggests that many organizations do consider safety and health management a prime social responsibility. Exceptional safety records stand as proof of this commitment. For example, between March 1974 and April 1980, Du Pont's Chattanooga plant accumulated 48 million continuous working hours in which not a single employee was absent from work because of occupational illness or injury.[1]

The extent to which an organization demonstrates social responsibility is part of the firm's public image, and a positive safety record can contribute to positive public relations. But genuine humanitarian concerns are reflected in a commitment to employee health and safety as well. These concerns are expressed in the feelings people have for each other when an illness or accident causes serious injury or death, and in the sense of purpose displayed by those responsible for safety and health programs. Certainly, the effects of a job-related illness or injury go far beyond the economic loss to the organization and extend to long-term consequences to workers and their families.

Influence of Labor Unions

Historically, labor unions have generally been active in matters of health and safety and have pressed management to improve working conditions. An example of current union concern is expressed in the increasing number of industrial hygienists employed by labor unions to monitor the working conditions of their members, particularly in the chemical, rubber, oil, auto, and primary-metals industries. This development is due to pressure from rank-and-file members, as well as from union leadership, and is aimed at identifying health hazards and securing corrective action.

Unions also tend to bargain strenuously for health and safety provisions in labor contracts. For example, a recent study of labor-management agreements found that 94 percent of the contracts in manufacturing firms contained safety and health clauses. Safety equipment was mentioned in 43 percent of all contracts surveyed.[2]

Moreover, unions are increasingly requesting membership on plant safety and health committees and asking that workers be paid by the company for time devoted to meetings. Provisions for joint management-union committees are found in 48 percent of labor contracts; pay for time spent on committee activities is specified in about one-third of the clauses providing for joint committees.[3] In addition, many unions are asking for company contributions of several cents per hour for safety and health research and for compensation for time spent accompanying government occupational safety and health officers on plant-site inspections. In support of these efforts, the AFL-CIO established a Department of Occupational Safety and Health to work with industry in identifying problem areas and reducing industrial accidents and personal injuries.[4]

Costs   The costs to an organization of accidents, injuries, and occupational diseases are both tangible and intangible. The tangible costs are the measurable financial expenses. The intangible costs include lowered employee morale, less favorable public relations, and weakened ability to recruit and retain employees.

Frequently, organizations ignore or are not aware of the tangible but "hidden" costs of occupational illness or injury. The following list gives some idea of the costs associated with a single accident in the workplace:

- The cost of wages paid to workers who are attracted to the accident site and therefore not working
- Equipment or work in process that is interrupted, spoiled, or damaged; slowdowns at later production stations caused by interruptions in the work of the injured person as well as the work of those who came to the scene
- The repair of damaged equipment or work in process
- Cleanup costs
- Payments to the injured employee in excess of workers' compensation
- Dispensary services provided by the plant nurse, company infirmary, and so on
- The diminished productivity of the injured person after his or her return to the job but before full work output can be sustained
- Cost of supervisory time (incurred because accidents must be investigated, and reports must be made and processed)
- Extra overtime costs occasioned by the initial interruption of work
- Costs associated with the recruitment, selection or transfer, and training of a replacement for the recuperating worker
- Costs associated with the higher scrap, spoilage, or generally lower efficiency of the replacement
- Legal costs for advice with respect to any potential claim
- Costs of rental equipment placed temporarily in service while unsafe equipment is repaired or replaced[5]

The National Safety Council estimated that 75 million days were lost in 1990 as a result of new and previous accidents in the workplace in the United States. The council also estimated that another 100 million days would be lost in future years because of the accidents that occurred in that year. The 1990 costs were estimated at $63.8 billion. A single death was estimated to cost $730,000.[6]

Public Awareness   Extensive media attention, widespread concern about environmental pollution, pressure from advocacy groups, rising levels of education, and the availability of information have heightened public awareness of health and safety issues in the workplace. For example, in 1985 the media reported that Ralph Nader's Health Research Group found through a review of recently released government documents that some 250,000 employees ran higher-than-normal risks of developing various diseases, including cancer, from exposure to toxic substances at work. The group reported that some 59,000 foundry workers risked cancer and respiratory diseases because of exposure to such substances as metal fumes and coal tar. Some 50,000 miners exposed to silica and uranium dust had increased risks of silicosis and lung and respiratory cancer.[7] As another example, the government has reported that among certain asbestos-factory workers cancer death rates of 40 to 45 percent have occurred, and lung abnormalities have been found in 38 percent of some asbestos workers' family members.[8]

Media coverage of a number of major disasters has intensified public awareness in recent years. Here are a few, some of which are mentioned in Chapter 3:

- Poisonous chemical release at Bhopal, India, 1984 (4,000 deaths and 30,000 to 40,000 serious injuries)
- Nuclear blast at Chernobyl in Ukrainian SSR, 1986 (more than 2,000 people killed by radiation poisoning and nearly 100,000 resettled; disastrous effects continue including substantial increase in number of rare childhood cancers)
- Release of hydrogen fluoride from a ruptured tank, Texas City, Texas, 1987 (800 people treated for breathing disorders and skin problems, 3,000 residents evacuated for three days)
- Conflagration on North Sea oil rig, 1988 (167 workers killed)
- Chemical plant explosion outside Houston, Texas, 1989 (23 workers killed)
- Leakage of chemicals from an electronics plant into a water reservoir, Kumi, South Korea, 1991 (hundreds, perhaps thousands, become violently ill)
- Blaze in a chicken-processing plant, Hamlet, North Carolina, 1991 (25 workers killed by fire and smoke)[9]

Such reports tend to heighten public awareness. In turn, public awareness tends to result in pressure on organizations to develop more effective health and safety programs. Public pressure has also prompted some organizations to provide more health and safety information to employees and to the public. After the disaster at the Union Carbide plant in Bhopal, India, for example, Monsanto Company announced it would immediately start publicizing information about the toxic products the company makes within the communities where these products are made.[10]

Legal Obligations

Workers' Compensation

Organizations have extensive legal obligations with regard to health and safety. One major obligation is paying workers' compensation insurance premiums under state workers' compensation laws. This insurance provides benefits to workers who suffer occupational injuries regardless of fault. In many states organizations have an incentive to improve safety conditions since their insurance premiums are affected by the number of claims made by their employees. For many organizations, the cost of workers' compensation insurance premiums is a major driving force behind their safety programs.

For decades, workers' compensation benefits were paid only in cases in which a worker suffered physical impairment as a result of a work accident. In recent years, however, state laws and court decisions have increasingly brought emotional and physical impairment due to job stress within the arena of compensable claims. For example, the California labor code allows compensation for injuries caused by "repetitive mentally or physically traumatic activities extending over a period of time, the combined effect of which causes any disability or need for medical treatment." Thus, employers' legal liability is being extended into the emotional and mental health area.[11]

Labor Laws   Various labor laws also refer to worker health and safety. For example, the Walsh-Healey Act states that no part of a government contract shall be performed "under working conditions which are unsanitary or hazardous or dangerous to the health of employees engaged in the performance of said contract. Compliance with the safety, sanitary, and factory inspection laws of the State in which the work or part thereof is to be performed shall be prima-facie evidence of compliance with this subsection."[12] The Federal Mine Safety and Health Act of 1977 (previously called the Coal Mine Health and Safety Act) goes into considerable detail about such matters as dust concentration, ventilation, roof supports, the use of explosives, emergency procedures, and inspections.[13]

Supreme Court   Supreme Court rulings also create legal obligations for employers, and, in the case of at least one decision, can create difficult dilemmas. In the 1991 decision in *UAW v. Johnson Controls*, the Court ruled that employers could not bar women of childbearing age from specified jobs (in this case, working with automobile batteries containing lead) because of potential danger to unborn children. The Court left open the question of how organizations might legally protect workers in high-risk jobs and at the same time protect the organization from liability. One likely consequence is that organizations will sharply increase health and safety protections for employees on hazardous jobs.[14] (See also Chapter 3.)

Criminal and Civil Penalties   In addition, various laws provide for civil and/or criminal penalties for violations. For example, under the Federal Mine Safety and Health Act, a mine operator can be fined $25,000 or imprisoned for a year, or both, for a willful violation of a health or safety standard. In 1984 prosecutors of the state of Illinois obtained a grand jury indictment charging five top officers of a company with the murder of an employee, Stefan Golab, who died from cyanide poisoning. Golab was employed by Film Recovery Systems, a company that specialized in extracting silver from used film. The prosecutors alleged that the company officials were fully aware of the dangers of cyanide and failed to ensure the protection of workers by providing the proper equipment. In June of 1985 a Cook County judge found three of the corporate officials guilty of murder in Golab's death — the former president, plant manager, and plant foreman of the now defunct company.[15]

In 1988 a California jury found the Reliance Steel and Aluminum Company and two of its executives guilty of a criminal misdemeanor in the death of an employee. The jury found that the company had not properly trained the employee in the use of a steel-slitting machine by providing only three hours of training when the normal practice was to provide thirty days of training.[16] In 1989 the president of Elliott Plumbing & Heating, a South Dakota firm, was sentenced to six months in jail and a $21,452 fine for failing to comply with trenching standards under the Occupational Safety and Health Act. Two employees of the firm had been killed when a trench they were digging collapsed.[17] In the case cited earlier of a North Carolina chicken-processing plant where a fire in 1991 killed twenty-five workers and injured fifty-six more, the owner was sentenced to nearly twenty years in prison for involuntary manslaughter. The company, Imperial Food Products Inc., was fined $808,150. Among other violations of state health and safety laws, exit doors had been locked and there was no fire alarm or sprinkler system.[18] Such prosecution is part of a growing trend of criminal prosecutions at both the state and federal levels for workplace safety violations.[19]

Probably the most far-reaching legal obligations of employers in health and safety matters have been established by the Occupational Safety and Health Act. This important law and its implications for human resources management are described in the next section.

The Occupational Safety and Health Act

In 1969, in the aftermath of a tragic explosion that claimed the lives of seventy-eight coal miners and amid reports of a high incidence of black-lung disease among miners, Congress passed the Coal Mine Health and Safety Act. The following year, continuing public and government concern about safety and health in the workplace was reflected in passage of the **Occupational Safety and Health Act (OSH Act).** The law's purpose was to establish and enforce safety and health standards to reduce the incidence of occupational injury, illness, and death.

The act covers nearly all employees; exempted are miners, who are covered by the Federal Mine Safety and Health Act, and government agencies that are covered by other laws. (If, however, those agencies do not regulate health and safety in specific areas, OSH Act standards apply.) Gradually, OSH Act standards are superseding those established under various laws, such as the Walsh-Healey Act and the Construction Safety Act.[20]

Administration   Administration of the OSH Act is through the **Occupational Safety and Health Administration (OSHA)** in the U.S. Department of Labor (DOL). The agency establishes and enforces occupational safety and health standards through inspections, citations, and fines; it also provides consultation services. State OSHA programs are found in those states that have assumed responsibility for administration of the act. Under special plans negotiated with the DOL, states agree to establish programs of inspection, citation, and training that meet or exceed the minimum standards enforced on the federal level.[21]

Rights of Employees and Employers   Both employees and employers have certain rights under the act. Included in the rights of employees or their representatives are the rights to do the following:

- Review copies of appropriate standards, rules, regulations, and requirements that the employer should have available at the workplace

- Request information from the employer on safety and health hazards in the workplace, precautions that may be taken, and procedures to be followed if an employee is involved in an accident or is exposed to toxic substances

- Have an authorized representative, or themselves, review the Log and Summary of Occupational Injuries (OSHA No. 200) at a reasonable time and in a reasonable manner

- Object to the abatement period set by OSHA for correcting any violation in the citation issued to the employer by writing to the OSHA area director within fifteen working days from the date the employer receives the citation

- Have access to relevant employee exposure and medical records

- Request the OSHA area director to conduct an inspection if they believe hazardous conditions or violations of standards exist in the workplace

- Have an authorized employee representative accompany the OSHA compliance officer during the inspection tour

- Respond to questions from the OSHA compliance officer, particularly if there is no authorized employee representative accompanying the compliance officer on the inspection "walkaround"

- Observe any monitoring or measuring of hazardous materials and see the resulting records, as specified under the Act, and as required by OSHA standards

- Submit a written request to the National Institute for Occupational Safety and Health (NIOSH) for information on whether any substance in the workplace has potentially toxic effects in the concentration being used, and have names withheld from employer, if that is requested

- Be notified by the employer if the employer applies for a variance from an OSHA standard, and testify at a variance hearing, and appeal the final decision

- Have names withheld from employer, upon request to OSHA, if a written and signed complaint is filed

- Be advised of OSHA actions regarding a complaint and request an informal review of any decision not to inspect or to issue a citation

- File a Section 11(c) discrimination complaint if punished for exercising the above rights or for refusing to work when faced with an imminent danger of death or serious injury and there is insufficient time for OSHA to inspect; or file a Section 405 reprisal complaint under the Surface Transportation Assistance Act (STAA)[22]

In addition, OSHA has issued an elaborate set of regulations called "Hazard Communication," which, along with state regulations, are more commonly referred to as **right-to-know laws.** Under these rules, employers in basic industries must provide information about hazardous substances in the workplace. More than a thousand different chemicals and compounds have been identified as hazardous under the regulations. Information must be provided by employers through material safety data sheets, container labels, and training programs for employees. Originally, the OSHA regulations applied only to manufacturers, but a suit brought by the United Steelworkers resulted in a federal court order to OSHA to extend the rules to nonmanufacturers. (Besides representing many steel mill employees, the steelworkers union also represents employees in such diverse settings as retailing firms, warehouses, police departments, hospitals, schools, and distributorships.)[23]

The rights of employers include the rights to do the following:

- Seek advice and off-site consultation as needed by writing, calling or visiting the nearest OSHA office

- Apply to OSHA for a temporary variance from a standard if unable to comply because of the unavailability of materials, equipment or personnel needed to make necessary changes within the required time

- Request and receive proper identification of the OSHA compliance officer prior to inspection

- Be advised by the compliance officer of the reason for an inspection

- Have an opening and closing conference with the compliance officer

- File a Notice of Contest with the OSHA area director within fifteen working days of receipt of a notice of citation and proposed penalty

- Apply to OSHA for a permanent variance from a standard if you can furnish proof that your facilities or method of operation provide employee protection at least as effective as that required by the standard

- Take an active role in developing safety and health standards through participation in OSHA Standards Advisory Committees, through nationally recognized standards-setting organizations and through evidence and views presented in writing or at hearings

- Be assured of the confidentiality of any trade secrets observed by an OSHA compliance officer during an inspection

- Submit a written request to NIOSH for information on whether any substance in your workplace has potentially toxic effects in the concentrations being used[24]

Inspections OSHA inspections are conducted by **compliance officers.** These inspectors are men and women from the safety and health field who have attended at least four weeks of specialized training at OSHA's Training Institute near Chicago. They also take additional specialized training once each year in areas such as industrial hygiene, construction, or maritime safety and health.[25]

OSHA's blanket authority to enter and inspect a workplace was tempered by a Supreme Court decision in 1978. In the case of *Marshall, Secretary of Labor, et al.* v. *Barlow's Inc.,* the Court ruled that an employer could require OSHA to obtain a search warrant before entering for inspection.[26]

The inspection process starts with the compliance officer presenting his or her credentials and asking to see the appropriate employer representative. If the inspection has resulted from an employee complaint, the compliance officer should give to the employer a copy of the complaint with the complainant's name withheld, as well as copies of any applicable laws and safety and health standards. The inspector may also want to see the organization's safety and health records.[27]

Before an **inspection tour,** the compliance officer will want to meet with a representative of the employees if the company is unionized. If it is not, an employee selected by the members of the plant safety committee might be appropriate, or the employees may be asked to select a representative. Both an employee representative and an employer representative typically accompany the compliance officer during the inspection. The compliance officer may also want to interview various employees at his or her discretion about safety and health conditions. The act gives the compliance officer the right to take photographs, make instrument readings, and examine records. Trade secrets observed by the compliance officer are kept confidential, however. Violation of this principle could result in the inspector being subject to a $1,000 fine and/or one year in jail.[28]

After the inspection, procedures call for the officer to discuss his or her observations with the employer and review possible violations. The employer should indicate the time needed to correct any hazardous conditions noted by the officer. Citations and penalties are not issued at this time, nor can the officer order that an establishment or part of it be closed down immediately. If an imminent danger exists, the compliance officer will ask the employer to abate the hazard and remove endangered employees. If the employer does not comply, OSHA administrators can go to the Federal District Court for an injunction prohibiting further work as long as unsafe conditions exist.[29]

Violations and Citations

If after the inspection tour an OSHA standard is found to have been violated, the area director determines what citations and penalties, if any, will be issued, as well as a proposed time period for abatement.[30] If an employer believes the citation is unreasonable or the abatement period is insufficient, he or she may contest it. The act provides an appeal procedure and a review agency, the Occupational Safety and Health Review Commission, which operates independently from OSHA.

Civil penalties from $60 to $10,000 may be imposed for each violation. Criminal penalties are levied in the most serious cases. For example, a willful violation that results in the death of an employee can bring a court-imposed fine of up to $250,000 (or $500,000 if the employer is a corporation) or imprisonment for up to six months, or both. A second conviction can result in these penalties being doubled. Falsifying records can result in a fine of up to $10,000 and six months in jail.[31] Multiple violations or failure to correct prior violations can add up to enormous fines. OSHA fines in the millions of dollars have been levied, although settlements have tended to be less than the proposed fines. The Doe Run Company agreed to a $1.3 million settlement to settle OSHA allegations that the company violated federal health and safety standards at its Herculaneum, Missouri, smelter. OSHA originally proposed penalties of $2.8 million, alleging 313 violations, 283 of them willful.[32] The Phillips 66 Company agreed to a $4 million settlement after OSHA had proposed a $5.7 million fine for some 575 willful and serious safety violations.[33]

Occupational Accidents

Accident prevention is a major goal of safety and health management. OSHA requires employers to keep a log of on-the-job accidents, and accident investigation and measurement can supply useful data for developing effective safety programs and improving working conditions. These data can be useful to safety specialists as well as to worker-management safety committees.

Variables Related to Accident Rates

To develop strategies for reducing accidents, it is important to understand the conditions associated with high accident rates. A good deal is known about those conditions. For example, size of organization, work schedules, type of industry and occupation, and worker behavior have been shown to be related to accident rates.

Size of Organization

Research has shown that the highest accident rates occur in firms with at least fifty but fewer than one hundred employees. In such businesses, the operations are large enough so that the owner or manager may not personally appear in the production areas very often and may not have firsthand knowledge of dangerous conditions. Further, such businesses are ordinarily too small to warrant the employment of a full-time, experienced safety officer, and safety management tends to be the responsibility of a manager who has a wide variety of other duties. In contrast, the small-business operator may also be a producing craftsperson who is frequently on the shop floor and keeping an eye on safety conditions.[34]

Work Schedules   There is some contradictory evidence, but studies generally show that accidents occur more frequently on night shifts. This may be because night workers are more likely than day workers to have been active for extended amounts of time before reporting to work and thus become fatigued more quickly. Moreover, a high proportion of night-shift workers sleep less than day workers and their sleep is of a less restful quality.[35]

Research has also found that workers on rotating shifts tend to have more accidents and generally experience more problems than employees who work on regular schedules. Although the number of sick days taken is not significantly different from the number taken by nonrotated employees, the problems tend to be more serious and chronic.[36] (See also the discussion in Chapter 8 on shift work.)

Type of Occupation   Some occupations are inherently more dangerous than others. Deep-shaft mining and urban law enforcement, for example, all too often provide settings for tragedy. However, crab fishing in Alaska waters is the most dangerous occupation of them all.[37]

Table 20.1 shows the relative dangers of employment in different major industry categories in 1991. Looking at the *death rates* — deaths per thousand workers — one sees that agriculture, which includes forestry and fishing, is the most dangerous of the broad categories, followed closely by mining and quarrying. The death rate in construction and transportation and public utilities is also relatively high. Overall, however, deaths due to occupational accidents declined 81 percent between 1912 and 1991.[38]

There are also high risks associated with certain industrial processes and settings like infrequently used stairways. Falls are the third most common cause of work injuries.[39] Table 20.2 shows the most common types of disabling work injuries by industry category. Overall, overexertion resulted in the most workers' compensation cases in 1988 (31 percent), followed by being struck or being struck against something (24 percent), and then by falls on the job (17 percent of injuries). This relative ranking holds across industries, but, as could be expected from Table 20.1, the proportion of cases of being struck by or struck against is substantially higher in agriculture, construction, and mining than in some of the other industries.

Worker Behavior   Individual workers have a good deal of control over their own safety. Workers can injure themselves through carelessness, use of improper techniques, unwise decisions in situations with obvious risk, and use of inappropriate tools or inadequately maintained equipment. If records show that a given worker is committing unsafe acts or reporting injuries frequently, the most common approach to the problem is counseling. Increased supervision, transfer to a less hazardous job, and special training are other common approaches.[40]

Accident Prevention   Accident prevention is a complicated matter, requiring control of all the variables described in the previous section. Experience has shown that safety training, protective equipment, and emergency plans are particularly important in accident-prevention efforts.

TABLE 20.1 Work deaths, injuries, and death rates by industry division, 1991

	WORKERS[a] (000)	DEATHS	DEATH RATES[a]	DISABLING INJURIES[a]
All industries	116,400	9,900[b]	9	1,700,000
Agriculture[c]	3,200	1,400	44[b]	140,000
Mining, quarrying[c]	700	300	43	30,000
Construction	5,900	1,800	31	180,000
Manufacturing	18,200	800	4	310,000
Transportation and public utilities	6,000	1,300	22	140,000
Trade[c]	26,800	1,000	4	320,000
Services[c]	37,800	1,700	4	330,000
Government	17,800	1,600	9	250,000

Source: National Safety Council estimates (rounded) based on data from the National Center for Health Statistics, state vital statistics departments (see page 16), and state industrial commissions. Numbers of workers are based on Bureau of Labor Statistics data and include persons aged 14 and over.

[a]Deaths per 100,000 workers in each group.

[b]About 3,500 of the deaths and 100,000 of the injuries involved motor vehicles.

[c]Agriculture includes forestry and fishing. Mining and quarrying includes oil and gas extraction (preliminary MSHA reports indicate 115 deaths in coal, metal, and nonmetal mining in 1991). Trade includes wholesale and retail trade. Services includes finance, insurance and real estate.

Agriculture rate excludes deaths of persons under 14 years of age. Rates for other industry divisions do not require this adjustment. Deaths of persons under 14 are included in the agriculture death total.

Source: National Safety Council, 1992. *Accident Facts, 1992 Edition*, p. 34. (Itasca, IL: National Safety Council). Reprinted by permission.

Safety Training and Communications

In an accident-prevention program, safety training must be an ongoing concern, starting with orientation to the job and continuing over the course of a worker's employment, particularly in the more hazardous industries. In addition, the importance of accident prevention should be reinforced through various communications with employees. Most organizations have ongoing programs to promote safety awareness. Some of the communications methods they use to promote this awareness are posters, meetings, fire drills, articles in employee publications, booklets and handbooks, slogans, safety awards, and guest speakers.[41]

Most organizations provide safety training to both supervisors and employees, and, when provided, this training is usually mandatory. Further, a high proportion of organizations require that employees pass proficiency tests before they are allowed to use hazardous equipment.[42]

According to a survey by the Bureau of National Affairs, company safety specialists are responsible for safety training in three-fifths of organizations with safety programs, but supervisors are also used in two-fifths of the programs. Outside trainers, community fire department officials, Red Cross representatives, and medical professionals are also used in about two-fifths of the safety programs.[43] Good safety performance is recognized through formal safety award programs in more than a third of the organizations surveyed.

Protective Equipment

Some of the most frequently used personal safety devices are earplugs, hard hats, safety goggles or glasses, safety boots, gloves, face shields, hairnets, safety belts, respiratory equipment, and protective clothing. Devices commonly used to make the job environment safer are machine guards, emergency first-aid equipment, heat and

TABLE 20.2 Work injuries involving disability by type of accident and industry division, 1988

TYPE OF ACCIDENT	ALL INDUSTRIES	AGRICULTURE[a,b]	MINING[b]	CONSTRUCTION	MANUFACTURING	TRANS. AND PUB. UTIL.	TRADE[b]	SERVICES[b]	PUBLIC SECTOR
Total	100.0%	100.0%	100.0%	100.0%	100.0%	100.0%	100.0%	100.0%	100.0%
Overexertion	31.3	24.2	24.1	25.1	34.7	31.1	31.1	34.4	29.0
Struck by or struck against	24.0	29.4	26.9	29.0	25.2	18.6	26.7	20.0	19.6
Falls	17.1	17.3	16.0	21.9	11.7	18.3	18.1	19.1	18.1
Bodily reaction	7.6	7.2	5.9	6.6	6.8	8.3	6.9	8.1	10.3
Caught in or between[c]	5.2	6.5	10.1	4.1	8.3	4.5	4.4	3.7	2.9
Contact with radiation, caustics, etc.	3.1	4.8	5.5	2.6	3.4	2.2	1.8	3.6	4.5
Motor-vehicle accident[c]	3.1	2.7	2.7	2.0	1.0	9.6	2.6	3.3	5.2
Rubbed or abraded	2.0	2.9	1.9	3.5	2.6	1.5	1.6	1.4	1.4
Contact with temperature extremes	2.0	1.1	2.1	1.8	1.8	0.8	3.3	1.6	1.6
Other, nonclassifiable	4.6	3.9	4.8	3.4	4.5	5.1	3.5	4.8	7.4

Source: Bureau of Labor Statistics Supplementary Data System, based on 1,047,055 cases involving disability from 14 states, 1988.
[a]Excludes farms with less than 11 employees.
[b]Agriculture includes forestry and fishing; mining includes quarrying and oil and gas extraction; trade includes wholesale and retail; services includes finance, insurance, and real estate.
[c]Caught in or between includes caught under. Motor-vehicle accident includes highway only.

Source: National Safety Council, 1992. *Accident Facts, 1992 Edition.* (Itasca, IL: National Safety Council), p. 36. Reprinted by permission.

fire detectors, shower facilities, and the marking of exits and aisles. Motivating employees to use safety equipment properly, of course, is more complicated than just providing the equipment. The worker and the group have a great deal of control over the extent to which protective equipment is used properly.

Emergency Plans Some risks to employee safety, plant security, and community safety are posed by chance occurrences. Geological catastrophies, such as earthquakes and volcanic eruptions, vandalism and arson, equipment failure, and such medical emergencies as heart attacks are unpredictable. The intensity of hurricanes, typhoons, and river flooding may be slightly more predictable. Yet organizations must be prepared to attend to the needs of employees and citizens in the surrounding community if catastrophes occur. The Bhopal disaster in India in 1984 pointed up inadequacies both in plant safety procedures and in the plant's ability to protect the lives and health of the people in the surrounding area. The nuclear plant accident at Three Mile Island in 1979 clearly demonstrated the wisdom of having carefully developed emergency plans and may have pointed up the need for even more reliable equipment and procedures. Emergency planning by microelectronics companies in the San Francisco Bay area paid huge dividends in the major earthquake of 1989. Companies like Intel had taken precautions such as bolting machine tools to shop floors and installing computer sensors linked to shutoff valves in the pipes that ran throughout their plants. As a result, damage was minimal.[44] Managers of chemical plants in hurricane- or tornado-prone areas have long known the importance of disaster plans. (See also the discussion of crisis management teams in Chapter 10, and *Contemporary Issues* on page 537.)

Organizations must be prepared to provide competent first aid at a moment's notice or even to evacuate employees and nearby residents from the site. Such contingency preparation necessitates training, and emergency procedures must also be coordinated with the outside community through the police, firefighters, and hospitals.

Occupational Disease

Occupational disease can be defined as a job-induced disturbance of the normal functioning of the body or a person's mental and emotional capacities. Examples of common occupational diseases are silicosis from breathing silica dust, rashes from handling insecticides, impaired hearing from exposure to noisy machines, and lead poisoning from exposure to lead in paint. Excessive and prolonged job stress, which is beginning to be recognized as a serious problem in many contemporary organizations (see next section), can also be considered an occupational disease.

Potential lawsuits and criminal charges are reason enough for organizations to be very interested in the prevention of occupational disease. The economics of occupational disease are also of major concern. It has been estimated that American business and industry pay half of the nation's health care bills, and any reasonable preventive measures organizations can take would seem to make economic sense.[45]

Common Health Hazards Health hazards on some kinds of jobs have been mentioned throughout this chapter. In general, some of the common causes of occupational illness are exposure to toxic substances and dangerous chemicals, radiation, cigarette smoke, harmful fumes and

Contemporary Issues

When Disaster Strikes: Putting People First

Hurricane Andrew — the third strongest storm to hit the United States this century — plowed across southern Florida in August [1992], leaving behind a path of destruction.

Area employers faced the gargantuan task of not only getting their business back on track, but also caring for their most important asset: their employees. Miami-based Burger King was one of several companies that responded quickly to the disaster.

First Things First

After the hurricane ravaged its headquarters, Burger King immediately set up a temporary office at a nearby resort, explained Dennis Liberson, vice president of human resources services at Burger King. Then, the company worked to address its primary concerns: the psychological well-being of its employees and their basic needs, such as food, water and shelter. Burger King employs about 750 people at its headquarters. About 300 employees, including Liberson, lost their homes during the killer hurricane.

"In order to get Burger King back on its feet, we had to get our people on their feet," Liberson said. "[The employees] wanted to know if the company was going to stay in Miami, if they still had a job and if they would be paid. It was announced right away that Burger King would rebuild its headquarters on the existing site."

To reassure employees, the company set up several toll-free telephone lines. Callers to one number listened to a recorded message from CEO Barry Gibbons who gave a daily update on what was being done to get Burger King back on its feet. Another telephone number was set up to answer employees' questions and offer assistance. The company also bought the services of a voice

mail line, since its own voice mail system was not operating, to enable employees to communicate among themselves.

Burger King also assured its employees that they would be paid. Even though the storm hit on Monday, August 24, payroll ran on that Thursday. "Once people knew that they had a job and that they would be paid, they could concentrate on their families," Liberson said. "We wanted people to take care of their personal needs without worrying about their jobs."

Since many people were left homeless and without food, Liberson explained that Burger King served meals all day long — the company's specialty of Whoppers and french fries — in front of its damaged headquarters.

The company also sent construction crews — ones it had contracted with to work on its restaurants — to repair employees' homes, and put down deposits on several apartments in the area so that employees left homeless would have someplace to live.

In addition, the company suspended its managed healthcare program, as well as its emergency room deductible, after the hurricane hit. This allowed employees to use other area hospitals and seek emergency room treatment for non-emergency ailments when they couldn't find doctors.

"We learned that being flexible was the most important way to approach this in order to address everyone's needs quickly," Liberson said. "We told [the people putting together the relief services] that if it felt right, to do it."

Spotlighting Services

On September 1, one week after Andrew hit, Burger King held a mass meeting for employees and their families that included an exposition to spotlight available benefits and services. Various representatives offering medical, financial and legal assistance were on hand to help employees and answer their questions. For example, a credit union provided emergency loans, benefits personnel answered questions about payroll, public adjusters addressed housing questions, relocation consultants offered advice on buying homes and

psychological counselors were available to help employees, their spouses and children overcome the disaster's effects.

---

vapors aggravated by poor ventilation, excessive noise, and inadequate lighting. The rapidly growing use of visual display terminals (VDTs) is associated with such ailments as eyestrain, neck pain, and disorders of the hand and wrist nerves, including carpal tunnel syndrome, a painful wrist disorder caused by repeated hand or wrist motions.[46]

In some ways, avoiding occupational disease is more difficult for organizations than avoiding accidents. In the first place, occupational diseases are frequently diagnosed only in their advanced stages. Workers may not notice the small, incremental changes in their physical condition that may occur from week to week or even year to year. Second, there is no opportunity to identify with certainty the precise moment the problem began and what the precise circumstances were. A third problem is whether an occupational disease is attributable to repeated exposure and progressive debilitation over time, or whether one exposure produced the disease. Thus, the strategy for minimizing health risks may need to be very complex and may be very expensive.

Minimizing Health Risks

When the nature of a health hazard is understood, a hierarchy of approaches, in order of preference, has been suggested:

1. Substitution of materials that are less toxic
2. Enclosure of the process, with automatic or remote operation as far away as possible
3. Isolation of the harmful process from the rest of the facility, while also providing special protection for all who must work in that operation
4. Exhaust ventilation (local)
5. Ventilation (general)
6. Wet methods (to keep dust down)
7. The use of personal protection devices, with special emphasis on personal respiratory protective gear
8. Decreased daily exposure through shorter work periods or rotating job assignments
9. Personal hygiene, including the use of protective creams
10. High standards of housekeeping and general maintenance
11. Warnings and publicity[47]

Obviously, several approaches might be used at one time.

As more is learned about the connections between industrial environments and medical consequences, employers will undoubtedly be required to shoulder more of the responsibility for both initial and cumulative exposure prevention, as well as for compensation of victims. It is also likely that health and safety departments will need to devote more time and expense to (1) maintaining records of industrial exposures faced by employees, (2) monitoring cumulative exposure effects on a routine basis, and (3) checking the degree to which safety measures are routinely applied.

Other Health Problems

Alcohol and drug abuse, prolonged job stress, and emotional illness are among the enormously costly problems that need to be addressed through programs within organizations as well as through broader community programs. Alcohol and drug abuse, in particular, appear to be growing problems of incredible magnitude. The Alcohol, Drug Abuse and Mental Health Administration estimates that alcohol and drug abusers cost the country more than $140 billion per year in direct costs. One hundred billion dollars of this is lost productivity.[48] Excessive job stress is estimated to cost American business and industry some $75 to $100 billion each year.[49] Mental health problems have been estimated to cost employers $17 billion annually.[50] These costs are of various kinds, and they include losses stemming from absenteeism, lowered productivity, and treatment expenses. What cost figures do not show, of course, is the mental and emotional anguish these problems cause fellow workers, family members, and others. Obviously, drug, alcohol, and emotional problems off the job carry over into the job setting, and vice versa.

Substance Abuse

It is estimated by the National Institute on Drug Abuse and the National Institute on Alcohol Abuse and Alcoholism that at least 10 percent of the work force is afflicted with drug addiction or alcoholism. Another 10 to 15 percent is affected by the substance abuse of a member of the immediate family. At least one in every four members of the work force, then, is directly affected by substance abuse.[51] Clearly, alcohol and drug abuse are so extensive as to constitute a potential major health and productivity problem for any organization.

Increasingly, alcohol abuse is seen as a disease. The majority of companies surveyed in one study reported that, in cases where alcohol or drug abuse was suspected, the employee was referred for counseling prior to being subject to disciplinary action.[52] In discharge cases involving alcoholism, arbitrators tend to disapprove of the imposition of severe penalties unless counseling and treatment have been tried first. On the other hand, arbitrators tend to support discipline in cases involving drugs.[53]

Most major employers offer counseling and treatment for alcohol or drug abuse as part of their employee benefit packages. Most medium-sized and large organizations also work with government and community agencies such as Alcoholics Anonymous, and some have established their own employee assistance programs (see Figure 20.1 and the discussion of EAPs later in the chapter). Often various kinds of family support are part of the total program because it has been recognized that the affected person's total environment must be supportive if change is to occur. The union and management must also work together to make sure the employee is not ostracized by the work group. It is essential, however, that appropriate performance standards be maintained.

Table 20.3 outlines some suggested steps in dealing with an employee whose performance is below standard and when alcohol or drug abuse is suspected. Notice that there is an emphasis on job performance throughout the process.

Denial is a typical response of the alcoholic or addicted person. But the problem must be confronted before treatment can be effective. One expert advises this approach:

> As job performance is adversely affected, the person is confronted, and offered the program to help with problems that may be causing the performance deterioration. Increasing pressure is applied as performance continues to deteriorate, and the final step is "either-or" which is crucial to any program. The alcoholic is given a choice — either to go to the program and cooperate fully with it, or be terminated.
>
> This crisis is the reason for the success of occupational alcoholism programs. It forces the alcoholic, often for the first time, to be open to the program and to treatment. The recovery rates in occupational programs are higher than through any other approach.[54]

According to William Mayer, psychiatrist and member of the Alcohol, Drug Abuse and Mental Health Administration, the employee's supervisor "plays an important role in bringing the troubled employee into treatment."[55]

The Drug-Free Workplace Act

Recognizing the huge direct and indirect costs of substance abuse to the American society, late in 1988 Congress passed a law that is having far-reaching implications for human resources management in organizations with federal contracts. The Drug-Free Workplace Act of 1988 (a subsection of the Anti-Drug Abuse Act) requires federal contractors to establish policies and procedures to ensure that their organizations are free of drug abuse and to make a "good-faith" effort to sustain a drug-free working environment.

Under this act, contractors must publish company rules prohibiting the "manufacture, distribution, dispensation, possession, or use" of controlled substances in the workplace; establish a drug-free awareness program; and administer appropriate discipline or require participation in a rehabilitation program in the event an employee is convicted of violating any criminal drug statute in the work setting. In the awareness program, employees must be informed of (1) the dangers of drug abuse in the workplace; (2) the organization's policy of maintaining a drug-free workplace; (3) any available drug counseling, rehabilitation, and employee assistance programs; and (4) the penalties that the employer may impose for drug abuse violations. Employees are required to notify the employer within five days after any substance abuse conviction, and the employer is required to notify the appropriate federal government agency within ten days after receiving notice from the employee of any such conviction.[56]

Although the Drug-Free Workplace Act does not specifically mention drug testing, it is likely that compliance with the law will result in the establishment or enlargement of drug-testing programs by government contractors. Drug testing — a highly controversial area — will be discussed next.

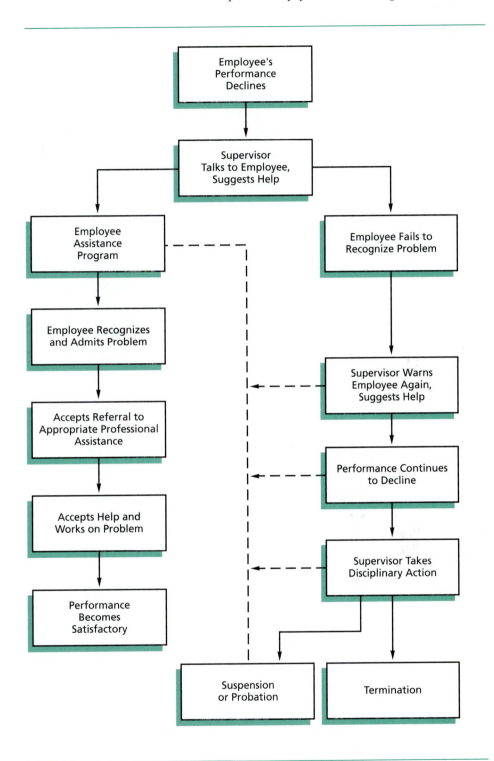

FIGURE 20.1   Employee assistance program: the supervisor's role

Source: Edwin J. Busch, Jr., "Developing an Employee Assistance Program," © September 1981. Reprinted with the permission of *Personnel Journal*, Costa Mesa, California; all rights reserved.

TABLE 20.3 Guidelines for supervisors in approaching the troubled employee

HOW TO APPROACH A TROUBLED EMPLOYEE

1. Establish levels of work performances you expect.
2. Be specific about supportive behavioral criteria, i.e., absenteeism, poor job performance and others.
3. Be consistent.
4. Try not to diagnose the problem.
5. Restrict criticism to job performance.
6. Be firm.
7. Be prepared to cope with the employee's resistance, defensiveness or hostility.
8. Try to get the employee to acknowledge the problem.
9. Show him [or her] he [or she] cannot play you against higher management and/or union.
10. Point out the availability of counseling services.
11. Discuss drinking only if it occurs on the job or the employee is obviously intoxicated.
12. Get a commitment from the employee to meet specific work criteria and monitor this with a plan for improvement based on work performance.
13. Explain that the employee must decide for himself [or herself] whether or not to seek assistance.
14. Emphasize confidentiality of the program.

Source: Christine A. Filipowicz, "The Troubled Employee: Whose Responsibility?" Reprinted with the permission of HR Magazine (formerly Personnel Administrator) published by the Society for Human Resource Management, Alexandria, VA.

Drug Testing   Increasingly, private-sector employers are developing drug-testing policies. Of 1,633 firms polled by the American Management Association in 1990, 63 percent reported drug testing programs. The most common use of drug tests — 54 percent of firms — was in the screening of job applicants. Twenty percent of the firms periodically tested employees for drug use, whereas 38 percent tested only when drug use was suspected. Practices from firm to firm varied widely when drug testing was positive, with some firms terminating employees and others using suspension or probation. In general, however, the most common practice — 68 percent of firms — was to refer employees who tested positive for counseling and treatment.[57]

In 1988 the U.S. Department of Transportation ordered an extensive, random, drug-testing program for 4 million nongovernment workers, including interstate truck and bus drivers; airline pilots, navigators, flight attendants, and mechanics; subway engineers and bus drivers in mass transit systems; railway engineers, brakemen, and conductors; seamen with Coast Guard licenses; and pipeline workers. Employers would arrange testing through independent laboratories and would be required to remove workers who tested positive from their jobs. Reinstatement could occur after treatment and after passing the tests. In 1989 the Supreme Court, in the *Skinner* case, upheld federal regulations permitting railroad management to test an employee when there is reasonable suspicion that the employee is under the influence of alcohol or drugs. They also upheld regulations requiring railroad management to give such tests to crew members in the case of a major accident.[58]

Unions, however, generally have not been supportive of random drug testing. In some instances, it has taken a tragedy to change the minds of union leaders. After a 1991 New York subway disaster that killed five people and injured more than two hundred, the president of Transport Workers Local 100 announced that he and the members of the local would support random testing for both drugs and alcohol. The motorman operating the train admitted that he had been drinking before reporting to work and that he was falling asleep at the controls. He was later convicted of manslaughter.[59]

The legal issues on drug testing are complex and still evolving. In the public sector, some of the issues center on constitutional rights pertaining to search and seizure, privacy, and due process. In the private sector, some of the legal issues center on equal employment opportunity laws, disability discrimination laws, and liability for defamation and wrongful discharge. What is clear is that courts tend to approve drug testing when there is a "reasonable individualized suspicion" that an employee's performance is being affected by drugs.[60]

Stress

Concern about stress and how to manage it have recently become major issues in safety and health. Hans Selye, one of the foremost authorities on this subject, defines **stress** as follows:

> . . . by stress the physician means the common results of exposure to any stimulus. For example, the bodily changes produced whether a person is exposed to nervous tension, physical injury, infection, cold, heat, X-rays, or anything else are what we call stress.[61]

The problem is not stress itself but **prolonged** and unchecked **stress.** When the body remains in an excited state after a crisis has passed, harmful effects begin to set in.

Studies indicate that prolonged stress is linked to subsequent physical injury, debilitation, and disease, including heart disease. Cardiovascular diseases are responsible for more than half of all deaths in the United States, and heart attacks are the leading cause of death among males over the age of thirty-five. Further, there are links between stress and gastrointestinal diseases, arthritis, and rheumatism, which are major sources of employee disability.[62] In 1989 stress claims accounted for 15 percent of all workers' compensation cases.[63]

Some of the causes of excessive stress in organizations are unresolved conflict, overdemanding superiors, harassment of various kinds, and intense and prolonged competition. In particular, according to one researcher, excessive stress tends to occur in jobs in which there are heavy psychological demands but the worker has little control over how to get the job done. Examples are machine-paced jobs such as garment stitcher, assembly-line worker, and freight handler. Other examples are service jobs in which the employee has little control over how to relate to the client, such as telephone operator, nurse's aide, and cashier.[64] Postal work appears to be a high-stress job. Stress appears to be a factor in — and certainly a result of — the homicides that have occurred at post offices. Over a period of a decade, 10 postal workers have shot and killed 34 co-workers. (During 1980–85, homicide was the third leading cause of work-place death.)[65]

Numerous stress-reduction techniques are available, including individual, group, and organizational approaches. Some of the individual approaches are exercise and physical activity, diet and nutrition, and meditation and relaxation techniques. Support groups of various kinds probably have valuable stress-reduction benefits. Organizational approaches cover a wide range. More open communications can foster discussion about things that are causing distress; job duties can

Increasing awareness of the effects of stress on the body has prompted companies to provide their employees with access to stress reduction techniques.

be clarified; and jobs can be restructured to provide more autonomy. Shifts can also be made in organizational climate toward more support and the working through of conflict. Providing exercise facilities, health profiling (through such means as questionnaires and physical examinations), and making available employee assistance programs (EAPs), discussed later in this section, are additional ways in which companies can help employees reduce their stress level.[66] Other approaches include life and career planning and counseling (see Chapter 10).

AIDS   The rapid and tragic spread of **Acquired immune deficiency syndrome (AIDS)** has created a serious problem for employers. (The term *HIV* is frequently used in connection with AIDS and means "human immunodeficiency virus." AIDS arises from the effects of systemic infection with the virus. Most employers wish to create and maintain a safe working environment for their employees and to protect their customers and clients. At the same time, most employers, after dealing with their initial fears about AIDS, want to treat victims with compassion. Probably all wish to avoid discrimination suits.[67]

Concern about discrimination suits is well founded. The Americans with Disabilities Act (ADA) now protects persons with AIDS from discrimination.[68] Earlier, twenty-one states, the District of Columbia, and a number of municipalities had declared AIDS-based discrimination to be contrary to law. Further, the federal Vocational Rehabilitation Act of 1973 — applying to employers with government contracts and institutions receiving financial assistance from the government — prohibits discrimination against otherwise qualified persons *solely* on the basis of their disability. In addition, the employer is expected to make "reasonable accommodation" to help such employees.[69] (See Chapter 3 on the ADA and reasonable accommodation.) The Office of Personnel Management of the federal government has established policies pertaining to the entire 2.1 million federal work force that bar discrimination against AIDS-afflicted employees and provide for disciplinary action for fellow workers who refuse to work with such employees.[70]

Although there is no known risk that employees with AIDS will transmit the infection to coworkers, consumers, or clients in ordinary employment situations, there do appear to be risks in some occupations. The U.S. Centers for Disease Control (CDC) finds the greatest risk of transmission in health care situations where there is an invasive procedure or wound and transmission of infected blood from one person to another. As a result, the CDC recommends precautionary procedures, such as wearing gloves, for health care workers in a number of circumstances.[71]

Since there is no medical evidence of danger of infection from AIDS in normal workplace settings, most employers can apply their present medical and health benefit practices to the AIDS situation. IBM, for example, has the following policy:

> If an IBM employee becomes ill with AIDS, he or she will be treated like any employee with any other chronic illness. Such employees will continue to be eligible for all medical benefits. They will be allowed to work as long as their condition permits them to perform the duties of their job.[72]

Employee Assistance Programs

Of all the companies responding to a 1989 survey by a publication of the Society for Human Resource Management, 79 percent reported that they provided an **employee assistance program (EAP).**[73] These programs have been defined as "more or less structured programs that utilize technical, administrative, and professional human services and personnel people, on either a contractual or employment basis, to meet the needs of troubled employees."[74] The counseling conducted usually focuses on such problems as mental health, stress, alcohol and drug abuse, compulsive gambling, family and marital matters, legal or personal financial difficulties, and job adjustment.[75]

Employee assistance programs for larger firms are typically offered within the organization. For cost reasons, however, many small and medium-sized firms have formed consortia to offer such services. In a consortium arrangement, EAP services are available to the employees of all the cooperating organizations.[76] Numerous entrepreneurial EAPs have also been formed, with the EAP organization managing assessment and referral, and sometimes diagnosis and counseling.[77] Still another alternative is for organizations to refer employees to outside agencies and to pay all or some fraction of the costs.

Most organizations may not be able to afford full-time counselors, clinical psychologists, or psychiatrists, but some can. Certainly, a significant proportion of firms could afford the part-time services of such specialists. In any event, it would seem that every enterprise should be prepared to refer seriously troubled employees to outside specialized agencies. In organizations large enough to have a human resources department, members of that department, in particular, should have knowledge about such services and be skilled in making referrals.

Ideally, every supervisor should have skills in effective listening and enough knowledge of nondirective counseling to give "emotional first aid." Such interviewing can not only help the employee's general mental health and reduce stress in the organization; it can also enhance communications between superior and subordinate.

Managing Safety and Health Programs

Managing safety and health is one of the more difficult areas of management. One reason for this difficulty is that influencing the attitudes and behaviors that contribute to accidents is an extremely complex matter. Most harmful events result from failure to apply known principles to control these events. The challenge of safety management is to influence people to apply these principles.[78] Experience seems to show that this challenge can be met most effectively if there is extensive employee participation in establishing safety and health goals and in recommending changes in procedures to minimize risks. Another reason safety and health management is a difficult area is that there is insufficient knowledge about the long-term effects of exposure to materials such as metals, solvents and fuels, pesticides, and a variety of air pollutants.[79]

Elements of Sound Safety and Health Programs

According to the Occupational Safety and Health Administration, an effective occupational safety and health program, regardless of the size of the organization, includes the following four basic elements:

1. The manager or management team leads the way, especially by setting policy, assigning and supporting responsibility, setting an example, and involving employees.
2. The worksite is continually analyzed to identify all hazards and potential hazards.
3. Methods for preventing or controlling existing or potential hazards are put in place and maintained.
4. Managers, supervisors, and employees are trained to understand and deal with worksite hazards.[80]

Another item should be added, although it may be implicit in the above:

5. A comprehensive, ongoing effort is made to help employees at all levels manage stress.

The relationship between stress and accidents and stress and illness is well documented; therefore, organizations must pay careful attention to the psychological and emotional climate of the work setting, as well as to mechanical and physical conditions.[81]

Top-Management Commitment

One of the most important factors influencing safety and health management is commitment from the top. This level of support is necessary so that those directly responsible can effectively carry out their mission.

Top management demonstrates commitment by providing employee and supervisory training programs, taking safety and health management into account in evaluating the performance of supervisors, establishing safety committees, and allocating sufficient financial resources to the safety and health program. In addition, top-management commitment is demonstrated through a strong policy statement about safety and health.[82] (For an example of a policy statement, see Figure 20.2.) In many organizations, top management's commitment to safety and health extends to providing comprehensive wellness programs.

Wellness Programs

Wellness programs are growing in popularity, particularly among mid-sized to large companies. Typically, these programs provide access to some or all of the following facilities: gymnasiums, weight rooms, athletic fields, rooms for aerobic exercises, and swimming pools. Some of the courses or programs offered within the broader wellness programs include weight loss, smoking cessation, organized exercise, stress management, and back-problem management.[83]

Role of Supervisors

The supervisor plays a central role in safety and health management. In fact, as three experts state it, "Everything that everybody else does is worthless if the supervisor does not do his [or her] job."[84] Four key tasks are seen as making up the supervisor's role in the safety program:

1. *Investigating* all accidents to determine underlying causes
2. *Inspecting* his or her area routinely and regularly to uncover hazards
3. *Coaching* (training) his or her people so they know how to work safely
4. *Motivating* his or her people so that they want to work safely[85]

Supervisors also have an important role in employee health. In particular, through a coaching, supportive, participative leadership style, they can reduce stress and enhance the health of subordinates. They also play a key role in making referrals to employee assistance programs, and they can be alert to health hazards in the workplace. It is important that the performance appraisal of supervisors include effectiveness in these safety and health tasks.

Specialists

The safety and health department usually consists of a manager and various specialists, inspectors, and technicians. The most common location for this unit is in the human resources or personnel department, with the safety and health manager reporting to its director.

This is consistent with the recommendation of experts that "health, safety, and environmental control must be under one department head who in turn reports to no less than one position below the chief executive officer."[86]

Frequently there are three levels of safety practitioners in large organizations. First is the **safety director** or safety manager, who is responsible for organizing, stimulating, and guiding the safety program and for serving as a spokesperson to management and the union. A second category of practitioner is the **safety engineer.** This person is the "one who analyzes exposures to physical injury or illness hazards, analyzes the capabilities and limitations of the human organism as related to the operation of equipment and processes, and tries to design the job and workplace to fit the real people who must work there."[87] A third category of practitioner is the **safety inspector.** This job is usually an entry-level position and involves auditing compliance with policies and procedures.[88]

Other practitioners are **health and industrial hygienists.** The job of these specialists is to maintain the health of the work force by preventing or controlling occupational and nonoccupational diseases and disabilities. Industrial-hygiene specialists deal with the identification, evaluation, and control of chemical, biological, and physical agents and psychological stresses in the workplace that may affect employees' health.[89] An important role of these specialists is to ensure that exposure limits on toxic chemicals as established by OSHA are not exceeded. The scope of this responsibility is suggested by the fact that, in 1989 alone, OSHA set or toughened workplace exposure limits on 376 toxic chemicals.[90]

Our safety and health program will include:

- Providing mechanical and physical safeguards to the maximum extent possible.

- Conducting a program of safety and health inspections to find and eliminate unsafe working conditions or practices, to control health hazards, and to comply fully with the safety and health standards for every job.

- Training all employees in good safety and health practices.

- Providing necessary personal protective equipment and instructions for its use and care.

- Developing and enforcing safety and health rules and requiring that employees cooperate with these rules as a condition of employment.

- Investigating, promptly and thoroughly, every accident to find out what caused it and to correct the problem so that it won't happen again.

- Setting up a system of recognition and awards for outstanding safety service or performance.

We recognize that the responsibilities for safety and health are shared:

- The employer accepts the responsibility for leadership of the safety and health program, for its effectiveness and improvement, and for providing the safeguards required to ensure safe conditions.

- Supervisors are responsible for developing the proper attitudes toward safety and health in themselves and in those they supervise, and for ensuring that all operations are performed with the utmost regard for the safety and health of all personnel involved, including themselves.

- Employees are responsible for wholehearted, genuine cooperation with all aspects of the safety and health program including compliance with all rules and regulations — and for continuously practicing safety while performing their duties.

FIGURE 20.2   Model safety and health policy statement

Source: U.S. Department of Labor, *OSHA Handbook for Small Businesses*, Occupational Safety and Health Administration, Safety Management Series, OSHA 2209 (rev.), 1990, pp. 50–51.

Role of the Human Resources Department

A 1990 survey of 839 organizations of all types found 93 percent with formal safety and OSHA compliance programs. In 74 percent of the organizations with such programs, personnel or human resources departments were partly or fully responsible for the programs. Seventy-six percent of the organizations had employee assistance or counseling programs, and, of these, 93 percent assigned such programs either solely or jointly to the personnel or human resources department. Fifty-one percent of the organizations had in-house medical services; in 65 percent of these, the personnel or human resources department had either sole or joint responsibility for the activity. Sixty percent had health and wellness programs, and in 90 percent of these the personnel or human resources department had sole or joint responsibility.[91] Clearly, the human resources department has a major role in the management of safety, health, and employee assistance programs. (See *International Perspective* on page 550 for some of the unusual responsibilities of the HR department in international operations.)

In addition to directing and coordinating the activities of the various safety, health, and employee assistance specialists, the human resources director has a major role in linking these activities to other human resources processes. For example, information about these activities needs to be incorporated in employee orientation and training programs. Supervisors and higher managers need training in effective listening and in making referrals to employee assistance specialists. Effective safety and health practices need to be considered in performance appraisal systems and in making reward decisions. In the unionized setting, safety and health matters are areas for collective bargaining and, ideally, should become areas for collaborative problem solving. Safety and health need to be considerations in job design, work rules, and schedules. Disciplinary procedures need to be developed for serious infractions of safety rules.

The human resources director also has a major role in interpreting the needs of the safety, health, and employee assistance programs to top management. This includes the ability to convince top management of the value of long-range preventive programs as well as to secure immediate support for and cooperation in taking corrective action when necessary.

Finally, the human resources department has a broad communications responsibility in the areas of safety, health, and employee assistance. It is important that employees, supervisors, and all other members of management be kept informed of the status of ongoing programs and of changes in programs.

Summary

There are numerous compelling reasons for being concerned about safety and health practices in organizations. These involve humanitarian considerations, labor relations, legal and contractual compliance, public awareness, and cost.

The Occupational Safety and Health Act establishes safety and health standards affecting most organizations and provides for inspections that can lead to citations and penalties. Both employers and employees have certain rights under the act.

Some of the variables affecting accident rates are organization size, type of industry, and work schedules. Training and increasing awareness are important partial remedies.

Occupational disease is a particularly difficult problem for many reasons, including the fact that the onset of some diseases is gradual and hard to detect. It is likely that organizations will be required to shoulder more responsibility for prevention of both initial and cumulative exposure in the future.

Substance abuse is a significant problem in many organizations. Increasingly, alcoholism is seen as a disease. In handing down awards under labor-management contracts, arbitrators typically insist that companies offer counseling and treatment before discharging workers for poor performance stemming from alcohol abuse. Arbitrators are less sympathetic with respect to drug use. The Drug-Free Workplace

International Perspective

In Times of Global Crisis, Call on HR

For an expatriate employee thousands of miles away from home, the company is the family. "Whenever something goes wrong, and it will; he or she will naturally turn to the company for help," says Jay Hornsby, Dow Chemical Co.'s vice president of human resources.

Global human resources managers have been called on to assist employees based abroad with a wide and often difficult range of problems. Some of these problems include medical emergencies, natural disasters, wars, revolutions and other international crises . . . .

Medical emergencies occur fairly frequently. Ralph W. Stevens, vice president of personnel and employee relations for Hamilton Oil Corp., recalls the case of a high-ranking technical manager who suffered a stroke while on business in Korea, where the company maintains no office. Operating long-distance, Stevens managed to find a first-rate physician, set the employee up in a well-regarded hospital and transfer sufficient funds to cover his medical bills, while comforting the manager's frantic family.

Cleveland-based Ferro Corp. has provided ongoing medical protection for both its U.S. expatriates and its non-U.S. employees by forging close links with the international department of the Cleveland Clinic, which is affiliated with other top-ranked medical facilities and physicians worldwide.

A couple of years ago, the teen-age daughter of a senior Ecuadorian manager was involved in a serious car accident. Local doctors expected the girl to lose her eye, so she was flown to the U.S. where surgeons at the Cleveland Clinic saved her vision. "It was a somewhat dramatic, but enormously heartwarming incident," recalls David B. Woodbury, Ferro's vice president of human resources.

Because of its extensive operations in Latin America, Ferro has long had contingency plans in place for another kind of emergency: terrorist kidnappings. Luckily, nothing adverse has ever happened, which is why the company still strives to maintain a politically neutral and noncontroversial image when it operates in potential international trouble spots . . . .

Various contingency plans, including means and methods to evacuate workers if necessary, are in place for most U.S. companies currently operating in the Persian Gulf. CPC International Inc., for example, has a food processing plant in Saudi Arabia that was still going full speed when PERSONNEL JOURNAL went to press. "Naturally, we have contingency procedures approved and ready, although we would rather not discuss them," says Richard P. Bergeman, the company's vice president of human resources.

During its more than 100-year history, Fluor Daniel has had to deal with almost every kind of international crisis. "Earthquakes, hurricanes, uprisings, we've probably had employees caught in all of them," says Tom Blackburn, the company's director of international administration.

To Blackburn, more difficult and wrenching than politically induced crises are instances when an expatriate employee dies abroad. He once had to coordinate the transport of a worker's coffin from an international site back to the U.S., giving what solace he could to the man's grieving widow. "You know, a human resources manager is a lot like a priest sometimes," says Blackburn.

Source: Excerpted from Ellen Brandt, "Global HR," *Personnel Journal* 70 (March 1991):43.

Act requires federal contractors to establish policies and programs to ensure a drug-free work environment. Drug testing by employers is growing rapidly. The legal issues are complex and still evolving, but it is clear that courts tend to approve drug testing when there is a "reasonable individualized suspicion" that an employee's performance is being affected by drugs.

Prolonged stress is associated with enough health and accident problems for stress to be an important area of concern for organizations. A wide variety of programs is currently being used to help organizations and employees manage or reduce stress.

The spread of AIDS has created difficult health management problems for employers, who have the dual responsibility of avoiding discrimination against victims and providing safe working conditions. Since there is no medical evidence of danger of infection from AIDS in the ordinary workplace, most employers can apply their present medical and health benefit practices pertaining to chronic illness in the event that an employee becomes ill with AIDS. The Americans with Disabilities Act (ADA) now protects persons with AIDS from discrimination.

Employee assistance programs (EAPs) offer help to the troubled employee. Human resources department members and all supervisors and managers need to be skilled in referring people suffering from emotional illness or from family or other crises to employee assistance specialists.

Top-management commitment is important to the success of any safety and health program in the organization. Increasingly, top-management support is extending to include broad wellness programs. Supervisors also have key roles in safety and health management.

In organizations large enough to employ specialists, the safety and health department typically reports to the human resources department. The human resources director has significant responsibilities in coordinating safety, health, and employee assistance activities with the management of other human resources processes. Ideally, this coordination is highly interactive and draws on the expertise and involvement of organization members at all levels. Excellence in safety and health matters requires high-quality teamwork.

Ethical Dilemma

Tony Hills is a plant supervisor with Glossy Alloy Metal Cleaning and Etching. He has a rush order to clean a small batch of metal parts using a chemical that is known to be highly toxic and suspected to cause cancer if worker exposure is prolonged. The ventilation system in the cleaning room is malfunctioning, but the customer must have the parts that afternoon. Charles Dunn, the operator who will clean the metal, comments on the lack of ventilation, but Tony tells him to go ahead, saying "A little bit of exposure won't hurt you. Besides, this is an important customer we've got to keep."

Comment on the ethics of Tony's directive. What should Charles do? What would you have done in Tony's place?

Key Terms

Occupational Safety and Health
   Act (OSH Act)
Occupational Safety and Health
   Administration (OSHA)
right-to-know laws
compliance officer
inspection tour
occupational disease
stress
prolonged stress

acquired immune deficiency
   syndrome (AIDS)
employee assistance program
   (EAP)
wellness programs
safety director
safety engineer
safety inspector
health and industrial hygienists

Review Questions

1. Provide several reasons why organizations must be concerned about safety and health management.
2. Discuss some of the hidden costs of job accidents.
3. Explain the major features of the Occupational Safety and Health Act and discuss the impact of the law.
4. Discuss some of the rights that both employees and employers have under the Occupational Safety and Health Act.
5. Describe some common accident-prevention methods.
6. List some approaches to minimizing health risks from toxic or dangerous chemicals.
7. What are employee assistance programs, and what is their purpose?
8. Describe an effectively managed safety and health program.
9. What steps are recommended for inclusion in an alcohol abuse program?
10. What policies and procedures would seem wise relative to AIDS? (a) In a bank? (b) In a hospital?

Opening Case Questions

Case 20.1   Can We Afford a High-Quality Safety Program?

1. What appear to be the reasons for the top management of Magic Compounds to be reviewing the company's safety program at this time?
2. What kinds of safety violations at Magic Chemicals could result in criminal proceedings?

Case 20.2   Just Whom Am I Protecting?

1. Is it possible that Jill and Bob's experiment to catch Jerry "in the act" will be unsuccessful? Why or why not?
2. What can Jill and Bob do now?

Comprehensive Case

Drug Testing

Over the past decade, testing employees and job applicants for drugs has rapidly become standard practice for many organizations. According to a recent survey by the American Management Association (AMA), about three-quarters of large American companies now use drug tests, a 250 percent increase in just five years. Of the surveyed firms, over half now test all job applicants for drugs, and the AMA estimates that about one-third of the people applying for jobs in 1992 were tested for drugs.

Some of the reasons for such testing are fairly straightforward: people who abuse alcohol and other drugs cost their employers an estimated $120 billion a year. Compared with their clean and sober peers, substance abusers are absent more than twice as often, file five times as many medical claims, and are four times as likely to be involved in accidents on the job or off the job.

Reports from a number of different quarters indicate that the percentage of positive drug-test results is dropping. SmithKline Beecham, a maker of pharmaceuticals, reported that 8.8 percent of 2.2 million tests in 1991 came back positive, down from 11.1 percent in 1990 and 18.1 percent in 1987. The AMA survey indicated that the positive rate for job applicants in 1991 was 4.6 percent, versus 5.8 percent the year before. Increased public awareness and corporate education and assistance programs no doubt have contributed to this decrease, as has the simple fact that companies are now testing more people, not just suspected abusers. The AMA survey showed that companies that coupled testing with drug prevention programs had a much lower rate of positive tests than did companies without prevention and education efforts. Despite these encouraging figures, SmithKline notes that its tests turned up 56,000 positive tests for cocaine — still a sizable number.

The question of what to do with applicants or employees who test positive is a quagmire of legal, moral, and business issues. Especially during the early years of drug tests, some people who tested positive successfully challenged the testing on the basis of the tests' high error rates. When the Centers for Disease Control studied thirteen drug-testing laboratories in 1988, it concluded that none of them was reliable and that the worst labs made mistakes up to two-thirds of the time.

Because errors can be made at any stage of the drug-testing process — from the collection of the specimen to the reporting of the results — groups like the National Institute on Drug Abuse (NIDA) recommend that organizations carefully follow certain guidelines in selecting a testing laboratory and carrying out the testing process. First, if at all possible, the lab should be NIDA-certified, especially because the rapid expansion of the drug-testing business has encouraged the growth of less reputable labs in the last few years. Of the twelve hundred or so drug-testing laboratories operating in the United States in 1992, only about eighty were NIDA certified. Using NIDA-certified labs may be somewhat more expensive than using uncertified labs, but since the average jury award for a wrongful termination suit is $750,000, companies should think twice before saving a few dollars on drug testing.

Companies are also encouraged to check the credentials of the laboratory's staff, conduct their own tests of the lab's quality control measures, and carefully review the "chain of custody" — the handling of each urine or blood specimen, which should be documented step by step. For a lab to be certified by the NIDA, the lab's director must have the kinds of expertise and state certification that will make the director a persuasive legal ally if a lab test is challenged in court.

Most organizations check initial positive tests with a second, more accurate test and then have a doctor interview the employee to see if the employee might have some valid reason for testing positive. After that, the NIDA recommends that the organization have a flexible policy about how to handle the employee, a policy that may include termination, referral to an employee assistance program, or temporarily changing the employee's duties while the employee undergoes rehabilitation.

Although many companies are becoming more careful about the way they handle drug testing, unresolved issues and questions persist about the practice. The constitutional right of privacy does not extend to private companies, but many people feel that testing employees for drugs is an unwarranted invasion of privacy. Indeed, some state and local governments — notably the city of San Francisco — have barred employers from testing employees unless they have good evidence that a suspected drug user endangers others. The possibility of a false-positive test result ruining a person's career still worries many job applicants, and some organizations continue to reject job applicants solely on the basis of a first, inexpensive, and often inaccurate test. And because many companies ignore the two substances that cause the most deaths and damage — tobacco and alcohol — some advocates of civil liberties question whether the current wave of drug testing is really more an act of social policing than an attempt to make the workplace safer and more productive.

The change in the political climate may bring a reassessment of drug testing in the 1990s. And some experts think that in the future more companies will use performance testing, which shows whether an employee's ability to work is diminished — whether by illegal drugs, legal substances, or other factors like sleeplessness or stress.

Sources: Rob Brookler, "Industry Standards in Workplace Drug Testing," *Personnel Journal* 71 (April 1992):128–132; George R. Gray and Darrel R. Brown, "Issues in Drug Testing for the Private Sector," *HRfocus* 69 (November 1992):15; Eric Rolfe Greenberg, "Test-Positive Rates Drop As More Companies Screen Employees," *HRfocus* 69 (June 1992):7; Laura A. Lyons and Brian H. Kleiner, "Managing the Problem of Substance Abuse . . . WITHOUT ABUSING EMPLOYEES," *HRfocus* 69 (April 1992):9; and "Workers Testing Positive for Drugs Declined in '91," *Wall Street Journal*, February 11, 1992, p. A8.

Discussion Questions

1. What are some of the pitfalls in drug testing?
2. What are some ways to improve the accuracy of drug testing?

CHAPTER 21

Participative Strategies for Organization Improvement

LEARNING OBJECTIVES

- Describe the goals and objectives of participative strategies for organization improvement.
- Characterize the conditions under which an organization improvement strategy is likely to succeed.
- Explain the role of a qualified facilitator in resolving conflicts between individuals and groups.
- Describe several techniques for improving teamwork in a group setting.
- Identify major features of each of the comprehensive improvement strategies described in this chapter: organization development programs, quality-of-work-life projects, and total quality management.

CASE 21.1   What Caused That Fiasco?

Emily Page, human resources director at Bayshore Technical Products Corporation, was annoyed and disappointed. In an effort to involve employees more directly in improving quality and productivity, she had encouraged the company to initiate a program called "Employee Participation in Quality and Productivity Improvement" (or the "EP program" for short). Things had not gone well, and Emily was discussing the results with Sterling Jones, a consultant who had been hired by the company president, Mark Andrews. The hope was that Sterling would be able to help get the EP program back on track. Mark had given him only a short briefing and then referred him to Emily. As Mark put it, "It's really Emily's program. She got us going in this direction, and we're behind her, but I want her to be the company expert as well as the coordinator of the EP effort."

"We started with groups of about twelve employees in each of three departments," Emily explained to Sterling. "One group is coming up with good recommendations, but the other two have really bombed out. In fact, one group doesn't meet anymore. Apparently a couple of outspoken people started dominating that group and nobody else could get a word in edgewise. People lost interest, and almost everyone dropped out. With only two or three people showing up and the rest making excuses, there didn't seem to be any point in continuing."

"What about the other two groups?" Sterling asked.

"Well, take the group that's limping along," Emily began. "They've been meeting for an hour each week for two months now, but I can't say that they're really accomplishing anything. They seem to be floundering, and I think they're pretty discouraged. At the supervisor's suggestion, the members elected one of the hourly workers as the chairperson, but I don't think she knows much about running meetings. The group that is beginning to generate really good ideas seems to be working well together. My hunch is that it's because they like the supervisor, who also seems to know how to run meetings."

"Well, it seems to me that maybe you've made a better start than you realize," said Sterling. "One group seems successful, and one group can probably be salvaged. I'd have to do some informal chatting with the supervisor and the employees in the disbanded group to see if anything can be done to resurrect it. But before I go poking around in the organization, I've got quite a few questions for you. For example, who's behind this program so far? What's the prevailing leadership style in the organization? Is the union involved? How much training have group leaders had? Who reviews recommendations? What do employees see as the end product of the program? What are the incentives to participate, to cooperate?"

"I guess you're covering all the angles," Emily responded. "Let's start with who's behind the program. But before we finish talking today, I hope you can give me some ideas on how we could have avoided that one fiasco."   ◄

CASE 21.2   Appreciations and Concerns

Linda Carr, an experienced management consultant and group dynamics trainer, had been hired by Paul Silverstein to conduct some "team building" sessions with the top management group of his division. Paul's division manufactured motorcycles, and his was the largest, most profitable division of Transport Systems, Inc. The other divisions manufactured snow vehicles, all-terrain vehicles, and special vehicles for the military.

Paul had been feeling for some time that teamwork and cooperation weren't as high in his management group as they had once been. He also sensed that his group wasn't as innovative as the management groups in some of the other divisions. Although the group had been together for several years — the newest member, the division controller, had come aboard three years ago — they really didn't know each other very well. At least, that's the way it seemed to Paul.

When Paul had discussed some of these concerns with the division managers at a recent staff meeting, one manager had suggested holding a retreat so the group could get together in a comfortable environment and discuss where things stood, suggest improvements, and make plans for the future. Paul said he felt the group should hire a specialist in team building to run the workshop if such a retreat were to take place, and he was pleased with the generally enthusiastic response to this idea. A committee was appointed to interview consultants with expertise in group work, and Linda Carr was unanimously recommended. When Paul met with Linda, he too was favorably impressed. He arranged for her to start interviewing each of the seven managers in the group on an individual basis, a procedure she had recommended.

Several things were evident to Linda when she reviewed her notes from the interviews. One clear theme was that each member of the group had some concerns about the way two or three other members were going about their jobs but that these concerns were not particularly serious. Linda sensed that the problems could probably be worked through fairly easily, but for some reason or other, people were keeping their concerns to themselves. Another clear theme was that people were feeling tired, unappreciated, and taken for granted. Still another theme was that Paul's subordinates liked him and basically supported his managerial approach, but a number of them wished he would be more direct with them about how he saw their performance.

When the group met with Linda at the two-day retreat, held at a resort in a rustic setting, the first thing she did was tell the members about the themes she had identified from the interviews. She also elaborated a little on each theme and showed how they tended to be interrelated. She then proposed a sequence of issues for the group to work on based on the themes, starting with interpersonal and group issues and ending with long-range planning items. The group seemed satisfied with the design, and Linda gave them their first assignment.

"What I would like you to do," Linda said, "is to take a pencil and paper and jot down one to three concerns that you have about how each person in the group is handling his or her job. The concerns can be little ones or major ones. Be as descriptive as possible about what the person is doing, and comment on how it affects you or your work. Then, after you have done that, jot down one to three things you appreciate about each member of the group."

After about fifteen minutes, when it appeared that each person had finished making notes, Linda said, "We'll deal with concerns first. The rule will be that you can ask for clarification, but you can't argue with what someone says until after you have heard from everyone. Who wants to be the first to receive some feedback?" "I'll go first," Paul volunteered. "I probably make the most mistakes." One member of the group immediately shot back, "That's right, boss. None of the rest of us ever make mistakes. I figure I'm more or less perfect." Everybody laughed.

One of the concerns expressed to Paul was echoed by several members of the group. It went something like this: "When you review my work, your criticisms are all so vague that I don't know which areas really concern you. In addition, I don't get a clear sense of which aspects of my work you think are outstanding. I'd like to hear specific feedback more often." One person said, "I know you're awfully busy, but when you flip through your appointment book or look at your watch when we're meeting together, I get anxious and start hurrying through things — and then I get even more anxious when I sense I'm not presenting things well."

Paul and the others found the morning intense and engrossing. The time seemed to go by quickly. Six people had received feedback by lunchtime. Linda noticed that each had taken notes on the comments, and all had asked some questions to clarify what was said about them.

During lunch the conversation focused on politics and sports. Nothing was said about the exercise, although as people were getting up from the table everyone laughed when someone asked, "OK, which of the last two people is going to be in the barrel next?"

After each person had been the focal point of the discussion, Linda said, "Now let's do some contracting before we move into the appreciation part of the exercise. Jot down what you are willing to do differently, and indicate what help you need from specific individuals and the group if you are to do these things successfully." After several minutes of making notes, each person, in turn, asked for various kinds of assistance from different individuals. Linda made notes on flip-chart paper about each agreement that was made. "I'm going to ask you to review these agreements and how things are going about three months from now," she said.

The appreciation exercise seemed to be unusually rewarding for some members of the group. For example, the manufacturing manager was visibly moved when several colleagues commented on how much they appreciated his willingness to listen and help. "Thanks a lot," he said, "that's better than a pay increase. Well, maybe not better, but just as good." Everyone laughed and the moment was gone. But the sense of being appreciated stayed with the manager for a long time.

Although the first day's session had been intense, people seemed to be lively and full of energy during the second day of the retreat. They tackled some major issues in a constructive way — including how to improve their relationships with the other divisions — and moved on to do some long-range planning before they adjourned. Paul was very pleased with the results, as were other members of the group. They agreed to hold a one-day follow-up session with the consultant in three months and to monitor ongoing progress during regular staff meetings as well. ◀

These cases describe efforts to increase overall organizational effectiveness through employee participation. The efforts are components of what can be labeled **participative improvement strategies** because they aim to increase active and constructive involvement by employees in the achievement of organizational goals. Underlying these strategies is the belief that employees can and want to make contributions to organizational effectiveness beyond what is required of them in a job description. The assumption is that employees can help increase the effectiveness of their own work groups in solving problems and can help build teamwork and cooperation that facilitate the attainment of shared goals.

As Case 21.1 illustrates, effective employee participation in organizational improvement is not easily achieved. Participative strategies cannot work unless employees are equipped with participative skills, and the greater the level of participation, the greater the need for interpersonal, group, intergroup, and leadership skills. It is possible that the limited success of the EP program at Bayshore Corporation can be attributed to a shortage of such skills, although there may be other problems such as lack of top management involvement, lack of clarity as to the purposes of the program, or lack of incentives for employees to support the program. Assuming that lack of group and team leadership skills are part of the problem, the consultant may recommend a systematic training program in group skills for each of the EP groups and as new groups are formed. The consultant might want to work with each group *as a group* in teaching new skills.

Case 21.2 illustrates how an experienced consultant goes about diagnosing problems in a particular work group and encouraging those involved to confront these problems in a direct, constructive fashion. Through interviews with individual staff members, Linda Carr was able to identify issues that affected the functioning of the group. For example, one problem was an avoidance of dealing with interpersonal concerns; another was a withholding of appreciation when someone did something well. Linda then conducted a concerns-and-appreciation exercise designed to improve interpersonal relationships as a first step in improving the overall effectiveness of the group. By the end of the retreat, the group had made substantial progress in identifying ways of increasing their contributions to organization improvement.

When employees do participate effectively in organization improvement efforts, the payoff in enhanced morale and performance can be substantial. That is why many organizations today seek to give employees more opportunities for participation and to help develop the skills with which to participate effectively. This chapter discusses various kinds of improvement strategies that build on the relationship between participative skills and overall effectiveness. The role of the human resources department in implementing these strategies is also described.

Organization Improvement and Employee Participation

Improvement strategies represent organizational responses to challenges posed by the rapidly changing world in which we live. From the organization's perspective, the challenge is to achieve more effective and efficient production of goods and services. From the employee's perspective, the challenge is to enhance the quality of work life so that the organization is an attractive and satisfying place to work. Providing opportunities for meaningful participation is a way of meeting both challenges at once.

Current Attitudes Toward Participation

A survey of 785 "opinion leaders" a few years ago concerning innovative and promising trends in human resources management found that the clearest trend was employee participation and participative management. This was also seen as the major change needed by organizations in the foreseeable future.[1]

As John Naisbitt suggests in his book *Megatrends:*

The ethic of participation is spreading bottom up across America and radically altering the way we think people in institutions should be governed. Citizens, workers, and consumers are demanding and getting a greater voice in government, business, and the marketplace.[2]

In a follow-up book, *Re-inventing the Corporation*, Naisbitt and Patricia Aburdene provide numerous organizational implications, including the following:

The top-down authoritarian management style is yielding to a networking style of management, where people learn from one another horizontally, where everyone is a resource for everyone else, and where each person gets support and assistance from many different directions.[3]

These shifts toward more participation, according to Naisbitt, are occurring at a time when there is a "confluence of both changing values and economic necessity." The economic necessity he is referring to stems from lagging productivity and quality and increased competition.[4]

Clearly, many leading corporations are moving in the directions Naisbitt is describing. In particular, an emphasis on high participation and involvement through the development of effective teams and delegation of major responsibilities to these teams is evident in such companies as Xerox Corp., Levi Strauss, Apple Computer, and Monsanto Company.[5]

Under What Circumstances Is Employee Participation Effective?

The important question may not be, does participation work? but rather, *Under what circumstances does employee participation contribute to organizational outcomes such as effectiveness, efficiency, development, and participant satisfaction?* As Naisbitt implies, because of societal and economic changes, participation may be almost an imperative. The old authoritarian ways simply do not work. On the other hand, there are all kinds of participation and many contexts in which participation can occur. Some participative approaches may have little or no benefit — for example, pseudoparticipation, in which decisions have already been made before employees are asked for their input — whereas others may be highly successful in the view of all parties concerned.

In general, *effective* participation — not just participation — can yield many benefits. After an exhaustive review of the research literature, Marshall Sashkin concludes as follows:

Decades of research shows conclusively that given half a chance — with competent implementation under appropriate conditions — participative management can assuredly benefit organizations in terms of hard criteria of performance and productivity.[6]

Although some authors have reached less optimistic conclusions,[7] Sashkin's summary seems correct. Note that, according to Sashkin, participative management produces benefits "under appropriate conditions" and "with competent implementation." Some of the conditions under which participative approaches lead to constructive outcomes are discussed a little further in this chapter. First, however, we need to consider some of the various degrees and forms of participation.

Different Degrees and Kinds of Participation

The degree to which employees participate in problem solving and decision making and their effectiveness in this participation are a function of many variables. The degree and skill will vary with the type of problem or decision that must be dealt with, the extent to which the work group is experienced and trained in participative skills, and the willingness of management to delegate authority to employees. The degree of participation also varies from one organizational setting to another, depending on the organizational culture, management philosophy, prevailing leadership style and expertise, and union-management relations.

There are also different kinds of participation. Participation can vary in the extent of employee authority, the number and configuration of people interacting, whether participation is direct or representative, and whether it is voluntary or mandatory.

Extent of Authority

Supervisors and managers are usually selective about what decisions will include employee participation. In some instances, employees may have an equal say in a decision; at other times, their involvement may be limited to providing information and ideas so that the manager can make an informed decision. As participative skills are developed, employees may gradually be given more and more authority in decision making. In time, some decisions may be made completely by employees.

Figure 4.3 in Chapter 4, which illustrates the continuum of manager-nonmanager behavior, shows the various ways authority can be shared between subordinates and managers. At one extreme, there is no employee participation in the decision-making process; at the other extreme, managers and employees engage in joint decision making, which implies genuine participation and considerable authority on the part of employees.

Number and Configuration of People Interacting

Participation can involve an entire work group meeting to address particular problems, or it can take place in a one-on-one situation, such as a performance review discussion between a supervisor and subordinate. The interpersonal dynamics are quite different under each of these circumstances (see Figure 4.4 in Chapter 4) and will tend to evoke different participative skills from those involved. When an **intact work group** (group members plus their supervisor) meets, more information can be shared and ideas can be discussed more thoroughly than if just two people are meeting. But because of the number of people involved, there are more complexities to manage than when a supervisor and subordinate meet together.

When several groups are brought together to address shared concerns or when employees participate in a large conference, the complexities multiply. Conducting a meeting of several intact groups or running a large conference requires much more preplanning of both the agenda and the physical arrangements than does a small-group meeting or a one-on-one discussion.

Direct or Representative Participation

In **direct participation,** employees interact directly with those in authority; in **representative participation,** employees elect representatives to take part in decision making with higher levels of management. An example of the indirect, representative kind of participation popular in Europe is **co-determination,** in which union representatives sit on boards of directors. Another example is the proposal for **works councils** considered by the European Commission. In these councils, at least three worker representatives would meet with top management at least once per year to discuss ongoing issues. Management would be expected to consult with works councils on an ongoing basis concerning decisions that might affect workers.[8] Still another example of representative participation, familiar in America, is the union bargaining committee that meets with management to negotiate a labor contract.

Voluntary or Obligatory Participation

A meeting of a supervisor with his or her subordinates to solve a production problem is ordinarily a voluntary matter on the part of the supervisor and the organization. (The subordinates, however, may be required to attend the meeting.) In contrast, the mechanisms for worker participation under co-determination in Germany are established by law.[9]

The participative improvement strategies described in this chapter do not involve representative or obligatory kinds of participation. Most of the strategies we discuss have a strong element of group problem solving; some focus on relationships between groups. All the improvement strategies treated here involved firsthand rather than representative participation and participation that is usually undertaken on a voluntary basis.

Conditions for Success

Effective participation is not easy to achieve, and many consultants and researchers are still trying to improve the way participation is fostered in the organizational setting. But experience with participative improvement strategies suggests a number of conditions that need to be present for these strategies to succeed over the long term.

We are not referring to short-term improvements relative to running meetings, listening to subordinates, involving subordinates in decision making, or using an occasional task force. Although these improvements are important and may be steps in an overall, long-term change process, what we are referring to are long-term, continuous change processes and the conditions for their success. A number of conditions follow, some of which overlap. Probably all are interrelated.

Top Management and Union Support and Involvement

An overriding condition is top-management support and involvement. Unless top management supports the improvement effort and allocates financial resources and time and effort to the process, it is unlikely the process will go very far. It is important that top management leads by example and provides the recognition and support that organizational members will need in the change effort.

Similarly, in a unionized firm, support and involvement of union leaders is essential, particularly with respect to that segment of the work force that is unionized. It is vital that management and union leaders minimize adversarial stances and shift to distributive bargaining modes if participative strategies are to work.

A Sense of Need for Improvement

In general, organization improvement efforts are undertaken when top management or heads of major units within the organization feel that major aspects of organizational performance (such as productivity, product quality, internal cooperation, or employee satisfaction) are not as high as they could be. Accompanying this feeling is a sense of urgency — a sense that addressing organizational problems in a direct and constructive fashion is the only way to eliminate their negative effects on performance.

Employee Support

Obviously, participative approaches will not work if employees fail to support them. David Levine and Laura Tyson analyzed successful participatory systems in the United States and abroad and found that four characteristics are necessary for long-term employee support. The firms chosen included large Japanese firms, the Mondragon group of worker-owned cooperatives in the Basque region of Spain, large firms in Sweden, and a representative American company, Hewlett-Packard Co.

The four characteristics Levine and Tyson emphasize as necessary for sustained employee support are as follows:

1. *Some form of profit sharing or gainsharing.* Although participation may provide its own rewards for many employees, in the long run effective and sustained participation requires rewards for extra effort and a share in any increased profits.
2. *Long-term employment relations and job security.* Workers are more likely to cooperate in increasing efficiency if they are not fearful that this will lead to layoffs. Further, employees with job security are more likely to focus on long-term improvements, and group-based rewards are more likely to be effective motivators as the employee sees an ongoing relationship with a work group. In addition, high-participation firms typically need to make large investments in employee selection, socialization, and training, and these costs are more likely to be recovered in a long-term relationship.
3. *Reduced pay and status differentials.* Large differentials in pay and status tend to inhibit trust and cooperation. Bonuses based on group output provide incentives to attain group goals and to discourage "free riders."
4. *Guaranteed individual rights.* Effective participatory systems usually have policies and procedures to safeguard the rights of employees, particularly the right to dissent and the right of due process. Further, "just cause" is required for dismissal in contrast to company reliance on the "at will" doctrine.[10]

Lack of Coercion

Organization improvement strategies work best when employees choose to participate instead of being coerced. Forcing people to exercise more initiative is a contradiction in terms, and it tends not to work. Occasionally, managers will try to require employee involvement in various programs, but when people feel coerced or manipulated, their participation tends to be lackluster or ineffective. Therefore, it is important that management be sensitive to how much people want to be involved. Usually, employees feel they do not have enough involvement, and they are willing and frequently eager to participate in matters affecting their jobs, their work groups, and the organization.

Follow-up

It is important that people be persevering enough to work through problems. Changing human relationships in an organization is a complicated process, and those involved need to exercise patience in working things through. Sometimes managers and subordinates want a "quick fix" to a problem; most organization improvement efforts cannot be quick fixes and require a serious commitment of time and effort to succeed.[11]

Organization improvement efforts also require systematic follow-up to ensure lasting gains. In many instances, participative techniques yield immediate, positive results. But these improvements tend to "disappear into the woodwork" if the change effort is not viewed as an ongoing process.

Qualified Facilitators

Another condition that needs to be present for many participative improvement efforts to be successful is a qualified facilitator. A **facilitator** (or *consultant-facilitator*) is a professional who has been specially trained in participative skill development. Although their backgrounds vary, most facilitators have extensive training in group dynamics, social psychology, counseling or clinical psychology, and consultation skills. Linda Carr, in Case 21.2 is employed in the facilitator role.

Facilitators may come from outside or from within the organization. For example, TRW Electronic Systems Group and Polaroid Corp. have trained a number of their own human resources professionals for the facilitator role; these individuals are called upon from time to time to act as consultants to various departments and divisions. It is important, however, that facilitators come from outside the units they are trying to help. Experience suggests that it is next to impossible for a facilitator to be sufficiently objective if he or she is part of the ongoing dynamics of the unit. This is not to say that a well-trained person cannot be helpful to his or her own group, but optimal effectiveness in the facilitator role requires enough detachment so that, for example, the facilitator can confront a group (including the boss) with whatever issues the group may be avoiding.[12]

A Systems View

Organization improvement efforts generally embrace a systems view of the organization and its problems. According to this perspective, changes in one organizational relationship or process need to be sustained and reinforced by changes in other areas.[13] Suppose, for example, that an intact work team agrees that holding weekly meetings will be important for smooth operation of the unit and for effective problem solving. The supervisor's boss, however, believes that meetings are "silly and a waste of time" and communicates this to the supervisor. The outcome is predictable. The supervisor is going to be very reluctant to hold the meetings and probably will not schedule them. As another example, if the improvement process requires effective teamwork but the appraisal and compensation systems recognize only individual efforts, cooperation and teamwork are not likely to be strong. A systems view is required so that changes can be made simultaneously in many organizational variables.

Viewing Effective Participation as a Long-Term Process

Although we will occasionally use the word *program* in describing participative improvement efforts, in order for these change efforts to succeed, management and employees alike need to view the efforts as long-term processes — not as programs with specific ending points. There may be many short-term goals and achievement points, but organization improvement needs to be viewed as a continuous process through which individuals, groups, and the total organization keep finding ways to make the organization more effective. (This is consistent with the Japanese concept of *kaizen*, or continuous improvement. See *International Perspective* on page 578.)

Building Interpersonal Skills and Teamwork While Solving Problems

Common goals of many organization improvement strategies are to elicit greater cooperation and teamwork among employees while at the same time making progress in solving problems. To achieve these goals, certain techniques can be used to improve the way individual workers relate to other people in one-on-one situations. Other useful techniques focus on the individual's ability to function effectively as part of a team, and still others emphasize how an entire group relates to another group. This section provides an overview of some specific techniques with which to build a comprehensive strategy for organization improvement.

Two-Person Techniques   Techniques that involve two people attempt to develop fundamental interpersonal skills that employees need to participate effectively. The purpose of these techniques is to improve communication and understanding between two people so they can interact more effectively and manage their differences constructively.

Active Listening   One of the most fundamental communication skills is **active listening,** which involves listening carefully to the words and feelings being expressed and feeding these back in such a way that the speaker knows he or she has been understood. An important part of this skill is checking on meaning, or paraphrasing, in which the listener says back to the speaker what he or she senses the speaker is trying to communicate. To paraphrase accurately, the listener must suspend judgment and prejudice and focus on the feelings underlying the message. As Edgar Schein puts it, the listener must concentrate on "relaxing the critical mind."[14]

Active listening is crucial in any participative effort because misunderstanding and inability to communicate will damage or destroy any human relationship or cooperative undertaking. Therefore, training in active listening and exercises that develop paraphrasing skills are an important part of many organization improvement strategies.

Two-Person Conflict Resolution   When serious disagreement arises between two people — for example, about how work should be done or about goals, resources, roles, or authority — conflict that interferes with organizational performance can result. A facilitator is often effective in helping to resolve these conflicts and in restoring more constructive relationships.

Active listening is one of the most fundamental communication skills essential for good human relations and the improvement of any organization.

As a neutral third party, the facilitator can help both parties listen to each other and work through whatever problems exist. A technique like the following might be used.

STEP 1 The facilitator asks each person to develop two lists:
  a. Things appreciated or liked about the relationship and the way the other person carries out his or her responsibilities.
  b. Things that concern the person about the relationship and the way the other person carries out his or her responsibilities.

STEP 2 Each person shares with the other what he or she has listed. The facilitator discourages any arguing and helps the two people focus on listening and understanding. The facilitator might, from time to time, ask each person to paraphrase what the other is saying.

STEP 3 Each person offers information that might help to clarify matters.

STEP 4 The parties negotiate changes with each other. The facilitator lists the agreements and notes unresolved issues.

STEP 5 The parties and the facilitator plan how to work on the unresolved issues and arrange a follow-up session.[15]

The success of this conflict-resolution technique depends on the desire of the two parties to improve the relationship and their willingness to work hard at it. Obviously, success also depends on the skill of the facilitator and the extent to which he or she earns the two parties' trust.

Group Techniques

Experience and research in organization improvement indicate that when all members of a work group, including the supervisor, work together on common problems, the overall functioning and morale of the group improve dramatically. More effective teamwork can be fostered through such approaches as participative staff meetings, team-building techniques, sensing, team MBO, and quality circles. (For some of the reasons teams are not always productive, see *Contemporary Issues* on page 567.)

Staff Meetings

Supervisors and managers can build teamwork by encouraging greater employee participation in regular staff meetings. A staff meeting is a logical setting in which to build participative skills in group problem solving and decision making. But there are other ways to improve participation even before the meeting is held. For example, the supervisor can solicit agenda items from group members beforehand and give priority to those items during the meeting. If the group is large — say, beyond eight members or so — the supervisor can ask members to meet in smaller groups to discuss certain problem areas and to develop recommendations that can be reported back to the entire group during the staff meeting. In this way, more people are likely to have a chance to participate, and the total group can make use of the resources of all of its members.

Team Building

Team building is the name commonly given to a one- to three-day diagnostic, problem-solving meeting involving an intact work group and a facilitator. The facilitator works collaboratively with the members of the group and the formal leader to identify both strengths and problem areas and to assist in making plans for improvement. The group could include all of the members of management in a small

Contemporary Issues

Why Teams Aren't Always More Productive

Despite all the efforts by companies to use teams to enhance productivity and competitiveness, it seems that the individuality of employees and the structure of most organizations prevent teams from being as effective as these businesses would hope. So says the Wilson Learning Corp., a training and development firm located in Eden Prairie, Minnesota, which recently conducted a survey of teams in more than 500 organizations. According to Wilson Learning, the vast majority of survey respondents indicated that there are both individual and organizational factors that limit team performance.

Ways in which individuals can limit a team's productivity include:

- An unwillingness of team members to set aside position and power

- Diverse levels of ability, knowledge and skill among group members, placing more burden on some members than on others

- Challenges to and conflicts arising from individual members' personal beliefs.

The organizational barriers to team performance mentioned most frequently by study participants include:

- Rewards and compensation that focus on individual performance only

- Performance appraisals that ignore the employee's team performance

- Unavailability of pertinent information

- Lack of commitment of top management

- Internal competition that limits effectiveness.

Source: Dawn Gunsch, "For Your Information," *Personnel Journal* 72 (February 1993):16.

---

company, or even all of the employees in a very small organization. Linda Carr's work with the management group in Case 21.2 is an example of team building.

Typically, the facilitator interviews each member of the group, including the supervisor, asking questions like, "What things are going well in this group?" and "What things are getting in the way of the group's effectiveness?" The facilitator takes notes during the interviews and later extracts themes that are fed back anonymously to the group at the beginning of the workshop or retreat. These themes form the agenda around which the workshop is designed. Table 21.1 lists some themes from interviews with a fictional group — themes that are not at all unusual in consulting experience.

Many techniques can be used in team building. For example, suppose that "Our staff meetings aren't as effective as we'd like" is a high-priority problem. If the group consists of eight to twelve people, the facilitator may ask them to break into two or three smaller groups to tackle this assignment: "Describe what is wrong with staff meetings." After the responses have been shared and major similarities have been noted on flip-chart paper, the facilitator might ask small groups (with the same or different members) to develop recommendations for changing the meetings. These recommendations are then reported back and, through discussion, consensus is reached on what actions to take to achieve needed changes.

TABLE 21.1 Sample themes from team-building workshops

Our goals are unclear.
We are unclear about the roles of the purchasing manager and the administrative assistant.
Our staff meetings aren't as effective as we'd like.
There is a conflict between _____ and _____ that is getting in the way.
We don't do a good job of listening to each other.
Trust and mutual support are too low.
We don't follow up on decisions we make.
How are we going to organize for project X?
First-line supervisors have difficulty communicating with us.

As another example, suppose a high-priority problem is lack of clarity about various roles, such as the role of purchasing manager and the role of administrative assistant. The facilitator might sound out the purchasing manager and the administrative assistant about their willingness to participate in a **role analysis process (RAP).** If they appear to be fairly comfortable with the idea, the facilitator will then ask for one of the two to volunteer to be first. The process, which involves discussion of various aspects of a particular job as seen by members of a group, will then be explained to the group, and, ideally, several other members will volunteer to have their roles discussed.

Assuming the purchasing manager volunteers to go first, the group will be asked to respond to the question, "If the purchasing manager were operating in an optimally effective way, what would he or she be doing?" The purchasing manager listens while answers are recorded on flip-chart paper. The purchasing manager can ask questions for clarification but cannot debate any item until the listing is completed. Following this step, the purchasing manager is given the opportunity to respond, and discussion and any agreements about changes follow.

Typically, what happens through the role analysis process is a renegotiation of several aspects of the role to the satisfaction of all concerned, including the incumbent, his or her peers, and the supervisor. The flip-chart material becomes a kind of dynamic job description that role incumbents frequently tape on the walls of their offices or have typed for convenient reference.[16] (See Table 21.2 for the steps of this process.)

Sensing   Another technique that involves groups — but in this case not intact work groups — is **sensing.** In their book on managing, Jack Fordyce and Raymond Weil provide a clear illustration of this technique in which groups of workers interact with members of top management. The general manager of an organization employing two thousand people wants to find out what matters are of the most concern to employees so he or she can address these concerns, and how they might be alleviated, in the annual report to employees. The manager asks the personnel director to schedule a series of meetings with a cross section of employees so that he or she can find out what is on people's minds.

The human resources director selects four groups of twelve employees each. One group is drawn from nonsupervisory shop, technical, and office employees. A

TABLE 21.2 Procedure for using role analysis process (RAP)

ROLE ANALYSIS PROCESS

1. Role incumbent listens while members of the group answer this question:
   If the (Job Title) were operating in an optimally effective way, what would he or she be doing?
2. All responses are listed on flip-chart paper.
3. Role incumbent may ask questions for clarification but may not argue until Step 2 is complete.
4. Role incumbent responds.
5. Discussion takes place and any changes are agreed upon.

Source: Based on Wendell L. French and Cecil H. Bell, Jr., *Organization Development: Behavioral Science Interventions for Organization Improvement,* 4th ed. (Englewood Cliffs, N.J.: Prentice-Hall, 1990), chap. 10; and I. Dayal and J. M. Thomas, "Operation KPE: Developing a New Organization," *Journal of Applied Behavioral Science* 4 (1968):473–506.

second group is drawn from among professional employees and staff specialists. A third group is selected from among the supervisors. A fourth group is made up of a cross section of employees from various departments and levels.

Before selecting the participants and scheduling the meetings, the human resources director talks with the supervisors of prospective participants to explain the process, to assure them that no direct actions affecting their units will be taken as a result of the meetings, and to secure their cooperation. Before each meeting, the human resources director meets for half an hour with the participants to brief them on the general manager's purpose and to help them begin to talk about some of their concerns as a way of warming up to the task. During the meeting, the general manager mostly listens but occasionally asks questions for clarification. Occasionally, he or she expresses thoughts or plans already made about some of the topics raised.[17]

The sensing process is valuable because it can open up direct communication across the organizational hierarchy. There is some risk, however, that the role of the supervisor will be undermined, especially if employees by-pass their immediate superiors and reserve their recommendations only for the sensing session. Moreover, management response to significant concerns must be evident to employees in order to maintain their support of and participation in the process.

The sensing process is similar to the use of **focus groups** in market research: panels of consumers are assembled, usually for a modest fee, and asked to respond to selected questions or topics. Focus groups, however, usually consist of strangers, whereas sensing groups are members of the same organization. In addition, the agenda for focus group discussions is usually narrow, whereas the agenda in sensing sessions may be whatever employees wish to talk about.[18]

Team MBO   **Team MBO** is similar to traditional management-by-objectives programs except for some additional features (see Chapter 13). One such feature is that group objectives are developed by the team and progress on them is reviewed by the team. Another feature is that individual objectives are discussed with the team as well as with the supervisor, thus opening up the process to peer interaction and influence. Progress on these objectives is also reported to and discussed with peers.

Team MBO obviously requires a strong commitment on the part of team members to work together and to help each other. The success of this approach also depends on the group becoming relatively skilled in active listening and in group problem solving.[19]

Quality Circles   **Quality circles** are largely a Japanese synthesis of American ideas pertaining to statistical quality control and group dynamics. Americans like W. Edwards Deming and Joseph Juran brought quality control expertise to Japan in the 1950s. By the 1960s Kaoru Ishikawa of Tokyo University, inspired by the works of American behavioral scientists, added the notion of small groups of workers formed to address problems in their work areas.[20] The outcome, quality circles, is currently popular nationally and internationally. However, many of these circles have failed because not enough attention has been paid to conditions for their success, as described earlier in the chapter regarding participative improvement efforts.

Basically, a quality circle is a group of employees — usually from seven to ten — from the same unit who voluntarily meet together regularly, usually for one hour a week, to identify, analyze, and make recommendations about quality problems and other production problems in their area. The meetings are typically chaired by the supervisor, but sometimes the chairperson is elected, as in one of the groups in Case 21.1. Occasionally, the chair is rotated among members of the group. Recommendations developed by the quality circle are typically reported to a management committee that is part of the regular decision-making structure of the organization.

To ensure full participation, leaders of quality circles are often trained in group dynamics so that they can lead effective group discussions. One technique for ensuring full participation is for the leader to ask each person around the table, in turn, to provide one idea about a matter. Additional comments can be made after each person has had a turn. Group members may also be given a background in group dynamics and are sometimes taught certain analytical techniques (such as statistical quality-control methods) to help them make more informed decisions about quality and production.

Frequently, organizations using quality circles appoint a qualified member of the human resources department as a coordinator or a facilitator for the quality circle groups. This person can provide training in group methods and can sit in on meetings and be of assistance when groups need help.

To be successful, the quality circle approach to organization improvement (like other participative approaches) must be compatible with management's philosophy about how to relate to employees. In addition, success requires management support and involvement. Management must be heavily involved in evaluating recommendations emerging from groups and providing recognition for workable and useful ideas.

As part of a broader employee involvement (EI) program at the Ford Motor Co., quality circles have improved product quality and reduced production costs and absenteeism. With the support of the United Auto Workers, thousands of Ford employees in eighty-six of the company's ninety-one plants and depots meet once a week in small groups to deal with quality, production, and work-environment problems. The broader EI program has included vendors and dealers in a comprehensive quality improvement program.[21] Typically, as at Ford, the more successful quality circle programs have been part of a broader participative management system.

Study Action Teams   There are numerous other techniques and approaches for employee involvement in organization improvement efforts — for example, **study action teams,** used at Xerox and discussed in Chapter 18. These teams of about eight members included managers, engineers, and hourly employees who were assigned full-time for six months to investigate a specific problem affecting their whole work area. Essentially, these teams were cross-functional and multilevel task forces. Team recommendations, when implemented, resulted in reductions in departmental operating costs of up to 25 percent. An important by-product of the teams' work was improved labor-management cooperation.[22]

Intergroup Problem Solving and Conflict Management

Intergroup relationships are very important to the success of the organization. Groups must be able to cooperate in solving shared problems and to manage differences that arise during day-to-day operations. Thus, it is important that the manager and subordinates of each unit pay some attention to the quality of their relationships with other units.

If a relationship between groups has deteriorated because of an unresolved conflict, or if two groups simply wish to improve an already good relationship, a participative technique similar to the third-party peacemaking advocated for two-person conflict resolution can be immensely helpful. This technique, called **intergroup problem solving,** is outlined below.

STEP 1 The facilitator asks each group to develop three lists about the other group: (1) a positive list — things liked about the other group; (2) a negative list — things the other group is doing that reduce the effectiveness of one's own group or of the organization as a whole; and (3) a list of predictions about what the other group will include on its first two lists. The two groups meet in separate rooms to prepare their lists, which are recorded on flip-chart paper.

STEP 2 The two groups return to a common room and present what they have listed. The rules imposed by the facilitator are the same as in two-party conflict resolution: no arguing is allowed during the presentation phase; only questions to gain clarification are permitted.

STEP 3 The groups again meet separately to discuss the implications of what they have heard. Frequently, the groups find that their differences are not as great as they had imagined and that a good deal of misunderstanding is based on inadequate information and inaccurate perceptions. Each group develops a list of priority concerns that need to be addressed.

STEP 4 The groups share their new lists and, with the facilitator's help, make a composite list of what both groups agree are priority matters.

STEP 5 The procedure may vary, but a likely next step is for the facilitator to appoint subgroups composed of members of both groups. Each subgroup is then asked to meet and further diagnose an assigned problem and to report back to a general session of all the participants with recommendations for action. During this general session, an attempt is made to reach consensus on action steps, and individuals are given specific assignments with agreed-upon completion dates. Action steps and assignments are recorded.

STEP 6 A follow-up session is held involving both groups or the leaders of both groups. Progress is reviewed and further action plans are made if necessary.[23]

Ideally, this approach is used only after both groups have had some experience with team building in their own units. Sometimes, however, misunderstandings and conflict become so crippling to organizational effectiveness that it is wise for management to engage a facilitator and move directly into the conflict situation. But this requires at least a modest level of understanding and acceptance of the process. Obviously, the facilitator must earn the trust of both groups to be effective.

Survey Feedback   The dynamics of **survey feedback** are similar to those of team building except that questionnaires rather than interviews are used to gather data from employees. The questionnaire typically surveys employees from several departments or all employees within the organization. Ordinarily, in team building, data are obtained from only one unit at a time.

The survey feedback process typically unfolds this way:

1. The top management of the organization is involved in preliminary planning. Usually, the human resources director is given responsibility for coordinating the effort with consultant help.

2. It is decided to collect data about organizational climate and perceptions about human resources policies and practices from all organization members.

3. A questionnaire is purchased from a publisher or consulting firm and adapted for the particular organization. (See Chapter 4 for reference to climate surveys.)

4. The questionnaire is filled out anonymously. Participation is voluntary, but organization members are encouraged to participate.

5. Data are tabulated and results fed back to the top-management team and then down through the hierarchy. Floyd Mann calls this an "interlocking chain of conferences."[24] Specific data obtained from each unit are fed back to the particular unit, usually along with more general data about the whole organization or division. (Specific data from other, comparable units are usually not provided to prevent one unit from blaming or embarrassing another.)

6. Each manager presides at a meeting or workshop with his or her subordinates during which (a) subordinates are asked to participate in interpreting the data, (b) problems are identified and further diagnosed, (c) action plans are made for remedying deficiencies and making constructive changes, (d) plans are made for interacting with other groups to solve problems that involve more than one unit, and (e) plans are made for discussing the data at the next lower level.

7. Most feedback sessions involve a consultant-facilitator who helps prepare the superior for the meeting and who serves as a resource person to the group.[25]

This process is quite different from that where top management administers a questionnaire and then tries to interpret the results and take action.

Comprehensive Improvement Strategies

When viewed individually, the techniques described thus far are somewhat limited in scope. It is true that many of them can be used to solve problems and improve relationships within the organization on an ad hoc basis. But improvement in morale and overall performance can be more extensive and lasting when participative techniques are carefully chosen and implemented in the context of an organization-wide improvement strategy.

Three comprehensive improvement strategies are described in this section: organization development programs (OD); quality-of-work-life (QWL) projects; and total quality management (TQM). In actual use, improvement efforts similar to any one of these — or an improvement effort that combines two or more of these — may carry a different label. Thus, it is necessary to examine the specific techniques being applied in an organization improvement effort to understand exactly what strategy is being used.

These three strategies, which are used extensively both in the United States and abroad, share some common features. However, they place different emphases on what might be called the human or social system processes versus the technological processes and structure. As shown in Figure 21.1, organization development strongly emphasizes interpersonal, group, intergroup, and organizational processes. Examples would be learning more about group dynamics and running meetings while at the same time solving problems being faced by the unit. Total quality management programs, on the other hand, are likely to stress statistical quality control,

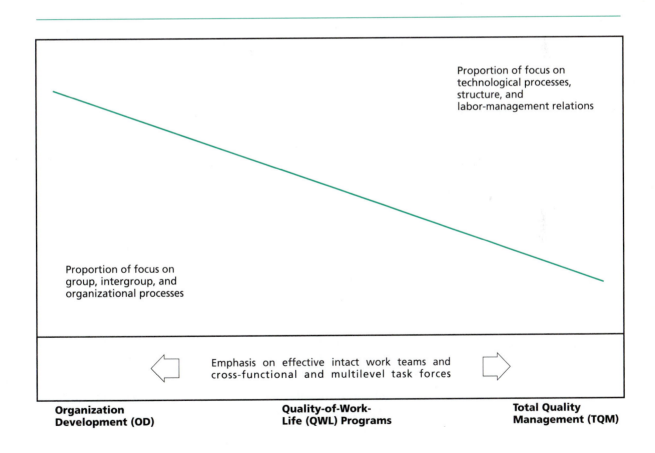

FIGURE 21.1 Emphases in different participative improvement strategies

simplifying work-flow processes, and doing things right all the way from product design to serving the customer.

The common features of these strategies relate to developing and using effective teams. The effective use of intact work groups and cross-functional and multilevel task forces is a major component of all three strategies. Further, both QWL and TQM programs may use such OD approaches as team building and sensing techniques. Conversely, action plans coming out of team building and intergroup problem solving in OD programs may include recommendations about adopting QWL and TQM approaches. The three strategies, therefore, are by no means mutually exclusive and, in practice, may overlap considerably.

Organization Development Programs

Organization development efforts typically include a number of the techniques and approaches described earlier in the chapter. Team building, in particular, tends to have central importance. Survey feedback, which uses questionnaires in contrast to the interviews, has many similarities to team building, and can also be crucial. Sensing and interpersonal and intergroup conflict management techniques are frequently used as well.

As a broad strategy, **organization development (OD)** can be defined as follows:

> Organization development is a top-management-supported, long-range effort to improve an organization's problem-solving and renewal processes, particularly through a more effective and collaborative diagnosis and management of organization culture — with special emphasis on formal work team, temporary team, and intergroup culture — utilizing the assistance of a consultant-facilitator and the use of the theory and technology of applied behavioral science, including action research.[26]

To a large extent, the focal point of most OD programs is the prevailing culture of various groups and of the organization as a whole. There is a conscious effort to examine beliefs, values, norms, and goals to see which are useful and which need to be changed. The genius of this approach is that improvements in the culture of the organization are made simultaneously with the solving of substantive problems.

The above definition also refers to **action research:** the process of gathering information, feeding it back, and developing plans for implementing desired changes. In a typical OD program, action research involves gathering information (usually through interviews and questionnaires), making that information visible (for example, reporting interview themes to a group on flip-chart paper), and then facilitating employee participation in a diagnostic and problem-solving effort. Figure 21.2 illustrates action research in the context of team building or survey feedback.

When top management or some key person in the organization senses that there are deficiencies in the way the organization is functioning that are due partly to an inappropriate organizational culture, an OD program may be initiated. The process might go something like this:

1. A qualified consultant (or possibly a team of consultants) is selected. The consultant acts as a facilitator to intact work teams and helps manage the entire OD process as it unfolds.
2. Team building (or a combination of survey feedback and team building) starts with the top team and is extended gradually to subordinate teams as it is found helpful and as managers request this assistance.

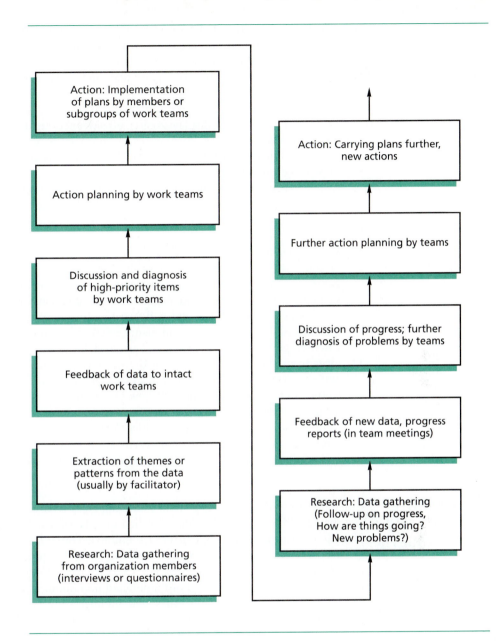

FIGURE 21.2   The action research model

3. The team building is supported with individual and group training in group process and leadership skills. Some of this training will occur during team-building workshops; some of it may occur in special training sessions.
4. Intergroup problem-solving sessions are held when data gathering reveals conflicts and misunderstanding between groups.
5. Other techniques, such as sensing, are used as relevant.

6. A steering committee, representing a cross section and all levels of the organization, is appointed early in the process. This committee advises top management and the consultant(s) on the next steps in the process.

7. There is extensive follow-up of action plans in regular unit or department meetings.

8. As organization members develop their participative skills through the OD process, they begin to display greater effectiveness in their interpersonal and group interactions. They become better equipped to solve problems and cope with issues that affect the entire organization, such as developing new markets, improving products, and so on.

9. As teamwork, support, and openness increase, participative management of the organization's culture becomes the norm. Rather than treating the organizational culture as a given, all members of the organization can play an active role in shaping the desired culture.

10. Human resources policies and management practices are revised as necessary to be congruent with and supportive of the emerging culture. For example, the organization may adjust its compensation policy to reward effective participation by individuals and groups; managers may recognize and reward employees for their skills in cooperation and collaborative problem solving along with their technical skills; and training and management development programs may give a new emphasis to interpersonal and group skills.

11. Organization members apply what they have learned to changing opportunities and challenges in the organization's external environment — to user response to the organization's products, to new technology, to changing economic conditions, and so on.

12. Action research becomes a way of life. When it is relevant to do so, systematic efforts are made to find out what organization members are perceiving, feeling, and thinking in order to maintain increased efficiency and high morale.[27]

Quality-of-Worklife Projects

Collaborative efforts by management and employees to improve both productivity and the conditions of working life are called **quality-of-worklife (QWL) projects.** Many of these projects are implemented in unionized organizations as a result of integrative bargaining between companies and unions. QWL projects are not limited to the unionized setting, however. A few years ago, Richard Walton estimated that there were at least a thousand plants, both union and nonunion, using QWL programs in the United States, with "many times that number somewhere in the transitional stage," that is, beginning to use some participative programs like quality circles.[28]

Features

Some of the common features of QWL and OD programs include a focus on intact work teams, problem-solving sessions by work teams ranging over many aspects of work life, the availability of additional training, the availability of facilitators, and increased responsiveness by supervisors and managers to employees (both a feature and an outcome). Overall, there tends to be a heightened level of participation and involvement by employees in matters affecting their work. But in contrast with many OD programs, which tend to start at the managerial and professional levels, QWL efforts tend to be focused on supervisory and production employees. Ideally, an organization improvement strategy will blend features of OD and QWL and encompass the entire organization.

At General Motors Corp., QWL projects have included these characteristics:

- Union agreement with and participation in the process
- Voluntary participation on the part of employees
- Assurance of job security (no loss of jobs as a result of the program)
- Training programs in team problem solving
- The use of quality circles through which employees meet to discuss problems affecting the plant's performance and their work environment
- Encouragement of job rotation and skill development within work teams
- Availability of skills training
- Work-team involvement in forecasting staffing needs, in work planning, and in team-member and team-leader selection
- Periodic plant and team meetings to discuss such matters as quality, schedules, safety, and customer orders
- Responsiveness to employee concerns[29]

Results and Limitations   Many QWL projects have had at least modest success, but frequently there have been difficulties in sustaining or expanding the process beyond a few years. Research suggests that there are reasons for the limited success of some QWL projects. First, changes in union (or management) leadership can destroy the continuity of a QWL program. Second, expectations about how fast improvements would occur may have been too high. Third, these efforts are often aimed at the production or clerical work force, with little attempt to change the culture at the managerial and professional levels. Finally, there has usually been insufficient attention to long-term financial rewards for the participants.[30]

Total Quality Management

Total quality management (TQM), sometimes called "continuous quality improvement," is a combination of a number of organization improvement techniques and approaches, including statistical quality and process control, quality circles, self-managed teams, and task forces, and extensive participatory management. Much of the impetus for TQM has come from a growing awareness by American managers of the critical need for American corporations to compete on a global scale. In particular, it has become obvious that Americans must compete with the Japanese, who have had great success in managing quality. (For some of the history of continuous improvement programs in Japan, see *International Perspective* on page 578.)

Features   The following features tend to characterize total quality management. The list is based largely on a special issue of *Business Week*, entitled *The Quality Imperative*, and on "total quality" conferences held in the United States and abroad by the Conference Board.[31]

- *Primary emphasis on customers.* The development of an organizational culture in which employees at all levels, including the CEO, treat customer needs and expectations as paramount.
- *Daily operational use of the concept of "internal customers."* Emphasis on the concept that work flow and internal interdependencies require that organizational members treat each other as valued customers within units and across functional lines.

International Perspective

Continuous Improvement Programs in Japan

Continuous improvement programs (CIPs) unleash employee experience and creativity to improve both products and processes. They are often cited as the most important difference between the Japanese and Western management styles and as a major factor in Japan's economic success. Yet the CIP was conceived, developed, and brought to maturation in the United States. After World War II, the U.S. government helped to export it to Japan, where it was well received and promptly flourished. Despite the long history and well-documented benefits of such systems, few U.S. companies have invested effort in CIPs equivalent to that of their Japanese competitors.

Japanese companies have put almost forty years into the development and refinement of CIPs, or *kaizen* programs as they are known in Japan, and have brought the art and science of managing them to new levels of sophistication. The aim of these programs is precisely to design and implement a system whose natural equilibrium is constant improvement and change. How can a company that does not have such a program compete with one that does?

Source: Excerpted from Dean M. Schroeder and Alan G. Robinson, "America's Most Successful Export to Japan: Continuous Improvement Programs," *Sloan Management Review* 32 (Spring 1991):67.

- *An emphasis on measurement using both statistical quality control and statistical process control.* (**Statistical quality control** is a method of measuring and analyzing deviations in manufactured products; **statistical process control** is a method of analyzing deviations in manufacturing processes.)[32]

- ***Competitive benchmarking.*** Continuous rating of the company's products and practices against the world's best firms, including other organizations in other industries.

- *Continuous search for sources of defects, with the goal of eliminating them entirely (zero defects.)* (The Japanese call this *kaizen*.)[33]

- *Participative management.* This includes extensive delegation and involvement, and a supportive, coaching leadership style.

- *An emphasis on teams and teamwork.* Typically, this includes self-managed teams. Cross-functional and multilevel task forces are used extensively.

- *A major emphasis on continuous training.* This means learning new and better ways of doing things and adding new skills. In many organizations, this approach will be reinforced by changes in the compensation system — for example, the introduction of skill-based pay.

- *Top-management support on a continuous basis.* This requires a long-term perspective on the part of top management, and a long-term commitment to providing supportive leadership.

Extent of Use   Some version of total quality management is being used in virtually all types of organizations, including manufacturing (for example, basic metals, chemicals, automobiles, semiconductors, and electronics), software development, railroads, airlines, insurance, and retail sales. Organizations as diverse as hospitals and navy aircraft carriers are becoming involved.

Results   At the request of members of Congress, the U.S. General Accounting Office (GAO) assessed the impact of total quality management programs in companies selected from among the highest-scoring applicants for the **Malcolm Baldrige National Quality Award.** Established under a law named for a former secretary of commerce, this award is designed to recognize companies that have successfully implemented total quality management systems. The GAO reported the following results:

> Companies that adopted quality management practices experienced an overall improvement in corporate performance. In nearly all cases, companies ... achieved better employee relations, higher productivity, greater customer satisfaction, increased market share, and greater profitability.[34]

The GAO further found that total quality management is as relevant to small companies as to large ones and that sufficient time needs to be allowed for gains to appear. On the average, companies improved their performance in two and one-half years. Thus, TQM requires a long-term perspective; it is a long-term, continuous process.[35]

Problems   Some of the problems experienced by companies attempting to implement TQM are common to many organization improvement efforts that require a major change in the culture of the organization. For example, there can be initial union resistance, as experienced at the Inland Steel Bar Company, particularly when there has been a history of adversarial relations.[36] Further, first-line and middle managers may be threatened by the need to delegate extensive responsibility to self-managed teams and/or task forces and may resist shifting to more of a coaching and supporting role. And, as is the case in all major organization improvement efforts, new ways of doing things may not compensate for major strategic blunders.[37] (For more on TQM, see Figure 22.3 on page 613, Chapter 22.)

Legal Aspects of Employee Involvement Programs

Late in 1992 the National Labor Relations Board ruled that "action committees" set up by the management of the Electromation Company of Elkhart, Indiana, were illegal under the National Labor Relations (Wagner) Act of 1935. Passed when it was assumed that labor-management relations were essentially adversarial, the law prohibits companies from establishing, dominating, or interfering with labor organizations (see Chapter 2). In the Electromation case, an NLRB administrative judge, and later the four-member board, ruled that the committees formed by Electromation constituted a "labor organization" and were therefore a company-dominated union. The board ordered the committees disbanded.[38]

In the Electromation case, the board found that the company had dominated the groups in the way they were structured: each had about five workers and one or two management officials as members. Further, the company had involved the committees in discussing such issues as wages and work rules, areas that the union contended — and the board agreed — were the province of collective bargaining.[39]

Early interpretations of the NLRB ruling suggest that various kinds of employee involvement programs, such as quality circles, are not necessarily prohibited, provided they are "structured carefully," as one board member stated. Another board member wrote the following in his concurrence with the decision:

> I find nothing in today's decision that should be read as a condemnation of cooperative programs. Indeed, in this age of increased global competition I consider it of critical importance that management and employees be able, indeed, are encouraged, to engage in cooperative endeavors to improve production methods and product quality.[40]

In 1993, the NLRB made a decision that, in the eyes of the business community, added to the murkiness and uncertainty in the labor law stemming from the Electromation case. In this case, involving DuPont's Chambers Works plant in New Jersey and the plant's Chemical Workers Association, the NLRB ordered DuPont to disband seven committees formed to deal with safety and recreation issues. One likely consequence will be a major effort in Congress to amend the National Labor Relations Act in the direction of supporting worker involvement, not curtailing it. Further, Labor Secretary Robert Reich has repeatedly said he would seek such legislation if NLRB rulings served to stifle worker-management teams.[41]

The lesson for management at the moment, then, is to follow guidelines such as the following until there are further NLRB cases and/or the law is changed. The following guidelines, written after the administrative judge ruled and before the full board ruled on the Electromation and DuPont cases, are attributed to Don Zimmerman, a Washington lawyer and former NLRB member:

- Make participation strictly voluntary.
- Have committees focus on such areas as improving productivity, product/customer service quality, or supplier relations.
- Avoid meetings that appear to be negotiations between management and labor over issues that could be considered terms and conditions of employment.
- Do not establish these committees when the company is facing a union organizing campaign.[42]

Role of the Human Resources Department

Some indication of the extensive involvement of human resources professionals in participative strategies for organization improvement can be seen in recent surveys. For example, in one survey of 490 organizations, 82 percent had organization development programs. The personnel or human resources department had responsibility for the program in 38 percent of these organizations and shared the responsibility with other departments in another 51 percent. Overall, then, the HR department had a major role in 89 percent of the programs.[43]

Planning and Managing Participation

Experience indicates that optimal success in organization improvement efforts requires joint planning and development of the process by human resources professionals and managers at all levels of the organization. Top-management support and involvement are crucial. In addition, union support and involvement are crucial in the unionized organization. The talents and insights of middle managers and first-line supervisors are essential as well. If these people are not extensively involved, not only is a major resource being underused, but they will also tend to thwart or undermine the program because of misinformation or an understandable desire to protect themselves against changes over which they have no control.

The human resources department needs to be extensively involved because that department houses those people who advocate careful and thoughtful attention to the development and use of *all* the human talent in the organization. Further, the human resources department needs to be heavily involved in any major improvement effort so that human resources policies and practices are congruent with the thrust of the effort. The reverse is also important: the human resources department needs to be involved so that improvement efforts are not launched that are inconsistent with the organization's philosophy and policies with respect to human resources.

The human resources department is the logical unit to employ one or more professionals trained in participative approaches to organization improvement. For example, one or two members of that department, depending on its size, might be hired partly because of their team-building skills or might be given training to develop those skills. Similarly, the department might develop a staff member to become the coordinator and facilitator for a quality circle program. As another example, the human resources department is likely to coordinate training programs in statistical quality and process control to help launch and sustain a total quality management program.

Sustaining Participation

In organizations where management wishes the culture and climate to become more participative, it would seem that all human resources professionals could profit from training and experience in action research methods. Skills in interviewing, in designing and administering questionnaires, and in running workshops can be immensely helpful in the context of broad organization improvement strategies.

Members of the human resources department can also profitably use action research methods in reviewing and improving various personnel practices. For example, if the human resources department or top management wishes to investigate the potential usefulness of a plant-wide productivity incentive program of some kind, gathering data through such mechanisms as interviews, questionnaires, and meetings can be very helpful in diagnosing what problems need to be solved and deciding whether such an incentive system might be appropriate for solving them. Members of personnel departments all too frequently sell management on a new program of some kind without careful diagnosis of organization strengths and weaknesses. Top management is prone to do the same thing, and the human resources department can provide a major service by helping managers do a better job of diagnosing problems and soliciting employees' ideas about solutions.

Finally, it is important that the human resources department anticipate, and help other managers be aware of, the various implications and ramifications of changes that are proposed or started. For example, launching a cost-cutting program without thinking through its impact on jobs and people is very shortsighted, but it is sometimes done. The human resources director needs to be persuasive in convincing managers that consultation with the human resources department on major changes would be wise. Being helpful when the problem is brought to the human resources department is obviously important if managers, including top management, are to continue to consult with that department.

Summary

This chapter has dealt with participative strategies and techniques for organization improvement. The trend is toward more opportunities for participation by employees in meaningful aspects of their work. This suggests the need for more effective participation. Participation can vary in the extent of freedom, the number of people interacting, whether the participation is direct or through representatives, and whether it is voluntary or has some legal or contractual basis.

The techniques that have been described include active listening, two-party conflict resolution, team building, role analysis process (RAP), sensing, team MBO, quality circles, intergroup problem solving, and survey feedback. Comprehensive strategies that may include many of these techniques are organization development (OD), quality-of-work-life projects (QWL), and total quality management (TQM). A participative, team approach underlies most of these techniques and strategies. Action research is fundamental to OD and can be very useful in QWL and TQM programs.

A number of conditions are necessary for optimal success in the use of the various improvement techniques and strategies described: voluntary participation, qualified facilitators, key people sensing a need for organization improvement, a willingness on the part of all participants to work through problems and to follow up on action steps that are taken, and a systems view of the organization and its problems.

Some of the reasons for difficulties in sustaining participative improvement programs have included changes in union and management leadership, expectations that are too high, lack of attention to the culture at the top of the organization, and insufficient attention to long-term financial rewards for the participants. Resistance to these programs by supervisors and middle managers has also been a problem in some instances.

Legal aspects of employee participation programs, such as quality circles, are evolving. It is important that union cooperation be obtained, and that such programs be voluntary and not appear to be negotiations between management and labor over terms and conditions of employment.

Optimal success in organization improvement efforts requires joint planning and development of the process by human resources professionals and managers at all levels of the organization. Top-management support is crucial. The human resources department needs to be heavily involved in any major improvement effort to ensure that change efforts are congruent with the organization's philosophy and policies with respect to human resources.

The human resources department is the logical unit to employ one or more professionals trained in participative approaches to organization improvement. Further, if the organization wishes to become more participative, human resources professionals can make extensive use of action research methods. Finally, the human resources department needs to have a systems view of change and improvement in order to help manage improvement efforts effectively.

Ethical Dilemma

A county government agency located in Southeast City is planning to survey all employees with an extensive organizational climate survey, followed by a major organizational improvement effort. By law, the agency must solicit proposals from several consultants or consulting firms. With the agency manager's concurrence, the personnel director has essentially preselected a firm whose principals are long-time friends of the personnel director. Proposals are solicited from a four-state area and the preselected firm is hired. The losing proposals are turned over to the winning firm by the personnel director with the comment, "You can probably pick up some good ideas from these."

Discuss the ethics of what has occurred. If the losing firms learned how the contract was awarded, how might they react?

Key Terms

participative improvement strategies
intact work group
direct participation
representative participation
co-determination
works councils
facilitator
active listening
team building
role analysis process (RAP)
sensing
focus groups
team MBO

quality circles
study action teams
intergroup problem solving
survey feedback
organization development (OD)
action research
quality-of-work-life (QWL) projects
total quality management (TQM)
statistical quality control
statistical process control
competitive benchmarking
Malcolm Baldrige National Quality
    Award

Review Questions

1. Describe several different forms of participation.
2. What conditions are necessary for the success of a participative improvement effort?
3. Explain the role of a qualified facilitator in change programs and in resolving conflicts.
4. Describe several techniques for improving teamwork using group methods.
5. What is team building? How does this differ from survey feedback?
6. Describe the major features of organization development, quality-of-work-life projects, and total quality management.
7. What appear to be the legal constraints on employee involvement programs?
8. What is the role of the human resources department in organization improvement efforts?

Opening Case Questions

Case 21.1   What Caused That Fiasco?

1. How would you respond to Emily's question about how the fiasco could have been avoided?

2. If you were the consultant, what recommendations would you have for Emily at this point?

Case 21.2   Appreciations and Concerns

1. Why was the exercise in concerns and appreciations Linda's first assignment to the group?
2. What seem to be some of the values and assumptions of an organization development program?

Comprehensive Case

The Role of Human Resources Managers in Total Quality Management

The term *total quality management (TQM)* covers a variety of approaches to reaching one overriding goal — customer satisfaction. TQM's advocates generally espouse "continuous improvement," empowering and involving employees, just-in-time manufacturing techniques, and the use of cross-functional teams. Generally seen as a Japanese phenomenon although its origins are American, TQM has had some notable successes in American business. Recent surveys, however, show that only a minority of the companies using TQM feel that it has helped them become more productive and profitable. Although the focus of TQM is often on production, the involvement of human resources managers is crucial if an organization is to implement TQM successfully and to avoid the kinds of problems that have made TQM less than a total success in many American companies.

Experts cite a number of ways that human resources managers can help achieve total quality management.

1. Institute TQM in the human resources department. The department can then lead the way, providing a model of what TQM can accomplish for the organization as a whole.
2. Assess thoroughly the organization's climate and make sure that all innovations take the current climate into account. The climate will change under TQM, but the change will fail if it is too radical or too rapid.
3. Provide a systems perspective. While people in such areas as marketing, production, and facilities may become totally involved in how TQM is affecting their own departments, human resources managers can provide everyone with a sense of how the program is affecting the whole and how the parts fit together.

4. Help managers who were promoted for their technical skills to improve their abilities to coach, empower, counsel, and in general provide the kind of flexible, diverse management that TQM often requires.
5. Assist in change management by helping employees improve their communication skills, persuading them to buy into the new management system, or even preparing them to be let go.
6. Develop the new hiring, evaluation, and reward systems made necessary by a shift to TQM.
7. Assist management in finding and training the personnel needed to fill new supervisory positions created by TQM.
8. Prepare employees to work effectively in teams and help build team spirit and cohesiveness.
9. Avoid the pitfalls of a process focus. Sometimes in the enthusiasm for a TQM system, managers call for extensive training and organizational changes without clearly specifying the need for the training or the desired results of the changes. Human resources professionals can be more effective if they keep one eye focused on the long-term effects of the training they are being asked to provide.
10. Find ways to reward team effort. TQM sometimes fails because an organization's system for rewarding individuals is inconsistent with TQM's emphasis on teamwork.
11. Rely on organization development more than on training.
12. Assist managers in exploring the issues in their own departments, defining desired results, and designing methods to assess success.
13. Help to develop structures, systems, and culture for the organization that will help it fulfill its new vision.

14. Time the changes in the personnel system to follow, not precede, changes in organizational structure, teamwork, and so forth. For example, the human resources department cannot institute incentives for teams until the teams are working together productively.

15. Provide the new types of training necessary for employees working under TQM. Many employees will need to learn how to collect, analyze, and present data relevant to their areas.

16. Revise evaluation systems so that they reflect customer and peer input, not just supervisors' evaluations.

17. Gather feedback from employees to gauge how the changes are being perceived and what different kinds of training or team building may be needed.

18. Train employees from various parts of the organization in how to conduct benchmarking studies — closely examining how corresponding parts of other organizations do their jobs well. At the same time, the human resources staff needs to make clear to everyone involved in benchmarking that many reasons besides lack of employee effort can cause a depart-

ment's employees not to be as productive as those in a corresponding department in another organization.

19. Conduct benchmarking studies of well-respected human resources departments in other organizations to determine if personnel could be deployed more productively.

20. Keep abreast of the latest innovative human resources techniques and ideas covering such areas as how to develop the best relationships with suppliers and customers and how most effectively to empower employees.

Sources: David Chaudron, "HR and TQM: All Aboard!" *HRfocus* 69 (November 1992):1–6; Michael S. Leibman, "Getting Results from TQM," *HRMagazine* 37 (September 1992):34–38; Otis Port, "Quality," *Business Week*, November 30, 1992, pp. 66–72; and Jonathan D. Weatherly, "Dare to Compare for Better Productivity," *HRMagazine* 69 (September 1992):42–46.

Discussion Questions

1. Briefly describe how a human resources department might lead the way in establishing TQM in an organization.

2. What kinds of training appear to be necessary for successful TQM efforts? How does that training differ from organization development?

CHAPTER 22

International Human Resources Management

LEARNING OBJECTIVES

- Define international human resources management.
- Describe a number of complexities of IHRM.
- Understand the meaning of a wide variety of terms used in IHRM.
- Describe a number of dimensions along which cultures differ.
- Identify several HRM practices of foreign companies operating in the United States that might differ from those of U.S. firms.
- Identify a number of HRM practices in foreign countries that differ from U.S. practices.

The following two letters deal with Tom, a young U.S. citizen, going to work for a Japanese firm. Tom is working for this Japanese firm to help prepare himself for graduate school. He has not been to Japan before. The cultural shock Tom experiences is applicable to any organization that recruits a national from another country. The human resources department can be the catalyst to ensure a smoother transition.

CASE 22.1   Tom Goes to Work in Japan

Dear Mom and Dad,

I can't believe that I am actually in Japan! I arrived in Nagoya twelve hours after leaving L.A. and got quite a reception. The plant manager and four department heads greeted me formally with deep bows and names spoken so hastily that I barely caught them. This was not a problem since they gave me their business cards (mEE-she), printed on one side in Japanese and on the other in English. Only a few awkward words of English were spoken by my welcoming committee, who then settled into Japanese, leaving my "Japanese for Travelers" cassette skills far behind. I had just enough time to glance at their cards before we were whisked off to two waiting taxis.

My hosts pointed out various sights as we made our way through the congested streets, and then we arrived at my new home on the side of a lush, tree-covered hill about twenty minutes from the city by car. The house was pleasant, with a traditional Japanese tile roof and a little backyard overrun by bamboo. As we stepped through the front door, my forehead collided with the upper door frame, and as I stood up inside the entryway after removing my shoes in proper Japanese fashion, my head encountered a hanging lamp suspended from the ceiling. The house was obviously not built for a 6′2″ American. I had been prepared to do a lot of bowing in Japan, but I had not expected to have to bow whenever I walked through my house!

After a cursory explanation in Japanese about the appliances and other household items, such as the Japanese bath and the futon, and pointing down the street to a restaurant, my welcoming committee departed. (My first meal in that restaurant will be another story!) One of my colleagues was scheduled to stop by the next morning to escort me to the neighborhood train station and on to the auto plant. My job, as you know, will consist of teaching conversational English to managers and supervisors and helping with English documents and manuals.

I was thinking about the approaching day as I unpacked, when I discovered that there was little space to hang my clothes — just enough for a couple of suits. There was plenty of closet space, but equipped only with a large shelf in the middle. Never mind. In the morning I would ask my coworker how to handle this dilemma.

After sleeping very little because of the change in time, I arose early. My coworker arrived at 6:30, introduced himself with a bow and took off his shoes in the entryway as he handed me his card. Somehow I communicated to him my concerns about the closet problem and he tried vainly to explain in Japanese and gestures. Finally, he picked up some of my clothes and demonstrated that the suits should be hung, but the shirts folded, put in drawers, and ironed before wearing. He pointed to his watch, so I grabbed my briefcase and we headed out, donning our shoes as we left.

As we started our walk to the train station, my guide gestured toward two places on the road and said, "Dust." This baffled me and since he spoke little English and I spoke even less Japanese, it took the entire ten-minute walk for me to figure out that he was showing me where to put the trash for pickup! Both of us were thrilled at this triumph of communication, but it was short-lived as I soon discovered just how meager my Japanese skills were. The name of the train station was in English, but all other signs were in incomprehensible Japanese.

The station was a mass of pushing people. It made the New York subway at rush hour seem positively tranquil! No sooner had my escort purchased our tickets than the train arrived and the waiting mob surged forward, sweeping me helplessly along in its current.

Somehow I managed to squeeze through the door behind my colleague and discovered why people sometimes lose shoes on Japanese trains. There was already an enormous number of people crowded into the train when it arrived at our station, and people waiting on the platform were determined to join them. They kept moving forward, compressing the crowd tighter and tighter, and just when I thought that we would surely perish in the press, the conductor pushed on even more people, causing muffled grunts and groans throughout the overloaded car. The conductor sounded his whistle, the doors closed, and the overburdened train lumbered impossibly forward. I wasn't quite sure if both of my shoes were still on.

Ten minutes and four stations later, I began to wonder why I had bothered to press my suit that morning. We arrived at another station and suddenly most of the crowd swept forward, my colleague among them. Confirming the presence of my briefcase and both shoes, I plunged into the tide.

My arrival at the plant was quite an event (to me, at least). Ten minutes after I entered the large office, which housed all the supervisors' and managers' desks, I found myself standing at one side of my desk doing stretching exercises with my coworkers. When the exercises were completed, with all the employees still standing next to their desks, the plant manager approached me and made a few comments in Japanese. Bowing deeply to me, as did the rest of the people in the office, he stepped back, with everyone looking expectantly at me. After an awkward moment, someone near me mumbled the equivalent of "Speech." *Speech? Speech?!!*

Somehow I managed to say a few appropriate things (I hoped) in English about how honored I was to have been chosen to come to the plant, and how I hoped I could be an asset to the corporation. After a hasty *domo aragato* (thank you very much) and bowing deeply, I breathed a sigh of relief as my coworkers turned to their desks and the day's tasks. I was just sitting down when the plant manager approached me and gestured that I should follow him. "Speech" he said, and led me to a balcony above the factory floor. *Speech.?!*

Love,
Tom ◀

CASE 22.2   "Learning the Lines" in a Japanese Company

Dear Mom and Dad,

I've been here a week now, and am slowly beginning to get the hang of things. I've met many new people and am doing more exciting things than I have in any other week in my life. Yes, I survived the speech — loudspeakers and all — in front of the entire plant (about 2,500 workers) and the plant manager expressed his sincere appreciation. He then invited me over to his house for dinner on the following evening.

The dinner went well, and I even remembered to bring a gift, per Japanese custom. The plant manager appeared to be delighted with the L.A. Dodgers baseball hat that I gave him, and wore it through the entire meal. We drank beer and sake, and — you'll be proud of me, Mom — I tried everything on the table, even the sushi and sashimi. Most of it was delicious.

More dinners and parties followed throughout the week, with the most memorable evening ending at a local karaoke bar — a "singing" bar where the patrons sing solos to the music of their favorite songs. I even mustered the courage to sing the Beatles' "Let It Be" to the obvious entertainment of everyone!

Sometime during the evening, a distinguished man introduced himself, handed me his mEE-she and explained in broken English that his daughter is attending UCLA. He explained that he is the personnel director of a large electronics company and hoped that I would visit the plant for a tour sometime soon. I thanked him for his kind offer and our conversation ended just in time for us to join in a rousing chorus of a Japanese song. This apparently required the voices of all of the patrons in order to achieve the desired effect.

The dinners and parties have made it difficult for my still jet-lagged body to remain awake throughout the 8:00 a.m. to 8:00 p.m. workday. While my contract states that I have to work only until 5:00 p.m., it quickly became evident that my contract omitted several important items.

Everyone has been kind and helpful and, despite the absence of a formal company orientation, I am "learning the lines," as one of my Japanese friends puts it. Early on, I was given an inside tip by one of my new friends that I am expected to go out with my "group" for after-work drinking. When I asked why all activities seem to center around our group or section, I received the rather patronizing answer that everyone is part of a group and would be nothing without the other members. I learned from another friend that a person who doesn't participate in group activities never gets promoted and sometimes even gets fired. Most of the members of my section lead harried lives, many of them leaving for work at about 6:00 a.m., before their families arise, and returning home around midnight, after everyone has gone to bed. Some supervisors and managers see their children only on weekends.

Another matter not spelled out in the contract was my lunch hour. "Hour" is a euphemism. Lunch "fifteen minutes" is more accurate, since everyone hurries through lunch in order to get back to work. This has been a bit difficult for me, because the lunches in the plant cafeteria are still boiling when the food arrives on one's tray. How my coworkers can devour a near-boiling bowl of ramen, rice, or stir-fried vegetables is beyond me. Since my reason for being here is preparation for graduate school and I don't plan a long-term career here, I decided to live on the edge and take a half hour to eat my lunch. I still burn my mouth daily!

Well, I'd better run. Japan is a fascinating country — there is so much to learn here! Next time I'll tell you about my credit card and banking problems.

Love, Tom ◀

T om's experiences during his first week in Japan working for a Japanese firm give us some hints about the complexities and challenges of international human resources management. For example, in his letters home, he provides some information about working rules and norms — the exercises at his desk, the lunch "hour," the long day, and the expectations about socializing. He describes the physical facilities (the low ceilings in the doorways in his assigned house) and the difficulties of commuting by rail. He seems to have adjusted to some of the food, but we sense that he is somewhat overwhelmed by not being able to read or understand much Japanese. We learn a little about promotion policies, and what Tom is beginning to experience regarding the balance between work and personal life makes us wonder what tensions this creates in Japanese homes. Further, Tom is having credit card and banking problems. (For more on banking problems abroad, see *Contemporary Issues* on page 592.)

Tom's experiences have important implications for international human resources management. For example, when a company recruits a national from another country, it should select the individual carefully so that the new employee does not quickly resign due to culture shock. Intensive language training may be necessary, and certainly there will be a great need for a thorough orientation process, and so on. The human resources policies and practices of Tom's employer will greatly affect Tom's motivation and effectiveness, the employer's future ability to recruit from abroad, and the organization's overall effectiveness.

This chapter deals with some of the terminology and complexities of international human resources management and considers some of the dimensions along which different cultures can be contrasted. The chapter also discusses briefly a few HRM practices of foreign companies in the United States and concludes with a lengthier description of selected HRM policies or practices in various countries around the globe. We turn first to a definition of international human resources management.

What Is International Human Resources Management?

International human resources management (IHRM) *is the systematic planning and coordination of the fundamental organizational processes of job and work design, staffing, training and development, appraising, rewarding, and protecting and representing the human resources in the foreign operations of an organization.* Obviously, IHRM is highly interdependent with the human resources processes of the parent organization. Simply put, IHRM is HRM that cuts across national boundaries. But as Tom's case illustrates, it is not simple. IHRM can be very complex.[1]

Tom's situation is only one of an extensive variety of situations that have implications for IHRM. Globalization has created an array of employment scenarios based on such variables as citizenship, location, to whom the person reports, and the term of the assignment. Table 22.1 indicates some of these scenarios. For instance, category 2 sums up the situation of an employee of an American firm sent to work for a foreign **affiliate** (a branch or subsidiary). Category 9 describes the situation of an employee of a foreign affiliate assigned to work in the United States. Category 10 covers the situation of an employee of an American affiliate abroad who is a citizen of the host country. And so on. The employees in categories 2 and 9 are **expatriates,** that is, they are employees assigned to work in another country. (See the definitions in Figure 22.1.) The term is also frequently used to describe anyone who has chosen to work in a foreign country.

Contemporary Issues

Expatriate Banking — The Forgotten Detail

Quite often one of the most important details for a successful international relocation is overlooked . . . both by expatriates and their corporations. In all the frenzied activity and confusion that surrounds an international relocation, the banking needs of expatriates are seldom considered.

Unlike other elements of a relocation, banking services must be provided for on a continuous basis, both in the country of assignment and back in the United States, because many of expatriates' U.S.-based obligations such as mortgages, insurance or credit cards continue during their stay abroad.

Companies, even the more experienced ones, rarely consider their expatriates' banking needs until funds are lost in transit, checks start to bounce and credit ratings are damaged. As a result, the banking problems experienced by expatriates soon become the companies' problems, when their employee's productivity declines as more and more time is spent in trying to unravel their international woes.

Therefore, personal banking is one relocation detail that should be carefully considered and planned before expatriates leave on assignment. To minimize banking problems, corporations and expatriates should consider retaining a bank that is familiar with the needs of individuals who will be on overseas assignment and offers specialized programs to fulfill these specific U.S.-based banking needs.

Here are some areas to consider when selecting an expatriate banking program:

If expatriates are paid in the United States, then they will need a U.S.-based bank account to receive these funds, and they will require access to these funds for their overseas living expenses during their assignment. It is important to have a bank skilled in making overseas transfers of funds to consumers.

Many banks have set up systems for movement of large amounts of money for corporations, but few are equipped to move and track down the small amounts that consumers frequently want to transfer. Be careful. It can take a bank, inexperienced in such matters, months to find a transfer that has gone astray.

Expatriates may have need of moving funds to other financial institutions in the U.S. for children boarding in a U.S. school or to complete real estate, stock or financial transactions. Make sure that the bank can set up automatic transfers on an ongoing basis.

If U.S.-based obligations such as mentioned above are maintained, then make sure that the bank has a comprehensive set of bill-payment services.

Some questions to consider when choosing a banking program abroad:

- **Does the bank have a separate unit with a staff of personal bankers experienced in handling the unique banking needs of the expatriate?**
  The staff should be familiar with time zones, exchange rates, overseas funds delivery time, correspondent host banks and expatriates' special requirements.

- **Does the bank offer expatriates banking services to all of its customers or only to "high-net-worth" customers?**
  Many banks will only accommodate expatriates who maintain five- or six-figure balances. Check minimum requirements and fees.

- **Does the bank offer limited transaction services (international transfers), or can it provide a comprehensive package such as time deposits, brokerage services, mutual funds, foreign currency deposits and credit?**

- **Does the bank protect you from unauthorized access to accounts through the use of a PIN (personal identification code)?**
  These two questions are important to answer because it is extremely important to avoid fraud and maintain confidentiality when expediting telephone instructions.

- **Will the bank allow you to issue special or standing instructions by telephone or fax, or must you only use tested telexes or letters?**
  Tested telexes can be inconvenient and/or costly, and letters take considerable time in the

mail (if and when they arrive at all!). Neither of these is desirable when money is quickly needed.

- **Does the bank have an extensive consumer network overseas?**
  A global consumer network will facilitate transactions between the U.S. bank and the host bank, as well as assist expatriates in setting up an account at the overseas location.

Source: Helen Benjamin, "Expatriate Banking — The Forgotten Detail." Reprinted with the permission of HRNews (formerly Resource) published by the Society for Human Resource Management, Alexandria, VA.

TABLE 22.1 Categories of international personnel

Category	Description	Example
1 Parent local national	The traditional 'local hire': A local national working for the parent company	An American working for the American parent in the United States
2 Parent expatriate	Employee sent by the parent company, under control of the parent, to work in a foreign affiliate	An American temporarily assigned by the parent company to work in the Mexican affiliate.
3 Parent headquartered foreign national	A foreign affiliate employee transferred to the parent; coming under the control of the parent	A Mexican employee permanently transferred to the American headquarters
4 Affiliate local national (top mgmt)	Foreign affiliate employee of foreign nationality, controlled by the parent company	The Mexican manager of the Mexican affiliate, reporting directly to the American parent company
5 Local hire of foreign nationality	Employee hired by the parent to work in the parent company, coincidentally of foreign nationality	An employee hired in the U.S. to work in the parent company, who happens to be of foreign nationality
6 Affiliate based parent TCN*	Traditional TCN: Controlled by the parent, working in a foreign affiliate, whose nationality is of neither the parent nor affiliate country	The manager of the Mexican facility who is of British nationality and reports to the parent company
7 Affiliate employee in parent company	Employee controlled by the affiliate, of parent company nationality, working in the parent company	An American executive, of American nationality, responsible for representing the affiliate within the parent company, reporting directly to the management of the Mexican affiliate

TABLE 22.1 Categories of international personnel (*Cont.*)

Category	DESCRIPTION	EXAMPLE
8 Affiliate headquartered foreign national	Employee of parent company nationality, working in the affiliate and under the control of the affiliate	An American employee permanently transferred to the Mexican affiliate
9 Affiliate expatriate	Affiliate employee, of affiliate nationality, assigned to work in another country	A Mexican employee temporarily assigned by the Mexican affiliate to work in the United States
10 Affiliate local national	The traditional 'local hire': A local national working for the affiliate	A Mexican, hired by the Mexican affiliate, to work in Mexico
11 Parent based affiliate TCN	Controlled by the affiliate, working in the parent, whose nationality is of neither the parent nor affiliate	A British national, hired by the Mexican affiliate, and assigned to the United States
12 Local hire of foreign nationality	Employee hired by the affiliate to work in the affiliate, coincidentally of foreign nationality	An employee hired in Mexico to work in the Mexican affiliate, who happens to be of foreign nationality

*A TCN is a third-country national (see Figure 22.2)

Source: From S. Barnett, B. Toyne, & M. Mendenhall (1992). "A Three Dimensional Classification Schema for the Study of International Human Resources," presented at the annual meeting of the Academy of Management, Las Vegas, Nevada, August 9–12, 1992. Reprinted by permission of the authors.

Tom's situation is closest to categories 5 and 12 — "local hire of foreign nationality." (Typically, a **local hire** is a person hired from the local community where the plant or office is located.) But Tom is a little different. Tom is a U.S. citizen, recruited in the United States to work temporarily for a company based in a foreign country. Another example, similar to the one for category 5, is an American hired to work for a foreign company that has a plant or office in the United States. Americans working at the Japanese Nissan Motor Co. plant in Smyrna, Tennessee, or at the German BMW plant in Spartanburg, South Carolina, illustrate this situation, which is becoming very common in the United States. Because of federal and state laws, as well as competitive pressures, many of the HRM practices in such companies will resemble those found in American-owned firms; however, there may be a number of differences, some very subtle.

In another common scenario, which fits category 10, local hires are used extensively by an American firm that has a plant or office in a foreign country. Local hires are likely to make up the bulk of the work force in such foreign branches for a number of reasons. Not only do many countries have laws requiring a high proportion of employees to be **nationals** (or local nationals — see Figure 22.1); they further restrict the employment of foreigners by requiring visas and work permits. Besides, it probably makes good sense to utilize people who are familiar with the region or country and who may also be less costly to hire than employees sent from the United States.

What should the pay scale be for these nationals? Should they be paid at a rate similar to those paid by the company in the States (perhaps incurring the wrath of

Do You Speak the Language of International HRM?

Aguinaldo: (Mexico) A mandatory annual bonus of 15 to 30 days' pay, normally paid at Christmas time.

Antiquidates: (Venezuela) Half-a-month bonus for service indemnity.

Assignment: Refers to the period of time an employee is an expatriate. Special types include:

- **Assignment Completion:** The process of closing out an assignment and returning to the home-country and/or point-of-origin.

- **Business Trip:** Normally for a short period, generally less than one month in duration.

- **Extended Business Trip:** Normally longer than one month and may be up to two to three months' duration.

- **Foreign Assignment:** Additional emphasis that the assignment is at an overseas location rather than domestic.

- **Permanent Status:** In very few cases is an assignment truly "permanent." In most cases, an assignment of one or more years' duration is called "permanent."

- **Temporary Assignment:** Refers to a shorter assignment period of longer than two to three months, but normally shorter than one year in duration.

Balance Sheet Approach: A compensation approach that identifies the gains and losses of a particular assignment due to taxes, cost-of-living, etc., and attempts to even out windfalls and shortfalls to achieve the desired incentive level.

Base Salary: The expatriate's or TCN's salary only; this excludes the allowances and deductions associated with foreign service. Unless otherwise noted, it is the amount upon which future salary adjustments are calculated.

Bilateral Tax Agreement: Between the U.S. and foreign government that defines the personal income tax arrangements for U.S. expatriates assigned to that foreign country.

Completion Allowance: Additional compensation paid annually or at completion of assignment. Often used at remote hardship locations to encourage employees to remain for the full assignment period.

Cost Differential: A payment to compensate employee for differences in living costs (housing, goods, and services) between host- and home-countries . . . .

Danger Pay: At assignment locations where there is physical danger (war, etc.), often a special additional salary payment is made.

Dual Employment Contracts: An employee resides and works in one country, but travels to and works in another country. Two employment contracts cover this arrangement.

Employee Categories: Refers to the various types of international employees. Some of the examples of employee categories include:

- **Local Hire:** An employee hired in-country for work in that country. Often has the special meaning that the employee is not a national of that country, i.e., an American hired in country X for employment in country X. However, the American's employment package is that of a local national, not a U.S. expatriate.

- **Local National or National:** An employee hired for employment in his or her own country.

- **HCN:** Host-Country National.

- **PCN:** Parent-Country National.

- **TCN:** Third-Country Nationals; often refers to expatriate employees who are not U.S. citizens, but citizens of a "third" country.

- **Inpatriate:** Foreign manager in the U.S. Can also be used for U.S. expatriates returning to an assignment in the U.S.

- **Expatriate (Expat):** Normally a professional /managerial employee moved from one country to, and for employment in, another country.

- **Foreign Managers in the U.S.** An "expatriate" in the U.S. where the U.S. is the host-country and the manager's home-country is outside of the U.S.

- **International Staff:** Expatriate employees from home-countries other than the U.S.

FIGURE 22.1   Terminology in IHRM

- **Foreign National:** Frequently refers to the special case of a non-U.S. citizen assigned to the U.S. as an expatriate.

- **Indigenous Employee:** An alternate term for "local national/national" not often used because of prejudice concerns.

Expatriate Allowance: Payment to employee for undertaking an international assignment.

Fiscal Clearance: Prior to a foreign resident departing a host country, many countries require a document issued by the local Tax and/or Treasury department verifying that host-country income taxes have been paid.

Foreign Tax Credit: Because U.S. citizens/residents are taxed on their worldwide income, expatriates often pay foreign tax and the U.S. government allows a credit against a U.S. tax liability.

Hardship Allowance: An extra ongoing allowance paid to expatriates for TCNs assigned to locations with abnormally difficult or hazardous living or working conditions.

Home Leave: Paid roundtrip from assignment location to point and/or country of origin. Frequency often tied to degree of hardship at assignment location . . . .

Iron Rice Bowl: (China) The regular non-contract employment bond between employer and worker that is almost indestructible.

Localization: The process of replacing expatriates (normally higher cost) with local national employees.

Market Basket: A selection of typical shopping items used to compare cost-of-living differences between host- and home-countries.

MNC: A multinational corporation . . . .

Negative Differentials: Situation where a calculation for an allowance such as a cost differential shows negative, i.e., costs of assignment location are less than home-country costs.

Overbase Compensation: Additional payments over and above base salary to compensate for hardship, danger, extended workweek, and so forth.

R & R: At remote and hardship locations and/or where an employee is on an unaccompanied basis, provision is made to leave the assignment location for a short break.

Repatriation: The process of return to the home country at completion of assignment . . . .

Settling-In Allowance: Reimbursement for living costs at the assignment location until the arrival of personal and household effects shipment and movement into permanent accommodation.

Split Pay: where pay is delivered in a combination of host- and home-country currencies.

Split Payroll: Where an employee is on two payrolls, with each paying only a portion of the salary, to reduce income taxes in the host country.

Tax Equalization: A technique by which the U.S. and foreign taxes paid by or on behalf of the expatriate are reconciled to the tax burden that would have been incurred if the employee had remained in the U.S. In this process, "windfall" gains are recovered from the employee . . . .

Thirteenth Month: Compensation bonus-type arrangement where one month's extra salary is paid once a year . . . .

Visas: In overseas countries, there are a variety of visa types and formalities as follows:

- **Dependent Visa:** permits a family to accompany or join employee in country of assignment.

- **Exit Visa:** permits a foreign resident to leave the host country.

- **Exit/Re-entry Visa:** permits a foreign resident to leave and then re-enter the host country . . . .

- **Multiple Entry Visa:** permits multiple entries to a country without the need to obtain a new visa each visit.

- **Single Entry Visa:** permits a one-time entry into a country. Another visa is required for any further visits.

- **Residency Visa:** permits entry and allows person to take up permanent residency in the country.

- **Work Permit:** authorizes paid employment in a country.

- **Work Visa:** authorizes entry into a country to take up paid employment.

White Book: issued to green card holders going outside the U.S. on an international assignment to document intent to return and remain as U.S. resident aliens. . . .

FIGURE 22.1   *(Continued)*

Source: Selected from Patrick V. Morgan, "Do You Speak the Language of International HRM?" Reprinted with the permission of HRNews (formerly Resource) published by the Society for Human Resource Management, Alexandria, VA.

other employers in the host country if U.S. wages are much higher)? Should they be paid the average of the going rate for the locality, or better than average? If some star performers emerge in this foreign plant or office, what are the opportunities for promotion within the firm, and perhaps to the head office in the United States? What compensation package should be offered to an American manager sent to one of these plants? What training should that person have before leaving? What assistance on returning? Or should a local national be promoted to the top job in the foreign plant? These are some of the questions with which international human resources management must grapple.

The cultural subtleties affecting IHRM may be the most challenging. For example, Tom's housing is not built for people over six feet tall. What should Tom do? What are the norms for making a suggestion or registering a complaint? What is the employer prepared to do, if anything? Tom was given some gifts on arrival. Does he reciprocate and give gifts in return and, if so, how expensive should they be? Does his employment and good relations with fellow trainers require that he spend many nights at the sushi bars?

Although the discussion in this chapter does not provide definitive answers to such dilemmas, it alerts the reader to some of the complexities of international human resources management. And awareness can be a stimulus to planning and preparedness, whether the individual involved is a supervisor or manager, a human resources specialist, or a new employee in a multinational corporation.

Multinational Corporations (MNCs)

It is clear that the **multinational corporation (MNC)** is playing an increasingly major role in the world economy; such a corporation is usually defined as *a company with operations in more than one country.*[2] Generally, this means that the company has significant assets in terms of plants and/or offices in one or more foreign nations and derives some of its profits from these operations.

Some of the factors cited in Chapter 3 as contributing to globalization are accelerating the development of MNCs. The drive toward a common market in Europe, the momentum toward ratifying a North American free trade agreement; and the end of the Cold War, along with the breakup of the U.S.S.R. into separate nations and the advance of eastern European nations toward democracy and free markets are all helping spawn MNCs. Other spurs to the growth of multinationals include India's rapid progress toward free enterprise, and China's movement by fits and starts toward the same goal;[3] Japan's commercial expansion in Southeast Asia;[4] and the spread of Korean business into Europe.[5] Additional strong stimuli favoring the rise of multinationals are joint enterprises between firms of the major industrial nations, innovations in communications and transportation, and the dissemination of management and technical knowledge.

The activities of some MNCs have an interesting twist. For example, the Ford Motor Co. is investing more than $1 billion in a plant in Valencia, Spain, to build small engines for cars that will be manufactured elsewhere in Europe. The engine was designed and developed for Ford by Yamaha of Japan.[6] Toyota Motor Corp. is building station wagons in Georgetown, Kentucky, for sale in its home country, Japan.[7]

Probably all of the five hundred largest industrial corporations in the world in terms of sales, as identified by *Fortune* magazine, are multinationals. Certainly, the

The movement toward globalization has created vast opportunities for employees of multinational corporations. And, in turn, the HRM role has become an international one.

largest companies in the countries having the most representation on *Fortune's* 500 list are multinationals. They include General Motors Corp. (United States), Toyota (Japan), British Petroleum Co. (Britain), Daimler-Benz (Germany), Elf Aquitaine (France), Volvo (Sweden), Samsung Group (South Korea), Nestlé (Switzerland) Broken Hill Proprietary (Australia), and Northern Telecom (Canada).[8] One needs only to drive a short distance on a main thoroughfare in a U.S. city to see products or advertisements from many of these MNCs: automobiles from Japan and Germany, gasoline and oil sold by a British company, chocolate from Switzerland's Nestlé, and so on. These organizations have significant assets in terms of plants and/or other facilities in the United States.

The number of MNCs of small or modest size is also increasing.[9] These companies face many of the same international human resources challenges as the larger firms. However, the large MNCs are likely to have well-developed programs managed by IHRM specialists such as managers of international human resources, managers who focus on expatriate compensation and benefits, and training people who manage **cross-cultural training** programs.[10] For example, Du Pont, with its twenty or more years of experience in cross-cultural training, recently developed comprehensive training activities for the South American and Asian Pacific regions. Du Pont's program includes "expatriate selection, predeparture training, assistance in settling in, ongoing cross-cultural team-building seminars, and repatriation counseling."[11]

Cultural Dimensions

In Chapter 4, organizational culture is defined as including values, beliefs, assumptions, myths, norms, goals, and visions that are widely shared in the organization. The term *culture* as applied to nations, regions, or ethnic groups has a similar meaning.

Expatriates face so many cultural differences that the term **culture shock** is often used to indicate the overall sense of difficulty in coping in a foreign locale and sometimes upon returning home as well. A manager transferred from a U.S. plant to one in another English-speaking country, such as Great Britain or New Zealand, may not have much trouble adjusting to modest differences in culture; yet even in these cases there may be some momentary shocks — like forgetting to drive on the left-hand side of the road, using incorrect procedures in placing a long-distance telephone call, or not handling a knife and fork in the manner of the local people. Sometimes the term *culture shock* is also used when employees move from one company to another in their own country, for organizational cultures can vary greatly, as we have seen. (The problem of blending business practices across national boundaries is sometimes referred to as "culture clash." See *International Perspective* on page 600.)

According to Philip Harris and Robert Moran, differences in culture — particularly national or ethnic culture — can be contrasted along ten dimensions.[12] The following list summarizes their findings:

- *Sense of self and space.* Self-identity and appreciation is shown by a humble demeanor in one culture, macho behavior in another. One culture emphasizes group cooperation, whereas another stresses independence and creativity. Americans like more physical space between individuals, while Latins and Vietnamese prefer to be much closer.

- *Communication and language.* Within any one language group there are different dialects, accents, slang, and jargon. Some nations have fifteen or more spoken languages. Various gestures have different meanings in different cultures.

- *Dress and appearance.* Garments and body decorations vary by culture. The Englishman's bowler and umbrella and the Polynesian sarong are examples. Suits worn for business and blue jeans worn by young people are seen across many cultures.

- *Food and eating habits.* Different cultures may have distinctive ways of selecting, preparing, and eating food. Beef, a favorite of many Americans, is forbidden in the Hindu culture, and pork, eaten extensively by the Chinese and others, is normally forbidden in Moslem and Jewish cultures or subcultures. The manner of eating also varies across cultures: in some eating with one's hands may be customary, whereas in others the rule may be to use chopsticks or a full set of cutlery.

- *Time and time consciousness.* The sense of time varies among cultures. Germans are precise about time, whereas Latins are more casual. In some areas of the world, people think in terms of spring, summer, fall, and winter; in some other areas, they may think in terms of rainy and dry seasons.

- *Relationships.* Family living arrangements vary from small to large, and there are often variations in the importance attributed to one sex or the other, or to age. For example, in a Hindu household, the mother, father, children, parents, uncles, aunts, and cousins may live under one roof. In some cultures, the accepted marriage relationship is monogamy (one spouse), whereas other cultures accept polygamy (one husband, several wives) or polyandry (one wife, several husbands). In some cultures, the elderly are honored; in others, they are ignored. In some cultures, women must wear veils and appear deferential, but in others they are viewed as equal or superior to men.

International Perspective

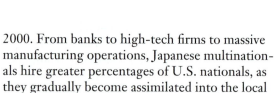

The U.S./Japanese HR Culture Clash

HR professionals who work for Japanese companies that have expanded into the U.S. market are adapting to HR management based on teamwork and loyalty.

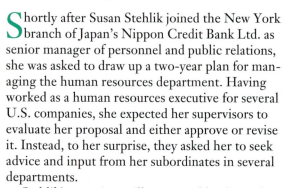

Shortly after Susan Stehlik joined the New York branch of Japan's Nippon Credit Bank Ltd. as senior manager of personnel and public relations, she was asked to draw up a two-year plan for managing the human resources department. Having worked as a human resources executive for several U.S. companies, she expected her supervisors to evaluate her proposal and either approve or revise it. Instead, to her surprise, they asked her to seek advice and input from her subordinates in several departments.

Stehlik's experience illustrates a blending of U.S. and Japanese business practices: Nippon was using Japanese shared decision-making — called *ringi* — to implement a written human resources management policy, which is a distinctly American phenomenon. The incident also shows how differently Japanese firms approach human resources management. In contrast with U.S. firms, in which leadership and direction tend to come from upper management, Japanese managers attempt to foster consensus on business decisions.

Human resources management is becoming a vital part of globalization for Japanese corporations. Because of the surge in Japanese direct investment in the U.S. during the last few years, the number of U.S. workers employed by Japanese subsidiaries in the U.S. also is increasing. Japanese direct investment in the U.S. is growing at an average rate of 35% a year, from approximately $5 billion in 1980 to $85 billion today, according to the U.S. Commerce Department's Bureau of Economic Analysis.

HR experts estimate that Japanese subsidiaries employ 350,000 U.S. nationals, and predict that the number could grow to one million by the year 2000. From banks to high-tech firms to massive manufacturing operations, Japanese multinationals hire greater percentages of U.S. nationals, as they gradually become assimilated into the local economies.

"There's no question that there has been a concentrated effort among Japanese firms here to increase the localization of the work force," says Alan Parter, president of Parter International Inc., a New York City-based consulting firm that advises companies on good corporate citizenship. Like other multinationals that are doing business in the U.S., he says, "these companies realize that to succeed, they need to become more American."

A greater proportion of the employees of large manufacturing operations tend to be local residents, while organizations in the service sector tend to have more Japanese expatriates on staff. At some of the Japanese automobile factories in the U.S., for example, more than 95% of the employees are U.S. nationals. In Japanese banks, on the other hand, generally only 25% to 40% of the employees are U.S. nationals.

At the heart of these changes is human resources management. Because Japanese companies traditionally approach personnel management differently from their U.S. counterparts, virtually all of them are finding that they must make changes to adjust to the U.S. business environment. Some pattern their human resources policies closely after U.S. models, while others retain many Japanese elements. But for many of these companies, HR management is in a state of flux, because they're still maturing as multinationals and only now are building a global work force.

Consequently, assimilation hasn't been easy. Some Japanese companies have drawn criticism for the way they handle employees who are U.S. nationals. Numerous sexual- and racial-discrimination suits have been filed against Japanese firms operating in the U.S. Another complaint is that the companies refuse to promote U.S. nationals to senior positions.

In response to such criticism, many Japanese government officials and executives are promoting *good corporate citizenship* as a way to ease tension between the U.S. and Japan. The term is used broadly to include HR management practices as well as community involvement and philanthropic donations. Because personnel management is one of the most visible aspects of a corporation, it can contribute to — or detract from — the company's image.

Japanese firms emphasize the team. Historically, the Japanese corporation has played a societal role that is different from that of the U.S. corporation, in that it supplies lifetime employment and social welfare for its employees. Although the tradition is changing, HR experts estimate that as many as 80% of the workers in Japan are given lifetime employment.* In addition, many Japanese companies provide housing and social activities for their workers, as well as day care and assistance in planning their children's education.

In Japanese firms, the emphasis is on the corporate team rather than on individual performance. Business decisions, for example, are made through consensus building, or *nemawashi*. Loyalty, rather than individual initiative, is rewarded by Japanese companies.

"The Japanese human resources system is based on the assumption that employees have a strong loyalty to the company, so that even if they aren't paid high wages in their younger days,

they'll work hard, because they know their future will be protected," says Yasaharu Yoneda, senior vice president for strategic planning at the New York City branch of the Industrial Bank of Japan. He says such long-term loyalty is difficult to cultivate among U.S. workers, who are accustomed to greater career mobility.

Many Japanese companies recognize the critical role of HR management in building their international business. "As a global bank, we need to have the best human resources we can throughout the world," says Yoneda, adding, "Among all the departments, human resources is the most important for the bank." Indeed, many Japanese corporate leaders do a stint in HR administration on their way to the top in their companies.

But Japanese companies see HR management less as a specialty or profession than as an important skill for all departments. "They don't really see HR as a science. They see it as something everyone needs to know for good management," says Michael E. Pilnick, who for four years was manager of training and development at Secaucus, New Jersey-based Matsushita Electric Company of America, and now is manager of training and development at Edison, New Jersey-based Sea-Land Inc.

U.S.-based Japanese subsidiaries frequently hire U.S. human resources professionals because they need seasoned local HR managers to be pathfinders or ambassadors between the Japanese headquarters and the local work force. These managers also must interpret the labyrinth of personnel laws in the U.S. Japanese companies face far greater legal constraints on human resources policies here, driving many of them to develop written policies for the first time.

*For a more conservative figure, see "Japan", p. 605

Source: Excerpted from Elizabeth Klein, "The U.S./Japanese HR Culture Clash," *Personnel Journal* 71 (November 1992):30–31.

- ■ *Values and norms.* What is valued varies among cultures. Whereas those operating at a survival level value the gathering of food and shelter, people in more affluent cultures may value luxuries and titles. Some place a high value on the acquisition of material possessions. However, in some Pacific-island cultures, the greater one's status the more one is expected to share possessions or to give them away.

Customs pertaining to gift giving, birth, death, marriage, showing respect, and expressing good manners also differ from culture to culture.

- *Beliefs and attitudes.* Religious beliefs and practices vary among cultures. Western culture tends to be largely influenced by Judeo-Christian-Islamic traditions. Eastern or Asian cultures, on the other hand, appear to be strongly influenced by Buddhism, Confucianism, Taoism, and Hinduism.

- *Mental processes and learning.* Different cultures reward and punish for learning or not learning certain information or learning or not learning it in a particular way. For example, the Germans stress logic, while the Japanese and the Navajo Indians reject this Western idea. Some cultures emphasize abstract thinking and conceptualizing, whereas others emphasize rote memorization.

- *Work habits and practice.* Cultures vary in terms of attitudes toward work, the dominant types of work, the division of work, and work practices, such as promotions and rewards. Some cultures have a particularly strong work ethic; in others it is less strong. Methods of giving praise range from presenting war bonnets to testimonial dinners, commendations, and medals.[13]*

Cross-cultural training for potential expatriates is vital in order to avoid mistakes and to minimize stress for both the individual and the family. A former manager of projects for Control Data in such diverse places as England, Iran, and Romania believes that most expatriate failures occur because of problems in adjusting to a particular culture. He says, "People aren't fired because they lack technical competence; they're fired because they can't get along."[14] Experts can provide training that is specific to a particular culture. Such training teaches many of the important "dos and don'ts" that the potential expatriate needs to be aware of. Figure 22.2 indicates a few of these cross-cultural dos and don'ts.

HRM Practices in Foreign Companies in the United States

Because of prevailing federal, state, and local laws and customs, HRM practices of foreign MNCs with plants and offices located in the United States tend to be similar to practices in American-owned companies. However, there are some exceptions.

Japanese managers in the United States, for example, are more likely to emphasize teamwork and consensus decision making than many of their American counterparts. The Germans are more likely to sponsor apprenticeship programs than are U.S. firms. To illustrate German practice, the Robert Bosch Corporation of Stuttgart, Germany has established three-year apprenticeship programs at its Charleston and Anderson, South Carolina, plants and at its New Bern, North Carolina, facility to train craft workers.[15]

Some practices have a negative side. Thus, U.S. citizens employed in management jobs in foreign plants or offices in the United States have frequently complained that they are not sufficiently included in policy decision making and are

---

Cross-cultural Dos

- Provide plenty of background information when working with Germans. They have a saying, "You have to start with Charlemagne," which means they require detail and a historical perspective on issues before feeling comfortable making decisions.

- Remember that the Japanese are interested in long-term relationships that generally are based on trust, friendship, service and quality, rather than price.

- Remember to use formal titles with the French until you've known them for a considerable length of time. The quick familiarity of Americans can be offensive to them.

- Realize that in Latin countries it isn't what you do that counts, but to whom you're related. Americans tend to rank each other by occupation, but Latin Americans will want to know who your father is. In Germany, on the other hand, credentials are what matter. Forget about the importance of being a "self-made man." It's where you went to school that counts.

- Offer a gift when invited to a Japanese home. Gifts must not be lavish, but in good taste and nicely wrapped. Don't use white wrapping paper, however. It's a sign of death.

- Feel free to make physical contact — a pat on the back, a long handshake or even a kiss on the cheek — with your associates in Europe and Latin America. These gestures are almost always acceptable in a business setting. On the other hand, in India and Pakistan, no type of touching is acceptable. People simply bow.

- Dress conservatively in Japan and avoid cologne and perfume. They aren't used in that country traditionally and could be offensive.

Cross-cultural Don'ts

- Don't ask a French person, "Where do you live?" or "What do you do?" It's similar to asking an American, "How much money do you make?"

- Don't suggest casually to a German individual, "Let's get together for lunch sometime," unless you mean it. Taking the comment literally, the German is apt to take out a calendar to schedule a time.

- Don't stand more than a foot away from a business associate in Saudi Arabia. Too much distance is a sign of rejection.

- Don't expect your Latin American counterparts to stick to an agenda or start meetings exactly at the scheduled time. They're more flexible with time and regard it as a long-term commodity.

- Don't make the mistake of not knowing whether a person you're working with in Czechoslovakia or Poland is aligned with the old communist system or the new generation of free enterprise. Values, goals and expectations between the two groups are apt to be very different.

- Don't say "no" to the Japanese. Because of their desire for saving face and maintaining harmony, Japanese people have an aversion to this word. To avoid being impolite, they'll either simply not respond, or they'll give an evasive answer such as "It's very difficult."

- Don't cross your legs or expose the heel of your foot during a business meeting in the Middle East. This gives the signal to your host that they're worthy of being stepped on.

- Don't hold up your hand, palms outward, in Africa. Such a gesture is considered rude and inappropriate.

FIGURE 22.2 Cross-cultural dos and don'ts

Source: Excerpts from Shari Caudron, "Training Insures Success Overseas," *Personnel Journal* 70 (December 1991):28, 29.

often barred from promotion. In 1990 only 31 percent of senior managers in Japanese subsidiaries in the United States were Americans.[16]

On the positive side, foreign plants in the United States are a source of innovative ideas about plant operations. To use just one example, the Toyota Motor Corp. installed cords that flash a light, signaling to a team leader that a worker needs help. If the problem is not resolved in one minute, the assembly line automatically stops. Most problems are solved within the minute; the line keeps running about 93 percent of the time.[17]

HRM Practices and Environment in Foreign Countries: Selected Examples

This section offers some illustrations of HRM practices and the HRM environment on the international scene. They are relevant in the sense that international managers and IHRM practitioners need to be alert to such matters as (1) what some of the expectations of local nationals might be, (2) issues of congruence or incongruity with company philosophy, (3) differing legal requirements around the world, (4) motivational and cost aspects of the differing practices, and (5) what foreign practices are particularly innovative and might have application in the United States.

However, there is no attempt in this discussion to evaluate individual practices. Any given HRM practice must be evaluated in terms of a specific organization's entire fabric of HRM practices, as well as in terms of the broader societal context in which it is found — especially its economic, legal, and cultural context. A seemingly bizarre or extreme practice might be perfectly understandable in this broader context. But, just because a practice is understandable does not necessarily mean it will be effective in the long run. The practice of "shaming" in China and the pattern of mutual favors and lack of performance review in state-run enterprises in Hungary are two such examples. Dictatorial practices in some plants in the former Soviet bloc of nations, or child labor practices in India will also have long-term adverse consequences in terms of labor relations and health.

In the ensuing pages, the varied practices of many lands are grouped according to the broad human resources processes described in earlier chapters. As we have seen throughout the book, many of these categories overlap.

HR Planning: Legislative and Labor Force Aspects

Great Britain   Like most of Europe, England does not have laws barring age discrimination, and it is common practice for employers to run ads seeking workers under the age of forty. Forced early retirement is common. However, some firms in Great Britain, as well as in France and Germany, are actively seeking "mature entrants."[18]

Sweden   Eighty-one percent of all women in Sweden are in the work force. They hold one-third of the supervisory jobs. Wage differences between men and women have narrowed considerably, but starting salaries are lower in "women's occupations."[19]

Germany   Skilled laborers from other countries — Polish metalworkers, Russian bricklayers, Czech welders, and Croatian mechanics — are working in German, French, Italian, and British factories for a fraction of the wages paid locals. Most send much of their hard currency home to eastern Europe.[20]

Italy   Italian organizations are facing a serious shortage of engineers and nurses. The health ministry has approved five thousand temporary employment contracts for Filipino and Polish nurses, provided they have similar qualifications as Italian nurses. To promote equality in the workplace, the Italians passed legislation in 1991 giving firms incentives to employ women.[21]

Switzerland   In 1990 foreigners made up 26 percent of Switzerland's total labor force and 55 percent of the labor force in the clothing, textile, leather, and shoe industries.[22]

Japan   The system of "lifetime employment," which up to now was enjoyed by about 30 percent of the work force — mostly male university graduates in large firms — is on the decline. Competition from MNCs is a major factor in this decline, and one result is the rapid growth of an executive search industry.[23]

Singapore   The government intends to seek stronger punishment for employers who illegally hire foreign workers. In 1989 a law made caning a mandatory punishment for employers who violated the law, but only illegal workers have been caned thus far.[24]

China   Although an "enterprise law" of 1988 gives managers ultimate decision making in management matters, many factory managers find it prudent to thrash out policies in a tripartite system involving the Communist party factory committee, union representatives, and management.[25] (On a visit to the U.S.S.R. just before the dissolution of the Soviet state, your author found the same kind of tripartite factory governance.)

India   It is estimated that over half of the world's child laborers are found in India. Although India's Parliament has passed a number of laws to prohibit child labor or to ameliorate conditions, poor families often have no alternative to employing children at home (cottage industries) or to making them available to exploitative employers.[26]

Pakistan   In 1988 total female participation in the work force, in terms of paid work, was between 4 and 6 percent. Traditionally, women are not permitted to seek work outside the home, except in family fields, which are deemed an extension of the home.[27]

Israel   The number of Soviet Jewish immigrants rose from 12,900 in 1989 to 184,400 in 1990. The immigration rate slowed during the Gulf War but increased afterward. This immigrant labor force is highly educated, has high technical knowledge, a high labor participation rate, and a high percentage of women workers.[28]

Job and Work Design

Canada   Work sharing is increasing as companies and employees take advantage of a program sponsored by the federal government. When production must be cut, an employee's hours can be reduced to as little as two days per week and the worker can claim unemployment insurance for the remaining three days for up to twenty-six weeks.[29]

Great Britain   Annualized hour systems, under which a worker's hours are calculated for a full year, are spreading and now include 6 percent of British employees. Such systems, negotiated with unions, give employees the security of a monthly paycheck, but permit flexible scheduling of five-day workweeks so that companies can operate seven days a week without paying overtime.[30]

Sweden   Self-directed work teams are commonplace in the Swedish auto industry — along with frequent job rotation and job enrichment.[31]

France   French unions objected to the strict appearance code Euro Disney applied to job candidates at its new theme park near Paris. Detailed rules pertaining to hair styles, jewelry, and clothing were made part of the terms of employment by the Walt Disney Company. It also made clear its expectations regarding cleanliness, illustrating them by means of a video shown to applicants.[32]

Russia   Russian factories are in the throes of redesigning assembly lines and jobs as they convert from the manufacture of military equipment to civilian production. For example, one large factory in St. Petersburg (formerly Leningrad) is shifting from making tanks to the production of oil-drilling equipment, machine tools, and steam irons.[33]

Japan   Japanese employees work much longer hours than workers in other industrial societies, but this pattern is shifting due to competitive pressures and changing attitudes of younger people. In 1992 a five-day workweek replaced a six-day one for public employees. By then, some 12 percent of private employers were already on this work schedule. About two-thirds of private employers had been partially moved to a five-day week by scheduling it once per month.[34]

A common mistake made by American managers in Japan is to divide up work into tasks and then to assign these segments to individuals. The Japanese prefer to assign work to groups and to let the group figure out how to carry it out.[35]

Another version of autonomy is Sony Corp.'s program of "self-promotion" in which enterprising engineers are encouraged to seek out projects of interest to them without informing their supervisors. If they can land a new position elsewhere in the company, the supervisor is expected to allow the transfer. Sony employs four hundred women engineers in Japan.[36]

Korea   In 1990 the average Korean worked 48.3 hours per week, an hour less than the previous year. The workweek has been declining in recent years; Korean workers once worked the longest hours in the world.[37]

Staffing: Recruitment, Selection, Transfers, Promotions, and Separations

Ireland   Part-time employment is a growing trend, accounting for seventy-two thousand workers in 1988, or nearly 8 percent of total employment. About twenty thousand workers are not covered by protective legislation (unemployment compensation, protection against unfair dismissal, maternity leave, and so on) because they work less than eighteen hours per week. Women constitute 80 percent of this group.[38]

Portugal   Dismissing employees is next to impossible because employers are required to defend dismissals as legal actions. Further, significant mandatory termination expenses are imposed in Portugal, as well as in other European Community countries. In Portugal, an employee aged forty-five, earning a salary of $50,000 (U.S.), and with twenty years' service would be entitled to $83,000 in statutory dismissal benefits.[39]

Malaysia   Malaysia attracts a large number of workers from Indonesia and the Philippines. Workers from Thailand are also employed in the northern part of Malaysia. A large number of Malaysians work in Singapore — perhaps as many as a hundred thousand — primarily in construction, manufacturing, and retailing. Some are supplied housing by their employers in Singapore, but large numbers commute daily between Johor Baharu and Singapore.[40]

Hong Kong   Hewlett-Packard Co. — one of the largest employers among some three thousand electronics manufacturers in the sixteen square miles of Hong Kong — is forced to pay high salaries to counter employee attrition and the high cost of living. To buy a two-bedroom apartment can cost $1 million.[41]

China   Although Chinese workers are supposed to have greater freedom in finding their own jobs than in the past, in practice there is little labor mobility because employers provide housing, health care, and retirement insurance, which can be lost or reduced by a move. Most students graduating from universities and demobilized soldiers are assigned jobs.[42]

Egypt   Egyptian law prohibits a private enterprise from dismissing a worker because of the company's financial difficulties or because of the employee's poor performance unless there is a lengthy probation and termination process in either case. In practical terms, government and public-sector workers cannot be terminated either.[43]

Training and Development

Mexico   In partnership with the Japanese firm Mazda Motor Corporation, Ford Motor Co. built a clone of a Mazda plant at Hermosillo, five hours by car from Tucson. Mexican workers were sent to Spain and Japan for training during the plant start-up. To become employed, the candidates — called *becarios*, or scholarship students — must pass a seven-week course with a grade of 80 percent or better. Workers are called "operators" or "technicians." Manufacturing productivity and quality are very high.[44]

France   As in Spain and Italy, worker training tends to be centralized through government policy. For example, French companies must pay a training tax based on the number of employees.[45]

After General Electric Co. took over the medical-equipment manufacturer Cie. Generale de Radiologie, GE held training seminars for the French company's European managers. Participants were urged to wear GE T-shirts emblazoned with the "Go for One" GE slogan to indicate they were "members of the team." The French managers wore the T-shirts at the seminar, but grudgingly. One French manager recalled: "It was like Hitler was back, forcing us to wear uniforms. It was humiliating."[46]

Germany   The German apprenticeship system annually enrolls 70 to 80 percent of the young people not destined for universities, and provides on-the-job and classroom training in 380 recognized occupations, covering some 20,000 different kinds of jobs found in Germany. Apprenticeships are generally for three years, and apprentices receive lower wages than fully trained craft workers.[47]

Japan   Each year, several hundred employees of Japanese firms have been sent to the United States and Europe to pursue MBA degrees, primarily to develop their understanding of Western business practices and their facility with the English language. Since the MBA degree is not particularly valued as an avenue of promotion within fairly rigid corporate structures, some returning MBAs look for better jobs. As a result, some companies have cut back on their sponsorships; others require employees to pay back tuition if they leave the firm within three to five years after returning.[48]

Although in 1986 the Japanese Diet (parliament) passed legislation barring sex discrimination in the workplace, only 1 percent of employed women held managerial jobs in 1991. Women constitute 40 percent of the Japanese work force.[49]

Morocco   A high proportion of clerical jobs are staffed by women, but increasingly "a cadre of high-powered women business executives" is appearing in Morocco — particularly in Casablanca. BCM, Morocco's largest private bank, employs some four hundred women, out of a total of about sixteen hundred employees. Its publications run regular features about the women executives and other female employees.[50]

Performance Appraisal and Review

Hungary   As a carryover from the previous Communist rule, there is little pressure for high standards of individual performance in state-owned enterprises. Some state enterprises have performance appraisal systems, but personnel directors find it difficult to persuade managers to carry out evaluations. This is changing in private enterprises, but the situation is confounded by the long-standing custom of supervisors awarding bonuses based on haggling with subordinates about job assignments. Any use of effective appraisals is vitiated by managers turning a blind eye to employee use of organizational resources and to absenteeism.[51]

Uzbekistan   During a visit there, I saw bulletin boards at factory entrances publicly scolding managers for inadequate performance. Banners urging workers toward higher productivity were evident throughout the factories visited.

China Shaming is used as a form of control over performance. The harshest level is "criticism," or the leader railing "against the worker's behaviors, character, and beliefs" in front of comrades.[52]

Compensation and Reward: Pay, Incentives, Benefits, and Informal Rewards

Canada On January 1, 1990, a pay equity act went into effect in Ontario requiring all private and public sector employers with more than five hundred workers to post plans for remedying pay inequalities between men and women.[53]

Mexico Because the Mexican minimum wage of 11,000 pesos, or about $4 per day, is so low, many MNCs voluntarily pay more. However, factory wages in Mexico — varying from an average of $2.99 per hour in Matamoros to $1.51 per hour in Piedas Negras — are so much lower than in the United States that the wage differentials are a matter of friction in U.S. management-employee relations, particularly when the wage differentials lead to a U.S. manufacturing plant moving to Mexico.[54]

European Community The European Court of Justice ruled in 1990 that European companies cannot set different pension benefits for women and men. The most impact is in Britain, where women receive full retirement benefits at age sixty and men at sixty-five. This ruling also affects MNCs with subsidiaries in Europe.[55]

At Midland Bank in Britain, and at Swift, a fund transfer network in Belgium, more men than women take advantage of company-sponsored daycare centers. Denmark Radio's parental leave plan allows fathers to take ten weeks off after the birth of a child.[56]

Belgium Workers are entitled to ten days of leave without pay to deal with family emergencies, such as the illness of a child.[57]

Sweden The average Swedish worker was absent for illness twenty-six days in 1988 and received full pay for all sick days. This absenteeism for illness compares with about fifteen days in the rest of Europe and ten to twelve days in the United States. Some of the larger Swedish firms report that it is not unusual for one-fourth of all employees to be absent on a given day.[58]

Hungary Workers are inclined to demand a bonus if asked to work on a task force that involves no overtime pay. As a result, managers hold back some bonus money to cover such demands.[59]

Russia Under Mikhail Gorbachev's regime, the general director of the Orekhovo-Zuevo Textile Factories Association decentralized the management of the association's sixteen factories, placed some three hundred engineers and technicians on a merit-pay scheme, and instituted a variable pay plan for employees based on output. Output and profits have grown, and wages, while low, are three times the average for industrial jobs in Russia. The general director and his managers "are eager to become controlling owners" under Russian President Boris Yeltsin's program of privatization of industry.[60]

Japan The basic compensation system for new regular employees is a monthly salary pegged to the person's level of educational attainment, not to job assignment.

The monthly salary rises automatically, at least once per year, on the basis of length of service rather than level of performance. It is also customary to pay bonuses twice a year, in June and December.[61]

Sumitomo Bank, Nomura Securities, and other financial institutions with offices in other countries offer special leaves for their young bachelor expatriates to return to Japan to court prospective brides. The bachelors usually work with the assistance of matchmakers, who arrange a series of meetings with prospects. Typically, the companies pay full roundtrip airfare for the first trip back to Japan, and if the first try is unsuccessful, half fare for a second trip.[62]

Singapore   The National Wage Council has been pressing firms to adopt "flexi-wage" systems under which annual wage increases are kept small and supplemented by a variable year-end bonus based on profitability and productivity.[63]

Indonesia   Social security, unemployment, and sickness benefits do not exist at the national level. Employers are expected to be responsible for the health and well-being of workers and their families.[64]

China   In a blend of Communism and capitalism, factories in Daqiuzhuang, a village of about 4,400 people near Tianjin, are so successful that the per capita income is ten times the national average. These factories are careful to track costs and use complex incentive systems, including piece rates. Unlike most villages, which have a Communist party secretary, a village leader, and plant managers, at Daqiuzhuang all three are combined in one person, who acts as the chief of a giant holding company.[65]

Australia   All Australians are entitled to an 85 percent rebate of medical fees based on schedules set by the government. They are also entitled to free admission and treatment in public hospitals. Corporations may supplement this coverage by buying private insurance based on a community rating principle, under which the insurer may not differentiate according to state of health, sex, or age.[66]

Morocco   Employees in Moroccan companies receive ten statutory holidays — some national, some religious. The national holidays are March 3, Throne Day; May 1, Labor Day; May 23, National Day; August 14, Saharan Provinces Day; November 6, Green March Day; and November 18, Independence Day. The religious ones are Eid al-Fitr (end of Ramadan); Eid al-Adha (feast of the lamb); Muslim New Year; and Idul Maoulid Annabaoui (the Prophet's birthday). More than one day off is customary for some of these holidays.[67]

Argentina   Because of inflation, minimum wages set by the government become irrelevant almost immediately. In June 1989 a tripartite commission set the minimum wage at 20,000 australs, which had a $62 (U.S.) value at that time. In September 1990 the commission raised the minimum by 3,500 percent.[68]

Turkey   Various fringe benefits (bonuses, premiums, meal allowances, and other payments) comprise about two-thirds of the total remuneration of Turkish industrial workers. Direct wages constitute about one-third.[69]

Labor Relations

Mexico   Strikes in 1992, such as the ones at the General Motors prize-winning plant in Ramos Arizpe and the Volkswagen AG plant in Puebla, are making Mexican officials suspect that U.S. unions are helping Mexican unions in order to raise the cost of manufacturing cars south of the U.S. border. U.S. unions deny helping to organize strikes in Mexico but do acknowledge providing financial aid.[70]

Germany   In 1992 the Public Workers' Union (OTV), which includes most flight attendants and ground-service personnel at Lufthansa A.G. airline, protested the airline's plans to cut as many as seven thousand employees from the payroll. The OTV insisted that Lufthansa first slim down bulging administrative and management payrolls.[71]

Denmark   It is estimated that 80 percent of all wage earners are organized into trade unions. Further, the labor market features a high level of vocational training, which includes both apprenticeship programs and the retraining of adult workers.[72]

France   French law requires all enterprises with fifty or more employees to have works councils. Through these councils, open to both union and nonunion members, employees are consulted on working conditions and on policies regarding company-financed recreation facilities.[73]

Poland   The government of Poland has called on managers of state-owned enterprises to dismiss striking workers who walked off the job before talks were concluded. The strikes are seen by the government as crippling its push to restructure enterprises and to move further toward a market economy. There is considerable ambivalence about firing strikers, however, because it was strike action in 1988 and 1989 that forced the Communist regime to relinquish power.[74]

South Africa   Job security is growing in importance to South Africa's unions in their negotiations with employers. Unions are increasingly insisting that all aspects of layoffs be negotiated, including training and dismissal packages. A marked rise in labor violence occurred in 1990, particularly in the form of striking workers' attacks on nonstrikers.[75]

Peru   While Peruvian law and the constitution guarantee freedom of association, freedom of collective bargaining, the right to strike, and freedom from compulsory labor, in practice it is very difficult to organize a union because of limitations and restrictions. For example, registration and government recognition are required.[76]

Safety and Health

Great Britain   Contract workers on North Sea oil rigs have been seeking union recognition from the major oil companies. Their campaign was spurred by a disastrous explosion on the Piper Alpha rig in 1988, in which a large number of workers lost their lives. The contract workers claimed that any workers questioning health and safety practices could be victimized because they had no union to speak for them. Campaign tactics included sit-ins on oil platforms during the summer and early fall of 1990.[77]

Ukraine Childhood thyroid cancer has accelerated from about four cases per year to about sixty in Belarus as a result of the 1986 explosion of the Chernobyl nuclear power plant. In the area first hit by radiation, Gomel, the thyroid cancer rate is about 80 times the world average.[78]

Japan Because company loyalty has traditionally been measured by how long one works each day and each week, many salaried workers may be literally killing themselves through heart attacks or strokes. The Japanese call this *karoshi* — meaning death from overwork. Related to this phenomenon is the extensive nighttime socializing of salaried workers. The government is now campaigning to reduce the workweek and to encourage a more balanced lifestyle. Major companies, such as Matsushita Electric and Sony, are requiring employees to take their full vacations.[79]

Employee Rights

Japan The first sexual harassment (called *saku-hara*) case won in Japan was against a small publishing company in 1991. A female employee claimed that her supervisor spread rumors about her alleged promiscuity and then fired her when she complained.[80]

Other issues relating to women's rights are emerging in Japan. For example, Hitachi Ltd. is facing a wage discrimination suit, in which nine women allege that men with similar histories of employment were paid 10 to 74 percent more. Sumitomo Life Insurance Company is defending itself against charges by two dozen women that the company delays the promotion of married women.[81]

Thailand Labor Department officials acknowledge that small businesses continue to violate flagrantly Thai worker safety and labor laws. In the Bangkok area, there are only two thousand inspectors responsible for tens of thousands of companies.[82] More than 200 people were killed and 500 injured in a 1993 fire in a Bangkok toy factory.[83]

Saudi Arabia A claim in U.S. courts by an American citizen that the Arabian American Oil Company (Aramco) discriminated against him on the basis of race, religion, and national origin was dismissed. The Fifth Circuit Court of Appeals ruled that Title VII of the Civil Rights Act, as amended, does not apply to U.S. citizens working in foreign countries for American companies.[84]

Organization Improvement

Canada Many Canadian, German, and Japanese firms, along with U.S. firms, have pursued total quality management (TQM) programs in recent years. (See Figure 22.3.) Although there have been many positive results overall, the United States, in particular, is lagging in some industries in terms of employee involvement and attention to customer satisfaction levels.[85]

Commonwealth of Independent States Some managers in the former Soviet Union doubt whether participative approaches can work in their countries. One manager said, "There has always been a priest, czar, bureaucrat, or apparatchik to tell people what to do."[86]

Japan New employees are taught that problems are "golden eggs": that it is good to identify problems, be "discontented" with one's job and company products,

Employee Participation TQM environments allow all employees to participate in helping achieve organizational quality goals. All employees are held accountable for quality and are given tools and training to fulfill this responsibility. TQM is based on the assumption that the employees closest to a particular organization's daily operating procedures are in the best position to understand and improve the quality of those procedures.

Brief History of Total Quality Management
Quality has always been an important element of competitive success. U.S. companies have traditionally used a combination of final inspections and post-production adjustments to ensure quality. Quality was generally not viewed as the responsibility of all employees, however. Specialization within U.S. companies separated the quality function from such areas as planning, design, production, and distribution.

Quality Management in Post-War Japan In contrast to the specialized approach traditionally used in the United States, a number of Japanese companies, rebuilding from post-war devastation, adopted an innovative, integrated approach to achieving quality. Several leading applied statisticians and quality experts — most notably Drs. W. Edwards Deming and Joseph M. Juran — introduced quality management principles to Japanese industry. The Union of Japanese Scientists and Engineers, a private organization formed by engineers and scholars, provided a forum for the widespread dissemination of statistical quality control techniques. In 1951 the group established the Deming Prize, with the intention of raising the quality levels of Japanese industry. Many of the management techniques developed since then form the foundation of the TQM principles that are gaining popularity in the United States today.

Total Quality Management in the United States Using an integrated approach to quality, a number of Japanese firms sharply improved their quality levels and began to penetrate U.S. markets. In the late 1970s and early 1980s, this enhanced competition stimulated attention in the United States to the role of TQM systems in activating quality improvement. U.S. companies began to seek out quality management experts to try to understand what was happening and to fashion an appropriate response. Many U.S. experts contributed to the understanding of quality management. Among these experts were Deming, Juran, Armand V. Feigenbaum, and Philip B. Crosby. We noted the increasing interest in TQM in our March 1988 analysis of the growing Japanese presence in the U.S. auto industry. In that report we noted that U.S. auto manufacturers, "reacting to competitive pressures . . . began to change the way they were doing business . . . . Many of the features which made the Japanese model a success are now being tried and implemented by U.S. automakers."

The increased interest in Japanese management methods was also accompanied by research in the United States that documented that firms can reduce their costs by improving quality. Quality management practitioners began citing the large, hidden costs that companies were incurring due to producing substandard products and services. These costs, known as the "cost of nonconformance," included appraisal, inspection, rework, and warranty fees as well as the cost of replacing customers driven away by poor quality. Some experts estimated that manufacturing costs could be reduced by over 30 percent simply by eliminating scrap and rework that occurs from correcting defects in the manufacturing process.

FIGURE 22.3   The pursuit of TQM

Source: U.S. General Accounting Office, *Management Practices: U.S. Companies Improve Performance Through Quality Efforts,* GAO/NSIAD–91–190, May 1991, pp. 10–11.

and seek constructive ways to improve them. In addition, there is a structured mechanism for expediting problem-finding activity. Workers are given problem-finding cards, on which they can write down whatever dissatisfies them about their jobs. Workers can then place these cards on a wall poster in the column marked "problems" so that others can see their "golden eggs." If other workers notice a problem posted that is of interest to them, they will join forces to help solve it.[87]

Summary and Role of the HRM Department

The IHRM aspects of human resources management in the multinational corporation obviously require a global perspective. The difference between domestic HRM and IHRM is one of complexity. This complexity affects all the major HRM processes.

There are many varieties of employment situations around the globe: foreign locals working for a U.S. plant or office abroad, American expatriates working for U.S. firms in foreign countries, foreign citizens working for U.S. firms at the U.S. headquarters, and so on.

Multinational corporations (MNCs), usually defined as companies with operations in more than one country, are growing in numbers and complexity. An example of this complexity is the Ford Motor Co. building an engine plant in Spain to produce engines designed by Yamaha of Japan for automobiles to be sold in Europe and the United States.

Expatriates may experience many cultural differences in such matters as the sense of self and space, communications and language, dress and appearance, food and eating habits, time and time consciousness, relationships, values and norms, beliefs and attitudes, mental processes and learning, and work habits and practice.

Foreign MNCs with operations in the United States are likely to have human resources practices similar to those of American-owned firms here. However, there can be differences along such dimensions as degree of participation, decision making, delegation, and opportunity for advancement. Foreign plants in the United States can be good sources of innovative ideas.

Both human resources practices and the environment in which they exist vary widely around the world. Some of the salient issues — areas of difficulty or controversy or areas of widely differing philosophy or practice — across many countries are as follows:

- Job security
- The recruitment and selection of qualified specialists and managers
- The status and rights of women and minorities
- Utilization of refugee and migrant workers
- Utilization of older workers
- Child labor
- Safety and health of employees
- Balancing work, leisure, and the family
- Flexibility in scheduling work
- The use of teams versus individual assignments
- The extent to which the government mandates employee benefits

- The extent to which businesses and governments support training and apprenticeship programs

- In eastern Europe and elsewhere, the kinds of HRM practices that will be tolerated and at the same time enhance the shift to democratic, market economies

Clearly, the HRM department and HRM professionals have many complexities and challenges to manage in IHRM. Here are just a few areas that require the attention and expertise of the HRM professional working in cooperation with other managers:

- *Human resources planning.* The laws of the host country pertaining to hiring, compensation, and termination must be followed.

- *Staffing.* Criteria for the selection of expatriates and foreign managers need to be developed. Decisions have to be made as to the balance between the use of local nationals and the use of U.S. managers.

- *Training and development.* Cooperation between the U.S. company and local educational and training institutions needs to be fostered. Strategies should be designed regarding the career paths and advancement opportunities of both expatriates and foreign managers and employees. Locals need to be trained in effective leadership and human resources practices. Potential expatriates and their families require cross-cultural training.

- *Performance appraisal and review.* Appraisal procedures should take into account local culture and history, but at the same time they must shift toward emphasis on performance, particularly in places where minimal performance has been tolerated.

- *Compensation.* The HRM professional must work with experts in international finance in developing compensation schemes that must balance a number of sometimes conflicting factors, including rapid shifts in currency values, local wage and benefit levels, moving and living costs for expatriates, and inflation.

- *Labor relations.* Besides complying with local labor law, expatriate managers must adapt bargaining strategies to local customs.

- *Safety and health.* It is important that HRM specialists and other managers adhere to or exceed U.S. standards when local standards are inadequate. Human resources are the organization's most important resources, regardless of national borders.

- *Organization improvement.* It is important to assume that people, in general, will want to help improve organizational effectiveness if they see and experience positive returns to themselves, their families, and their communities. Changing the culture of a given plant or facility will require patience, skill, and a shared vision.

Ethical Dilemma

Yankee Electronics is a large manufacturer of communication, television, radio, and vehicle electronic equipment. The company has plants in twelve countries — mostly countries with lower wage scales than in the United States. Yankee's human resources philosophy and practices in the United States are considered very advanced. Practices in Yankee's foreign plants are much more advanced than local practices, but this is not the case in many of the subcontractor plants with which these foreign plants do business. Safety practices are frequently abysmal, working hours excessive, and benefits absent or minimal. Worst of all, there is frequent use of child labor. Some managers and employees in the United States are starting to be concerned. Yankee Electronics has no direct control over the human resources practices of the foreign subcontractors. Further, to insist on higher standards could be politically awkward and could drive the costs of some Yankee products up to the point that some products might not be competitive in world markets.

Discuss this situation in terms of ethics. What, if any, responsibility does Yankee Electronics have regarding the welfare of employees in foreign subcontractor plants? For providing employment in its own foreign plants?

Key Terms

international human resources
   management (IHRM)
affiliate
expatriate
local hire

national
multinational corporation (MNC)
cross-cultural training
culture shock

Review Questions

1. What is the difference between HRM and IHRM?
2. What is an expatriate?
3. What are some of the key dimensions that can be used to contrast and compare different cultures?
4. What is meant by culture shock?
5. What might be some cultural problems faced by a local hire employed by a U.S. firm in Asia? What kind of training or other activities might assist local hires?
6. What might be some problems faced by an American working in a foreign-owned and foreign-managed plant or office located in the United States? What kind of training or other activities should the foreign company provide to minimize these problems?
7. What are some of the common HRM issues that appear in a number of countries around the world?

Opening Case Questions

Case 22.1 Tom Goes to Work in Japan

1. What problems did Tom face when he arrived in Japan?
2. How could Tom's Japanese employer have assisted him with some of these problems? What might Tom have done to prepare himself better?

Case 22.2 "Learning the Lines" in a Japanese Company

1. What norms did Tom experience in this company?
2. What norms and/or human resources practices being experienced by Tom were probably dysfunctional for the organization? Why? Which ones were probably useful? Why?

Comprehensive Case

Indirect Compensation Under the Guatemalan Labor Code

In the United States, we are used to relatively simple labor-management relations. The employer has to pay a minimum wage and contribution for Social Security and Unemployment Compensation, but most other obligations are a matter of contract, either with the union or with the individual employee. The Guatemalan Labor Code has the Government play a much greater role in labor-management relations.

For example, you hire an employee, Juan Perez, and agree to pay him 20 quetzales per day. If he is working full time, i.e. 5 or 6 days a week, his legal pay is 600 quetzales per month. Juan gets paid for Sunday even though he is not working. Saturday he works half a day for a full day's wages.

Even though you agreed to pay Juan by the day, he is entitled to an "incentive bonus" of 30 centavos per hour. If Juan works the statutory maximum of 44 hours per week, you would pay him an additional Q 57.60 per month, but it wouldn't be used to calculate his other benefits.

Sometime during the year, you are required to pay Juan's salary for 15 working days of vacation. Many companies have established a tradition of paying an additional 2 weeks bonus. If you establish this tradition, it becomes an "acquired right." Juan could win a case in court if, for example, earnings were down and you didn't pay him the bonus.

In December each year, Juan is entitled to a "Christmas bonus," i.e. an additional paycheck. This "aguinaldo" is as much of an obligation as the Q 20 you pay for each day, but again it isn't used to calculate his other benefits.

Social Security is much like the obligation in the United States. Almost everyone employed by a company is required to pay it. Juan pays 3 percent or 4.5 percent of his pay, depending on whether he works in an area which has a Social Security hospital. You pay 11.3 percent, i.e.

Q 67.80 per month for Juan who is earning Q 20 per day.

The new Law of Compensation for Time of Service is being challenged in court. The major issue is when it took effect. The law says you have to deposit an amount equal to 8.33 percent of Juan's monthly earnings in an account at the Banco de Trabajadores for Juan to withdraw when he leaves his job. You would be depositing Q 49.98 each month.

What if you close the company? Since this would be a matter outside Juan's control, he is being separated "unjustly." That means that Juan would be entitled to an additional month's pay for each year he worked. If you have provided any "economic benefits" like meals, bus service, etc., which employees normally pay themselves, the law says you have to add 30 percent to Juan's normal pay to compensate him for the loss of these benefits, i.e. Juan's monthly salary is Q 20 3 30 3 130 percent or Q 780. It doesn't matter that the actual cost of providing these services was much lower. If Juan had worked for you for 10 years, with "economic benefits," he would be entitled to Q 7886.67 in economic compensation. Any bonus you paid him, like the vacation bonus, would be added to his salary when the Government calculates the compensation. This debt takes precedence over all others.

The final "indirect benefits" is even more intangible. For example, what if your company is doing well and a group of employees organizes to request a raise. Knowing that would raise all of their separation pay [since separation pay is calculated on the last 6 months salary], you refuse. Juan can then go to the labor court with an "economic grievance." The court does not consider whether Juan is earning more than he would with the competition — it only looks to see if you have the economic means to pay him. If the court recommends you give Juan a raise and you don't, he then has a right to strike. If the strike is later found to be justifiable (using the same criteria about economic means), you have to pay Juan while he was on strike. If he decides to work during the strike, you have to pay him double.

For a comparison, let's look at what it costs an employer to hire John Doe in the United States for $20 per day (which means he could work only about 5 hours at the minimum wage) and the cost of employing Juan Perez in Guatemala for Q 20 per day. In the following we will assume that both are paid for 15 working days of vacation which is more than many Americans would receive.

Paid for one year's salary	$5200	Q 8526.40
Employers payment for Social Security	$738.40	Q 822.64
Compensation/Separation Pay	0	Q 1395.34

Source: *Guatemala*, American Embassy, Guatemala City, U.S. Department of Labor, Bureau of International Affairs, FLT 91–18, 1990, pp. 10–11.

Discussion Questions

1. What is your impression of the overall simplicity of managing human resources under the Guatemalan Labor Code?
2. What would you need to know and/or calculate, to have a good understanding of the advantages and disadvantages of operating a plant in Guatemala?
3. What kind of specialized assistance would you want to obtain, if any, if you were the plant manager of a U.S. firm working in Guatemala?

CHAPTER 23

Looking Ahead in Human Resources Management

LEARNING OBJECTIVES

- Explain the increased status of the modern human resources department.
- Characterize some of the current ethical issues faced by human resources directors.
- Identify the means by which human resources professionals can develop their careers.
- Describe future roles of the human resources department.
- Characterize some of the significant future directions in human resources management.

CASE 23.1   ## We've Got to Look to the Future

Karen and Frank King owned a rapidly growing firm that specialized in manufacturing stylish sports clothes. Between them, they handled all of the responsibilities of president of the company and chairman of the board. Business was good and was getting better. Karen and Frank had assembled a group of highly talented people in design, marketing, and manufacturing, and profits had grown steadily during each year of operation.

Karen and Frank had shared human resources management responsibilities since they started the business five years ago, but the firm was getting too large and growing too fast for them to devote sufficient attention to these matters. In particular, they realized that they were being less thorough in recruiting and checking references for professional and managerial people and that they were spending too little time making compensation and promotion decisions. So far, they had not made any major mistakes, but they were afraid they might. In addition, they realized they had not developed a statement about their management philosophy, nor had they developed a comprehensive set of human resources policies that could be applied uniformly in the organization. They had talked from time to time about hiring a human resources director, but their busy schedules had interfered with making a final decision in the matter.

Today they were having lunch together, and the conversation went like this:

"Frank, we've got to decide on the qualifications and hire a human resources director. We're not keeping up with the recruiting, let alone planning for the future."

"You're right, Karen, things are getting a bit haphazard in the people side of the business. We're doing lots of things without much thought. Mostly what we do seems to turn out all right, but I would have more peace of mind if we had someone to help us really think through a total human resources program."

"To pick up on that idea, Frank, I think it's probably crucial that we develop sound policies and practices that will take us where we think we'd like to be in the next, say, five to ten years. Maybe we should develop some ideas about what high-performing organizations in our business might look like in the future as part of an overall strategic plan and then hire a personnel director with the qualifications to help take us there." Karen then added, "But no matter whom we hire, that person has got to be committed to our philosophy about how people should be managed."

"I agree," said Frank, "but exactly what is our philosophy? I think we generally see eye to eye, but maybe it's time we tried to put our philosophy in writing. We need a draft of a statement that others could react to. Here's a suggestion: let's get our top staff members out of the office for a day sometime over the next two weeks and hammer out the first draft of a statement of philosophy and some broad guidelines about personnel policies and practices. Then we'll have some coherent statements about people management that we can use when we advertise and interview for our new human resources director. Once on board, the new person can suggest changes and help us refine our various policy and procedure statements."

Karen's response was immediate. "Let's do it," she said. ◄

CASE 23.2   The Retreat

In a regular meeting with all of the corporate officers and department heads — a total of eighteen people — Karen and Frank discussed their conclusions about the need to select a human resources director. Most comments were supportive and the only criticism was an implied "it's a move that is overdue."

Frank and Karen then proposed their idea of a retreat to develop a corporate human resources philosophy statement and some broad guidelines for human resources policies and practices. Their idea had now grown to a day and one-half meeting at a beach resort, starting at noon on a Friday, with work until early evening, followed by a social hour and dinner. Models would display some of the new sports lines after dinner. Discussions would continue at 8:00 the next morning, with adjournment at 4:00 p.m. Karen and Frank also indicated they might use a consultant they knew who was good at designing workshops and helping to run meetings.

It seemed to Karen and Frank that there was unanimous support for these ideas, and any complications centered on timing. "I don't see how we can all get away at the same time," one department head said. Another countered with, "Surely we can all donate a Saturday within the next few weeks, and also delegate running the organization for a Friday afternoon. Our subordinates might just like to get us out of their way for a while." "What if they don't want us back?" someone added, and was joined in laughter by the rest.

At the retreat, Karen and Frank made some brief opening statements, summarized as follows: "We believe we have an outstanding management team. We appreciate your being here and devoting this time. We hope you will be candid and participate actively. Let's try to work through any disagreements by consensus. And hopefully we can have some fun."

The consultant then divided the group into three heterogenous subgroups and gave them their first assignment: "Take flip charts, marking pens, and masking tape and go to separate rooms. Try to reach consensus on what kind of culture, climate, and relationships *you* want to have in this organization. Use short phrases. We're going to start with ourselves. Define culture, climate, and relationships any way you want. You have an hour and a half before you are to report back here. Appoint a spokesperson. Come back here to get coffee and tea or fruit juice whenever you want. Are there any questions?"

There was one question: "I suppose we'll agree on many things, but what if we do disagree on something?" The consultant answered: "That's OK. Try to resolve any differences, but when you can't, report on both sides of the disagreement. You don't need to identify who said what."

In an hour and a half, and after a short break, the subgroups reported to the total group. The major items on the three flip charts were as follows:

GROUP A	GROUP B	GROUP C
Openness	Cooperation	Listening
Customer focus	Contributions rewarded	Candor
Mutual support	Open door (anybody's)	Teamwork (ourselves and
Rewards for performance	Candor, no secrets	throughout Company)
A piece of the action	The customer is key	Withhold judgment on
Teamwork	Equal employment	creative ideas

GROUP A	GROUP B	GROUP C
Latitude to try new things	Good listening skills	Get out to see the customer
Consensus decision making	Team support	Rewards based on contribution
Valuing diversity	Organic characteristics	Informality
Informality	Strong support for innovation and creativity	Devil's advocate and options
Recognition for past contributions	Being goal oriented	Problems brought to team
Keeping an eye on the competition	Minimum of red tape	Fun
System 4T	Being training and development oriented	Evolution not revolution
	Participative (and more retreats like this)	Team skills
		Appreciating and capitalizing on diversity

Spokespersons for each group elaborated on each item. Evaluative comments from the total group were postponed until after all questions of clarification had been addressed.

"Well, what are your reactions?" the consultant asked the group. Several commented on the commonality across the groups. Some wanted further discussion of the meaning of some of the brief terms or phrases. Karen's reaction was, "This is great! There's a lot of agreement across the three groups." Frank concurred. "I'm really pleased at the similarity," he said. "Now we've got to take these general statements and figure out how to push forward."

"That's right," the consultant added. "I think the next step is to see if we can agree on a composite list, and see if there is anything we want to add. Then we'll have a framework for beginning to work on a statement of human resources philosophy. We can get a lot done by the end of the afternoon. Tomorrow we'll see if we can hammer out some specifics of what all of this means in terms of hiring, training, compensation, and so forth. And then, before we adjourn, we ought to spend some time talking about the implications for hiring a human resources director." ◄

The chapter-opening cases suggest that people in charge of organizations and of the human resources within those organizations need to give thought to the future and prepare accordingly. A conscious effort to anticipate change, instead of merely reacting to change as it happens, makes management a far-sighted, goal-oriented process in which careful analysis of significant trends within and outside the organization is a key component.

In Case 23.1, Karen and Frank are beginning to think seriously about which human resources policies and practices would help ensure the future success of their company. They realize that they would be the key architects of those policies and practices and that the need to develop a comprehensive human resources program could no longer be ignored. In addition, they recognize that this program must be coordinated with a clear statement of management philosophy and their strategic plans for the entire operation.

In case 23.2, the top management retreat reflects Karen and Frank's convictions that managers throughout the organization have a great deal of responsibility and control over both the quality of working life and the quality of human resources practices in a particular setting. The consultant's sequence of assignments reflects the consultant's belief that a good guide to developing a philosophy of human resources management for the organization might be the way they, as top managers, would like to be treated.

Implicit in both cases is the idea that management has a great opportunity and challenge to manage organizations in such a way that human needs and aspirations are met at the same time as economic, quality, and productivity objectives are met. In terms of the long-range success of the organization, these objectives are inseparable. And the extent to which all of these objectives are attained is a measure of how well the organization is performing as a whole.

Management — owners, managers, supervisors, and boards of directors — must pay careful attention to the effective use of human resources, along with financial, technological, and physical resources, if organizations are to achieve desired outcomes. At the same time, management must pay careful attention to the outside environment. The talent and motivation represented by the organization's human resources are the keys to how effectively the organization relates to that external environment and to how effectively financial, technological, and physical resources are used in the pursuit of organizational goals.

This chapter presents some ideas about how organizations over the next ten or twenty years will need to manage human resources to create this successful integration. First, the chapter summarizes the current importance and responsibilities of human resources departments and outlines job and career opportunities in the field itself. It then describes possible future roles for the human resources department and suggests the kinds of changes that might be anticipated in each of the major processes in human resources management.

The Modern Human Resources Department

As discussed in Chapter 2, the personnel, or human resources, department emerged around 1912, when several specialists were brought together in one department: the employment agent, the social or welfare secretary, the labor department specialist, the wage or rate clerk, the pension administrator, the safety director, the company physician, and the training specialist. It was an important department then; today it has even greater stature and importance.

Importance   Until about twenty years ago, human resources departments were perceived by many executives as performing routine support activities; now they are perceived as performing activities central to the ongoing health and vitality of organizations. Symptomatic of that shift in perception are the responses given in a nationwide survey cited in Chapter 21 of 785 opinion leaders, including corporate officers and human resources executives in some of the nation's largest firms, faculty and placement directors in major universities, leading consultants in management and human resources management, and editors of major business journals. The respondents were asked, "On the whole, how much importance would you place on human resources policies and practices as a factor in business success?" Of those interviewed, 92 percent answered "utmost importance," or "very important."[1]

In another study, eighteen chief executive officers were asked to rank four management responsibilities — financial, people, marketing, and operations — in order of importance. "People" received eight first choices, "marketing" five first choices, "operations" two, and "financial" one first choice. Two executives made no ranking.

One of the CEOs who made no ranking said, "There needs to be a proper balance between all four areas. All four areas are like vital organs of the human body. Who is to say that one is more important than the other to survival and good health?"[2] Although there is no question that all four areas are vital management responsibilities, the overall impression given by these interviews is that top management considers human resources management extremely important.

Responsibilities   Table 23.1 shows the activities for which personnel or human resources departments are typically responsible. This table reports the results of a survey in which human resources and employee relations executives in 599 organizations of all types were asked to indicate whether their department had sole responsibility, shared responsibility, or no responsibility for each of the 68 activities listed. A particularly good indication of the extent of personnel department involvement can be derived by adding the two columns "HR Dept. Only" and "HR and Other Dept(s)." After

TABLE 23.1   Human resource activities

Activity	Company Has Activity	(No. of Cos.)	RESPONSIBILITY FOR THE ACTIVITY IS ASSIGNED TO:[1]		
			HR Dept. Only	HR and Other Dept(s).	Other Dept(s). Only
Employment and recruiting					
Interviewing	99%	(597)	37%	60%	3%
Recruiting (other than college recruiting)	98	(584)	72	27	1
Pre-employment testing (except drug tests)	77	(460)	88	10	2
College recruiting	65	(391)	78	20	2
Training and development					
Orientation/induction	99	(593)	58	40	2
Skills training, non-management	96	(578)	22	51	27
Performance appraisal, management	96	(577)	50	45	5
Performance appraisal, non-management	96	(575)	48	48	4
Supervisory training	95	(569)	44	48	8
Management development	90	(539)	45	47	9
Tuition aid/scholarships	82	(492)	82	14	4
Career planning/development	73	(438)	46	49	5
Compensation					
Wage/salary administration	99	(590)	80	18	2
Payroll administration	97	(581)	27	32	41
Job descriptions	97	(580)	59	39	1
Job evaluation	95	(568)	64	34	3
Job analysis	92	(553)	72	27	1
Executive compensation	78	(469)	51	30	19
Incentive pay plans	70	(417)	45	41	14

TABLE 23.1   Human resource activities *(Continued)*

Activity	Company Has Activity	(No. of Cos.)	HR Dept. Only	HR and Other Dept(s).	Other Dept(s). Only
			RESPONSIBILITY FOR THE ACTIVITY IS ASSIGNED TO:[1]		
Benefits					
Vacation/leave processing	99	(595)	74	24	2
Insurance benefits administration	99	(592)	88	9	3
Unemployment compensation	98	(585)	87	8	5
Pension/retirement plan administration	94	(562)	71	22	6
Flexible spending account administration	56	(338)	79	16	5
Flexible benefits plan administration	51	(303)	81	15	4
Profit sharing plan administration	38	(229)	62	27	12
Stock plan administration	27	(162)	61	20	19
Employee services					
Recreation/social programs	87%	(524)%	58%	30%	12%
Employee assistance plan/ counseling	77	(459)	81	12	7
Legal services	72	(431)	16	32	53
Relocation services	69	(411)	77	18	5
Food service/cafeteria	66	(395)	36	8	56
Credit union	57	(341)	53	11	36
Outplacement services	54	(323)	93	7	1
Pre-retirement counseling	51	(306)	91	6	3
Child care center	8	(45)	51	9	40
Employee relations					
Disciplinary procedures	99	(592)	43	55	2
EEO compliance/affirmative action	97	(581)	88	11	1
Complaint procedures	96	(575)	54	44	2
Exit interviews	96	(574)	86	12	2
Award/recognition programs	94	(561)	66	29	5
Employee communications/ publications	93	(557)	42	40	18
Productivity/motivation programs	81	(483)	29	59	11
Suggestion systems	68	(405)	47	36	17
Attitude surveys	59	(354)	78	17	6
Union/labor relations	43	(260)	65	30	4
Personnel records					
Personnel recordkeeping	99	(595)	87	13	*
Promotion/transfer/separation processing	98	(589)	68	30	2
Human resources information systems	93	(560)	68	29	3

TABLE 23.1   Human resource activities *(Continued)*

Activity	Company Has Activity	(No. of Cos.)	HR Dept. Only	HR and Other Dept(s).	Other Dept(s). Only
			Responsibility for the Activity is Assigned to:[1]		
Health and safety					
Workers' compensation administration	99	(593)	76	13	11
Safety training/OSHA compliance	94	(562)	42	35	23
Health/wellness program	63	(376)	79	14	7
Drug testing	62	(372)	83	12	5
In-house medical services	51	(306)	63	12	25
Strategic planning					
Human resource forecasting/ planning	89	(532)	55	40	5
Organization development	82	(490)	38	51	11
Mergers and acquisitions	39	(232)	40	47	13
International personnel/ HR administration	20	(120)	73	18	9
Company operations					
Purchasing	97	(582)	4	8	88
Administrative services	97	(579)	17	20	64
Maintenance/janitorial services	95	(571)	8	6	86
Security/property protection	92	(550)	23	21	56
Public/media relations	90	(542)	16	24	60
Community relations/contribution programs	90	(538)	30	36	34
Risk management/business insurance	90	(538)	15	17	69
Travel/transportation services	87	(523)	10	13	77
Office/clerical services	73	(435)	24	28	48
Library	42	(254)	24	9	68

*Less than 0.5 percent.

[1]Percentages are based on companies providing data on where responsibility for the activity is assigned, as shown by the first column of numbers in parentheses. Percentages may not add to 100 due to rounding.

Source: Reprinted with permission from *Bulletin To Management* (BNA Policy and Practice Series), BNA Survey No. 57, pp. 2–3 (June 25, 1992). Copyright 1992 by the Bureau of National Affairs, Inc. (800-372-1033.)

Contemporary Issues

SHRM Code of Ethics

As a member of the Society for Human Resource Management, I pledge to:

- Maintain the highest standards of professional and personal conduct.
- Strive for personal growth in the field of human resource management.
- Support the Society's goals and objectives for developing the human resource management profession.
- Encourage my employer to make the fair and equitable treatment of all employees a primary concern.
- Strive to make my employer profitable both in monetary terms and through the support and encouragement of effective employment practices.
- Instill in the employees and the public a sense of confidence about the conduct and intentions of my employer.
- Maintain loyalty to my employer and pursue its objectives in ways that are consistent with the public interest.

- Uphold all laws and regulations relating to my employer's activities.
- Refrain from using my official positions, either regular or volunteer, to secure special privilege, gain or benefit for myself.
- Maintain the confidentiality of privileged information.
- Improve public understanding of the role of human resource management.

This Code of Ethics for members of the Society for Human Resource Management has been adopted to promote and maintain the highest standards among its members. Adherence to this code is required for membership in the Society and serves to ensure public confidence in the integrity and service of human resource management professionals.

Source: *Who's Who in HR, 1993 Directory* (Alexandria, Va.: Society for Human Resource Management, 1993), p. 5.

---

all, in actual practice the management of most human resources activities is shared to some extent between the human resources department and other managers, even when the human resources department is formally assigned the prime responsibility. By adding across, it is apparent that a very high proportion of HR departments had at least shared responsibility for most of the activities listed down to "company operations." HR involvement in general operations such as purchasing, maintenance, and transportation is relatively rare.

For another view of the role of the human resources department, see Figure 23.1. This is a position description for the top human resources position at Erie Insurance Group, a position currently having the rank of executive vice president. The position reflects the wide range of responsibilities typically assigned to the human resources department.

Current Ethical Issues

Ethics, as defined in Chapter 4 as a system of moral principles, is of considerable concern to human resources executives. In the 1991 survey cited in that chapter,

ERIE
INSURANCE
GROUP

EXEMPT POSITION DESCRIPTION		

<table>
<tr><td rowspan="8">POSITION INFO</td><td colspan="2">COMPANY TITLE
Division Officer - Human Resources</td><td>DATE
2-1-84 R</td></tr>
<tr><td colspan="3">FUNCTIONAL (GENERIC) TITLE
Division Officer</td></tr>
<tr><td colspan="3">INCUMBENT</td></tr>
<tr><td colspan="2">REPORTS TO (NAME/POSITION)
Chairman of the Board/President</td><td>E/P/A ☐
O/T ☐
S/P/M ☐</td></tr>
<tr><td>DIVISION

Human Resources</td><td>DEPARTMENT ☐
SECTION ☐
UNIT ☐</td><td>GRADE</td></tr>
</table>

BASIC FUNCTION	Responsible for developing, implementing, coordinating, and reviewing the ERIE's personnel policies, practices, procedures, and programs and the like. Specific personnel practices under the general direction of the incumbent are: recruitment, selection, orientation and placement of employees; compensation administration, employee relations, health and welfare, training and development, safety, security, communications, employee services, and all other related personnel functions.

PRINCIPAL FUNCTIONAL RESPONSIBILITIES

1. Directs and coordinates the implementation of all new and revised personnel policies, practices, procedures, programs, and the like in conformance with the ERIE's personnel philosophy and compliance with the letter and spirit of federal, state, and local law.

2. Monitors the day-to-day application of all personnel policies, practices, procedures, programs, and the like to assure uniformity and conformity to the ERIE's philosophy and compliance with the letter and spirit of federal, state, and local law.

3. Plays a key role in developing new or revising tne ERIE's personnel philosophy.

4. Develops or directs the development of personnel policies, practices, procedures, and programs consistent with the ERIE's and employee needs.

5. Implements or directs the implementation of all new and revised personnel practices to meet the needs of the ERIE and employees.

6. Keeps the Office of the Chairman and other executives informed of the effectiveness of present personnel policies and practices. Recommends changes as required. Keeps others informed as to the possible effects on the ERIE of developments and changes taking place in the nation, government, region, and the industry.

7. Supervises and coordinates the activities of personnel directing the functions of communications, employee relations, employment practices, education, compensation, employee welfare and related services.

8. Directs and maintains various managerial activities designed to maintain the division's personnel at a high level of cooperation with resulting operational effectiveness and efficiency.

9. Directs the preparation and maintenance of such reports as are necessary to maintain the activities of the Division. Prepares and presents reports to the Office of the Chairman, or others as requested or required.

10. Represents the ERIE on all employment practices inquiries, investigations, etc., when interacting with people not employed by the ERIE.

11. Directly or indirectly represents the ERIE in any types of negotiations involving or affecting personnel policies and practices.

12. See also "General Responsibilities for Management Positions."

FIGURE 23.1   Position description for a senior personnel administrator

Source: Designed by M.P. Eisert, Erie Insurance Group.

TABLE 23.2 The 10 "most serious" ethical situations reported by HR managers in the 1991 SHRM/CCH survey

Situation	PERCENT
Hiring, training or promotion based on favoritism (friendships or relatives)	30.7
Allowing differences in pay, discipline, promotion, etc., due to friendships with top management	30.7
Sex harassment	28.4
Sex discrimination in promotion	26.9
Using discipline for managerial and nonmanagerial personnel inconsistently	26.9
Not maintaining confidentiality	26.4
Sex discrimination in compensation	25.8
Nonperformance factors used in appraisals	23.5
Arrangements with vendors or consulting agencies leading to personal gain	23.1
Sex discrimination in recruitment or hiring	22.6

"Percent" is the percent responding with 4 or 5 on 5-point scale measuring "degree of seriousness" (5 = "very great").

Source: Reproduced with permission from *Human Resources Management 1991 SHRM/CCH Survey*, June 26, 1991 Part II, published and copyrighted by Commerce Clearing House, Inc., 4025 W. Peterson Ave. Chicago, Illinois 60646.

1,078 respondents — mostly human resources vice presidents or directors — found that the most serious ethical problems faced by today's human resources professionals have to do with managers making personnel decisions based on factors other than performance. Dealing with favoritism and bias was reported as the most serious ethical problem area.[3]

Table 23.2 lists the ten "most serious" ethical situations reported by these human resources managers. In addition to a number of these having potential legal consequences, we can predict that all of these ethical problems will give rise to perceptions of inequity on the part of other employees. In turn, these perceptions are likely to affect adversely both performance and morale, ultimately reducing the effectiveness of the organization. (See the discussion of equity theory in Chapter 5 and the model of organizational performance in Chapter 4.) Thus, a major, ongoing challenge for human resources managers is to develop and monitor policies and practices that reduce or eliminate such problems. Besides helping establish standards for ethical behavior, the human resources professional can also make a strong impact by pointing out the dysfunctional consequences of unethical actions. (See also *Contemporary Issues* on page 627 for the code of ethics of the members of the Society for Human Resources Management.)

Career Opportunities and Professional Development

The importance accorded human resources management and the lengthy list of activities in which most human resources departments are involved suggest that there are extensive career opportunities in the human resources field. The following sec-

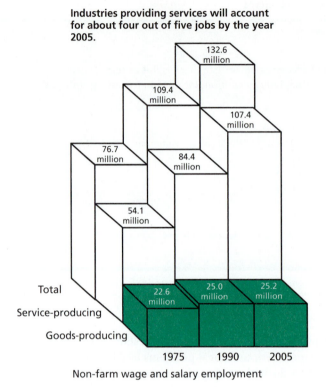

Industries providing services will account for about four out of five jobs by the year 2005.

132.6 million
109.4 million
107.4 million
76.7 million
84.4 million
54.1 million

Total
Service-producing
Goods-producing

22.6 million
25.0 million
25.2 million

1975   1990   2005

Non-farm wage and salary employment

FIGURE 23.2   Industries providing services will account for about four out of five jobs by the year 2005

Source: U.S. Department of Labor, *Occupational Outlook Handbook, 1992–93. Edition.* Bureau of Labor Statistics, Bulletin 2400, May 1992, p. 10.

tions describe employment opportunities and professional development opportunities available to those who wish to enter the field or add to their training.

Employment Opportunities   Some idea of the employment opportunities in human resources management can be obtained by looking at government projections of employment in this field and by examining the various specialties and typical entry jobs. Salary data may also be of interest.

The Bureau of Labor Statistics projects that through the year 2005 the number of specialists and managers in personnel or human resources, training, and labor relations will grow faster than the average for all occupations.[4] Overall, a large proportion of the growth in personnel jobs will be in the service-producing industries because these industries are expected to account for four out of five jobs by the year 2005.[5] (See Figure 23.2.)

TABLE 23.3 Specialties of the personnel and industrial relations field as defined by ASPA (now Society for Human Resource Management)

1. **Staffing.** Screening; interviewing; recruitment; testing; personnel records; job analysis; job description; staffing tables; promotion; transfer; job enlargement.
2. **Personnel Maintenance.** Counseling; personnel appraisal inventories; turnover; health services and accident prevention; employee benefits and services.
3. **Labor Relations.** Group relationships with organized or unorganized employees; negotiations; contract administration; grievances; arbitration; third-party involvement; mutual aid pacts.
4. **Training/Development.** Job training; supervisor and foreman training; managerial and executive development; pre-employment and special purpose training; retraining.
5. **Compensation.** Wage and salary surveys; incentive pay plans; profit-sharing; stock ownership; financial and non-financial rewards; job enrichment; wage and salary controls.
6. **Employee Communications.** House organ [company newsletter]; employment handbook; rumor control; listening; attitude; morale and expectation surveys; feedback analysis.
7. **Organization.** Structural design, planning, and evaluation; innovation; utilization of formal and informal; reducing conflict; overcoming resistance to organizational change.
8. **Administration.** Explanation and interpretation of options — authoritative, consultative, participative self-management styles; assistance in change.
9. **Personnel Policy and Planning.** Defining organizational goals; policy guidelines and strategies; identifying, translating, and complying with public manager policy; forecasting manpower needs; selecting optional courses.
10. **Review Audit Research.** Program reporting/recording; evaluation of policies and programs; theory testing; innovation; experimentation; cost/benefit studies.

Source: Gary B. Hansen, "Professional Education for Careers in Human Resource Administration," January 1984 issue of *Personnel Administrator*. Reprinted with the permission of HRMagazine (formerly Personnel Administrator) published by the Society for Human Resources Management, Alexandria, VA.

Specialties and Entry Jobs

Table 23.3 shows ten specialty areas within human resources management identified by the American Society for Personnel Administration (ASPA), which is now called the Society for Human Resource Management. In small organizations, human resources professionals are likely to be responsible for all or several of these areas. In larger organizations, there may be one or more specialists for each area. For example, in the staffing area, large organizations are likely to employ interviewers, test specialists, college recruiters, and job analysts. In the employee communications area, there might be an editor for the company magazine and one or more people who specialize in writing handbooks and manuals. Specialties may be combined in various ways. For example, trainers employed in the training unit might also write and edit special publications, such as employee benefit pamphlets or handbooks on safety.

There is no single entry job in human resources management; the type of entry job depends on the size of the organization. Typical entry-level positions are employment interviewer, personnel assistant, job analyst, and training specialist. If the job of employment interviewer is any indication, there should be substantial opportunity for securing entry-level positions over the next decade.

Organizations show no definite pattern of recruiting from within or from outside in filling entry-level personnel jobs. It is clear, however, that additional work experience and education can give an applicant an edge over those with less experience and/or education.

Salaries

Salaries for human resources management jobs vary greatly, depending on such factors as the number of employees in the organization, type of industry, the level of responsibility, the specialist's level of education and amount of experience, whether the person has international as well as national responsibilities, and geographic location. For example, a 1991 survey sponsored by the Society for Human Resource Management found human resources executives in companies with more than 10,000 employees averaging $158,000 in base salary and $203,000 in total compensation. Those in companies with fewer than 250 employees earned an average base salary of $92,000 and $105,000 in total compensation. (Total compensation includes base salary plus bonus.) The highest compensation for human resources executives was in Silicon Valley of California and in New York City. Compensation averaged substantially lower in Tampa and Indianapolis.[6]

A survey by the same organization a year earlier found human resources executives in the wholesale/retail trade to be the highest paid. Their total compensation averaged $158,000; 95 percent of these executives were eligible for bonuses. In contrast, those in service and nonprofit organizations averaged $83,000 in total compensation, partly reflecting the fact that only 40 percent were eligible for bonuses.[7]

The particular assignment of human resources specialists also influences pay. Another 1990 study found the median annual income of training directors to be $50,351; benefits supervisors, $39,827; and recruitment and interviewing specialists, $35,572.[8]

Development of Human Resources Professionals

There are many avenues by which one can further one's career or professional standing in the human resources management profession. Career-development opportunities are available through academic training, attendance at professional association meetings and seminars, accreditation by a professional agency, and reading professional journals and books.

College and University Courses

A high proportion of colleges and universities offer courses in human resources management, and many schools offer majors or fields of concentration in this area at the undergraduate or graduate level. A survey of 130 members of the Personnel/Human Resources Division of the Academy of Management, whose members are mostly professors in business schools, found that 77 percent of the schools responding offered one or more personnel and industrial relations courses at the undergraduate level, and 65 percent offered one or more courses at the graduate level.[9] The human resources or personnel management major typically includes additional specialized courses, such as wage and salary administration, recruitment and selection, and training and development. Courses in such disciplines as psychology, sociology, statistics, and labor law are frequently recommended as electives.

Professional Associations and Seminars

Professional associations allow persons who are active in the human resources field to keep up with current trends and developments through conferences, publications, seminars, workshops, and research projects. The Society for Human Resource Management, with more than eighty thousand members, is one of the largest

Associations such as the Society for Human Resource Management provide a forum for HR professionals to net-work and keep up with current trends in the field. In addition, the organization has student chapters at colleges and universities.

professional associations to which human resources professionals may belong. This organization has chapters in all fifty states and the District of Columbia, Guam, and Puerto Rico, as well as in Bermuda, the Virgin Islands, Canada, Korea, and Mexico. There are chapters in most metropolitan areas throughout the United States, as well as student chapters at nearly 230 colleges and universities in most of the states and in the District of Columbia and Puerto Rico.[10]

Another example of a large professional association is the International Personnel Management Association (IPMA), which draws its membership largely from human resources professionals in municipal, county, state, and federal government employment. IPMA has both individual memberships and agency memberships. Personnel professionals in some 1,100 government agencies are members by virtue of agency membership. IPMA has about fifty chapters throughout the nation.

Still another large professional association, the Industrial Relations Research Association, tends to focus on labor-management relations, but many of its sessions and reports overlap or are relevant to the broad field of human resources management. The IRRA has fifty-six local chapters across the United States, two in Canada, and one in France. There members meet with colleagues from private, public, and federal organizations, college and university faculties, and with third-party neutrals. Other professional associations, such as the American Society for Training and Development and the American Compensation Association, tend to draw their memberships from particular specialties within the field.

Most of these associations hold national or regional conferences annually; their local chapters may meet more often. Most sponsor or cosponsor conferences abroad from time to time. Most of them also offer specialized one- to three-day seminars. The American Management Association, various private consulting firms, and many colleges and universities also offer seminars on both general and specialized aspects of human resources management.

Accreditation   **Accreditation** is a way of recognizing a specified level of competence within a particular field. The Human Resource Certification Institute (HRCI) — formerly the Personnel Accreditation Institute — was incorporated in 1975, after three years of research and development by a task force established by the American Society for Personnel Administration (now the Society for Human Resource Management). The purposes of the accreditation, as described in the original PAI handbook, are as follows:

- To recognize individuals who have demonstrated expertise in particular fields
- To raise and maintain professional standards in the field
- To identify the body of knowledge as a guide to practitioners, consultants, educators, and researchers
- To aid employers in identifying qualified practitioners
- To provide an overview of the field as a guide to self-development[11]

The HRCI has two levels of accreditation: professional in human resources (PHR) and senior professional in human resources (SPHR). Passing a comprehensive examination is a requirement for both designations. In addition, the PHR designation requires four years of professional human resources experience at the exempt level, or two years professional service and a bachelor's degree, or one year of professional service and a graduate degree. The SPHR designation requires eight years of professional exempt experience, or six years professional experience and a bachelor's degree, or five years professional human resources experience and a graduate degree.

Journals   There are many respected journals that allow both human resources professionals and other managers to add to their store of knowledge about human resources management. These journals are an important source of timely information about changes and developments in the field, and men and women making career decisions may find it useful to browse through some of them.

Here is a sample of some well-known journals that specialize in human resources management:

- *ACA Journal* (American Compensation Association)
- *Arbitration Journal*
- *British Journal of Industrial Relations*
- *Compensation & Benefits Management*
- *Compensation and Benefit Review*
- *Employee Benefit Plan Review*
- *Employee Relations Law Journal*
- *HRfocus* (formerly *Personnel*)
- *HRMagazine* (formerly *Personnel Administrator*)
- *HRNews* (formerly *Resource*)
- *Human Resource Management*
- *Human Resource Management Review*
- *Human Resource Planning*
- *Industrial and Labor Relations Review*
- *Industrial Relations*
- *Industrial Relations Journal*
- *Industrial Relations Law Journal*
- *International Journal of Conflict Management*
- *International Journal of Human Resource Management* (United Kingdom)
- *Journal of Collective Negotiations*
- *Journal of Individual Employment Rights*
- *Journal of Industrial Relations* (Australia)
- *Journal of Management Development* (United Kingdom)
- *Journal of Occupational and Organizational Psychology* (United Kingdom)
- *Labor History*
- *Labor Law Journal*
- *Monthly Labor Review*
- *Occupational Health & Safety*

- *Occupational Outlook Quarterly*
- *Personnel Journal*
- *Personnel Management*
- *Personnel Management Abstracts*
- *Personnel Psychology*

- *Personnel Review* (United Kingdom)
- *Public Personnel Management*
- *Training: The Magazine of Human Resources Development*
- *Training and Development Journal*

Numerous business and management publications periodically include articles on human resources management or articles that are highly relevant to the field. Some of these are as follows:

- *Academy of Management Executive*
- *Academy of Management Journal*
- *Academy of Management Review*
- *Across the Board*
- *American Journal of Sociology*
- *American Psychologist*
- *Business Horizons*
- *Business Week*
- *California Management Review*
- *Fortune*
- *Group & Organization Studies*
- *Harvard Business Review*
- *Human Relations*
- *Journal of Applied Behavioral Science*
- *Journal of Applied Psychology*

- *Leadership & Organization Development Journal*
- *Long-Range Planning*
- *Management Review*
- *National Productivity Review*
- *OD Practitioner*
- *Organization Development Journal*
- *Organizational Behavior and Human Decision Processes*
- *Organizational Dynamics*
- *Sloan Management Review*
- *Supervision*
- *Supervisory Management*
- *The Wall Street Journal*
- *Work and Occupations*
- *Working Woman*

Future Roles of Human Resources Professionals

A recent survey of 615 top executives in both industrial and service companies of various sizes found that product quality, service quality, and productivity were the most critical competitive issues facing their firms. When asked to rate ways of strengthening competitiveness, 50 percent chose internal management actions, including educating and training employees, over public policy changes such as trade regulation or tariffs. When asked to elaborate on means of improving quality, the executives rated highly motivation, changes in corporate culture, and employee education. Clearly, these are human resources issues and have important implications for future roles of human resources professionals.[12]

To achieve a progressive, innovative culture within the organization — and to cope with the critical challenges that the future might bring — human resources professionals are likely to assume certain roles with greater frequency, in addition to managing the many activities shown in Table 23.1. These emerging roles are the consultant-adviser role, the catalyst-facilitator role, the diagnostic role, and the assessment role. The roles overlap.

<table>
<tr><td>

The Consultant-Adviser Role
</td><td>

A crucial role that overlaps the others is the **consultant-adviser role**. In particular, the top human resources executive will increasingly play a major role in advising the CEO and the top management team about the human resources implications of broad organizational strategy, both nationally and globally.[13] Further, the human resources department will be called upon more and more to advise management at all levels about the motivational, morale, and legal implications of various present and proposed policies and practices. Finally, as pressures for heightened quality and productivity intensify, the human resources department can help ensure that management remains aware of the need to protect, develop, and reward organizational members appropriately.
</td></tr>
</table>

The Catalyst-Facilitator Role

The human resources director has a unique opportunity to serve in a **catalyst-facilitator role** in stimulating a top-management discussion about management philosophy, leadership style, and organizational culture and climate. It is important that management develop a clear view of these interrelated matters and that management be self-conscious about them on an ongoing basis. If these areas are not consciously examined and managed, the organization and the people in it can become victims of dysfunctional values, beliefs, assumptions, myths, norms, and practices rather than being masters of these dimensions. The human resources director is the logical person to make these dimensions priority concerns of top management. In addition, the human resources director can serve as a resource person about these concepts and their links to organizational outcomes such as effectiveness, efficiency, development, and participant satisfaction.

The Diagnostic Role

Increasingly, human resources professionals are expected to be experts in the **diagnostic role;** that is, they are expected to identify the underlying causes of an organizational problem as distinct from its symptoms and to come up with solutions — or systems for solving the problem — that correspond with the diagnosis. All too often, programs of various kinds, like MBO, job enrichment, incentive systems, quality circles, and so on, are proposed by managers or human resources people and then "bought" as quick cures without consideration for their effects on existing systems and on other aspects of organizational life. What is usually needed is an accurate description of the problem to be solved, a careful analysis of the dynamics of that problem, and a close look at alternative solutions and their ramifications before a program is implemented.

The Assessment Role

One of the most difficult roles for human resources professionals is the **assessment role,** in which they assess the effectiveness of various human resources policies and practices. A comprehensive evaluation of the effectiveness of an organization's human resources policies and practices is called a **human resources management audit** or personnel management audit. At least three kinds of measurements can be used regularly or as part of a comprehensive human resources management audit: (1) informed management judgment, (2) perceptions of employees, and (3) statistical and cost analysis.

Among the most valuable sources of information in the evaluation of human resources programs are the informed reactions and judgment of supervisors and managers. Simply asking supervisors and managers how a particular program or practice is going and what might be done to make it better can be an extraordinarily valuable way of evaluating and improving programs. Such measurement needs to be systematic and thorough enough so that the human resources department does not rely on the impressions of just one or two managers. Similar means of measurement are questionnaires or a series of interviews soliciting employees' perceptions of the impact of particular practices or programs.

A statistical or cost analysis of other practices can also be very useful. For example, a company might wish to analyze the relative merits of recruiting professionals through campus visits and through newspaper advertisements and interviews in large cities. Only careful analysis will reveal some of the hidden costs of some practices or outcomes. An illustration is Wayne Cascio's analysis of the costs of absenteeism. Hidden costs include substantial losses in supervisory salaries resulting from time spent managing problems of absenteeism, such as instructing replacement employees and counseling and disciplining absentees.[14] A comprehensive human resources audit might use all of these methods and analyze a wide array of human resources practices and outcomes.

Summary: Future Directions in Human Resources Management

It is projected that in the near future effective human resources management will move in the specific directions noted further in this section. Already evident in some of the world's leading organizations,[15] these directions, viewed together, constitute a fabric of mutually reinforcing philosophies, policies, and practices.

By and large, these directions are consistent with the discussion in Chapter 4 of Burns and Stalker's notions of an organic system (with an appropriate balance of mechanistic characteristics depending on the technology) and Likert's concept of a System 4T. In the latter, we need to recall, the "T" stands for "Total model," which includes high performance goals and high technical competence. *The thrusts listed below must be made in the context of high standards of performance and increasingly innovative and excellent technology if they are to succeed and be sustained.*

There is always a risk that these directions will be abandoned when an organization's top leadership changes or when top management is faced with a major crisis. In times of crisis, top managers sometimes revert to autocratic, punitive, or adversarial behaviors, which tend to destroy trust. High trust between people is indispensable in high-performance organizations.

The human resources executive and the human resources department will have a major co-leadership role in these directions:

Leadership Philosophy and Style

- A simultaneous focus on technology, the customer, and the social system of the organization
- Top management clarifying and developing management philosophy, examining its own leadership style, and setting an example for both effective teamwork and "staying close to the customer"
- More appreciation of diversity in the work force and in management
- An accelerated shift toward participative team-leadership styles
- Supervisors and managers at all levels becoming better listeners, coaches, and participative problem solvers

- Increased delegation to effective teams (intact work teams with a formal leader, self-managed teams, task forces, cross-functional teams, and so on)
- Boards of directors taking a more active interest in these matters

Internationalization

- More expertise pertaining to the language and culture of host countries
- More expertise in the subtleties and complexities of effective human resources practices in other countries (see *International Perspective* on page 639).

Human Resources Planning

- More linking of human resources planning to the strategic planning processes of the organization
- Careful attention to demographic and legal trends

Job Design and Work Rules

- Increased application of alternative forms of work schedules, such as flextime, telecommuting, permanent part-time work, and peak-time employment
- Designing work to capitalize on effective team and interteam creativity and cooperation
- Reconceptualizing the roles of supervisors to emphasize expediting, coordinating, coaching, and training
- More effective use of people with disabilities

Staffing

- Intensified attention to the employment, utilization, and career development of a diverse work force
- Greater understanding of and attention to career transitions, including entry, promotion, transfer, and separation
- More openness and information about the various staffing processes (for example, more frequent use of job posting and career ladders)

Training and Development

- Increased training in group and leadership skills for supervisors, managers, and teams at all levels
- Increased training in statistical quality control and statistical process control

Performance Appraisal and Review

- More emphasis on participative goal setting and ongoing interaction about progress
- More attention to team goal-setting and review processes

Compensation and Benefits

- Extensive application of gainsharing plans
- Increased emphasis on developing bias-free job evaluation methods
- Increased use of skill-based pay
- Revitalization of suggestion systems and a shift toward team rewards
- Increased employee stock ownership
- Rapid spread of employer-sponsored or subsidized daycare centers
- Increased attention to family-care benefits, including unpaid leave
- Major attention to controlling health care costs — health care, in particular — and increased use of flexible benefits programs
- More attention to equity in the compensation and benefits of part-time employees

International Perspective

In Search of Today's Euro-Executive
Successful Euro-executives won't fit into the traditional mold.

As U.S. companies expand into Europe, they are facing a new staffing challenge — how to hire the Euro-executive.

A recent study of 200 HR managers and other executives found that 54 percent of the surveyed companies are looking to expand into Western Europe within the next five years.

These executives see the challenge of staffing European operations as a major issue. Some 46 percent cited barriers such as culture and language, and 38 percent expressed concern about their ability to find qualified nationals.

Euro-Executive

What are the characteristics of a successful Euro-executive?

For many companies, Europe is an uncharted frontier. While it is often possible to create a standardized manual for opening new offices in Cincinnati, San Diego or Portland, the exact opposite is true in Europe. Thus, the Euro-executive thrives on breaking new ground.

Of course you do not want the kind of executive who sets his or her sights on a goal and lets nothing interfere with the plan for achieving it. Flexibility of thought and behavior is critical.

A successful Euro-executive relishes the idea of absorbing one or more cultures and designing new procedures that match the needs of each situation. Because European-based executives are more likely to have their far-away — and sometimes exotic — activities heavily scrutinized by a home office that prefers the way things have always been done, they also must carry a lion's share of courage to defend their convictions.

HR's Role

One challenge HR will face is convincing management that it cannot apply the rules of hiring for a relatively homogeneous environment, as exists in the United States, to the job of recruiting for the loosely knit confederation of divergent cultures that make up Europe.

While a complete and carefully developed job description leads to finding a better candidate under any conditions, it is absolutely crucial to finding the right Euro-Executive.

As you work with management to write these descriptions, be prepared to indicate when a mix of operational responsibilities does not make sense from a people-skills standpoint. For example, when companies start new offices, it is common to ask executives to wear several hats until growth reaches a certain critical mass. This happens because Americans seldom comprehend the complexity of managing in mixed cultures. Consequently, international staffing requests often have so many requirements of expertise and cultural knowledge that no one individual could ever meet them all.

Take, for example, a U.S. executive who opens a new Atlanta office for the company and oversees both sales and operations. Her region covers a six-state territory, and manufacturing is done in yet another state. She travels two-thirds of the time. In addition, she is required to understand the English language and American labor law.

Now look at her European counterpart. He opens an office in France. His sales territory includes Italy, Germany and the United Kingdom. His manufacturing is done in Spain. He travels two-thirds of the time. In addition, he is required to understand five languages and cultural mores, and the labor laws of two countries.

Thus, HR must convince management to write a very detailed job description for each European position so that you can research the multi-cultural requirements and return with an assessment of the practicality of the position as defined.

What may be very practical in the United States can be a design for failure abroad. As the human resource manager, you can play a major role in preventing such mistakes.

Source: Max Messmer, "In Search of Today's Euro-Executive." Reprinted by permission of publisher, from *Personnel*, July/1991 © 1991. American Management Association, New York. All rights reserved.

Labor Relations
- Increasing numbers of comprehensive, cooperative labor-management programs focusing on employee involvement in quality, productivity, and quality-of-work-life matters
- NLRB and/or congressional affirmation of the legality and necessity of a wide range of employee-involvement programs

Employee Rights
- More and more commitment to the concept of organizational due process
- Continued and enlarged protections pertaining to race, national origin, sex, age, lifestyle, and disability status under the Civil Rights Act and related legislation
- More and more organizations voluntarily adopting rules to protect employee privacy and to prevent misuse of employee records
- More and more enforcement of prohibitions against all forms of harassment — particularly sexual, age, ethnic status, national origin, religious, and lifestyle harassment

Safety and Health
- Increased attention to workplace safety and health hazards
- Increased skill and attention in confronting substance-abuse problems
- Rapid growth in employee assistance programs
- Heightened attention to protecting the rights of AIDS victims
- Growth in wellness programs

Organization Improvement
- Greater understanding of the systems ramifications that must be managed in organizational improvement efforts
- More successful integration of various kinds of participative improvement strategies, such as OD, QWL, and TQM
- Greater use by human resources professionals of participative, action research methods in keeping their own departments at peak effectiveness to better assist the total organization

What lies ahead for all managers in the area of human resources management is exciting and demanding. The personal and career rewards will be high for those managers and human resources professionals who can help their organizations weave the fabric of policies and practices necessary for a high quality of work life and successful competition. The broader context is the rapidly changing world.

Ethical Dilemma

CEO Anita Kelley has endorsed the concept of self-managed teams in the company's factories. She wasn't too keen on the concept, but urging from the manufacturing vice president and industry reports of successful applications convinced her. The human resources vice president had reservations, but did not voice them out of fear of being perceived as resistant to change. Explanatory meetings, chaired by the vice president of manufacturing, were held with middle managers in the factories, followed by a series of meetings with supervisors, chaired by selected middle managers. In effect, supervisors were told to delegate more decision making to employees and to take on more of a coaching role. There was little training beyond that. Some effective self-managed teams emerged over the first six months of the program, but there was a great deal of confusion and resistance on the part of both supervisors and employees. Middle managers were less than enthusiastic, though not openly resistant, in progress meetings with the manufacturing vice president.

What are the ethical issues in this situation, if any? Assuming that self-managed teams would be desirable in this company's factories, what processes or steps might be followed to give the concept more chance of success?

Key Terms

ethics
accreditation
consultant-adviser role
catalyst-facilitator role

diagnostic role
assessment role
human resources management audit

Review Questions

1. What are the reasons for the increased status of the human resources department?
2. What are several of the most serious ethical issues faced by human resources executives?
3. Identify ways in which human resources professionals may enhance their professional development.
4. Describe several future roles that seem to be emerging for human resources professionals.
5. Identify at least one significant future direction, as noted in this chapter, in each of the major human resources processes.

Opening Case Questions

Case 23.1   We've Got to Look to the Future

1. Why does Karen bring up the company's philosophy when she talks about hiring a human resources director and implementing a human resources program?
2. Which one of the emerging roles for human resources professionals — consultant-adviser, catalyst-facilitator, diagnostic, and assessment — is likely to occupy the most time of Karen and Frank's soon-to-be-hired human resources director in the immediate future?

Case 23.2   The Retreat

1. What are some of the common themes across the three subgroups in terms of the culture, climate, and relationships that the participants would like to have in the organization?
2. Discuss how each of these themes could be related to some policy or practice in human resources management.

Comprehensive Case

Managing Diversity

Most organizations' efforts to increase diversity in their work forces began as responses to societal and governmental pressures. Worried about the possibility of lawsuits or loss of federal contracts, companies tried to hire new recruits based on affirmative action guidelines. While such policies opened the door for many women and members of minorities who had been shut out before, they did not solve the underlying problem: the vast majority of people in control of the country's organizations continued to be white males.

Today the attention that organizations pay to diversity has shifted, in response both to the successes and problems of affirmative action programs and to the changing demographics of the United States. Most organizations now recognize that simply hiring minority employees does not ensure a diverse work force. Without changes in the organization's structure and culture, women and minority members often get stuck at the lower levels of the organization and choose to leave in disproportionate numbers. So organizations already committed to becoming more diverse have begun focusing on making their cultures more supportive of diversity. They have also started opening the doors of the corner offices and boardrooms to those who have traditionally found them shut.

Many organizations that responded to affirmative action grudgingly are now realizing that creating a more diverse work force is not just the politically correct thing to do but also makes good business sense. In fact, consultants on work force diversity stress that employees are likely to support diversity only if they see that it is consistent with a company's business goals. Evidence of diversity's positive effect on business abounds: companies sell more successfully when their employees' age, sex, and race match their customers'; input from a wide range of people helps make better decisions than input from a homogeneous group; innovation flourishes when ideas are drawn from a diverse group of people; and women and minority employees are more productive when they do not feel isolated and estranged from the people around them. The American population is becoming older, and nonwhites will become a majority in the next century. Organizations not prepared for these demographic changes will be at a disadvantage.

Faced with these realities, organizations are scrambling to find ways to manage diversity — to make a diverse work force a strength rather than a problem. A major step for many companies is to recognize that they must undergo a radical cultural change, and that such a change must be led by managers at all levels. Many companies now regularly enroll all employees in programs that teach them to confront their own prejudices, understand the value of diversity, and try to see the world from other perspectives. Avon, for instance, sends a racially and ethnically diverse group of 25 managers at a time to the American Institute for Managing Diversity at Morehouse College, where for three weeks they confront their differences and learn to listen to other viewpoints. Levi Strauss invests $5 million each year in a program titled "Valuing Diversity," which includes a three-and-a-half-day workshop for senior managers. Burger King has sent all 170 senior managers and 700 employees at its headquarters through a three-day basic training in diversity awareness.

To help management deal sensitively and productively with diversity issues, many organizations have also established multicultural advisory groups. Avon calls its group the Multicultural Participation Council. U S West has eight employee resource groups, organized by employees who share backgrounds or interests, such as Native Americans, veterans, gays and lesbians, and people with disabilities.

To address specifically the difficulty many women and minority employees have faced in rising above a certain level, some organizations establish incentives for upper managers. Xerox Corp. holds division and group managers accountable for meeting diversity goals for upper-level jobs. Managers at U S West who promote only white males or in other ways do not support the company's pluralism efforts may lose their bonuses or see their salaries fall. U S West also looks to its employee resource groups to provide lists of candidates ready for advancement. Recognizing that holding one of a number of key positions seems to be almost a prerequisite for managerial advancement, many companies have started ensuring that women and minority members get a better shot at such important jobs.

Perhaps the most telling insight about managing diversity has come from Xerox. Studying how its managers could better manage diversity, Xerox found that the real problem was not training managers to work with minorities; the managers needed to improve their skills in managing *anyone*. So what started out as a desire to help the company deal with a diverse work force should translate into an improvement in management across the board.

Sources: Lawrence M. Baytos, "Launching Successful Diversity Initiatives," *HRMagazine* 37 (March 1992):91–97; Shari Caudron, "U S West Finds Strength in Diversity," *Personnel Journal* 71 (March 1992):40–44; Alice Cuneo, "Diverse by Design," *Business Week Reinventing America 1992*, p. 72; R. Roosevelt Thomas, Jr., "From Affirmative Action to Affirming Diversity," *Harvard Business Review* 68 (March–April 1990):107–117; and Lena Williams, "Scrambling to Manage a Diverse Work Force," *New York Times*, December 15, 1992, p. A1.

Discussion Questions

1. What factors are persuading many companies to inaugurate "managing diversity" programs?
2. What are some of the components of diversity programs?

NOTES

CHAPTER 1

1. Howard V. Hayghe, "Volunteers in the U.S.: Who Donates the Time?" *Monthly Labor Review* 114 (February 1991):17–23.
2. Margaret Magnus, "Personnel's Increasing Management Role," *Personnel Journal* 68 (February 1989):6; Roy Foltz, Karen Rosenberg, and Julie Foehrenbach, "Senior Management Views the Human Resource Function," *Personnel Administrator* 27 (September 1982): 37–50; and American Society for Personnel Administration, "The Changing Role of the Human Resource Professional," *1984 ASPA Annual Report*, p. 7.
3. "'Human Resources' Gains as a Function Title," *Resource*, January 1986, p. 2; Edward F. McDonough III, "How Much Power Does HR Have, and What Can It Do to Win More?" *Personnel* 63 (January 1986):19; and Donna Brown, "HR is the Key to Survival in the '90s," *Personnel* 68 (March 1991):5.
4. David Ulrich and Arthur Yeung, "A Shared Mindset," *Personnel Administrator* 34 (March 1989):38–45.

CHAPTER 2

1. Frederick Winslow Taylor, *The Principles of Scientific Management* (New York: Harper & Brothers, 1919), Copyright © 1911, pp. 21–37, 130.
2. Frank B. Gilbreth, *Motion Study* (New York: Van Nostrand, 1911).
3. Lillian M. Gilbreth, *The Psychology of Management* (New York: Macmillan, 1914).
4. E. Dorothea Pround, *Welfare Work* (London: G. Bell and Sons, 1916), p. 5.
5. Henry Eilbirt, "The Development of Personnel Management in the United States," *Business History Review* 30 (Autumn 1959):349.
6. Ibid., pp. 348–349.
7. Hugo Münsterberg, *Psychology and Industrial Efficiency* (Boston: Houghton Mifflin Company, 1913), pp. 63–75.
8. Ibid., Chapter 10. For further discussion of Münsterberg, see Frank J. Landy, "Hugo Münsterberg: Victim or Visionary?" *Journal of Applied Psychology* 77 (December 1992):787–802; and Merle J. Moskowitz, "Hugo Münsterberg: A Study in the History of Applied Psychology," *American Psychologist* 32 (October 1977):824–842.
9. B. Von Haller Gilmer, *Industrial Psychology* (New York: McGraw-Hill, 1961), pp. 21–22. For more on the history of industrial-organizational psychology, see Raymond A. Katzell and James T. Austin, "From Then to Now: The Development of Industrial-Organizational Psychology in the United States," *Journal of Applied Psychology* 77 (December 1992):803–835.

10. Howard W. Johnson, "The Hawthorne Studies: The Legend and the Legacy," in Eugene L. Cass and Frederick G. Zimmer, eds., *Man and Work in Society* (New York: Van Nostrand Reinhold Company, 1975), pp. 273–275.
11. F. J. Roethlisberger and W. J. Dickson, *Management and the Worker* (Cambridge, Mass.: Harvard University Press, 1939); and T. North Whitehead, *The Industrial Worker* I-II (Cambridge, Mass.: Harvard University Press, 1938)
12. Sanford Cohen, *Labor in the United States* (Columbus, Ohio: Charles E. Merrill, 1960), p. 70.
13. Ibid., p. 449.
14. Foster Rhea Dulles, *Labor in America*, 2nd rev. ed. (New York: Thomas Y. Crowell, 1960), pp. 126–149.
15. Ibid., pp. 150–165.
16. Arthur A. Sloane and Fred Whitney, *Labor Relations*, 4th ed. (Englewood Cliffs, N.J.: Prentice-Hall, 1981), p. 91. See also *Business Week*, May 6, 1961, pp. 90–91.
17. Dulles, *Labor in America*, pp. 195–196; and George S. Gibb and Evelyn H. Knowlton, *The Resurgent Years, 1911–1927: History of Standard Oil Company (New Jersey)* (New York: Harper & Brothers, 1956), p. 136.
18. *Business Week*, September 3, 1979, pp. 26–28.
19. Paul P. Van Riper, *History of the United States Civil Service* (Evanston, Ill.: Row, Peterson, 1958), pp. 96–112.
20. Ordway Tead and Henry C. Metcalf, *Personnel Administration* (New York: McGraw-Hill, 1920).
21. Eilbirt, "The Development of Personnel Management," p. 352.
22. C. V. Carpenter, "The Working of a Labor Department in Industrial Establishments," *Engineering Magazine* 25 (April 1903):1–9.
23. F. W. Taylor, "Shop Management," *Transactions*, American Society of Mechanical Engineers, 24 (1903):1399–1404.
24. William F. Willoughby, *Workingman's Insurance* (New York: Thomas Y. Crowell, 1898), p. 282.
25. Thomas G. Spates, *Human Values Where People Work* (New York: Harper & Brothers, 1960), p. 73.
26. Louis A. Boettiger, *Employee Welfare Work: A Critical and Historical Study* (New York: Ronald Press, 1923), pp. 127–133.
27. Gibb and Knowlton, *The Resurgent Years*, pp. 572–577.
28. Abraham B. Shani and Ord Elliott, "Sociotechnical Systems Design in Transition," in Walter Sikes, Allan Drexler and Jack Gant, eds., *The Emerging Practice of Organization Development* (Alexandria, Virginia: NTL Institute for Applied Behavioral Science; and San Diego, California: University Associates, 1989), p. 188.
29. Wendell L. French, *The Personnel Management Process*, 6th ed. (Boston: Houghton Mifflin Company, 1987), pp. 652, 653.

CHAPTER 3

1. Susan E. Shank, "Women and the Labor Market: The Link Grows Stronger," *Monthly Labor Review* 111 (March 1988):6.
2. U.S. Department of Labor, *Occupational Outlook Handbook, 1992–93*, Bureau of Labor Statistics, Bulletin 2400, May 1992, pp. 8, 9.
3. *Working Age*, American Association of Retired Persons, Special Issue 1991, p. 6.
4. *Fortune*, April 20, 1992, p. 20; and Michael W. Horrigan and James P. Markey, "Recent Gains in Women's Earnings: Better Pay or Longer Hours?" *Monthly Labor Review* 113 (July 1990):11.
5. Howard N. Fullerton, Jr., "Labor Force Projections: 1986 to 2000," *Monthly Labor Review* 110 (September 1987):19–29. See also *New York Times*, April 11, 1991, p. A14; and *Business Week*, December 21, 1992, pp. 29–30.
6. *Occupational Outlook Handbook*, p. 9.
7. Joel Dreyfuss, "Get Ready for the New Work Force," *Fortune*, April 23, 1990, p. 165; and *Working Age*, 1991, p.1.
8. William F. Rothenbach and Alan G. Rash, "Difference in Work Force Expectations," *Personnel Administrator* 29 (May 1984):122–128.
9. Richard E. Walton, "Criteria for Quality of Working Life," in *The Quality of Working Life*, ed. Louis E. Davis and Albert B. Cherns (New York: The Free Press, 1975), 1:91–104.
10. Ibid., p. 93.
11. Ibid., pp. 94–95.
12. *Fortune*, February 12, 1990, pp. 44–54.
13. *New York Times*, December 7, 1992, p. A4; *New York Times*, September 18, 1992, p. C5; *New York Times*, September 21, 1992, p. A1; Carla Rapoport, "Europe Looks Ahead to Hard Choices," *Fortune*, December 14, 1992, pp. 144–153; and Louis R. Bechtel, "Traveling in the European Superstate," *Across the Board* 28 (April 1991):53–54.
14. *Fortune*, April 19, 1993, pp. 95–102.
15. *Los Angeles Times*, December 18, 1991, p. 1.
16. See *Business Week*, March 16, 1992, p. 134; *New York Times*, December 9, 1991, pp. A1, A4; and *Business Week*, April 15, 1991, pp. 46–58.
17. *Fortune*, April 22, 1991, p. 14.
18. Koh Sera, "Corporate Globalization: A New Trend," *Academy of Management Executive* 6 (February 1992):89.
19. *New York Times*, May 16, 1991, p. C3.
20. See *New York Times*, September 17, 1992, p. 1.
21. *Seattle Post-Intelligencer*, September 22, 1988, p. 4.
22. *Fortune*, April 22, 1991, pp. 157–164.
23. *New York Times*, September 16, 1992, p. A8.
24. *Fortune*, December 17, 1990, p. 121; and *Business Week*, October 28, 1991, pp. 120–121.
25. *Wall Street Journal*, October 2, 1992, p. B8.
26. *Occupational Outlook Handbook*, pp. 10–11.
27. *New York Times*, December 30, 1991, p. C3; and *Fortune*, June 1, 1992, p. 171.
28. *Business Week*, March 4, 1991, pp. 60–61; and Arthur Neef and James Thomas, "International Comparisons of Productivity and Unit Labor Trends in Manufacturing," *Monthly Labor Review* 111 (December 1988):27–33.
29. *Fortune*, February 25, 1991, pp. 72–84. See also *Wall Street Journal*, August 12, 1992, p. A1.
30. *Fortune*, October 19, 1992, pp. 54–55.
31. Douglas L. Fleuter, *The Workweek Revolution*, (Reading, Mass.: Addison-Wesley, 1975), pp. 73–75.
32. *Fortune*, February 11, 1991, p. 113; and *Fortune*, May 20, 1991, pp. 113–114.
33. *Fortune*, April 9, 1990, pp. 56–62. See also *Chicago Tribune*, May 28, 1991, sec. 3, p. 1.
34. *Monthly Labor Review* 107 (August 1984):39.
35. Bureau of National Affairs, *Labor Relations Reporter*, Special Supplement to Vol. 138, No. 11, November 11, 1991, pp. S1–S19.
36. Section 201–210, Civil Rights Act of 1991, as approved by the House and Senate, November 7, 1991.
37. *Wall Street Journal*, March 21, 1991, p. B1.
38. David Israel and Greg McConnell, "New Law Protects Older Workers," *HRMagazine* 36 (March 1991):77–78.
39. U.S. Department of Justice, Civil Rights Division, *The Americans with Disabilities Act: Questions and Answers*, Office of the Americans with Disabilities Act, 1991, p. 1.
40. Ibid., p. 3.
41. U.S. Department of Justice, *Handbook for Employers: Instructions for Completing Form 1–9*, Immigration and Naturalization Service, May 1987.
42. Amy M. Nice, "Skilled Workers Find Easy Access," *Personnel* 68 (March 1991):3–4.
43. U.S. Department of Labor, Wage and Hour Division, "Regulations, Part 4: Labor Standards for Federal Service Contracts," WH Publication 1267, rev. October 1986, p. 35.
44. *Monthly Labor Review* 107 (April 1984):48.
45. Paul D. Staudohar, "New Plant Closing Law Aids Workers in Transition," *Personnel Journal* 68 (January 1989: 87–90.
46. Leonard Saxe, Denise Dougherty, and Theodore Cross, "The Validity of Polygraph Testing," *American Psychologist* 40 (March 1985):356.
47. Bureau of National Affairs, *Bulletin to Management* 39 (June 30, 1988):1.
48. Drug-Free Workplace Act of 1988 (Subtitle D of Anti-Drug Abuse Act of 1988).

CHAPTER 4

1. *Fortune*, April 22, 1991, p. 67.
2. Fremont E. Kast and James E. Rosenzweig, *Organization and Management: A Systems and Contingency Approach*, 4th ed. (New York: McGraw-Hill, 1985), p. 14.
3. "The Toughest Job in Business: How They're Remaking U.S. Steel," *Business Week*, February 25, 1982, p. 53.
4. Based on the definition in *The American Heritage Dictionary of the English Language*, 3rd ed., Boston: Houghton Mifflin Company, 1992. See also Richard

T. DeGeorge, *Business Ethics*, 3rd ed. (New York: Macmillan Publishing Company, 1990), pp. 14–18; Manuel G. Velasquez, *Business Ethics: Concepts and Cases* (Englewood Cliffs, N.J.: Prentice-Hall, 1982), pp. 6–7; and William A. Wines and Nancy K. Napier, "Toward an Understanding of Cross-Cultural Ethics: A Tentative Model," *Journal of Business Ethics* 11 (November 1992):831–841.

5. Commerce Clearing House, "1991 SHRM/CCH Survey," *Human Resources Management* service, June 26, 1991, p.1.

6. Douglas McGregor, *The Human Side of Enterprise* (New York: McGraw-Hill, 1960), pp. 33–34, 47–48.

7. Ibid., pp. 35, 43–49; see also Warren Bennis, "Douglas McGregor's *The Human Side of Enterprise*," *New Management* 3 (Summer 1985):60–61; and James O'Toole, *Vanguard Management* (Garden City, N.Y.: Doubleday, 1985), p. 98.

8. From *Hewlett-Packard Statement of Corporate Objectives*, October 1987 (pamphlet).

9. John P. Kotter, *A Force for Change: How Leadership Differs From Management* (New York: The Free Press, 1990), pp. 4, 5.

10. Ibid., p. 7.

11. See Ricky Griffin, *Management* (Boston: Houghton Mifflin Company, 1984), p. 421.

12. See Shelley A. Kirkpatrick and Edwin A. Locke, "Leadership: Do Traits Matter?" *Academy of Management Executive* 5 (May 1991):48–59.

13. Edwin A. Fleishman and Edwin F. Harris, "Patterns of Leadership Behavior Related to Employee Grievances and Turnover," *Personnel Psychology* 15 (Spring 1962):43–44; Robert L. Kahn, "Productivity and Job Satisfaction," *Personnel Psychology* 13 (Autumn 1960):275–287; and Robert R. Blake and Jane S. Mouton, *The Managerial Grid* (Houston: Gulf Publishing, 1964).

14. Jay W. Lorsch and John J. Morse, *Organizations and Their Members* (New York: Harper & Row, 1974); and Fred E. Fiedler and Martin M. Chemers, *Leadership and Effective Management* (Glenview, Ill.: Scott, Foresman and Company, 1974).

15. Robert Tannenbaum and Warren H. Schmidt, "How to Choose a Leadership Pattern," *Harvard Business Review* 36 (March–April 1958):95–101.

16. Ibid. For more on leadership, see Edwin P. Hollander and Lynn R. Offermann, "Power and Leadership in Organizations," *American Psychologist* 45 (February 1990):179–189; Harold J. Leavitt, *Corporate Pathfinders* (New York: Penguin Books, 1987); Warren Bennis and Burt Nanus, *Leaders: The Strategies for Taking Charge* (New York: Harper & Row, 1985); and David A. Van Seters and Richard H. G. Field, "The Evolution of Leadership Theory," *Journal of Organizational Change Management* 3, No. 3 (1990):29–45.

17. Marshall Sashkin, *A Manager's Guide to Participative Management* (New York: American Management Associations, 1982), pp. 60–61.

18. See Edwin A. Locke and David M. Schweiger, "Participation in Decision-Making: One More Look," in *Research in Organizational Behavior*, ed. Barry M. Staw (Greenwich, Conn.: JAI Press, 1979), 1: 265–339.

19. See Robert R. Blake and Jane Srygley Mouton, "Theory and Research for Developing a Science of Leadership," *The Journal of Applied Behavioral Science* 18 (No. 3 1982):290; and J. L. Cotton, D. A. Vollrath, K. L. Frogatt, M. L. Lengnick-Hall, and K. R. Jennings, "Employee Participation: Diverse Forms and Different Outcomes," *Academy of Management Review* 13 (January 1988):8–22.

20. Sashkin, *A Manager's Guide to Participative Management*, pp. 60–61.

21. Paul R. Lawrence, C. A. Vlachoutsicos, Igor Faminsky, Eugene Brakov, Sheila Puffer, Alexander Naumov, Elise Walton, and Vitale Ozira, *Behind the Factory Walls* (Boston: Harvard Business School Press, 1990), p. 276.

22. *The Arizona Republic*, January 28, 1985, p. C1.

23. Homer J. Hagedorn, "Everybody Into the Pool," *Across the Board* 21 (October 1984):26.

24. Pascale, "The Paradox of 'Corporate Culture,'" p. 26. For more on organizational culture, see Edgar H. Schein, *Organizational Culture and Leadership* (San Francisco: Jossey-Bass, 1985); and Edgar H. Schein, "Organizational Culture," *American Psychologist* 45 (February 1990):109–119.

25. Based on George H. Litwin, John W. Humphrey, and Thomas B. Wilson, "Organizational Climate: A Proven Tool for Improving Performance," in *The Cutting Edge: Current Theory and Practice in Organization Development*, ed. W. Warner Burke (La Jolla, Calif.: University Associates, 1978), pp. 187–205. See also Steve W. J. Kozlowski and Mary L. Doherty, "Integration of Climate and Leadership: Examination of a Neglected Issue," *Journal of Applied Psychology* 74 (August 1989):546–553.

26. George H. Litwin and Robert A. Stringer, *Motivation and Organization Climate* (Boston: Graduate School of Business Administration, Harvard University, 1968), pp. 81–82.

27. Tom Burns and G. M. Stalker, *The Management of Innovation* (London: Tavistock, 1961), pp. 119–120.

28. Wendell L. French and Cecil H. Bell, Jr., *Organization Development: Behavioral Science Interventions for Organization Improvement*, 4th ed. (Englewood Cliffs, N.J.: Prentice-Hall, 1990), p. 236.

29. Burns and Stalker, *The Management of Innovation*, pp. 119–125.

30. French and Bell, *Organization Development*, pp. 237–238.

31. Joan Woodward, *Industrial Organization: Theory and Practice* (London: Oxford University Press, 1965), p. 71.

32. Paul R. Lawrence and Jay W. Lorsch, *Organization and Environment: Managing Differentiation and Integration* (Boston: Graduate School of Business Administration, Harvard University, 1967), p. 32.

33. Lorsch and Morse, *Organizations and Their Members*, pp. 79–83, 105–107.

34. James C. Taylor and David G. Bowers, *Survey of Organizations: A Machine-Scored Standardized Questionnaire Instrument,* Institute for Social Research (Ann Arbor: University of Michigan, 1972), pp. 3–4.

35. Based on Rensis Likert and Jane Gibson Likert, *New Ways of Managing Conflict* (New York: McGraw-Hill, 1976), pp. 21–32; Rensis Likert, *The Human Organization: Its Management and Value* (New York: McGraw-Hill, 1967), pp. 3–10; Rensis Likert, *New Patterns of Management* (New York: McGraw-Hill, 1961), pp. 223–233; and David G. Bowers, *Systems of Organization* (Ann Arbor: University of Michigan Press, 1976), pp. 101–107.

36. Likert and Likert, *New Ways of Managing Conflict,* pp. 48–50, 75.

37. William F. Dowling, "At General Motors: System 4 Builds Performance and Profits," *Organizational Dynamics* 4 (Winter 1975):23–38; and Likert, and Likert, *New Ways of Managing Conflict,* pp. 71–86.

CHAPTER 5

1. A. H. Maslow, *Motivation and Personality,* 2nd ed. (New York: Harper & Brothers, 1970), chap. 3–7.

2. Clayton P. Alderfer, *Existence, Relatedness, and Growth: Human Needs in Organizational Settings* (New York: The Free Press, 1972), pp. 6–13, 133; and Clayton P. Alderfer, "Theories Reflecting My Personal Experience and Life Development," *Journal of Applied Behavioral Science* 25, No. 4 (1989):351–365.

3. D. C. McClelland, *The Achieving Society* (Princeton, N.J.: Van Nostrand, 1961); and D. C. McClelland, *Assessing Human Motivation* (New York: General Learning Press, 1971).

4. David C. McClelland and David H. Burnham, "Power Is the Great Motivator," *Harvard Business Review* 54 (March–April 1976):100–110.

5. Frederick Herzberg, Bernard Mausner, and Barbara Snyderman, *The Motivation to Work,* 2nd ed. (New York: John Wiley & Sons, 1959), pp. 59–62, 60–74; and Frederick Herzberg, "One More Time: How Do You Motivate Employees?" *Harvard Business Review* 65 (September–October 1987):109–120.

6. D. P. Schwab, W. H. DeVitt, and L. L. Cummings, "A Test of the Adequacy of the Two-factor Theory as a Predictor of Self-report Performance Effects," *Personnel Psychology* 24 (Summer 1971):293–304.

7. Based on Walter R. Nord, "Beyond the Teaching Machine," in *Concepts and Controversy in Organizational Behavior,* ed. Walter R. Nord, 2nd ed. (Pacific Palisades, Calif.: Goodyear Publishing Company, 1972), pp. 151–174.

8. George C. Homans, *Social Behavior: Its Elementary Forms* (New York: Harcourt, Brace & World, 1961), chap. 12; and Robert D. Bretz, Jr. and Steven L. Thomas, "Perceived Equity, Motivation, and Final-offer Arbitration in Major League Baseball," *Journal of Applied Psychology,* 77 (June 1992):280–287.

9. Jerald Greenberg, "Equity and Workplace Status: A Field Experiment," *Journal of Applied Psychology* 73 (November 1988):606–613; Jerald Greenberg, "Employee Theft as a Reaction to Underpayment Inequity: The Hidden Cost of Pay Cuts," *Journal of Applied Psychology* 75 (October 1990):561–568; William M. Evan and Roberta G. Simmons, "Organizational Effects of Inequitable Rewards: Two Experiments in Status Inconsistency," *Administrative Science Quarterly* 14 (June 1969):224–237.

10. David A. Nadler and Edward E. Lawler III, "Motivation: A Diagnostic Approach," in *Perspectives on Behavior in Organizations,* ed. J. Richard Hackman, Edward E. Lawler III, and Lyman W. Porter (New York: McGraw-Hill, 1977), pp. 27–29. For an overview of the major theories of motivation, see Raymond A. Katzell and Donna E. Thompson, "Work Motivation: Theory and Practice," *American Psychologist* 45 (February 1990):144–153.

11. For a study on predispositions toward job satisfaction, see Elaine D. Pulakos and Neal Schmitt, "A Longitudinal Study of a Valence Model Approach for the Prediction of Job Satisfaction of New Employees," *Journal of Applied Psychology* 68 (May 1983):307–312.

12. See Nadler and Lawler, "Motivation: A Diagnostic Approach," p. 36; and Edward E. Lawler III and Lyman W. Porter, "The Effect of Performance on Job Satisfaction," *Industrial Relations* 7 (October 1967):20–28. See also Cheri Ostroff, "The Relationship Between Satisfaction, Attitudes, and Performance: An Organizational Level Analysis," *Journal of Applied Psychology* 77 (December 1992):963–974.

13. Nadler and Lawler, "Motivation: A Diagnostic Approach," p. 29.

14. Paul Spector, "Relationships of Organizational Frustration with Reported Behavioral Reactions of Employees," *Journal of Applied Psychology* 60 (October 1975):635–637.

15. "Navy Identifies Plan Saboteurs," *The Seattle Times,* September 23, 1980, p. A4; Bob Smith, "The Dark Side of Corporate America," *HRfocus* 69 (October 1992):1, 8.

16. Richard M. Steers and Susan R. Rhodes, "Major Influences on Employee Attendance: A Process Model," *Journal of Applied Psychology* 63 (August 1978):391–407. See also Robert Eisenberger, Robin Huntington, Steven Hutchison, and Debora Sowa, "Perceived Organizational Support," *Journal of Applied Psychology* 71 (August 1986):500–507.

17. M. C. Knowles, "Labour Turnover: Aspects of Its Significance," *Industrial Relations* (Australia) 18 (March 1976):67–75.

18. Jon R. Katzenbach and Douglas K. Smith, "The Discipline of Teams," *Harvard Business Review* 71 (March–April 1993):112.

19. See F. J. Roethlisberger and William J. Dickson, *Management and the Worker* (Cambridge, Mass.: Harvard University Press, 1939; reprinted 1956), pp. 417–423.

20. Martin Patchen, "Supervisory Methods and Group Performance Norms," *Administrative Science Quarterly* 7 (December 1962):275–294.

21. Robert L. Kahn, "Productivity and Job Satisfaction," *Personnel Psychology* 13 (Autumn 1960):285.

22. Robert Schrank, *Ten Thousand Working Days* (Cambridge, Mass.: The MIT Press, 1978), p. 82.

23. See Rensis Likert, *New Patterns of Management* (New York: McGraw-Hill, 1961), pp. 172–177; and Kenneth Benne and Paul Sheats, "Functional Roles of Group Members," *Journal of Social Issues* 4 (Spring 1948):41–49.

24. This discussion is drawn partly from Likert, *New Patterns of Management*, pp. 166–167.

25. Based on Robert R. Blake, Herbert A. Shepard, and Jane S. Mouton, *Managing Intergroup Conflict in Industry* (Houston: Gulf Publishing, 1964), pp. 19–41; Muzafer Sherif, *Group Conflict and Cooperation* (London: Routledge and Kegan Paul, 1966); and Robert R. Blake and Jane S. Mouton, "Reactions to Intergroup Competition Under Win-Lose Conditions," *Management Science* 4 (July 1961):420–435.

CHAPTER 6

1. For more on mission statements, see John A. Pearce II and Fred David, "Corporate Mission Statements: The Bottom Line," *Academy of Management Executive* 1 (May 1987):109–116.

2. *Business Week*, September 17, 1984, p. 66. For more on strategic planning, see Peg Anthony and Lincoln Akin Norton, "Link HR to Corporate Strategy," *Personnel Journal* 70 (April 1991):75–86; and Christine D. Keen, "Strategic Planning for the HR department," *HR News*, May 1993, p. A19.

3. James W. Walker, *Human Resource Planning* (New York: McGraw-Hill, 1980), pp. 11–22.

4. Ibid. For more on human resources planning, see Susan E. Jackson and Randall S. Schuler, "Human Resource Planning: Challenges for Industrial/Organizational Psychologists," *American Psychologist* 45 (February 1990):223–239.

5. For more on succession planning, see James E. McElwain, "Succession Plans Designed to Manage Change," *HRMagazine* 36 (February 1991):67–71; *Wall Street Journal*, January 8, 1989, p. 1; and Robert J. Sahl, "Succession Planning—A Blueprint for Your Company's Future," *Personnel Administrator* 32 (September 1987): 101–106.

6. For information on the extent of computer use in various aspects of human resources management, see Morton E. Grossman, "The Growing Dependence on HRIS," *Personnel Journal* 67 (September 1988):53–67.

7. U.S. Department of Labor, Bureau of Labor Statistics, *Occupational Outlook Handbook, 1992–93*, Bulletin 2400, p. 274.

8. Ibid., 12.

9. Ibid.

10. *Time*, April 9, 1990, p. 28; Karen Matthes, "Attracting and Retaining Hispanic Employees," *HRfocus* 69 (August 1992):7. See also *Monthly Labor Review* 115 (August 1992):2.

11. Mack A. Player, *Federal Law of Employment Discrimination* (Saint Paul, Minn.: West Publishing, 1976), p. 116.

12. David P. Twomey, *Equal Employment Opportunity Law*, 2nd ed. (Cincinnati, Ohio: Southwestern Publishing Co., 1990), p. 34; and Robert D. Gatewood and Hubert S. Feild, *Human Resource Selection* (Chicago: The Dryden Press, 1990), p. 45.

13. Bureau of National Affairs, *Labor Relations Reporter, Fair Employment Practices Manual*, 451 (October 1987):1–5; Title VII, Civil Rights Act of 1964, Sections 706–707.

14. Civil Rights Act of 1991, Section 102; and Bureau of National Affairs, *Labor Relations Reporter*, Special Supplement to Vol. 138, No. 11, November 11, 1991, pp. S1–S19.

15. *Resource* (February 1984):12.

16. *Impact* (Prentice-Hall), 7, no. 8, January 19, 1983, p. 8.

17. *Wall Street Journal*, March 24, 1988, p. 2.

18. *HR News*, Society for Human Resource Management, May 1990, p. 15.

19. *Wall Street Journal*, December 5, 1990, p. B6.

20. *New York Times*, April 29, 1992, p. A15.

21. U.S. Department of Labor, *Dictionary of Occupational Titles*, 4th ed., Employment and Training Administration, 1991.

22. American Society for Personnel Administration, *Fair Employment Digest* (December 1971):3.

23. *U.S. News and World Report*, December 1, 1980, p. 79.

24. *Wall Street Journal*, June 6, 1972, p. 1.

25. *USA Today*, December 31, 1990, p. 2A.

26. *New York Times*, April 28, 1993, p. A1; and *Wall Street Journal*, April 29, 1992, p. A4.

27. "Women in Work—Facts and Fictions," *Newsletter*, Institute for Social Research, University of Michigan, Autumn 1972, pp. 4–5; and Patricia Voydanoff, "Women's Work, Family, and Health," *Working Women*, ed. Karen S. Koziara, Michael H. Moskow, and Lucretia D. Tanner, Washington D.C.: Bureau of National Affairs, 1987, Industrial Relations Research Series, pp. 69–96.

28. Donald P. Schwab and Herbert G. Heneman III, "Effects of Age and Experience on Productivity," in *Academy of Management Proceedings*, ed. Robert L. Taylor, Michael J. O'Connell, Robert A. Zawacki, and D. D. Warrick, Proceedings of the 36th Annual Meeting of the Academy of Management, Kansas City, Missouri, August 11–14, 1976, pp. 281–283.

29. See, for example, *New York Times*, May 21, 1991, p. A10; and David V. Lewis, "Make Way for the Older Worker," *HRMagazine* 35 (May 1990):75–77.

30. Stephen J. Cabot, "Living with the New Amendments to the Age Discrimination in Employment Act," *Personnel Administrator* 32 (January 1987):53–55.

31. Irene Pave, "They Won't Take It Anymore," *Across the Board* 27 (November 1990):19.

32. *Wall Street Journal*, November 2, 1990, p. B10.

33. *Monthly Labor Review* 108 (March 1985):49.

34. *Wall Street Journal*, June 3, 1987, p. 12.

35. "Wounded Executives Fight Back on Age Bias," *Business Week*, July 21, 1980, p. 109; *Wall Street Journal*, August 27, 1991, p. B6; *Wall Street Journal*, August 28, 1992, p. B7; *New York Times*, September 18, 1992, p. C3; and *Personnel Journal* 71 (April 1992):31.

36. Peter M. Jamero, "Handicapped Individuals in the Changing Workforce," *Journal of Contemporary Business* 8 (November 4, 1979):33–42.

37. Julie Wysock and Paul Wysock, "An Employer's Guide to Employment and Disability," *Journal of Contemporary Business* 8 (November 4, 1979):59–66.

38. Jamero, "Handicapped Individuals in the Changing Workforce," p. 36.

39. *Affirmative Action for Disabled People: A Pocket Guide*, The President's Committee on Employment of the Handicapped (pamphlet, no date); and Steven Fox, "Employment Provisions of the Rehabilitation Act," *Personnel Journal* 66 (October 1987):132–135ff.

40. See U.S. Department of Justice, Civil Rights Division, *The Americans with Disabilities Act: Questions and Answers*, Office of the Americans with Disabilities Act, 1991, pp. 1–8; *Wall Street Journal*, February 28, 1991, p. 12; and *Business Week*, April 12, 1993, p. 72.

41. James Ledvinka and Vida G. Scarpello, *Federal Regulation of Personnel and Human Resource Management*, 2nd ed. (Boston: PWS-Kent Publishing Company, 1991), p. 110.

42. Bureau of National Affairs, "Employment and Accommodation of Individuals with Disabilities," *Bulletin to Management*, 42 (January 31, 1991):3–5.

43. Kenneth L. Sovereign, *Personnel Law* (Reston, Va.: Reston Publishing Company, 1984), p. 81.

44. U.S. Department of Labor. *OFCCP: Making EEO and Affirmative Action Work*, Office of Federal Contract Compliance Programs, January 1987 (pamphlet). See also David Ankeny and David Israel, "Completing an On-Site OFCCP Audit," *HRMagazine* 38 (March 1993):89–93.

45. *New York Times*, November 22, 1991, p. A11.

46. Equal Employment Opportunity Commission, "Affirmative Action Guidelines," *Federal Register*, Friday, January 19, 1979, p. 4425.

47. *Wall Street Journal*, April 15, 1980, p. 6.

48. *Wall Street Journal*, July 16, 1980, p. 13.

49. David P. Twomey, *A Concise Guide to Employment Law: EEO & OSHA* (Cincinnati, Ohio: South-Western Publishing Company, 1986), pp. 63–67.

50. *Wall Street Journal*, March 26, 1987, p. 3.

51. Ibid.

52. *Monthly Labor Review* 107 (August 1984):39.

53. *Wall Street Journal*, March 26, 1987, p. 3.

54. Bureau of National Affairs, *Labor Relations Reporter*, Special Supplement to Vol. 138, No. 11, November 11, 1991, pp. S1–S19; and "Race in the Workplace: Is Affirmative Action Working?" *Business Week*, July 8, 1991, pp. 50–63.

55. *New York Times*, November 22, 1991, p. A11.

56. Betty Southward Murphy, Wayne E. Barlow, and D. Diane Hatch, "Employer Obligations Regarding Military Leave," *Personnel Journal* 69 (November 1990):15; and *Wall Street Journal*, April 5, 1991, p. A16.

57. Dave Jensen, "Iraqi Crisis Leaves HR Departments Scrambling," *Personnel Journal* 69 (October 1990):118–120.

58. *St. Petersburg Times*, March 16, 1990, p. 11A. See also Christine Klingberg, "Violations of Child Labor Laws Up 250 Percent," *HR News*, March 1990, p. 9.

59. *New York Times*, August 19, 1992, A16.

60. Bureau of National Affairs, "The Personnel/Human Resources Department: 1989–1990," *Bulletin to Management*, SHRM-BNA Survey No. 54, June 28, 1990, p. 2.

61. Kenneth F. Misa and Timothy Stein, "Strategic HRM and the Bottom Line," *Personnel Administrator* 28 (October 1983):27–30.

CHAPTER 7

1. J. Richard Hackman and Greg R. Oldham, *Work Redesign* (Reading, Mass.: Addison-Wesley, 1980), pp. 77–80.

2. Ibid., pp. 3–21.

3. Ibid., p. 20.

4. Ibid., pp. 82–88. See also Tom D. Taber and Elisabeth Taylor, "A Review and Evaluation of the Psychometric Properties of the Job Diagnostic Survey," *Personnel Psychology* 43 (Autumn 1990):467–500.

5. Hackman and Oldham, *Work Redesign*, pp. 103–129. See also pp. 275–315 for a copy of the JDS scoring key and guidelines for use.

6. Robert N. Ford, "Job Enrichment Lessons from AT&T," *Harvard Business Review* 51 (January–February 1973):96–106.

7. Ibid., pp. 96–106. See also Ricky W. Griffin, "Effects of Work Redesign on Employee Perceptions, Attitudes, and Behaviors," *Academy of Management Journal* 34 (June 1991):425–435.

8. William J. Paul, Keith B. Robertson, and Frederick Herzberg, "Job Enrichment Pays Off," *Harvard Business Review* 47 (March–April 1969):61–78.

9. M. Scott Myers, "Every Employee a Manager," *California Management Review* 10 (Spring 1968):9–20.

10. M. Scott Myers, *Every Employee a Manager* (New York: McGraw-Hill, 1970), pp. 74–87.

11. Peter G. Gyllenhammar, *People at Work* (Reading, Mass.: Addison-Wesley, 1977); and A. Mikalachki, "The Effects of Job Design in Turnover, Absenteeism and Health," *Industrial Relations* 30 (August 1975):377–388. For more on the self-managed team concept, see James Kochanski, "Hiring in Self-Regulating Work Teams," *National Productivity Review* 6 (Spring 1987): 153–159.

12. E. L. Trist, G. W. Higgin, H. Murray, and A. B. Pollock, *Organizational Choice* (London: Tavistock Publications, 1965).

13. A. K. Rice, "Productivity and Social Organization in an Indian Weaving Shed," *Human Relations* 6 (1953): 297–329.

14. *Business Week*, August 17, 1992, pp. 86–91. See also Thomas A. Stewart, "The Search for the Organization of Tomorrow," *Fortune*, May 18, 1992, p. 94.

15. Nancy K. Austin, "Making Teamwork Work," *Working Woman*, January 1993, pp. 28, 70; *Fortune*, October 19, 1992, p. 113; and Jana Schilder, "Work Teams Boost Productivity," *Personnel Journal* 71 (February 1992):67–71.

16. Paul Robertson, and Herzberg, "Job Enrichment Pays Off," pp. 61–78.

17. Ford, "Job Enrichment Lessons from AT&T," pp. 96–106.

18. Myers, *Every Employee a Manager*, pp. 74–87; and *Business Week*, April 27, 1968, p. 60.

19. Mikalachki, "The Effects of Job Design," pp. 377–388.

20. Trist et al., *Organizational Choice*, p. 294; and Rice, "Productivity and Social Organization," pp. 297–329.

21. See David A. Whitsett and Lyle Yorks, "Looking Back at Topeka: General Foods and the Quality-of-the-Work-Life Experiment," *California Management Review* 25 (Summer 1983):93–109; Richard E. Walton, "Innovative Restructuring of Work," in *The Worker and the Job*, ed. Jerome E. Rosow (Englewood Cliffs, N.J.: Prentice-Hall, 1974), p. 162; and Richard E. Walton, "Work Innovations at Topeka: After Six Years," *Journal of Applied Behavioral Science* 13 (July–August–September 1977):422–433.

22. U.S. Department of Labor, "Job Redesign: Some Case Histories," *Manpower* (May 1973):8–19; and *Business Week*, May 13, 1991, p. 70.

23. Seminar with Ake Magnusson of Stockholm School of Economics, November 14, 1975, Graduate School of Business Administration, University of Washington, Seattle, Washington. For a research study that found employees in autonomous work groups in a minerals processing plant to have more favorable attitudes than workers in more traditional jobs, but higher absenteeism and turnover, see John L. Cordery, Walter S. Mueller, and Leigh M. Smith, "Attitudinal and Behavioral Effects of Autonomous Group Working: A Longitudinal Field Study," *Academy of Management Journal* 34 (June 1991):464–476.

24. Ernesto J. Poza and M. Lynne Markus, "Success Story: The Team Approach to Work Restructuring," *Organizational Dynamics* 8 (Winter 1980):3–21.

25. See Ernest J. McCormick, "Job and Task Analysis," in *Handbook of Industrial and Organizational Psychology*, ed. Marvin D. Dunnette (Chicago: Rand McNally, 1976), pp. 652–654. See also Jai V. Ghorpade, *Job Analysis: A Handbook for the Human Resource Director* (Englewood Cliffs, N.J.: Prentice-Hall, 1988); and Frank J. Landy and Joseph Vasey, "Job Analysis: The Composition of SME Samples," *Personnel Psychology* 44 (Spring 1991):27–49.

26. Ernest J. McCormick, Paul R. Jeanneret, and Robert C. Mecham, "A Study of Job Characteristics and Job Dimensions as Based on the Position Analysis Questionnaire (PAQ)," *Journal of Applied Psychology Monograph* 56 (August 1972):347–368.

27. Ibid., pp. 363–366. See also Robert J. Harvey, Milton D. Hakel, Lee Friedman, and Edwin T. Cornelius III, "Dimensionality of the Job Element Inventory, A Simplified Worker-Oriented Job Analysis Questionnaire," *Journal of Applied Psychology* 73 (November 1988):639–646.

28. Wayne F. Cascio, *Applied Psychology in Personnel Management* (Reston, Va.: Reston Publishing Company, 1978), pp. 141–142.

29. U.S. Supreme Court, *Willis S. Griggs et al. v. Duke Power Company*, March 8, 1971.

30. *Wall Street Journal*, May 6, 1983, p. 1.

31. *Ideas & Trends in Personnel*, Commerce Clearing House, No. 69, July 13, 1984, p. 108.

32. *Business Week*, October 22, 1990, p. 87.

CHAPTER 8

1. Bureau of National Affairs, *Bulletin to Management*, BNA Policy and Practice Series 43 (October 8, 1992):320.

2. Perry Garfinkel, "Smoker Seg," *Across the Board* 21 (July–August 1984):29. See also Robert J. Nobile, "Putting Out Fires with a No-Smoking Policy," *Personnel* 67 (March 1990):10.

3. *Wall Street Journal*, January 25, 1983, p. 25.

4. *Wall Street Journal*, May 16, 1991, p. A5.

5. *Wall Street Journal*, May 8, 1990, p. B1.

6. "Absenteeism and Lateness," *Personnel Policies and Practices* (Prentice-Hall, 1981), p. 16.

7. Susan R. Mendelson and Anne E. Libbin, "Employee Alcohol- and Drug-Testing Programs," *Personnel* 65 (September 1988):66; and Michael R. Carrell and Christina Heavrin, "Before You Drug Test..." *HRMagazine* 35 (June 1990):64–66.

8. Bureau of National Affairs, "Employee Discipline and Discharge," *Personnel Policies Forum* 139 (January 1985):17–18. Companies lose billions to employee theft. See *Wall Street Journal*, October 5, 1992, p. B2.

9. *Wall Street Journal*, March 30, 1982, p. 1.

10. See Karen L. Vinton, "Documentation That Gets Results," *Personnel* 67 (February 1990):42–46.

11. David N. Campbell, R. L. Fleming, and Richard C. Grote, "Discipline Without Punishment—At Last," *Harvard Business Review* 63 (July–August 1985):162–164, 168, 170.

12. For more on progressive discipline, see Walter Kiechel III, "How to Discipline in the Modern Age," *Fortune*, May 7, 1990, pp. 179–180; and Martin Levy, "Discipline for Professional Employees," *Personnel Journal* 69 (December 1990):27–28.

13. Robert W. Fisher, "When Workers Are Discharged—An Overview," *Monthly Labor Review* 96 (June 1973):8.

14. Bureau of National Affairs, *Bulletin to Management*, June 19, 1975. See also "Older Employees Fight Back," *Personnel* 65 (January 1988):6.

15. O. L. Harvey, "The 10-Hour Day in the Philadelphia Navy Yard, 1835–36," *Monthly Labor Review* 85 (March 1962):258–260.

16. Douglas L. Fleuter, *The Workweek Revolution: A Guide to the Changing Workweek* (Reading, Mass.: Addison-Wesley, 1975), p. iv.

17. *Monthly Labor Review* 111 (August 1988):11; and *Monthly Labor Review* 114 (March 1991):68.

18. U.S. Department of Labor, "Hours of Work: A Brief History," *Employment and Training Report of the President* (Washington, D.C.: Government Printing Office, 1979), pp. 77–79.

19. See U.S. Department of Labor, Wage and Hour Division, *Handy Reference Guide to the Fair Labor Standards Act*, WH Publication 1282, rev. April 1990.

20. *Federal Register*, Vol. 58, No., 39, Wednesday, February 27, 1991, p. 8250; and David S. Gold and Beth Unger, "DOL Makes Final Rule on Computer-Worker Exemption," *HR News*, December 1992, p. A7.

21. W. P. Colquhoun and J. Rutenfranz, *Studies of Shiftwork* (London: Taylor & Francis, Ltd., 1980), p. ix.

22. *Wall Street Journal*, March 26, 1990, p. 8A.

23. Peter Finn, "The Effects of Shift Work on the Lives of Employees," *Monthly Labor Review* 104 (October 1981):31.

24. Colquhoun and Rutenfranz, *Studies of Shiftwork*, p. 5.

25. *Wall Street Journal*, April 10, 1990, p. A1.

26. Jon L. Pierce, John W. Newstrom, Randall B. Dunham, and Alison E. Barber, *Alternative Work Schedules* (Boston: Allyn and Bacon, 1989), p. 93; and Bureau of National Affairs, "Wage and Salary Administration," *Personnel Policies Forum*, Survey No. 147, June 1990.

27. Ibid. See also *Wall Street Journal*, April 10, 1990, p. A1.

28. Graham L. Staines and Joseph H. Pleck, "Nonstandard Work Schedules and Family Life," *Journal of Applied Psychology* 69 (August 1984):515–523. See also Charlene M. Solomon, "HR is solving shift-work problems," Personnel Journal 72 (August 1993):36–48.

29. Finn, "The Effects of Shift Work on the Lives of Employees," p. 34. See also Richard M. Coleman, "Shiftwork Scheduling for the 1990s," *Personnel* 66 (January 1989):10–15; and Richard M. Coleman, "Twelve-Hour Shift Schedules," *HRfocus* 69 (May 1992):16–17.

30. U.S. Department of Labor, "Hours of Work: A Brief History," pp. 77–79.

31. Herman Z. Levine, "Alternative Work Schedules: Do They Meet the Workforce Needs? Part 1," *Personnel* 64 (February 1987):57–62.

32. U.S. Department of Labor, *Employment and Training Report of the President*, 1979, p. 84.

33. Kenneth E. Wheeler, Richard Gurman, and Dale Karnowieski, *The Four-Day Week* (New York: American Management Associations, 1972), pp. 1–3.

34. Douglas L. Fleuter, *The Workweek Revolution: A Guide to the Changing Workweek* (Reading, Mass.: Addison-Wesley, 1975), pp. 12–15; and Allan R. Cohen and Herman Gadon, *Alternative Work Schedules: Integrating Individual and Organizational Needs* (Reading, Mass.: Addison-Wesley, 1978), pp. 49–64. See also Randall B. Dunham, Jon L. Pierce, and Maria B. Castaneda, "Alternative Work Schedules: Two Field Quasi-Experiments," *Personnel Psychology* 40 (Summer 1987):215–242.

35. Research Institute of America, *Employment Coordinator* 5 (June 16, 1986):C-17, 652.

36. Earl F. Mellor, "Shift Work and Flexitime: How Prevalent Are They?" *Monthly Labor Review* 109 (November 1986):14–21; and Stanley D. Nollen, *New Work Schedules in Practice* (New York: Van Nostrand Reinhold Company, 1982), p. 6.

37. *Resource* (February 1989):2.

38. *Wall Street Journal*, January 19, 1993, p. A1; and "Flexible Work Hours Gather Momentum," *U.S. News & World Report*, September 28, 1981.

39. Fleuter, *The Workweek Revolution*, pp. 73–102.

40. Based on Fleuter, *The Workweek Revolution*, pp. 77–84; R. T. Golembiewski, R. Hilles, and M. S. Kagno, "A Longitudinal Study of Flex-Time Effects," *Journal of Applied Behavioral Science* 10 (October 1974):503–532; Simcha Ronen and Sophia B. Primps, "The Compressed Work Week as Organizational Change: Behavioral and Attitudinal Outcomes," *Academy of Management Review* 6 (January 1981):61–74; and *Resource* (February 1989):2.

41. Ibid.

42. *U.S. News & World Report*, October 4, 1982, p. 74.

43. For example, see R. A. Winett and M. S. Neale, "Results of Experimental Study on Flexitime and Family Life," *Monthly Labor Review* 103 (November 1980):29–32. See also David A. Ralston, "How Flextime Eases Work/Family Tensions," *Personnel* 67 (August 1990):45–48. For more on European experience, see Paul Bernstein, "The Ultimate in Flexitime: From Sweden, by Way of Volvo," *Personnel* 65 (June 1988):70–74.

44. Richard S. Belous, "How Human Resource Systems Adjust to the Shift Toward Contingent Workers," *Monthly Labor Review* 112 (March 1989):7–12.

45. Kathleen Christensen, "Flexible Staffing and Scheduling in U.S. Corporations," *The Conference Board Research Bulletin No. 240* (1989):7; and Kathleen Christensen, "Here We Go Into the 'High-Flex Era,'" *Across the Board* 27 (July–August 1990):22–23.

46. *Resource* (August 1984):2; and *Seattle Business Journal*, August 20, 1984, p. 11.

47. *Wall Street Journal*, February 8, 1983, p. 1.

48. *Wall Street Journal*, February 12, 1985, p. 1.

49. Stanley Nollen, *New Patterns of Work* (Scarsdale, N.Y.: Work in America Institute, 1979), pp. 5–6. See also Pierce, et al., *Alternative Work Schedules*, pp. 72–91.

50. *Wall Street Journal*, June 2, 1982, p. 48. See also Pierce, *Alternative Work Schedules*, pp. 72–76.

51. Nollen, *New Patterns of Work*, p. 6. See also William G. Kuchta, "Part-Year vs. Part-Time Employment," *Personnel Administrator* 33 (May 1988):60–63; and Robert B. Moberly, "Temporary, Part-Time, and Other Atypical Employment Relationships in the United States," *Labor Law Journal* 38 (November 1987):689–696.

52. Howard E. Miller and James R. Terborg, "Job Attitudes of Part-Time and Full-Time Employees," *Journal of Applied Psychology* 64 (August 1979):380–386.

53. See Michael Frease and Robert A. Zawacki, "Job Sharing: An Answer to Productivity Problems," *Personnel Administrator* 24 (October 1979):35–38.

54. David Clutterbuck, "Why a Job Shared Is Not a Job Halved," *International Management* 34 (October 1979):45–47.

55. Nollen, *New Work Schedules in Practice* (New York: Van Nostrand Reinhold, 1982), pp. 141–147.

56. James O'Toole, *Vanguard Management: Redesigning the Corporate Future* (Garden City, N.Y.: Doubleday, 1985), p. 121. For more on job sharing, see Alan Deutschman, "Pioneers of the New Balance," *Fortune*, May 20, 1991, pp. 60–68.

57. Frease and Zawacki, "Job Sharing," pp. 35–37, 56; and Clutterbuck, "Why a Job Shared Is Not a Job Halved," pp. 45–47.

58. *Business Week*, May 3, 1982, p. 66.

59. Kathleen Christensen, "A Hard Day's Work in the Electronic Cottage," *Across the Board* 24 (April 1987):17–23. See also Dori Sera Bailey and Jill Foley, "Pacific Bell Works Long Distance," *HRMagazine* 35 (August 1990):50–52.

60. *Wall Street Journal*, December 22, 1989, p. B1.

61. See *Business Week*, May 3, 1982, p. 66; *Wall Street Journal*, February 13, 1985, p. 31; and William H. Wagel, "Telecommuting Arrives in the Public Sector," *Personnel* 65 (October 1988):14–17.

62. Carol-Ann Hamilton, "Telecommuting," *Personnel Journal* 66 (April 1987):91–101; *Wall Street Journal*, December 22, 1989; and *Business Week*, January 23, 1984, p. 99.

63. Janice Castro, "Disposable Workers," *Time*, March 29, 1993, pp. 43–47.

64. *Wall Street Journal*, February 13, 1985, p. 31.

65. *Puget Sound Business Journal*, February 21–27, 1992, p. 10.

66. Betty Southward Murphy, Wayne E. Barlow, and D. Diane Hatch, "Manager's Newsfront," *Personnel Journal* 71 (October 1992):27–28.

CHAPTER 9

1. Shari Caudron, "Focus: Recruitment," *Personnel Journal* 71 (June 1992):121.

2. Milan Moravec, "High Tech Job Posting—by Computer," *Personnel Journal* 70 (November 1991):64–68; and William C. DeLone, "Telephone Job Posting Cuts Costs," *Personnel Journal* 72 (April 1993):115–118. See also Milan Moravec, "Effective Job Posting Fills Dual Needs," *HRMagazine* 35 (September 1990):76–80.

3. Edith F. Lynton, *Corporate Experiences in Improving Women's Job Opportunities* (New York: The Conference Board, 1979), pp. 36–39; and Bureau of National Affairs, "Recruiting and Selection Procedures," *Personnel Policies Forum* 146 (May 1988):5.

4. Ibid., p. 6.

5. Ibid., p. 7.

6. Shari Caudron, "Recruit Qualified Employees from

7. For more on executive recruiting, see Norman E. Van-Maldegiam, "Executive Pursuit," *Personnel Administrator* 33 (September 1988):95–98.

8. Mary E. Scott, "Internships Add Value to College Recruitment," *Personnel Journal* 71 (April 1992):59–63.

9. U.S. Department of Labor, *Job Seeking Methods Used by American Workers*, Bulletin No. 1886 (Washington, D.C., 1975), pp. 1–10.

10. Bureau of National Affairs, "Recruiting and Selection Procedures," pp. 6–7.

11. U.S. Department of Labor, *Occupational Outlook Handbook 1990–91*, Bureau of Labor Statistics, Bulletin 2350, April 1990, pp. 8, 9.

12. Charlene Marmer Solomon, "Careers Under Glass," *Personnel Journal* 69 (April 1990):96.

13. Schaeffer and Lynton, *Corporate Experiences*, p. 42.

14. Bureau of National Affairs, "EEO Policies and Programs," *Personnel Policies Forum* 141 (May 1986):11.

15. U.S. Department of Justice, Civil Rights Division, *The Americans with Disabilities Act: Questions and Answers*, Office of the Americans with Disabilities Act, 1991, p. 3.

16. Society for Industrial and Organizational Psychology, *Principles for the Validation and Use of Personnel Selection Procedures*, 3rd ed. (College Park, Md., 1987), pp. 6–18.

17. Frank L. Schmidt, John E. Hunter, Robert C. McKenzie, and Tressie W. Muldrow, "Impact of Valid Selection Procedures on Work-Force Productivity," *Journal of Applied Psychology* 64 (December 1979):609–626.

18. "Uniform Guidelines on Employee Selection Procedures," Section 3, D, *Federal Register*, Vol. 43, No. 166 (Friday, August 25, 1978), p. 38297.

19. Betty Southward Murphy, Wayne E. Barlow, and D. Diane Hatch, "Supreme Court Decisions Impact Title VII and ADEA Claims," *Personnel Journal* 70 (June 1991):30–32.

20. See Hannah R. Rothstein, Frank W. Erwin, Frank L. Schmidt, William A. Owens, and C. Paul Sparks, "Biographical Data in Employment Selection: Can Validities be Made Generalizable?" *Journal of Applied Psychology* 75 (April 1990):175–184.

21. For more on the weighted application blank, see D. G. Lawrence, B. L. Salsburg, J. G. Dawson, and Z. D. Fasman, "Design and Use of Weighted Application Blanks," *Personnel Administrator* 27 (March 1982):47–53.

22. Washington State Human Rights Commission, Olympia, Washington, *Pre-Employment Inquiries and Screening*, August 1988 (pamphlet).

23. Bureau of National Affairs, "Recruiting and Selection Procedures," p. 22.

24. Norma R. Fritz, "When Talk Isn't Cheap," *Personnel* 65 (March 1988):8.

25. *HR News*, April 1991, p. 15.

26. Rosemary M. Collyer and Victoria L. Eastus, "Reference Checking: The Sources to Use and Pitfalls to Avoid," *Legal Report*, Society for Human Resource

Management, Summer 1991, pp. 1–4; and *New York Times*, May 8, 1993, p. 17. See also Betty Southward Murphy, Wayne E. Barlow, and D. Diane Hatch, "Job Reference Liability of Employers," *Personnel Journal* 70 (September 1991):22.

27. Kenneth L. Sovereign, "Pitfalls of Withholding Reference Information," *Personnel Journal* 69 (March 1990):116. See also Caleb S. Atwood and James M. Neel, "New Lawsuits Expand Employer Liability," *HRMagazine* 35 (October 1990).

28. See National Commission on State Workmen's Compensation Laws, *Report of the National Commission on State Workmen's Compensation Laws* (Washington, D.C., 1972). See also *Wall Street Journal*, January 3, 1989, p. B2.

29. U.S. Department of Justice, *The Americans with Disabilities Act: Questions and Answers*, p. 5. See also Gene Carmean, "Tie Medical Screening to the Job," *HRMagazine* 37 (July 1992):85–87; and Jonathan A. Segal, "Pre-employment Physicals Under the ADA," *HRMagazine* 71 (October 1992):103–107.

30. Robert M. Madigan, K. Dow Scott, Diana L. Deadrick, and Jil A. Stoddard, "Employment Testing: The U.S. Service is Spearheading a Revolution," *Personnel Administrator* 31 (September 1986):102. See also Paul L. Blocklyn, "Preemployment Testing," *Personnel* 65 (February 1988):66–68. Charlene Marmer Solomon, "Testing is Not at Odds with Diversity Efforts," *Personnel Journal* 72 (March 1993):100–104.

31. Telephone call to Seattle office of the U.S. Department of Labor, June 19, 1991; Justin Martin, "Workplace Testing: Why Can't We Get It Right?" *Across the Board* 27 (December 1990):39; and *Congressional Record*, Vol. 137, No. 158, October 30, 1991, p. 315476.

32. Graphology—handwriting analysis—does not appear to have much research support for measuring personality dimensions or for predicting job success. See Gershon Ben-Shakhar et al., "Can Graphology Predict Occupational Success?" *Journal of Applied Psychology* 71 (November 1986):645–653.

33. See Thomas Moore, "Personality Tests are Back," *Fortune*, March 30, 1987, pp. 74–82; and David Kiersey and Marilyn Bates, *Please Understand Me: Character and Temperament Types* (Del Mar, Calif.: Prometheus Nemesis Book Company, 1984).

34. Bureau of National Affairs, "Recruiting and Selection Procedures," p. 19. See also Marick F. Masters, Gerald R. Ferris, and Shannon L. Ratcliff, "Practices and Attitudes of Substance Abuse Testing," *Personnel Administrator* 33 (July 1988):72–78.

35. FEP Commission, State of Illinois, *Myart v. Motorola* (1964).

36. U.S. Supreme Court, *Griggs v. Duke Power Company*.

37. See *Fair Employment Digest*, American Society for Personnel Administration, March 1978, p. 2.

38. Thomas L. Bright and Charles J. Hollon, "State Regulation of Polygraph Tests at the Workplace," *Personnel* 62 (February 1985):50.

39. Tori DeAngelis, "Honesty Tests Weigh in with Improved Ratings," *The APA Monitor* 22 (June 1991):7.

40. *Personnel Journal* 70 (May 1991):17.

41. Susan R. Mendelsohn and Kathryn K. Morrison, "Testing Applicants for Alcohol and Drug Abuse," *Personnel* 65 (August 1988):57–60.

42. Betty Southward Murphy, Wayne E. Barlow, and D. Diane Hatch, "DOT Finalizes Drug Testing Rules," *Personnel Journal* 69 (March 1990):17.

43. *Seattle Times/Seattle Post-Intelligence*, July 26, 1992, A12; and "Survey Finds Employers Out of Step When It Comes to AIDS Policies," *Personnel* 68 (July 1991):23.

44. Mark A. Johnson, "Lights, Camera, Interview," *HR Magazine* 36 (April 1991):66–68.

45. Brooks Mitchell, "Interviewing Face-to-Interface," *Personnel* 67 (January 1990):23–25.

46. For more on interviewing, see Diane Arthur, *Recruiting, Interviewing, Selecting & Orienting New Employees*, 2nd ed. (New York: AMACOM, 1991); Robert W. Eder and Gerald R. Ferris, eds., *The Employment Interview: Theory, Research, and Practice* (Newbury Park, Calif.: Sage Publications, 1989); James M. Jenks and Brian L. P. Zevnik, "ABCs of Job Interviewing," *Harvard Business Review* 67 (July–August 1989):38–42; and Michael M. Harris, "Reconsidering the Employment Interview: A Review of Recent Literature and Suggestions for Future Research," *Personnel Psychology* 42 (Winter 1989):691–726.

47. *Wall Street Journal*, October 7, 1992, p. B1.

48. U.S. Department of Justice, Immigration and Naturalization Service, *Handbook for Employers: Instructions for Completing Forms 1–9*, May 1987, pp. 1–17 (pamphlet). See also James G. Frierson, "National Origin Discrimination: The Next Wave of Lawsuits," *Personnel Journal* 66 (December 1987):97–108.

49. *Wall Street Journal*, June 27, 1988, p. 17.

50. Erie Insurance Group, form HR B-1, November 1987.

CHAPTER 10

1. Susan Berger and Karen Huchendorf, "Ongoing Orientation at Metropolitan Life," *Personnel Journal* 68 (December 1989):28–35.

2. Maureen Reidy Witt and Sandra R. Goldman, "Avoiding Liability in Employee Handbooks," *Employee Relations Law Journal* 14 (Summer 1988):17.

3. Ibid.

4. Earl R. Gomersall and M. Scott Myers, "Breakthrough in On-the-Job Training," *Harvard Business Review* 44 (July–August 1966):62–72.

5. Ibid., pp. 66–68.

6. John P. Cotter, "Managing the Joining-Up Process," *Personnel* 49 (July–August 1972):46–56. For a broad look at the "socialization" process, see Edgar H. Schein, "Organizational Socialization and the Profession of Management," *Sloan Management Review* 30 (Fall 1988):53–65.

7. Joyce E. Santora, "How Alfa-Laval Got Employees Moving," *Personnel Journal* 70 (January 1991):42.

8. Neville C. Tompkins, "GTE Managers on the Move," *Personnel Journal* 71 (August 1992):86–91.

9. See Craig C. Pinder, "The Dark Side of Executive Relocation," *Organizational Dynamics* 17 (Spring 1989):48–58; Walter Kiechell III, "When the Boss Wants You to Move," *Fortune*, April 13, 1987, pp. 125, 126; and Lionel Tiger, "Is This Trip Necessary? The Heavy Human Costs of Moving Executives Around," *Fortune*, September, 1974, pp. 139–141ff.

10. For more on dual-career couples, see Arlene A. Johnson, "Relocating Two-Earner Couples: What Companies Are Doing," *The Conference Board Research Bulletin*, No. 247, 1990, 26 pp.; Linda Thornburg, "Transfers Need Not Mean Dislocation," *HRMagazine* 35 (September 1990):46–48; and Douglas T. Hall and Judith Richter, "Balancing Work Life and Home Life: What Can Organizations Do to Help?" *Academy of Management EXECUTIVE* 2 (August 1988):213–223.

11. *Wall Street Journal*, August 19, 1992, p. B1.

12. Wendell L. French, *The Personnel Management Process*, 6th ed. (Boston: Houghton Mifflin Company, 1987), p. 409. For more on the dual ladder concept, see Robert W. Goddard, "Lateral Moves Enhance Careers," *HRMagazine* 35 (December 1990):69–74; and Cliff Hakim, "Boost Morale to Gain Productivity," *HRMagazine* 38 (February 1993):46–49. See also Gilbert Fuchsberg, "Parallel Lines," *Wall Street Journal*, April 21, 1993, p. R4.

13. Bureau of National Affairs, "Employee Promotion & Transfer Policies," *Personnel Policies Forum* 120 (January 1978):12–13.

14. *Fair Employment Digest*, American Society for Personnel Administration, December 1980, p. 2.

15. See, for example, Allen I. Kraut, "Prediction of Managerial Success by Peer and Training-Staff Ratings," *Journal of Applied Psychology* 60 (February 1975):14–19.

16. Barbara B. Gaugler, Douglas B. Rosenthal, George C. Thornton III, and Cynthia Benston, "Meta-Analysis of Assessment Center Validity," *Journal of Applied Psychology Monograph* 72 (August 1987):493.

17. Douglas W. Bray, "The Assessment Center and the Study of Lives," *American Psychologist* 37 (February 1982):180–189; and Ann Howard, "An Assessment of Assessment Centers," *Academy of Management Journal* 17 (March 1974):115–134.

18. William E. Dodd, "Attitudes Toward Assessment Center Programs," in *Applying the Assessment Center Method*, ed. Joseph L. Moses and William C. Byham, (New York: Pergamon, 1977), pp. 169–170.

19. Richard Klimoski and Mary Brickner, "Why Do Assessment Centers Work? The Puzzle of Assessment Center Validity," *Personnel Psychology* 40 (Summer 1987):243–260. See also Richard J. Ritchie and Joseph L. Moses, "Assessment Center Correlates of Women's Advancement into Middle Management: A 7-Year Longitudinal Analysis," *Journal of Applied Psychology* 68 (May 1983):277–231; and Gaugler et al., "Meta-Analysis of Assessment Center Validity," pp. 493–511.

20. Douglas T. Hall and Francine S. Hall, "What's New in Career Management," *Organizational Dynamics* 5 (Summer 1976):23–24.

21. See *Time*, March 15, 1993, p. 55, for example.

22. *Wall Street Journal*, December 10, 1991, p. C1; and *Wall Street Journal*, June 6, 1991, p. B1.

23. Eleanor Johnson Tracy, "Parachutes A-Popping," *Fortune*, March 31, 1986, p. 66.

24. William R. Walter and Anthony J. Obadal, "Layoffs: The Judicial View," *Personnel Administrator* 20 (May 1975):13–16. See also Bernie Siebert, "Downsizing: An Overview of Legal Considerations," *Proceedings of the 1992 Spring Meeting*, Industrial Relations Research Association, 1992, pp. 483–487.

25. Douglas F. Seaver, "The *Stotts* Decision: Is It the Death Knell for Seniority Systems?" *Employee Relations Law Journal* 10 (Winter 1984–1985):497–504.

26. Janisse Klotchman and Linda L. Neider, "EEO Alert: Watch Out for Discrimination in Discharge Cases," *Personnel* 60 (January–February 1983):64.

27. Ibid., p. 65; and Cecil G. Howard, "Strategic Guidelines for Terminating Employees," *Personnel Administrator* 33 (April 1988):106–109. See also James G. Frierson, "How to Fire Without Getting Burned," *Personnel* 67 (September 1990):44–48; and Jonathan A. Segal, "Firing Without Fear," *HRMagazine* 37 (June 1992):125–130.

28. *HR News*, June 1991, p. A2. See also Walter Kiechel III, "The Art of the Exit Interview," *Fortune*, August 13, 1990, pp. 114–115.

29. *Working Age*, American Association of Retired Persons, September/October 1990, p. 5.

30. For more on early retirement and retirement planning, see Allen T. Steinberg, "Best Bets for Retirement," *HRMagazine* 37 (January 1992):47–50; and William J. Bowman, "Ten Steps to Retirement," *HRMagazine* 37 (August 1992):86–87.

31. Jeffrey M. Miller, *Innovations in Working Patterns: Report of the U.S. Trade Union Seminar on Alternative Work Patterns in Europe* (Washington, D.C.: The Communications Workers of America and the George Marshall Fund of the United States, 1978), p. 17. See also Frank P. Louchheim, "Executive Retirement: Change Trauma Into Opportunity," *Personnel Journal* 69 (March 1990):26–32.

32. See Donna Brown, "Preretirement Planning and the Bottom Line," *Personnel* 68 (June 1991):4.

33. Stephen L. Fink, Joel Beak, and Kenneth Taddeo, "Organizational Crisis and Change," *Journal of Applied Behavioral Science* 7 (November 1, 1971):15–37. See also Ian I. Mitroff, Paul Shrivastava, and Firdaus E. Udwadia, "Effective Crisis Management," *The Academy of Management EXECUTIVE* 1 (November 1987):283–292.

34. Gary B. Hansen, "Innovative Approach to Plant Closings: the UAW-Ford Experience at San Jose," *Monthly Labor Review* 108 (June 1985):34–37.

35. G. James Francis, John Mohr, and Kelly Andersen, "HR Balancing: Alternative Downsizing," *Personnel Journal* 72 (January 1992):71–78.

36. D. Quinn Mills, *The IBM Lesson: The Profitable Art of Full Employment* (New York: Times Books, 1988), p. 50.

37. *USA Today*, January 7, 1993, p. 1B; *Wall Street Journal*, February 25, 1993, p. B8; and *New York Times*, July 28, 1993, p. A1.
38. Lawrence M. Brammer and Frank E. Humberger, *Outplacement & Inplacement Counseling* (Englewood Cliffs, N.J.: Prentice-Hall, 1984).
39. *Wall Street Journal*, May 29, 1984, p. 1.
40. Bill Saporito, "Cutting Costs Without Cutting People," *Fortune*, May 25, 1987, p. 27.
41. *HR News*, October, 1992, p. A26.
42. Bruce R. Ellig, "Pay Policies While Downsizing the Organization: A Systematic Approach," *Personnel* 60 (May–June 1983):26–35. See also Robert M. Tomasko, "Downsizing: Layoffs and Alternatives to Layoffs," *Compensation Review* 23 (July–August 1991):19–32; Edmund Faltermayer, "Is This Layoff Necessary?," *Fortune*, June 1, 1992, pp. 71–86; Anne T. Lawrence and Brian S. Mittman, "Downsizing on the Upswing," *Personnel* 68 (February 1991):14–15; and Kim S. Cameron, Sarah J. Freeman, and Aneil K. Mishra, "Best Practices in White-Collar Downsizing: Managing Contradictions," *Academy of Management EXECUTIVE* 5 (August 1991):57–73.
43. Stephenie Overman, "Crisis Management," *HR Magazine* 36 (November 1991):43–59. See also Charlene Marmer Solomon, "The LA Riots: An HR Diary," *Personnel Journal* 71 (July 1992):22–29.
44. Edgar H. Schein, *Career Dynamics: Matching Individuals and Organizational Needs* (Reading, Mass.: Addison-Wesley, 1978), p. 211.
45. From Wendell L. French and Cecil H. Bell, Jr., *Organizational Development*, 4th ed. (Englewood Cliffs, N.J.: Prentice-Hall, 1990), pp. 159–160.
46. See Herbert Shepard, "Life Planning," in *The Laboratory Method of Changing and Learning: Theory and Application*, ed. Kenneth D. Benne, Leland P. Bradford, Jack R. Gibb, and Ronald Lippitt (Palo Alto, Calif.: Science and Behavior Books, 1975), pp. 240–251.

CHAPTER 11

1. *HRfocus* 70 (February, 1993):14.
2. See Penny Moser, "The McDonald's Mystique," *Fortune*, July 4, 1988, p. 116; and *Wall Street Journal*, September 28, 1987, p. 31.
3. H. G. Flinn, Jr., "The Emerging Role of the Professional Educator in Business," *Harvard Graduate School of Education Bulletin* 23 (Spring 1979):31.
4. Based on John R. Hinrichs, "Personnel Training," in *Handbook of Industrial and Organizational Psychology*, ed. Marvin D. Dunnette (Chicago: Rand McNally, 1976), p. 832.
5. For more on the distinctions between training and development, see John Lawrie, "Differentiate Between Training, Education and Development," *Personnel Journal* 69 (October 1990):44; and Harry B. Bernhard and Cynthia A. Ingols, "Six Lessons for the Corporate Classroom," *Harvard Business Review* 66 (September–October 1988):40–48.
6. Robert W. Goddard, "The Crisis in Workplace Literacy," *Personnel Journal* 66 (December 1987):73. See also Nancy Lynn Bernardon, "Let's Erase Illiteracy from the Workplace," *Personnel* 66 (January 1989):29–32; and Richard G. Zalman, "The "Basics" of In-house Skills Training," *HRMagazine* 36 (February 1991):74–78.
7. Anthony Patrick Carnevale, *America and the New Economy* (Washington, D.C.: The American Society for Training and Development; and U.S. Department of Labor, Employment and Training Administration, 1991), p. 108.
8. Frank O. Hoffman, "The Hierarchy of Training Objectives," *Personnel* 62 (August 1985):12–16. See also Anthony P. Carnevale, Leila J. Gainer, and Ann S. Meltzer, *Workplace Basics: The Skills Employers Want* (Washington, D.C.: The American Society for Training and Development and U.S. Department of Labor, Employment and Training Administration, 1988); Irwin L. Goldstein and Patrice Gilliam, "Training System Issues in the Year 2000," *American Psychologist* 45 (February 1990):134–143; and Edward R. Del Gaizo, "Building a Curriculum That Works," *Personnel* 66 (November 1989):58–61.
9. See Stephenie Overman, "Retraining Puts Workers Back on Track," *HRMagazine* 37 (August 1992):40–43.
10. Jennifer J. Laabs, "How Federally Funded Training Helps Business," *Personnel Journal* 71 (March 1992):35–39.
11. For more on the Job Training Partnership Act, see Louis A. Ferman, Michele Hoyman, Joel Cutcher-Gershenfeld, and Ernest J. Savoie, *New Developments in Worker Training: A Legacy for the 1990s* (Madison, Wis.: Industrial Relations Research Association, 1990), pp. 236–256; and U.S. Congress, Office of Technology Assessment, *Worker Training: Competing in the New International Economy*, OTA-ITE-457 (Washington, DC: Government Printing Office, September 1990).
12. *Business Week*, January 20, 1992, pp. 70–71; Jeffrey A. Cantor, "The Job Training Act and Shipbuilding: A Model Partnership," *Personnel Journal* 65 (June 1986):118–125; and Craig Mellow, "Motown's Manpower Renewal," *Across the Board* 24 (June 1987):31–39.
13. D. Keith Denton, "Multi-Skilled Teams Replace Old Work Systems," *HRMagazine* 37 (September 1992):48–56.
14. Joyce E. Santora, "Keep up Production Through Cross-training," *Personnel Journal* 71 (June 1992):162–166.
15. For more on JIT, see Kenneth N. Wexley and Gary P. Latham, *Developing and Training Human Resources in Organizations* (Glenview, Ill.: Scott, Foresman and Company, 1981), p. 109; and Dean M. Schroeder and Alan G. Robinson, "America's Most Successful Export to Japan: Continuous Improvement Programs," *Sloan Management Review* 32 (Spring 1991):72. For more on OJT, see Stephen B. Wehrenberg, "Supervisors as Trainers: The Long-Term Gains of OJT," *Personnel*

Journal 66 (April 1987):48–51; and Office of Technology Assessment, *Worker Training*, 1990.

16. U.S. Department of Labor, *The National Apprenticeship Program*, Bureau of Apprenticeship and Training, 1982, pp. 1–9 (pamphlet).

17. Stephenie Overman, "Apprenticeships Smooth School to Work Transitions," *HRMagazine* 35 (December 1990):41. See also Margaret Hilton, "Shared Training: Learning from Germany," *Monthly Labor Review* 114 (March 1991):33–37, and *Wall Street Journal*, May 19, 1992, p. A1.

18. U.S. Department of Labor, *The National Apprenticeship Program*; and U.S. Department of Labor, *Apprenticeship: Past and Present*, Bureau of Apprenticeship and Training, 1987 (pamphlet).

19. Robert W. Glover, "Breadth of Training in Apprenticeship," *Monthly Labor Review* 98 (May 1975):46–47.

20. "Pre-Employment Training Catches on in U.S.," *Resource*, March 1985, p. 3.

21. Jeremy Main, "New Ways to Teach Workers What's New," *Fortune*, October 1, 1984, p. 85.

22. Stephen Schwade, "Is It Time To Consider Computer-Based Training?" *Personnel Administrator* 30 (February 1985):25–35. See also Ralph E. Ganger, "Computer-Based Training Works," *Personnel Journal* 69 (September 1990):85–91.

23. Joseph P. Giusti, David R. Baker, and Peter J. Graybash, "Satellites Dish Out Global Training," *Personnel Journal* 70 (June 1991):80–84. See also *Wall Street Journal*, May 18, 1992, p. R11; and *Fortune*, December 28, 1992, pp. 90–95.

24. *Business Week*, September 7, 1987, p. 108.

25. Patricia Sellers, "How IBM Teaches Techies How to Sell," *Fortune*, June 6, 1988, pp. 141–146.

26. Diane Filipowski, "How Federal Express Makes Your Package Its Most Important," *Personnel Journal* 71 (February 1992):40–46.

27. For more on some of the complexities of selecting and training present employees as trainers, see Marie A. Dumas and David E. Wile, "The Accidental Trainer: Helping Design Instruction," *Personnel Journal* 71 (June 1992):106–110.

28. "How to Measure Return on Training," *Impact* (June 22, 1983):4.

29. Harold E. Fisher, "Make Training Accountable: Assess Its Impact," *Personnel Journal* 67 (January 1988):73–75.

30. Donald L. Kirkpatrick, "Four Steps to Measuring Training Effectiveness," *Personnel Administrator* 28 (November 1983):19–25. For more on training evaluation, see Jac Fitz-enz, "Proving the Value of Training," *Personnel* 65 (March 1988):17–22.

31. Maynard A. Howe, Carman L. Dawson and Dee Gaeddert, "Expert Training That's Free," *Personnel Journal* 70 (March 1991):59–62.

CHAPTER 12

1. Largely based on Vicki S. Kaman and John P. Mohr, "Training Needs Assessment in the Eighties: Five Guideposts," *Personnel Administrator* 29 (October 1984): 47–53.

2. See also R. Bruce McAfee and Paul J. Champagne, "Employee Development: Discovering Who Needs What," *Personnel Administrator* 33 (February 1988): 92–98.

3. *Business Week*, February 3, 1992, p. 56.

4. See Dan L. Costley and Faye A. Moore, "The Subliminal Impact and Hidden Agendas of Training," *Personnel Journal* 65 (March 1986):101–105.

5. Glenn M. McEvoy and Paul F. Buller, "Five Uneasy Pieces in the Training Evaluation Puzzle," *Training and Development Journal* 44 (August 1990):42.

6. American Society for Personnel Administration, "Most Companies Offer Tuition Aid," *Resource*, August 1988, p. 3. See also Joan Birnbaum, "Tuition Aid Programs," *HRNews*, May 1992, p. A2.

7. Drawn from Caela Farren and Beverly Kaye, "The Principles of Program Design: A Successful Career Development Model," *Personnel Administrator* 29 (June 1984):109–118.

8. See William J. Rothwell, "Curriculum Design in Training: An Overview," *Personnel Administrator* 28 (November 1983):53–57.

9. Donald L. Kirkpatrick, "Effective Supervisory Training and Development, Part 2: In-House Approaches and Techniques," *Personnel* 62 (January 1985):52–56.

10. Lynn McFarlane Shore and Arvid J. Bloom, "Developing Employees Through Coaching and Career Management," *Personnel* 63 (August 1986):34. See also Roger D. Evered and James C. Selman, "Coaching and the Art of Management," *Organizational Dynamics* 18 (Autumn 1989):16–32.

11. Mary Settle, "Up Through the Ranks at McDonnell Douglas," *Personnel* 66 (December 1989):20.

12. Caela Farren, Janet Dreyfus Gray, and Beverly Kaye, "Mentoring: A Boon to Career Development," *Personnel* 61 (November–December 1984):20–24.

13. Ibid.

14. Ibid. For more on mentoring, see George F. Drehr and Ronald A. Ash, "A Comparative Study of Mentoring Among Men and Women in Managerial, Professional, and Technical Positions," *Journal of Applied Psychology* 75 (October 1990):539–546; James A. Wilson and Nancy S. Elman, "Organizational Benefits of Mentoring," *Academy of Management EXECUTIVE* 4 (November 1990):88–94; and Beth Rogers, "Mentoring Takes a New Twist," *HRMagazine* 37 (August 1992):48–52.

15. For more on computerized business simulations, see Thomas F. Pray, "Management Training: It's All in the Game," *Personnel Administrator* 32 (October 1987):67–72.

16. See George C. Thornton III and Jeanette N. Cleveland, "Developing Managerial Talent Through Simulation," *American Psychologist* 45 (February 1990):190–199.

17. For a description by the originators, see Paul Pigors and Faith Pigors, *Case Method in Human Relations: The Incident Process* (New York: McGraw-Hill, 1961).

18. See, for example, Peter Petre, "Games That Teach You to Manage," *Fortune*, October 29, 1984, pp.

65–72; and Larry J. B. Robinson, "Role Playing as a Sales Training Tool," *Harvard Business Review* 65 (May–June 1987):34–35.

19. For a contemporary endorsement of T-group training as a vehicle for learning about group processes, see Marvin R. Weisbord, *Productive Workplaces* (San Francisco: Jossey-Bass, 1987), pp. 334–335.

20. See Eric Berne, *Games People Play: The Psychology of Human Relationships* (New York: Grove Press, 1964), Chapters 1–2; and T. Harris, *I'm OK—You're OK* (New York: Avon Books, 1969).

21. For more on behavior modeling, see Paul F. Buller and Glenn M. McEvoy, "Exploring the Long-term Effects of Behaviour Modelling Training," *Journal of Organizational Change Management* 3, No. 1 (1990):32–45; and William M. Fox, "Getting the Most from Behavior Modeling Training," *National Productivity Review* 7 (Summer 1988):238–245.

22. For information on designing in-basket exercises, see Terri Burchett, "In-Basket Cases Keep Policies in Line," *Personnel Journal* 66 (May 1987):61–65.

23. Jennifer J. Laabs, "Team Training Goes Outdoors," *Personnel Journal* 70 (June 1991):56–63.

24. Marc S. Bassin, "Developing Executive Leadership: A General Foods Approach," *Personnel* 65 (September 1988):38–42.

25. Joel Dreyfuss, David Kirkpatrick, Patricia Sellers, and H. John Steinbreder, "Danger in the Wilderness," *Fortune*, September 14, 1987, p. 6. See also *Wall Street Journal*, December 4, 1990, p. B1.

26. For an essay on nurturing high-tech talent, see Laurence Hooper, "The Creative Edge," *Wall Street Journal*, May 24, 1993, p. R6.

27. *Wall Street Journal*, September 8, 1992; and Gary N. Powell, "Upgrading Management Opportunities for Women," *HRMagazine* 35 (November 1990):67. See also *Fortune*, September 23, 1991, p. 9; *Business Week*, June 8, 1992, pp. 74–81; and *Fortune*, September 21, 1992, pp. 44–56.

28. *Business Week*, August 6, 1990, p. 51.

29. Anne M. Morrison and Mary Ann Von Glinow, "Women and Minorities in Management," *American Psychologist* 45 (February 1990):205. See also Michelle Neely Martinez, "The High Potential Woman," *HRMagazine* 36 (June 1991):46–51; Linda K. Stroh, Jeanne M. Brett, and Anne H. Reilly, "All the Right Stuff: A Comparison of Female and Male Managers' Career Progression," *Journal of Applied Psychology* 77 (June 1992):251–260; and Jennifer J. Laabs, "The Sticky Floor Beneath the Glass Ceiling," *Personnel Journal* 72 (May 1993):35–39.

30. Morrison and Von Glinow, "Women and Minorities in Management," p. 205. See also Charlene Marmer Solomon, "Networks Empower Employees," *Personnel Journal* 70 (October 1991):51–54.

31. American Association of Retired Persons, *How to Train Older Workers*, Worker Equity Department 1988, p. 4 (pamphlet). See also Anthony Aamirez, "Making Better Use of Older Workers," *Fortune*, January 30, 1989, pp.

179–187; and *Wall Street Journal*, May 21, 1991, p. A1.

32. Olivia S. Mitchell, "The Relation of Age to Workplace Injuries," *Monthly Labor Review* 111 (July 1988):8–13.

33. See Florence Mintz, "Retraining: The Graying of the Training Room," *Personnel* 63 (October 1986):69–71.

34. Jennifer J. Laabs, "The Golden Arches Provide Golden Opportunities," *Personnel Journal* 70 (July 1991):52–57.

35. Michelle Neely Martinez, "Creative Ways to Employ People with Disabilities, *HRMagazine* 35 (November 1990):40–44.

36. Stephenie Overman, "Managing the Diverse Work Force," *HRMagazine* 36 (April 1991):32. See also Lloyd S. Lewan, "Diversity in the Workplace," *HR Magazine* 35 (June 1990):42–45; R. Roosevelt Thomas, Jr., "From Affirmative Action to Affirming Diversity," *Harvard Business Review*, 68 (March–April 1990): 107–117; Benson Rosen and Kay Lovelace, "Piecing Together the Diversity Puzzle," *HRMagazine* 36 (June 1991):78–84; and Taylor H. Cox and Stacy Blake, "Managing Cultural Diversity: Implications for Organizational Competitiveness," *Academy of Management EXECUTIVE* 5 (August 1991):45–56.

37. Shari Caudron, "U S West Finds Strength in Diversity," *Personnel Journal* 71 (March 1992):40.

38. Ibid., pp. 40–44. See also Lawrence M. Baytos, "Launching Successful Diversity Initiatives," *HR Magazine* 37 (March 1992):91–97.

39. Helen LaVan, Nicholas Mathys, and David Drehmer, "A Look at the Counseling Practices of Major U.S. Corporations," *Personnel Administrator* 28 (June 1983):76ff.

40. H. Wayne Smith and Clay E. George, "Evaluating Internal Advanced Management Programs," *Personnel Administrator* 29 (August 1984):118ff.

CHAPTER 13

1. Alan H. Locher and Kenneth S. Teel, "Appraisal Trends," *Personnel Journal* 67 (September 1988):139–145.

2. *Code of Federal Regulations*, 5, Administrative Personnel, rev., January 1, 1980.

3. Locher and Teel, "Appraisal Trends," pp. 139–140. See also Jeanette N. Cleveland, Kevin R. Murphy, and Richard E. Williams, "Multiple Uses of Performance Appraisal: Prevalence and Correlates," *Journal of Applied Psychology* 74 (February 1989):130–135.

4. Michael Beer, "Note on Performance Appraisal," in *Readings in Human Resource Management*, ed. Michael Beer and Bert Spector (New York: The Free Press, 1985), p. 315.

5. Richard D. Arvey, *Fairness in Selecting Employees* (Reading, Mass.: Addison-Wesley, 1979), p. 113.

6. William H. Holley and Hubert S. Field, "Performance Appraisal and the Law," *Labor Law Journal* 26 (July 1975):423–430.

7. David P. Twomey, *Equal Employment Opportunity Law*, 2nd ed. (Cincinnati: South-Western Publishing Co., 1990), pp. 35, 64–66.

8. Gerald V. Barrett and Mary C. Kernan, "Performance Appraisal and Terminations: A Review of Court Decisions Since *Brito v. Zia* with Implications for Personnel Practices," *Personnel Psychology* 40 (Autumn 1987):501; and David I. Rosen, "Appraisals Can Make—or Break—Your Court Case," *Personnel Journal* 71 (November 1992): 113–118.

9. Donald J. Campbell and Cynthia Lee, "Self-Appraisal in Performance Evaluation: Development Versus Evaluation," *Academy of Management Review* 13 (April 1988):302–314.

10. Irene H. Buhalo, "You Sign My Report Card—I'll Sign Yours," *Personnel* 68 (May 1991):23.

11. Gary P. Latham and Kenneth N. Wexley, *Increasing Productivity Through Performance Appraisal* (Reading, Mass.: Addison-Wesley, 1981), pp. 84–85.

12. Angelo S. DeNisi, W. Alan Randolph, and Allyn G. Blencoe, "Potential Problems with Peer Ratings," *Academy of Management Journal* 26 (September 1983):457–463.

13. Glenn M. McEvoy, Paul F. Buller, and Steven R. Roghaar, "A Jury of One's Peers," *Personnel Administrator* 33 (May 1988):94–101; and Carol A. Norman and Robert A. Zawacki, "Team Appraisals—Team Approach," *Personnel Journal* 70 (September 1991):101–104.

14. Antony J. Michels, "More Employees Evaluate the Boss," *Fortune*, July 29, 1991, pp. 12–13; and Joyce E. Santora, "Rating the Boss at Chrysler," *Personnel Journal* 71 (May 1992):38–45. See also Kate Ludeman, "Upward Feedback Helps Managers Walk the Talk," *HRMagazine* 38 (May 1993):85–93; and David Kirkpatrick, "Could AT&T Rule the World?" *Fortune*, May 17, 1993, p. 64.

15. Mark R. Edwards, "Implementation Strategies for Multiple Rater Systems," *Personnel Journal* 69 (September 1990):130–141.

16. Mark R. Edwards and J. Ruth Sproull, "Making Peformance Appraisals Perform: The Use of Team Evaluation," *Personnel* 62 (March 1985):28–32.

17. L. L. Cummings and Donald P. Schwab, *Performance in Organizations: Determinants & Appraisal* (Glenview, Ill.: Scott, Foresman and Company, 1973), p. 90.

18. Richard Henderson, *Performance Appraisal: Theory to Practice* (Reston, Va.: Reston Publishing Company, 1980), pp. 137–138.

19. For an early description of this technique, see John C. Flanagan and Robert K. Burns, "The Employee Performance Record: A New Appraisal and Development Tool," *Harvard Business Review* 33 (September–October 1955):95–102.

20. Donald P. Schwab, Herbert G. Heneman III, and Thomas A. DeCotiis, "Behaviorally Anchored Rating Scales: A Review of the Literature," *Personnel Psychology* 28 (Winter 1975):550.

21. Ibid., pp. 551–552, 560. See also Kevin R. Murphy and Joseph I. Constans, "Behavioral Anchors as a Source of Bias in Rating," *Journal of Applied Psychology* 72 (November 1987):573–577.

22. Uco Wiersma and Gary P. Latham, "The Practicality of Behavioral Observation Scales, Behavior Expectation Scales, and Trait Scales," *Personnel Psychology* 39 (Autumn 1986):619–628.

23. Robert Rodgers and John E. Hunter, "Impact of Management by Objectives on Organizational Productivity," *Journal of Applied Psychology* 76 (April 1991):322–336.

24. See Harry Levinson, "Management by Whose Objectives?" *Harvard Business Review* 48 (July–August 1970):125–134; and George Strauss, "Management by Objectives: A Critical View," *Training and Development Journal* 26 (April 1972):10–15.

25. Wendell L. French and Robert W. Hollmann, "Management by Objectives: The Team Approach," *California Management Review* 13 (Spring 1975):13–22; and Rensis Likert and M. Scott Fisher, "MBGO: Putting Some Team Spirit into MBO," *Personnel* 54 (January–February 1977):40–47.

26. H. Kent Baker and Philip I. Morgan, "Two Goals in Every Performance Appraisal," *Personnel Journal* 63 (September 1984):74–78.

27. E. Kay, J. R. P. French, Jr., and H. H. Meyer, *A Study of the Performance Appraisal Interview* (New York: Management Development and Employee Relations Services, General Electric Co., March 1962), pp. 17–27. See also Robert A. Baron, "Countering the Effects of Destructive Criticism: The Relative Efficacy of Four Interventions," *Journal of Applied Psychology* 75 (June 1990):235–245; and Barry R. Nathan, Allan M. Mohrman, Jr., and John Milliman, "Interpersonal Relations as a Context for the Effects of Appraisal Interviews on Performance and Satisfaction: A Longitudinal Study," *Academy of Management Journal* 34 (June 1991):352–369.

28. Edward E. Lawler III, Alan M. Mohrman, Jr., and Susan M. Resnick, "Performance Appraisal Revisited," *Organizational Dynamics* 13 (Summer 1984):20–35.

29. Charles H. Fay and Gary P. Latham, "Effects of Training and Rating Scales on Rating Errors," *Personnel Psychology* 35 (Spring 1982):105–116.

CHAPTER 14

1. *New York Times*, July 19, 1991, p. A10. For more on pay equity, see Jerry M. Newman and George T. Milkovich, "Procedural Justice Challenges in Compensation: Eliminating the Fairness Gap," *Labor Law Journal* 41 (August 1990):575–580.

2. Bureau of National Affairs, "Wage and Salary Administration," *Personnel Policies Forum Survey No. 147*, June 1990, pp. 3–4.

3. Ibid., p. 6.

4. Donald J. Treiman, *Job Evaluation: An Analytic Review*, Interim Report to the Equal Employment Opportunity Commission (Washington, D.C.: National Academy of Sciences, 1979), p. 22. See also Laurent Dufetel, "Job Evaluation: Still at the Frontier," *Compensation Review* 23 (July–August 1991):53–67.

5. J. D. Williams, *Public Administration* (Boston: Little, Brown and Company, 1980), pp. 436–438.

6. P. R. Jeanneret, "Equitable Job Evaluation and Classification with the Position Analysis Questionnaire," *Compensation Review* 12 (First Quarter 1980): 32–42; Robert C. Mecham, "Quantitative Job Evaluation Using the Position Analysis Questionnaire," *Personnel Administrator* 28 (June 1983):82–88, 124; and Donald J. Treiman and Heidi I. Hartmann, eds., *Women, Work, and Wages: Equal Pay for Equal Value* (Washington, D.C.: National Academy Press, 1981), pp. 125–126.

7. Ronnie J. Straw and Lorel E. Foged, "Job Evaluation: One Union's Experience," *ILR Report* 19 (Spring 1982):24.

8. Treiman, *Job Evaluation*, p. 11.

9. Straw and Foged, "Job Evaluation," pp. 24–26. For the effective use of job evaluation in mergers, see Mary A. Hopkinson, "After the Merger: Paying for Keeps," *Personnel Journal* 70 (August 1991):29–31.

10. Garry D. Fisher, "Salary Surveys—An Antitrust Perspective," *Personnel Administrator* 30 (April 1985): 87–97, 154. For more on problems with wage and salary surveys, see Reuben J. Sokol, "Seven Rules of Salary Surveys," *Personnel Journal* 69 (April 1990): 83–87; and Robert J. Sahl, "Job-Content Salary Surveys: Survey Design and Selection Features," *Compensation Review* 23 (May–June 1991):14–21.

11. Paul R. Reed and Mark J. Kroll, "Red-Circle Employees: A Wage Scale Dilemma," *Personnel Journal* 66 (February 1987):92–95; and Bureau of National Affairs, "Wage and Salary Administration," 1990, p. 23.

12. Bureau of National Affairs, "Wage and Salary Administration," 1990, pp. 11–12.

13. George T. Milkovich and Jerry M. Newman, *Compensation* (Plano, Tex.: Business Publications, 1984), p. 256.

14. Bureau of National Affairs, "Wage and Salary Administration," *Personnel Policies Forum Survey No. 131* (July 1981):17.

15. Bureau of National Affairs, "Wage and Salary Administration," 1990 *Personnel Policies Forum Survey No. 147*, p. 18.

16. *Wall Street Journal*, November 11, 1983, p. 5.

17. *New York Times*, August 24, 1992, p. C4.

18. *Wall Street Journal*, June 21, 1991, p. A4. For more on executive pay, see Beth Enslow, "Up, Up, and Away," *Across the Board* 28 (July–August 1991):18–25; and *Business Week*, May 4, 1992, pp. 142–148.

19. *Wall Street Journal*, April 13, 1981, p. 33.

20. Graef S. Crystal, "The Re-emergence of Industry: Pay Differentials," *Compensation Review* 15 (Third Quarter 1983):29–32.

21. Bureau of National Affairs, "Wage and Salary Administration," 1990 *Personnel Policies Forum Survey No. 147*, p. 18.

22. For more on the advantages and disadvantages of merit pay, see Edward E. Lawler III, *Strategic Pay* (San Francisco: Jossey-Bass Publishers, 1990), pp. 71–76; and Donald Brookes, "Merit Pay: Does It Help or Hinder Productivity?" *HRfocus* 70 (January 1993):13.

23. Richard E. Kopelman, Janet L. Rovenpor, and Mo

24. Cayer, "Merit Pay and Organizational Performance: Is There an Effect on the Bottom Line?" *National Productivity Review* 10 (Summer 1991):299–307.

24. *Fortune*, April 22, 1991, p. 218; and *Business Week*, May 13, 1991, p. 70. See also Thoms J. Krajci, "Pay That Rewards Knowledge," *HRMagazine* 35 (June 1990):58–60; Gerald E. Ledford, Jr., "Three Case Studies on Skill-Based Pay: An Overview," *Compensation Review* 23 (March–April 1991):11–23.

25. See Richard L. Bunning, "Models for Skill-based Pay Plans," *HRMagazine* 37 (February 1991):62–64.

26. *HRfocus* 69 (October 1992):6.

27. See William W. Seithel and Jeff S. Emans, "Calculating Merit Increases: A Structured Approach," *Personnel* 60 (September–October 1983):56–68.

28. For more on subjective factors in pay increase decisions, see Kathryn M. Bartol and David C. Martin, "When Politics Pays: Factors Influencing Managerial Compensation Decisions," *Personnel Psychology* 43 (Autumn 1990):599–614.

29. For more on the "pay-for-performance" concept and its pros and cons, see Thomas Rollins, "Pay for Performance: Is It Worth the Trouble?" *Personnel Administrator* 33 (May 1988):42–46; Edward E. Lawler III, "Pay for Performance: Making It Work," *Personnel* 65 (October 1988):68–71; and Marcia P. Miceli and Iljae Jung, Janet P. Near, and David B. Greenberger, "Predictors and Outcomes of Reactions to Pay-for-Performance Plans," *Journal of Applied Psychology* 76 (August 1991):508–521. See also Linda Thornburg, "Pay for Performance: What You Should Know," *HRMagazine* 37 (June 1992):58–64.

30. *Congressional Quarterly*, December 2, 1989, p. 3304; and U.S. Department of Labor, *The Fair Labor Standards Act of 1938, As Amended*.

31. *Monthly Labor Review* 105 (December 1982):50.

32. *Wall Street Journal*, February 20, 1990, p. A1; and *Wall Street Journal*, February 27, 1990, p. A3.

33. U.S. Department of Labor, "Equal Pay for Equal Work Under the Fair Labor Standards Act, Interpretative Bulletin," WH Publication 1209, p. 6.

34. George S. Roukis, "Protecting Workers' Civil Rights: Equality in the Workplace," *Labor Law Journal* 26 (January 1975):3–16.

35. *Business Week*, November 25, 1972, p. 44.

36. *Wall Street Journal*, July 23, 1984, p. 9.

37. *Business Week*, July 20, 1981.

38. *Business Week*, November 26, 1984, p. 92.

39. *Fortune*, April 20, 1992; and *Business Week*, October 28, 1991, p. 35.

40. Michael W. Horrigan and James P. Markey, "Recent Gains in Women's Earnings: Better Pay or Longer Hours?" *Monthly Labor Review* 113 (July 1990):11.

41. Benson Rosen, Sara Rynes, and Thomas A. Mahoney, "Compensation, Jobs, and Gender," *Harvard Business Review* 83 (July–August 1983):174.

42. Geraldine A. Ferraro, "Bridging the Wage Gap: Pay Equity and Job Evaluations," *American Psychologist* 39 (October 1984):1166–1167.

43. George T. Milkovich, "The Emerging Debate," in *Comparable Worth: Issues and Alternatives*, ed. E. Robert Livernash (Washington, D.C.: Equal Employment Advisory Council, 1980), p. 36; and George T. Milkovich, "The Nature of the Earnings Gap," in Dana E. Friedman, ed. "Pay Equity," *The Conference Board Research Bulletin* No. 219 (1988):8–10.

44. Helen Remick, "Strategies for Creating Sound, Bias Free Job Evaluation Plans," *Job Evaluation and EEO: The Emerging Issues* (New York: Industrial Relations Counselors, 1978), p. 91.

45. Helen Remick, "The Comparable Worth Controversy," *Public Personnel Management Journal* 10 (Winter 1981):377.

46. Ibid., p. 376.

47. Schwab, "Job Evaluation and Pay Setting," p. 68.

48. George H. Hildebrand, "The Market System," in *Comparable Worth*, p. 91.

49. Treiman, *Job Evaluation*, p. 46.

50. *Resource*, July 1985, p. 1.

51. *Wall Street Journal*, April 12, 1985, p. 52.

52. *Wall Street Journal*, September 6, 1985, p. 5.

53. Thomas H. Patten, Jr., *Fair Pay* (San Francisco: Jossey-Bass Publishers, 1988), pp. 64–69.

54. June Horrigan and Ann Harriman, "Comparable Worth: Public Sector Unions and Employers Provide A Model for Implementing Pay Equity," *Labor Law Journal* 39 (October 1988):704–711. See also *Business Week*, June 8, 1992, pp. 74–83.

55. Bureau of National Affairs, "Wage and Salary Administration," 1981, p. 23.

56. Edward E. Lawler III, "The Mythology of Management Compensation," *California Management Review* 9 (Fall 1966):11–12.

57. Jay Schuster and Jerome Colletti, "Pay Secrecy: Who Is For and Against It?" *Academy of Management Journal* 16 (March 1973):35–40.

58. Bureau of National Affairs, "Human Resources Activities, Budgets, and Staffs: 1991–92," *Bulletin to Management*, SHRN-BNA Survey No. 5, June 25, 1992, p. 2.

CHAPTER 15

1. Charles Peck, "Variable Pay: New Performance Rewards," *The Conference Board Research Bulletin No. 246*, 1990, p. 3. See also R. Bradley Hill, "Your Salary Administration is Out of Date," *HRMagazine* 37 (June 1992):55–57.

2. David W. Belcher, *Compensation Administration* (Englewood Cliffs, N.J.: Prentice-Hall, 1974), p. 317.

3. See Mary Cook, "Piecework vs. Daywork: The Big Dilemma," *Personnel Administrator* 18 (November–December 1973):2–4.

4. Edward Lawler III, *Strategic Pay* (San Francisco: Jossey-Bass Publishers, 1990), pp. 57–69.

5. Jerry McAdams, "Rewarding Sales and Marketing Performance," *Personnel* 64 (October 1987):8.

6. *Wall Street Journal*, June 19, 1984, p. 33.

7. Bureau of National Affairs, "Non-Traditional Incentive Pay Programs," *Personnel Policies Forum Survey No. 148*, May 1991, pp. 9–10.

8. See Suzanne L. Minken, "Does Lump-sum Pay Merit Attention?" *Personnel Journal* 67 (June 1988):77–83; and *Business Week*, November 3, 1986, pp. 30–31. See also Helen Huntley, "Christmas Bonuses Repackaged," *St. Petersburg Times*, December 25, 1989, p. 6.

9. *New York Times*, September 12, 1991, p. C2; and *Business Week*, October 7, 1991, p. 34.

10. Harlan Fox, *Top Executive Compensation, 1980 Edition* (New York: The Conference Board, 1980), p. 6.

11. Jude T. Rich and John A. Larson, "Why Some Long-Term Incentives Fail," *Compensation Review* 16 (First Quarter 1984):26–37.

12. *Business Week*, May 9, 1983, p. 80; and *Business Week*, April 2, 1984, pp. 99–100.

13. Valerian Anderson, "Kudos for Creativity," *Personnel Journal* 68 (September 1991):90.

14. Aubrey C. Daniels, "Want More Winners? Draw a Bigger Circle," *HRMagazine* 38 (February 1933):53–54.

15. Bureau of National Affairs, *Bulletin to Management*, No. 1798, September 20, 1984, p. 8.

16. *Business Week*, April 29, 1991, p. 56. See also Rebecca A. Grant, Christopher A. Higgins, and Richard H. Irving, "Computerized Performance Monitors: Are They Costing You Customers?" *Sloan Management Review* 29 (Spring 1988):39–45; and James R. Larson, Jr., and Christine Callahan, "Performance Monitoring: How it Affects Productivity," *Journal of Applied Psychology* 75 (October 1990):530–538; and Terri L. Griffith, "Teaching Big Brother to be a team player: computer monitoring and quality," *Academy of Management EXECUTIVE* 7 (February 1993):73–80.

17. *HRNews* January 1990, p. 15.

18. *Seattle Times*, October 5, 1990, p. A5.

19. See F. J. Roethlisberger and William J. Dickson, *Management and the Worker* (Cambridge, Mass.: Harvard University Press, 1956), chap. 18.

20. Grant, Higgins, and Irving, "Computerized Performance Monitors," p. 43.

21. *Wall Street Journal*, September 3, 1992, p. A41; *Business Week*, August 3, 1992, pp. 24–25; and *New York Times*, October 30, 1992, p. C3.

22. *Seattle Post-Intelligencer*, June 25, 1992, p. A12.

23. Ford S. Worthy, "Manipulating Profits: How It's Done," *Fortune*, June 25, 1984, pp. 50–54.

24. *Wall Street Journal*, July 15, 1982, p. 27.

25. *Wall Street Journal*, June 14, 1983, p. 1; and *Business Week*, November 29, 1982, p. 35.

26. Luis R. Gomex-Mejia, David B. Balkin, and George T. Milkovich, *Organizational Dynamics* 18 (Spring 1990): 62–75.

27. Donald O. Jewell and Sandra F. Jewell, "An Example of Economic Gainsharing in the Restaurant Industry," *National Productivity Review* 6 (Spring 1987):134–143; Brian E. Graham-Moore, "Productivity Gainsharing in the Service Sector," *Personnel Management: Compensation Service* (Paramus, N.J.: Prentice-Hall Information Services, 1987), pp. 367–371; and Michael R.

Dulworth and Brian L. Usilaner, "Federal Government Gainsharing Systems in an Environment of Retrenchment," *National Productivity Review* 6 (Spring 1987):144–152.

28. Edward J. Ost, "Team-Based Pay: New Wave Strategic Incentives," *Sloan Management Review* 31 (Spring 1990):19–27.

29. Brian E. Graham-Moore and Timothy L. Ross, *Productivity Gainsharing: How Employee Incentive Programs Can Improve Business Performance* (Englewood Cliffs, N.J.: Prentice-Hall, 1983), pp. 23–24.

30. James W. Driscoll, "Working Creatively with a Union: Lessons from the Scanlon Plan," *Organizational Dynamics* 8 (Summer 1979):61–80. See also Michael Schuster, "The Scanlon Plan: A Longitudinal Analysis," *Journal of Applied Behavioral Science* 20, no. 1 (1984):23–38; and Gary W. Florkowski, *HRMagazine* 35 (January 1990):36–38.

31. David W. Belcher, *Compensation Administration* (Englewood Cliffs, N.J.: Prentice-Hall, 1974), pp. 331–335. For more on Rucker plans as contrasted with other gainsharing plans, see Christopher S. Miller and Michael H. Schuster, "Gainsharing Plans: A Comparative Analysis," *Organizational Dynamics* 16 (Summer 1987):45–67.

32. A. D. Sharplin, "Lincoln Electric's Unique Policies," *Personnel Administrator* 28 (June 1983):8–10; David Jenkins, *Job Power* (London: William Heinemann, 1974), pp. 215–219; and Carolyn Wiley, "Incentive Plan Pushes Production," *Personnel Journal* 72 (August 1993):86–91. See also James W. Lincoln, *A New Approach to Industrial Economics* (New York: The Devin-Adair Company, 1961).

33. Kathryn A. DCamp and Robin A. Ferracone, "Spot Gain Sharing Provides High-Impact Incentives," *Personnel Journal* 68 (September 1989):84–88.

34. For a description of challenges and problems in the administration of a successful Scanlon plan, see Robert J. Schulhof, "Five Years with the Scanlon Plan," *Personnel Administrator* 24 (June 1979):55–62.

35. For an analysis of research studies that support these statements, see Edward E. Lawler III, *Pay and Organization Development* (Reading, Mass.: Addison-Wesley, 1981), pp. 146–152; and J. Kenneth White, "The Scanlon Plan: Causes and Correlates of Success," *Academy of Management Journal* 22 (June 1979):292–312. See also Prescott Behn, "An Answer to the Japanese Challenge," *HRMagazine* 35 (August 1990):76–79; and Kevin M. Paulsen, "Lessons Learned from Gainsharing, *HRMagazine* 36 (April 1991):70–74.

36. Edward M. Coates III, "Profit Sharing Today: Plans and Provisions," *Monthly Labor Review* 114 (April 1991):19–25.

37. *Business Week*, November 7, 1988, pp. 134, 136.

38. *Wall Street Journal*, November 5, 1984, p. 27. For an example of a successful application of profit sharing and other incentives in retailing, see John Huey, "Wal-Mart: Will It Take Over the World?" *Fortune*, January 30, 1989, pp. 52–61.

39. See *Wall Street Journal*, April 16, 1987, p. 27.

40. *Wall Street Journal*, August 25, 1988, p. 1.

41. *Wall Street Journal*, May 15, 1984, p. 1.

42. Steve Paloncy, "Team Approach Cuts Costs," *HRMagazine* 35 (November 1990):61–62.

43. Dawn Gunsch, "Employee Suggestions and Resulting Savings Continue to Increase," *Personnel Journal* 71 (August 1992):17.

44. Robert H. Waterman, Jr., *The Renewal Factor* (New York: Bantam Books, 1987), pp. 73–74.

45. *Business Week*, February 20, 1989, p. 55.

46. Paloncy, "Team Approach Cuts Costs," p. 61.

47. Dawn Gunsch, "Thousands for Your Thoughts," *Personnel Journal* 70 (August 1991):16.

48. Milton A. Tatter, "Turning Ideas into Gold," *Management Review* 64 (March 1975):5–6.

49. Gail Gregg, "The Power of Suggestion," *Across the Board* 20 (December 1983):30.

50. Gunsch, "Employee Suggestions," p. 17.

51. Gregg, "The Power of Suggestion," pp. 29–31.

52. Ibid., p. 31.

53. W. Clay Hamner and Ellen P. Hamner, "Behavior Modification on the Bottom Line," *Organizational Dynamics* 4 (Spring 1976):8–9.

54. Ibid.

55. Ibid.

56. Gina Ameci, "Bonuses and Commissions: Is Your Overtime Pay Legal?" *Personnel Journal* 66 (January 1987):107–108.

57. *Wall Street Journal*, November 23, 1983, p. 6.

58. Raymond E. Maejerus, "Workers Have a Right to a Share of Profits," *Harvard Business Review* 62 (September–October 1984):42, 43, 50

59. Richard I. Henderson, *Compensation Management: Rewarding Performance*, 3rd ed. (Reston, Va.: Reston Publishing Company, 1982), p. 351.

60. See Graham-Moore and Ross, *Productivity Gainsharing*, pp. 1–15. See also Nancy J. Perry, "Here Come Richer, Riskier Pay Plans," *Fortune*, December 19, 1988, pp. 50–58.

61. Bureau of National Affairs, "Human Resources Activities, Budgets, and Staffs: 1991–92," *Bulletin to Management*, SHRM-BNA Survey No. 57, June 25, 1992, pp. 2–3.

62. John Huey, "America's Most Successful Merchant," *Fortune*, September 23, 1991, pp. 46–59.

CHAPTER 16

1. *Wall Street Journal*, April 29, 1983, p. 27.

2. Paul N. Keaton and Michael J. Semb, "Shaping up the Bottom Line," *HRMagazine* 35 (September 1990): 81–86.

3. *J. K. Lasser's Monthly Tax Letter* 2 (December 1992):4.

4. Bureau of National Affairs, *Labor Policy and Practice*, 365: 5 July 1986. For more on unemployment compensation, see Catherine A. Shanklin, "Unemployment Insurance: Survive the System," *Personnel Journal* 69 (March 1990):84–89; and *Ideas & Trends*, Commerce

Clearing House, August 5, 1992, p. 126.

5. *New York Times*, April 11, 1991, p. C1.

6. *New York Times*, April 11, 1991, p. C1; and *Business Week*. October 19, 1992, p. 90.

7. U.S. Chamber of Commerce, *Employee Benefits, 1992 Edition*, p. 24.

8. This discussion is based on William J. Wiatrowski, "New Survey on Pension Benefits," *Monthly Labor Review* 114 (August 1991):8–22; and Edward J. Emering, "Defined Benefits Are in Jeopardy," *Personnel Journal* 70 (April 1991):104–109.

9. Wiatrowski, "New Survey on Pension Benefits," p. 9; and Karen Matthes. "Defined Benefit Pension Plans: An Uncertain Future," *HRfocus* 69 (May 1992):3.

10. U.S. Chamber of Commerce, *Employee Benefits, 1990 Edition*, p. 21.

11. Emering, "Defined Benefits Are in Jeopardy," p. 107.

12. Donald K. Odermahn, "Four Steps to a Successful 401(k) Plan," *HRMagazine* 36 (August 1991):44–46; and *Business Week*, December 21, 1992, p. 38.

13. See Nathaniel Gilbert, "Both Sides of the ESOP Story," *Personnel* 67 (April 1990):28–32; Charles G. Burck, "There's More to ESOP Than Meets the Eye," *Fortune*, March 1976, pp. 128–132ff.; and *Business Week*, August 8, 1988, p. 61.

14. Stephanie Lawrence, "ESOPS Show Record Growth," *Personnel Journal* 69 (May 1990):10.

15. *Fortune*, May 20, 1991, pp. 83–88: *Wall Street Journal*, March 22, 1991, p. 1–8; and *Business Week*, April 15, 1985, p. 94.

16. This discussion is based on Donald G. Carlson, "Responding to the Pension Reform Law," *Harvard Business Review* 52 (November–December 1974):133–144; and Robert Frumkin and Donald Schmitt, "Pension Improvements Since 1976 Reflect Inflation, U.S. Law," *Monthly Labor Review* 102 (April 1979):32–37. See also "Pension Portability," *HRMagazine* 37 (February 1992):99–100.

17. U.S. Chamber of Commerce, *Employee Benefits, 1992 Edition*, p. 28. See also David E. Ott, "Survivor Income Benefits Provided by Employers," *Monthly Labor Review*, 114 (June 1991):13–18.

18. David A. Weeks, *Rethinking Employee Benefits Assumptions* (New York: The Conference Board, 1978), p. 63; *Wall Street Journal*, March 26, 1985, p. 4; and Michael Bucci, "Health Maintenance Organizations: Plan Offerings and Enrollments," *Monthly Labor Review* 114 (April 1991):11–18.

19. Phyllis R. Yale, "Controlling the Uncontrollable," *Across the Board* 28 (April 1991):13–15; Ronald Henkoff, "Yes, Companies Can Cut Health Costs," *Fortune*, July 1991, pp. 52–56; and *Wall Street Journal*, January 29, 1991, p. B1.

20. *Wall Street Journal*, April 8, 1988, p. 17. See also *Business Week*, September 28, 1992, pp. 36–38.

21. *Wall Street Journal*, May 6, 1988, p. 44. For more on child-care programs, see *Fortune*, August 10, 1992, p. 50–53; Gopal C. Pati, "Child Care Options Abound,"

Across the Board 28 (January–February 1991):22–26; and Linda Thiede Thomas and James E. Thomas, "The ABCS of Child Care: Building Blocks of Competitive Advantage," (Winter 1990):31–41. See also Jennifer J. Laabs, "Family Issues Are a Priority at Stride Rite," *Personnel Journal* 72 (July 1993):48–56.

22. *New York Times* February 8, 1993, p. B1; *Wall Street Journal*, February 5, 1993, p. A5; *Oregonian*, February 5, 1993, p. D1; and *Maui News*, January 6, 1993, p. A7.

23. Roy S. Azarnoff, "Can Employees Carry the Eldercare Burden?" *Personnel Journal* 67 (September 1988): 60–62.

24. See Sherry E. Sullivan and J. Barry Gilmore, "Employers Begin to Accept Eldercare as a Business Issue," *Personnel* 68 (July 1991), pp. 3–4: *Wall Street Journal*, June 23, 1993, p. B1; and Jeff L. Lefkovich, "Business Responds to Elder-care Needs," *HRMagazine* 37 (June 1992):103–108.

25. U.S. Chamber of Commerce, *Employee Benefits, 1992 Edition*, p. 13.

26. *Business Week*, September 30, 1991, p. 41.

27. Bureau of National Affairs, "Paid Holiday and Vacation Policies," *Personnel Policies Forum* 142 (November 1986):1.

28. Kevin J. O'Donnell and Kathy A. Lawler, "Group Legal Services Plans," *Personnel Administrator* 32 (March 1987):92–97; and *HRfocus* 70 (January 1993):5.

29. *The 1993 Business Week 1000*, April 1, 1993, p. 49; *Wall Street Journal*, August 31, 1982, p. 1; and Jack N. Kondrasuk, "Corporate Physical Fitness Programs: The Role of the Personnel Department," *Personnel Administrator* 29 (December 1984):75–80.

30. "Visions," *HRMagazine* 36 (March 1991):81–82.

31. Chris W. Chen, "TRW's Housing Plan," *Personnel Journal* 70 (March 1991):83–86.

32. Posted on bulletin board, AMC Theatres, Tyrone Square, Saint Petersburg, Florida, November 25, 1989.

33. *Wall Street Journal*, July 15, 1980, p. 1.

34. *Wall Street Journal*, April 13, 1993, p. A1; Rita Dommermuth, "Commuter Subsidies Are Gaining Speed," *HRfocus* 69 (March 1992):9; and Charlene Marmer Solomon, "The Traffic Trap," *Personnel Journal* 69 (November 1990):65–70; and

35. *Wall Street Journal*, March 26, 1985, p. 39; and *Business Week*, December 10, 1990, p. 196.

36. *Wall Street Journal*, December 19, 1984, p. 31.

37. *Business Week*, March 13, 1978, p. 79.

38. *Wall Street Journal*, April 15, 1980, p. 1.

39. *Business Week*, November 2, 1981, p. 56.

40. Weeks, *Rethinking Employee Benefits Assumptions*, p. 87.

41. Ibid., p. 88.

42. *Wall Street Journal*, June 21, 1983, p. 1.

43. Barbara Anne Solomon, "A Company That Benefits from Child-Care Benefits," *Personnel* 62 (February 1985): 4–6.

44. Mark E. Haskins, "In-House Financial Planning for Employees," *Personnel Administrator* 64 (August 1985): 99–116.

45. *Wall Street Journal*, June 21, 1988, p. 1.

46. *Business Week*, June 24, 1991, p. 50.

47. Sal D. Rinella, "Burger King Hooks Employees With Educational Incentives," *Personnel Journal* 68 (October 1989):90.

48. *Fortune*, November 1, 1990, p. 223.

49. U.S. Chamber of Commerce, *Employee Benefits, 1992 Edition*, p. 16.

50. Joyce E. Santora, "American Airlines Opts for Flex," *Personnel Journal* 69 (November 1990):32–34; and M. Michael Markowich, "Flex Still Works," *Personnel Journal* 69 (December 1990):62–64.

51. Dennis H. Roberts, "Financial Education Enhances Cafeteria Benefits," *Personnel Journal* 69 (April 1990): 116.

52. Robert C. Wender and Ronald L. Sladky, "Flexible Benefit Opportunities for the Small Employer," *Personnel Administrator* 29 (December 1984):111–118.

53. Ibid., pp. 112–113; and Carolyn A. Baker, "Flex Your Benefits," *Personnel Journal* 67 (May 1988):54–61.

54. Susan J. Velleman, "Flexible Benefits Package That Satisfy Employees and the IRS," *Personnel* 62 (March 1985):33–41.

55. *Fortune*, August 8, 1983, p. 105. For more on flexible benefit plans, see Robert D. Heller, "Cafeteria Benefits Plans: A Simpler Approach," *Personnel* 65 (June 1988):30–35; Commerce Clearing House, *Flexible Benefits: Will They Work For You?* (Chicago: Commerce Clearing House, Inc., 1988); and Richard Gisonny and Steven H. Fein, "Benefits and Taxes," *HRMagazine* 36 (February 1991):37–42.

56. Bureau of National Affairs, *Bulletin to Management*, March 22, 1962, p. 8.

57. Judith F. Mazo, "Another Compliance Challenge for Employers: The Retirement Equity Act," *Personnel* 62 (February 1985):43–49.

58. Bureau of National Affairs, *Bulletin to Management*, ASPA-BNA Survey No. 39, January 24, 1980, pp. 1–12.

59. Buck Consultants, "Changes in Mandatory Retirement and Benefit Accruals Take Effect," *Personnel Journal* 66 (January 1987):24–25.

60. "Equal Employment Opportunity Commission Guidelines on Discrimination Based on Sex," amended April 4, 1972, Section 1604.9, Fringe Benefits. See also W. Thomas Reeder, Jr., "The Nondiscrimination Rules for Employee Health and Welfare Plans," *Legal Report*, Society for Human Resource Management (Winter 1992):1–5.

61. *Monthly Labor Review* 106 (September 1983):36.

62. American Society for Personnel Administration, *Washington Vantage Point*, May 1979, p. 1. See also *Business Week*, August 10, 1992, p. 42.

63. *Monthly Labor Review* 106 (August 1983):40.

64. Betty Southward Murphy, Wayne E. Barlow, and D. Diane Hatch, "COBRA Takes Effect," *Pesonnel Journal* 66 (January 1987):12.

65. Frederick I. Shick, "Tax Reform's Impact on Benefit Programs," *Personnel Administrator* 32 (January 1987): 80–88. See also Jack H. Schechter, "The Impact of Tax Reform on Employee Benefits: A Halftime Report," *Personnel* 65 (January 1988):46–51; and John M. Walbridge, Jr., "Finding Your Way Through Section 89," *Personnel* 66 (January 1989):16–20.

66. *Wall Street Journal*, January 25, 1985, p. 37.

67. *Wall Street Journal*, July 3, 1984, p. 7.

68. *Wall Street Journal*, October 19, 1992, p. B1.

69. J. Brad Chapman and Robert Otteman, "Employee Preference for Various Compensation and Fringe Benefit Options," *Personnel Administrator* 20 (November 1985), special insert, 6 pp. See also Thomas J. Bergmann and Marilyn A. Bergmann, "How Important Are Fringe Benefits to Employees?" *Personnel* 64 (December 1987):59–64.

70. Philip Kienast, Douglas MacLachlan, Leigh McAlister, and David Sampson, "The Modern Way to Redesign Compensation Packages," *Personnel Administrator* 28 (June 1983):127–133. See also Marie Wilson, Gregory B. Northcraft, and Margaret A. Neale, "The Perceived Value of Fringe Benefits," *Personnel Psychology* 38 (Summer 1985):309–320.

71. *Wall Street Journal*, September 25, 1984, p. 1.

72. *Wall Street Journal*, March 19, 1985, p. 1.

73. Bureau of National Affairs, *Bulletin to Management*, BNA Policy and Practice Series, vol. 42, no. 3, Part II, January 24, 1991, p. 5; and *Wall Street Journal*, October 28, 1992, p. B1.

74. *Wall Street Journal*, November 11, 1992, p. B1; Peggy Stuart, "Self-Insurance Cuts Health Care Cost," *Personnel Journal* 71 (July 1992):51–57; and Jennifer J. Laabs, "Deere's HMO Turns Crisis Into Profit," *Personnel Journal* 71 (October 1992):82–89.

75. Bureau of National Affairs, *Bulletin to Management*, No. 1811, December 20, 1984, p. 1.

76. Based on Morton E. Grossman, "Benefits: Costs & Coverage," *Personnel Journal* 65 (May 1986):74–79; and Bureau of National Affairs, "Controlling Health Care Costs: Crisis in Employee Benefits," *Bulletin to Management*, PPP BM No. 1759—Part II, December 15, 1983, p. 6. See also John S. Montgomery, "Shrink Mental Health Care Costs," *Personnel Journal* 67 (May 1988):86–91; and Carol J. Loomis, "The Killer Cost Stalking Business," *Fortune*, February 27, 1989, pp. 58–68.

77. Barron H. Harvey, Judy A. Schultze, and Jerome F. Rogers, "Rewarding Employees for Not Using Sick Leave," *Personnel Administrator* 28 (May 1983):55–59.

78. *Business Week*, March 21, 1983, p. 146.

79. Bureau of National Affairs, *Bulletin to Management*, No. 1794, August 23, 1984, p. 1.

80. *New York Times*, September 17, 1991, p. C15.

81. Elizabeth K. La Fleur and Walter B. Newsom, "Opportunities for Child Care," *Personnel Administrator* 33 (June 1988):146–154.

82. James F. White, "Preparing Benefit Statements," *Personnel* 63 (May 1986):13–18.

83. Anthony J. Barra, "Employees Keep Informed With Interactive Kiosks," *Personnel Journal* 67 (October 1988):43–51.

84. Jennifer J. Laabs, "Oliver: A Twist on Communication," *Personnel Journal* 70 (September 1991):79–82.

85. James Ledvinka, *Federal Regulation of Personnel and Human Resource Management* (Boston: Kent Publishing Company, 1982), pp. 235–238.

CHAPTER 17

1. E. Wight Bakke, "To Join or Not to Join," in *Unions, Management and the Public*, 3d ed., ed. E. Wight Bakke, Clark Kerr, and Charles W. Anroo (New York: Harcourt, Brace & World, 1967), pp. 85–92. See also Hoyt N. Wheeler and John A. McClendon, "The Individual Decision to Unionize," in *The State of the Unions*, ed. George Strauss, Daniel G. Gallagher, and Jack Fiorito (Madison, Wis.: Industrial Relations Research Association, 1991), pp. 47–83.

2. W. Clay Hamner and Frank J. Smith, "Work Attitudes as Predictors of Unionization Activity," *Journal of Applied Psychology* 63 (August 1978):415–421.

3. Robert McGlotten, "The Flip Side," *Personnel Administrator* 32 (July 1987):64.

4. For an article on the role of the shop steward in a steel mill, see *Wall Street Journal*, April 1, 1987, pp. 1, 12.

5. *New York Times*, April 16, 1992, p. A1; and *Wall Street Journal*, April 20, 1992, p. A3.

6. Based on Bureau of National Affairs, "Union Membership," *Bulletin to Management Datagraph*, February 28, 1991, pp. 60–62.

7. *Ibid*, p. 60.

8. *Wall Street Journal*, May 15, 1987, p. 44; and *Business Week*, June 29, 1987, p. 36.

9. Courtney D. Gifford, *Directory of U.S. Labor Organizations, 1988–89 Edition* (Washington, D.C.: Bureau of National Affairs, 1988), p. 42; and *Fortune*, February 8, 1993, p. 130.

10. Advisory Commission on Inter-governmental Relations, *Labor-Management Policies of State and Local Government* (Washington, D.C.), September 1969, pp. 8–9. For more on white-collar organizing, see John G. Kilgour, "The Odds on White-Collar Organizing," *Personnel* 67 (August 1990):29–34.

11. See Dudley W. Buffa, *Union Power and American Democracy: The UAW and the Democtratic Party, 1972–83* (Ann Arbor: The University of Michigan Press, 1984).

12. Courtney D. Gifford, *Directory of U.S. Labor Organizations, 1990–91 Edition* (Washington, D.C.: Bureau of National Affairs, 1990), p. 4.

13. For more on what management may and may not do relative to unionization or decertification drives, see Paul S. McDonough, "Maintain a Union-Free Status," *Personnel Journal* 69 (April 1990):108–114.

14. I. Chafetz and C. R. P. Fraser, "Union Decertification: An Elementary Analysis," *Industrial Relations* 18 (Winter 1979):68.

15. William J. Bigoness and Ellen R. Peirce, "Responding to Union Decertification Elections," *Personnel Administrator* 33 (August 1988):49–53.

16. Bureau of National Affairs, "Union Membership," p. 60; and *New York Times*, February 15, 1993, p. C6.

17. *Wall Street Journal*, January 29, 1991, p. A1.

18. *Seattle Times*, July 20, 1991, p. A1.

19. For information on women and unions, see Karen S. Koziara, Michael H. Moskow, and Lucretia D. Tanner, eds., *Working Women: Past, Present, Future* (Washington, D.C.: Bureau of National Affairs, 1987), p. 190.

20. Bureau of National Affairs, "Basic Patterns: Union Security," *Collective Bargaining Negotiations and Contracts*, 87: 1, March 9, 1989.

21. *Fortune*, October 24, 1988, p. 8.

22. AFL-CIO, *The Changing Situation of Workers and Their Unions:* A Report by the AFL-CIO Committee on the Evolution of Work (Washington, D.C.: AFL-CIO), February 1985, pp. 12–13.

23. Ibid., p. 13.

CHAPTER 18

1. Archibald Cox, "Rights Under a Labor Agreement," *Harvard Law Review* 69 (February 1956):606.

2. Labor Management Relations Act, 1947 (as amended, 1959), Section 8(d).

3. Robben W. Fleming, "The Obligation to Bargain in Good Faith," in *Public Policy and Collective Bargaining*, ed. Joseph Shister, Benjamin Aaron, and Clyde W. Summers (New York: Harper & Row, 1962), p. 63.

4. *H. K. Porter Co.* v. *NLRB*, 397 U.S. 99 (1970).

5. Fleming, "The Obligation to Bargain in Good Faith," pp. 63, 64.

6. Benjamin J. Taylor and Fred Whitney, *Labor Relations Law*, 4th ed. (Englewood Cliffs, N.J.: Prentice-Hall, 1983), p. 408.

7. *Los Angeles Times*, April 21, 1988, p. IV-6; and *Business Week*, June 27, 1988, p. 82.

8. For a discussion of distributive and integrative bargaining see Richard E. Walton and Robert B. McKersie, *A Behavioral Theory of Labor Negotiations* (New York: McGraw-Hill, 1965), pp. 4–6.

9. See *Wall Street Journal*, April 15, 1988, p. 30. See also Donald F. Ephlin, "Revolution by Evolution: The Changing Relationship Between GM and the UAW," *The Academy of Management EXECUTIVE* 2 (February 1988):63–66.

10. *Business Week*, July 26, 1993, p. 84.

11. *Honolulu Star-Bulletin*, December 23, 1987, p. C1; and *Wall Street Journal*, April 20, 1990.

12. Edgar Weinberg, "Labor-Management Cooperation: A Report on Recent Initiatives," *Monthly Labor Review* 99 (April 1976):17–18. For a description of a successful program in the public sector, see Ronald Contino, "Productivity Gains Through Labor-Management Cooperation at the N.Y.C. Department of Sanitation

Bureau of Motor Equipment," in *Teamwork: Joint Labor-Management Programs in America*, ed. Jerome M. Rosow (New York: Pergamon, 1986), pp. 169–186.

13. Peter Lazes, Leslie Rumpeltes, Ann Hoffner, Larry Pace, and Anthony Costanza, "Xerox and the ACTWU: Using Labor-Management Teams to Remain Competitive," *National Productivity Review* 10 (Summer 1991):339–349. See also *Business Week*, April 5, 1993, p. 26.

14. Daniel Quinn Mills, *Labor-Management Relations*, 2nd ed. (New York: McGraw-Hill, 1982), p. 264.

15. *Business Week*, May 4, 1992, p. 36; *Chicago Tribune*, September 27, 1992, sec. 7, p. 3; *Business Week*, August 10, 1992, p. 56; *New York Times*, April 21, 1992, p. A11; and *Wall Street Journal*, April 22, 1993, p. A15.

16. Mills, *Labor-Management Relations*, p. 246.

17. William H. Holley and Kenneth M. Jennings, *The Labor Relations Process*, 2nd ed. (Chicago: The Dryden Press, 1984), p. 175.

18. See Sam Kagel, "Combining Mediation and Arbitration," *Monthly Labor Review* 96 (September 1973):62.

19. *Wall Street Journal*, May 22, 1987, pp. 1, 7.

20. Bureau of National Affairs, *Collective Bargaining Negotiations and Contracts*, "Basic Patterns: Grievances and Arbitration," 51:5, February 9, 1989.

21. Ibid., 51:2.

22. Ibid., 51:1

23. Peter Feuille, Michael LeRoy, and Timothy Chandler, "Judicial Review of Arbitration Awards: Some Evidence," in *Proceedings of the 1990 Spring Meeting*, Industrial Relations Research Association, May 2–4, 1990, Buffalo, New York, p. 482.

24. Bureau of National Affairs, *Basic Patterns in Union Contracts*, 9th ed., 1979, p. 16.

25. Federal Mediation and Conciliation Service, *Thirty-Ninth Annual Report—Fiscal Year 1986*, pp. 25–26.

26. Frank Elkouri and Edna A. Elkouri, *How Arbitration Works*, 4th ed. (Washington, D.C.: Bureau of National Affairs, 1985), p. 138.

27. See Owen Fairweather, *Practice and Procedure in Labor Arbitration*, 2nd ed. (Washington, D.C.: Bureau of National Affairs, 1983).

28. See Jay E. Grenig, "Stare Decisis, Res Judicata, and Collateral Estoppel and Labor Arbitration," *Labor Law Journal* 38 (April 1987):195–205.

29. Harold W. Davey, *Contemporary Collective Bargaining*, 3rd ed. (Englewood Cliffs, N.J.: Prentice-Hall, 1972), p. 38.

30. George H. Friedman, "Correcting Arbitrator Error: The Limited Scope of Judicial Review," *Arbitration Journal* 33 (December 1978):9–16.

31. Thomas J. McDermott, "Arbitrability: The Courts vs. the Arbitrator," *Arbitration Journal*, 23 (January 1968):18–27.

32. Arthur A. Sloane and Fred Whitney, *Labor Relations*, 4th ed. (Englewood Cliffs, N.J.: Prentice-Hall, 1981), p. 225

33. Based on Thomas W. Jennings, "The Crossroads of the Future," *Labor Law Journal* 31 (August 1980):498–502.

34. Feuille, LeRoy, and Chandler, "Judicial Review of Arbitration Awards," p. 482.

35. Betty Southward Murphy, "The Chairman Looks at the NLRB," *Personnel Administrator* 21 (May 1976):26.

36. Tim Bornstein, "Interest Arbitration in Public Employment: An Arbitrator Views the Process," *Labor Law Journal* 29 (February 1978):79.

37. Ibid., pp. 77–86.

38. Paul D. Staudohar, "Results of Final-Offer Arbitration of Bargaining Disputes," *California Management Review* 18 (Fall 1975):57–61.

CHAPTER 19

1. William A. Kaplin, *The Law of Higher Education* (San Francisco: Jossey-Bass, 1979), p. 20.

2. Patricia A. Somers and Judith Clementson-Mohr, "Sexual Extortion in the Workplace," *Personnel Administrator* 24 (April 1979):27.

3. "Sexual Harassment Lands Companies in Court," *Business Week*, October 1, 1979, pp. 120–122.

4. Equal Employment Opportunity Commission, "Final Amendments to Guidelines to Discrimination Because of Sex," *Federal Register*, November 10, 1980, p. 74677.

5. Dawn Bennett-Alexander, "Sexual Harassment in the Office," *Personnel Administrator* 33 (June 1988):174–188; and Maria Morlacci, "Sexual Harassment Law and the Impact of *Vinson*," *Employee Relations Law Journal* 13 (Winter 1987–88):501–519.

6. Stacey J. Garvin, "Employer Liability for Sexual Harassment," *HRMagazine* 36 (June 1991):101; and "Hostile Environment Costs Employer $147,000," *HRNews*, April 1993, p. A19.

7. *Wall Street Journal*, December 2, 1991, p. B1; Allen I. Fagin and Myron D. Rumeld, "Employer Liability for Sexual Harassment," *Legal Report*, Society for Human Resource Management, Fall 1991, pp. 1–4; Ann Meyer, "Getting to the Heart of Sexual Harassment," *HRMagazine* 37 (July 1992):82–84; and Jonathan A. Segal, "Seven Ways to Reduce Harassment Claims," *HRMagazine* 37 (January 1992):84–85.

8. Eric Matusewitch, "Language Rules Can Violate Title VII," *Personnel Journal* 69 (October 1990):102.

9. *Wall Street Journal*, October 28, 1991, p. A16.

10. For more on "just cause," see Donald S. McPherson, "The Evolving Concept of Just Cause: Carroll R. Daugherty and the Requirement of Disciplinary Due Process," *Labor Law Journal* 38 (July 1987):387–403.

11. See Kenneth Sovereign, *Personnel Law* (Reston, Va.: Reston Publishing Company, 1984), p. 269.

12. David W. Ewing, *Freedom Inside the Organization* (New York: E. P. Dutton, 1977), pp. 108–110.

13. *Monthly Labor Review* 106 (June 1983):48.

14. Kenneth D. Walters, "Your Employees' Right to Blow the Whistle," *Harvard Business Review* 53 (July–August 1975):26–34.

15. Gregory J. Mounts, "Significant Decisions in Labor Cases," *Monthly Labor Review* 102 (April 1979):61.

16. Ewing, *Freedom Inside the Organization*, p. 233.

17. "Fight for Rights," *Wall Street Journal*, July 24, 1980, p. 38.

18. Ewing, *Freedom Inside the Organization*, pp. 101–102.

19. *Wall Street Journal*, December 31, 1984, p. 11.

20. *Wall Street Journal*, June 24, 1991, p. A4.

21. Bureau of National Affairs, "Communicating Policies," *Personnel Management: BNA Policy and Practice Series*, 207:584, October 1987.

22. Timothy R. Barnett and Daniel S. Cochran, "Making Room for the Whistleblower," *HRMagazine* 36 (January 1991):58–61. See also *Business Week*, June 3, 1991, pp. 138–139.

23. Ewing, *Freedom Inside the Organization*, p. 129. See also *Business Week*, September 4, 1989, pp. 74–82.

24. Bureau of National Affairs, "Employee Information and the Privacy Issue," *Personnel Management: BNA Policy and Practice Series*, 251:654, September 1987; and Philip Adler, Jr., Charles K. Parsons, and Scott B. Zolke, "Employee Privacy: Legal and Research Developments and Implications for Personnel Administration," *Sloan Management Review* 26 (Winter 1985):14. For more on privacy, see Barbara A. Bland-Acosta, "Developing an HRIS Privacy Policy," *Personnel Administrator* 33 (July 1988):52–59.

25. John G. Fox and Paul J. Ostling, "Employee and Government Access to Personnel Files: Rights and Requirements," *Employee Relations Law Journal* 5 (Summer 1979):70.

26. "Workplace Surveillance Risky Business," *Resource*, December 1989, p. 19.

27. Ibid., p. 19.

28. *Business Week*, January 15, 1990, p. 75.

29. Larry Reynolds, "Rights Groups Condemn Eavesdropping Supervisors," *Personnel* 68 (April 1991):19.

30. "Workplace Surveillance Risky Business," p. 19.

31. *Business Week*, January 15, 1990, p. 75. For more on computer monitoring, see *Fortune*, November 4, 1991, p. 131.

32. Commerce Clearing House, *Pension Plan Guide*, 1979, par. 9207. See also Commerce Clearing House, "Pension Plans—Welfare and Other Funds," *Labor Law Reports*, 6930.8501, 1987.

33. Peter F. Drucker, "The Job as Property Right," *Wall Street Journal*, March 4, 1980, p. 22.

34. Jack Stieber, "Most U.S. Workers Still May Be Fired Under the Employment-at-Will Doctrine," *Monthly Labor Review* 107 (May 1984):34–35.

35. Ibid., p. 35. See also Philip R. Voluck and Michael J. Hanlon, "Contract Disclaimers in Policy Documents," *Personnel Journal* 66 (August 1987):123–131. For more on employment at will, see David S. Hames, "The Current Status of the Doctrine of Employment-at-Will," *Labor Law Journal* 39 (January 1988):19–32.

36. See Nancy K. Kubasek and M. Neil Browne, "Recruiter Beware: The Oral Promise of Lifetime Employment May Be More Than a Mere Inducement,"
Labor Law Journal 42 (May 1991):273–284; William E. Fulmer and Ann Wallace Casey, "Employment at Will: Options for Managers," *Academy of Management EXECUTIVE* 4 (May 1990):102–107; and Robert J. Nobile, "Say it Legally," *Personnel* 68 (May 1991):11.

37. Bureau of National Affairs, "Employee Discipline and Discharge," *Personnel Policies Forum* 139 (January 1985):10. See also Douglas M. McCabe, *Corporate Nonunion Complaint Procedures and Systems* (New York: Praeger, 1988).

38. Douglas McCabe, "Grievance Processing: Non-Union Setting—Peer Review Systems and Internal Corporate Tribunals: A Procedural Analysis," *Labor Law Journal* 39 (August 1988):496–502. See also Richard Grote, "Peer Review May Keep You Out of Control," *Wall Street Journal*, August 14, 1992, p. A14.

39. In 1809 Sweden instituted an ombudsman who was appointed to report directly to Parliament. See Ewing, *Freedom Inside the Organization*, p. 167; Justin Martin, "New Tricks for an Old Trade," *Across the Board* 29 (June 1992):41.

40. Xerox Corp. appointed an ombudsman for managers and salaried employees in 1972. See *Business Week*, May 3, 1976, pp. 114–116. See also Lucinda Lamont, "Control Data's Review Process," *Personnel* 64 (February 1987):7–11; James T. Ziegenfuss, Jr., Mary Rowe, Lee Robbins and Robert Munzenrider, "Corporate Ombudsmen," *Personnel Journal*, 68 (March 1989): 76–79; and Junda Woo, "Ombudsmen Proliferate in the Workplace," *Wall Street Journal*, Frebruary 19, 1993, p. B12.

41. Ewing, *Freedom Inside the Organization*, pp. 166–170.

42. Bureau of National Affairs, "Policies for Unorganized Employees," *Personnel Policies Forum* 125 (April 1979):6.

43. Daryl G. Hatano, "Employee Rights and Corporate Restrictions," *California Management Review* 24 (Winter 1981):11.

44. Adler, Parsons, and Zolke, "Employee Privacy," p. 20.

45. Lawrence Z. Lorber, J. Robert Kirk, Kenneth H. Kirschner, and Charlene R. Handorf, *Fear of Firing: A Legal and Personnel Analysis of Employment-at-Will* (Alexandria, Va.: The ASPA Foundation, 1984), p. 22. See also Maureen R. Witt and Sandra R. Goldman, "Avoiding Liability in Employee Handbooks," *Employee Relations Law Journal* 14 (Summer 1988):5–18.

46. Bureau of National Affairs, "Employee Discipline and Discharge," pp. 26–27.

CHAPTER 20

1. National Safety Council, *Accident Facts, 1987 Edition* (Chicago: National Safety Council), p. 42

2. Bureau of National Affairs, *Collective Bargaining: Negotiations and Contracts* 95 (March 9, 1989):1–4.

3. Ibid., p. 4.

4. John E. Aberton, "Labor Unions and Accident Prevention: Champion or Adversary?" *Professional Safety* 25 (November 1980):19–20.

5. Dan Petersen, *Safety Supervision* (New York: Amacom, 1976), pp. 50–53.

6. National Safety Council, *Accident Facts, 1991 Edition* (Chicago: National Safety Council), p. 35.

7. *Wall Street Journal*, January 25, 1985, p. 10.

8. U.S. Department of Labor, "Health Hazards of Asbestos," Occupational Safety and Health Administration, Pamphlet 3040, 1979, p. 1.

9. Bhopal accident: *USA Today*, October 22, 1992, p. 4A; *St. Petersburg Times*, December 4, 1989, p. 16A; and *New York Times*, March 25, 1993, p. A7. Chernobyl blast: *Wall Street Journal*, September 3, 1992, p. B2; *Time*, April 9, 1990, pp. 68–70; and *St. Petersburg Times*, April 23, 1990, p. 11A. Texas City tank rupture: *New York Times*, June 19, 1991, p. A14. North Sea fire: *Business Week*, June 24, 1991, p. 104. Houston explosion: *Wall Street Journal*, August 23, 1991, p. B4. Kumi, South Korea, chemical leak: *New York Times*, April 16, 1991, p. C1. Hamlet, North Carolina, fire: *New York Times*, September 5, 1991, p. A15; and *New York Times*, September 15, 1992, p. A8.

10. *Resource*, March 1985, p. 6.

11. John M. Ivancevich, Michael T. Matteson, and Edward P. Richards III, "Who's Liable for Stress on the Job?" *Harvard Business Review* 64 (March–April 1985):60. See also David S. Allen, "Less Stress, Less Litigation," *Personnel* 67 (January 1990):32–35; and Mark O. Feter, "What to Do About Workers' Comp," *Fortune*, June 29, 1992, pp. 80–82.

12. Section 1 (e), The Walsh-Healey Public Contracts Act, as amended.

13. *U.S. Code, 1982 Edition* (Washington, D.C.: U.S. Government Printing Office, 1983), p. 120ff.

14. See Lawrence Z. Lorber and J. Robert Kirk, "UAW v. Johnson Control Fetal Exclusion Policies Struck Dow," *Legal Report*, Society for Human Resource Management, Summer 1991, pp. 5–8; and Martha Peak, "It's Not Just a Women's Issue," *Personnel* 68 (June 1991):15.

15. *Wall Street Journal*, June 17, 1985, p. 2.

16. Robert H. Sand, "Current Developments in OSHA," *Employee Relations Law Journal* 14 (Summer 1988):128.

17. *HRNews*, February 1990, p. A 11.

18. *Wall Street Journal*, September 15, 1992, p. B7.

19. Garth L. Mangum, "Murder in the Workplace: Criminal Prosecution v. Regulatory Enforcement," *Labor Law Journal* 39 (April 1988):220–231.

20. U.S. Department of Labor, *All About OSHA*, Occupational Safety and Health Administration, Pamphlet 2056 (rev.), 1985, p. 3.

21. U.S. Department of Health, Education, and Welfare, National Institute for Occupational Safety and Health, DHEW (NIOSH), Loren L. Hatch et al., *Self Evaluation of Occupational Safety and Health Programs*, Publication No. 78–187, October 1978, p. 1.

22. U.S. Department of Labor, *OSHA: Employee Workplace Rights*, Occupational Safety and Health Administration, Pamphlet 3021 (rev.), 1989, pp. 5–6.

23. *Wall Street Journal*, November 22, 1988, p. B2; and Bruce D. May, "Hazardous Substances: OSHA Mandates the Right to Know," *Personnel Journal* 65 (August 1986):128.

24. U.S. Department of Labor, *All About OSHA*, pp. 41–42.

25. U.S. Department of Labor, *OSHA Inspections*, Occupational Health and Safety Administration, Pamphlet 2098, 1989 (Revised), p. 5.

26. *Marshall, Secretary of Labor, et al. v. Barlow's Inc.*, May 23, 1978. Docket No. 76–1143.

27. U.S. Department of Labor, *OSHA Inspections*, 1989, pp. 4–6.

28. Ibid., p. 7.

29. Ibid., pp. 2–9.

30. U.S. Department of Labor, *All About OSHA*, p. 27.

31. U.S. Department of Labor, *OSHA Inspections*, 1989, pp. 10–11.

32. *Wall Street Journal*, March 7, 1988, p. 25.

33. *New York Times*, August 23, 1991, p. A16.

34. Robin L. Ballau and Roy M. Buchan, "Study Shows That Gender Is Not a Major Factor in Accident Etiology," *Occupational Health and Safety* 47 (September–October 1978):54–58.

35. David Margolick, "The Lonely World of Night Work," *Fortune*, December 15, 1980, pp. 108–114.

36. "Rotating Shift Work Causes Many Problems," *Occupational Safety and Health* 47 (September–October 1978): 21.

37. National Safety Council, *Accident Facts, 1992 Edition* (Itasca, Ill.: National Safety Council), p. 36.

38. Ibid., p. 34.

39. Bill Saporito, "The Most Dangerous Job in America," *Fortune*, May 31, 1993, pp. 130–140.

40. Bureau of National Affairs, "Safety Policies and the Impact of OSHA," *Personnel Policies Forum* 117 (May 1977):12.

41. Ibid., p. 7.

42. Ibid., p. 6.

43. Ibid., p. 8.

44. *Wall Street Journal*, October 19, 1989, p. A15; and *New York Times*, August 15, 1993, p. Y15. See also Robert B. Kelly, *Industrial Emergency Preparedness* (New York: Van Nostrand Reinhold, 1989).

45. William S. Cohen, "Health Promotion in the Workplace," *American Psychologist* 40 (February 1985):213–216.

46. *Business Week*, January 30, 1989, pp. 92–93, Elissa-Beth Chapnik and Clifford Gross, "Visual Display Terminals: Health Issues and Productivity," *Personnel* 64 (May 1987):10–16; *Wall Street Journal*, September 28, 1992, p. A1; Editors, "Safety Measures for Users of Computers," *HRNews* 36 (July 1991):77–78; and *Business Week*, July 13, 1992, p. 142.

47. Ward Gardner and Peter Taylor, *Health at Work* (New York: John Wiley & Sons, 1975), pp. 72–73. See also Office of Technology Assessment, Congress of the United States, *Preventing Illness and Injury in the Workplace* (New York: UNIPUB, 1985).

48. James T. Wrich, "Beyond Testing: Coping With Drugs at Work," *Harvard Business Review* 6 (January–February 1988):120.

49. Cohen, "Health Promotion in the Workplace," p. 215.

50. Donald W. Myers, *Establishing and Building Employee Assistance Programs* (Westport, Conn.: Quorum Books, 1984), p. 11.

51. Wrich, "Beyond Testing," p. 120.

52. Bureau of National Affairs, "Employee Discipline and Discharge," *Personnel Policies Forum* 139 (January 1985): 8.

53. G. J. Provost et al., "Alcohol or Drug Abuse on the Job: A Study of Arbitration Cases," *Employee Relations Law Journal* 5 (Autumn 1979):245–253.

54. Paul Sherman, as quoted in Robert D. Dugan, "Affirmative Action for Alcoholics and Addicts?" *Employee Relations Law Journal* 5 (Autumn 1979):240–241.

55. William Mayer, "Alcohol Abuse and Alcoholism: The Psychologist's Role in Prevention, Research, and Treatment," *American Psychologist* 38 (October 1983): 1119.

56. Drug-Free Workplace Act of 1988 (Subtitle D of the Anti-Drug Abuse Act of 1988). See also Robert J. Nobile, "The Drug-Free Workplace Act: Act on It!" *Personnel* 67 (February 1990):21–23.

57. Bureau of National Affairs, *Bulletin to Management* 42 (May 23, 1991):154. See also Dawn Gunsch, "Training Prepares Workers for Drug Testing," *Personnel Journal* 72 (May 1993):52–59.

58. American Society for Personnel Management, *Legal Report*, Spring 1989, pp. 1–6. See also Jonathan A. Segal, "To Test or Not to Test," *HRMagazine* 37 (April 1992):40–43.

59. *New York Times*, August 30, 1991, p. A1; and *New York Times*, October 16, 1992, p. A15.

60. Brian Heshizer and Jan P. Muczyk, "Drug Testing at the Workplace: Balancing Individual, Organizational, and Societal Rights," *Labor Law Journal* 39 (June 1988):342–357; G. John Tysse, "Is Now the Time to Drug Test?" *Legal Report*, Society for Human Resource Management, Fall 1991, pp. 4–7; and Rob Brooker, "Industry Standards in Workplace Drug Testing," *Personnel Journal* 71 (April 1992):128–132.

61. Hans Selye, *Stress Without Distress* (New York: The New American Library, 1974), p. 151.

62. Richard P. Sloan, Jessie C. Gruman, and John P. Allegrante, *Investing in Employee Health* (San Francisco: Jossey-Bass, 1987), pp. 240–242.

63. Helen LaVan, Marsha Katz, and Wayne Hochwarter, "Employee Stress Swamps Workers' Comp," *Personnel* 67 (May 1990):61–64.

64. *U.S. News and World Report*, September 5, 1983, p. 45.

65. *The Boston Sunday Globe*, May 2, 1993, p. 71; *The New York Times*, May 8, 1993, p. A1; and National Safety Council, *Accident Facts, 1992 Edition*, p. 40.

66. John M. Ivancevich and Michael T. Matteson, "Optimizing Human Resources: A Case for Preventive Health and Stress Management," *Organizational Dynamics* 9 (Autumn 1980):5–25. See also Gwendolyn Puryear Keita and James M. Jones, "Reducing Adverse Reaction to Stress in the Workplace," *American Psychologist* 45 (October 1990):1137–1141; John M. Ivancevich, Michael T. Matteson, Sara Freedman, and James S. Phillips, "Worksite Stress Management Interventions," *American Psychologist* 45 (February 1990): 252–261; and C. Brady Wilson, "U.S. Businesses Suffer from Workplace Trauma," *Personnel Journal* 70 (July 1991):47–50.

67. Robert S. Letchinger, "AIDS: An Employer's Dilemma," *Personnel* 63 (February 1986):58–63. See also Nancy L. Breuer, "AIDS Issues Haven't Gone Away," *Personnel Journal* 72 (January 1992):47–49; Vaughn Alliton, "Financial Realities of AIDS in the Workplace," *HRMagazine* 37 (February 1992):78–81; and *New York Times*, November 23, 1992, p. A1.

68. U.S. Department of Justice, *The Americans with Disabilities Act*, Civil Rights Division, Office of the Americans with Disabilities Act, booklet, 1991, p. 7.

69. Geralyn McClure Franklin and Robert K. Robinson, "AIDS and the Law," *Personnel Administrator* 33 (April 1988):118–121.

70. George Ruben, "Developments in Industrial Relations," *Monthly Labor Review* 111 (June 1988):62.

71. David L. Wing, "AIDS: The Legal Debate," *Personnel Journal* 65 (August 1986):114–119. See also Jonathan A. Segal, HIV: How High the Risk?" *HRMagazine* 38 (February 1993):93–100; and *New York Times*, December 4, 1991, p. A1. See also James Monroe Smith, "How to Develop and Implement an AIDS Workplace Policy," *HRFocus*, March 1993, p. 15.

72. *IBM Management Report*, September 1987, p. A124.

73. *Resource*, April 1989, p. 2.

74. Myers, *Establishing and Building Employee Assistance Programs*, p. 4.

75. Ibid., p. 16. See also Steve Bergsman, "Help Employees Who Help Themselves," *HRMagazine* 35 (April 1990):46–49; and Bob Smith, "Compulsive Gamblers: In Over Their Heads," *HRFocus* 69 (February 1992):3.

76. Harvey Shore, "SRM Forum: Employee Assistance Progams—Reaping the Benefits," *Sloan Management Review* 25 (Spring 1984):70.

77. Diane Kirrane, "EAPs: Dawning of a New Age," *HRMagazine* 35 (January 1990):32.

78. John V. Grimaldi and Rollin H. Simonds, *Safety Management*, 3rd ed. (Homewood, Ill.: Irwin, 1975), p. 5.

79. See Bernard Weiss, "Behavioral Toxicology and Environmental Health Science," *American Psychologist* 38 (November 1983):1174–1187.

80. U.S. Department of Labor, *OSHA Handbook for Small Businesses*, Occupational Safety and Health Administration, Safety Management Series, OSHA 2209 (rev.), 1990, p. 6.

81. See John W. Jones, David DuBois, and Lisa Wuebker, "Promoting Safety by Reducing Human Error," *Personnel* 63 (June 1986):41–44.

82. Grimaldi and Simonds, *Safety Management*, p. 107.

83. See Fred W. Schott and Sandra Wendel, "Wellness with a Track Record," *Personnel Journal* 71 (April 1992): 98–104; Deborah L. Gebhardt and Carolyn E. Crump, "Employee Fitness and Wellness Programs in the Workplace," *American Psychologist* 45 (February 1990): 262–272; Dennis Thompson, "Wellness Programs Work for Small Employers, Too," *Personnel* 67 (March 1990):26–28; and Shari Caudron, "A Low-cost Wellness Program," *Personnel Journal* 71 (February 1992):34–38.

84. F. W. Heinrich, Dan Petersen, and Nestor Roos, *Industrial Accident Prevention*, 5th ed. (New York: McGraw-Hill, 1980), p. 300.

85. Ibid., p. 300.

86. Reynold L. Hoover, Robert L. Hancock, Kevin L. Hylton, O. Bruce Dickerson, and George E. Harris, *Health, Safety, and Environmental Control* (New York: Van Nostrand Reinhold, 1989), p. 10.

87. William English, "What Is Safety Management?" *Professional Safety* 25 (September 1980):27.

88. Ibid., p. 27. See also Ted Ferry, "Guidelines for Hiring Safety Personnel," *Personnel Journal* 65 (September 1986):40–44.

89. L. L. Hatch et al., *Self-Evaluation of Occupational Safety and Health Programs*, U.S. Department of Health, Education, and Welfare, National Institute for Occupational Safety and Health, DHEW (NIOSH) Publication No. 78–187, October 1978, pp. 5–6.

90. *Wall Street Journal*, January 16, 1989, p. C16.

91. Bureau of National Affairs. "The Personnel/Human Resources Department: 1989–1990," *Bulletin to Management* (June 28, 1990):2–3. See also Richard Lock, "The Safety-HR Connection," *Personnel Journal* 71 (July 1992):18.

CHAPTER 21

1. S. William Alper and Russell E. Mandel, "What Policies and Practices Characterize the Most Effective HR Departments?" *Personnel Administrator* 29 (November 1984):120–124.

2. John Naisbitt, *Megatrends: Ten New Directions Transforming Our Lives* (New York: Warner Books, 1982), p. 159.

3. John Naisbitt and Patricia Aburdene, *Re-inventing the Corporation* (New York: Warner Books, 1985), p. 72.

4. Naisbitt, *Megatrends*, p. 183.

5. Brian Dumaine, "The Bureaucracy Busters," *Fortune*, June 17, 1991, pp. 36–50; and *New York Times*, June 25, 1991, p. C1.

6. Marshall Sashkin, *A Manager's Guide to Participative Management* (New York: American Management Association, 1982), p. 60.

7. See Edwin A. Locke and David M. Schweiger, "Participative Decision-Making: One More Look," in *Research in Organizational Behavior*, ed. Barry M. Staw (Greenwich, Conn.: JAI Press, 1979), pp. 265–339; Bennett Harrison, "The Failure of Worker Participation," *Technology Review* 94 (January 1991):74; and

Bryan Miller, "Not All It's Cracked Up to Be?" *Across the Board* 28 (November 1991):24–28.

8. Rebecca Rolfes, "Giving the EC the Works," *Across the Board* 28 (November 1991):15–16.

9. See Sar A. Levitan and Diane Werneke, "Worker Participation and Productivity Change," *Monthly Labor Review* 107 (September 1984):28–33; and Friederich Furstenberg, "Co-Determination and Its Contribution to Industrial Democracy: A Critical Evaluation," *Proceedings of the Thirty-Third Annual Meeting*, Industrial Relations Research Association, 1981, pp. 185–190.

10. David I. Levine, "Participation, Productivity, and the Firm's Environment," *California Management Review* 32 (Summer 1990):86–100.

11. For more on this, see Ralph H. Kilmann, *Beyond the Quick Fix: Managing Five Tracks to Organizational Success* (San Francisco: Jossey-Bass Publishers, 1984).

12. For more on the role of the facilitator, see Edgar Schein, *Process Consultation*, vol. 1 (Reading, Mass.: Addison-Wesley, 1988).

13. For some of the theory on this subject, see Kurt Lewin, *Field Theory in Social Science* (New York: Harper & Brothers, 1951); and Ludwig von Bertalanffy, *General Systems Theory* (New York: George Braziller, 1968).

14. Edgar H. Schein, "Improving Face-to-Face Relationships," *SMR Portfolio: The Art of Managing Change and Uncertainty*, a collection of reprints from the *Sloan Management Review*, 1983, p. 34.

15. Based on Jack Fordyce and Raymond Weil, *Managing with People* (Reading, Mass.: Addison-Wesley, 1971), pp. 114–116. See also Richard E. Walton, *Managing Conflict: Interpersonal Dialogue and Third-Party Roles*, 2nd ed. (Reading, Mass.: Addison-Wesley, 1987).

16. See Wendell L. French and Cecil H. Bell, Jr., *Organization Development: Behavioral Science Interventions for Organization Improvement*, 4th ed. (Englewood Cliffs, N.J.: Prentice-Hall, 1990), chap. 10.

17. Fordyce and Weil, *Managing with People*, pp. 143–146.

18. See Richard A. Krueger, *Focus Groups* (Newbury Park: Sage Publications, 1988), pp. 18–20.

19. For further elaboration, see Wendell L. French and Robert Hollmann, "Management by Objectives: The Team Approach," *California Management Review* 17 (Spring 1975):13–22; and Rensis Likert and M. Scott Fisher, "MBGO: Putting Some Team Spirit into MBO," *Personnel* 54 (January–February 1977):40–47.

20. William L. Mohr and Harriet Mohr, *Quality Circles* (Reading, Mass.: Addison-Wesley, 1983), p. 13.

21. *Business Week*, July 30, 1984, p. 80; and Lawrence Schein, *The Road to Total Quality: Views of Industry Experts*, The Conference Board Research Bulletin No. 239, 1990, p. 6. For more on quality circles, see Gregory P. Shea, "Quality Circles: The Danger of Bottled Change," *Sloan Management Review* 27 (Spring 1986): 33–46; Sandy J. Wayne, Ricky W. Griffin, and Thomas S. Bateman, "Improving the Effectiveness of Quality Circles," *Personnel Administrator* 31 (March 1986): 79–88; and Peter F. Drucker, "The Emerging Theory

of Manufacturing," *Harvard Business Review* 68 (May–June 1990):96.

22. Peter Lazes, Leslie Rumpeltes, Ann Hoffner, Larry Pace, and Anthony Costanza, "Xerox and the ACTWU: Using Labor-Management Teams to Remain Competitive," *National Productivity Review* 10 (Summer 1991):339–349.

23. Based on Robert Blake, H. A. Shepard, and Jane S. Mouton, *Managing Intergroup Conflict in Industry* (Houston, Tex.: Gulf Publishing, 1964); and Fordyce and Weil, *Managing with People*, pp. 124–130.

24. Floyd C. Mann, "Studying and Creating Change," in *The Planning of Change*, ed. W. G. Bennis, K. D. Benne, and R. Chin (New York: Rinehart and Winston, 1961), p. 609.

25. Based on Mann, "Studying and Creating Change," pp. 605–613; and French and Bell, *Organization Development*, chap. 13. For more on survey feedback, see Jack W. Wiley, "Making the Most of Survey Feedback as a Strategy for Organization Development," *OD Practitioner* 23 (March 1991):1–4; and Tom Standing, Jerry Martin, and Milan Moravec, "Attitude Surveys: A Catalyst for Cultural Change," *HRfocus* 68 (December 1991):17–18.

26. French and Bell, *Organization Development*, p. 17.

27. For more on organization development, see Wendell L. French, Cecil H. Bell, Jr., and Robert A. Zawacki, eds., *Organization Development: Theory, Practice, and Research*, 3rd ed. (Homewood, Ill.: BPI and Richard D. Irwin, 1989).

28. Richard E. Walton, "From Control to Commitment in the Workplace," *Harvard Business Review* 64 (March–April 1985):84.

29. Stephen H. Fuller, "How Quality-of-Worklife Projects Work for General Motors," *Monthly Labor Review* 103 (July 1980):37–39; and Irving Bluestone, "How Quality-of-Worklife Projects Work for the United Auto Workers," *Monthly Labor Review* 103 (July 1980):39–41. See also Alfred S. Warren, "Quality of Work Life at General Motors," in *Teamwork: Joint Labor-Management Programs in America*, ed. Jerome M. Rosow (New York: Pergamon, 1986), pp. 119–132; and *Wall Street Journal*, January 12, 1989, pp. 1, 7.

30. Paul S. Goodman, "Quality of Work Life Projects in the 1980s," *Labor Law Journal* 31 (August 1980):487–494. See also Mitchell W. Fields and James W. Thacker, "Influence of Quality of Work Life on Company and Union Commitment," *Academy of Management Journal* 35 (June 1992):439–450.

31. *Business Week*, special issue "The Quality Imperative," October 25, 1991, 216 pp.; Barbara H. Peters and Jim L. Peters, *Total Quality Management*, The Conference Board Report No. 963, 1991, 63 pp.; and Jeremy Main, "How to Win the Baldrige Award," *Fortune*, April 23, 1990, pp. 101–116.

32. *Business Week*, special issue, *The Quality Imperative*, October 25, 1991, p. 9. See also "The Benchmarking Boom," *HRfocus* 70 (April 1, 1993):1, 6–7.

33. *Ibid.* See also Business Week, April 12, 1993, p. 93.

34. U.S. General Accounting Office, *Management Practices: U.S. Companies Improve Performance Through Quality Efforts*, National Security and International Affairs Division, May 1991, p. 2.

35. Ibid., p. 4.

36. Alan L. Wilgus, "Forging Change in Spite of Adversity," *Personnel Journal* 70 (September 1991):60–67.

37. Frank Rose, "How Quality Means Service Too," *Fortune*, April 22, 1991, pp. 97ff. For more on TQM, see Marshall Sashkin and Kenneth J. Kiser, *Total Quality Management* (Seabrook, Md.: Ducochon Press, 1991); and *Business Week*, special report "Quality," November 30, 1992, pp. 66–67.

38. *New York Times*, December 18, 1992, p. A15; and *Wall Street Journal*, December 18, 1992, p. A12.

39. Ibid.

40. *Wall Street Journal*, December 18, 1992, p. A12.

41. *Wall Street Journal*, June 7, 1993, pp. A2 and A14; *New York Times*, June 8, 1993, p. A11; and *Wall Street Journal*, June 9, 1993, p. A14.

42. Larry Reynolds, "Old NLRB Rule Could Jeopardize Quality Programs," *HRfocus* 68 (December 1991):1–2.

43. Bureau of National Affairs, "Human Resources Activities, Budgets, and Staffs: 1991–92," SHRM-BNA Survey No. 57, June 25, 1992, p. 3.

CHAPTER 22

1. See also Peter J. Dowling and Randall S. Schuler, *International Dimensions of Human Resource Management* (Boston: PWS-Kent, 1990), pp. 4–16.

2. See Michael E. Porter, *The Competitive Advantage of Nations* (New York: The Free Press, 1990), p. 18.

3. *Wall Street Journal*, May 4, 1992, p. A20; *Business Week*, September 28, 1992, p. 58; and Brenton Schlender, "China Really Is on the Move," *Fortune*, October 5, 1992, pp. 114–122.

4. *Wall Street Journal*, September 4, 1992, p. A1.

5. *Business Week*, August 24, 1992, p. 43.

6. *Financial Times* (London), July 7, 1992, p. 1.

7. *New York Times*, September 8, 1992, p. C2.

8. *Fortune*, July 27, 1992, p. 176.

9. Porter, *The Competitive Advantage of Nations*, p. 62.

10. See Calvin Reynolds, "Are You Ready to Make IHR a Global Function?" *HRNews*, February 1992, pp. 1–2; and Alicia Kitsuse, "At Home Abroad," *Across the Board* 29 (September 1992):35–38.

11. Kitsuse, "At Home Abroad," p. 38.

12. Philip R. Harris and Robert T. Moran, *Managing Cultural Differences*, 3rd ed. (Houston: Gulf Publishing Company, 1991), pp. 206–211.

13. Ibid., pp. 206–211. For another classification scheme, see Endel-Jakob Kolde, *Environment of International Business*, 2nd ed. (Kent Publishing Company, 1985), pp. 420–428.

14. See Shari Caudron, "Training Ensures Success Overseas," *Personnel Journal* 70 (December 1991):27. See also Stephanie Derderion, "International Success Lies

in Cross-Cultural Training," *HRfocus* 70 (April 1993): 9.

15. Stephenie Overman, "Apprenticeships Smooth School to Work Transitions," *HRNews* 35 (December 1990):42–43.

16. *Fortune*, December 3, 1990, p. 107.

17. *New York Times*, May 5, 1992, p. A1.

18. *Wall Street Journal*, August 14, 1990, p. B1.

19. U.S. Department of Labor, Bureau of International Labor Affairs, *Foreign Labor Trends* 90–52, 1989, p. 11.

20. *Business Week*, January 27, 1992, pp. 44–45.

21. *Foreign Labor Trends*, 92–5, 1990–1991, pp. 4, 13.

22. *Foreign Labor Trends*, 91–45, 1990–1991, p. 5.

23. *Fortune*, May 21, 1990, p. 144; Harumi Befu and Christine Cernosia, "Demise of 'Permanent Employment' in Japan," *Human Resource Management* 29 (Fall 1990): 231–249; and *Business Week*, September 7, 1992, p. 46.

24. *Foreign Labor Trends*, 91–13, 1990, p. 4.

25. *Foreign Labor Trends*, 91–11, 1989–1990, p. 7.

26. *Foreign Labor Trends*, 92–7, 1990–1991, p. 5.

27. *Foreign Labor Trends*, 91–06, 1989–1990, p. 6.

28. *Foreign Labor Trends*, 91–49, 1990–1991, p. 3.

29. *Foreign Labor Trends*, 91–23, 1990, p. 12.

30. *Financial Times* (London), September 7, 1992, p. 8.

31. David I. Levine, "Participation, Productivity, and the Firm's Environment," *California Management Review* 32 (Summer 1990):88–90.

32. *New York Times*, December 25, 1991, pp. 1, 22.

33. *New York Times*, August 19, 1992, p. A4.

34. *Seattle Post-Intelligencer*, October 7, 1991, p. A2; and *Japan Times* (Tokyo), January 20, 1992, p. 22.

35. Magoroh Maruyama, "Changing Dimensions of International Business," *Academy of Management EXECUTIVE* 6 (August 1992), p. 89

36. *Fortune*, February 24, 1992, p. 78.

37. *Foreign Labor Trends*, 91–14, 1990–1991, p. 5.

38. *Foreign Labor Trends*, 91–25, 1990–1991, p. 5.

39. *HRfocus* 69 (August 1992):18.

40. *Foreign Labor Trends*, 91–62, 1990–1991, p. 15.

41. *Seattle Times/Seattle Post-Intelligencer*, August 30, 1992, p. C2.

42. *Foreign Labor Trends*, 91–11, 1989–1990, p. 7.

43. *Foreign Labor Trends*, 91–09, 1990, p. 4.

44. *Business Week*, March 16, 1992, p. 102.

45. Robert O'Connor, "New Training Approaches for Europe '93," *Personnel Journal* 71 (May 1992):97.

46. *Wall Street Journal*, July 31, 1990, p. A8.

47. *Foreign Labor Trends*, 91–48, 1990–1991, p. 7; and *Fortune*, June 19, 1989, p. 136.

48. *Wall Street Journal*, May 4, 1992, p. B1.

49. *Wall Street Journal*, June 6, 1991, p. A1.

50. *Foreign Labor Trends*, 92–2, 1990–1991, p. 6.

51. Jone L. Pearce, "From Socialism to Capitalism: the Effects of Hungarian Human Resources Practices," *Academy of Management Review* 5 (November 1991):75–88.

52. James A. Wall, Jr., "Managers in the People's Republic of China," *Academy of Management EXECUTIVE* 4 (May 1990):25.

53. *Foreign Labor Trends*, 91–23, 1990, p. 21.

54. *New York Times*, September 1, 1992, pp. A1, C4.

55. *Wall Street Journal*, June 26, 1990, p. A1.

56. Rebecca Rolfes, "Workforce Europe: Are Women Coming in From the Cold?" *Across the Board* 27 (September 1990):60.

57. *Foreign Labor Trends*, 92–1, 1990–1991, p. 8.

58. *Business Week*, July 9, 1990, p. 14; and *Foreign Labor Trends*, 90–52, 1989, p. 8.

59. Pearce, "From Socialism to Capitalism," p. 81.

60. *Business Week*, July 27, 1992, p. 48–53.

61. *Foreign Labor Trends*, 90–14, 1989, p. 11.

62. *Fortune*, June 19, 1989, pp. 9, 12.

63. *Foreign Labor Trends*, 91–13, 1990, p. 3.

64. *Foreign Labor Trends*, 91–34, 1990–1991, p. 8.

65. *New York Times*, November 10, 1992, p. A7.

66. Buck Consultants, "Healthcare 'Down Under": Australia Considers Reforms," *HRfocus* 69 (June 1992):10.

67. *Foreign Labor Trends*, 92–2, 1990–1991, p. 6.

68. *Foreign Labor Trends*, 91–15, 1990, p. 5.

69. *Foreign Labor Trends*, 91–37, 1990–1991, p. 5.

70. *Business Week*, August 31, 1992, p. 39.

71. *Business Week*, September 1992, p. 80.

72. *Foreign Labor Trends*, 92–6, 1991, p. 2.

73. *Foreign Labor Trends*, 91–26, 1990–1991, p. 10.

74. *New York Times*, August 31, 1992, p. A4.

75. *Foreign Labor Trends*, 91–29, 1990, p. 8.

76. *Foreign Labor Trends*, 91–31, 1990–1991, p. 8.

77. *Foreign Labor Trends*, 91–60, 1990–1991, p. 5.

78. *Time*, September 14, 1992, pp. 17, 20.

79. *Business Week*, August 3, 1992, p. 35; and John P. Young, "From the Editor," *Academy of Mangement EXECUTIVE* 5 (February 1991):4.

80. *Business Week*, July 13, 1992, p. 42.

81. Ibid.

82. *Foreign Labor Trends*, 91–36, 1990–1991, p. 12.

83. *The Seattle Times*, May 11, 1993, p. A7; and *Wall Street Journal*, May 13, 1993, p. A13.

84. *Personnel Journal* 69 (June 1990):23.

85. *Wall Street Journal*, May 14, 1992, p. B1.

86. John M. Ivancevich, Richard S. DeFrank, and Paul R. Gregory, "The Soviet Enterprise Director: an Important Resource Before and After the Coup," *Academy of Management EXECUTIVE* 6 (February 1992):46.

87. Min Basadur, "Managing Creativity: A Japanese Model," *Academy of Management EXECUTIVE* 6 (May 1992):33.

CHAPTER 23

1. S. William Alper and Russell E. Mandel, "What Policies and Practices Characterize the Most Effective HR Departments?" *Personnel Administrator* 29 (November 1984):120–124.

2. Roy Foltz, Karen Rosenberg, and Julie Foehrenbach, "Senior Management Views the Human Resources Function," *Personnel Administrator* 27 (September 1982):37.

3. Commerce Clearing House, "1991 SHRM/CCH Survey," CCH *Human Resources Management* service, June 26, 1991, pp. 1–12.

4. U.S. Department of Labor, *Occupational Outlook Handbook, 1992–93 Edition*, Bureau of Labor Statistics, Bulletin 2400, May 1992, pp. 52–53.

5. *Ibid.*, p. 10.

6. L. Kate Beatty, "Pay Goes Up as HR Jobs Broaden," *HRMagazine* 36 (September 1991):55–58.

7. L. Kate Beatty, "What's Driving Your Pay," *HRMagazine* 35 (July 1990):45–48.

8. Steven Langer, "What You Earn and Why," *Personnel Journal* 70 (January 1991):25. See also Kenneth Labich, "The New Pay Game . . . And How You Measure Up," *Fortune*, October 19, 1992, pp. 116–119.

9. Donald P. Rogers, "The Basic Course in Personnel Administration/Industrial Relations," *Collegiate News and Views* 38 (Fall–Winter, 1984):5–7. See also Donald W. Myers, "Business Schools Lag in HR Offerings," *HRMagazine* 35 (August 1990):72–74.

10. Telephone call to headquarters, Society for Human Resource Management, November 13, 1991; *Who's Who in HR, 1993 Directory* (Alexandria, Va: Society for Human Resource Management 1992); and HR Certification Institute, *Register of Certified Human Resource Professionals*, Society for Human Resource Management, June 1992, p. ii.

11. Personnel Accreditation Institute, *Accreditation for Personnel and Human Resource Professionals*, p. 1 (pamphlet; P.O. Box 19648, Alexandria, Va. 22320.)

12. Y. K. Shetty and Paul F. Buller, "Regaining Competitiveness Requires HR Solutions," *Personnel* 67 (July 1990):8–12.

13. See Audrey Freeman, *The Changing Human Resources Function*, Conference Board Report No. 950, 1990, p. 18.

14. Wayne F. Cascio, *Costing Human Resources: The Financial Impact of Behavior in Organizations* (Boston: Kent Publishing Company, 1982), pp. 45–55. See also Joel Lapointe and Jo Ann Verdin, "How to Calculate the Cost of Human Resources," *Personnel Journal* 67 (January 1988):34–45.

15. See, for example, Robert Levering and Milton Moskowitz, *The 100 Best Companies to Work For in America* (New York: Doubleday, 1993).

GLOSSARY OF KEY TERMS

Numbers in parentheses refer to the chapters in which key terms appear.

Absenteeism   Failure to report to work. *(5)*

Accreditation   A way of recognizing a specified level of competency within a particular field. *(23)*

Acquired immune deficiency syndrome (AIDS)   A disease of the immune system in which the victim has impaired ability to fight off infections. *(20)*

Across-the-board pay increases   General percentage pay increases for employees, usually to accommodate pressures from inflation. *(14)*

Action research   The process of gathering information, feeding it back, and developing plans for implementing desired changes. *(21)*

Active listening   Careful listening to words and feelings being expressed and reflecting them back to speakers in such a way that they know they have been understood. *(21)*

Ad hoc arbitration   Arbitration in which an arbitrator is appointed for each case. *(18)*

Adverse impact   Disproportionate selection of any legally protected group, leading to conclusions of discrimination. *(9)*

Affiliate   A subsidiary, joint venture, or branch of a company located in another country. *(22)*

Affirmative action   A remedial concept that requests employers and labor unions to take voluntary, positive steps to improve the work opportunities for women, racial and ethnic minorities, disabled workers, and others who have been deprived of job opportunities. The provision of equal opportunity for minority and female employees. *(3, 6)*

Age harassment   A type of harassment in which an older worker is subject to derogatory remarks and is denied the opportunity to learn new tasks. *(19)*

Agency shop   A workplace in which nonunion members of the bargaining unit must contribute to the union an amount usually equivalent to the regular dues. *(17)*

Appraisal interview   An interview in which the results of a performance appraisal are verbally communicated to the employee. *(13)*

Apprenticeship programs   Programs in which trainees learn by working with people already skilled in particular jobs. *(11)*

Appropriate bargaining unit   A group of employees who share common employment conditions and interests and who may reasonably act together for purposes of collective bargaining. *(17)*

Arbitration   Outside appeal to a neutral party in an attempt to resolve a dispute between labor and management. *(18)*

Arbitrator   A neutral third party, selected by management and the union, who hears a dispute and hands down a decision that is final and binding. *(18)*

Assessment center   Information about an employee's promotability and career development needs is gathered systematically and analyzed as the candidate participates in a series of tests, interviews, and exercises. *(10)*

Assessment role   The role of evaluating the effectiveness of various human resources policies and practices. *(23)*

Attrition   A reduction in the number of employees through normal retirements and resignations. *(6)*

Behavioral modeling   Presenting or showing participants a particular behavior or way of doing something, followed by practice of the behavior through role playing. *(12)*

Behavioral observation scales (BOS)   Scales on which several behaviors are listed individually for each performance dimension. The rater is required to assess the individual on *each* behavior. *(13)*

Behavioral sciences   The social and biological sciences pertaining to the study of human behavior. *(2)*

Behaviorally anchored rating scales (BARS)   Scales that focus on specific job behaviors rather than on traits or characteristics. Scales are used for each important area of job behavior. *(13)*

Behavior modification   The process of shaping behavior through reinforcement. Also known as *operant conditioning*. *(5)*

Benefit survey   A survey of the benefits offered by other firms. *(16)*

Benchmarking   (See Competitive benchmarking)

Bid   To enter the competition for a particular job opening. *(9)*

Biodata   Biographical data. *(9)*

Bona fide occupational qualification   A legal, justifiable personnel decision based on sex, religion, or national origin. *(6)*

Bottom-line-principle In the Uniform Guidelines on Employee Selection Procedures, a stipulation that as long as the firm's employee selection process does not produce an adverse impact, federal agencies generally will not challenge particular components of that process. *(9)*

Boycotts Organized refusals to buy products from certain companies to express protest. *(2)*

Bumping A system that permits the demotion of more senior employees to replace the more junior employees who have been laid off. *(10)*

Business agent An employee of a craft union who negotiates and administers the labor contract and handles the union's day-to-day business affairs. *(17)*

Cafeteria benefit plan (See Flexible benefit plan)

Career crisis A traumatic event in terms of a career change, such as demotion, transfer to an undesirable job or location, layoff, discharge, or unemployment for any length of time. *(10)*

Career management The planning of staffing policies and systems. *(6)*

Career progression ladders Charts that illustrate the horizontal and vertical movement of employees from one job to another within an organization. Also called *job ladders, promotion ladders,* or *career paths.* *(7, 10)*

Case studies The analyses of written or videotaped problem situations. *(12)*

Catalyst-facilitator role The role of stimulating a top-management discussion about management philosophy, leadership style, and organizational culture and climate. *(23)*

CEO Chief executive officer *(1)*

Check list method An appraisal method in which the rater is presented with a list of positive or negative adjectives or descriptive behavioral statements and asked to check off all those that apply to the person being rated. *(13)*

Chronobiologists Scientists who study the biological rhythms of the human body. *(8)*

Circadian cycles The rhythmic biological cycles recurring approximately every twenty-four hours. *(8)*

Classification method A method of job evaluation that starts with one-paragraph descriptions of a predetermined number of levels, grades, or "classes" of jobs, each of which corresponds to a pay grade. *(14)*

Climate surveys Questionnaires used to measure individual perceptions of the prevailing climate in the organization. *(4)*

Closed shops Companies that hire only union members. *(2, 17)*

Coaching The frequent helping of a subordinate by a superior. *(12)*

Coaching and development goals Uses of performance appraisal for counseling and coaching employees to improve their performance, developing commitment to the organization, motivating employees, strengthening superior-subordinate relations, and diagnosing individual and organizational problems. *(13)*

Co-determination Indirect representative participation in which union representatives sit on boards of directors. *(21)*

Coercive secondary boycott Example: The picketing by a union of an organization that uses, buys, or deals with products or services from the organization with which the union has a dispute. *(18)*

Collective bargaining The process by which a formal agreement is established between a union and management regarding wages, hours, working conditions, and similar matters. *(2, 18)*

Commission A bonus given according to the number of items or dollar volume sold. *(15)*

Commuter marriage A marriage in which each spouse may work three to five days a week in a different location. *(10)*

Compa ratio A calculation that tells to what degree the jobs within a pay grade will average out near the midpoint of the range. *(14)*

Comparable worth The concept that women should receive the same compensation as men in the same organization for work of comparable worth as well as for work of equal worth. *(14)*

Compensation and reward A process that determines what wages, salaries, and incentives are paid and what supplemental benefits and nonfinancial rewards are provided. *(1)*

Competition Involves common goals and a good deal of common interest, along with limited opposing behaviors. *(5)*

Competitive benchmarking Continuous rating of the company's best products and practices against the world's best firms. *(21)*

Compliance officers Men and women from the safety and health field who have attended at least four weeks of specialized training at OSHA's Training Institute and who conduct OSHA inspections. *(20)*

Compressed workweek A work schedule in which employees work the same number of hours per week but in fewer days than they previously worked. *(8)*

Computer-assisted instruction   Programmed training of employees by computers. *(11)*

Computer-assisted interview   An interview in which an applicant answers questions presented on a video screen. *(9)*

Computer simulation models   Simulation programs that approximate various business situations. *(12)*

Concessionary bargaining   A form of integrative bargaining in which labor actually gives up something it previously had won. *(18)*

Conciliation   A procedure whereby a third party helps labor and management develop and adhere to an agenda, as well as gives them encouragement to address as objectively as possible the issues on which they are divided. *(18)*

Conflict   Opposing behaviors between two or three people or groups who have incompatible goals. *(5)*

Consent election   An election to determine whether a majority of employees favor a particular union to act as their bargaining representative. *(17)*

Construct validity   The extent to which a selection device measures an abstract trait, such as numerical aptitude. *(9)*

Consultant-adviser role   The role of advising management at all levels about the motivational, morale, and legal implications of various policies and practices. *(23)*

Content validity   The relationship between behaviors measured by a selection device and behaviors involved in the job. *(9)*

Contingency plans   Options that can be implemented to minimize negative effects on a company's human resources should an organizational crisis arise. *(10)*

Contingent workers   Workers who are on the payroll of an organization in a part-time or temporary capacity, or who are subcontractors, consultants, or leased employees. *(8)*

Contract rights   The rights of employees for which they have contracted with management. *(19)*

Contract trainers   Outside trainers hired when staff trainers are not available. *(11)*

Craft union   A group of workers who possess the same skill or perform essentially the same task or function. It attempts to organize all the practitioners of that craft who are employed by the same employer or located within a particular area. *(17)*

Criterion-related validity   The correlation between scores on a selection device and ratings on a particular criterion of job performance; expressed as a correlation coefficient. *(9)*

Critical incidents   Worker behaviors that characterize either very good or very poor performance. *(7)*

Critical-incidents technique   A record, kept by the appraiser, of unusually favorable or unfavorable occurrences in an employee's work. *(13)*

Cross-cultural training   Training to assist in understanding and accommodating to specific cultures; sometimes includes team building with persons from more than one culture. *(22)*

Cross-functional teams   Groups comprising specialists from different functions, such as accounting, engineering, manufacturing, marketing, personnel, and so on. *(21)*

Culture shock   An overall sense of difficulty in coping in a foreign locale. *(22)*

Decertification election   An election held to determine whether a majority of employees want to end their affiliation with a union. *(17)*

Decision-making leave   A one-day, paid leave during which the employee is to think through his or her commitment to the organization and willingness to solve an immediate problem. *(8)*

Defined benefit pension plan   A pension plan that specifies the amount of the pension that will be received by the retiree; it is usually based on a combination of salary and length of service. *(16)*

Defined contribution pension plan   A pension plan that features a specified formula for contributions going into the plan but does not specify the amount to be received by the retiree. *(16)*

Demotion   A reduction in job responsibilities, usually accompanied by a reduction in hourly pay or salary. *(8, 10)*

Deregulation   Reduction or elimination of governmental regulation and control of particular industries. *(3)*

Development   An organizational outcome: the extent to which individual employees, groups of workers, and the total organization are developing in their capacity to meet future opportunities and challenges. *(4)*

Diagnostic role   The role of identifying the underlying causes of an organizational problem and developing solutions—or systems for solving the problem—that correspond with the diagnosis. *(23)*

Differential piece-rate plans   Plans in which the worker who exceeds standard production is compensated for all work at a higher rate than workers who satisfy only the minimum standard. *(15)*

Direct participation   The direct interaction of employees with those in authority in a collaborative effort to achieve organizational goals. *(21)*

Discharge   Management action in which an employee is separated from the organization and the payroll for violation of company rules or inadequate performance. *(8, 10)*

Disciplinary action   The penalty or punishment associated with violation of a rule. *(8)*

Disciplinary layoff   The temporary separation of an employee from the organization and the payroll, usually for a rule violation. *(8)*

Disciplinary review board   A committee—usually three or more managers and sometimes a psychiatrist or psychologist—that reviews instances of disciplinary action and can correct or amend a penalty that an employee considers to be unfair or too harsh. *(19)*

Discrimination   Employment decisions based on racial, sexual, age, handicapped status or other kinds of prejudice. *(3, 6)*

Distributive bargaining   A form of collective bargaining that involves the distribution of things that exist in limited quantity, such as wealth and power. *(18)*

Diversity, managing cultural   A term broadly applied to the recruitment, selection, promotion, and training of minorities and the training of all employees in more cultural awareness and appreciation. *(3, 12)*

Docking   The withholding of wages from an employee for time missed at work due to absenteeism or tardiness. *(8)*

Documentation   In the context of work rules violations, careful recording of the facts of the situation. *(8)*

Downsizing   Layoffs. *(10)*

Dual-career couple   A couple in which both spouses are employed. *(10)*

Dual ladders   Parallel avenues for advancement; for example, opportunities for scientists to be promoted to more complex technical positions in contrast to managerial posts. *(10)*

Due process   In organizations, fair and orderly procedures carried out in accordance with established rules and principles that acknowledge the rights of individual employees. *(19)*

Economic strike   A strike over wages, hours, or conditions of work. *(18)*

Effectiveness   An organizational outcome: the extent to which organizational goals are achieved. *(4)*

Efficiency   An organizational outcome: the ratio of outputs to inputs, or of benefits to costs. *(4)*

Elder care   An employee benefit that provides assistance in the care of elderly relatives. *(16)*

Employee assistance programs (EAPs)   Counseling programs in organizations that focus on such problems as mental health, stress, alcohol and drug use, and legal and financial difficulties. *(20)*

Employee association   A professional association that advances the professional interests of its members and engages in collective bargaining with employers. *(17)*

Employee benefits   The services and programs offered workers by organizations, ranging from legally required benefits, such as social security payments, to various optional benefits, such as time off with pay for personal business, vacation, and health insurance. *(16)*

Employee-centered behavior   A type of managerial behavior that includes being friendly and approachable, listening to subordinates, and involving them in planning or decision making. *(4)*

Employee referrals   Suggestions from employees or friends of the organization as to likely candidates for jobs. *(9)*

Employee stock ownership plan (ESOP)   A plan in which employees may purchase company stock through payroll-deduction or installment plans, usually below market price. *(16)*

Employment agents   In organizations around the turn of the century, clerks who handled much of the recruiting and initial screening of applicants. *(2)*

Employment-at-will rule   A doctrine specifying that an employer in a private institution may dismiss an employee, with or without specific cause, in the absence of a written employment agreement. Sometimes called a *termination-at-will rule* or the *absolute right to discharge*. *(19)*

Employment eligibility   The legal right to accept a job in the United States. *(9)*

Empowerment   The enhanced autonomy, creativity, and productivity of subordinates, achieved through training, delegation, involvement, and support. *(4)*

Equal employment opportunity   Equal consideration of all qualified job applicants regardless of sex, race, age, religion, national origin, or handicapped status. *(6)*

Equity   The quality of being just or fair. *(5, 6)*

Error of central tendency   An error that occurs when an appraiser tends to rate the performance of all or most of the persons being appraised around the center of the rating scale. *(13)*

Essay method   A method of appraisal in which the appraiser writes a free-form essay describing subordinates' performances in a number of broad categories. *(13)*

Ethics   A system of moral principles pertaining to the standards of a particular group, profession, or culture. One way to consider the ethics of a given action is to assess the extent of its constructive consequences to others versus the extent of its harmful or destructive consequences. *(4, 23)*

Evaluation goals   Uses of performance appraisal (a) to provide feedback to employees; (b) to develop valid data for pay and promotion decisions; (c) to help the manager make retention and discharge decisions and provide a means for warning employees about unsatisfactory performance. *(13)*

Executive search firm   A private employment agency that specializes in searching out top-level executives to fill critical corporate positions. *(9)*

Exempt employees   As defined by the Fair Labor Standards Act, employees who are exempt from being paid overtime. *(8, 14)*

Exit interview   An interview, usually conducted by a representative of the personnel department, to determine why an employee is leaving. *(10)*

Expatriate   An employee assigned to work in another country, or anyone who has chosen to work in a foreign country. *(22)*

Expedited arbitration   An accelerated form of arbitration in which the two parties in the dispute do not file prehearing or posthearing briefs, no stenographic record is taken, awards are made within five days of the end of the hearing, and the arbitrator's opinions, when required, are kept very short. *(18)*

Extrinsic rewards   External reinforcements such as pay, recognition, or promotion. *(5)*

Facilitator   A professional who has had special training in participative skill development, in structuring and moderating problem-solving meetings, and in the use of action research. *(21)*

Fact-finding   A procedure in which a neutral party, either an individual or a panel, is appointed to determine the facts in a dispute, then makes a report that will provide the parties engaged in the dispute with a more accurate understanding of the situation and thus increase the likelihood that an agreement can be reached. *(18)*

Fallback position   A position with the same status and pay as a promoted employee's original job, to which the employee may be transferred if the promotion proves unsuccessful. *(10)*

Family leave   Leave of absence for taking care of an infant, a family member who is ill, or elderly relatives. *(16)*

Featherbedding provisions   Labor contract provisions that force the employer to hire unnecessary employees. *(2)*

Feedback   Information provided to employees concerning how well they are doing their jobs. *(13)*

Field recruiting   The sending of recruiters into the field—college campuses, meetings of professional associations, and the like—to locate prospective employees. *(9)*

Final-offer arbitration   A procedure in which each party submits a package of contract provisions to an arbitrator, who must make a choice. Sometimes called *last-offer ballot* or *forced-choice arbitration*. *(18)*

Flexible benefit plan   A benefit plan that allows employees to choose a particular mix of benefits that add up to a certain dollar amount. Also called a *cafeteria benefit plan*. *(16)*

Flextime   A schedule under which employees may choose when to arrive at work and when to depart; includes a core time when everyone must be on the job. *(8)*

Focus groups   Small groups of consumers (or employees) assembled to respond to selected questions and/or topics by market (or organizational) researchers. *(21)*

Formal groups   Groups established by management, such as a work group, a special committee, or a task force. *(5)*

Functionally illiterate   Unable to read, write, calculate, or solve problems at a level that enables one to cope with even the simplest organizational tasks. *(11)*

Gaming simulation   A management development exercise in which participants are given background information, instructions about conditions and rules to follow, and perhaps roles to play. *(12)*

Garnishment   A legal proceeding in which a creditor of an employee gets a court order requiring the company to turn over some fraction of that employee's wages. *(8)*

Glasnost Russian term meaning openness; used to characterize former Soviet President Mikhail Gorbachev's campaign for more openness. *(3)*

Glass ceiling Invisible barrier to advancement confronting women and minorities. *(3, 9)*

Glass wall Invisible barrier to lateral mobility confronting women and minorities. *(9)*

Globalization A focus on international competition and interdependency. *(2)*

Golden parachute Severance pay, often quite generous, at the executive level. *(10)*

Graphic rating scale method A rating scale that concentrates on specific employee behaviors or characteristics as they relate to work performance. *(13)*

Green-circle jobs Jobs identified as being underpaid when wages or salaries are plotted against job evaluation points. *(14)*

Grievance A formal complaint filed by an employee following an established grievance procedure. *(17)*

Grievance-arbitration procedures Systematic, union-management deliberations of a complaint filed either by an employee or by management at successively higher organizational levels and potentially by a neutral third party. *(18)*

Group incentive plans Individual plans applied to small groups of workers, to encourage the teamwork and cooperation needed to attain high productivity or performance. *(15)*

Group interview An interview of a number of job candidates at once. Generally the applicants are allowed to discuss job-related matters among themselves while their performance is rated by one or more observers. *(9)*

Group maintenance behaviors Behaviors that pertain to the emotional life of the work group. *(5)*

Group task behaviors Those group member behaviors that relate directly to the task such as initiating, information giving, and summarizing. *(5)*

Halo effect The tendency for an interviewer to be influenced by a particular area in which the applicant looks impressive, to the exclusion of other matters. *(9)*

Halo error A situation in which a supervisor generalizes from one dimension of a person's job performance to all dimensions of performance. *(13)*

Hazing The harassment of a new employee with unnecessary tasks or practical jokes. *(10)*

Health and industrial hygienists Specialists who assist in maintaining the health of the work force

by preventing or controlling occupational and nonoccupational diseases and disabilities. *(20)*

Health maintenance organization (HMO) Organization offering total health care, including such services as general practitioner, specialist, laboratory, surgical, hospital, consulting-nurse, emergency-room, and pharmacy services. *(16)*

Home-based work Working at home for an employer. *(8)*

Honesty tests Pencil and paper questionnaires that inquire into a job applicant's attitudes about theft. *(9)*

Horizontal restructuring A method of job enlargement that involves broadening the scope of the job to include tasks that previously preceded or followed in the flow of the work. *(7)*

Horn effect The tendency for an interviewer to turn one negative characteristic of a job candidate into the conclusion that the candidate is weak in all areas. *(9)*

Hostile environment sexual harassment A form of sexual harassment in which an unwelcome or hostile environment is created *(19)*

Hot cargo (or hot goods) agreement An illegal agreement between a company and a union to cease handling the products of, or cease doing business with, other firms or persons. *(18)*

Human relations movement A movement focusing on group behavior and on workers' feelings as they relate to productivity and morale. *(2)*

Human resources The people who work for a business or service organization, combining their efforts, talents, and skills with other resources, such as knowledge, materials, and energy, to create useful products and services. *(1)*

Human resources management The philosophy, policies, procedures, and practices related to the management of people within an organization; includes human resources planning, job and work design and analysis, staffing, training and development, performance appraisal and review, compensation and reward, employee protection and representation, and organization improvement. *(1)*

Human resources management audit A comprehensive evaluation of the effectiveness of an organization's human resources policies and practices. *(23)*

Human resources planning The process of assessing an organization's human resources needs in relation to organizational goals and making plans to ensure that a competent, stable work force is employed. *(1, 6)*

Hygiene factors   In Herzberg's motivation-hygiene theory, the factors whose absence or negative qualities result in dissatisfaction: company policy and administration, supervision, salary, interpersonal relations, and working conditions. *(5)*

Illegal bargaining issues   Bargaining issues that would conflict with the law and therefore may not be made a part of a labor contract, even if both sides agree to do so. *(18)*

Immigration Reform and Control Act   Legislation requiring employers of four or more workers to hire only U.S. citizens and aliens authorized to work in the United States. *(9)*

Impasse   A deadlock in negotiations. *(18)*

Implied contract   An inferred understanding of the conditions of continued employment. *(19)*

Improshare   A productivity gainsharing plan that focuses on the number of hours saved for a given number of units produced. *(15)*

In-basket training   A method that consists of giving trainees a set of memos, letters, and other items that managers might find in their in-baskets upon arriving at work and that they are required to respond to by delaying a decision about the issue, referring the issue to someone else in the organization, or making a decision about the issue. *(12)*

Incentive plans   Reward systems that provide financial or nonfinancial compensation to employees who make substantial contributions to organizational effectiveness. *(15)*

Incident process   Specialized form of case method focusing on a dilemma. *(12)*

Individual incentive plans   Reward systems tied to the performance of individual employees. *(15)*

Industrial-organizational psychology   A scientific discipline that focuses on such subjects as assessment methods, aptitudes, motivation, leadership, group dynamics, and decision making. *(2)*

Industrial psychology   Early forms included application of techniques for measuring differences in aptitude and mental ability between people to problems of employee selection and placement. *(2)*

Industrial union   A union composed mainly of unskilled workers in a given industry no matter what jobs these workers perform. *(17)*

Industrial welfare movement   Attempts of employers around the turn of the century to improve working conditions in their own factories. *(2)*

Informal groups   Groups in an organization that have not been established by management but that form spontaneously as a result of individuals' proximity or similarity of work, mutual interests, mutual need fulfillment, or combinations of reasons. Also called *shadow groups*, because they tend to be less visible to management than formal groups. *(5)*

Injunctions   Court orders that prohibit workers and unions from certain actions during labor disputes. *(2)*

Inspection tour   A compliance officer's inspection of a workplace to check safety and health conditions. *(20)*

Insubordination   The refusal to carry out instructions from a superior. *(8)*

Intact work teams   Members of a work group plus the supervisor. *(4, 21)*

Integrative bargaining   A form of collective bargaining in which both sides engage in problem solving and benefit from an agreement because both labor and management share common goals and concerns. *(18)*

Interactive video (IAV)   A video that allows for interaction; uses a computer and keyboard, video screen, material stored on a videodisc, and video camera and tape. *(11)*

Interest arbitration   A procedure that involves submitting to an arbitrator any point that the parties cannot agree on in negotiating a contract. *(18)*

Intergroup problem solving   A participative technique for solving problems between two groups, involving both groups and a facilitator. *(21)*

Internal tribunals   Committees—usually including one or more fellow workers, management representatives, and representative of the human resources department—who arbitrate complaints or grievances of workers and hand down binding decisions consistent with company-published policies and procedures. Also called *peer review panels*. *(19)*

International human resources management (IHRM)   The systematic planning and coordination of job and work design, staffing, training and development, appraising, rewarding, and protecting and representing the human resources in the foreign operations of an organization. *(22)*

Intrinsic rewards   Internal reinforcements, such as a feeling of accomplishment or self-worth. *(5)*

Inverse seniority   A system in which the most senior workers are given the first opportunity to elect layoff. *(10)*

Involuntary transfer   An organization-initiated reassignment of an employee from one job to another, one department to another, one shift to another, or one geographic location to another. *(10)*

Job analysis An outgrowth of job design, the process of investigating the tasks and behaviors associated with a particular job. *(1, 7)*

Job and work design Specifies the tasks to be performed by individuals and groups within an organization and establishes the rules, schedules, and working conditions under which people perform those tasks. *(1)*

Job content The set of activities to be performed on the job, including the duties, tasks, and job responsibilities to be carried out; the equipment, machines, and tools to be used; and the required interactions with others. *(7)*

Job description Written summary, sometimes called a *position description*, of the basic tasks associated with a particular job. *(7)*

Job design The process of determining the specific tasks and responsibilities to be carried out by each member of an organization. *(7)*

Job Diagnostic Survey (JDS) An instrument used to determine whether there is a need to redesign work and whether doing so is feasible, given the existing structure of the jobs and existing conditions in the organization. *(7)*

Job enlargement The addition of more and different tasks to a job. Sometimes called *horizontal restructuring*. *(7)*

Job enrichment The process of enhancing job characteristics for the purpose of increasing worker motivation, productivity, and satisfaction. Sometimes called *vertical restructuring*. *(7)*

Job evaluation The systematic determination of the relative worth of jobs within an organization to establish wages and salaries. *(7, 14)*

Job factors Factors, such as responsibility, skill, effort, or working conditions, that are considered appropriate dimensions for determining relative job worth, or value to an organization. *(14)*

Job instruction training (JIT) Determination of training needs, recognition of the needs of the trainee, feedback from the trainee, frequent appraisal, and correction. *(11)*

Job posting The announcement of job openings to all current employees. *(9)*

Job relatedness The extent to which selection or appraisal standards are relevant to performance on the job. *(9)*

Job satisfaction A person's emotional response to aspects of work (such as pay, supervision, and benefits) or to the work itself. *(5)*

Job Service In most states, an agency responsible for assistance in job placement. *(9)*

Job sharing The splitting of a job into two four-hour segments that are shared by two people, or the splitting of a job so that one person works full days for part of a week and another person works the other days. *(8)*

Job specifications The qualifications needed to perform a job, frequently listed as part of a job description. *(7)*

Job Training Partnership Act (JTPA) Legislation that created a federal program that helps retrain workers. *(11)*

Job worth The value of a job to an organization. *(14)*

Joint Apprenticeship Committees Joint management-union committees to plan and manage local apprentice programs. *(11)*

Jurisdictional strikes Strikes organized to force an employer to assign work to one union, trade, or craft instead of to some other. *(18)*

Just cause Valid, job-related reasons for terminating employment. *(19)*

Key job A job that is found in many organizations and that has relatively stable content. *(14)*

Knowledge-based pay (See Skill-based pay)

Labor department specialists In turn-of-the-century organizations, a person responsible for responding to complaints from union employees and for monitoring working conditions and wage policies. *(2)*

Labor union An organization that bargains for employees over wages, hours, and other terms and conditions of employment. *(2, 17)*

Laboratory training Experience-based learning workshops that generally emphasize interaction between trainers and trainees. *(12)*

Layoff The temporary or indefinite removal of employees from the payroll. *(10)*

Layout and physical arrangements The design of the workplace itself, the technology and equipment made available for completing tasks, and other characteristics of the organization's physical environment. *(4)*

Leadership The process of influencing individual and group behavior toward the attainment of organizational goals. *(4)*

Leniency error An error made when an appraiser gives employees higher ratings than they deserve. *(13)*

Local hire An employee hired from the local community where the plant or office is located. *(22)*

Lockout Literally, a locking out of employees by managers in the hope that the employees, or the union that represents them, will be more eager to reach agreement if the workers no longer have an income. *(2, 18)*

Maintenance behaviors Those group member behaviors that relate to the emotional life of the group and its development, such as harmonizing, gate keeping, and encouraging. *(5)*

Maintenance of membership requirements Clauses in union contracts that require workers who belong to a union at the beginning of a contract's term to remain members throughout the period covered by the contract (except for a specified interval near the contract's expiration date, when withdrawal is permitted). *(17)*

Make-work provisions Labor contract provisions that create jobs with no substance or purpose. *(2)*

Malcolm Baldrige National Quality Award Established by Congress to recognize companies that have successfully implemented total quality management (TQM) systems. *(21)*

Management and career development Efforts to increase an organization's present and future ability to meet its goals by educating managers and all employees above and beyond the immediate technical requirements of their jobs. *(12)*

Management by objectives (MBO) A system that features an agreement between a superior and a subordinate on the subordinate's objectives for a particular period and a scheduled review of how well the subordinate has achieved those objectives. *(13)*

Management game (See gaming simulation)

Management philosophy The set of ideas and beliefs held by executives about how people should be managed. *(4)*

Management systems Procedures and devices for channeling organizational activities such as planning, goal setting, staffing, purchasing, marketing, accounting, communicating, and the like. *(4)*

Managing diversity (See Diversity, managing cultural)

Mandatory bargaining issues Items about which unions and management must negotiate, including wages, hours, and conditions of work. *(18)*

Mandatory benefits Employee benefits that organizations are required by law to provide. *(16)*

Mandatory retirement A retirement required by the organization. *(6)*

Measured day-rate plan An individual incentive plan under which employees are rated every two or three months on several factors, such as productivity, quality of work, dependability, and versatility. *(15)*

Mechanistic system A managerial system including such features as high task specialization, extensive reliance on each hierarchical level for coordination and control, conservative communications, emphasis on vertical interactions, insistence on loyalty, and a one-on-one leadership style. *(4)*

Med-arb A combination of mediation and arbitration in which union and management agree that a third party will mediate, but will then decide issues that cannot be settled through mediation. *(18)*

Mediation A procedure in which a third party suggests specific alternatives for the consideration of labor and management and assists the two sides in reaching agreement. *(18)*

Mentor A person more senior in position or experience who is available to a junior person for coaching or counseling concerning job and career progress. *(12)*

Merit Quality performance that deserves reward. *(14)*

Merit pay Pay increase based on job performance. *(14)*

Merit-pay plan Under this plan, pay raises are determined by job performance. Employees who achieve a certain level of performance relative to established standards or relative to the performance of others earn an increase in their regular rate of pay. *(14)*

Mission statement A written statement of an organization's overall purpose, or mission. *(6)*

Motivated behavior The desire and willingness of employees to expend effort to reach and sustain high levels of performance. *(4)*

Motivation The desire and willingness of a person to expend effort in order to reach a particular goal or outcome. *(5)*

Motivators In Herzberg's motivation-hygiene theory, the key factors in motivation and satisfaction: achievement, recognition, the work itself, responsibility, and advancement. *(5)*

Multinational corporation (MNC) A company with operations in more than one country. *(22)*

Multi-skilling Training employees to have multiple skills. *(11)*

National A citizen of the country where the plant or office exists. *(22)*

National emergency dispute A strike that could threaten the economic well-being of the nation or imperil the national defense. *(18)*

Needs forecasting The process of determining an organization's future demand for human resources. *(6)*

Negligent hiring A situation where an employer does not reasonably investigate the background of a potential employee and thus exposes others to the risk of harm or injury. *(9)*

Nondirective interview An interview in which the interviewer asks minimal, open-ended questions; reflects or restates the feeling expressed by the applicant; and avoids arguments, taking sides, or moralizing. *(9)*

Nonexempt employees Employees protected by the Fair Labor Standards Act relative to overtime payment. *(8, 14)*

Occupational disease A job-induced disturbance of the normal functioning of the body or of a person's mental and emotional capacities. *(20)*

Occupational Safety and Health Act (OSH Act) A federal law that established and enforces safety and health standards to reduce the incidence of occupational injury, illness, and death. *(20)*

Occupational Safety and Health Administration (OSHA) An agency within the U.S. Department of Labor that establishes and enforces occupational safety and health standards through inspections, citations, and fines; it also provides consultation services. *(20)*

Ombudsman A person who handles the investigation and resolution of employees' complaints. *(19)*

On-the-job-training (OJT) Specific procedures for delivering training to an employee. *(11)*

One-on-one interview A type of interview in which the job candidate meets privately with a single interviewer to discuss his or her qualifications for the job. *(9)*

Open-door policy A way of handling grievances in which employees are given access to their superiors so that problems can be brought into the open and resolved in a mutually satisfying way. *(19)*

Organic system A managerial system including such features as a continuous reassessment of tasks through interaction; authority and control stemming from expertise; very open and extensive communications, with encouragement of diagonal and horizontal, as well as vertical, communications; commitment to the organization's mission; and a team leadership style. *(4)*

Organization development (OD) A long-range, comprehensive organizational improvement strategy featuring extensive use of action research and a focus on interpersonal, group, intergroup, and organizational processes. *(21)*

Organization improvement The flow of events that determines the strategies by which organizations attempt to improve their effectiveness, increase employee satisfaction, or otherwise enhance the organizational environment. *(1)*

Organizational climate The measurable, collective perceptions of organization members about those aspects of their working life that affect their motivation and behavior—in particular, the culture of the organization, the prevailing leadership style, the degree of structure, and the personnel policies and practices. *(4)*

Organizational culture Those values, beliefs, assumptions, myths, norms, and goals that are shared widely in the organization. Also includes *management philosophy. (4)*

Organizational due process Established procedures for handling employee complaints and grievances; protection against punitive action for using these procedures; and systematic and thorough review of complaints and grievances by unbiased or neutral parties. *(3, 19)*

Organizational goal An organization's long-term, broad purpose or aim. *(6)*

Organizational hierarchy The grouping of workers into units (such as departments and divisions) and levels to determine who is held accountable to whom. *(4)*

Organizational objective An organization's short-term purpose or aim. *(6)*

Organizational outcomes Measures of performance: effectiveness, efficiency, development, and participant satisfaction. *(4)*

Organizational psychology Aspects of the behavioral sciences that focus on the dynamics of leadership, group behavior, and motivation. *(2)*

Organizational responsibilities Responsibilities relating to the overall organization that each employee is expected to carry out. *(7)*

Orientation A program designed to acquaint new employees with the organization and help them begin their jobs productively. *(10)*

Outdoor-based programs Management and employee development programs that use a permanent conference center with both indoor and outdoor facilities for learning. *(12)*

Outplacement Assistance, for employees who have been laid off or otherwise terminated, from the organization in locating jobs elsewhere in the community. *(10)*

Overtime work Work performed beyond the regularly scheduled workday or workweek as defined by the organization or by law. *(8)*

Panel interview A type of interview in which one job candidate meets with a panel of two or more representatives of the firm, who take part in the questioning and discussion. *(9)*

Parallel ladders Opportunities for professional employees to be either promoted into more complex technical jobs or promoted into jobs with supervisory or managerial responsibility. *(10)*

Participant satisfaction An organizational outcome: employees' emotional response to their work and jobs. *(4)*

Participation Employee involvement in organizational problem solving and decision making. *(3)*

Participative improvement strategy An effort to increase overall organizational effectiveness through employee participation. *(21)*

Pay for performance A pay and incentive plan that attempts to create a direct link between employee performance and compensation. *(14)*

Pay grade A numbered or lettered pay range (such as Grade VIII) to which a number of jobs are assigned. *(14)*

Peak-time employees Permanent part-time workers with whom businesses supplement their staffs at peak periods, such as noon hours. *(8)*

Peer ratings The evaluations of an employee's performance or potential for advancement by other employees of equal rank. *(10)*

Peer review panels Sometimes called *internal tribunals*, these are groups of management representatives and fellow employees whose task is to hand down a binding decision in nonunion grievance procedures. *(19)*

Pension A regularly paid retirement income. *(10)*

Pension administrators In turn-of-the-century firms, persons who managed the pension and insurance plans. *(2)*

Perestroika In the late '80s, Soviet term for the restructuring of the U.S.S.R. economy, including the fostering of private enterprise. *(3)*

Performance appraisal The formal, systematic assessment of how well employees are performing their jobs in relation to established standards, and the communication of that assessment to employees. *(13)*

Performance appraisal and review The ongoing evaluation of individual and group contributions to an organization, and the communication of those evaluations to the persons involved. *(1)*

Performance management The planning of broad organizational matters, such as quality of work life, and of specific human resources management processes, such as performance appraisal and reward structures. *(6)*

Performance standards Statements that make explicit the quantity and/or quality of performance expected in the basic tasks set forth in the job description. *(7)*

Permanent part-time employee A permanent member of the staff who works only part-time. *(8)*

Permanent umpire system A system in which labor and management agree to use a particular arbitrator, or several arbitrators in rotation, for the life of the labor contract. *(18)*

Phased retirement Part-time work or job-sharing approaches that allow employees nearing retirement gradually to reduce the number of hours they work per day, per week, or per year. *(10)*

Picketing The act of protesting publicly by carrying placards, usually in front of the workplace. *(2)*

Piece-rate plan An incentive system in which compensation is based on the number of units produced. In most piece-rate plans, the worker is guaranteed a base rate, or minimum hourly wage that assumes a certain rate of production, and is paid extra for production above that rate. *(15)*

Piecework system See piece-rate plan.

Point-factor method A method of job evaluation that uses several factors common to the jobs being evaluated. *(14)*

Polygraph testing The measurement of a subject's physiological changes (such as heart rate) in reaction to a structured set of questions. *(3, 9)*

Portability An employee's ability to transfer vested benefits to another employer or to an individual retirement account. *(16)*

Position Analysis Questionnaire (PAQ) A job analysis device in which the analyst rates the job against approximately 190 job elements, usually on a 0- to a 5-point scale. *(7)*

Positive reinforcement programs Programs in which the principles of behavior modification and operant conditioning are used to influence worker behavior. *(15)*

Postemployment surveys Surveys that ask separated employees to supply reasons for their resignations, several weeks after their departure. *(10)*

Predictive validity The degree to which an aptitude or mental ability test accurately predicts job success. *(2)*

Preemployment training Training by an organization in which job seekers are tested and instructed in employment fundamentals without pay. *(11)*

Preferred provider organization (PPO) A network of doctors and hospitals who have agreed to provide health care at discount and practice according to a set of guidelines. *(16)*

Process An identifiable flow of interrelated events moving toward a specified goal, consequence, or end. *(1)*

Production bonus An incentive system in which workers who surpass minimum production standards are given a bonus payment that is based on cost savings associated with higher productivity. *(15)*

Production-centered behavior A type of behavior required for effective leadership, in which the leader focuses on task-oriented aspects of work. *(4)*

Productivity Total amount of worker output. *(3)*

Productivity bargaining A form of integrative bargaining in which wage increases are tied to the union's acceptance of work practices that will increase efficiency. *(18)*

Productivity gainsharing (PG) plan An incentive plan based on the productivity of an organization or a plant as a whole. *(15)*

Profit-sharing plan An incentive system in which some portion of the organization's earnings is distributed to employees to supplement their usual wages or salaries. *(15)*

Program planning The planning of organizational programs through performance management and career management. *(6)*

Progressive discipline A means of administering work rules to current problems early to avoid the last-resort step of discharge. The management responds to an employee's first offense with some minimal action, such as an oral warning, but treats subsequent offenses with more serious penalties, such as disciplinary layoff or discharge. *(8)*

Prolonged stress Unchecked stress, in which the body remains in an excited state after a crisis has passed and which can lead to harmful effects. *(20)*

Promotion The reassignment of an employee to a position that offers higher pay and greater responsibilities, privileges, and potential opportunities. *(10)*

Protection and representation Formal or informal processes of protecting and representing employees faced with arbitrary and impulsive treatment or physical danger and health hazards. *(1)*

Protests Public displays, by workers as a group, of disapproval over conditions of employment. *(2)*

Quality circle A group of employees who meet regularly to discuss ways to improve products and work methods. *(3, 21)*

Quality of work life The degree of excellence in organizational life as measured by adequate and fair compensation, safe and healthy working conditions, opportunity to use and develop human capacities, opportunity for continued growth and security, social integration, constitutionalism, balanced role of work, and socially beneficial work. *(3)*

Quality-of-work life (QWL) project A comprehensive improvement strategy—often implemented as a result of integrative bargaining—in which labor and management make a collaborative attempt to improve the working lives of employees and enhance their ability to produce. *(18,21)*

Quasi-judicial Analogous to or approaching the role of a judge; used to describe an arbitrator's role. *(18)*

Quid pro quo sexual harassment The phrase (the Latin words mean "something for something") describes the situation where a supervisor offers something in return for sexual favors. *(19)*

Ranking method A method of job evaluation where raters rank various jobs using overall judgments of worth rather than determining the critical factors in each job. *(14)*

Rate ranges The lower and upper dollar limits assigned to a pay grade. *(14)*

Reasonable accommodation Any modification or adjustment to a job or the work environment that will enable a qualified applicant or employee with a disability to perform essential job functions. *(3, 9)*

Recall The rehiring of laid-off employees. *(10)*

Recruitment The process of finding qualified people and encouraging them to apply for work with the firm. *(9)*

Red-circle job Jobs identified as being overpaid when wages or salaries are plotted against job evaluation points. *(14)*

Reduction in force (RIF) Separation or layoff of a proportion of a work force. Term frequently used in Great Britain, e.g., "I've been riffed." *(3)*

Reinforcement   The process of influencing behavior through rewards and punishments, according to a theory based largely on the work of B. F. Skinner. *(5)*

Reference checks   Communication with previous employers and others who can provide information about a job applicant. *(9)*

Reliability   Consistency of the results produced by a test or other selection device. *(9, 13)*

Relocation   The transfer of an employee from one location to another. *(10)*

Representative participation   The interaction of elected employee representatives with higher levels of management to make organization-wide decisions. *(21)*

Resignation   The voluntary separation of an employee from an organization. *(10)*

Restrictive work rules   Regulations that impose tight control over employees' behavior; usually associated with union-management agreements that limit broadening the scope of individual jobs. *(8)*

Retirement   The systematic separation of older workers from an organization. *(10)*

Retraining   Developing new skills and knowledge as a result of technological or organizational changes. *(11)*

Reverse seniority   A system in which the most senior employee is the last to be laid off and the first to be recalled. *(10)*

Right-to-know laws   "Hazard communication" regulations established by the Occupational Safety and Health Administration, specifying that employers in basic industries must provide information about hazardous substances in the workplace. *(20)*

Right-to-work laws   State laws that outlaw closed shops, union-shop provisions in contracts, and maintenance of membership requirements. *(2, 17)*

Role analysis process (RAP)   A team-building technique in which members of a work group discuss various aspects of a particular job as they see it. *(21)*

Role playing   An activity in which participants assume the role of specific persons in a situation, act out the event, and then discuss the implications. *(12)*

Run-off election   A union representation election held if there are more than two choices on a ballot and no single union receives a majority of votes on the first ballot. *(17)*

Sabotage   The deliberate damaging of equipment or products. *(5)*

Safety director   A safety practitioner (also known as *safety manager*), who is responsible for organizing, stimulating, and guiding a company's safety program and who serves as a spokesperson to management and the union. *(20)*

Safety engineer   A safety practitioner who studies workers' exposure to injury or illness and tries to design job procedures and the workplace to fit workers' capabilities and limitations. *(20)*

Safety inspector   An entry-level safety practitioner who audits compliance with safety policies and procedures. *(20)*

Safety specialists   Persons who help ensure safe working conditions in industrial firms. *(2)*

Salary   A weekly, monthly, or yearly rate of pay. *(14)*

Salary compression   A narrowing of the differentials between job levels that is created when inflation drives up beginning wages and salaries. *(14)*

Salary reduction plan   A pension benefit program under which an employer may establish a retirement savings plan to which employees can contribute through payroll deductions. The employee's contributions reduce the employee's taxable income, and no income taxes are paid until the employee starts drawing from the fund after retirement. Also known as *401(k) plan*. *(16)*

Scanlon plan   A productivity gainsharing plan featuring bonuses to employees for reducing labor costs relative to productivity, extensive union-management cooperation, and committee participation by employees at all levels. *(15)*

Scientific management   A movement during the late 1800s and early 1900s that concentrated particularly on job design, selection, and compensation. Frederick W. Taylor developed this view of management as a science. *(2)*

Screening   A process, usually conducted by the human resources department, that determines which job applicants will be sent to department heads or other managers for final evaluation. *(9)*

Selection   The process of choosing among people who apply for work with an organization. *(9)*

Selective strikes   Strikes against only some of a large employer's plants. *(18)*

Self-managed team   A work group that essentially manages itself with very little supervision. *(7)*

Seniority   An employee's length of service with the department or organization. *(10)*

Sensing   A technique used to foster more effective communications, in which selected groups of workers interact with members of top management. *(21)*

Severance pay A lump-sum payment to an employee at the time of permanent separation from an organization. *(10)*

Sexual harassment Sexual advances toward an employee, usually a subordinate, often with hints of advancement or threats to job status; or the creation of an environment that is hostile, abusive, or intimidating to the opposite sex. *(19)*

Shift work Regular employment that occurs sometime between 7 p.m. and 7 a.m. *(8)*

Shop steward A union member, operating at the department or line level, who represents fellow union members and serves as a link between the union members and the officers. *(17)*

Sitdown strike A strike in which workers literally sit down in the plant and refuse to work.

Situational-problem interview A type of interview in which the candidate is given a specific problem to solve or a project to complete. *(9)*

Skill-based pay The wages paid to individual members of a work group according to the number of tasks they can perform or the number of skills they have mastered. Also called knowledge-based pay. *(7, 11, 14)*

Skills inventories Computerized systems in which information on each employee's skills, educational background, work history, and other important factors is stored in a data base, which can then be used to identify employees with the qualifications needed for a particular job. *(9)*

Slowdown A reduction in productivity by workers. *(18)*

Social, or welfare, secretary An employee, in organizations around the turn of the century, who helped with employee finances, housing, health, recreation, education, and other matters. *(2)*

Social security Employee benefits provided through the federal Old-Age, Survivors, Disability, and Health Insurance (OASDHI) program. *(16)*

Sociotechnical programs Efforts to link the social aspects of the factory, mine, and office with the technology used. *(7)*

Specialist A practitioner, consultant, educator, or researcher, accredited at the senior level, who has in-depth expertise in one area of a field.

Specialization Expertise in a particular area, or set of tasks. *(1)*

Spot bonus A cash award for extraordinary achievement or performance. *(15)*

Spot gainsharing (SGS) plans Productivity gainsharing plans with a fixed time frame and adapted to solving specific problems. *(15)*

Staff trainers Full-time training specialists on an organization's payroll, or members selected to do part-time training. *(11)*

Staffing The process that results in the continuous assignment of workers to all positions in the organization. *(1)*

Standard-hour plan A production-bonus incentive system under which "standard time" for completing a particular job or task is established. *(15)*

Statistical process control A method of measuring and analyzing deviations in manufacturing processes. *(21)*

Statistical quality control A method of measuring and analyzing deviations in manufactured products. *(21)*

Stereotypes Assumptions about people that prevent fair consideration of personal qualifications. *(9)*

Steward An employee of the company and member of the union, whose union assignment is to make sure that the labor contract is being followed. *(17)*

Stock appreciation rights (SARs) One version of the stock option, under which an executive can relinquish the right to purchase the company's stock and receive instead an amount equal to the increased value of the stock from the date the stock option was granted. *(15)*

Stock option An incentive plan under which an executive, manager, or professional is granted the right to buy a certain number of shares of the company's stock at a given price and by a specified date. *(15)*

Strategic plan A plan for conducting an organization's business as profitably and successfully as possible. *(6)*

Stress Bodily response to exposure to a stimulus. *(20)*

Strike The refusal of workers, as a group, to work due to disapproval of working conditions. *(2, 18)*

Strikebreakers Nonunion workers who are willing to replace striking employees. *(2)*

Structure The arrangements in an organization through which the activities and behavior of its employees are directed toward desired goals. *(4)*

Structured, or patterned, interview A type of interview in which the interviewer follows a standard list of questions to be asked of all applicants. *(9)*

Study action teams Cross-functional and multi-level task forces temporarily assigned full-time to study a particular problem within a work area. *(18, 21)*

Submission agreement An agreement, sometimes called a *stipulation* or an *agreement to arbitrate*, which is signed by both labor and management representatives and describes the dispute and the authority that the arbitrator can exercise. *(18)*

Succession planning The process of anticipating future managerial staffing needs and making plans for the development of managers to meet those needs. *(6)*

Suggestion plan An incentive system under which employees are rewarded by cash payment, merchandise, or travel if they offer useful ideas for improving organizational effectiveness. *(15)*

Supplemental unemployment benefits (SUB) Company payments to laid-off workers, designed to extend or enlarge the unemployment benefits provided under state law. *(10)*

Support groups Groups formed, for example, by minorities and women, for career guidance and psychological support. *(12)*

Survey feedback A comprehensive improvement strategy in which employees in several departments—or all employees within the organization—complete questionnaires about the workplace; results are fed back to groups in a series of problem-solving workshops. *(21)*

System A particular set of procedures and devices designed to control a process in a predictable way. *(1)*

Systems 1–4T A typology of management systems developed by Rensis Likert and colleagues featuring measurable characteristics along several dimensions, including leadership style, direction of communications flow, location of control, use of rewards versus punishment, and so on. *(4)*

System 4T System 4 plus such dimensions as high performance goals and high technical competence (*T* refers to "Total model"). *(4)*

Systems theory A theory that emphasizes the relationships among the many parts or aspects of some totality, such as an organization. *(2)*

Task behaviors Behaviors bearing directly on getting the task done. *(5)*

T-groups Small groups, of ten to twelve, that, under the guidance of a trainer, learn to deal with feelings, learn how to communicate feelings, and learn from the perceptions and reactions of others. *(12)*

Team A small group with complementary skills, commitment to common goals, and considerable interdependence and interaction. *(5)*

Team building A diagnostic, problem-solving meeting involving an intact work group and a facilitator. *(21)*

Team MBO A management-by-objectives program in which a work team develops group objectives and reviews individual and group progress on objectives. *(13, 21)*

Teamwork People's willingness and ability to work together to achieve organizational goals. *(4)*

Telecommuting A method of working at home for an organization through the use of computer and word processor equipment linked by telephone to the home office. *(8)*

Theory X From Douglas McGregor: the assumption that the average person dislikes work and responsibility, has little ambition, and primarily wants security, and thus that this person needs to be directed, controlled, coerced, and threatened with punishment in order to make him or her work toward organizational goals. *(4)*

Theory Y From Douglas McGregor: the assumption that work is as natural as play or rest, that people will exercise self-direction in working toward goals to which they are committed, and that commitment stems from the rewards associated with attaining those goals, and, accordingly, that people can learn to accept and seek responsibility and have more creativity and ingenuity than is usually recognized. *(4)*

Third-country national (TCN) An employee whose nationality is neither the country of the company's headquarters nor of the country where he or she is working. *(22)*

Time-and-motion study An analytical approach, based on laws of efficient motion, to efficiency in industry. *(2)*

Total quality management (TQM) A synthesis of a number of organization improvement approaches, including use of statistical quality and process control, quality circles, self-managed teams, task forces, and extensive use of participatory management. *(21)*

Totality of conduct A combination of actions that may violate the duty to bargain in good faith. *(18)*

Training Organizationally directed experiences that are designed to further the learning of behaviors that will contribute to organizational goals. *(11)*

Training and development A complex mixture of activities—including skill development programs, coaching by a supervisor, general management courses, and training seminars—intended to improve the performance of individuals and groups within an organization. *(1)*

Training objectives The desired outcomes of a training program. *(11)*

Training specialists Persons who staff formal training programs offered by organizations. *(2)*

Transactional analysis (TA) A procedure that focuses on viewing the interactions between individuals and between groups as transactions. *(12)*

Transfer The reassignment of an employee from one job, one department, one shift, or one geographic location to another. *(10)*

Turnover The ratio of separations to total work force for some period. *(5, 10)*

Two-tier wage scale A wage scale for new hires that is significantly lower than that for employees already on the payroll. *(18)*

Understudy assignment The assigning of an inexperienced manager to work for a more experienced manager, often on an "assistant to" basis. *(12)*

Unemployment compensation An employee benefit administered under state and federal laws that provides emergency income to people when they are unemployed. *(16)*

Uniform Guidelines on Employee Selection Procedures Guidelines developed by the Equal Employment Opportunity Commission and three other federal agencies to help employers develop legally acceptable selection standards. *(9)*

Union shop provisions Provisions in contracts that make union membership a requirement for all workers in a bargaining unit. *(2, 17)*

Valence The degree of attractiveness or value of a potential outcome to a specific individual. *(5)*

Validity The degree to which the scores or rankings on a test or other selection device relate to success on the job. *(9, 13)*

Value Something that is prized or esteemed. *(4)*

Valuing diversity (See Diversity, managing cultural)

Variable pay Compensation other than base wages or salaries in which payment fluctuates according to some standard. *(15)*

Vertical restructuring Job enrichment that involves the addition of some activities previously performed by the supervisory level, including some of the planning. *(7)*

Vestibule training The practice of giving skills training to individuals after they are hired but before they are assigned to specific jobs. *(11)*

Vesting Entitlement of an employee—based on minimum standards established by law—to receive the employer's contributions to a pension fund even if he or she leaves the job before retirement. *(16)*

Videoconferencing Two-way satellite transmission of training sessions or staff meetings. *(11)*

Videotape interviewing The videotaping of selection interviews, which can then be reviewed, transported, or shown in a different sequence. *(9)*

Vision A broad image or view of what organization members want the organization to be like in the future. *(4)*

Voluntary bargaining issues Bargaining issues that are lawful but not mandatory. *(18)*

Wage or hourly pay The pay basis used most frequently for production and maintenance employees (blue-collar workers). *(14)*

Wage and salary surveys Surveys carried out by mail, telephone, or interview concerning the wages and salaries paid for selected jobs in other organizations. *(14)*

Wage, or rate, clerk In turn-of-the-century organizations, an employee of a labor department who set wage rates based on time-and-motion studies and an analysis of job tasks. *(2)*

Warnings Notices that inform an employee that a more severe penalty (frequently specified) will be applied at the next infraction of the rules. *(8)*

Weighted application form An application form in which some items that are judged important are given more predictive weight than others. *(9)*

Weighted check list A check list on which each item—a positive or negative adjective or a descriptive behavioral statement—is weighted based on its perceived importance to successful job performance. *(13)*

Wellness programs Programs that promote the health and well-being of employees. *(20)*

Whipsawing A negotiating tactic in which the union that represents the employees in all of the company's plants insists that an advantage gained at one plant should be applied to all the others. *(18)*

Whistle blowing Speaking out about an organization's involvement in illegal, immoral, or irresponsible practices. *(19)*

Wilderness programs Management and employee development programs held in a wilderness area and involving such activities as river rafting or mountain climbing, with debriefing occurring at the campsite. *(12)*

Work banking   The hiding of present production in order to demonstrate productivity up to some standard or quota at some future time. *(5)*

Work group   A number of persons, usually reporting to a common superior and having some face-to-face interaction, who have some degree of interdependence in carrying out tasks for the purpose of achieving organizational goals. *(5)*

Workers' compensation   An employee benefit that provides payments—and also medical and rehabilitation services—to workers or dependents in the event of job-incurred injury, illness, or death. *(2, 16)*

Work rules and regulations   The standarized procedures for controlling, rewarding, and punishing employees' behavior. *(4)*

Works council   Familiar in Europe, an elected body of worker representatives that meets periodically with top management about issues affecting workers. *(21)*

Yellow-dog contract   An agreement between management and a worker under which the worker agrees not to join a union, in exchange for continued employment. *(2)*

AUTHOR INDEX

SUBJECT INDEX (INCLUDING COMPANIES)